# The Cultural Study of Work

# The Cultural Study of Work

Edited by
Douglas Harper and
Helene M. Lawson

ROWMAN & LITTLEFIELD PUBLISHERS, INC.
*Lanham • Boulder • New York • Toronto • Oxford*

ROWMAN & LITTLEFIELD PUBLISHERS, INC.

Published in the United States of America
by Rowman & Littlefield Publishers, Inc.
A wholly owned subsidiary of The Rowman & Littlefield Publishing Group, Inc.
4501 Forbes Boulevard, Suite 200, Lanham, MD 20706
www.rowmanlittlefield.com

P.O. Box 317, Oxford OX2 9RU, UK

British Library Cataloguing in Publication Information Available

**Library of Congress Cataloging-in-Publication Data**

The cultural study of work / edited by Douglas Harper and Helene M. Lawson.
    p.   cm.
  Includes bibliographical references and index.
  ISBN 0-7425-1917-1 (cloth : alk. paper)—ISBN (invalid)
0-7425-1917-8 (pbk. : alk. paper)
    1. Work—Sociological aspects.  2. Industrial sociology.  I. Harper,
Douglas.   II. Lawson, Helene M., 1937–
HD6955.C86  2003
306.3′6—dc21                                                        2003009704

Printed in the United States of America

♾ ™ The paper used in this publication meets the minimum requirements
of American National Standard for Information Sciences—Permanence of
Paper for Printed Library Materials, ANSI/NISO Z39.48-1992.

*To the memory of*
*Everett Cherrington Hughes, Ph.D.*
*1897–1983*

# Contents

# Introduction

*Douglas Harper and Helene M. Lawson*

This book applies the concept of culture to the study of work. James Spradley, an anthropologist, suggested that "culture" consisted of the categories and plans for action shared by a group. Howard Becker, a sociologist, defined culture as the "shared understandings people use to coordinate their activities."

We take "work" to indicate purposeful activities that people do to live. Once that was directly connected to getting material subsistence; now most of us work in a complex economy and society where our work has little to do with providing us directly with food or shelter. Still, most everyone in all societies understands instinctively what "work" refers to.

We use Becker and Spradley's definitions because they recognize that culture consists of categories made by people who see the world in similar ways and agree upon words to describe these parts. When that shared world surrounds work, we can speak of a work culture. The second parts of both Spradley's and Becker's definitions remind us that people not only collectively define the world but also manage it. Managing a culture involves strategies and activities that are coordinated with others who share our work cultures.

## WHAT'S UNUSUAL ABOUT OUR APPROACH?

Sociologists began to study work in the earliest decades of the discipline. At the core of Marx's sociology is the consideration of how work confirms and extends human capabilities or denigrates and dehumanizes us. Max Weber studied how the cultural definition of work changed under Protestantism, giving rise to the development of capitalism. The subtext of Weber's study is an understanding of how modern work drives us ceaselessly and takes over more and more of our lives.

Emile Durkheim approached work as part of the study of the division of labor. In earlier, village societies (which he referred to as having mechanical solidarity), work was an expression of one's sameness to others; in modern societies (which Durkheim referred to as exhibiting organic solidarity), work represented the differences between people. The evolving division of labor was, for Durkheim, the key to understanding how and why societies change.

Although work was at the core of issues that compelled these and other sociologists' writing in the first decades of our discipline, almost no sociologists studied the cultural definition of work; none entered the factory, farm, or firm to understand how work was defined and managed by those who work. The closest thing to an ethnography of work in the early period of sociology was Frederick Engels's incredible book, *The Condition of the Working Class in England,* written in 1845 when the author was twenty-four years old. This book, which inspired Marx, was based on what we would now call intensive field research in the working-class slums and factories of industrial England. What is not generally known is that Engels, the son of a factory owner, was guided into the dark neighborhoods and oppressive factories by his working-class Irish girlfriend. All fieldworkers need an entry to the field!

The cultural study of work emerged in the United States during the 1920s as part of what was called the Chicago School of Sociology. At the University of Chicago's sociology department, sociologists did in-depth field studies of many institutions of urban society, including those surrounding work. One of these scholars was Everett Hughes, who earned his Ph.D. at the University of Chicago in 1927 for a study of the Chicago real estate board. Hughes later became the most important figure in the tradition we refer to as the "cultural study of work." If the subdiscipline has parentage, Hughes is its father.

Hughes's early research examined how occupations evolve into professions and how professions evolve and develop in different economic and social systems. During the 1930s and early 1940s, Hughes worked primarily in the areas of ethnicity and social psychology, returning to the study of work after he assumed the sociology chair at the University of Chicago in the late 1940s. Hughes became editor of the *American Journal of Sociology* in 1952 and devoted his first issue to the cultural study of work. His editorial foreword to that issue spoke of the "double burden" of sociologists to analyze the processes of human behavior free of time and place while also becoming "ethnologists of their own societies." Hughes spoke to the need to seek variety and contrast in case studies that would allow sociologists to study similar sociological processes from several vantage points. He was especially interested in his earlier question of how occupations claimed the status of a profession, and how those claims were typically contested, denied, or gained in small steps.

The first volume of the *AJS* under Hughes included papers that became classics in the subdiscipline. Donald Roy (1952) studied what he called "goldbricking" in the machine shop, whereby workers determined rates of production and kept those who produced too much in line. William Kornhauser (1952) studied the conflicting roles of Black union officials in a White union in which the officials' constituencies expected them to advance their cause and their supervisors expected the officials to keep their constituencies in line. Eli Chinoy (1952) examined the ideology of opportunity and the reality of limited job mobility among automobile workers who eventually shift their expectations of social mobility to their children. Howard Becker (April 1952) studied the vertical and horizontal mobility of Chicago schoolteachers in the context of the external factors that shape their profession. Finally, Ray Gold (1952) studied how janitors do the dirty work of clients whose incomes often are less than theirs.

These studies were among the first in American sociology to study work close up. This involved immersion in the setting for extended time, and observation and in-depth interviewing rather than surveying with written questionnaires. The cultural study of work extended the awareness that had developed during the heyday of the Chicago School of Sociology that social life could be profitably studied in concrete detail, by close observation, and with intuitive musings as well as analytical deduction.

## A BRIEF HISTORY OF THE
## CULTURAL STUDY OF WORK

Prior to the pioneering efforts of Hughes and his colleagues, a small number of cultural studies of work had found their way to publication. William Foote Whyte (1949) studied the social structure of the restaurant, and Oswald Hall (1948) analyzed the subjective construction of medical doctors' careers. Both of these themes—that is, the study of the coordinated lines of work that constitute the social structure of a work environment, and the study of the career as defined inwardly as well as by the calendar—became streams in the cultural study of work. Similarly, these studies showed the utility of examining what Hughes called "the humble and the proud," that is, the cultures of the most highly trained professionals in the society and the most mundane of service jobs.

The 1950s were dominated by the contributions of Hughes and, to a great extent, his student, Howard S. Becker. Hughes's contributions were largely theoretical. Among his insights was the understanding that in all work settings there was an ongoing struggle over who would control productive output. Donald Roy (1953, 1955) and others examined this phenomenon in the setting of the industrial machine shop. Becker studied jazz musicians and their relationship to audiences (September 1952), and the means by which public school teachers managed their clients and their careers (April 1952). Robert Wilson (1954) applied Whyte's perspective on teamwork in the restaurant to the operating room; and Fred Davis (1959) offered the first of many studies of the client and provider in a fleeting relationship, in this case in the taxicab. Becker and Blanche Geer (see chapter 3) examined the development of professional ideology in medical school. The study of occupations grew to include sailors, retail furriers, salesmen, garment workers, lawyers, and funeral directors. The 1950s established the sociology of work, and many of the studies noted here were subsequently read by several generations of sociologists. One senses in these studies the recognition that in the study of work, sociology could approach the concrete while examining theoretical issues.

During the 1960s, the cultural study of work in part followed sociology's increasingly critical orientation. Ethnomethodologists such as Egon Bittner (1967; see chapter 11, this volume) studied how the police on skid row keep the peace in settings where most denizens are lawbreakers. Jerry Jacobs's (1969) study of a social welfare agency applied Weber's understanding of rationalization to life in a bureaucracy. Studies of industrial work were developed in Eli Chinoy's study of assembly-line workers (1964), and Hughes's focus on the relationship between occupations and professions in several papers captured the interest of scholars studying law or medicine, funeral directors, and others. Important books included Becker and Hughes et al.'s 1961 study of occupational socialization in medical school, which began the decade, and Shostak's study of blue-collar life (1969), which ended it.

In the 1970s, Blanche Geer and Howard Becker studied occupational socialization in a five-year research project, "Educational Experiences for Non-college Youth," which eventually led to Geer's 1972 edited volume on work socialization. This was the first comparative study of work socialization, and it recalled Hughes's suggestion that the cultural study of work should be built from detailed case studies and comparisons between them.

In 1974 a journal devoted to the study of work, *Sociology of Work and Occupations*, published its inaugural issue. The journal has remained open to all sociological approaches to work, and several important cultural studies of work have found their way to print in the journal.

Several scholars who subsequently became major contributors to the subfield first published in the 1970s, including John Van Maanen, Robert Faulkner, Robert Bogdan, Jack Haas, and Gary Fine. The study of so-called deviant occupations, such as strippers and prostitutes, became common during the 1970s, and others studied how deviant activity such as theft or drug use were integrated into nondeviant work roles. Hochschild's study of the emotion work of airline stewardesses (1983) was the seminal study of emotion work. Subsequent studies of emotions on the job focused on how workers managed boredom, fear, anger, and love as part of the cultural mastery of work.

During the 1980s, sociologists began to study the impact of greater gender equality in the workforce. For example, Vaught's examination of women's experience of degrading initiation rituals in an underground coal mine (1980; see chapter 5, this volume), previously experienced only by men, opened up the question of the cultural effects of gender integration in specific occupations. Other women-oriented research examined the work experiences of female lawyers, truckers, assembly plant workers, seminary students, and corrections officers, as well as the impact of shift work on family life. Hochschild's concept of emotion work was applied to the study of sales, convenience store clerking, and professional sports. Several sociologists studied work in the arts, often focusing on the cultural definition of the career. Graham Tomlinson (1985; see chapter 9, this volume) studied how encyclopedia writers bend and break rules to produce their expected output, in fact making up truth as a way of processing the work demands of that job. Sociological attention was paid to the cultures of police, smokejumpers, psychiatrists, social workers in the ghetto, high steel workers (iron workers on skyscrapers), meat cutters, immigrant workers, and folk singers.

The decades of the 1970s and 1980s produced at least fifteen book-length studies of work cultures. These included Jonathan Imber's 1986 study of how medical doctors define and manage the concept of abortion in a practice that is designed to sustain and protect life. Mary Lorenz Dietz (1983) showed how professional hit men define and manage the violence that is at the core of their work. Douglas Harper, one of the editors of this volume, documented in his 1982 volume how railroad tramps were a hidden part of the migrant labor force in the agricultural West.

The most recent past, the 1990s until the present, has seen the continuing development of durable themes, such as professionalization, in the context of the developing professions. Researchers during this time continued to study how deviant activity is often part of nondeviant work cultures. Researchers began to study not only the integration of women into men's work but also the integration of men into what was previously women's work. In addition, researchers began to study jobs and occupations such as child care (including the work of nannies), female car sales, and low-status service jobs in fast-food restaurants and convenience stores that were usually gender specific.

Our brief overview has revealed certain patterns. Early studies concentrated on industrial and professional work. Of course, this was at a time before deindustrialization, and blue-collar life was a vital subject for sociological study. Similarly, the question of what role professions would have in the rapidly developing post–World War II society led sociologists to raise the question of the nature of professions in situ.

In the decades that followed, sociologists have studied most, but certainly not all, occupations listed in the census. Early emphasis was on themes such as the social organization of work and occupational socialization. The themes of routinization, dehumanization, and alienation have been explored in settings ranging from meat-packing plants to computerized clerking. Growing feminist orientation in sociology has led to the subject of domestic work (that is, what was previously termed "housework") and subsequently to the work experiences of women who broke gender barriers and entered work previously dominated by men. In recent years, researchers have turned to occupations and work settings that have traditionally been dominated by women, such as domestic service, childcare, and other "caring" professions. Finally, the study of emotion work that began with Hochschild's research has been widely applied to the cultural study of work.

## WHAT IS MISSING FROM THE CULTURAL STUDY OF WORK? WHAT REMAINS TO BE DONE?

There is no greater issue in the current configuration of work than globalization. Although the term is in vogue and thus is used sloppily, we find it has rather precise meaning in the context of work. We note that globalization sometimes moves modern jobs such as computer programming to people in places of the world, such as India, that are mostly still village cultures. In these circumstances, we imagine that third world computer programmers enter the modern work world through their modems. What work culture means in this context is not yet known, for no sociologists have studied this phenomenon.

We also recognize that globalization means moving jobs that have been defined as unacceptable in the United States and Europe to areas of the world where the heavy hand of international capital may still create factories in the mode of the mid-nineteenth century with long working hours, child labor, no unionization, plus low pay. Sociologists have made their way into some of these work settings and have produced studies such as Angelo Soares's (1991) study of work organization in Brazilian data processing centers. These work settings beg for more attention from sociologists and anthropologists.

Finally, globalization means the destruction of local work cultures. This might be Italian farmers whose specialty of mozzarella made with buffalo milk does not meet uniform standards imposed by the European community. In this instance, ethnographers might salvage at least the memory of these local work cultures. At best, ethnographic work will tell the story of work cultures that may, on second thought, fight their way into continued existence.

These and other matters of globalization may be easily considered a new mandate for those interested in the cultural study of work. It will mean getting access to work settings beyond the borders of the United States, researching in languages other than English, and seeing the dual mandates of comparative and ethnographic focus in a worldwide context. Since nearly all humans must work, it would appear that the intimate study of work in a global context is utterly appropriate for the expansion of international sociology.

Table I-1. Journal Articles and Significant Book Chapters on the Cultural Study of Work, by Decade

| 2000–2001 | 1990–1999 | 1980–1989 | 1970–1979 | 1960–1969 | 1950–1959 | 1940–1949 | 1930–1939 |
|---|---|---|---|---|---|---|---|
| 9 | 56 | 60 | 52 | 21 | 18 | 4 | 2 |

*Source:* Douglas Harper and Helene M. Lawson

## IMAGES OF WORK

The cover photograph and the photographs that appear at each part's introduction were taken by Douglas Harper, one of the coeditors of this book. Doug has been interested in photography since he was an undergraduate and has been long involved with using photography in sociology.

Most of these photographs were taken on sociological research projects, often outside the United States. Doug uses these images to suggest that the cultural processes of work exist cross-culturally and to remind us of the need to make sociology less ethnocentric. The sociology of work is still, unfortunately, mostly the sociology of U.S. work, and we hope that these photos will help encourage that to change.

We encourage students who are interested in the sociology or work and photography to become active in the International Visual Sociology Association (IVSA—visit our website at www.visualsociology.org) and to explore their own methods, perhaps visual, for studying the culture of work.

## CITED AND RECOMMENDED READING

Becker, H. S. "Social-Class Variations in the Teacher-Pupil Relationship." *Journal of Educational Sociology* 25 (April 1952): 451–65.

————. "The Professional Dance Musician and His Audience." *American Journal of Sociology* 57 (September 1952): 136–44.

Bittner, Egon. "The Police on Skid Row." *American Sociological Review* 32 (1967): 699–715.

Chinoy, Eli. "The Tradition of Opportunity and the Aspirations of Automobile Workers." *American Journal of Sociology* 57, no. 5 (1952): 453–59.

Davis, Fred. "The Cabdriver and His Fare." *American Journal of Sociology* 63, no. 2 (1959): 158–65.

Dietz, Mary Lorenz. *Killing for Profit: The Social Organization of Felony Homicide.* Chicago: Nelson-Hall, 1983.

Engels, Friedrich. *The Condition of the Working Class in England.* Leipzig: O. Wigand, 1845.

Geer, Blanche, ed. *Learning to Work.* Beverly Hills, Calif.: Sage, 1972.

Hall, O. "The Stages of a Medical Career." *American Journal of Sociology* 53 (March 1948): 327–36.

Harper, Douglas. *Good Company.* Chicago: University of Chicago Press, 1982.

Hughes, E. C. *Selected Papers on Work, Self and the Study of Society.* Bk. 2, *The Sociological Eye.* Chicago: Aldine, 1972.

Imber, Jonathan B. *Abortion and the Private Practice of Medicine.* New Haven, Conn.: Yale University Press, 1986.

Jacobs, Jerry. "Symbolic Bureaucracy: A Case Study of a Social Welfare Agency." *Social Forces* 47 (June 1969): 413–22.

Kornhauser, William. "The Negro Union Official: A Study of Sponsorship and Control." *American Journal of Sociology* 57, no. 5 (1952): 443–52.

Roy, Donald. "Quota Restriction and Goldbricking in a Machine Shop." *American Journal of Sociology* 57 (March 1952): 427–43.

————. "Work Satisfaction and Social Reward in Quota Achievement: An Analysis of Piecework Incentive." *American Sociological Review* 18 (October 1953): 507–14.

————. "Efficiency and 'The Fix': Informal Intergroup Relations in a Piecework Machine Shop." *American Journal of Sociology* 60 (1955): 255–66.

Soares, Angelo S. "Work Organization in Brazilian Data Processing Centers: Consent and Resistance." *Labour Capital and Society* 24, no. 2 (1991): 154–83.

Whyte, William Foote. "The Social Structure of the Restaurant." *American Journal of Sociology* 54 (January 1949): 302–10.

Wilson, Robert N. "Teamwork in the Operating Room." *Human Organization* 12 (winter 1954): 9–14.

# I

# WORK AS SOCIAL INTERACTION

*Netherlands Jazz*

The work of musical improvisation is based on intimate social interaction: initiating, listening, taking turns, building energy, and taking pause. Jazz performers are soloists and at the same time members of a team. They move between these roles with a glance or gesture or musical communication that few outside the jazz world would recognize. The improvisation is based on scales that derive from the chords that make up the song, so beneath the appearance of unbounded creativity is a structure of expectations and constraints. It is a good metaphor for the idea of social interaction in work.

Photo: Bimhus, a jazz club in Amsterdam, 1991, by Douglas Harper

A ll work is fundamentally rooted in social interaction. Work involves not only the organized interaction among individuals (such as people rowing a boat together) but also the unorganized, fleeting interaction between people, some who may be patients, customers, students, or clients of others. In fact, given that much of the work of modern society involves serving each other, communicating with each other, and convincing each other to do something, it is this dimension of interaction that preoccupies us in part I. This inquiry, however, should be placed into the context that reaches into earlier forms of work interaction.

If we think of work as physical problem solving that insures the survival of the group, it is easy to imagine preindustrial groups hunting, planting, harvesting, or building. Although work is a complex composite of small, integrated activities, the common gloss for such analysis is the division of labor. The division of tasks and the assigning of some tasks to one individual rather than another are both formal and informal. The formal division of labor in preindustrial groups may be on the basis of gender or age, whereas the informal assignment of task may be based on skill or opportunity. The division of labor makes it possible to achieve tasks that individuals alone could not accomplish. But although the division of labor may be rudimentary, the actual forms of cooperation are often complex.

Work interaction, even in its most physical manifestations, is partly cognitive. Physically working together leads to likeminded thinking. Workers share words, thus forming categories of meaning about work they do together. The importance of communicating is to coordinate activities. This leads to specialized vocabularies and eventually to larger and larger worldviews. Durkheim referred to this as the collective conscience that arises from simple divisions of labor. We now extend that to mean that work becomes the basis of stories, which become the fantasy of folktales. Constructing the folklore of work is one of its informal elements.

The interaction of work always combines formal and informal elements. There are the activities one is expected to do (if one works voluntarily) and the things one is compelled to do (if one works involuntarily), but these do not cover the range of activities that constitute work interaction. More informal elements of worker interaction take place in what sociologists have for a long time called "informal work groups." The organization of work interaction on the assembly line, for example, is rigid, but workers informally organize to lighten the burden of the line. The work group might, for example, work double time for short periods, allowing a worker an unofficial break. Although this might seem insignificant, it amounts to workers wresting control from the machines of production and the bureaucracy that drives them to pace their bodies at varying and thus more humanly dimensioned rates. Or the informal work group may be secretaries who decide together which of those for whom they work they will apply strict interpretations of rules and regulations. In this instance, it is the work group that collectively defines how the work will actually be accomplished for no rules are exhaustive and all are open to interpretation.

The organization of worker interaction is sometimes physical and rudimentary. The bodies all pulling oars on a ship, mimicked in the modern rowing scow, sense the rhythm of the stroke with little outside help. One guesses that the eventual pattern of movement has to do with the breathing pattern of the collective work group. The physical rhythm might be organized by song or chant, similar to how it happens when soldiers or schoolchildren march. Little modern work, however, is physical, collective, and not tied to the rhythm of a machine. Those who have experienced such physical, collective interactive work, however, often speak of the social identity and pleasure that arises from the experience.

Work interaction, however, is usually more complex, requiring more elaborate patterns and modes of communication. Think, for example, of the double-play combination in baseball, where infielders coordinate their actions to achieve a collective end. The players are trained to expect a set of movements that might take one of several versions, depending on where the ball is hit. The crack of the bat galvanizes four people to split-second movements to ball or base: a hard throw or an underhanded flip, an acrobatic jump over a sliding base runner, and a twisting spike across the baseball diamond. It is one of the most celebrated moments in sports. It seems automatic and lasts only for a second. Yet the choreographed interaction is guided by expression, movement, and gesture that take several minutes to describe.

We have spoken to this point about the physical interaction of work. Work interaction, however, might be purely mental. In an electronic age, this might be most fully embodied by two or more people, perhaps separated by thousands of miles, working through the Internet to solve any of a range of problems. The nonphysical interaction takes, in this and most cases, the form of dialogue. All who have "brainstormed" (a word that is probably derived from "barnstorming"—the freewheeling acrobatics of stunt pilots) have experienced the complexity and stimulation of the interplay of two or more minds collectively seeking new knowledge or at least new definition. This is certainly work as social interaction, but it is seldom studied as such.

We have considered work interaction directed to a common goal. The way we think of teamwork, for example, suggests the value we assign to the cooperative achievement of a common work goal, which is the topic of Wilson's 1954 article, included in this volume (see chapter 1). Work interaction, however, is not always directed to a common end, as we recognize ourselves as slaves on the galley, workers on the line, or small cogs in large organizations.

There are intermediate steps in which interacting parties might be only partly organized to gain the same end. That is the way it is with teaching. The teacher presumably wants to impart knowledge that students want to gain. All who have been a teacher or a student, however, know this description to be at best incomplete. One party is generally less interested in the interaction than the other. Perhaps young children are eager to learn and the teacher is weary. Or adolescents may feel the compulsion of bureaucratic mandate to remain against their wishes in school. Presumably in colleges and universities, the balance is more equal; students attend because they want to learn, and professors have gained their job of choice and are happy to be in the classroom. The complexities of learning in any classroom environment are, of course, much greater. The word "work" derives from the Greek "to bring forth." This infers dialogue, interaction, redefinition by both parties, and further interaction. But the idea that the teacher as well as the student learns from the interaction of teaching is a radical one. One can say that when the teacher stops learning (e.g., by delivering a written lecture to an anonymous hall of students), the interaction is over; education is no longer a dialogue, and most parties speak of boredom, meaninglessness, and alienation.

Work interaction includes bargaining. As we live increasingly in a contractual world, bargaining seems a quaint and out of place concept. If we travel to a nonindustrial country, we may be confronted, for the first time, with verbal haggling over prices that precede all fixed pricing in the marketplace. But bargaining has a larger meaning. Thinking of the interaction of work, the bartender bargains when he or she exchanges pleasant talk or feigns interest for a tip. The more expensive the item being sold, the more serious the interpersonal bargain. Thus the customer buying a new automobile may feel that he or she has entered into a relationship with a salesman or saleswoman that extends beyond the showroom floor. The salesperson must "cool out the mark" when the sale is complete; the relationship must be transferred to the service manager, but not completely. The salesperson wants, of course, for the buyer to retain just enough interest in their relationship to return when it is time again to buy a car. The relationship between editors and authors is sometimes similar. Authors, particularly after experiencing rejection by several editors, seek to establish relationships that exceed the narrow professional interests that tie them together. This, of course, changes when the authors become well-known; suddenly it is the editors who cultivate relationships in which subtle, off-the-record bargaining takes place. The nannies and au pairs studied by MacDonald (1998; see chapter 2) explore some of the bargains that extend into the emotional regions of family life.

These introductory remarks suggest some of the myriad of ways we might think of work as social interaction. The selections we've chosen show these ideas in the concrete circumstances of work or, in Howard Becker's phrase, "doing things together."

## CITED AND RECOMMENDED READING

Bell, M. "Tending Bar at Brown's: Occupational Role as Artistic Performance." *Western Folklore* 35 (1980): 93–107.

Bigus, Odis. "The Milkman and His Customers." *Urban Life and Culture* 1 (1972): 131–65.

Bjarnason, T., and T. Thorlindsson. "In Defense of a Folkmodel: The 'Skipper Effect' in the Icelandic Cod Fishery." *American Anthropologist* 95 (1992): 371–94.

Brass, Jay. "Dunners and Defaulters: Collectors' Work as a Context for Naming." *Urban Life* 12 (1983): 49–73.

Butler, William R., and William Snizer. "The Waitress-Diner Relationship: A Multimethod to the Study of Subordinate Influence." *Sociology of Work and Occupations* 3, no. 2 (May 1976.): 209–22.

Henslin, James, and Mae Briggs. "The Sociology of the Vaginal Examination." In *Down to Earth Sociology,* edited by James Henslin, 193–204. New York: The Free Press, 2001.

Miller, Stephen J. "The Social Basis of Sales Behavior." *Social Problems* 12 (1964): 15–24.

Murray, Susan B. "Child Care Work: Intimacy in the Shadows of Family Life." *Qualitative Sociology* 21, no. 2 (1998): 149–68.

Prus, Robert. "Pursuing Commitments: An Analysis of the Influence Work Involved in 'Closing Sales.'" *Qualitative Sociology* 11, no. 3 (fall 1988): 194–214.

Ronai, Carol Rambo. "Sketching with Derrida: An Ethnography of a Researcher/ Erotic Dancer." *Qualitative Inquiry* 4, no. 3 (1998): 405–20.

———. "The Next Night Sous Rature: Wrestling with Derrida's Nemesis." *Qualitative Inquiry* 5, no. 1 (1999): 114–29.

Roth, Julius. "The Treatment of Tuberculosis as a Bargaining Process." In *Human Behavior and Social Processes,* edited by A. M. Rose, 575–88. Boston: Houghton Mifflin, 1962.

Sanders, Clinton R. "Psyching out the Crowd: Folk Performers and Their Audiences." *Urban Life and Culture* 3, no. 3 (1974): 264–81.

Stein, Leonard J. "The Doctor-Nurse Game." *Archives of General Psychiatry* 16 (1964): 699–703.

# 1

## Teamwork in the Operating Room

*Robert N. Wilson*

Like all dramas, a surgical operation has certain important plots and sub-plots, a cast of characters, and a spatial setting. In narrative form, surgery at a large general hospital often occurs in a sequence such as the following:

"At seven o'clock in the morning, nurses have arrived on the surgical floor. They find maids finishing the cleaning of the operating suites and corridors. Notices of scheduled operations for the day are posted in prominent places, listing the patient's name, type of case, operating surgeon, and appropriate operating room. Orderlies and nurses aides are wheeling small tables into the rooms, with sterile equipment laid out ready to use. The charge nurse assigns to their respective cases the scrub nurses (who will actually assist the surgeon) and the circulating nurses (who will perform general tasks around the operating room such as fetching water and counting sponges).

"As the hour of surgery, eight o'clock, approaches, the scrub nurses are washing hands and arms in the small scrub rooms next to the operating rooms; when they are thoroughly washed, according to specific procedures and an allotted time, they slip into sterile gowns and gloves. Their scrubbing must precede that of the doctors, since the nurses will be expected to assist the latter in their scrubbing and gowning. The first patients are in the corridor or preparation room where they have been wheeled by an orderly, and they are already in a semi-conscious state from drugs of a sedative type.

"With the arrival of M.D.'s on the scene, the tempo of preparation increases. Nurses are now untying the sterile bundles and spreading instruments out for instant use. Usually, orderlies and the charge nurse are checking lights, suction hoses, etc. The anesthetist is setting up his tanks and dials at the head of the operating table. Internes and their more advanced colleagues, the surgical residents, are ordinarily scrubbing before the operating surgeon appears. Much joking and chatter occur between these younger doctors and the nurses. When the operating surgeon, an older and more dignified M.D., starts to scrub, the tone of levity may decrease markedly. His appearance signals an even more alert and faster level of preparation on the part of other members of the operating team. The nurses assist the doctors in dressing for surgery; they hold gowns ready for the doctors to step into when scrubbed, and when the gowns are on they tie them securely. They hold rubber gloves up so that the doctors can put them on more easily. At this stage, before the incision has even been made, the motif of watchful cooperation has been established between nurses and doctors in the process of gowning.

"Now the patient has been wheeled into the room and the anesthetist is busily caring for him, making him comfortable and applying anesthetic. (The anesthetist is the patient's direct 'companion' in this venture, the person who reassuringly sedates him and establishes a close personal connection.) In a difficult case, the surgeon has perhaps previously consulted a colleague about the technique he plans to use and what conditions he expects to find. As the moment of cutting draws nearer, however, he is 'on his own' as the captain of the team; his lonely responsibility is mitigated by the presence of younger doctors and nurses, but he must be the key decision-maker.

"At the signal from the anesthetist that the patient has reached a proper depth of unconsciousness, the surgeon makes his first incision. (The patient has already been draped and painted by the cooperation of house staff and nurses, under the surgeon's direction). Immediately, by spoken word or conventional hand-signals, the surgeon calls on the nurse for sponges and instruments; the young doctors assisting at the operation are brought into play to hold retractors and clamps which staunch the flow of blood and keep visibility good in the operative field. At each stage in events, the surgeon consults the anesthetist to keep check on the patient's condition. Some portions of the operation may actually be performed by the surgeon's assistants, although he is always in close supervision and handles the critical moves himself. It is a mark of status to be allowed to work in the operative field, and actual surgery is done only by well-trained resident doctors. Nevertheless, the familiarity gained by simply holding the wound open for the surgeon is a vital part of the young interne's experience.

"There are two parallel status lines at work in the room. The surgeon passes on commands to the senior resident, who in turn passes them to junior residents and internes. The scrub nurse likewise initiates action for the circulating nurse and any students present. These chains of authority are criss-crossed by orders from the surgeon to the scrub nurse, and from any doctor to any of the nurses; however action is seldom if ever initiated in reverse; nurses do not issue orders to any doctors, and the lower echelons rarely direct the activities of the higher.

"The operating surgeon, after finishing his major task, consults the anesthetist again with respect to the patient's general condition and the length of time required to close the wound. As the closing process begins, there is a visible relaxation of tension and vigilance; joking becomes more frequent, and the pace of work more leisurely. Before a stitch can be taken, however, the nurse must count the sponges used in the operation, as a safeguard against leaving foreign objects in the patient's body. Here, at least, the nurses do initiate action, for the surgeon waits for their assurance that the sponge count is correct.

"During the sewing-up phase, the junior members of the surgical team usually take a more prominent role than they have in earlier stages. Often the chief surgeon will remove his gloves and stand around chatting, or even leave the room entirely. The resident is left in charge, and he and the internes proceed to apply the finishing touches. After the sutures are all in place, the anesthetist takes charge of dressing the patient and moving him from the table to a cart which will return him to his bed. In this he is assisted by nurses and, usually, an orderly; sometimes the junior doctors will help out, but the chief surgeon is not engaged in this phase.

"At length the patient, anesthetist, and doctors leave the room. The nurses are last to leave, as they were first to arrive. They pick up the doctors' discarded gowns and gloves, and prepare the room for the next case. The whole process, requiring from 30 minutes to six or more hours, has included a large cast of characters exhibiting much communication. Yet they are so familiar with their jobs that the number of spoken words may have been slight."

A marvelous example of teamwork has taken place. Although innumerable orders have been given, most of them have flowed from the dictates of the patient's presence and condition. In a very real sense, few of the directives issued during surgery are arbitrary decisions on the surgeon's part. Rather, in the last analysis, the patient's needs have been the controlling element in the entire situation. Thus the person who seems to have been least capable of exerting authority—the prone, unconscious "object"—has in fact assumed the star role and has exercised the preponderant influence on the course of the drama.

In the days before modern techniques of asepsis had been developed, but after the idea of cleanliness had begun to be accepted in medicine, it was the custom to spray the operating area with an antiseptic solution. A certain noted surgeon, therefore, used to pause before the operation and intone, "Brethren, let us spray." Somehow this irreverent remark typifies an important aspect of life in the surgery; where the job to be done is intrinsically abnormal and fraught with anxieties, the atmosphere is deliberately made as mundane and casual as possible. In this most serious of situations, efforts are directed toward pulling the psychological climate into "normalcy." Like the small boy whistling past the graveyard, the inhabitants of the room make things prosaic; further, there is reason to think that energies must be mobilized for the work itself, not allowed to drain off in unproductive fear and trembling. While operating rooms are not truly places of levity, and *Ars Chirurgica* advises the surgeon to be "fearful in dangerous things," the pattern of joking and small talk is perhaps the most striking feature of surgery to the outsider. There is drama, but only a fraction of total operating time looks anything like the Hollywood stereotype of tight-lipped tenseness and mute solemnity. The self-consciousness which one would expect to characterize a person invading another's body, and literally "holding a life in his hands," is for the most part dispelled by technical considerations; a job must be done, a careful exacting task, and this is the focus of energy and intellect. Operating rooms, then, are workmanlike. The first impression dispels any thought of "constant crisis."

Every operating room is:

    A.  like *all* other operating rooms
    B.  like *some* other operating rooms
    C.  like *no* other operating rooms

This logical scheme was originally applied to the field of personality, but it fits the operating room equally well. In fact, it might well be said that the surgery *has* a personality of its own, a distinctive blend of characteristics setting it apart from the rest of the hospital. It is perhaps a misnomer to speak of "the" operating room; rather, there are probably many types of which may be classified in several ways.

## EVERY OPERATING ROOM IS LIKE
## *ALL* OTHER OPERATING ROOMS

What do all operating rooms share as identifying marks? At least the following features are proposed.

### Drama, Excitement, Intensity: An Air of Importance

Surgery is so obviously worthwhile and effective that it may be trite to comment on its importance. Yet there are many other aspects of medicine, and many aspects of every job, which lack the immediacy and lauded purpose of surgery. In the operating room, there can be no doubt that what is being done is dangerous and vital. Because we all share a belief in the importance of the body, because it is a basic part of the human being's security, any drastic manipulation (such as cutting) is cause for excitement. Further, the power to enter and change the body[1] signifies an immense responsibility on the surgeon's part, and insures that the atmosphere shall include a sense of awe. And there is an element of drama, despite the stricture that it does not resemble the movie version. Each operation is a problem, a challenge, whose course can be plotted but not thoroughly predicted. One piano chord in the old-fashioned cinema announced that "something is going to happen." Just so, in an operating room everyone knows that "something is going to happen."

As one graduate nurse expressed it:

> Down here you have the patient at the most critical time of his life and you know by the time he leaves the operating room what his chances are. You feel as if you are really important in his life. You're only with him a little while but still it's the critical time so far as he is concerned.

We have stressed the mundane aspects of operating room life, and pointed out the joking air which often precedes and follows the surgery, One can hear much talk of fishing trips, much mutual kidding, etc. All these contribute to a reduction of tension. But the tension exists; everything is *not* sweetness and light. A recurrent index of tension is the tendency to quick flareups of "temperament," of irritated and antagonistic remarks. Some impression of this index is gained from a record of part of an operation by an observer seated in the gallery.

"At this point, we have an interesting piece of interaction between the scrub nurse and Dr. M. The nurse hands him one swab, retaining another in her hand. He takes the swab as she hands it to him, and throws it angrily on the floor on the other side of the operating table. He asks, 'Is this phenol?' (referring to the swab left in her other hand). The nurse replies (pointing disgustedly to the floor) 'That one was phenol. This one is alcohol.' Dr. M.: 'When I called for phenol twenty minutes ago, I *meant* phenol. I've got to swab that whole end off. Now get me some phenol.' The nurse then fills a small cup with phenol and hands it to Dr. M. with a swab. This procedure he accepts.

"Dr. M. is now under great tension. It shows. His remarks become more brusque, irritated, profane. When the nurses have trouble getting a hose fixed up, he says, 'Let's get going here. Dammit, it takes twenty minutes to do a thing and there is one way to do it right.' The nurses begin to count sponges in a fairly loud voice. M. shouts to them, 'Stop counting sponges! Don't do *anything* until I stop this bleeder.' A moment later he shouts at Y (the assistant resident), 'Pull back those fingers, Jesus, let's see this thing'"

## Emphasis on Teamwork and Cooperation

It might be said that every operation is a *co*-operation. In surgery, no one can "go it alone"; each person is dependent on many others, and the patient is of course dependent on all members of the team. So necessary is team-work, in the nature of the job, that even individuals who are personally antagonistic often act in concert during the course of surgery. (In this, the operating team is like a jazz band or baseball club. Legend has it that the members of the famous double-play combination of Tinker to Evers to Chance did not speak off the field for many years.) The individuals compos-ing an operating team are so close-knit, and understand the task at hand so thoroughly, that verbal signals are often unnecessary. A language of gesture has developed whose meanings are crystal clear to persons following the operation intently. Perhaps the outstanding examples of intuitive co-operation occur in these pairs of team members:

surgeon—nurse
surgeon—anesthetist
surgeon—assistant surgeon

To the nurse, the intimate comprehension of the surgeon's technique, and his recognition of her competence, may become a prime reward of her job. The desirability of a close harmony is recognized as is illustrated by the comments of an operating nurse and a surgeon respectively:

"Morale is high in the operating room because there is a team spirit. The finest point in the nurses' life comes when she is finally taken in and fully accepted as a member of the team. On a certain day, everything changes. There is almost a clean break with the past. . . . The surgeon will recognize you and call you by name. A kind of emotional block is broken, and you know you are accepted. Any nurse feels very wonderful about this. The main reward for doing operating-room nursing lies in a special relationship with the surgeon."

"Both instruments and nurses have to be worked with for a couple of years before you know them. If she (nodding at nurse) stayed with the same guy for two years she would do everything before he even asked for it."[2]—A senior resident

It is obvious that the surgeon and anesthetist must work together. The degree of anesthesia to be given a patient depends on the type of operation and the various stages in its progress. Conversely, the surgeon must be kept informed of changes in his patient's condition. One interview note states:

"We then got into a discussion of how the anesthetist works. Dr. D. described as perhaps the most important point a close cooperation with the operating surgeon. He said it is desirable that the anesthetist know the sur-geon well, know his technique, and be able to co-operate with him almost automatically."

## Technical Criteria and "the Religion of Competence"

All operating rooms place great stress on efficiency and expertness. In part, this is due to the complicated nature of surgical work; the fact that it rests on an exacting knowledge of multiple factors. The irascible surgeon who is highly skilled, and thereby gains respect, is a familiar figure. Unpleasant personal characteristics may often be overlooked if competence is high enough. The judgment of colleagues and nurses soon enough labels any doctor according to the degree of mastery he is observed to exercise, and the palm goes to the expert.

In part, too, the importance of cleanliness contributes to a desire for efficiency. The rituals connected with sterility promote a precise mode of behavior which infuses the nonsterile portions of technique. Surgical work is, by definition, careful.

The surgical job itself is such a demanding one in terms of exactitude that it draws all related jobs into the orbit of mechanical perfection. Because surgery must be orderly, the tasks which facilitate it are also orderly. "A neat job," then, can describe everything from a virtuoso performance by a heart surgeon to the measured folding of towels by a nurse's aide.

In the surgery, all tasks are "obvious" and can be quickly judged by ideal criteria; nowhere is the American talent for the admiration of "know-how" more clearly expressed. It is plain that the emphasis on technique and precision is necessary to high-level effort in surgery. Yet we may also mention the possibility that some portion of this emphasis serves a subsidiary function: it keeps the hands and mind busy on detail in a setting where excess imagination or sensitivity might interfere with the psychological boldness required. Inspection, not introspection, is the imperative of operating room activity.

## The Surgeon's Authority

> The surgeon is like the captain of a ship. He is ultimately responsible for everything that happens in the operating room.
>
> —Chief of surgery

Huge responsibilities demand huge grants of power, for responsibility and power must be in some way commensurate. The surgeon's authority is unquestioned, it would seem, because of three interrelated factors. First, there is the right relation between authority and responsibility; a person held to account for something must, fairly, be in a position to affect the process by which the thing comes about. Second, the surgeon stands at the very top of a skilled hierarchy. He is not a replaceable part, and, ideally, he knows more about the job at hand than anyone else in the room. Therefore, it is natural that he would be vested with the authority to direct the work on grounds of competence. Third, there is an aura of magic and reverence surrounding the figure of the surgeon; this aura has its roots in the ancient connection of priest and healer. When the three factors are combined, one sees a potent basis of authority. Although the authority is mitigated in several ways, it is a "constant" characteristic of the surgery. Relaxation of power may occur when long acquaintance and close work relations, especially those between doctor and nurse, have visited the third factor, the priestly aura or "charisma." Implicit or explicit resistance (or rarely, transgression) to authority often stems from a surgeon's failure to fulfill wholly the standards of competence, so that respect is weakened. At any rate, the overpowering nature of the surgeon's position is almost certain to produce an undercurrent of resentment among lower-status members of the work team. This is illustrated in the exasperated aphorism of an operating room nurse: "Nurses spend half their lives waiting on doctors, and the other half waiting *for* them."

## Physical and Psychological Isolation from the Rest of the Hospital

For reasons of sterility and general work flow considerations, the operating suite is always separated from the hospital as a whole. It has its own floor, or part of a floor, and is for most purposes a "closed system." Although patients must be brought to surgery and taken back to their beds when the operation is over, this task is performed by orderlies, and other hospital personnel rarely visit the surgery. Of course casual visiting is prohibited, since nonessential onlookers would tend to disrupt the precision of work, and might increase the danger of infection.[3]

The isolation of the operating room means that, in the eyes of other employees, this area is strange and forbidding. All nonsurgical people are in a fundamental sense on the "outside" and may be curious about what occurs in the sanctum. They have, further, a definite attitude of awe and admiration for the activities that go on there and the "initiates."

Conversely, the surgical staff, from doctors to maids, develop a strong feeling of camaraderie. They recognize their status and role as a special group. Their world is the surgery, not the hospital. This implies great warmth and cohesion, as well as agreement on a variety of values. They must and do learn to live together as an elite corps.

## EVERY OPERATING ROOM IS LIKE *SOME* OTHER OPERATING ROOM

There seem to be a number of types of operating room, which share certain secondary characteristics. These qualities are like an overlay, supplementing and modifying, but not drastically changing the conditions noted above.

## The Extent of Teaching Carried On

On this factor, operating rooms may vary from those that include no personnel in training to those that involve students, nurses, internes, and residents. Obviously, in the teaching situation, part of everyone's energy must go into the initiation process. The presence of students keeps people on their toes, keeps an air of questioning and striving alive, which infuses the surgery. Out-dated and incompetent elements, be they surgeons, nurses, or surgical techniques, have little chance of survival.

Methods and attitudes undergo constant changes, as the operating room keeps pace with the advance of medical science. And the surgery is "conscious" of its work, measuring and evaluating it in the light of high criteria of excellence. The stress on *competence* is heightened because every case is in one sense a model for the learners.

Division of labor is pushed further in teaching hospitals. For one thing, more hands are available; for another, there is a constant effort to split off suitable practice tasks which can give a student experience and afford him a gradual introduction into the core of the operation. Both nurses and doctors in training follow a series of stages, whereby they approach ever more closely the condition of standard excellence. Nurses move from circulating duties to scrub nurse, from easy to hard cases. Internes and residents progress from holding retractors and stitching incisions to the actual work of the operating surgeon. The accentuated division of labor means that coordination of all the parts is more difficult to achieve, and therefore planning is essential. Since a very large number of people are involved, interpersonal relations take on added significance; morale and skill must be high to insure smooth functioning.

Differences in prestige are multiplied in the teaching situation. The ladder of status has many extra rungs, within both medical and nursing staffs. Thus we find not only the invariant distinction between surgeon and nurse, but finer distinctions between scrub nurse and circulating nurse, between chief surgeon, assistant surgeon, resident, and interne. These gradations have the advantage of inducting "raw" individuals through manageable stages, so that they are not thrust from student to full professional in a single immense jump. However, they also tend to increase social distance and multiply the opportunities for friction. An amusing account of status-laden behavior, as told by two operating room nurses, will illustrate the theme:

"They asked the question, 'Who is the first person to leave the operating room after an operation? And immediately answered it with, 'The surgeon, of course.' They said first the surgeon steps back from the table, takes off his gown and gloves, throws them in a heap on the floor and walks out of the room. Then the lesser fry close up the incision and then they leave, also stripping off their gowns and gloves and dropping them in a heap any place on the floor. They described how even the young resident will rip off a towel from the operating table, perhaps with several instruments on it, and just throw it to the floor while preparing the patient to go back downstairs, and then the resident will wait for the nurse to untie his gown and stalk away. After everyone has gone, the nurse or nurses and the anesthetist are left to clear up the place and to get the patient back downstairs. Miss R. exclaimed, 'After the great big doctors are all finished, who do you think moves the patient back on the stretcher to take him downstairs? The nurse of course.' At this point Miss M. interjected, 'Yes that is what happens. They just walk out after shouting at you for two solid hours.'"

The fact of teaching means that each stage in surgery itself will be carefully scrutinized and explained. Although not all surgeons converse during the course of an operation, it is usual for the surgeon, his assistant, and/or the senior resident to carry on a running commentary, describing the significance of the work at hand. In recent years there has been a shift away from didactic teaching in medicine: one demonstrator or lecturer confronting a mass of students. The stress now falls on clinical teaching which introduces material to the student through his active participation in a case. Thus the learners at an operation will be scrubbed up and actually assisting, rather than watching from the gallery. (Few operating rooms are now being constructed with amphitheaters, as a result of this trend.)

Problems are introduced by the teaching emphasis, many of them concerning the amount of participation allowed to the student. In surgery, only one man can operate; in the teaching of medicine, multiple diagnoses of the same individual may be made for practice purposes. There is a story of a young interne which points up the dilemma. After a particularly impressive piece of surgery, the doctors retired to the surgeons' lounge just off the operating room. The chief, who had performed the operation, began discussing it with his team. At length, turning to a very young interne whose duty at the operation had been to hold the distal end of the retractor, the great man asked, "And what did you learn from this operation, my boy?" The interne replied, "I think I have definitely established, sir, that the assistant resident has a terrible case of dandruff." Yet a chief of neurological surgery has commented that in his own experience the gradual progression up the ladder of responsibility was an excellent introduction to his specialty. He noted especially the fact that the slow rise to a central position in the operating team insured that he would not feel too much pressure when he at length held full authority, that he would not feel "on the spot" in his first cases as operating surgeon.

Non-teaching hospitals lack the special difficulties involved in this sort of on-the-job education. On the other hand, they also lack the detailed explanations to members of the team, and the general air of competence and easy expertness which the presence of distinguished chiefs instills.

It might also be pointed out that non-teaching hospitals have no scapegoats as ready at hand as students. A latent function of student nurses and internes would seem to be found in their position as legitimate targets for the impatience and anxieties of graduate nurses or surgeons. Without disrupting the rapport of key team members, it is possible to vent anger at the circulating nurse who trips over her own feet, or the interne who is woolgathering when he should be watching the operation.

## The Difficulty of the Case in Progress

The relative seriousness of an operation determines many features of an operating room. For instance, in general terms, more difficult cases imply the involvement of more personnel, greater lengths of time, greater number of instruments, etc. In these important ways, a chest operation in Hospital X will be more nearly like a chest operation in Hospital Y than like a hemorrhoidectomy in Hospital X. While it is true that no two pieces of surgery are ever exactly alike, the major varieties show definite similarities.

In a fairly easy case, the atmosphere of the room tends to be rather relaxed and the requirements of strict attentiveness and speed on the part of all concerned are less rigorous. The tension which introduces friction into casual interaction is largely absent. However, in avoiding the extremes of pressure, the operating team misses the excitement and feeling of importance that accompany a major challenge to skill. Thus there may be complaints that the work is dull or routine, that the challenge is not great enough to hold one's interest at a high, sustained level.

Because fewer people work on a minor operation, the need for precise coordination is also less pronounced. In the teaching hospital, these cases are often used as opportunities for the young student to begin testing his own skills. A surgical resident may be given a vein ligation as his first solo flight, or a student nurse may serve as scrub nurse on the same type of operation. It is not true that these cases are taken "casually," but they do include a greater margin for error and seldom require split-second timing.

Since minor cases are usually short, the factor of fatigue is also less critical. In a long exacting surgical effort, physical exhaustion may cause outbursts of temper; mistakes may be less well tolerated toward the close of a lengthy job. Often a long case will involve shifts of personnel, especially nurses, thus adding to the need for tight coordination. The more difficult work, sometimes requiring six or even eight consecutive hours, points up the need for physical endurance in surgical personnel. A noted surgeon once remarked the possession of "good legs" as one of the qualities of a competent surgeon, since long hours of standing are so often necessary.

These two characteristics—the extent of teaching and the nature of the operation—may be viewed as scales having various values. Any operation will fall at a certain point on each scale, and share the qualities of that point with other operating rooms to form a "type." Thus we might speak of "major surgery in a teaching hospital," or "minor surgery in a small, non-teaching hospital," and find many elements in common within the designated category. There are undoubtedly other characteristics which contribute to a classification of operating rooms (for instance, whether the surgical staff is "open" or "closed") but these seem to be the most critical.

## EVERY OPERATING ROOM IS LIKE
## *NO* OTHER OPERATING ROOM

Three elements appear to account for the unique quality of each operating room—and, for that matter, of each single operation. They are

1. the personality of the surgeon.
2. the personality of the nurse.
3. the creative course of surgery itself.

Certain facets of the surgeon and nurse's personality have already been discussed, those features which seem to be invariant. Such, for example, are the factors associated with tension and fatigue (stereotypes of the "irritable" surgeon or the "snippy" nurse) or connected with formal lines of status and authority (the "authoritarian" surgeon, or "subservient" nurse). But over and above these behaviors which seem to be determined by "the situation" are a host of actions, attitudes, and traits which make each individual, in surgery or anywhere, unique.

An interview with a clinical instructor, a graduate nurse, provided an interesting illustration of the variations introduced by the surgeon's particular tastes in the matter of talking and joking during an operation:

" 'The operating room,' said Miss D, 'takes its tone from the personality and attitude of the surgeon. It is not a joking place if the surgeon does not make jokes, and not a talking place if the surgeon does not like to talk while operating.' She described several different staff members and their variations in operating-room leadership and atmosphere. She said that Dr. T's operating room was always very friendly and filled with witty exchanges, while Dr. H's, although friendly, was strictly business. One distinguished surgeon allows no talking whatever in his room, while another is so jovial that he always remarks during an operation that he considers himself very lucky to have been given the very best nurses available for *his* operation."

Nurses, too, may be impersonal or warmly involved, although they do usually follow the surgeon's lead. When a nurse and surgeon are extremely well-acquainted, and have between them the bond of countless shared experiences, their mutual personality adjustment may greatly enhance the technical efficiency of the team.

Surgery takes a different course each time it is performed. This is natural, since the bodies of patients are by no means uniform. But the truly individual character of some few operations stems from the creative element in new types of surgery. Perhaps a maneuver is being performed for the first time; perhaps the operation is exploratory and uncovers an unexpected cancer; perhaps a dramatic turn of events provokes an unanticipated crisis. In any event, something has been added to routine, and the operating room acquires a distinctive aura of excitement and discovery. In surgery, as in any other creative activity, there is room for novel aspects which thwart the attempt at rigid classification. Part of the peculiar charm and attraction of the operating room lies in this creative facet, the fact that routine may always be upset. If there were no possibility for innovation and inspiration, if surgery were really "routine," it is unlikely that it would attract the caliber of persons who *are* attracted to an operating room team.

## NOTES

Reprinted from *Human Organization* 12 (winter 1954): 9–14. Used with the permission of the Society for Applied Anthropology.

The material on which this article is based was gathered when Dr. Wilson was a research associate (1951–1954) at the New York State School of Industrial and Labor Relations, Cornell University, engaged in a field study of several hospitals. The study was part of a larger project sponsored by the American Hospital Association. The research was under the general direction of Temple Burling, M.D. Miss Edith M. Lentz was the field work supervisor and senior research associate. The Carnegie Corporation of New York has provided the major support for this study.

1. It has been remarked by many observers that in some sense the body on the table is no longer a human being in his fullest significance. The "person" becomes an "object," so that a complete emotional response to him (it) is no longer necessary or possible. As the chief surgeon once remarked to an observer seated in the gallery of the operating room: "This is a man; just wait, we'll put him back together and you'll see."

2. It should be noted that this comment, while perhaps not "typical," illustrates more than a simple stress on intimacy and experience. It expresses also the prestige difference between the two main hospital roles, with the surgeon implicitly derogating the nurse role by comparing her with an "instrument" or tool of the doctor.

3. The separate, confined spatial arrangement of the surgery may, in some cases, contribute to the surgeon's feeling of tension. He, the captain, is alone with the heavy responsibility of a difficult job. In one hospital, perhaps inadvertently, the physical

arrangement was such that fellow surgeons might drop by the open door to the scrub room for a casual chat and for consultation. The door leading to the hospital corridor remained closed, but the scrub room entrance, always open, provided easy access for interested colleagues. Numerous observations demonstrated convincingly that certain elements of support were derived from this "open-door" situation.

# 2

## Manufacturing Motherhood: The Shadow Work of Nannies and Au Pairs

*Cameron L. Macdonald*

Contemporary working mothers and child care providers are actively involved in a process of redefining motherhood. The nexus of this redefinition involves the negotiation of child-rearing practices, of who does what and what that division means. This transformation results in part from what Arlie Hochschild (1989) terms the second half of the "Stalled" industrial revolution. In the early 19th century, working men moved out of their home-based economies into the wage labor market.[1] More than a century later, large numbers of women in the United States, including mothers of young children, have moved into the paid labor force.[2] During the first half of the stalled revolution, market-bound fathers were replaced as a presence in the family by homebound, omnipresent mothers; during the second half, working mothers are frequently replaced by paid caregivers.

This article explores how women defined what it means to delegate "mother-work" to a paid child care provider, and how working mothers and paid caregivers negotiate the division of mothering labor.[3] In this research I define mother-work as those daily tasks involved in the care and protection of small children. For example, in interviews with mothers and paid caregivers, I asked about various mothering practices, including feeding, diapering, bathing, disciplining, putting children to bed, and playing with them. I also asked them about the relational tasks involved in mother-work: the soothing, stimulating, and connecting that are part of the everyday practices of connecting with infants and toddlers.[4] This definition of mother-work excludes other important aspects of mothering, such as conceiving, gestating, and

21

bearing children. Although separate from motherhood as a social role or identity, mother-work represents a large component of what it *means* to be a mother and to experience mothering. Therefore, the practice of delegating mother-work in relationship with a paid caregiver might fundamentally challenge our understanding of what it means to mother (Saraceno 1984; Uttal 1996).

Yet this delegation of mothering to paid child care providers is practiced within a cultural context that paradoxically values "intensive mothering" (Hays 1996). Sociologist Anne Oakley (1974: 187) referred to his "myth of motherhood" as the belief that "all women need to be mothers."[5] Clearly this view of motherhood offers no legitimate place for other caregivers, and paid child care is at best a necessary evil. Yet this belief system, and particularly its emphasis on the singular mother-child bond, contradicts the lived experience of most mothers. Despite the predominance of "intensive mothering" as a cultural value, in 1995, 60% of children under 6 were in nonparental child care, and 79% of those children were cared for by a nonrelative (U.S. Bureau of the Census 1996: 400). The practice of mother-work in the 1990's for most women obviously includes the use of paid caregivers. We live in a unique historical moment: full-time, at-home mothering is no longer the dominant mothering practice, even for middle- and upper-class women, yet the ideology associated with this practice is still powerful.

This research does not investigate whether or not children should be in child care, whether mothers work, or what form of child care is best suited to small children. Instead, it asks, given that the majority of women work outside of the home, and given that the dominant values concerning child rearing hearken back to the 1950s when the majority of middle-class mothers stayed home, how do working mothers and paid child care providers make sense of their shared mother-work?

The division of mother-work is an "ongoing interactional accomplishment" (DeVault 1991: 95). Working mothers and mother-workers must negotiate a shared understanding of what delegated mother-work means. Just as West and Zimmerman (1987) have argued that men and women "do" gender as "situated doing, carried out in the virtual or real presence of others who are assumed to be oriented to its production," we can understand the negotiations between mothers and paid caregivers as one aspect of "doing" motherhood (West and Zimmerman 1987: 127). Of course, the negotiation of the division of mother-work with paid caregivers is only one of the ways that mothers "do" motherhood: they interact with their children, their partners or co-parents, their extended families and friends, their social relations within the work place, and with themselves. All of these relationships entail some form of "display" that constitutes the self as a mother (Goffman 1976: West and Zimmerman 1987). Further these displays are shaped by social, cultural, and economic constraints. Mothers perform mothering tasks within a given context; social class, ethnicity, marital status, urban or rural environment, all shape how a woman "does" motherhood and how she negotiates divisions of mother-work with others (Glenn 1994).

Nannies and mothers "do" motherhood as a set of caregiving practices, but their negotiations also involve creating the rules and policies that structure an employer-employee relationship. Both nannies and mothers "consent," for different reasons, to an implicit work relation that "manufactures" an image of the mother to coincide with the tenets of intensive mothering (Burawoy 1979). In so doing, they reinforce a particular idealized version of motherhood, and simultaneously obscure the underlying reality of the practice of shared mother-work. Further, mothers and nannies manufacture this image of motherhood in tacit agreement, although their working relations are replete with conflict and contradiction. Finally, this belief in intensive mothering, and in the need to manufacture a view of mother-work that coincides with that belief, creates demands for what I term "shadow motherhood" on the part of child care workers. For child care workers, "shadow motherhood" means not only performing mother-work, but masking the fact that they are doing so. Mothers and child care providers collude in shoring up the myth of nuclear family self-sufficiency (Hertz 1991), by creating an image of the mother that coincides with the "intensive mothering" ideal (Hays 1996), and which obscures the everyday reality of shared mother-work.

## RESEARCH DESIGN

This article is part of a larger study examining how working mothers and child care providers negotiate the division of mothering labor within the context of in-home care:[6] who does what mothering tasks and, more importantly, what meanings are assigned to those tasks. This research emerges out of several lines of inquiry in recent scholarship on the family and the work of the home. Scholars have explored how caregiving work is both socially devalued and personally fulfilling (Abel and Nelson 1990; DeVault 1991). Others have examined the changing conditions of mothering as more mothers with young children work outside of the home (Garey 1995; Hays 1996; Uttal 1996). Research on domestic workers (Colen 1989; Dill 1988; Glenn 1986; Rollins 1985; Romero 1992) and on child care workers (Colen 1995; Enarson 1990; Joffe 1977; Murray 1995; Nelson 1990; Rutman 1996; Saraceno 1984; Wrigley 1995) has revealed a great deal about their working conditions and the power dynamics in their negotiations with their employers. This study focuses on the intersection of commodified caring work, the changing experience of mothering, and the role of paid caregivers in producing family life: specifically, it explores the production and negotiation of a particular type of shared mother-work.

To explore these issues, I conducted in-depth interviews with fifty-eight women: thirty-six child care providers and twenty-two working mothers who employ them. In twenty-eight cases, I interviewed the child care provider and the mother from the same family. The child care providers in this study represent the range of in-home care: one-third were European au pairs, one-third were American women working as nannies, and one-third were immigrants—both legal and illegal, primarily women of color.[7] The mothers were predominantly white, professional-class women, and all were married. Of the twenty-two mothers interviewed, three were women of color. Approximately one-half of the caregivers worked on a live-in basis, while the others worked full-time in their employers' homes but maintained their own residences.

I focused specifically on in-home child care, arrangements with nannies, au pairs, and full-time babysitters because these child care situations present a one-to-one negotiation between parent and provider in its most crystallized form. Unlike either center-based or family day care arrangements, only in the in-home care arrangement is there a direct, unmediated, negotiation between parent and provider over the terms of the child care arrangement.[8] I also limited the study to certain types of in-home care arrangements. I looked for working mothers who worked at least thirty hours per week outside of the home, and so had to rely on a child care provider for thirty-five or more hours per week, because these mothers are faced with having to delegate a large portion of their mother-work to someone else and to depend on that person in a way that mothers who can work at home, or who can work part-time, are not.

Because the study focuses in part on the effects of the ideology of intensive mothering, I limited the study to families with at least one child under school age at the time that they used in-home care. Most advice exhorting women to stay home from work with their children focuses on the period from birth to age three (Belsky 1990; Fraiberg 1977). I also limited the study to arrangements in which the caregiver's work is defined as child care only, rather than housekeeping with a child care component.[9] Finally, I limited the study to commodified care arrangements—that is, child care relationships that began as employer-employee relationships, rather than child care relationships with friends, neighbors, or kin.

All of the interviews were taped, transcribed, and then coded. The majority of the interviews took place at the respondent's home or workplace. I interviewed some respondents two to three times over a period of years, but most were interviewed once. Interviews ranged from 90 minutes to four hours in length and covered a number of topics, ranging from the choices that led them to their current situation, to the events of a typical day, to their feelings and beliefs about their child-rearing relationships. Although I followed the same interview topic guide for all of the interviews, the interviews were loosely structured, allowing room for respondents to raise questions and issues that they deemed salient.

I located respondents using a variety of means: advertising in local newspapers, visiting playgrounds, contacting nanny agencies, and posting flyers. Most respondents, however, were contacted through a modified snowball method. In order to avoid too much overlap among respondents, I interviewed no more than three women from the same social network. A research assistant fluent in Spanish recruited and interviewed Latin American immigrant nannies.[10] Although the sample was primarily a sample of convenience, I used a theoretical sampling strategy to ensure that respondents represented the broadest possible range within the universe of commodified in-home care (see Glaser and Strauss 1967: 45–77). For example, I sought nannies and au pairs from various backgrounds and with differing levels of experience. I also interviewed working mothers with children at various stages of development and with differing on-the-job pressures and demands. Nevertheless, the nature of the child care relationship limited the sample primarily to mothers with professional and managerial careers, who were predominantly white and married.[11]

## INTENSIVE MOTHERING

During the latter half of the twentieth century, "the ideology of intensive mothering" became a widely accepted belief system (Hays 1996: 9). This set of child-rearing guidelines encompasses the view that child rearing should be "child centered, expert guided, emotionally absorbing, labor intensive, and financially expensive," and should be performed by the mother alone (Hays 1996: 69). The concept of intensive mothering is psychologically defined— that is, we understand it as resulting from a set of child-rearing practices aimed at creating a psychological bond with a young child. For example, under the dictates of this belief system, mothers of small children should breast feed, not only for nourishment, but for the purposes of bonding; they should provide age-appropriate stimulation and interaction; and they should carefully monitor their child's cognitive and emotional development.

Intensive mothering is also considered a full-time job, at least during the first three to four years of life. It assumes that children require one primary caregiver: the biological or adoptive mother. It further assumes that the umbilical connection in some sense goes unsevered: that as the primary caregiver, the mother is ideally best suited to comprehend her child's needs and can interpret and respond to those needs intuitively. In return, her child should prefer her above all others. Consequently, the child rearing ideology of white middle-class America conceives of the care of young children as indivisible, and as exclusively the mother's terrain, with perhaps the addition of an enlightened participatory father or partner. Household employees and child care workers are conspicuously absent from this child rearing model.

The stakes are high for women who embrace the tenets of intensive mothering. The grown child is the "finished product" of the mother's labor, and a reflection on her worth and ability as a mother. The child rearing literature advocating this model of motherhood states that if mothers are to transmit to their children a sense of security and well-being, and ensure their accomplishment as mothers, they must successfully perform all of these activities during the critical phases of infancy and early childhood. And, if a child experiences difficulties later in life, it is often assumed that these difficulties stem from some lack or failure on the mother's part during this early period.

The working mothers in this study are generally professional or managerial workers whose partners have equally demanding careers. They do not represent working mothers generally, but instead they are upper-middle-class mothers who have more financial resources than most working mothers. They also hold "male careers" in which they face the expectation that childbearing will not interfere with their devotion on the job (Hertz 1986; Hochschild 1975; Schwartz 1989). They do, however, embody a particular ideal: they represent what Hochschild (1989) has termed "the woman with the flying hair," briefcase in one hand, child's hand in the other, striding confidently out into the day. One of the myths that has emerged concerning this "superwoman" typology is that she manages to balance a demanding career with equally demanding expectations about mothering without showing the strain and without any help (Hertz 1986). To a large extent, the mothers that I have selected represent the women who have come closest to this mythical ideal. The mothers I have interviewed also represent a class of women for whom the transition to working motherhood is most jarring. All but four of the mothers I interviewed were raised by at-home mothers when they were young. So unlike poor working mothers whose own mothers may have worked outside of the home even during the heyday of the housewife, these mothers engage in a mothering practice that is at odds with how they were raised and, to some degree, with their own child-rearing values.

These working mothers negotiate a compromise between demanding careers and their desire to provide the best possible care for their children by hiring a mother-surrogate to take their place during the working day. They cite as key benefits of in-home child care the flexibility of having a nanny "on call" who can adapt her work schedule to the exigencies of their careers, and the sense of control over their children's care that comes from bringing a provider to live and work under their supervision. So at least for the hours that they are at work, these mothers seek to *hire* an individual who will provide a nurturing environment for their children, rather than to *be* that nurturing individual themselves. Yet this compromise has emotional and psychological costs, particularly for those mothers who believe in the value of intensive mothering.

## CHILD CARE AS SHADOW WORK

Ivan Illich coined the term "shadow work" to refer to "that entirely different form of unpaid work which an industrial society demands as a necessary complement to the production of goods and services" (Illich 1981: 99–100). Often referred to as reproductive labor, or "women's work," shadow work is devalued, frequently invisible, and unpaid. Arlene Kaplan Daniels (1987) elaborates this distinction. She argues that reproductive labor is "invisible work" in part because much of it is difficult to conceptualize in market exchange terms. Thus, our common-sense understanding of what "counts" as work obscures work that is unpaid, work that takes place in the private sphere, and interactive work traditionally performed by women (Daniels 1987; Macdonald 1996).

Many activities included in reproductive labor are also viewed as "naturally feminine" and therefore not as skilled labor, but instead as the simple enactment of innate propensities. Therefore, we tend not to view many of women's skills as valuable or as requiring effort (Daniels 1987: 408). Thus we expect women to be "naturally" good listeners; similarly, nannies' employers expect them to "naturally" love the children in their care. As Daniels argues, relegating these qualities to the realm of "natural" human behavior further obscures the effort entailed in producing them (Daniels 1987: 410). Our failure to recognize the performance of certain tasks as work thus deprives those who undertake them of important validation. Daniels (1987: 408) further notes that "any recognition of an activity as work gives it a moral force and dignity—something of importance in a society." Therefore, conceptual distinctions between productive and reproductive labor, labor for money and labor for love, market work and shadow work, devalue tasks not easily commodified or understood as part of an economy based on market exchange. Ironically, many of the tasks understood as shadow work, far from being inconsequential, are in face absolutely essential to the maintenance of family life.

Mothering represents a paradoxical form of shadow work, however, because unlike other forms of housework, it is both demeaned *and* celebrated. Politicians and child-rearing experts have routinely referred to the work of raising young children as the most important job in the world, and as women's "sacred mission." During the 19th century, middle-class white women were urged to make a change from delegating child rearing tasks to domestic help to delegating to them all housework *but* child care, saving the precious work of molding young minds for themselves (Ehrenreich and English 1978; Green 1983; Hofferth 1989). This shift represents, in part, what Dorothy Roberts (1997) has termed the split between "spiritual" and "menial" housework. She argues that not only is work divided into productive and reproductive labor, but the reproductive labor of the home is divided into the spiritual, generally performed by middle-class white women, and the menial, generally relegated to women of color and working-class women. Thus, the southern mammy and the northern immigrant domestic worker took on the menial tasks of the home and were considered suitable to assist in raising their employers' children only because they were under the moral supervision of a white woman. Further, this split fostered a notion of domesticity that gave white women's mothering a moral purpose and the home the aura of a sacred haven.

> The notion of a purely spiritual domesticity could only be maintained by cleaning housework of its menial parts. The ideological separation of home from market then, dictated the separation of spiritual and menial housework. Housework's undesirable tasks had to be separated physically and ideologically from the moral aspects of family life (Roberts 1997: 55).

Splitting the work of the private sphere into spiritual and menial housework, and assigning race and class attributes to that division, Roberts argues, perpetuates both racial and class hierarchies among women, and the continuing devaluation of women's work.

As we move into the present day, this spiritual/menial split persists, allowing one class of women to enter the workforce and maintain the "spiritual" aspects of motherhood precisely because another class of women is available at low wages to fill in for them at home performing the "menial" motherhood of daily interaction with children.[12] Hierarchies of race, class, and immigration status structure the labor market for domestic workers (Colen 1995; Glenn 1986; Rollins 1985; Romero 1992). As Roberts points out, "Hiring a domestic worker leaves the employer free to both work outside of the home and to devote herself to the spiritual aspects of being a wife and mother" (Hertz 1986; Roberts 1997: 57). The working mothers I interviewed reinforce the spiritual/menial split by defining "spiritual motherhood" as selecting and supervising the child care worker, spending "quality time" with children, and retaining primary parent status regardless of how responsibility for care is distributed.

Motherhood is a paradoxical case, however, in the division of housework into the "spiritual" and the "menial," especially in an era in which intensive mothering is the norm. For example, Roberts points out that wet-nursing by slaves epitomized the paradoxes of menial housework in the antebellum south. Although today, breastfeeding signifies the ultimate maternal-child 'bond,' Roberts argues, in the slaveholding South,

The physical labor of breastfeeding was disengaged from its spiritual attributes to permit its performance by a morally inferior slave. . . . Thus the servant could conveniently do the mistress's work without appropriating the mistress's spiritual attributes. In other words, the nature of the work—whether spiritual and menial—depended on the status of the woman performing it (Roberts 1997: 56).

However, under the tenets of intensive mothering, mother-work is defined as a set of practices aimed at establishing a bond with a small child, and is therefore understood as accruing to the person with whom the child has bonded. Given this understanding of the relationship between mother-work and motherhood, between the often menial tasks and the spiritual identity, how do women who set out to purchase a one-to-one bond with a paid caregiver for their child maintain themselves as *the* mothers in their own families?

Delegating mother-work to a paid employee creates quite a tension in the "spiritual/menial" split, because it is precisely those tasks associated with "menial" motherhood mothering, e.g. feeding, holding, disciplining, etc., that are understood to create the bond constitutive of motherhood. How do working mothers delegate the menial tasks of mothering, yet maintain "spiritual" motherhood, especially if they believe in the importance of psychological bonds? And what delineates the line between themselves as mother and the nanny as "not mother"? Because the nanny represents the medium through which the mother's child rearing beliefs and practices are transmitted, she is viewed as an extension of that mothering practice, not as an individual with her own particular relationship with the children. To the extent that her particular relationship with the children emerges, it is often viewed as a rupture of this understanding of her job as an extension of the mother.

Because of these tensions, the mothers I interviewed frequently wanted a "shadow mother"; an extension of themselves who would stay home as if she were the mother, but who would vanish upon the *real* mother's return, leaving no trace of her presence in the psychic lives of the children they shared. One mother described this expectation concerning her relationship with her one-year-old son's au pair:

I wanted her to love him and adore him during the day when she was with him, and at night or any time that I was home, I wanted her to *not* be loving and adoring towards him. I wanted her to just take a step back and be very "hands off." Which is sort of impossible to ask a person to shut off all the time, but I think she was very understanding and really tried to help me with that.

This kind of self-erasure, or "shutting off," is one of many aspects of child care workers' shadow labor.

Nannies and other child care workers are "shadow laborers" on several levels. Most obviously, they perform the work of the home, the reproductive labor that is the antithesis of market work. Hidden in households and in child care centers, many are denied basic workers' rights and access to fair pay because their work is not defined as part of the realm of the adult labor force (Phillips, Howes, and Whitebook 1991; Silbaugh 1996). Further, they perform reproductive labor *in place of* the person socially ascribed these tasks—the mother. To call attention to themselves or their work would mean revealing that their employer depends on their labor to maintain the super-woman mystique. They are the "man behind the curtain" in the Oz of the dual earner family; we pay no attention to them. Therefore employers expect them to make themselves invisible, both in the psychic lives of the children in their care and in the social lives of the families that are their workplace. The "shadow motherhood" of nannies and au pairs, therefore, is not so much their recognized, paid labor of physical care for children, but the work of simultaneously building and concealing affective ties, and the work of maintaining family functioning while at the same time shoring up the myth of nuclear family self-sufficiency (Hertz 1986, 1991; Macdonald 1996).

## MANUFACTURING MOTHERHOOD

For both mothers and nannies, the work of "manufacturing motherhood" involves establishing and implementing interpretive rules. These rules are, for the most part, created by the mother, and put into action by the mothers and caregivers. Beyond the day-to-day negotiations over the actual care of children, caregivers and their employers also create a symbolic order that re-defines their division of mother-work so that it approximates the intensive-mothering ideal. They assign specific meanings to particular tasks and events to create an idealized version of the mother-child relationship: specifically, to magnify mother's significance in the home and to minimize the nanny's. Mothers and nannies "manufacture" a certain image and experience of motherhood. This image-making work falls into three major categories: defining the nanny as peripheral to the family; enhancing the mother within the family; and monitoring the division of mother-work through a system of "keeping the books."

### Defining Nannies Out

*Invisibility*

Mothers relegate nannies to the realm of "shadow motherhood" by ren-dering them invisible in several ways. For example, for many mothers, the nanny's departure signals the beginning of "family time," and they often expect her to physically disappear when her work day has ended to facilitate this. In this way, the nanny's presence or absence, and her engagement or disengagement with children, performs important "boundary work" distinguishing between parents' home and work lives (Nippert-Eng 1995). Because the nanny's presence signifies the antithesis of family life, many mothers devise strategies and rules to ensure that nanny and mother do not overlap. For example, Suzanne, a high-tech executive, spoke of how she chose live-out care as a way of safeguarding her family time, fearing that if she had live-in care, her own work day would extend indefinitely, blotting out her time with her daughter:

> We've talked about having somebody live-in, but I'm almost hesitant to do that, because that would—like right now, there's some structure that artificially or not—there is this sort of time in my mind when I'm really shooting to try and be home and I think that that would sort of like—blend out if I had somebody . . . here all the time.

Suzanne feared that if she had a live-in nanny, she would lose the important boundary created by the end of her nanny's work day. Without the "boundary work" of the nanny's departure, she feared that work life would "blend out" to home life and potentially obliterate it.

For other mothers, the nanny's arrival and departure became a poignant reminder that they were not the only mother-figure in their children's lives:

> She's out of here for the weekend, but she comes home on Sunday nights. Sometimes she'll be home like 6, and I'm so sad that she's home because it means my special time with him is over. And it reminds me that I have to leave him. It reminds me that he's going to be so excited to see her. That um, now he's not gonna want me, he's gonna want her.

Therefore they want their child care workers to wait in the wings until they are required.

The expectation from mothers that child care workers should recede into the wallpaper upon the mother's return from work left some nannies feeling excluded and unwanted. They balked at being asked, however implicitly, to assist in demarcating the line between "family" and "not-family" by defining themselves out. This was not a problem for caregivers who had homes and families of their own to go to, but for live-in workers, the pressure to give the family private time was acutely felt. Because they were young and far from home, the au pairs in this study for example, wanted to be considered part of the family, but instead found that at the end of the workday they were expected to perform the extra work of vanishing to help create "family time." As one au pair lamented in reference to her employer, "I always get the feeling, 'oh, she's going out. Yippee!'"

Employers also rendered nannies invisible in descriptions of the family.

The nanny's status as a putative family member was invisible. Although many mothers, especially those employing live-in workers referred to the nanny as "one of the family," in all my visits to employers' homes, I never once saw pictures of nannies with children on display. This was a striking omission in two ways. Many mothers offered to show me family pictures, while others had portraits of themselves, their children, and extended kin prominently exhibited, but in every case the nanny was conspicuously absent. On the other hand, when I visited nannies in their homes, or in their living quarters within their employers' homes, photographs of children currently and formerly in their care were highly visible. Generally nannies had one set of photos of their biological kin and a second display area for photographs of all of the children in their care. In other cases, depictions of biological kin and employment kin were intermingled. These photographs and family portraits represent a striking distinction between the displayed importance of the nanny-child relationship from the divergent perspectives of mother and child care provider. Although the nanny's labor is viewed as an extension of the mother's parenting work, and therefore an essential component of family life, she is invisible in documented portrayals of the family.

*Maximizing and Minimizing*

The mothers I interviewed simultaneously maximized and minimized the importance of their children's bonds with paid caregivers. On one hand, mothers frequently stressed the success of the nanny-child bond, stating that their nanny and child were "really attached" and that the child "really loved" his or her caregiver. On the other hand, they defined nannies out of the family by minimizing the importance of the nanny-child bond, particularly in discussions of nanny turnover. Although the need to feel good about her child care arrangement can lead a mother to maximize the nanny-child bond, to state that her provider is "great" and that her children "love" the nanny, this same need can lead her to minimize the effects of nanny turnover on her children's emotional well-being.

For example, Jane, a corporate vice president, described the departures of various nannies as not a problem for her sons. She said that because her older son (age 8) had been in day care, "he deals with transitions incredibly well, so for him if a person is living there it isn't that big an issue." She said that her younger son and his first nanny, who was with him from birth to 18 months, "adored each other," but at the same time described the nanny's departure as no big deal:

> Well he's young enough so that, you know, he talks about her all the time. I mean he understands and says that Andrea went home to be with her mommy and daddy. I think he missed her, but it doesn't seem to have had any huge impact on his overall well-being. . . . I guess my sense has always been if *family*

*life* is stable enough, that the transitions of *child care people*, as long as they're not constant changes, aren't going to have any terrible effects.

Jane's distinction between "family life" and "child care people" reveals how the nanny is situated in her child's life: although she spent more time with him than anyone else during the first year-and-a-half of his life, she is not an integral part of his family, psychologically or symbolically. This mother's strategy, therefore, was to simultaneously *maximize* the bond with the nanny in terms of how much her son benefited from it, and *minimize* the bond in terms of how much its loss would affect him. Not surprisingly, mothers and nannies often disagreed in their appraisals of the effects of nanny turnover. Sarah, the nanny who worked for Jane at the time of our interview, interpreted Andrea's departure much differently:

> I think Matthew (2 1/2 year old) is having a hard time because he's been through so many nannies. I mean he still talks about his other nannies. I was good friends with Andrea, his first nanny, and I have a picture of her upstairs and he'll go and see it and ask when she's coming back. And the same for Cindy, his second nanny. He wants to know why they left and I can't—well, it's like they had to go home, but he doesn't really understand why they left him. And he also asks me when I'm leaving. So you know, he's already—and Brian (8 year old) is that way too. Brian isn't willing to get close to anybody because he knows that eventually they're going to leave.

Some of the mothers I interviewed minimized the effects of the nanny-child bond on their children, but also diminished its impact on their child care providers. For example, Amy, a personnel manager, was exasperated at her au pair's emotional departure at the end of her one-year stay:

> The last month with our first au pair was VERY difficult for me. I mean, I would come from work and she would be CRYING because she realized that her time was coming to an END, you know, she was having a very difficult time with the fact that she was going to be replaced. . . . I was getting to the point where it was like "OK, we've gone through this already, you have to leave, it's not a choice." She said to us at one point, "I can't imagine anyone taking care of the baby but me." And I was like, hello, I'M her mother? And she was like "Oh no that's not what I mean."

Like several mothers in this study, Amy also minimized the potential for too much attachment between her baby and her caregiver by explicitly choosing a form of child care that would end after one year. She explained her choice this way:

> I think a year is a good amount of time. I'm also selfish, it also means that the baby still connects with you because this person is only here for twelve months.

And that person turns over. So, the baby knows who I am and that I'm always there. And that's important, I think I feel a little less secure in my work and balancing routine if this person could potentially be there for five years of her life.

There were other mothers, however, who did not seek to discount the nanny-child bond, either through managing the rate of turnover, or through minimizing its effects. Although they were in the minority, these mothers sought to keep caregivers with their families for as long as they wished to stay, and once they had gone, took pains to remain in contact. Nonetheless, for many employers, managing the frequency of nanny turnover, as well as how to interpret its significance, was a primary means of "defining nannies out" of the family. Further, given the constraints placed on them by adherence to the logic of intensive mothering, minimizing the nanny's long-term importance was a key means of maintaining control of the primary caregiver position.

## Self-erasure

Given the constraints of the "shadow motherhood" imperative, nannies often find that not only is their importance in the children's lives unrecognized, they are also expected to contribute to the process of rendering themselves invisible. The nanny's job requires that she perform acts of self-erasure. Child care providers perform self-erasure primarily by following the "detached attachment" rule. Margaret Nelson (1990: 76) coined this term to describe the "feeling rules" concerning the emotional labor of family day care providers. Emotional labor is defined as work that "requires one to induce or suppress feeling in order to sustain the outward countenance that produces the proper state of mind in other" (Hochschild 1983: 7). For child care workers, the detached attachment rule assures that, while a caregiver display *enough* warmth and affection to make the child feel loved and the parent satisfied with the quality of care, she is also careful not to display *too much* love, to prevent the child from becoming overly attached and to avoid seeming to usurp the parent's place in the child's affections. Lura, a veteran nanny with over 11 years' experience, described it this way:

> I never got attached to them like the first one. And I think it's because you don't let yourself because you know how hard—how much it hurts when you have to leave them. And so you love them, you know, and you get, you get attached to them some, but you don't, you don't let them get wedged right into your heart. They're kind of there on the outside, but they don't get clear in there! You know, you love them, but not like your own. So, you treat them like your own, but you don't love them like your own. And it's hard to do.

It was particularly hard for younger nannies who had no children of their own, and lacked the motivation to distinguish between children who are "theirs," and "not theirs." As one nanny remarked, "Some nannies consider the kids theirs, and I felt the same way, I felt those kids were mine."

For the most part, the nannies and au pairs I interviewed did not strive for emotional detachment; on the contrary, they wanted recognition for the degree and efficacy of their emotional attachment and its importance in children's lives. In most cases, however, they were careful not to make waves. As Esther, a nanny from China, noted,

> I always try to not to let the parents uh, uhm—see that we are too affectionate? Because I don't know—I don't know whether they have any feelings that maybe I love her more than I should? I don't know.

Esther's remarks reflect the anxiety and confusion expressed by many caregivers about the line between "attached enough" and "too attached." Generally, the nannies I interviewed developed a level of attachment that they found emotionally satisfying, and that they believed would be beneficial to the children, but were also careful not to let it show. Given the constraints of the "detached attachment" rule, they often found that not only was their importance in the children's lives unacknowledged, they were expected to take part in the process of denying themselves the recognition they desired.

Caregivers did employ the "detached attachment" rule to protect themselves and the children in their care from the pain of eventual separation. This was more of a concern for the au pairs I interviewed, who faced a predetermined end to their relationships with children, than it was for the nannies, who did not.[13] Still, since all child care arrangements eventually come to an end, the work of separating from children as painlessly as possible often fell to the child care provider. For example, at the time of our interview, Valerie knew she had only a few months remaining on her contract. She described her separation plan this way:

> Within the next couple of weeks, I don't want to get too attached—or, I am already attached, but try to slowly break that attachment without them realizing it. Like before I used to give them hugs all the time for doing something good. Now it's just only when I see them in the mornings and maybe when they come home from school. I'm doing it gradually.

Like Valerie, many nannies found that transitioning out of a job required a great deal of emotion management as a form of self-protection. More importantly, they viewed protecting the children from the pain of an inevitable yet abrupt separation as a critical job responsibility. At the same time, since many parents did not recognize a nanny's departure as a significant event, caregivers frequently found that they needed to devise and implement their departure management plans without parental assistance. Even in leave-taking, they were to leave no footprints.

## Enhancing Mothers

### Engineering Quality Time

Because mothers were conscious of how little time they had at home during the work week, they wanted help from their partners and from their caregivers to make the time they had with their children special. Suzanne described needing to get in "face time" with her child, and spoke appreciatively about her husband's sensitivity to that need:

> I think that he um, is very sensitive about my need to feel like I'm getting a lot of face time and bonding time with my daughter, so he will often—[pause]— make sure that I get the time, you know he'll say, "do you want to give her her bath?" or "why don't you go and play with her while I clean up," or something like that.

This emphasis on quality time was not only motivated by guilt or a sense of scarce mother-child bonding time, but also by the belief that their children deserved and required a consistently present, focused, and attentive caregiver at all times. In an effort to emulate the intensive mothering ideal, these mothers hired nannies so that their children could have nonstop quality time in rotating shifts. Jessica, a management consultant, described this belief:

> He has Anabel [the au pair] all day and I think because he sleeps 5 hours a day, she's 100% energy with him when he's awake. And then at night when we get home, we're so excited and energized to see him, he has Mom and Dad at that same peak performance.

Mothers often mentioned the "peak performance" concept when they compared their current child care situation with what it might be like if they stayed home. Better the child should have multiple caregivers at peak performance than only one who might be burned-out or bored.

The crucial point, however, is that mothers also wanted to ensure that the *ultimate* peak performance occurred during their "shift." To bring this about, mothers often instructed nannies to engineer the child's day to produce high-quality time for them. Much negotiation and behind-the-scenes work went into producing the picture-perfect parent-child reunion at the end of the work day: the child waiting with excited anticipation, having been reminded that "mommy and daddy are coming home," wearing fresh clothes, having been fed his or her dinner, and ready for family time to commence. This arrangement was as much for the parents' benefit as it was for the child's, and it took a lot of work on both sides to bring it to fruition.

Mothers and caregivers often clashed over the need to engineer quality time. For example, several mothers and nannies spoke of frustrations around creating and enforcing nap schedules that would meet mothers' needs for quality time with their children after returning from work. These nap policies ranged from no naps to multiple naps, but the aim was always to organize the child's day to ensure stress-free, quality time at night. One mother explained her nap strategy this way:

> Scheduling of naps and deciding when the baby should or shouldn't have a nap was something that became an issue. See, the baby can take one nap during the day and be fine until about five o'clock when the au pair's done. If she *doesn't* have *two* naps, her miserable time is not while the au pair is taking care of her, her miserable time is between you know six, and eight-thirty, when *we* get her. . . . Our time with her in terms of quality was horrible because she was so upset and tired that we couldn't enjoy our period of time with her because she only had one nap during the day. So that was something we quickly had to deal with.

To solve this dilemma, she instructed her au pair to wake the baby after one hour of her morning nap so that she would be tired enough in the afternoon to take a second nap. She acknowledged that implementing this policy might be a hardship for the au pair:

> I mean it's tough to wake up the baby. She's cranky when you wake her up, but it's important so that she'll take her second nap. It wasn't acceptable to me, to work her schedule so that it was short-changing me . . . and it would really upset me when um, the arrangement worked out so that she would miss her second nap, and I would get the lousy time of the day with her.

The shadow work in this au pair's job was to engineer the baby's day to ensure that the best "quality time" would occur during the mother's at-home hours.

Similarly, a nanny described being instructed to prevent the three-year-old in her care from taking naps, so that she would not be fussy when her parents put her to bed in the evening. She noted:

> I think Courtney really needs naps. Especially on days when she goes to school she comes home exhausted. She falls asleep in the car. She falls asleep eating her lunch, and I have to get her in activity to keep her busy. . . . Whenever she's cranky they blame it on either she's hungry or she needs an activity, not she needs a nap. So she eats all the time and she's constantly driving me up a wall because I have to find things for her to do all the time and you just run out of things.

In this case, the nanny felt resentful, not only because the "no nap" policy meant that she had to work twelve-hour shifts without a break, but also because she felt she was not able to do what was best for the child.

Engineering the child's day can become complicated by the fact that the parents are on one type of schedule, while the children and consequently, their caregivers, are on another. Tamara Hareven (1982), in describing the transition from an agrarian to an industrial economy, distinguished between the experiences of "industrial time," with its fixed schedules and rigid time clock, and "family time," which was more flexible. Often, conflicts between mothers and caregivers over engineering the day emerged out of a conflict between the constraints of the mother's "industrial time" schedule and the nanny's adherence to what I will call "baby time," in which the day is paced by their perceptions of the child's needs. In the cases discussed here, the mothers needed regularly scheduled quality time with their children during the evenings, because they needed to fit their "family time" into a rigid "industrial time" schedule.

Joan, a corporate executive, described her frustration at coming home one evening to find that her one-year-old was asleep at six o'clock, which was not part of the agenda she had set with her nanny. She confronted the nanny about this scheduling lapse, because the baby would be fussy during the night as a result. Her nanny responded with a "baby time" rationale. Joan recounted:

> Melanie said "you know my philosophy is that I go with Charlotte's needs and she was really tired and really cranky and this is not the normal thing but for some reason she wanted to go to sleep. So I let her." . . . I said well you need to understand what is going on with me. When I come home and she's sleeping at six o'clock, I know she's going to wake up at seven, and then I'm going to be up with her all night, and I have a big meeting at seven thirty the next morning. That is what I'm going through.

Hochschild (1997) uses the distinction between "family time" and "industrial time" (cf. Hareven 1982) to contrast the experiences of at-home and working mothers. She describes at-home mothers who perceive themselves as building "spacious temporal castles" around their children's lives and who perceive working mothers as time-keeping "prison wardens" (Hochschild 1997: 77). Yet the working mothers interviewed here were not "prison wardens." Although they may have been imprisoned by the demands of their work lives, they did not choose to pass that regimentation on to their children. After all, they had hired a nanny precisely so their children could enjoy the flexibility of family time. They chose a one-on-one caregiver who could go with their children's schedule, not a day care center that would impose its own routines on their children. And when they were home, they consciously shifted into the relaxed pace of family time with their children. Still, many of the mothers I interviewed did impose an "industrial time" schedule on their nannies, and by extension, on their children in order to create the possibility of "family time" for themselves. Ironically, although they had hired an in-home caregiver precisely to avoid placing their children on the workday time schedule, they often rigidly engineered the child's day in order to ensure quality time at the end of it.

*Patrolling the Mother/Not-Mother Boundary*

Nannies also enhanced the mother's status by helping to ensure that the boundary between the mother and themselves was clearly delineated. Because of the importance of maintaining the mother's place as "primary caregiver," both mother and provider worked to negotiate and demarcate the boundary between mother and "not mother." The nannies and au pairs in this study were aware that job loss could be the penalty for failing to adequately maintain the mother/not mother boundary, and some of them believed that they had been fired by previous employers precisely because of this failure. On the other hand, mothers were very appreciative of nannies who helped them reinforce this boundary. For example, Joan noted:

> I think that she's sensitive to her relationship with me, she's sensitive to the fact that I'm the mom and she's not the mom. . . . I mean Melanie is very much like "well go say Hi to mom," and "let's tell mom what we did today" and I mean it's very kind of like that. I've never seen her be possessive with the baby. . . . She's pretty deferential to me when I'm there. That I'm kind of the primary person and she's the secondary person.

In discussions with mothers and nannies concerning the boundary between them, the following two issues were crucial. First, that the nanny defer to the mother, not only in decision-making, but in status. This deference took the form of symbolic acts reinforcing the assumption that the mother was the child's "primary" or "special" person, and that the nanny, no matter how beloved, was always secondary. Melanie displayed this deference to Joan's primary status, for example, when she made a scrapbook of the baby's first year: on one page she placed pictures of herself with Charlotte under the heading, "It Must Be Love"; on the facing page, she placed photos of Joan and Charlotte together with the caption "The Greatest Love of All."

Second, mothers expected nannies to help children distinguish between the mother and themselves, especially when children were beginning to talk. The word "mommy" and its usage were crucial. Anne, a Jamaican nanny, told me how she helped the children in her care learn her name to dissuade them from calling her mommy. Despite her efforts, she said,

They *still* call me mommy. Right in front of the parents. And I know—I know because every time—well. They know Carol is different. They know Carol is their mommy or whatever, but they can call everybody else's name—and you know, every time [they call me "mommy"]. I say "It's Anne, Anne." But to them it's "mommy, mommy." You know. And sometimes Carol said "oh— that's so nice. You know, if you wasn't taking good care of them, [they wouldn't call you mommy]." You know? She kind of laughs it off. Now some people would fire me a long time ago because they would say I'm trying, whatever— and this child shouldn't be calling me mommy because I'm Anne. But me, Carol and Alan, we try to [correct] them when they say mommy.

As Anne noted, some nannies could be fired for transgressing the mother/ not-mother boundary, no matter how innocently. On the other hand, some mothers, like Carol, viewed a young child's name confusion as a sign that the nanny was doing a good job, provided the nanny took pains to correct them.

Some nannies viewed the boundary between the mother and themselves as an artificial construct, especially in the eyes of the children in their care. For example, one nanny noted:

There was a while when Zachary thought I was his mom. . . . Elaine got all happy and excited when he started saying mamma and he said it on a weekend and when I got there on Monday it was the big thing, "Zachary says mommy now"—well he says it to me too, so I don't think he knows. . . . Elaine doesn't spend any more time with him than what I do. . . . Zachary's going both ways now, sometimes he wants me sometimes he wants her, and sometimes he even wants [his dad]—[his dad] can't understand it because [he] doesn't think Zachary even knows who he is.

Nonetheless, most were aware that creating a boundary between the mother and themselves as "not-mother" in the eyes of the children, arbitrary or not, was an essential job responsibility.

Nannies spoke of feeling both accused and guilty when a child in their care would violate the mother/not-mother boundary. This boundary viola- tion could take the form of calling the nanny "mommy," as in the case above, or of displaying a preference for the nanny over the mother, as noted below:

Sometimes Bonnie [the mother] seemed in a rush for me to get out of there. And she'd get *very* miffed if Rebecca would choose me—like she'd want me to carry her, hold her hand, or whatever—Bonnie would get very upset about it. You couldn't help but notice, because her facial expression would just go down.

Regardless of the arbitrary nature of the mother/not-mother boundary, or of how innocently it was transgressed, the nannies I interviewed often felt responsible for the transgression. Further, they felt it was their duty to restore the mother to her rightful place as primary caregiver.

> Typically, no matter how much I was fed up with a lot of things that Bonnie did and a lot of ways she treated me, I would still feel bad for her. I felt like, "No Rebecca, come on, it's your *mom*." And I'd feel terrible.

This nanny disliked her employer and found her difficult to work for, but nonetheless felt she should intervene to reinforce the mother's primary caregiver status, and to shore up the boundary between them. Not only do nannies patrol and reinforce the mother/not-mother boundary, but in doing so, they create a symbolic order to reinforce the mother's status as primary caregiver.

### Keeping the Books

Finally, mothers and caregivers worked at manufacturing mothering by monitoring the system, or keeping the books. As employers, mothers kept a careful accounting of the division of mother-work, and more importantly, the *meanings* assigned to that division. Given that all of the nannies in this study spent more time with the children during their waking hours, this imbalance needed to be countered with other strategies, such as the emphasis on quality time or the demand for detached attachment. Still, these strategies needed to be measured, and both mothers and caregivers kept track of the caregiving "ledger" to ensure that the mother's side always had the higher total.

This process was not without its conflicts, however. Numerous silent battles took place over whose tasks were the most important. Mothers often seemed to view the child's attachment as a zero-sum game—love for the nanny being automatically subtracted from the mother's side of the ledger. Nannies countered with the view that their bond with the children in their care was *almost* as important as the mother-child bond, but since mothers were clearly the primary parents, they were mistaken to worry about their relative status. Nannies and au pairs frequently compared their hours per week with the children to the time spent by their employers, as evidence that they really were de facto "third parents" in the family. Mothers countered by citing the importance of "quality time" or by tallying mothering tasks in to ensure that they had the higher total. For example, Leigh, a physician, said:

> One of the little mind games I played with myself when they were very young was about feeding them. I figured out that I fed them one more meal a week than the au pair did. And then I said, "Oh my god, how childish of you!" But I felt like, "So?" I had to come to terms with being a working mother.

Another mother counted the hours she spent with her child:

> I mean you know she [the nanny] spends ten hours a day with her, you know, which means I spend fourteen, but ten of those are sleeping hours.

Mothers created a distinction between weekends, when they were home, as family time, and weekdays, when they were not, as work time to demarcate the division between themselves and their caregivers. They often noted that, although the nanny might spend more total hours with the children, they were "during the week," and thus not during family time.

## Re-defining "Firsts"

The mothers I interviewed also balanced the ledger through a selective definition of childhood milestones. Leigh related this story:

> I remember coming home from work and the nanny said, "He took his first step." And I'm like that's great, I'm really happy for her. But in my mind he had *not* taken his first step because I hadn't seen him take it. When he took his first step and I saw it, *that* was the one that went down in the baby book. Spiteful of me? I don't know whether that was selfish or not.

Child care experts (Meltz 1991) reinforce this view, suggesting, for example, that child care providers avoid telling parents about important "firsts" that occur in their absence; instead, they argue, providers should say, "I bet she's going to walk any time now. I can't wait if she does it tonight at home!"[14] Many mothers appreciated this sleight of hand. For example, Pat, a military officer, noted:

> You know, Dagmar saw Timmy take his first step. But instead of her telling us, she was so considerate, she just waited and after we had seen it a couple times, I said, "Well how long has he been walking?" Not being stupid to think that he'd only done it on my time. And she just said, "Oh about a week. But I didn't want to tell you."

Whether, like Leigh, a mother chose not to recognize a "first" that occurred on the nanny's "time," or, like Pat, she preferred to find out when the event had occurred, most of the mothers I interviewed tracked developmental milestones by "shift."

Nannies were equally aware of the symbolic importance of witnessing firsts. For example, Melanie considered herself "lucky" that one-year-old Charlotte had performed all of her firsts on evenings and weekends. She hoped her employer would be understanding if the long-awaited first step occurred during a weekday, but she told me, "I hope she just does everything with them and then they get to tell me about it." Part of keeping accounts entailed ensuring that developmental milestones occurred during the parents' "shift." Consequently, most nannies and au pairs told me that they would either lie to parents about these events, like the nanny who noted, "I just let her see for herself so she can be happy," or they simply crossed their fingers and hoped that every milestone occurred on a weekend.

*Mother-only Tasks*

Mothers also balance the ledger by choosing specific tasks to designate as "mother-only" (Wrigley 1995).[15] The fact that certain events were likely to occur on the nanny's shift, or that her shift might be longer than the mother's, could be off-set by the fact that only the mother could or should perform certain child-rearing tasks. Breast-feeding is the most commonly cited example, not simply because of its inherent nutritional or emotional value, but because, as Leigh noted,

> This is the only thing I can do that the au pair or the nanny can't do. We had a nanny at the time who came in every day. She can do everything else. She can care and bond with him. This is the one thing I can do. And it was a little mental game that I played (laughs) with myself. It's like, "Baby, I really am your Mom because I'm the only one who can do this." Even though it was the biggest pain working and having to pump at work and that whole thing and getting up during the night. Because my husband couldn't get up for them, I had to do that. . . . And I think it helped me. It helped me deal with the fact that somebody else was home with them.

Given that Leigh is a physician, we might expect her to focus on the nutritional value of breast-feeding, but instead she emphasizes its symbolic importance as a marker designating her as "the mother."

Other mothers chose bathing, bedtime rituals, or breakfast preparation as their designated task. Aside from the example of breast-feeding, the nature of these tasks in themselves was unimportant. What was crucial was that they were sanctified as "mother-only" tasks, and that the "mother-only" restriction was strictly observed. Pat described a typical conflict concerning a mother-only task. She had chosen bathing as her designated ritual, and had asked her nanny not to give the baby a bath during the day:

> This was what MOM wanted to do, where my ego was, at least I thought it was. . . . And so (sighs) we laugh about this now. We know she humored me for about two weeks, and I came home and I would bathe Timmy. Finally one night I rolled in about 8:30. I was mad at myself. I was just mad at the world. I mean I hadn't gotten home in time to see Timmy before he went to bed. I didn't bathe him. I mean all these things, you know. And my husband wasn't there. He was on another travel assignment. And I come in and I'm like "Oh, I'm sorry,

Dagmar. I didn't get Timmy bathed."—She said, "That's OK. I bathed him this morning."—So then I was *really* mad.

After a "good cry and a drink," Pat thought about what to do. At first she considered letting the nanny go, noting that friends had fired nannies for similar transgressions, but she also acknowledged how attached Dagmar and Timmy had become. Then she reconsidered:

> And I sat down and I thought about it and I basically came away with "Wait a minute. The whole reason I'm upset is because I made the decision that that's what a Mom should do." OK? Because that's what my mom did. Well that doesn't necessarily mean that I'm one, a bad mother because I didn't bathe my child. And two, my son did get bathed. He just was being bathed at nine in the morning instead of eight at night.

Pat described her solution as a decision to

> disassociate my beliefs of what a mom should do with an infant and what nanny should be doing with an infant because I will always be the children's mother, no matter what. And they will always be the children's nanny. And the children may develop the same or similar or very very close relationships with them. But I'm ALWAYS gonna be their mom. And at that point, what we call my "bathing thing" was over.

Ultimately, Pat decided to stop keeping score. Her solution is significant because it represents a decision to be more flexible regarding her adherence to the tenets of intensive mothering, and to make a conscious choice to mother differently. She broke free from the constraints of an ideology that had created emotional and cognitive stress. She chose a common sense approach in lieu of intensive mothering. Her new approach represents a choice to distinguish her perceptions of her child's actual needs from a codified, idealized, version of motherhood.

Her assertion that she would *always* be the mother, regardless of who gave the bath represents a shift from the notion that the only mothering practices that "count" are those performed by the mother herself. Instead, Pat decided that as long as the children's needs were met by a loving caregiver, it didn't matter if *she* was the person to meet these needs. Pat's decision was also significant because it was so rare among the stories told to me by both mothers and caregivers.

## CONCLUSION

All of the interpretive strategies described above are aimed at creating an image of the mother that is in line with the tenets of intensive mothering. It is important to note that the work of "manufacturing motherhood" has very little to do with the actual quality of child care, or with the work of caring for children. Instead, it represents an extra dimension of work for both mother and nanny—work that is in the service of a belief system, rather than in the service of the children themselves. Further, "manufacturing motherhood" reinforces an idealized "image" of motherhood, and seeks to assuage mothers' feelings of inadequacy with respect to this image, but does not necessarily serve mothers' interests. Finally, "manufacturing motherhood" must be understood as work in the service of an "image" of the self-sufficient nuclear family, not in the service of concrete family needs.

One of the primary consequences of the belief in the intensive mothering ideology for the mothers I interviewed was that, paradoxically, by creating interpretive rules concerning the boundary between mother and not-mother, they reinforce the belief that children in non-maternal care are somehow deprived, regardless of the quality of that care. They therefore shore up a belief system that is the source of their guilt and discomfort. It is also important to note that these mothers do not create the interpretive rules discussed above out of arbitrariness, or a lack of consideration for their child care workers, but because they feel squeezed between their beliefs about good mothering and their working conditions. Most of the mothers I interviewed had very little maternity leave, and almost none had access to family-friendly work schedules such as part-time work or flextime. As a result, they often felt painfully disconnected from what went on at home during the day, and needed their child care providers to help them bolster their sense of being the primary caregiver within their own families.

For nannies and au pairs, "shadow motherhood" meant that they were expected to erase, or at least detach from, those aspects of child care that were the most meaningful to them. Some received recognition for their work because their employers did not view their connection to the children in their care as threatening. Most, however, did not receive the recognition they desired. Yet, as stated above, nannies and au pairs colluded in their own self-erasure, even when it was a source of frustration. They did so because, like their employers, they, too, believed in and adhered to the tenets of "intensive mothering." This belief lead them to act and feel in contradictory ways: on one hand, they held that the biological mother *should* be the primary parent, and thus they worked to reinforce that image; on the other hand, they believed in the value of bonding, and of their own bonds to the children in their care, and so they resented being "defined out" of the family realm.

Working in concert with and in opposition to their employers, nannies and au pairs forge a particular type of shared mothering. This shared mothering is created, however, within the context of a dominant cultural ideology that values only intensive mothering performed by the biological or adoptive mother, and not by a hired provider. As a result, mothers and nannies perform an extra dimension of interpretive work designed to mask the fact that their mother-work is, in fact, shared.

## NOTES

Reprinted from Cameron L. Macdonald, *Qualitative Sociology* 21, no. 1 (1998): 25–53. Courtesy of Kluwer Academic/Plenum Publishers.

The author would like to thank the following individuals for their valuable comments on earlier drafts of this chapter: Jean Elson, Faith Ferguson, Anita I. Garey, Karen V. Hansen, Rosanna Hertz, Henry Rubin, Carmen Sirianni, Gregory L. Williams, and two anonymous reviewers.

1. See, for example, Jessie Bernard (1981). This is not, however, to suggest that women did not work outside of the home during this period, only that white, middle-class *married* women tended to be housewives. (See Ammott and Matthei 1996; Kessler-Harris 1982.)

2. The changes described here apply primarily to white, middle-class women, since poor women and women of color have rarely had the opportunity to be at-home mothers.

3. Molly Ladd-Taylor (1994: 2) coined the term "mother-work" to refer to both "child-rearing in the home, and the maternalist reform activity characterized as 'social motherhood.'" This research focuses on the first component of mother-work.

4. Because of the sample design, almost all of the children discussed in the study were under age four.

5. See also Glenn (1994), Margolis (1984), and Thurer (1994), among others, for further critiques of the various "myths" of motherhood.

6. In-home care is care in the employer's home rather than in a center or the provider's home. This may be provided on a live-in or live-out basis, and the women who do this work are generally referred to as nannies, au pairs, or babysitters. For the purposes of this article, I refer to the child care workers I interviewed generally as nannies, although I refer to those working through foreign exchange programs as au pairs.

7. Au pairs, who come to the United States on a one-year tourist visa, work an average of 45 hours per week. Those I interviewed earned $100–$125 per week in addition to room and board, a plane ticket, and minimal health insurance. The nannies I interviewed earned salaries ranging from $80–$450 per week, generally without insurance or other benefits, for a 45–70 hour work week. The wide range in nanny salaries results from the wage difference between documented and undocumented workers.

8. This is not to suggest that relationships between parents and caregivers in day care centers and family day care homes do not present some of the same issues and conflicts. For more on these types of caregiving situations, see Joffe (1977), Murray (1995), Nelson (1990), Rutman (1996), Uttal (1996), and Wrigley (1995).

9. These three methodological choices distinguish this study from the work of Uttal and Wrigley, for example. By narrowing the focus of the analysis to one-on-one commodified child care arrangements in which the caregiver's primary charge is

to look after a child under school age, I highlight those aspects of the employer-caregiver relationship that are most informed by the ideology of intensive mothering.

10. I owe special thanks to Sandra Olarte for her diligent work on this aspect of the project. Her participation was valuable, not only because of her excellent language skills but also because of her ability to generate trust with respondents who were undocumented immigrants and because of her ability to comprehend and translate cultural metaphors used by women from various Latin American countries. (For more on the question of cross-cultural interviewing, see Reissman 1987).

11. Although one family was going through a divorce at the time of the study, and a few nannies worked for single mothers, the vast majority of family situations were dual-career married couples. In addition, although I sought ethnic variation, the majority of mothers were white (the study includes interviews with one Chinese American mother, one Latin American mother and one African American mother). In general, I found that women of color who used in-home care employed relatives or neighbors as caregivers, thus making them ineligible for this study.

12. Of course, we can see the same phenomenon in reverse in the assumptions underlying welfare reform: that the children of AFDC recipients would be better off in day care than they are with their mothers.

13. Most of the nannies I interviewed had one-year contracts that were up for annual renewal and renegotiation and that could extend indefinitely. Au pairs are limited to a one-year stay in the United States by the nature of their visas.

14. Although the article refers to day care workers, the same advice clearly applies to in-home child care providers.

15. Wrigley argues that parents keep "crucial aspects of care to perform themselves," but refers primarily to class-based tasks, such as reading to children or supervising their homework, tasks that middle-class parents often do not trust "class subordinate" caregivers to perform adequately (1995: 121).

## REFERENCES

Abel, E. and Nelson, M. 1990. *Circles of Care: Work and Identity in Women's Lives.* Albany: SUNY Press.

Ammott, T. and Matthei, J. 1996. *Race, Gender, and Work: A Multi-cultural Economic History of Women in the United States.* Boston: South End Press.

Belsky, J. 1990. "Parental and Nonparental Child Care and Children's Socioemotional Development: A Decade in Review." *Journal of Marriage and the Family* 52 (November): 885–903.

Bernard, J. 1981. "The Good Provider Role: Its Rise and Fall" *American Psychologist* 36:1: 1–12.

Burawoy, M. 1979. *Manufacturing Consent: Changes in the Labor Process under Monopoly Capitalism.* Chicago: University of Chicago Press.

Colen, S. 1995. "'Like a Mother to Them': Stratified Reproduction and West Indian Childcare Workers and Employers in New York." In Ginsburg and Rapp, eds., *Conceiving the New World Order: The Global Politics of Reproduction.* Berkeley: University of California Press, 78–102.

————. 1989. "Just a Little Respect: West Indian Domestic Workers in New York City." In Chaney and Castro eds., *Muchachas No More: Household Workers in Latin America and the Caribbean*. Philadelphia: Temple University Press.

Daniels, A. K. 1987. "Invisible Work." *Social Problems*. 34: 403–15.

DeVault, M. 1991. *Feeding the Family: The Social Organization of Caring as Gendered Work*. Chicago: University of Chicago Press.

Dill, B. T. 1988. "'Making Your Job Good Yourself': Domestic service and the construction of Personal Dignity." In Bookman and Morgen, eds., *Women and the Politics of Empowerment*. Philadelphia: Temple University Press.

Ehrenreich, B. and English, D. 1978. *For Her Own Good: 150 Years of the Experts' Advice to Women*. Garden City, N.Y.: Doubleday.

Enarson, E. 1990. "Experts and Caregivers: Perspectives on Underground Day Care." In Abel and Nelson, eds., *Circles of Care: Work and Identity in Women's Lives*. Albany: SUNY Press.

Fraiberg, S. 1977. *Every Child's Birthright: In Defense of Mothering*. New York: Basic Books.

Garey, A. I. 1995. "Constructing Motherhood on the Night Shift: 'Working Mothers' as 'Stay at Home Moms.'" *Qualitative Sociology* 18:4: 415–37.

Glaser, B. and Strauss, A. 1967. *The Discovery of Grounded Theory*. New York: Aldine de Gruyter.

Glenn, E. N. 1986. *Issei, Nisei, War Bride: Three Generations of Japanese American Women in Domestic Service*. Philadelphia: Temple University Press.

————. 1994. "Social Constructions of Mothering: A Thematic Overview," in Glenn, E., Chang, G. and Forcey, R. eds., *Mothering: Ideology, Experience, and Agency*. New York: Routledge.

Goffman, E. 1976. "Gender Display." *Studies in the Anthropology of Visual Communication* 3: 69–77.

Green, H. 1983. *The Light of the Home: An Intimate View of the Lives of Women in Victorian America*. New York: Pantheon.

Hareven, T. 1982. *Family Time and Industrial Time*. New York: Cambridge University Press.

Hays, S. 1996. *The Cultural Contradictions of Motherhood*. New Haven, Conn.: Yale University Press.

Hertz, R. 1991. "Dual-Career Couples and the American Dream: Self-sufficiency and Achievement." *Journal of Comparative Family Studies*. 22:2: 247–63.

————. 1986. *More Equal Than Others: Women and Men in Dual-Career Marriages*. Berkeley: University of California Press.

Hochschild, A. 1997. *The Time Bind: When Work Becomes Home and Home Becomes Work. New York*: Henry Holt.

————. 1989. *The Second Shift: Working Parents and the Revolution at Home*. New York: Viking Penguin.

————. 1983. *The Managed Heart: Commercialization of Human Feeling*. Berkeley: University of California Press.

————. 1975. "Inside the Clockwork of Male Careers." In Howe, ed., *Women and the Power to Change*. New York: McGraw-Hill, 47–80.

Hofferth, S. 1989. *Private Matters: American Attitudes toward Childbearing and*

*Infant Nurture in the Urban North 1800–1860*. Urbana: University of Illinois Press.

Illich, I. 1981. *Shadow Work*. Boston: M. Boyars.

Joffe, C. 1977. *Friendly Intruders: Child Care Professionals and Family Life*. Berkeley: University of California Press.

Katz Rothman, B. 1989. *Recreating Motherhood: Ideology and Technology in a Patriarchal Society*. New York: W. W. Norton.

Kessler-Harris, A. 1982. *Out to Work. A History of Wage-earning Women in the United States*. New York: Oxford University Press.

Ladd-Taylor, M. 1994. *Mother-work: Women, Child Welfare, and the State, 1890–1930*. Urbana: University of Illinois Press.

Macdonald, C. L. 1996. "Shadow Mothers: Nannies, *Au Pairs* and Invisible Work." In Macdonald and Sirianni, eds., *Working in the Service Society*. Philadelphia: Temple University Press.

Margolis, M. 1984. *Mothers and Such: Views of American Women and Why They Changed*. Berkeley: University of California Press.

Meltz, B. 1991. "When Jealousy Strikes the Working Parent." *Boston Globe*, March 15: 74.

Murray, S. 1995. "Child Care Work: The Lived Experience." Ph.D. diss., University of California, Santa Cruz.

Nelson, M. K. 1990. *Negotiated Care: The Experiences of Family Day Care Providers*. Philadelphia: Temple University Press.

Nippert-Eng, C. 1995. *Home and Work: Negotiating Boundaries through Everyday Life*. Chicago: University of Chicago Press.

Oakley, A. 1974. *Woman's Work: The Housewife, Past and Present*. New York: Random House.

Phillips, D., Howes, C., and Whitebook, M. 1991. "Child Care as an Adult Work Environment." *Journal of Social Issues* 47:2: 49–70.

Reissman, K. 1987. "When Gender Is not Enough: Women Interviewing Women." *Gender and Society* 1:2 (June): 172–207.

Roberts, D. 1997. "Spiritual and Menial Housework." *Yale Journal of Law and Feminism* 51.

Rollins, J. 1985. *Between Women: Domestics and Their Employers*. Philadelphia: Temple University Press.

Romero, M. 1992. *Maid in the U.S.A.* New York: Routledge.

Rutman, D. 1996. "Child Care as Women's Work: Workers' Experiences of Powerfulness and Powerlessness." *Gender and Society* 10: 629–49.

Schwartz, F. 1989. "Management Women and the New Facts of Life." *Harvard Business Review*. (January-February): 65–76.

Saraceno, C. 1984. "Shifts in Public and Private Boundaries: Women as Mothers and Service Workers in Italian Day Care." *Feminist Studies* 10:1 (Spring): 7–29.

Silbaugh, K. 1996. "Turning Labor into Love: Housework and the Law." *Northwestern University Law Review* 91:1: 1–86.

Thurer, S. 1994. *The Myths of Motherhood: How Culture Reinvents the Good Mother*. Boston: Houghton Mifflin.

U.S. Bureau of the Census. 1996. *Statistical Abstract of the United States*. Washington, D.C.: Author.

Uttal, L. 1996. "Custodial Care, Surrogate Care, and Coordinated Care: Employed Mothers and the Meaning of Child Care." *Gender and Society* 10:3: 291–311.

West, C. and Zimmerman, D. 1987. "Doing Gender." *Gender and Society* 1:2: 125–51.

Wrigley, J. 1995. *Other People's Children.* New York: Basic Books.

# II

# SOCIALIZATION AND IDENTITY

*Venice Barmaid*

**Our students in the United States often work as bartenders and barmaids. They tell us that there is great status difference between the two: bartenders dispense drinks to people sitting at the bar and control the scene: they can have rowdy customers thrown out or give away free drinks. In the past, they were all men; now, increasingly, women are found in these work roles. Barmaids, almost always women, visit tables, take orders, and ply their customers for tips.**

Photo: A barmaid in Venice, Italy, 2001, by Douglas Harper

I n this section, we study the merging of the person into the roles demanded by work. We have separated the topic into three parts: occupational socialization, which is learning the work role; the creation of a work identity, which indicates the extent to which work becomes our master identity; and careers, through which we study the subjective experience of work as successively defined throughout one's life.

The view of socialization that dominated early sociology held that humans come into the world a blank slate, then in rather clear steps become functioning members of the social system. People who are not properly socialized are "role failures" or deviants.

The perspective in tune with a cultural view of social life recognizes reality as ever evolving. The table on which one's computer rests is a loosely coordinated set of molecules, atoms, neutrons, and quarks (and whatever the new lens on the microscope discovers) holding each other in place through bonds of attraction and repulsion. The physical world can best be understood through the metaphor of change and movement; thus the social world, certainly more ephemeral than the physical, should be similarly understood. It is true that the individual is born a baby, defenseless and incompetent, and in reasonably consistent patterns gains the ability to walk, talk, listen to others, form abstract arguments, and eventually consider moral issues. Individuals learn, however, through interaction: taking the role of the other and making up lines of action, understanding the symbolic as well as the natural universe.

The most important distinction between these perspectives lies in the idea that socialization, from the first point of view, is largely finished by the time a child gains physical maturity. The cultural perspective understands that socialization takes place throughout one's lifetime—as we gain competencies necessary to interact in one group after another.

## FORMAL OCCUPATIONAL SOCIALIZATION

We call the specialized training for jobs or occupations we get in schools or training programs "formal occupational socialization." These range from training programs in trade schools to graduate schools for medicine, law, or other professions. These programs teach skills and knowledge, but they also teach informal and subtle aspects of an occupation almost by accident and certainly not as announced parts of curricula. Sociologists are not deeply interested in how technical skills and knowledge are transmitted in formal occupational socialization, and we recognize that the informal socialization also takes during work itself. Thus, our emphasis is on the informal processes of socialization that take place during formal training as well as on the job.

"Informal socialization" takes place as people learn informal vocabularies of jobs; as people learn to present themselves as legitimate members of a profession or occupation; as people go through rites of passage that mark entry into a job; as new workers learn norms as well as rules of the job; and, finally, as workers internalize the ideology of their job or profession. We will briefly discuss each of these aspects of occupational socialization.

## Informal Vocabularies

Formal socialization into a job almost always involves learning a set of terms that communicate the special knowledge of the job. These might be rather simple, such as a police recruit learning parts of his or her weapon, or they might be more elaborate and even require a different language, such as the Latin terminology the medical student learns. To be socialized into the job is not only to know these terms but also to be able to use them convincingly. The full socialization of a person into an occupation teaches neophytes the proper inflection, nuance, and phrasing and even in what circumstances one is expected to use a specific word or phrase. Sociologists have described how new recruits use occupational terminology too zealously and thus mark themselves as the opposite of what they are trying to claim.

Most of the actual language socialization is learned unconsciously from watching others. The new doctor learns how to speak to patients by watching the experienced doctors on the rounds in a hospital. The police officer learns how to interact with the public by being assigned to a toughened officer that he or she tries to emulate. One of the difficulties of college teaching is that there is so little opportunity to watch others teach and interact with students; thus, new teachers must learn a great deal of their real occupational language on their own and on a trial and error basis. We always remember how teachers we admired inspired us and dealt with us outside of the classroom, and our actions mimic those often long-past events.

Thus language is the first form of occupational socialization, but it is necessary to study informal language used in the job itself as well as technical vocabularies of work. Understanding the actual performance of the language is also a part of this study.

## Presentation of Self

To be socialized into a job involves learning how to present oneself by adopting the appearance expected in an occupation. In medieval cities, all guilded trades wore special uniforms and paraded through towns in their own colors. Our world today is not so different than this, but this is often not recognized. For example, Robert Granfield (1991) learned that working-class law students needed to replace their scruffy jeans and flannel shirts with suits—and suits of a specific brand (Brooks Brothers) and color (navy blue, gray, or black)—to be successful in job interviews. The clothes marked aspiring lawyers as legitimate to potential employers, and they also influenced how the new lawyers felt about themselves. It proved to be difficult for previously radical working-class students to maintain a working-class orientation toward the capitalist system while dressed as part of the class one is supposedly trying to subvert. Moreover, the same outfit—a navy Brooks Brothers suit—would hardly be the proper attire for a professor on an interview. Here the level of formality is lower, but still quite specific.

Some jobs come with uniforms: the UPS driver arrives in rather smart brown shorts and shirts that match his or her truck. Many uniforms are less obvious. Corporate businesspeople, lawyers, and politicians are expected to wear black, gray, or navy blue suits, cold colors that imply an analytic and unemotional perspective. Analysts noted that Ronald Reagan could wear the warm colors of brown and green and yet assert a charismatic presidential role. College professors, when they do dress up, usually wear sport coats and khaki pants in warm colors such as brown, olive green, and blue. As women have entered the previously male professions, a new look has emerged that largely mimics the male business suit. The color coding for women is largely the same as for men. In other words, colors are strong cultural indicators, both inward (that is, to others on the job) and outward (to the public).

It is not just the types of clothes one wears but also the way clothes are worn that indicates proper socialization into the job. Haas and Shaffir (1977) discovered that medical students gain what they call a "cloak of competence" by adjusting the extent to which their white smocks are rumpled and unbuttoned. Either extreme—bloody, dirty, and disheveled or crisply clean and ironed—sends the wrong message. The marks of wear on the smock show experience, and this inspires confidence, but sloppiness or evident filth would certainly not. Variations on this theme are found throughout the occupational world. Jeffrey Riemer (1977) tells us that experienced electricians are wary of an electrician with a shiny hard hat, for the newness of the hat marks one as an apprentice whose lack of experience may be dangerous. Riemer also noted that apprentices often burden themselves with too many tools of a less preferred brand, whereas experienced electricians are often identified by the sparseness of their tools, the tools' well-worn patina, and their proper brand. To be socialized into a job, therefore, is to learn how to use and display these props that are partly technical and partly symbolic. One of our students presented himself in different ways to the customers he delivered pizzas to in different social class neighborhoods. To the rich, he put on a clean apron and acted deferentially; in middle-class neighborhoods, his smock showed the tomato sauce stains that came with his job, and in these neighborhoods he complimented people on their houses, cars, and other possessions; and in working-class neighborhoods, his smock was even less well kept. To the working-class customers, he described his job as part of an attempt for social mobility, and his garb communicated solidarity with their class. He had learned that the informal part of his "uniform" communicated messages his various customers wanted to hear, and that resulted in higher tips.

In sum, socialization for a job involves learning how to present oneself in a way that is consistent with the image the public and the other members of the occupation expect. These may be strict uniforms and objects that convey legitimacy, or they may be subtle aspects of the presentation of self that are unconscious and not generally recognized. The result of learning how to present oneself as part of an occupation or job gives confidence to the people one interacts with as part of that job. As workers adopt these aspects of work, they adopt their own connection to an occupation. The previously radical law students who donned Brooks Brothers suits were changing the way they felt about the world as well as convincing their recruiters that they would behave in their jobs in the expected way.

## Rites of Passage

Most schools and training centers have a ritual that marks the end of training and the beginning of work. These are typically graduation ceremonies in which one dons special apparel and receives certifications that indicate the completion of training. The clothes, such as robes and special hats with particular pieces of cloth or cord, carry on a tradition that may be hundreds of years old. Although these ceremonies continue to be an important part of how one takes on the identity of a job, as society becomes more bureaucratized, they are less frequent and less rich in ceremony.

Occupational socialization, however, includes informal rites of passage that are integrated into work routines. These may involve humiliation and degradation, as in the case presented by Charles Vaught (1980, included in this volume; see chapter 5). The coal mine is dangerous, and the work crews survive through teamwork. The new miner must be "made a miner" through a rather violent rite that is easily interpreted as physical and sexual harassment. The miner is humiliated until he acknowledges the primacy of the group. Given that the recruits to the mine are stubborn, strong, and individualistic working-class men, the rite is severe. The men have to be broken as recruits in boot camp. But as women have entered the mines, the rites of passage have had to be reexamined. What may work as a male-to-male ritual has an entirely different meaning when men do the same things to female workers.

## Rules and Norms

Occupational socialization involves learning both the formal rules and informal norms of a setting. These rules are always incomplete, and sometimes the norms of the workplace contradict the rules. When we became professors, for example, we received the rules and regulations of our new workplaces. These were written in a legalistic prose and proclaimed to be policies of the trustees of our universities. Learning these formal norms had little to do with learning how to do our jobs successfully. In fact, few (if any) new professors spent much time with these intimidating documents. The informal norms were much more important. They were concerned with such issues as how to achieve tenure—that distant goal that dominated even the beginning professor's consciousness. We learned from our peers whether to concentrate on teaching or publication, what committees to seek assignments on, which administrators exercised genuine power, and which exercised only symbolic power. None of these informal norms of professorial life is written down; all are learned from peers. They become the stuff of organizational culture, changing as policies change and individuals in power come and go.

In many cases, learning the informal norms of the workplace involves learning what formal norms to break. This may mean holding back such as by giving less than one's potential or by actually breaking rules and laws. Many of the earliest studies of the culture of work observed precisely the means by which workers were informally taught to work to the norms of the workers rather than to the rules of formal expectations of management.

## Ideology

Becoming socialized into a job involves accepting the worldview of the occupational group, which is often called an "ideology." These ideologies may take over most of an individual's beliefs, such as in the case of the priesthood or other jobs that become lifelong commitments. Many professions that have what Everett Hughes called a license and mandate to know secrets, or to do extraordinary things such as seeing, touching, or cutting into people's bodies, are justified through ideologies. Becker and Hughes's early research on medical training first defined the importance of these ideologies. One learns these ideologies and adopts the worldviews they imply both in training and on the job. There are tremendous variations in the extent to which they influence workers, and they change through time. As society becomes more individualized as well as bureaucratic, occupational ideologies may recede in importance. An example of this is a medical doctor performing the same operation over and over for an HMO. Such doctors may come to see themselves as salaried workers and, as such, as more interested in the salary than the larger role the medical professional used to have.

One enters a job with a set of ideas that have developed through one's social class, family, and education. In many cases, the occupational socialization extends and further develops these forms of socialization. The child of a police officer, doctor, or cook likely has picked up fragments of his or her parents' occupational socialization and more easily adopts the beliefs of the profession as a new recruit. Or occupational ideologies may fly in the face of ideological orientations that a recruit brings to the job. Gary Fine's (1985) study of the occupational socialization of professional cooks, which is included in this volume (see chapter 4), makes this point. The cooks, recruited from working-class backgrounds, must reject the tastes—the unconscious aesthetic judgments—they grew up with to become successful cooks in settings that can afford their services. They become connoisseurs of sauces, crisply cooked vegetables, and rare meat. Because they serve a social class higher than their own, they must internalize at least part of the social world of those they will serve. This transformation of values has effects that may go beyond the experience of the workplace. One can imagine, for example, the experience of the young cook returning home to pass judgment on his mother's meatloaf and mashed potatoes after a few semesters of training! Robert Granfield's working-class law students defined their experiences at an elite law school in class terms. Granfield found, unlike Gary Fine, that the students entered law school proud of their working-class values, but they were willing to set them aside when the ideological expectations of the law profession so dictated.

Sherryl Kleinman's (1984) study of female seminary students at a humanistic seminary shows how ideologies on the job are often unconsciously part of gender consciousness. In the humanistic seminary, students draw upon values such as empathy and nonauthoritarian modes of presentation and decision making. The seminary itself inculcates a skeptical humanism instead of a fundamentalist view of Christianity. When the female graduate ventures into the occupational role of the minister, she has been trained to believe in values and methods that are often inconsistent with the expectations of congregations and church bureaucracies. For the female minister to survive, both she and the clients must adjust their expectations of each other.

## IDENTITY

If we consider occupational socialization as the means by which we are formally trained and informally acculturated to a job, we can understand identity as the result of that process. But our orientation focuses more on social process; and we understand that socialization to a job or occupation goes on throughout the job, and that the extent to which one's identity is consistent with one's occupation varies over time and by social location.

For much of the history of American sociology, work was thought of in the context of what were called "roles," considered to be building blocks of the social structure. A working society socialized people to fit the expectations of work roles, which were defined to address social needs. If socialization worked well, workers embraced their various positions in the society, social needs were met, and society functioned smoothly.

However, this view was always understood to be overly simple and blind to the factors that would influence why one job would seem to invite more identity than another. The articles in part II of this book and the recommended readings explore the problematic way in which occupational identities are created, sustained, and rejected.

From one perspective, the matter of roles and identities can be thought of as a continuum. In a small handful of occupations, the self is expected to merge with the job. Consider priests, for example. Although the role of the priest is, in fact, an occupation, it is supposed to be something greater, a master identity that encompasses all aspects of an individual's identity. The violation of this identity when priests molest children is felt so keenly not because the public is particularly religious, but because a role assumed to be beyond the individual is proved to be humanly made and thus fallible.

Sociologists have referred to strong but less than total identification with an occupation as "role closeness." Naturally, this often occurs in occupations that provide high status and financial rewards. But the concept is certainly not necessarily associated only with gaining rewards. One of the editors of this volume (Harper, 1987) studied the work of a rural mechanic, and certainly the most striking thing about this individual's strong and resilient work identity was its lack of dependence on financial reward. Among others we have studied, such as dairy farmers, the extent to which people feel closely integrated with their work role may be inversely correlated with their material rewards. The most traditional farmers, who made the least amount of money, appeared to have internalized the work role most deeply (Harper, 2001). Those who have jobs that provide contradictory bases for status and reward require that workers find complicated paths to a partial work identity (Ronai and Cross's study of strippers, included in this volume, tells this story well; see chapter 6).

The problematical aspects of getting one's identity from one's work has been called "role distance." The famous sociologist Erving Goffman described the ways people express their disdain or rejection of jobs they must have but don't want to. Of course, all societies devalue particular kinds of work, and people who find themselves in those jobs must create extreme role distance to sustain a positive sense of self aside from the work identity. The people who clean rotted roadkill from our highways see their role as a specialized service, which indeed it is. When occupations require truly heinous activities (say, for example, a member of a security or police force who must torture victims to extract information), workers must be extremely creative in separating themselves from their role, assuming they have not given in to the darkness of these officially deviant work roles.

The general perspective has come to be known as "identity work," that is, the recognition that identity is achieved, provisional, and always in some degree of change. One claims or rejects identity from work through strategies that are not at all obvious and are more easily understood by symbolic interactionists than role theorists.

## EXPERIENCING THE CAREER

The discussion of the career is an extension of the subject of occupational socialization. People in their late teens and early twenties, while preparing for their life's work, tend to think that their long struggle up the mountain of education will lead to a plateau called Adult Life, with Grown-up Work that may have a few gradual changes in elevation but mostly stays the same. The reality of modern life is, of course, quiet different. The pattern of one's life work may be clearly discernable and predictable, or it might be erratic and ever changing.

The career can be thought of as a scenario played differently by different actors. The metaphor of a stage is enticing; one sees the individual moving across the stage, aging, changing, and facing traumas and different possibilities: experiencing different things as important, finally finishing, and dying.

The idea of a career is tied in with the beginning of bureaucratic organization in public administration, the military, and the Christian church. The beginning of the career marked the modern era in which both individuals and institutions began to plan their futures explicitly. It might mean, for the institution, being able to project the costs of long-term institutional life. For the individual, the career provides not only a plan around which to organize one's working life but also a plan for the period when the work life is over. Rational saving for retirement, merged into the activities of work, is but a logical extension of the bureaucratic organization of one's life. Although in the traditional sense, the bureaucratic organization of the career provides for security and stability, it is also said that it is deadening and suffocating to know the contours and expectations of one's forty-year work life when one begins his or her job. Hoff's 1999 study of the careers of medical doctors in an HMO tells this story well.

These introductory comments view the career as an element of social structure. Our readings show the career as it is perceived and experienced.

One begins with the realization that there are vastly different types of careers, as we categorize them on the basis of such sociological constructs as "contingencies." Certainly, the classic Weberian sense of career still holds for such occupations as the civil service, the military, and in some cases academic life. One begins these careers with a clear understanding of the possibilities for one's future. One's performance is regularly monitored, and meritorious service (i.e., fulfilling institutional expectations) is awarded with raises, promotions, and more responsibilities. Systematic savings, initiated by the organization, make the transition to retirement as organizationally natural as were the movements through the various stages of the career. The subjective nature of passage through these types of careers has been studied by Edgar Sachein (1984).

Many jobs and occupations, however, do not form into a bureaucratically organized career. Perhaps the free farmer and the trader are the oldest examples of workers whose individual work life trajectory is based on individual effort and fortune rather than organizational mandate. With the rise of an entrepreneurial class, the concept of career took a different course: although the success or failure of the business depended on his or her actions outside of a larger organizational structure (in the sense, for example, that the continuation of the business is made possible by profits rather than tax revenues), the businessperson's long-term success led to larger businesses that provided careers, in the more traditional sense, for others.

We know little of how the career is perceived at the beginning. Becker and Carper's studies of graduate students in philosophy, engineering, and physiology ("The Development," 1956; "The Elements," 1956; 1957) are exceptions. We learn of the contrasting orientation to work futures among these three groups as well as their differing attitudes toward their training, their mentors, and their professors. The study whets one's appetite for a follow-up and a wider comparative framework in order to identify more general patterns of career perception at beginning, middle, and end.

The nature of the career is influenced by the particular type of effort that lies at its basis. If the effort is intellectual, a person may become more and more adept as he or she grows older. The professor, the doctor, and the judge presumably gain in competence as they gain in experience. This, of course, is a simplification that is at odds with the nature of these careers for many. The concept of "burnout" is applied to professionals who are done in by the pressure or, ironically, the routinization of their work.

If the skill that lies at the basis of the career is physical, the way it is for a ballet dancer (Federico, 1983) or an athlete (Gallmeier, 1987), the contours of the career are entirely different. One enters the career through competition and holds the job only by demonstrating in the work that one is better than those trying to take the job for themselves. In the case of the athlete or the dancer, the length of the career may be limited to a very short period: that of peak physical capacity. There are, however, vast differences even in these occupations. The average career of the professional football player is less than five years, and it is even shorter for baseball players (although rare stars play into their forties). Dancers seldom last more than ten years in a company, and because all but the stars are paid poorly and there are relatively few jobs on the periphery of the main career, most must leave the career completely when it is finished. Their identity earned through their work is reduced to fading newspaper or magazine articles, portfolios of photographs, and the few friends from the world of work they retain.

This leads to the question of the ends of careers, sequential careers, and careers of failed ambition. The issue of interest here is the way that these transitions are experienced by the people who often must in the years of their adulthood remake their identity. Some may be able to move into a new career on the periphery of the old—the baseball player may become a manager, or the dancer a choreographer—and thus retain their sense of self in their chosen world. Others must leave their chosen line of work (which they may have achieved at great odds and supreme effort) completely. Or one of the most interesting cases is of the worker who stops trying to achieve the most advanced form of an occupation because of what Howard Becker calls the "side bets"—the features of a person's life outside of work that take on more importance as one grows older. These may be family or lifestyle considerations that become more important as one gives up on the dreams of early adulthood. Or it might be, as Faulkner shows us (see chapter 8), that the individual chooses to play at a lesser orchestra in order to occupy a first chair, with its opportunities and honors. Given the complexity and significance of these issues (indeed, all of us experience the career and redefine ourselves in the process), it is surprising that so few sociologists have chosen it as subject matter. It remains fertile ground for the cultural study of work.

## CITED AND RECOMMENDED READING

Becker, Howard S., and James Carper. "The Development of Identification with an Occupation." *American Journal of Sociology* 61 (1956): 289–98.
———. "The Elements of Identification with an Occupation." *American Sociological Review* 21 (1956): 341–48.
———. "Adjustment of Conflicting Expectations in the Development of Identification with an Occupation." *Social Forces* 36 (1957): 51–56.
Becker, Howard S., and Blanche Geer. "The Fate of Idealism in Medical School." *American Sociological Review* 23, no. 1 (February 1958): 50–56.
Becker, H. S., and Anselm L. Strauss. "Careers, Personality and Adult Socialization." *American Journal of Sociology* 62 (November 1956): 253–63.
Coombs, R., et al. "Socialization for Death: The Physician's Role." *Urban Life* 4 (1975): 250–71.
Dressel, Paula, et al. "Becoming a Male Stripper." *Work and Occupations* 9, no. 3 (August 1982): 387–406.
Federico, Ronald. "The Decision to End a Performing Career in Ballet." In *Perform-*

*ers and Performances: The Social Organization of Artistic Work,* edited by Jack B. Kamermann and Rosanne Mortorella, 57–69. New York: Praeger, 1983.

Gallmeier, Charles. "Dinosaurs and Prospects: Toward a Sociology of the Compressed Career." In *Sociological Inquiry: A Humanistic Perspective,* edited by K. M. Mahmoudi, 1–21. Dubuque, Iowa: Kendall Hunt, 1987.

Geer, Blanche. "Learning to Work." *Sage Contemporary Social Science Issues* (1972): 48–109.

Geer, Blanche, et al. "Learning the Ropes: Situational Learning in Four Occupational Training Programs." In *Among the People,* edited by I. Deutcher and E. J. Thompson, 209–33. New York: Basic Books, 1968.

Granfield, Robert. "Making It by Faking It: Working-Class Students in an Elite Academic Environment." *Journal of Contemporary Ethnography* 20, no. 3 (1991): 331–51.

Haas, J., and W. Shaffir. "The Professionalization of Medical Students: Developing Competence and a Cloak of Competence." *Symbolic Interaction* 1 (1977): 71–88.

Haas, Jack, and William Shaffir. "The 'Fate of Idealism' Revisited." *Urban Life* 13, no. 1 (April 1984): 63–81.

Hafferty, Frederick W. "Cadaver Stories and the Emotional Socialization of Medical Students." *Journal of Health and Social Behavior* 29 (December 1988): 344–56.

Hall, O. "The Stages of a Medical Career." *American Journal of Sociology* 53 (March 1948): 327–36.

Harper, Douglas. *Working Knowledge: Skill and Community in a Small Shop.* Chicago: University of Chicago Press, 1987.

Harper, Douglas. *Changing Works: Visions of a Lost Agriculture.* Chicago: University of Chicago Press, 2001.

Heyl, Barbara. "The Madam as Teacher: The Training of House Prostitutes." *Social Problems* 24 (June 1977): 545–55.

Hickey, Joseph V., William E. Thompson, and Donald L. Foster. "Becoming the Easter Bunny: Socialization into a Fantasy Role." *Journal of Contemporary Ethnography* 7, no. 1 (1988): 67–95.

Hoff, T. J. "The Social Organization of Physician-managers in a Changing HMO." *Sociology of Work and Occupations* 26, no. 3 (1999): 324–51.

Jurik, N. C. "Getting Away and Getting By: The Experiences of Self-employed Home Workers." *Sociology of Work and Occupations* 25, no. 1 (1998): 7–35.

Kleinman, Sherryl. "Women in Seminary: Dilemmas of Professional Socialization." *Sociology of Education* 25 (October 1984): 210–19.

Ladinsky, Jack. "Careers of Lawyers, Law Practice, and Legal Institutions." *American Sociological Review* 28, no. 1 (February 1963): 47–54.

Levintin, T. E. "Role Performance and Role Distance in a Low-status Occupation: The Puller." *Sociological Quarterly* 5 (summer 1964): 251–60.

Miller, M. L., and J. Van Maanen. "Getting into Fishing: Observations on the Social Identities of New England Fishermen." *Urban Life* 11 (1982): 27–54.

Reitzes, Donald C., et al. "The Decision to Retire: A Career Perspective." *Social Science Quarterly* 79, no. 3 (September 1998): 607–19.

Riemer, J. W. "Becoming a journeyman electrician: Some implicit indicators in the apprenticeship process." *Sociology of Work and Occupations* 4: 87–98.

Roy, Donald. "Quota Restriction and Goldbricking in a Machine Shop." *American Journal of Sociology* 57 (March 1952): 427–43.

Sachein, Edgar H. "Culture as an Environmental Context for Careers." *Journal of Occupational Behavior* 5, no. 1 (January 1984): 71–81.

Simpson, I. H. "Patterns of Socialization into Professions: The Case of Student Nurses." *Sociological Inquiry* 37 (winter 1967): 47–54.

Skipper, J. K., et al. "Stripteasers: The Anatomy and Career Contingencies of a Deviant Occupation." *Social Problems* 17 (1970): 391–404.

Stebbins, R. A. "Career: The Subjective Approach." *Sociological Quarterly* 11 (winter 1970): 32–49.

Van Maanen, J. "Breaking in: Socialization to work." In *Handbook of Work, Organization and Society,* edited by R. Dubin, 67–130. Chicago: Rand McNally, 1976.

Van Maanen, John. "Observations on the Making of Policemen." *Human Organization* 32, no. 4 (1973): 407–17.

Woods, C. "Students without Teachers: Student Culture in a Barber College." In *Learning to Work,* edited by Blanche Geer, 19–29. Beverly Hills, Calif.: Sage, 1972.

# 3

# The Fate of Idealism in Medical School

*Howard S. Becker and Blanche Geer*

It makes some difference in a man's performance of his work whether he believes wholeheartedly in what he is doing or feels that in important respects it is a fraud, whether he feels convinced that it is a good thing or believes that it is not really of much use after all. The distinction we are making is the one people have in mind when they refer, for example, to their calling as a "noble profession" on the one hand or a "racket" on the other. In the one case they idealistically proclaim that their work is all that it claims on the surface to be; in the other they cynically concede that it is first and foremost a way of making a living and that its surface pretensions are just that and nothing more. Presumably, different modes of behavior are associated with these perspectives when wholeheartedly embraced. The cynic cuts corners with a feeling of inevitability while the idealist goes down fighting. *The Blackboard Jungle* and *Not as a Stranger* are only the most recent in a long tradition of fictional portrayals of the importance of this aspect of a man's adjustment to his work.

Professional schools often receive a major share of the blame for producing this kind of cynicism—and none more than the medical school. The idealistic young freshman changes into a tough, hardened, unfeeling doctor; or so the popular view has it. Teachers of medicine sometimes rephrase the distinction between the clinical and pre-clinical years into one between the "cynical" and "pre-cynical" years. Psychological research supports this view, presenting attitude surveys which show medical students year by year scoring lower on "idealism" and higher on "cynicism."[1] Typically, this cynicism is seen as developing in response to the shattering of ideals consequent on coming face-to-face with the realities of professional practice.

In this paper, we attempt to describe the kind of idealism that characterizes the medical freshmen and to trace both the development of cynicism and
the vicissitudes of that idealism in the course of the four years of medical
training. Our main themes are that though they develop cynical feelings in
specific situations directly associated with their medical school experience,
the medical students never lose their original idealism about the practice of
medicine; that the growth of both cynicism and idealism are not simple
developments, but are instead complex transformations; and that the very
notions "idealism" and "cynicism" need further analysis, and must be seen
as situational in their expressions rather than as stable traits possessed by
individuals in greater or lesser degree. Finally, we see the greater portion of
these feelings as being collective rather than individual phenomena.

Our discussion is based on a study we are now conducting at a state medical school,[2] in which we have carried on participant observation with students of all four years in all of the courses and clinical work to which they
are exposed. We joined the students in their activities in school and after
school and watched them at work in labs, on the hospital wards, and in the
clinic. Often spending as much as a month with a small group of from five
to fifteen students assigned to a particular activity, we came to know them
well and were able to gather information in informal interviews and by over-
hearing the ordinary daily conversation of the group.[3] In the course of our
observation and interviewing we have gathered much information on the
subject of idealism. Of necessity, we shall have to present the very briefest
statement of our findings with little or no supporting evidence.[4] The problem of idealism is, of course, many-faceted and complex and we have dealt
with it in a simplified way, describing only some of its grosser features.[5]


## THE FRESHMEN


The medical students enter school with what we may think of as the idealistic
notion, implicit in lay culture, that the practice of medicine is a wonderful
thing and that they are going to devote their lives to service to mankind.
They believe that medicine is made up of a great body of well-established
facts that they will be taught from the first day on and that these facts will
be of immediate practical use to them as physicians. They enter school
expecting to work industriously and expecting that if they work hard enough
they will be able to master this body of fact and thus become good doctors.

In several ways the first year of medical school does not live up to their
expectations. They are disillusioned when they find they will not be near
patients at all, that the first year will be just like another year of college. In
fact, some feel that it is not even as good as college because their work in
certain areas is not as thorough as courses in the same fields in undergraduate

school. They come to think that their courses (with the exception of anatomy) are not worth much because, in the first place, the faculty (being Ph.D.s) knows nothing about the practice of medicine, and, in the second place, the subject matter itself is irrelevant, or as the students say, "ancient history."

The freshmen are further disillusioned when the faculty tells them in a variety of ways that there is more to medicine than they can possibly learn. They realize it may be impossible for them to learn all they need to know in order to practice medicine properly. Their disillusionment becomes more profound when they discover that this statement of the faculty is literally true.[6] Experience in trying to master the details of the anatomy of the extremities convinces them that they cannot do so in the time they have. Their expectation of hard work is not disappointed; they put in an eight-hour day of classes and laboratories, and study four or five hours a night and most of the weekend as well.

Some of the students, the brightest, continue to attempt to learn it all, but succeed only in getting more and more worried about their work. The majority decide that, since they can't learn it all, they must select from among all the facts presented to them those they will attempt to learn. There are two ways of making this selection. On the one hand, the student may decide on the basis of his own uninformed notions about the nature of medical practice that many facts are not important, since they relate to things which seldom come up in the actual practice of medicine; therefore, he reasons, it is useless to learn them. On the other hand, the student can decide that the important thing is to pass his examinations and, therefore, that the important facts are those which are likely to be asked on an examination; he uses this as a basis for selecting both facts to memorize and courses for intensive study. For example, the work in physiology is dismissed on both of these grounds, being considered neither relevant to the facts of medical life nor important in terms of the amount of time the faculty devotes to it and the number of examinations in the subject.

A student may use either or both of these bases of selection at the beginning of the year, before many tests have been given. But after a few tests have been taken, the student makes "what the faculty wants" the chief basis of his selection of what to learn, for he now has a better idea of what this is and also has become aware that it is possible to fail examinations and that he therefore must learn the expectations of the faculty if he wishes to stay in school. The fact that one group of students, that with the highest prestige in the class, took this view early and did well on examinations was decisive in swinging the whole class around to this position. The students were equally influenced to become "test-wise" by the fact that, although they had all been in the upper range in their colleges, the class average on the first examination was frighteningly low.

In becoming test-wise, the students begin to develop systems for discovering the faculty wishes and learning them. These systems are both methods for studying their texts and shortcuts that can be taken in laboratory work. For instance, they begin to select facts for memorization by looking over the files of old examinations maintained in each of the medical fraternity houses. They share tip-offs from the lectures and offhand remarks of the faculty as to what will be on the examinations. In anatomy, they agree not to bother to dissect out subcutaneous nerves, reasoning that it is both difficult and time-consuming and the information can be secured from books with less effort. The interaction involved in the development of such systems and shortcuts helps to create a social group of a class which had previously been only an aggregation of smaller and less organized groups.

In this medical school, the students learn in this way to distinguish between the activities of the first year and their original view that everything that happens to them in medical school will be important. Thus they become cynical about the value of their activities in the first year. They feel that the real thing—learning which will help them to help mankind—has been postponed, perhaps until the second year, or perhaps even farther, at which time they will be able again to act on idealistic premises. They believe that what they do in their later years in school under supervision will be about the same thing they will do, as physicians, on their own; the first year had disappointed this expectation.

There is one matter, however, about which the students are not disappointed during the first year: the so-called trauma of dealing with the cadaver. But this experience, rather than producing cynicism, reinforces the student's attachment to his idealistic view of medicine by making him feel that he is experiencing at least some of the necessary unpleasantness of the doctors. Such difficulties, however, do not loom as large for the student as those of solving the problem of just what the faculty wants.

On this and other points, a working consensus develops in the new consolidated group about the interpretation of their experience in medical school and its norms of conduct. This consensus, which we call *student culture*,[7] focuses their attention almost completely on their day-to-day activities in school and obscures or sidetracks their earlier idealistic preoccupations. Cynicism, griping, and minor cheating become endemic, but the cynicism is specific to the educational situation, to the first year, and to only parts of it. Thus the students keep their cynicism separate from their idealistic feelings and by postponement protect their belief that medicine is a wonderful thing, that their school is a fine one, and that they will become good doctors.

## LATER YEARS

The sophomore year does not differ greatly from the freshman year. Both the work load and anxiety over examinations probably increase. Though they begin some medical activities, as in their attendance at autopsies and particularly in their introductory course in physical diagnosis, most of what they do continues to repeat the pattern of the college science curriculum. Their attention still centers on the problem of getting through school by doing well on examinations.

During the third and fourth, or clinical years, teaching takes a new form. In place of lectures and laboratories, the students' work now consists of the study of actual patients admitted to the hospital or seen in the clinic. Each patient who enters the hospital is assigned to a student who interviews him about his illnesses, past and present, and performs a physical examination. He writes this up for the patient's chart, and appends the diagnosis and the treatment that he would use were he allowed actually to treat the patient. During conferences with faculty physicians, often held at the patient's bedside, the student is quizzed about items of his report and called upon to defend them or to explain their significance. Most of the teaching in the clinical years is of this order.

Contact with patients brings a new set of circumstances with which the student must deal. He no longer feels the great pressure created by tests, for he is told by the faculty, and this is confirmed by his daily experience, that examinations are now less important. His problems now become those of coping with a steady stream of patients in a way that will please the staff man under whom he is working, and of handling what is sometimes a tremendous load of clinical work so as to allow himself time for studying diseases and treatments that interest him and for play and family life.

The students earlier have expected that once they reach the clinical years they will be able to realize their idealistic ambitions to help people and to learn those things immediately useful in aiding people who are ill. But they find themselves working to understand cases as medical problems rather than working to help the sick and memorizing the relevant available facts so that these can be produced immediately for a questioning staff man. When they make ward rounds with a faculty member they are likely to be quizzed about any of the seemingly countless facts possibly related to the condition of the patient for whom they are "caring."

Observers speak of the cynicism that overtakes the student and the lack of concern for his patients as human beings. This change does take place, but it is not produced solely by "the anxiety brought about by the presence of death and suffering."[8] The student becomes preoccupied with the technical aspects of the cases with which he deals because the faculty requires him to do so. He is questioned about so many technical details that he must spend most of his time learning them.

The frustrations created by his position in the teaching hospital further divert the student from idealistic concerns. He finds himself low man in a hierarchy based on clinical experience, so that he is allowed very little of the medical responsibility he would like to assume. Because of his lack of experience, he cannot write orders, and he receives permission to perform medical and surgical procedures (if at all) at a rate he considers far too slow. He usually must content himself with "mere" vicarious participation in the drama of danger, life, and death that he sees as the core of medical practice. The student culture accents these difficulties so that events (and especially those involving patients) are interpreted and reacted to as they push him toward or hold him back from further participation in this drama. He does not think in terms the layman might use.

As a result of the increasingly technical emphasis of this thinking the student appears cynical to the non-medical outsider, though from his own point of view he is simply seeing what is "really important." Instead of reacting with the layman's horror and sympathy for the patient to the sight of a cancerous organ that has been surgically removed, the student is more likely to regret that he was not allowed to close the incision at the completion of the operation, and to rue the hours that he must spend searching in the fatty flesh for the lymph nodes that will reveal how far the disease has spread. As in other lines of work, he drops lay attitudes for those more relevant to the way the event affects someone in his position.

This is not to say that the students lose their original idealism. When issues of idealism are openly raised in a situation they define as appropriate, they respond as they might have when they were freshmen. But the influence of the student culture is such that questions which might bring forth this idealism are not brought up. Students are often assigned patients for examination and follow-up whose conditions might be expected to provoke idealistic crises. Students discuss such patients, however, with reference to the problems they create for the *student.* Patients with terminal diseases who are a long time dying, and patients with chronic diseases who show little change from week to week, are more likely to be viewed as creating extra work with extra compensation in knowledge or the opportunity to practice new skills than as examples of illness which raise questions about euthanasia. Such cases require the student to spend time every day checking on progress which he feels will probably not take place and to write long "progress" notes in the patient's chart although little progress has occurred.

This apparent cynicism is a collective matter. Group activities are built around this kind of workaday perspective, constraining the students in two ways. First, they do not openly express the lay idealistic notions they may hold, for their culture does not sanction such expression; second, they are less likely to have thoughts of this deviant kind when they are engaged in group activity. The collective nature of this "cynicism" is indicated by the fact that students become more openly idealistic whenever they are removed from the influence of student culture—when they are alone with a sociologist as they near the finish of school and sense the approaching end of student life, for example, or when they are isolated from their classmates and therefore are less influenced by this culture.[9]

They still feel, as advanced students, though much less so than before, that school is irrelevant to actual medical practice. Many of their tasks, like running laboratory tests on patients newly admitted to the hospital or examining surgical specimens in the pathology laboratory, seem to them to have nothing to do with their vision of their future activity as doctors. As in their freshman year, they believe that perhaps they must obtain the knowledge they will need in spite of the school. They still conceive of medicine as a huge body of proven facts, but no longer believe that they will ever be able to master it all. They now say that they are going to try to apply the solution of the practicing M.D. to their own dilemma: learn a few things that they are interested in very well and know enough about things to pass examinations while in school and, later on in practice, to know to which specialist to send difficult patients.

Their original medical idealism reasserts itself as the end of school approaches. Seniors show more interest than students in earlier years in serious ethical dilemmas of the kind they expect to face in practice. They have become aware of ethical problems laymen often see as crucial for the physician—whether it is right to keep patients with fatal diseases alive as long as possible, or what should be done if an influential patient demands an abortion—and worry about them.[10] As they near graduation and student culture begins to break down as the soon-to-be doctors are about to go their separate ways, these questions are more and more openly discussed.

While in school, they have added to their earlier idealism a new and peculiarly professional idealism. Even though they know that few doctors live up to the standards they have been taught, they intend always to examine their patients thoroughly and to give treatment based on firm diagnosis rather than merely to relieve symptoms. This expansion and transformation of idealism appear most explicitly in their consideration of alternative careers, concerning both specialization and the kind of arrangements to be made for setting up practice. Many of their hypothetical choices aim at making it possible for them to be the kind of doctors their original idealism pictured. Many seniors consider specialty training so that they will be able to work in a limited field in which it will be more nearly possible to know all there is to know, thus avoiding the necessity of dealing in a more ignorant way with the wider range of problems general practice would present. In the same manner, they think of schemes to establish partnerships or other arrangements making it easier to avoid a work load which would prevent them from giving each patient the thorough examination and care they now see as ideal.

In other words, as school comes to an end, the cynicism specific to the school situation also comes to an end and their original and more general idealism about medicine comes to the fore again, though within a framework of more realistic alternatives. Their idealism is now more informed although no less selfless.

## DISCUSSION

We have used the words "idealism" and "cynicism" loosely in our description of the changeable state of mind of the medical student, playing on ambiguities we can now attempt to clear up. Retaining a core of common meaning, the dictionary definition, in our reference to the person's belief in the worth of his activity and the claims made for it, we have seen that this is not a generalized trait of the students we studied but rather an attitude which varies greatly, depending on the particular activity the worth of which is questioned and the situation in which the attitude is expressed.

This variability of the idealistic attitude suggests that in using such an element of personal perspective in sociological analysis one should not treat it as homogenous but should make a determined search for subtypes which may arise under different conditions and have differing consequences. Such subtypes presumably can be constructed along many dimensions. There might, for instance, be consistent variations in the medical students' idealism through the four years of school that are related to their social class backgrounds. We have stressed in this report the subtypes that can be constructed according to variations in the object of the idealistic attitude and variations in the audience the person has in mind when he adopts the attitude. The medical students can be viewed as both idealistic and cynical, depending on whether one has in mind their view of their school activities or the future they envision for themselves as doctors. Further, they might take one or another of these positions depending on whether their implied audience is made up of other students, their instructors, or the lay public.

A final complication arises because cynicism and idealism are not merely attributes of the actor, but are as dependent on the person doing the attributing as they are on the qualities of the individual to whom they are attributed.[11] Though the student may see his own disregard of the unique personal troubles of a particular patient as proper scientific objectivity, the layman may view this objectivity as heartless cynicism.[12]

Having made these analytic distinctions, we can now summarize the transformations of these characteristics as we have seen them occurring among medical students. Some of the students' determined idealism at the outset is reaction against the lay notion, of which they are uncomfortably aware, that doctors are money-hungry cynics; they counter this with an idealism of similar lay origin stressing the doctor's devotion to service. But this idealism soon meets a setback, as students find that it will not be relevant for a while, since medical school has, it seems, little relation to the practice of medicine, as they see it. As it has not been refuted, but only shown to be temporarily beside the point, the students "agree" to set this idealism aside in favor of a realistic approach to the problem of getting through school. This approach, which we have labeled as the cynicism specific to the school experience, serves as protection for the earlier grandiose feelings about medicine by postponing their exposure to reality to a distant future. As that future approaches near the end of the four years and its possible mistreatment of their ideals moves closer, the students again worry about maintaining their integrity, this time in actual medical practice. They use some of the knowledge they have gained to plan careers which, it is hoped, can best bring their ideals to realization.

We can put this in propositional form by saying that when a man's ideals are challenged by outsiders and then further strained by reality, he may salvage them by postponing their application to a future time when conditions are expected to be more propitious.

## NOTES

Reprinted from *American Sociological Review* 23, no. 1 (February 1958): 50–56.

Revision of paper read at the annual meeting of the Midwest Sociological Society, April 5, 1957, in Des Moines, Iowa.

1. Leonard D. Eron, "Effect of Medical Education on Medical Students," *Journal of Medical Education*, 10 (October, 1955), pp. 559–566.

2. This study is sponsored by Community Studies, Inc., of Kansas City, Missouri, and is being carried on at the University of Kansas Medical School, to whose dean, staff, and students we are indebted for their wholehearted cooperation. Professor Everett C. Hughes of the University of Chicago is director of the project.

3. The technique of participant observation has not been fully systematized, but some approaches to this have been made. See, for example, Florence R. Kluckhohn, "The Participant Observer Technique in Small Communities," *American Journal of Sociology*, 45 (November, 1940), pp. 331–343; Arthur Vidich, "Participant Observation and the Collection and Interpretation of Data," ibid., 60 (January, 1955), pp. 354–360; William Foote Whyte, "Observational Field-Work Methods," in Maria Johoda, Morton Deutsch, and Stuart W. Cook (editors), *Research Methods in the Social Sciences*, New York: Dryden Press, 1951, II, pp. 393–514; *Street Corner Society* (Enlarged Edition), Chicago: University of Chicago Press, 1955, pp. 279–358; Rosalie Hankey Wax, "Twelve Years Later: An Analysis of Field Experience," *American Journal of Sociology*, 63 (September, 1957), pp. 133–142; Morris S. Schwartz and Charlotte Green Schwartz, "Problems in Participant Observation," ibid., 60 (January, 1955), pp. 343–353; and Howard S. Becker and Blanche Geer, "Participant Observation and Interviewing: A Comparison," *Human Organization* (fall, 1957). The last item represents the first of a projected series of papers attempting to make explicit the operations involved in this method. For a short description of some techniques

used in this study, see Howard S. Becker, "Interviewing Medical Students," *American Journal of Sociology* 62 (September, 1956), pp. 199–201.

4. A fuller analysis and presentation of evidence will be contained in a volume on this study now being prepared by the authors in collaboration with Everett C. Hughes and Anselm L. Strauss. (*Editor's note:* That book was published as *Boys in White: Student Culture in Medical School* [Chicago: University of Chicago Press, 1961].)

5. Renee Fox has shown how complex one aspect of this whole subject is in her analysis of the way medical students at Cornell become aware of and adjust to both their own failure to master all available knowledge and the gaps in current knowledge in many fields. See her "Training for Uncertainty," in Robert K. Merton, George G. Reader, and Patricia L. Kendall, *The Student Physician: Introductory Studies in the Sociology of Medical Education*, Cambridge: Harvard University Press, 1957, pp. 207–241.

6. Compare Fox's description of student reaction to this problem at Cornell (op. cit., pp. 209–221).

7. The concept of student culture is analyzed in some detail in Howard S. Becker and Blanche Geer, "Student Culture in Medical School," *Harvard Educational Review* (winter, 1958), pp. 70–80.

8. Dana L. Farnsworth, "Some Observations on the Attitudes and Motivations of the Harvard Medical Student," *Harvard Medical Alumni Bulletin*, January, 1956, p. 34.

9. See the discussion in Howard S. Becker, "Interviewing Medical Students," op. cit.

10. This article was written in 1958, fifteen years before the U.S. Supreme Court decision *Roe v. Wade* (1973).

11. See Philip Selznick's related discussion of fanaticism in *TVA and the Grass Roots*, Berkeley: University of California Press, 1953, pp. 205–213.

12. George Orwell gives the layman's side in his essay, "How the Poor Die," in *Shooting an Elephant and Other Essays*, London: Secker and Warburg, 1950, pp. 18–32.

# 4

# Occupational Aesthetics: How Trade School Students Learn to Cook

*Gary Alan Fine*

Social scientists frequently distinguish between behavior that is instrumental and that which is expressive (Bales, 1953; Slater, 1955). Instrumental behavior is designed to achieve a goal, whereas expressive behavior reflects that constellation of motives that are personal, emotional, self-satisfying, and not directly related to achieving formal tasks. Such a dichotomy has appeared in the literature on work and occupations in the distinction between the "work" and that informal structure of work ("play") that makes work bearable (Bowman, 1983). The expressive side of work includes such activities as joking (Bradney, 1957), rites of initiation (Vaught and Smith, 1980), gossip (Davis, 1972), bingeing (Haas, 1972), and play (Nusbaum, 1978).

Although heuristically useful for some purposes, this distinction dissolves when we attend to the place of aesthetic display in work. Aesthetics are an integral part of most, if not all, human work, and comprise a particularly core component of those occupations that involve some measure of sensory evaluation, even when those occupations are not conventionally regarded as "artistic." For it is readily apparent that in most if not all occupations practitioners and clients are concerned not merely with the technical doing of tasks, but also with how the product looks and/or how the service is performed. In ignoring issues of work aesthetics, we ignore a critical factor in work generally and in the evaluation of occupational competency in particular. In this respect, then, aesthetic display involves expressive behavior that *is* instrumental behavior (Abrahams, 1978; Bell, 1976; Dargan and Zeitlin, 1983; Jones, 1975; McCarl, 1974; Terkel, 1975).

With the exception of research on occupations that are consensually defined as artistic, this aesthetic component of work has been little explored. Yet, setting aside the thorny philosophical question of what constitutes a work of art,[1] empirical evidence suggests that works, even those in industrial or service occupations, often treat their work as an aesthetic object—as something that can be judged in sensory terms (e.g., is it beautiful?). McCarl (1974: 245), for example, found that welders attend to the sensory characteristics of their creations, expressing this care in a concern with style:

> A craftsman creates a product by attempting to realize its ideal form, i.e., he decides consciously and unconsciously how the final product is supposed to look, feel, taste, smell, and sound, and then tries to create a material manifestation of his ideal based on the specific use to which the product will be put.

Sometimes this aesthetic emphasis is referred to as "craft," sometimes as "skill," sometimes as "professionalism," and sometimes, most directly, as "art."

This expressive orientation to one's work does not just happen. It must be taught and learned. The novice may wish to have an "aesthetic attitude" (Dickie, 1974), but may not recognize the criteria by which others (particularly those within the occupation) will define his or her work to support this claim; alternatively the novice may not, at first, be aware that any such aesthetic concerns apply.

In this article I will explore how occupational socialization involves an aesthetic component by examining institutional training for a single occupation—cooking. In the vocational school programs in restaurant and hotel cooking studied here, instructors and students are concerned, in addition to learning the technical requirements of the trade, with imparting and acquiring some measure of aesthetic sophistication. The careful distinction that we might otherwise make between "art" and "labor" is invalid. Students in the schools I observed learn the proper style of craftsmanship—what is "good" or "attractive"—along with the formal requirements of their work.

In this light, socialization into an occupation does not consist only of acquiring techniques for performing certain tasks; socialization also involves taking over specific standards, beliefs, and moral concerns. Students not only wish to do their work efficiently; they wish to do it well. In this respect, they develop a concern for form as well as with function (e.g., not only does the cake include all the proper ingredients, but does it look appetizing?). Technical skills are given a moral[2] lamination. So, unlike the approach that discerns "techniques" in the moral rhetoric of workers (Hughes, 1971: 340–341; Becker et al., 1961), finding reactions to constraints in the midst of culture, I examine how culture and value are found in the midst of techniques and constraints. Obviously, either perspective if pushed too far is invalid; I hope to reset the balance slightly.

Cooking is a particularly interesting occupation for an examination of the place of aesthetics in work. Cooking is not typically considered one of the fine arts (e.g., Osborne, 1977; Winterbourne, 1981), but food is judged in terms of its sensory components. Food not only provides calories and nutrients, but it can look, taste, smell, and feel "good." Indeed, the higher levels of the occupation do merge into the fine arts (Harris, 1979; Revel, 1982). Thus the issue of aesthetics is more self-consciously raised among cooks than is likely to be the case in many other occupations. From a formal perspective, cooking may be an art, but it need not be; cooks may be concerned with the sensory qualities of their food, but they need not be. Because of the tensions in the occupation, cooking provides a good case study of the relationship between instrumental and expressive concerns in an occupation, but for the same reason it cautions us in making generalizations to other occupations in which the issues are not drawn as clearly. Although the issue raised is applicable to other occupations, the resolution may differ from job to job.

## TRAINING COOKS

Cooks are trained through three different techniques of occupational socialization. The first, rarely found in America (at least in its pure form), is apprenticeship. This entrée to cooking, still practiced in some European kitchens, involves working under the supervision of a master chef for several years. This technique, emphasizing idiosyncratic role modeling rather than standardized learning, is too labor-intensive to be cost-effective in providing occupational recruits to take their place in a large, routinized industry. The second, numerically most common form of occupational socialization is on-the-job training. One of the most accessible and popular jobs for adolescents is working in a fast food restaurant. These food preparation jobs require little training and no previous experience. Although employees typically do not learn much about cooking, they acquire those food preparation skills necessary for doing their jobs. These skills may permit them to advance to better jobs and allow them to discover if they enjoy working in a kitchen. In addition, there is vertical job mobility within a restaurant for kitchen personnel. A new employee commonly starts as a busboy, this is promoted to dishwasher, then to cook's helper, and finally to cook. Most learning in such situations is through observation rather than formal instruction.

A third method of occupational recruitment, the one discussed in this article, is postsecondary education.[3] Over the past twenty years, many programs have been created to train students to take positions in the food preparation (or "hospitality") industry. The most prestigious of these is the Culinary Institute of America in Hyde Park, New York. Despite the existence of elite institutions, most programs have more modest goals, and are often located in state-run trade schools, community colleges, or privately operated vocational institutes. Students enroll in a one- or two-year program that teaches them the rudiments of food preparation, management, sanitation, and baking. In some schools, students operate a model restaurant open to the general public.

## RESEARCH SETTINGS

For this research I conducted participant observation research and in-depth interviews (of 35 students and 8 instructors) at two Twin Cities Technical Vocational Institutes. Both schools (named here: City TVI and Suburban TVI) are state-operated and both recruit students from the Twin Cities metropolitan area.[4] While the average SES of students who attend Suburban TVI is somewhat higher than that of those at City TVI, the similarities between the schools and the students outweigh their differences. In this analysis I shall not distinguish between the two schools.

City TVI, the school at which I conducted research most intensively, offers a 4-quarter (11-month) program (as opposed to 8 quarters at Suburban TVI).[5] In the first quarter students learn basic cooking skills, including baking, making sauces and stocks, and sautéing. During the second quarter the student does quantity cooking by preparing food for and then serving 300 students in the school's cafeteria. This quarter provides students with the opportunity to improve their cooking skills through repetition in an environment that attempts to simulate a working kitchen. In the third quarter students simulate working in a restaurant. The school operates a restaurant that serves breakfast to the public for 2 weeks each quarter and serves lunch for an additional 8 weeks. Each day students prepare 4 or 5 main courses (including such gourmet dishes as Beef Wellington and Pork Sate). During this quarter students are expected to learn techniques of cooking-to-order, the pressure of cooking several dishes simultaneously, how to wait on customers, and how to set up a dining room. In addition, students learn how to cut chicken and beef. The fourth quarter instructor teaches specialty cooking. This includes ice carving, chaud-froid buffet work (garde manger),[6] flambéing, specialty baking, and advanced sauces.

Both programs have a considerable drop out rate, as is true of vocational programs elsewhere (Golladay and Wulfsberg, 1981; London, 1978). The three classes I observed started with sixteen, thirteen, and eighteen students, and graduated seven, ten, and seven students respectively;[7] some of those who dropped out may eventually return to complete the program. The group that started out with sixteen students had only three who were still in the cooking industry one year after graduation. For better or worse, the socialization that is given doesn't "take" for most students. In this article I shall focus on successful socialization, recognizing that the tasks required and messages given do not satisfy all students.

Both chef training programs were located in postsecondary trade or vocational schools that offer a wide collection of specialized vocational training. A number of key features of the cooking programs at City TVI and Suburban TVI must be understood against the broader background provided by the social organization of such vocation or "trade" schools.

## DISTINCTIVE FEATURES OF TRADE SCHOOLS

Despite the large number of students who attend postsecondary trade or vocational schools[8] (nearly two million students in 1978–1979; Golladay and Wulfsberg, 1981: 29), there has been little ethnographic research on these institutions. With few exceptions (London, 1978; Notkin, 1972; Woods, 1972), sociologists have ignored vocational education, and none of these studies examines a public vocational-trade school. Because most research on postsecondary education has examined college and professional schools, it is important to recognize the significant differences between most college programs and most trade school programs: the rigid program requirements of trade school education, the postschooling employment focus (the absence of the rhetoric of education for its own sake), and the absence of a student subculture.

### Rigid Program Requirements

Students in each program have a fixed set of requirements that excludes electives. The course of study has been planned for the students by the administrators and instructors, and students have little control over their education in terms of what courses they must take (although sometimes they can choose the sequence of these courses). Students do, of course, negotiate with their instructors on assignments and decide collectively what they can reasonably be expected to know—much as has been described in medical school (Becker et al., 1961). Unlike college, where students have considerable free time interspersed with their classes, and where most students are in class no more than 15 hours a week, students at vocational schools have approximately 35 hours of classes each week. Also unlike college, in which much learning takes place outside of the classroom, at vocational schools there is little homework and few extracurricular activities. Vocational education is a cross between high school and apprenticeship.

## Employment Focus

With rare exceptions students attend vocational schools not to become good citizens or well-rounded persons (see London, 1978) but in order to obtain a job upon graduation. So, the primary thrust of vocational education is vocational. Students are encouraged to get a part- or full-time job when in school to supplement the training of the school, and to increase the likelihood of employment upon graduation (as well as to supplement their incomes). Students' heavy time commitment prevents the development of interests other than those that are vocational.

## Absence of Student Culture

Vocational schools are composed of different "occupationally specific programs." Students in any one program typically have little opportunity to meet students in other programs. In one school, cooking students had no classes with noncooks; in the second school, students had one class with a group of plumbers (1 hour/day for 12 weeks) only because it proved logistically impossible to schedule their Customer Relations classes at separate hours. With a few exceptions (a do-little student council, an occasional dance, and friendships made outside of the school), a student will not know students from other programs. Students rigidly segregate themselves at lunch by program. Neither school has a student newspaper and, with the exception of the cafeteria, neither school has a student lounge. One of the schools studied has 43 different occupational programs; the other has 45. One might reasonably consider each as composed of about 40 different schools housed under one roof with central budgetary authority. All this makes postsecondary trade schools structurally different from other postsecondary education.

## THE AESTHETICS OF FOOD

Most vocational students have not previously excelled in school, as trade school represents a career option that does not require finely honed academic skills. Although all students in these three classes had completed high school (or had received a high school equivalency diploma), most had no college training, and only two had completed college. The majority of students hope that trade school will provide an experience significantly different from their previous education, particularly in that it involves hands-on training.

Most students enter the chef training program largely unaware of what is involved in the occupation—even though all of them have cooked food previously (in some cases "professionally" for modest establishments). In their ignorance they are little different from medical students and other aspiring professionals (see Haas and Shaffir, 1982), except their expectations are much lower and their images dimmer. With few exceptions students do not have a clear idea of the aesthetics of professional cooking, and may not even know that there is an aesthetic, although from cooking at home (and eating elsewhere), students are implicitly aware of various folk aesthetics. Thus chef instructors face formidable tasks in training their charges to be professionals and in teaching them the dimensions of the aesthetics of professional cooking. This training is an eye-opening experience for most of the students.

As in most occupational training programs, students are not taught about the grand philosophy of the occupation (if such exists); rather, they are taught particular skills and techniques that contain within them the aesthetic rules that students must generalize to related tasks. Although students are exhorted to make their food look appetizing, because "people eat with their eyes," this bon mot tells students little about how to achieve this goal.

The aesthetic rules for cooking are potentially more intricate than those of many other productive activities in that cooking appeals to at least four of our five senses: sight, taste, texture, and smell. Even sound is a component of eating—as in the enjoyment of the sound of a crisp item (Vickers and Christensen, 1980). However, the visual component has first priority in the aesthetic canons of food preparation.

Most of the aesthetic training in trade schools consists of learning the practical details of cooking. Students are taught during their first week in school when learning to make French bread that they should cut four slits in the top of their unbaked French bread dough: "They serve as decoration more than anything. You can throw [poppy or sesame] seeds on if you want to" (field notes, City TVI). Students take this advice to heart as they make slits and add seeds; some students even top their loaves with both types of seed in order to make them look doubly nice. After the bread has been baked students comment on how impressed they are with how the loaves look. As one student remarks to a fellow student: "We did pretty good for rookies."

Such instruction was recurrent in learning to work with a variety of food-stuffs and techniques of cooking and baking. To bring out the red color in a cherry pie, for example, students are told to add red food coloring; cherries must be made to look like cherries. Although similar in some ways to home training in cooking, students are here taught "trade secrets" and are constantly reminded that they are cooking for paying customers, customers of whose taste they are unaware. As a result, students are taught that their standards must involve compromise—an attempt to hit the midpoint of taste. For example, one instructor tells his class that they must decide how much sugar to add to their whipped cream in that some enjoy the richness of the cream whereas others prefer the sweetness of the sugar: "Now sugar is a matter of personal taste. So we try to hit something in-between" (field notes, City TVI). The point is that cooks are constrained, however they might personally feel, to strive for the lowest common denominator—that level of food taste that will appeal to all of their customers. This assumes implicit knowledge of the tastes of their audience—tastes that will differ in different establishments.

As mentioned, cooking depends on four of the five senses: looks, taste, texture, and smell. Because there is more consensus on what looks nice than on what tastes good, much of the aesthetics of cooking is directed to visual appeal. And although smell is important in food appreciation, it is not often discussed separately from taste, and may not even be appreciated separately (Osborne, 1977); "taste" is thus the generic term for both smell and taste. To understand the conventions of the aesthetics of cooking, I shall examine looks, taste, and texture separately.

## LOOKS

In practice, the look of food is usually seen as its most important aesthetic dimension. Chef-instructors and cooking students believe that people judge food visually.

> PO: Is cooking an art?
> Student: It's visual. People eat with their eyes. Little children eat with their eyes. There are some things that, probably why I like Oriental foods. They use a combination of green things. When they cook so fast nothing bleeds out their color. . . . I'll say "Oh, the broccoli came out, it's so green". . . . You watch [people look at food], if it's ugly, if it's funny colored, if it doesn't look refreshing, they're not going to eat it [Interview, Suburban TVI].
> Student: Looks [is most important] because it's the first impression. I've fooled around with stuff like making frosting and you give someone vanilla white frosting and you color one batch red and one batch green and you say which one do you like the flavor best, and if they like cherries or strawberries, they're going to like the red one best, and if they like mint or something like that, they're going to like the green one best. There's no difference. It's the color. You taste what you see [interview, City TVI].

These students have learned that a diner's expectations affect enjoyment and evaluation. The competent chef must have his or her food look pleasing according to the standards of the customers.

Instructors often show slides of display work (platters and garde manger) that they and past students have made for food shows to introduce students to the aesthetics of looks. When they first see these elaborate and beautiful displays, students are taken aback and respond with murmurs of amazement.

They find it hard to believe that they will be able to create similar works. Most students report that they had absolutely no idea that cooks do things like that or could do things like that. Among the more impressive displays pictured were a loaf of pumpernickel bread baked to look like an alligator, a gum paste painting of Rembrandt's *Man in the Golden Helmet,* and exquisitely decorated chaud-froid salmons and turkeys. Although it may seem odd to some to refer to foodstuffs as "art" and as "beautiful," the viewer of such objects would surely be convinced that one needed artistic sensibility to produce such items. As one chef-instructor commented: "Some people are real masters in the art of the garde manger. Some are so perfect you wonder if it's real food. . . . This is art using food as a medium" (field notes, City TVI).

The concern with the visual aesthetics of food presentation is not only connected to the preparation of elaborate food platters, but applies to everyday issues of food preparation. Nowhere is this better illustrated than with garnishes, as one instructor comments:

> Everything is eaten first with the eye. They got to go hand-in-hand [taste and visual appeal]. Both add to each other. . . . A sprig of parsley is simple, but if used right is very nice. [Garnishes] give eye appeal. . . . Obviously there is a time and a place for something that's complex, also there's not a time and place for such things. Also, cost comes in. . . . Most of them are real common foods. . . . [Garnishes are], you know, just something a little different. Imagination. You can do anything with food. [He says of making a radish rose:] If you're getting $6.95 for a club house sandwich, you want the nice one; if you're getting $2.50, these [unimpressive-looking radishes] are fine [field notes, City TVI].

As this instructor explicitly states, in a trade like cooking (and even, one might add, in an art like sculpture), the cost of the object influences the amount of work and the quality of materials that one puts into it; cooking is not art for art's sake, but an occupation that needs to produce a marketable commodity for its not always sophisticated public. One cannot separate the self-image of the worker from the rewards he or she will obtain from the market. Aesthetic issues, therefore, are always seen as related to economic ones.

Even things as mundane as cooking chicken or making soup have an aesthetic associated with it. In making chicken students must learn how to eliminate those specks of cooked chicken blood from baked chicken, because "people see a little speck of chicken blood, it turns them off. They think it's raw" (field notes, City TVI). Although students are assured that this belief is nonsense, they learn that they must eliminate that chicken blood if they are to stay in business. In cooking cream of mushroom soup, one must not overcook one's roux;[9] as their instructor notes: "You don't want that roux to brown on you. Otherwise it will turn your soup a nice tan. You don't want that" (field notes, City TVI). Even though the cook is not part of an artistic elite but of a large, low-paid industrial workforce, he or she must acquire the definite visual sensitivity that every competent cook should know.

## TASTE

In emphasizing the primary importance accorded visual appeal, I do not mean to slight the aesthetic standards associated with taste. Taste is what most people imagine is most important in food and, even if it is not always so in fact, no restaurant will survive long if its customers don't like the taste of its products. Not only must every individual ingredient taste good, but there needs to be a "marrying of tastes." In discussing the way in which cooking is an art, one student comments that the most important part of cooking is "the combinations, using herbs and spices, blending them, that takes a lot of art, what spices go together, and what won't" (interview, Suburban TVI). One chef-instructor explains to his students why soup needs to be simmered for a long period of time: "The main purpose [of simmering] is to marry the tastes of the vegetables and the stock." He notes that one adds wine to soup because "the wine is in there for a particular fruit flavor, nothing else. It needs time to cook. Otherwise it tastes as if one has mixed one's wine and meal together. The wine is a seasoning, not a cocktail." He continues that students must learn to sample the soup and sauces they are cooking and that "you should learn to cook with your nose" (Field notes, City TVI).

As with the visual appeal of food, decisions that outsiders may see as inconsequential or irrelevant are defined as important. Students are taught that the type of fat that one uses affects the taste of one's product. The fat used in making roux for soup affects its flavor. As one instructor comments: "Some cooks use bacon grease in everything. It's fine in some things, but not good in others. You gotta watch it. . . . You gotta be a little fussy about what flavor you use" (field notes, City TVI). Likewise, the number of bay leaves that a student adds to a stew will affect its taste, and, hence, the product's salability and his or her reputation for competence.

As with looks, expectations influence taste; people often have unstated expectations for the way that food products should taste and are disappointed when they don't taste that way. This failing need not be the cook's fault; in some cases the public has the wrong impression. An instructor noted about veal, "It's a very delicate flavor. Some people don't like it, maybe because they assume that it's going to taste like beef" (field notes, City TVI). Cooks may add a robust gravy or may use their skills at menu writing to convey metaphorically what customers are likely to find when they order ("delicate," "milk-fed," "tender," or "light").

## TEXTURE

Texture is rarely given the credit it deserves in the culinary arts. Chef-instructors don't often tell their students how important texture is, although they may occasionally do so for individual products. However, when students are judged on the products they cook, they are often evaluated on the basis of the texture of their product. Unpleasant texture seems particularly central when a person describes why they dislike a food:

PO: What food don't you like?
Student: Kidney beans. Oh, I hate kidney beans.
PO: Why?
Student: Because the texture of them [is] so terrible. After you get past the skin the inside . . . feels terrible [interview, City TVI].
PO: What about peas don't you like?
Former Student: They're cooked too much. They're mush. I started eating them quite a bit when I was younger and they were mushy, bland [interview, City TVI].

Food can be spoiled when the texture is not right, whether this is due to natural circumstance or to the mistakes of cooks, as in overcooking vegetables; students were criticized for cooking "the hell out of them." Just as texture can detract from the aesthetic experience of eating, so can it enhance it, as when a cook crisps up parsley or takes care to produce velvety smooth sauces. Just as students are taught how to avoid ruining the texture of food, so too they must learn how to enhance it.

## LEARNING AESTHETICS

Cooking in a competent and professional fashion is not easy. Students must control the looks, taste, and texture of the food they cook. They had barely considered many of these issues before entering school; none of them consciously decided to become artists. They decided to enter trade school to learn a trade, to get a steady job; few students dreamt of becoming world-class chefs. Students hope to obtain entry-level cooking positions when they graduate, and those who already have positions hope to be promoted in rank and salary. However, by the end of their training the cooking students have become proud of their ability and proud of what they cook. They have learned to like what they cook, even if they can't always cook what they like.

At the beginning of the training program, students are self-conscious of their neophyte status. In one class, students referred to themselves as "rookies":

> After making pies a female student says to a male student: "They don't look too bad." The male comments: "Not for a bunch of rookies" [field notes, City TVI].

Often during the first few weeks students reminded themselves that they are "rookies" and this term enters the idioculture of the group (Fine, 1979). They use this term when modestly trying not to claim too much or excusing themselves when something has unexpectedly gone wrong. They are slowly developing a shared aesthetic. Throughout the year students regularly comment on the aesthetics of their own and their fellow students' work—the former typically with modest self-deprecation and the latter with collegial praise. Each evaluation slowly creates a shared aesthetic of cooking, of knowing what looks, tastes, feels, and smells "good."

The emerging aesthetic awareness of students is reflected in the expansion of their culinary tastes. Most students have previously had limited culinary experience. Many had never tasted such common upper-middle-class staples as artichokes, avocados, scallions, or scallops; some who had tasted such foods did not like them. Although some of these foods are not more expensive than others that are more common, they are not part of the taste repertoire of working-class Americans. Taste is stratified in complex societies like ours (Goody, 1982). Just as cultures and ethnic groups have their own culinary preferences, so do classes. Food has social meaning as well as taste.

An important latent function of these cooking programs is to expose students to these foods, cooked correctly, in a social setting in which they are rewarded for saying that they like them:

> The chef-instructor explains to students that their "taste buds haven't developed," which will take a while. He indicates that when he first became a cook he hated liver, clam chowder, and roquefort dressing. With regard to the latter, he comments: "I almost gagged. . . . I spit it out [the first time I tried it], but after a few times I came to like it. Then I started buying it for home. . . . I could have had a steak anytime I wanted, but it got boring. I was over dipping lettuce in roquefort dressing. [Students laugh loudly] In order to cook you have to like what you're cooking. . . . If you don't like it, fine, but I do want you to taste it" [field notes, City TVI].

Although cooks can and do cook things they dislike (many cannot abide liver or oysters), it does pose a problem when cooks must add something (like roquefort cheese or cayenne) "to taste." They must learn how to make food taste right, even when it tastes wrong to them. They learn standards of taste through the reactions of their instructors. Students are being socialized to expand their culinary horizons and to be proud of that which they prepare. As one student commented when he decided that he really did like eggplant: "I think I'm going to learn to like a lot of things I never liked before" (field notes, City TVI). The instructors' moral rhetoric is accepted as part of the student's development of a professional and artistic self.

Along with this expansion of sensory evaluation comes confidence in one's ability. At first students are pleased and a little surprised when they make something well. For example, the day that students first learned to cook vegetables and made a large vegetable platter was a memorable occasion:

> One student, highly impressed by another's broiled tomatoes with coriander, comments to me: "It's amazing how you can take something simple and make them look complicated. Like them tomatoes." Later this same student comments about how they learned to pipe Duchesse potatoes through a pastry bag: "I like what those things can do. Taking something that is ugly [i.e., mashed potatoes], they can make it pretty" [field notes, City TVI].

As their aesthetic judgments become more sophisticated, they become increasingly critical of food that is poorly prepared:

> One student who works at a local bar-restaurant explained proudly that one night recently when the regular cook was off duty, he made onion soup with real sliced onions, rather than with the dehydrated onions that they usually used. He said that the head cook on duty didn't want him to do this (implying that this man couldn't do it), but he did it anyway. He concludes: "It turned out really good soup. The customers commented on it" [field notes, City TVI]. One student tells the instructor: "That [is] a real problem of being a good chef, you would not like anyone else's food. You know, when I'm at home, my mom will come in with mushy vegetables, and I say I can do better than that" [field notes, City TVI].

Students also explain that they are no longer afraid or embarrassed to return food in restaurants when it is burned or undercooked. One student says: "I'm less appreciative [of food.] I know how it should be. There's no excuse for it being wrong." Another student expands, saying, "I'm more critical, but I'm also more appreciative of good food" (field notes, City TVI). They have entered the moral world of food preparation.

Perhaps the area in which cooking is most closely associated with art in the public mind is cake decoration. Everyone is impressed by wedding cakes. As the great nineteenth-century French chef Careme put it: "The fine arts are five in number—painting, sculpture, poetry, music, architecture—whose main branch is confectionery" (Willan, 1977: 130). At both schools students are taught how to decorate cakes, including making roses out of frosting, a skill that requires considerable practice and training.

Students discover that when they begin to make roses out of icing, they are faced with the same difficulty as when they started to cook: they do not do it very well. Students are freely critical of their roses. Actually with time, most students are able to master the skill. The most commonly used method is making a rose "on a nail." In this procedure, students use a long pastry nail, which has a head about an inch in diameter. After squeezing a small cylinder of frosting from their pastry bags, students squeeze out three small, think slabs of icing ("leaves") for the inside layer, four leaves for the middle layer, and five leaves for the outside. With time these roses can look quite realistic (although one would never confuse them with the flower) and beautiful.

Students almost always contend that a cake rose should look as much like a real rose as is possible and condemn those that do not:

PO: What do you look for in a really nice cake rose?
Student: How natural it is, the coloring, the texture; if it looks grainy, dry [it is not good]. . . . I want it really soft and creamy-looking [interview, Suburban TVI].
PO: What do you look for in a beautiful rose?
Student: Well, I noted at Target's [a discount department store with a bakery] and a lot of the bakeries, it just seems to be like the rose is one continuous motion. There is no identifiability of each petal, it didn't look like a rose, it looks like a glob of frosting that was kind of twisted like a rose.
PO: What would you look for in a good one?
Student: If you could see each petal, if it really looked like a rose [interview, City TVI].

In first learning to make roses, students have not mastered the hand movements that allow petals to look delicate, fresh, and sprightly; when movement is tentative, too much icing is released, making the rose petal appear thick and "clumpy." Students at City TVI came to refer to their poorer roses as "cabbages" and "boxes":

One student says about her own roses: "Everytime I start to get it, it turns to mush." A second turns to a third, joking: "That one looks like a cabbage. I don't want to pick on you. You just have to face the fact that that looks like a cabbage." Later when one student refers to her roses as looking like cabbages, another says: "Make big cabbage patches like mine. Big mongoloids" [field notes, City TVI].

Students at Suburban TVI use different metaphors, but with similar implications:

A student says of her roses that look squashed: "They look like they melted. They look like dying roses" [field notes, Suburban TVI].

Eventually students gain confidence in their work. In this case, because taste and smell are not relevant, students have a clear and stable aesthetic standard against which they can judge their work—the color, shape, and texture of the botanical rose. Developing an aesthetic consensus is quicker than in the production of other types of food products.

Cooking students, despite their "trade" orientation, know that they must be artistic to some degree. This is most evident in some parts of the courses, as in the fourth quarter at City TVI when they sculpt ice carvings and learn the performance art of flambéing. More generally, cooks recognize that their responsibility to decide how much of various ingredients to add places the taste, texture, smell, and looks of food in their hands. Recipes are never used as exact measures, but only as guidelines, and students are expected to add approximate amounts of ingredients and herbs and spices "to taste." This forces each student to make "creative" decisions:

> A student pours wine into his saucepan without measuring it. He turns to me: "That's all cooking ever was: a pinch here and there. Like artists have artistic license, I guess we have cooking license" [field notes, City TVI].

Whether or not the rhetoric of art is truly applicable (Fine, 1982), cooking provides an opportunity for cooks to express themselves aesthetically in what is essentially an industrial occupation.

Although students learn a recognized aesthetic consensus in cooking, they also learn that this consensus leaves room for some individuality; for example, there are no precise standards of what "to taste" means. When students were learning to make chocolate chip cookies, their instructor told them that "there will be no two batches which are alike" (field notes, City TVI). One student deliberately put in extra shortening because he wanted his cookies to be extra tender. Another remarks about the pies the class made: "We each have our own trademark. I can say this is Jim's pie or this ugly pie is mine. . . . It's more like an art form" (field notes, City TVI). One woman sprinkled cinnamon on top of her pie crust, not to meet an instructor's requirement but as a personal aesthetic statement.

Aspiring cooks who are unable or unwilling to be flexible and to change the recipes they use come to be ridiculed by their peers.

> Cathy jokes about how Ted attempts to follow all recipes exactly, even though the food may be overcooked or underdone. Laurie adds: "Ted checks everything by his watch. He'll do it for the full time, even if it's burning" [field notes, City TVI].

This recognizes that there is a style in cooking that individualizes this industrial process (see also Jones, 1975; McCarl, 1974). Although uniformity is a virtue, it can conflict with other values that are emphasized in trade school, such as expressing oneself through one's work. Cooking is an art because of the style that is involved in the process and because the eventual product will be subtly, undefinably different from all other dishes that go under its name. In this way the individual style of the cook-performer transcends the conventions of cooking, while still clinging to these conventions.

## LIMITATIONS OF COOKING AS ART

We must not overemphasize the aesthetic qualities of professional cooking or of the training that students receive. Much of the cooking that these students will be expected to do will not be recognized as artistic in either form or content. No matter how aesthetic a cook may make his or her product, in a matter of minutes it will be consumed and destroyed. Cooking is an activity that captures the moment, presenting food during that short period it is at the height of perfection. Because cooks typically work in a backstage area, one cannot even claim that cooking is a "performance art." The art in cooking is at best evanescent.

An equally important constraint of the aesthetic valuation of cooking is that one must please an audience, not one's peers. This paying audience may not share the cook's aesthetic standard, and may not even understand it, as these students did not before they entered the program. Cost often takes priority over the aesthetic niceties. Cooks may become frustrated with the "inappropriate" demands of their customers, as when customers ask for ketchup:

> One instructor complains: "Ketchup really bothers me, because people misuse it. You might as well eat a well-done hamburger, because it really covers it up. I've seen people put it on a prime rib. To me it makes zero sense. To me they're missing so much. They like it, but it bugs me and most chefs." One student asks how he feels about Heinz 57 and Worcestershire Sauce. The instructor continues: "I'm not gonna sit in judgment on what people like. Those are somewhat better than ketchup, but it bugs me." Later in the quarter, when students are eating French fried potatoes, a student asks for ketchup. A different instructor jokingly responds that she will use it only for her french fries and he brings it out [field notes, City TVI].

Cooking students learn through humorous social control simultaneously how to be good eaters (such as not using ketchup) and to expect the "indignity" of having their customers make "inappropriate" demands. They first must recognize that there exists a stratification of taste, and that they rank near the bottom—at least in the eyes of their instructors. Then they must overcome their culinary prejudices, and, once trained, must often cook for that same lowest common denominator (not making foods as spicy or sharp as might be aesthetically desirable—e.g., holding back on the anchovies in Caesar Salad). They must also consider the cost of the dish (e.g., replacing butter with margarine or shortening). Because cooking is a trade that has direct and immediate economic consequences, the aesthetic impulses of workers must be tempered by the economic constraints of the occupation. Although cooking involves aesthetics, it does not involve only aesthetics.

## CONCLUSION: LEARNING AESTHETICS IN TRADE SCHOOL

"Trades" as well as "fine arts" are concerned with the aesthetic quality of their products. Although consumers recognize that this should be the case with the arts, often the audience of the tradesperson is largely unaware of the aesthetic qualities on which workers judge their products or, indeed, may even be unaware that such standards exist. This public ignorance means that these artisans will have difficulty receiving public "credit" for their work and, lacking such credit, may not be able to obtain the resources and autonomy necessary to do their work well. Such is certainly the case among the cooks I studied. Although a small elite of cooks is publicly recognized for its art, most must accept low pay and public apathy, and feel some measure of resentment. Despite the finding in some studies of professional training that "idealism" and "values" are quickly lost (Becker and Geer, 1958; Haas and Shaffir, 1984), this research paints a somewhat different picture of cooks' training. These students arrive at trade school without any clear sense of the need for aesthetics or pride in their future occupation; most see cooking as a job. There they are taught that important aesthetic concerns exist that they, as cooks, should meet. Although there are many compromises a cook must make—aesthetics sometimes are sacrificed to shortcuts—cooking students have not lost their aesthetic concern by the end of their training. Just as some have been surprised by the "trade-like" qualities of some art schools (Adler, 1979; Mukerji, 1978; Strauss, 1970), many trade schools are more "art-like" than usually given credit for.

Despite the stereotype of vocational schools as locales in which only the technical components of an occupation are stressed (see London, 1978; Roberts, 1965), instructors and students in hotel and restaurant cooking programs are conscious of their aesthetic responsibilities and the boundaries of these responsibilities. Although my research has been limited to the observation of only one type of occupational training program, some of the same features described here may apply to other programs at vocational schools.

The question of art and aesthetics is relevant to cosmetology (e.g., Notkin, 1972), landscape design, advertising layout, architectural drafting, commercial art, television production, cabinetmaking, jewelry manufacturing, fashion merchandising, and upholstery—all programs at vocational schools. However, even in other programs less obviously connected with sensual issues, aesthetics is important in that the visual or tactile appeal of a finished product matters to the practitioners—beyond its instrumental qualities. Although these skills are partly learned on the job (e.g., Riemer, 1977), they also can be taught in school. Aesthetics are learned through on-the-job comparisons with fellow workers, through on-the-job comparisons with fellow workers, through direct instruction from teachers, and, of course, through the peer culture within the school program. These expressive values need not only reflect whether the item is produced efficiently or correctly, how well it serves its function, but may extend beyond that to what the product indicates about the worker's virtuosity, originality, or style.

Rather than emphasize how, in postsecondary training, students are drained of their naïve idealism and learn how to deal with the constraints of the real world of the occupation, I have focused on some positive values that are taught. Students seeking to learn this occupation in trade school enter the program with unformed attitudes and relatively low expectations. As a group they have not achieved much in high school and are searching for a steady job. From the first day in school they are informed that they have selected an occupation that has aesthetic standards and considerable possibilities for creativity. In some sense, they have stumbled into art. Although these students are taught some of the constraints they will face by the instructors and each other, the process of education seems different from the professional occupations often studied. From the opening day until graduation, students are taught and come to accept the fact that they should be making food that looks, tastes, smells, and feels good. Cooking may not be considered art in a formal sense, but students believe that it does have some of the characteristics we expect to find in art. It remains an open question whether my findings can be generalized beyond the kitchen; if they can, the distinctions drawn between artistic and nonartistic occupations, instrumental and expressive jobs, need to be narrowed.

Cooks derive satisfaction from more than seeing their customers fat and/or healthy. They are personally satisfied by meeting their own standards and those of their peers in the preparation of food. Focusing on how cooking students slowly learn these standards in the face of a society that generally does not recognize them reminds us that all aesthetic standards are socially situated and often involve subcultural values. The study of aesthetics should examine not only those who have critical advocates who proclaim the artwork for all to see, but to all toilers, who see in their toil some things of beauty.

## NOTES

Reprinted from Gary Alan Fine, *Journal of Contemporary Ethnography* (formerly *Urban Life*) 14, no. 1 (April 1985): 3–31. Copyright © 1985 by Sage Publications, Inc. Reprinted by permission of Sage Publications, Inc.

1. Formally, aesthetics refers to "those principles that are required for clarifying and confirming critical statements" (Beardsley, 1981: 3–4).

2. Following Hughes (1971), I use "moral" to indicate an implicit value orientation rather than to refer to narrow questions of ethics.

3. Some schools maintain high school foods programs, but these will not be discussed in this chapter.

4. Minnesota has an extensive system of vocational education; although the state ranks nineteenth in population, it ranks eleventh in the number of students in vocational education (41,181 students in 1978) and fourth in the number of technical vocational institutes. Of the 34 TVIs in the state, 18 have some kind of cooking program; 9 of these are chefs' training programs.

5. At Suburban TVI students take one quarter of management, one quarter of fundamentals of cooking, two quarters of quantity cooking, two quarters of international cuisine (in which they run a restaurant), and two quarters of bakery. There is some variation in the order that students take these quarters.

6. Chaud-froid refer to "cold sauces usually béchamel or a veloute with the addition of gelatine used to mask cold food platters for buffets" (Folsom, 1974: 499). Garde manger refers to cold meat work, usually fancy, decorated platters for display purposes.

7. The number of women in these classes were five, one, and nine respectively. Four, one, and four graduated, a higher rate than for males.

8. The terms "trade school," "vocational school," and "technical-vocational institute" will be used interchangeably in this analysis.

9. "Roux" is a cooked mixture of equal parts of fat (usually butter) and flour, used as the base for soups, sauces, and gravies.

## REFERENCES

ABRAHAMS, R. (1978) "Toward a sociological theory of folklore: Performing services," pp. 19–42 in R. H. Byington (ed.) *Working Americans: Contemporary Approaches to Occupation Folklore.* Los Angeles: California Folklore Society.

ADLER, J. (1979) *Artists in Office.* New Brunswick, NJ: Transaction.

BALES, R. F. (1953) "The equilibrium problem in small groups," in T. Parsons et al. (eds.) *Working Papers in the Theory of Action.* Glencoe, IL: Free Press.

BEARDSLEY, M. C. (1981) *Aesthetics: Problems in the Philosophy of Criticism.* Indianapolis: Hackett.

BECKER, H. S. (1982) *Art Worlds.* Berkeley: University of California Press.

—— and B. GEER (1958) "The fate of idealism in medical school." *Amer. Soc. Rev.* 23: 50–56.

—— C. HUGHES, and A. STRAUSS (1961) *Boys in White: Student Culture in Medical Schools.* Chicago: University of Chicago Press.

BELL, M. (1976) "Tending bar at Brown's: Occupational role as artistic performance." *Western Folklore* 35: 93–107.

BOWMAN, J. R. (1983) "The organization of spontaneous adult social play." Ph.D. diss., Ohio State University (sociology).

BRADNEY, P. (1957) "The joking relationship in industry." *Human Relations* 10: 179–187.

DARGAN, A. and S. ZEITLIN (1983) "American talkers: Expressive styles and occupational choice." *J. of Amer. Folklore* 96: 3–33.

DAVIES, K. (1972) *Human Behavior at Work: Human Relations and Organizational Behavior.* New York: McGraw-Hill.

DICKIE, G. (1974) *Art and the Aesthetic: An Institutional Analysis.* Ithaca, NY: Cornell University Press.

FINE, G. A. (1982) "Multiple socialization: The rhetorics of professional cooking." Presented to the American Educational Research Association, New York.

——. (1979) "Small groups and culture creation: The idioculture of little league baseball teams." *Amer. Soc. Rev.* 44: 733–745.

FOLSOM, L. A. (1974) *The Professional Chef.* Boston: CBI.

GOLLADAY, M. A. and R. M. WULFSBERG (1981) *The Condition of Vocational Education.* Washington, DC: National Center for Education Statistics.

GOODY, J. (1982) *Cooking, Cuisine and Class.* Cambridge: Cambridge University Press.

HAAS, J. (1972) "Binging: Educational control among high steel ironworkers." *Amer. Behavioral Scientist* 16: 27–34.

—— and W. SHAFFIR (1982) "Ritual evaluation of competence: The hidden curriculum of professionalization in an innovative medical school program." *Work and Occupations* 9: 131–154.

—— (1984) "The 'fate of idealism' revisited." *Urban Life* 13: 63–81.

HARRIS, J. (1979) "Oral and olfactory art." *J. of Aesthetic Education* 13: 5–15.

HUGHES, E. C. (1971) *The Sociological Eye.* Chicago: Aldine.

JONES, M. O. (1975) *The Hand Made Object and Its Maker.* Berkeley: University of California Press.

LONDON, H. B. (1978) *The Culture of a Community College.* New York: Praeger.

McCARL, R. (1974) "The production welder: Product, process, and the industrial craftsman." *New York Folklore Q.* 30: 243–253.

MUKERJI, C. (1978) "Distinguishing machines: Stratification and definitions of technology in film school." *Sociology of Work and Occupations* 5: 113–138.

NOTKIN, M. S. (1972) "Situational learning in a school with clients," pp. 49–58 in B. Geer (ed.) *Learning to Work.* Beverly Hills, CA: Sage.

OSBORNE, H. (1977) "Odours and appreciation." *British J. of Aesthetics* 17: 37–48.

REVEL, J. F. (1982) *Culture and Cuisine: A Journey through the History of Food.* New York: Doubleday.

RIEMER, J. W. (1977) "Becoming a journeyman electrician: Some implicit indicators in the apprenticeship process." *Sociology of Work and Occupations* 4: 87–98.

ROBERTS, R. W. (1965) *Vocational and Practical Arts Education.* New York: Harper and Row.

SLATER, P. (1955) "Role differentiation in small groups." *Amer. Soc. Rev.* 20: 300–310.

STRAUSS, A. (1970) "The art school and its students: A study and an interpretation," pp. 159–177 in M. C. Albrecht et al. (eds.) *The Sociology of Art and Literature.* New York: Praeger.

TERKEL, S. (1975) *Working.* New York: Avon.

VAUGHT, C. and D. L. SMITH (1980) "Incorporation and mechanical solidarity in an underground coal mine." *Sociology of Work and Occupations* 7: 159–187.

VICKERS, Z. M. and C. M. CHRISTENSEN (1980) "Relationships between sensory crispness and other sensory and instrumental parameters." *J. of Texture Studies* 11: 291–307.

WILLAN, A. (1977) *Great Cooks and Their Recipes: from Taillevent to Escoffier.* New York: McGraw-Hill.

WINTERBOURNE, A. T. (1981) "Is oral and olfactory art possible?" *J. of Aesthetic Education* 15: 95–102.

WOLFE, T. (1975) *The Painted Word.* New York: Bantam.

WOODS, C. (1972) "Students without teachers: Student culture in a barber college," pp. 19–29 in B Geer (ed.) *Learning to Work.* Beverly Hills, CA: Sage.

# 5

# Incorporation and Mechanical Solidarity in an Underground Coal Mine

*Charles Vaught and*
*David L. Smith*

Because of Durkheim's ambiguous evolutionary stance, only a few sociologists have looked for mechanical solidarity in modern American society. In discussing group reactions to disaster, Turner (1967) has suggested that mechanical solidarity is an essential substratum of social organization and is manifestly enacted whenever groups are being formed or reconstituted. Zurcher (1968) demonstrated the resurgence of mechanical solidarity in the disaster work crew and suggested that what was being enacted were ephemeral roles which functioned to support the shift back to organic solidarity. But what of groups which exist constantly on the edge of disaster? It is our contention that these groups will exhibit a continual concern with mechanical solidarity and develop behavioral patterns, beliefs, and sentiments in line with this concern.

Theoretically, there is good reason to expect that mechanical solidarity is, at least, an essential substratum of work groups and that it provides the necessary integration of workers. This observation establishes a theoretical link with the ubiquitous occurrence of informal work-group structure (Roberts and Dickson, 1947; Graves, 1958; Breed, 1955; Roy, 1953, 1960; Zurcher, 1965, 1967; Stoddard, 1968; Bryant, 1972a). The informal structure is the locus of mechanical solidarity.

Our fundamental hypothesis is a reformulation of Turner's (1967: 66) hypothesis VI: "Groups and organizations, the accomplishments of whose goal are precarious, will exhibit proportionately great preoccupation with mechanical solidarity." Our hypothesis states: *Work groups which operate under constant threat (danger) will exhibit mechanical solidarity as the dominant form of social integration.*

In his article we will illustrate the concern with mechanical solidarity in an underground coal mine by focusing upon the strategies of adaptation and incorporation which prepare the individual to meet the exigencies of a "hostile world" (Keesing, 1958) and to function as a member of a "society" (Durkheim, 1964: 105n) which requires that he or she subordinate his or her will to the will of the group (Lucas, 1969; Althouse, 1974). The subordination of individual will to group will is a means of ensuring the continued safety of the totality in a situation which is defined as being fraught with danger (Stone, 1946; Lucas, 1969; Althouse, 1974; McCarl, 1976). The dynamics by which this subordination is enacted is a more "archaic" form of gaming behavior than that typically witnessed in modern society.

## AN ENCAPSULATED ENCLAVE

The workers in an underground coal mine are effectively cut off from the world above from the time they enter the portal of the mine until they re-emerge some eight to ten hours later. In addition to being separated from the earth's surface by hundreds of feet of rock and shale, the miners must labor in dimly illuminated, confined areas which may be no more than 28 inches in height (depending upon the thickness of the coal seam). To the constant risk of working with electrified, mobile heavy equipment must be added the hazards of sudden cave-ins, upheavals, flooding, methane gas explosions, and the ever-present coal and rock dusts. In order to accomplish the extraction, haulage, and dumping of coal on a section, production crews must work as coherent "units." In fact, there are very few jobs in an underground mine which do not require a cooperative team effort.

Zurcher (1978), in conceptualizing the "encapsulated group," has noted that the term is not far removed from Goffman's concept of "total institution." The encapsulated group, however, differs from the total institution in certain significant respects: (1) the encapsulated group is smaller and less complex; (2) the encapsulated group has a short membership and makes no concerted effort to resocialize its members; (3) there is no procedure for impressing a new institutional status upon the "recruit"; and (4) the encapsulated group lacks a genuine work structure.

The "encapsulated enclave," as we have conceptualized it, contains features of both the encapsulated group and the total institution (Goffman, 1961a), as well as certain features of the "communal enclave" (Coleman,

1970): (1) membership is voluntary and may be ended at any time; (2) inter-action with the outside world is severely limited; (3) individual freedom is limited, and the will of the group takes precedence over the will of the individual (Durkheim, 1964); (4) the individual is seen as a "whole person" and is integrated into the group; (5) intense efforts are made to impress upon the individual the idea that he or she is occupying a different status in a "different world"; and (6) there is a full-blown authority structure designed to meet the aims of the formal organization. The underground coal mine is an encapsulated enclave which presents its inhabitants with certain unique environmental exigencies (Keesing, 1958) and fosters a more "primitive" type of mechanical solidarity than that which is usually found in American society.

## THE SETTING AND PLAY

The underground coal mine is contextually quite different from the majority of American work settings, and it has a divergent normative and valuative structure. Both workers and the public tend to characterize the miners as a "breed apart" from the rest of the populace (Boeth et al., 1978). The nature of the mining enterprise, with its dangerous, encapsulated environment tends to reinforce this notion among the workers (Gouldner, 1954; Lucas, 1969). Miners, like other relatively isolated groups in dangerous situations, must be able to react in terms of group expectations rather than to individual motivation (Hayner, 1945; Stone, 1946; Aran, 1974; McCarl, 1976). In a dangerous milieu, the strain of reacting to individual rather than to shared expectations would make the performance of hazardous tasks difficult. To reduce strain on the worker's psyche, it is necessary that he or she be able to "predict" the behavior of others in exigencies.

The observations utilized in this article were recorded by the senior author, a trained sociologist acting in the capacity of "complete participant" (Gold, 1958; Denzin, 1971). The senior author was employed at Paradise Four (pseudonym), a large, highly mechanized mine in western Kentucky owned by one of the nation's largest coal companies. All the observations and conversations contained in this article are from field notes taken between September 1974 and September 1977. Although field notes had to be recorded sometime after the end of each shift, the conversations reported are as close to exact wording as possible. The strength of the observations is bolstered by the fact that the observer worked approximately one year on each of the three shifts and held a variety of jobs within the mine. At the time of the study the mine was in the process of expansion, necessitating the hiring of some 280 workers (including fifteen females) during the three-year period.

The mine which was the locus of this study was organized to utilize the "conventional" method of "running" coal. The conventional mining method requires a series of sequential operations to be performed on the coal seam by different miners and machines (undercutting, drilling, blasting, loading, and bolting). This has two implications for the individuals working on any production unit: More workers are required to operate the section than would be required to operate a continuous mining section; and because of the noncontinuous, interdependent nature of the conventional enterprise, the workers have more free time to leave their equipment or assigned tasks to "visit" or horseplay (Roethlisberger and Dickson, 1947; Graves, 1958; Roy, 1953, 1960; Lucas, 1969; McCarl, 1976).

Mead (1934: 365–366) argued that the individual internalizes the attitudes of others largely through play, and it is by play and the game that an individual becomes an integrated member of a particular society. Play is frequently used to orient new members and to constrain others in order to maintain integration, cohesion, and solidarity (Bateson, 1958; Roberts and Sutton-Smith, 1962). The primary function of initiation games, ritual, and communications in the group is to reinforce shared sentiments and "therefore release the participants from the normal constraints of daily human interaction" (McCarl, 1976: 54). We shall attempt to show how these games operate to make significant and coherent adjustments to unusual work conditions by functioning to subordinate the will of the individual to the will of the group (see also Huizinga, 1955; Goffman, 1961b; Piaget, 1962; Roberts and Sutton-Smith, 1962; Zurcher, 1970; Steele and Zurcher, 1973). Deviant from the dominant cultural norms of individualistic achievement, and from norms of body privacy, they are nonetheless considered a normal and important part of this hostile work setting.

## A Different World

It is ironic that the openings of coal mines are termed "portals." Van Gennep (1960) noted that the erection of a portal is a complicated means of marking a boundary and is used symbolically in territorial passage. The act of moving through a portal may, in some cases, be seen as a direct rite of passage by means of which an individual journeys from one social world into another. The portal acts as a sort of "metaphorical membrane" (Goffman, 1961b: 66) beyond which the miners perceive a "different world" with different sentiments, expectations, and rituals (Zurcher, 1970: 183). The fact that they go to great lengths to stress this different world "texture of things" (Blumer, 1961: 11) was made clear to the senior author by the numerous references the workers made to "a whole different world," "we do things different down here," and "people outside just don't understand what it's like" (Turner, 1967: 61–63).

Several authors (Homans, 1941; Gouldner, 1954; Lucas, 1969; Aran, 1974) have discussed the function of ritual in promoting solidarity and reducing individual anxiety in unknown or potentially dangerous situations. The fact that each miner may have some degree of anxiety prior to entering the portal tends to foster a dependency upon the group, thereby increasing solidarity. At the same time, the act of going through routine procedures in the company of others lends an air of normalcy to the situation and acts as a tension-management mechanism (Aran, 1974).

Unlike inhabitants of a total institution, the miners go their own way at the end of each shift, necessitating a daily "reunion." The dressing ritual in the bathhouse takes place against a background of shouting, joking, and visitation which serves to reestablish the solidarity of the day before. Greetings are warm and boisterous as the miners enter the bathhouse and are reunited with their buddies. Individuals who "took one" the day before are met by laughter and shouts of "here come ol' part-time," and will be required to give an account of their adventures during their absence. The workers generally exchange experiences from the interim between shifts, as well as reminiscences of the prior shift. This exchange of experiences is a means of gaining reassurance and consolidating group solidarity (Aran, 1974: 130).

At the portal, the miners stand or sit with members of their own units or work crews, waiting for time to board the "man-trip" cars for the journey down the "slope." They laugh and joke among themselves, throw gravel at each other's knuckles, and shout insults to members of other units. If an individual strays away from his or her unit to talk with someone on another crew, he or she will soon be reminded to "come back over here with us where you belong." There is a strong identification with one's unit or crew, and most miners will express the sentiment that he or she works on the "best unit [or crew] in the mine." There is much friendly rivalry between units, some of which results in various form of horseplay. Although all miners are "brothers," the primary loyalty is to the unit. An interesting observation is the ease with which a unit will "forget" a member who has bid off the unit onto another job, and the ease with which the individual becomes an integral member of his or her new unit (see Durkheim, 1964: 149)

## TRANSITION AND INCORPORATION[1]

Every new miner at Paradise Four who passes through the portal for the first time has voluntarily doffed street clothing and donned the accouterments of the coal miner (McCarl, 1976). His external trappings are different from those of the older miners, however. Instead of the scarred black hard hat of the experienced miner, the "recruit's" hat is a bright orange. Although he wears the standard overalls or coveralls, mining belt, steel-toe boots, and self-rescuer, and carries the traditional round "miner's dinner bucket," they are all shiny and new.[2] The orange hat and the newness of his apparel serve to symbolically set him apart from the older workers as well as the outside world (Zurcher, 1967; McCarl, 1976). He assumes his seat on the man-trip to shouts of "new meat," and "Get a cap board, boys, we're going to get some ass this morning." Along with the catcalls will come such useful advice as "Keep your head down," and "Turn on your manlight, 'cause it's darker than Hell down there."

The orange hat makes a salient target once the "new man" is seated on the man-trip and will become the recipient of repeated blows from behind, administered by workers wielding hammers, "walking sticks," wrenches and other metallic objects which serve to create a ringing sensation in the individual's ears. Beating the hat, pulling the recruit's lamp cord and belt, kicking dents in his shiny new dinner bucket, and generally calling attention to the trappings of the occupation serve to remind the new worker that he is now a member of a "select" group which inhabits a different world, and that he will soon be occupying a new status (McCarl, 1976). Crowded onto the man-trip, his personal space invaded and his freedom of movement highly restricted by the close physical proximity of the other workers, he is lowered into an environment which is noisy, dusty, dank, and illuminated only by the shifting beams of miners' cap lamps. It is a world in which there are no familiar points of reference. His consciousness is bombarded by unfamiliar sights, sounds, and smells, which he is unable to logically relate to anything in his previous experience. He is in truth a "new man," experiencing the prototaxic "stream of consciousness" mode of sensory perception most often associated with infancy (Sullivan, 1977: 72). Despite the degree of self-reliance he experiences on the outside, he is now abjectly dependent upon these boisterous strangers to lead him around and show him what to do.

During this separation phase (Van Gennep, 1960) the new man has voluntarily placed his status in the outside world in abeyance, only to become a nonentity in the encapsulated enclave. Even though he must stay with an experienced individual or group, he is not a part of that group. Although the experienced miners do not treat him in a hostile manner, he may be largely ignored except for comments about safety and work techniques made for his benefit. For the first few shifts he will not be engaged in conversation to any great extent (Arble, 1976), and if he becomes the object of conversation he may be talked about as if he isn't present.

### Feeling Out

After the new man has survived a couple of shifts and indicated to the older miners that he has some "staying power," the workers begin a "conversational biographical sketching" (Fitzpatrick, 1974) aimed at filling in the new worker's background. It is at this time that the new man is defined in terms of what he did before. Although as with the carnival, the underground mine constitutes a type of "occupational foreign legion" (Bryant, 1972b), the workers tend to be very inquisitive about every facet of each other's private lives. The implication is that, though it really doesn't matter what one did before he came to the mine, or what he does on the outside, "we want to hear all about it, anyway." This feeling-out process begins the transition phase (Van Gennep, 1960) for the new man and serves several functions for the incorporation of the individual into the group. The background of the new worker forms a base upon which the older miners gradually construct a set of opinions about his reliability, his loyalty toward his "brothers," his attitudes toward the miner's work world, and his ability to control his temper in trying situations (Fitzpatrick, 1974). A "good 'ol boy" is one who accepts being the focus of horseplay with good grace, doesn't act as if he "knows it all the first day," pays attention when he's shown how to perform a task so he doesn't have to be shown repeatedly, and displays the proper receptiveness toward the "wisdom" the miners impart to him.

During the transition phase the new man gradually shifts to the parataxic (Sullivan, 1977: 72) mode of perception. Although he is not yet able to grasp the *gestalt* of the mine, he begins to relate events "in causal sequence." He has begun to use part of the rich occupational argot, although he may not know the precise meaning of some of the terms and often uses them in the wrong context. It is at this stage of the transition phase that the individual usually receives his nickname. The nickname is most often given as the result of some "greenhorn" gaffe or mistake, a peculiar observed personal trait, something unique in the person's background, or some "stunt" he is involved in after hiring in. The men sported such colorful monikers as "Chickenfucker," "Dick High," "Maggot Mouth," "Smooth Mouth," "Alice," "Loretta," "Dynamite," "Big Coon," "Plunger Lip," "Possum George," "Jackhouse Jones," and "Number Thirty-Five." The mine-specific name functions to further the other-world orientation by indicating to the individual and the group that one's name "outside" really doesn't tell very much about the person. Mine-specific names, on the other hand, are names the miners bestow on the new man in the process of being "reborn" (Weiss, 1967) and symbolize his ties to the group and the mine. He now has a name which has meaning within the group, and which indicates something about his character as a "total person." Many miners may work together for years without knowing each other's real names (Lucas, 1969).

## "Making a Miner"

The end of the transition phase is marked by the rite of "making a miner." This rite usually takes place (for the first time) during the first or second week the new worker is on the job. There are virtually no exceptions, and all new men are made a miner at least once early in their careers.

> The second week after hiring in, I was sent with the second shift timber crew to timber Number Three Unit's return air coarse. During a break, Henry Gibson asked me if I had been made a miner. When I replied that I had not, the men grabbed me and held me down while Henry gave me several swats with a cap board. "O.K., now if anybody asks you if you've been made a miner, you can tell them that the timber crew made you a miner."

New miners find rather quickly that once is seldom enough. The first time the senior author was sent to a production unit, he was again asked if he had been made a miner. When he replied that the timber crew had made him a miner, one of the men snorted: "Ha! The timber crew! What do them guys know about making a man a miner?" Whereupon the process was repeated to the satisfaction of the unit. If a new man takes umbrage at this summary treatment, which sometimes happens, the miners may decide that they did something wrong and repeat the rite until the victim expresses satisfaction with the results. The will of the group dominates.

> At dinner on Number Six, we decided it was time to make Lard Ass a miner. We held him down and Coach smoked him pretty good. He came up swinging when we turned him loose, so Coach decided he must not have done the job right. We grabbed Lard Ass and held him again, and Coach beat him until he told us we were doing a good job.

The act of being made a miner presents the new worker with a crucible for his conflicting emotional tendencies. On the one hand, he has come to idealize the men who have been virtually leading him around by the hand, teaching him the ways of the mine, and showing him how to avoid danger (Janis, 1968); on the other hand, they may have appeared callous about his personal feelings, making derogatory comments about his assessed individual worth, laughing at his gaffes, and giving him a name which he cannot repeat in polite company. They now force him to submit to a humiliating degradation of self (Garfinkle, 1956), confronting him with the solidarity of the group (Young, 1965) and forcefully impressing upon him the fact that he must give deference to group will.

## Incorporation

The process of incorporation is a diffuse phase and lasts an indefinite period of time, although, for all practical purposes, the end is marked when the miner has gained his first year of experience and is required to paint the orange hat another color. During this phase the new man learns the language, perceives the mine in the syntaxic mode (Sullivan, 1977), separating myth from fact, and begins to share the strong solidarity bond the miners have with each other. This harmonious collective attachment of wills is an essential feature of mechanical solidarity (Durkheim, 1964: 106). The direct bonding of individual and group makes practical the close cooperation necessary in those situations where danger is ever present and the actors do not have the requisite time and energy for analyzing each other's motives (McCarl, 1976).

Mechanically solitary groups faced with challenges to harmony of wills and boundary maintenance will increase their repressive activities (Inverarity, 1976, Erikson, 1966). The establishment and maintenance of this solidarity in the face of an influx of new members, each with his own vocabulary of motives (Mills, 1940; Zurcher, 1979), is problematic. In addition to threats to group solidarity in the form of new members to be incorporated, the actions of established group members often challenge group boundaries and from time to time even old miners may become the recipients of repressive horseplay. The games which we will discuss below may be seen to serve dual functions: On the one hand, they are rites of incorporation for new members; on the other hand, they can be seen as "punishment for the sake of punishment" which take on the diffuse, ritualistic character of rites of intensification (Durkheim, 1964).

## Penis Games

Although whipping, or "getting some ass," is the most prevalent body-centered game played by the miners, it is not so potentially degrading as the games which focus upon the reproductive organs. In American society, the genitals are the most sacrosanct area of the human body. In the initiation and reaffirmation games involving the penis, the miners are effectively stripping away the individual's old self-image and pride and underscoring the fact that he is helpless in the face of the encapsulated group's will. Indeed, submission to the group is the only way in which the individual may lay claim to group aid (in getting himself untied, for instance). Penis games are both body centered and group centered: First, few individuals voluntarily consent to having their penises handled by the workers. Therefore, it requires group effort to overcome the victim's resistance. Secondly, penis games provide the victim with a means of showing his prowess in combating his attackers and his skill in eluding capture. He may thus earn himself the reputation of being "a hard man to handle," thereby enhancing his prestige within the group (Goffman, 1961b).

One penis-oriented game which emphasizes the "different world" quality of the encapsulated enclave by caricaturing outside performances, and in which the participation is voluntary, is the "pretty pecker" contest. It takes on aspects of a beauty pageant with "judges" to decide the outcome and with prizes (usually a case of beer) awarded for the "prettiest pecker."

> During lunch on Number Four Unit the men decided to see whose "pecker" was the prettiest. After chipping in enough money to buy beer for the winner, they appointed Paw Paw, Lip, and Dirty Sally as judges. Five or six of the men then paraded their penises for perusal. After due deliberation the judges declared that Fast Fred's pecker was the "cutest little thing" they had ever seen and awarded him the prize.

"Greasing" takes on many of the qualities of an operating room scene, with a "doctor," "nurses," and various attendants. The nurses restrain the patient while the doctor operates (applies the grease), and the "anesthesiologist" administers the "anesthesia" (rock dust). In the account below, the greasing ceremony is used as a repressive social control mechanism, although on occasion greasing is done simply for the sake of greasing.

> One morning on Six Unit Chisel, a new man who had been assigned to us as a rib shoveler, was monopolizing the conversation. Coach commented to Rocky, "This boy's a real whiz; he's only been here a week and he already knows more about mining than I do." Rocky replied, "Yeah, I don't think anybody could be that wild this early in the morning unless he had crabs; I may have to operate." After enlisting the aid of several members of the unit, the men grabbed Chisel, held him down, and removed his pants. Rocky, the "Chief Surgeon" on the unit, ceremoniously donned a pair of rubber gloves, reached into a can of grease kept in the kitchen for such occasions, and began liberally coating Chisel's genitals. When Chisel began struggling violently, Rocky called for "anesthetic." Spanky, the anesthesiologist, threw several handfuls of rock dust on the greasy genitals. The nurses holding Chisel down began reassuring him that Rocky had never lost a patient on the operating table and requested him to "let them know" if he felt any pain. As Chisel's struggles subsided, Rocky yelled, "OH no! I'm losing him; quick! The stimulant!" Whereupon Coach gathered a handful of coal slack and dirt to add to the concoction.

All units and work crews have their "primitive law." These are unwritten prescriptions and proscriptions governing behavior in the group, i.e., "No pissing within 50 feet of the kitchen." "No lying on the man-trip." "Nobody but members of the unit can bring chicken for lunch." "Any non-member of the unit who works on the unit for three days must bring candy for the unit." "Hanging" takes the form of a public execution and usually follows some "serious" transgression of the "laws." The "condemned man" is bound securely, and his penis is then suspended from a wire attached to the roof supports. After the "prisoner" is secured by means of taping his hands and feet, the workers are free to sit around the scene and comment upon the action while the "executioner" completes the ceremony.

One night on third shift, Short Ruby, J. T., and I were dusting Number Three Unit. After we finished the job, Short Ruby stretched out in the bucket of the scoop and went to sleep. The mechanics, "mad" because he had gone to sleep on "their" unit before they had gotten a chance to, decide to hang him. After binding him from head to foot with electrical tape, they raised the bucket of the scoop, tied a length of shooting wire to his penis, secured the other end to a roof bolt overhead, and then lowered the bucket until the wire was stretched tight. The men then sat in a semicircle before the scoop bucket and tossed small rocks at the shooting wire. Each time a rock found its mark, the men were rewarded by an "ooh!" from Short Ruby. When Short Ruby began to worry aloud about what would happen if the hydraulics bled off the scoop, allowing the bucket to drop, one of the men suggested that "Maybe we'll have to change your name to Long Ruby."

"Hairing" and "jacking off" the individual are less ceremonious games than are hanging and greasing, and they are repressive social control mechanisms. Their function is much the same as the "binging" witnessed by Roberts and Dickson (1947). The miners resort to these summary (and painful) manipulations of the penis in order to "calm down" the individual who is getting too "wild"; i.e., working in a dangerous manner, working too fast, working too slow, exhibiting anger toward fellow workers, or being overexuberant in teasing.

One morning on Six Unit Spanky, the "general inside labor man" was pranking with Legs, one of the shuttle car drivers. Legs yelled for some of the men to hold Spanky for him. After they had succeeded in wrestling Spanky to the bottom, Legs reached into Spanky's pants and began pulling out tufts of pubic hair.

One afternoon on second shift Carbeurator, a car driver on Number Four Unit, became sullen about being teased and started "slow walking." Uncle Fuddly, the Face Boss, suggested that "What Carbeurator needs is jacking off with a handful of rock dust." The men flagged Carbeurator down, dragged him from his car, and held him down. Lip, the mechanic, began to masturbate Carbeurator while the men rubbed his shoulders and stomach to "Calm him down."

The "real man" in the encapsulated enclave is one who can engage in the sex dramas and homosexual buffoonery without being labeled, or seeing himself, a homosexual, and without experiencing role conflict (Reiss, 1961; Zurcher et al., 1966). Even the most primitive society has its deviants. In the mine, the deviant is one who fails to divest himself of his outside sex-role expectations and join in the games.

One night on third shift I was sitting beside Gentle Ben on the man-trip going in. The conversation turned to Junior, who was sitting in front of us. When I commented that Junior didn't seem to be able to "get into the spirit of things,"

Ben commented, "Yeah, that damned Junior's so square, I'll bet he jacks off in a bottle and pours it into his wife."

## Incorporating the "Coal Dust Queens"

The women, although not particularly attractive by American cultural standards of beauty, are exotics, and as such present the men with an intriguing new dimension to their games and conversations. Those females who are assigned to specific units or work crews are expected to stay with their crew, as are the males. The women who do not have specific crews are designated "general inside labor" and sit together near the other general inside laborers. Each woman can expect to "hold court" for several of the workers (and bosses), have pebbles flipped at her hard hat, and be the recipient of numerous less-than-honorable propositions.

> One morning as we were walking down to the portal, Coach surveyed the scene, noting the women, each surrounded by several "admirers." Shaking his head and chuckling, he commented to me, "Look at that. Ain't that something? There ain't a damned one of these women you would give a second glance on the street, but down here they're all queens."

Durkheim (1964: 283) identified a dialectic between the pressures that social units exercise upon one another to develop in increasingly divergent directions and the contrary pressure the common conscience exercises on each individual conscience. The first impels us to become distinct personalities, and the second demands our resemblance to everyone else. In the underground mine, with its status-based behavior expectations and previously all-male bonding, the collective conscience predominates. The advent of the females confronted the male miners with a "boundary crisis" (Inverarity, 1976; Erikson, 1966) which threatened the solidarity of the mine. The women were incumbents of quite different role-sets in the outside world and were entering a world in which the solidarity had been based in part on a variant of outside all-male role expectations. To be a miner was to be a "pinner-man," "scoopman," "beltman," and so on, to wear a "manlight," and ride a "man-trip" to the work place. The women, on the face of things, were not "like everyone else." The initial response of the male miners was to try to force the women out because "a coal mine's no fit place for a damn woman."

> Whirly Bird: Lydia wasn't the first girl to hire in here, Professor. We had another woman come a few days before she did. Ol' Hank [the mine foreman] took her with him to walk Number Four Unit's return air course. You know how low that is. Well, Hank walked her as fast as he could go in the low top,

and after about an hour she told him to take her to the bottom; she was going home. She never come back.

Professor: What about Lydia?

Whirly Bird: I tell you. I'm ashamed of the way we treated Lydia. No matter what was done to her during the shift, every day at the bottom while we waited for the trip out, into the sump she'd go. We'd souse her all the way under, too. She'd come up spluttering and crying, but she'd be back the next day. I reckon we finally got tired and decided, "Hell, if she wants the job that bad, she can have it."

As is true with military units (Anonymous, 1946) in cooperative work groups, the individual has only two alternatives: He or she either belongs to the group or is isolated. The initial tacit policy of Paradise Mining Company was to isolate the females as much as possible by assigning them "headers" to "watch." The "headerman," who tends the drive unit of a haulage belt, is one of the few workers in the mine who is along for much of the shift. The women, however, were as prone to sneak away from their lonely stations in search of companionship as were their male counterparts. The complete severance of accustomed social relations find compensation in the fortuitous acquiring of "buddies," with similarity of past background and interest being of little concern (Brotz and Wilson, 1946). Not long after the first women hired in at Paradise Four, they became frequent visitors to the various units and work crews near their headers.

Dirty Sally: I don't know how the company thought they would keep them women on the belts. Take ol' Lydia, for instance. Every day she would sneak up the belt to Number Seven Unit, and ol' Red [Face Boss] would let her get on a shuttle car. Pretty soon she could drive it as good as anybody. All she had to do then was wait for a car driving job to come open and bid on it.

Before long, the females had become members of units and work crews, and the males were faced with the problem of either incorporating them totally into the group or treating them as unique individuals.

With the exception of the first two women who hired in, the females were given names during the early transition phase. They began to answer to such nomina as "Big Bertha Butt," "Aunt Fanny Allcocks," "Drip Cock Freeby," "Hook Nose," "Grandma," and "Mack York." Nicknaming manifests an adjustment to new phenomena and situations, and it mirrors and reinforces the sense of solidarity (Elkin, 1946). The males began to assimilate the women by treating them as equals, "making them miners," chewing their ears, and expressing the sentiment that "as long as they do their job, they'll be o.k."

The first greasing of a female precipitated a minor crisis at Paradise Four, however.

Big Honky: I guess you was still on third shift when we greased ol' Drop Cock, Professor. She hadn't been here very long when Hank sent her and Super Trooper [a male orange hat] up here to shovel our belt. Well, you know we're the wildest unit in the mine. At that time we was greasing everybody who come on the unit. Well, at dinnertime here comes ol' Drop Cock and Super Trooper to visit. We greased Super Trooper and decided, "Hell! We've got four women working here now and they ain't a one of them been greased yet. We're just the boys to do it." Besides, we couldn't treat ol' Drop Cock any different. Well, we downed her and put the grease to her good.

Dirty Sally [Face Boss]: Yeah. I was up at the face. I came back to the kitchen and there she was; all spread out with that thing wide open. I said, "Damn Freeby, don't you know the company takes that grease out of my paycheck?" That didn't help matters any.

Whirly Bird: We had to hold ol' Legs back. His wife was about nine months pregnant and he hadn't had any in a while. He was tearing his coveralls off.

Spanky: Yeah. We should of let him screw her. That's what made her mad. She laid there all spread out for a long time after that we turned her loose and nobody would offer to put the meat to her.

Big Honky: Legs got down and helped her clean it off; he was real excited.

As a result of the greasing incident, and allegedly with the encouragement of Super Trooper, who was a former state policeman, she threatened suit against Paradise Mining Company and the members of Number Six Unit for several thousand dollars. The suit was still under consideration when the senior author joined Number Six Unit.

Dirty Sally: I had some people from the Human Rights Commission come down from Washington to talk to me just the other day. They wanted to know if that kind of thing went on all the time. I told them it did. They wanted to know if I ever got greased. I told them I got greased two or three times a week and got sent out naked the rest of the time. I also told them that when I saw Freeby in the kitchen she was laying there grinning. She didn't decide to get upset about things 'til Super Trooper convinced her she could get some money out of the company.

Big Honky: How the hell does a law court or the Human Rights Commission think they can have any idea of what goes on in a coal mine?

Drop Cock was ostracized by the men and overtly pressured by the other females to drop the suit idea. The topic turned to Drop Cock and the suit one day when Lydia had been sent to Number six Unit as a relief shuttle car driver.

Lydia: Some of the new women think Freeby ought to go ahead with the suit, but we're setting them straight. Us older women don't have anything to do with her except to tell her to drop the whole idea and not get our brothers in trouble. She was crying in the bathhouse the other day about how we treated her, and Babs slapped her and told her to drop her damned suit and behave herself and everything would be all right.

Today in the union meeting Drop Cock arose and tearfully apologized to her brothers and sisters for the hard feelings she had caused, and announced that she was dropping her lawsuit against the company and the men of Number Six Unit.

The group will dominated, and the women were accepted as miners with only slight alterations in belief and practices.

## SUMMARY

The sexual themes and dramatic performances recounted above may be viewed as perverse, brutal, and degrading if abstracted from the situated milieu in which they occur. Within the context of the encapsulated enclave, however, they are a powerfully integrating force for the group, a fact which each new individual (including the senior author) must learn from experience. Although the behavior we have been describing may be considered an extreme case, the underground mine and military units are not the only situational loci in which group sexual themes are played out. In less dangerous occupations, such as professional baseball and building tradesmen, group voyeurism has been observed. Rather than being pathological, it has served an integrating function (Bouton, 1970; Feigelman, 1974).

There are two congruencies in those situations where some type of "aberrant" sexual behavior has been observed taking place as a group enterprise. First, it occurs in those instances where groups are faced with the problem of maintaining their continuity despite turnover; and second, where close cooperation is necessary in order to get the job done in the easiest and best manner for the group (Anonymous, 1946). In contradistinction, encapsulated groups which are transitory in nature may have some sexual themes, but these seldom go beyond the level of joking with personnel, staring, and halfhearted attempts to strike up conversation. College fraternities utilize sex games as means of degradation in initiation rituals, but these are usually of short duration and not likely to be repeated once the individual has become an integral member of the group. Although some games, especially in fraternal initiations, may strongly violate the genital sanctity, these violations are not used as continual intensification and control mechanisms. Total institutions such as prisons and asylums may develop individually oriented sexual activities, but these are not games and are seldom carried out in group context. Asylums and prisons are not specifically work-goal oriented. The ship, although a total institution, is work-goal oriented and is the locus of group-oriented sexual themes (Zurcher, 1965).

Variant sex-role expectations in the encapsulated enclave emphasize the fact that the worker is faced with a different role-set than the role-set he or she performs on the outside. Instead of behavior which meets segmented role expectations, the individual is presented with status-based behavioral expectations. Those things of value in the wider sociocultural context, such as individualistic achievement and universalistic standards, are not only devalued inside, but are seen as threatening if adhered to by the individual. On the other hand, the particularistic ethic which strongly emphasizes group identity is highly valued. Miners habitually address each other as "buddy," express loyalty to their unit and their "brothers," and adhere to a code of "ethics" which strongly prohibits the violation of group norms. The "aberrant" sex roles acted upon inside are not seen as perverted as long as they are conducted in the "proper" context. The conflict occurs when the individual cannot abandon his or her outside role expectations and conform to the differing set of expectations in the mine.

There were two threats to the common conscience at Paradise Four: the steady influx of "new men," and the problem of how to deal with female miners. For these reasons, Paradise Four might be considered somewhat atypical in regard to the actual number of incorporation games being played during any given period of time, since the fewer new workers there are entering the setting, the fewer occasions there will be for "making a miner." The senior author, after hundreds of hours of swapping anecdotes with miners from several states, has concluded that the behavior reported here is not idiosyncratic to Paradise Four, however. All miners, for instance, seem to know that grease is used for more than lubricating the moving parts of mine machinery, and that cap boards have a function totally unrelated to their primary purpose of securing mine timers in place.

Interviews with miners in southwestern Virginia indicated that the frequency of horseplay was slightly greater for newer mines than for older mines with a more stable complement of workers (Wardell et al., 1979). This is in line with Inverarity's (1976) argument that the volume of diffuse, ritualistic "punishment for the sake of punishment" will increase as the boundaries of the collective conscience are threatened. The miners at Paradise Four were able to incorporate the new men and women without any basic changes in the solidarity of the mine. It is interesting to speculate, however, on what would have happened if there had been 150 females instead of 15. Durkheim (1964: 57) reminds us that the more mechanically solitary the society, the less social differentiation there is between males and females. With only a few women in the mine, most of the outside sex role baggage could be stripped away, and was. With an influx of a large number of women, though, there is a greater likelihood that outside role-sets would be imported into the encapsulated enclave, effectively weakening or changing the base of the collective conscience (Hayner, 1945). This is quite obviously a problem for further research.

In sum, we have suggested several different aspects of the interrelationship of individual and group in a dangerous milieu which serve to maintain rites demonstrating concern with mechanical solidarity: (1) threat to the existence of the group by turnover; (2) the need for reduction of anxiety in the individual; (3) management of tension occasioned by boredom or fear; (4) dependence of the individual upon others in the work setting; and (5) special need for shared expectations in dangerous work situations. We do not wish to argue that mechanical solidarity is only expressed in body-centered games, however (see Stoddard, 1968). Undoubtedly, each group characterized by a high degree of mechanical solidarity secures the loyalty of individuals in ways that have relevance in the milieu within which the group functions.

## THEORETICAL IMPLICATIONS

As social units exert ever more pressure upon one another, resulting in increased diversity, society moves toward organic solidarity (Smith and Snow, 1976). Durkheim expected the ancient corporations to be renewed and to fill the "moral" void left by changing community and family social solidarity. These corporations were to exert a power "capable of containing individual egos, of maintaining a spirited sentiment of common solidarity in the consciousness of all the workers" (Durkheim, 1964: 10). In most instances this has been only partially true; occupations have not become the basis for strong communal sentiments where the individual is viewed in holistic terms, rather than in terms of the segmented roles he or she plays in the larger societal context. However, the underground coal mine closely approximates the principle of Durkheim's speculations. Strong mechanical solidarity exists in most task-oriented groups which have elaborated a set of sentiments and beliefs, face some threat to their continued existence as a viable group, and are, in some sense, isolated from the larger society. Such groups would include submarine crews on missions, combat fighter squadrons, bomber crews, lumberjacks, military units in combat situations, pipeliners, construction crews, underground miners, and so on.

We may be aided in our conceptualizations if we consider mechanical and organic solidarity as existing on separate planes and tending to vary inversely (Collett et al., 1979). Organic solidarity at the group level refers to the volume and intensity of the common conscience which pressures the individual to "be like everyone else." The strength of the common conscience, then, would be expected to vary with the freedom of the individual to switch his or her allegiance to and from organizations. The more varying organizations are brought into play against one another, the less is the pressure of a single common conscience upon the individual. Nevertheless, we argue that mechanical solidarity is found to some degree in all but the most ephemeral groups, and that in work groups the locus of mechanical solidarity is the informal group structure. The greater the threats to the group, the greater will be the concern with mechanical solidarity.

## NOTES

Reprinted from Charles Vaught and David L. Smith, *Work and Occupations* 7, no. 2 (May 1980): 159–87. Copyright © 1980 by Sage Publications, Inc. Reprinted by permission of Sage Publications, Inc.

We are grateful for the constructive comments of Dr. Clifton Bryant, in whose seminar this idea originated. We especially acknowledge the efforts of Dr. Louis Zurcher, who spent several hours making detailed criticisms of two earlier drafts of this article. Our thanks also to two anonymous reviewers who suggested certain clarifications.

1. Because the "modern" underground mine has been exclusively a male domain until quite recently, we have chosen to treat the incorporation of females as a special case, hence the use of the masculine gender pronoun in the first part of this section.

2. The "dinner bucket" is round with removable compartments for food. The bottom of the bucket is designed to hold enough water to last the miners for several days in the event he or she is trapped. The "self-rescuer" is a small canister containing a breathing apparatus designed to filter out carbon monoxide in the event of a mine fire. It allows the miner approximately one hour of breathing time.

## REFERENCES

ALTHOUSE, R. (1974) *Work, Safety, and Life Style among Southern Appalachian Coal Miners.* Morgantown: West Virginia University, Office of Research and Development.

Anonymous (1946) "Informal social organization in the army." *Amer. of Sociology* 51 (March): 365–370.

ARAN, G. (1974) "Parachuting." *Amer. J. of Sociology* 80 (July): 124–152.

ARBLE, M. (1976) *The Long Tunnel.* New York: Atheneum.

BATESON, G. (1958) *Naven.* Palo Alto, CA: Stanford University Press.

BLUMER, H. (1961) *Symbolic Interactionism: Perspective and Method.* Englewood Cliffs, NJ: Prentice-Hall.

BOETH, R., J. LOWELL, and C. HARPER (1978) "Band of brothers." *Newsweek* 91 (March 6): 24–25.

BOUTON, J. (1970) *Ball Four.* New York: World.

BREED, W. (1955) "Social control in the newsroom: a functional analysis." *Social Forces* 33 (May): 326–335.

BROTZ, H. and E. WILSON (1946) "Characteristics of military society." *Amer. J. of Sociology* 51 (March): 371–375

BRYANT, C. D. (1972a) "Petroleum landmen: brothers in the oil fraternity," pp. 390–405 in C. D. Bryant (ed.) *The Social Dimensions of Work.* Englewood Cliffs, NJ: Prentice-Hall.

——— (1972b) "Sawdust in their shoes: the carnival as a neglected complex organization and work culture," pp. 180–205 in C. D. Bryant (ed.). *The Social Dimensions of Work.* Englewood Cliffs, NJ: Prentice-Hall.

CHILDERS, G. W., B. MAYHEW, Jr., and L. N. GRAY (1971) "System size and structural differentiation in military organizations: testing a base line model of the division of labor." *Amer. J. of Sociology* 76 (March): 813–830.

COLEMAN, J. S. (1970) "Social inventions." *Social Forces* 48 (December): 163–173.

COLLETT, J. S., D. WEBB, and D. L. SMITH (1979) "Suicide, alcoholism, and types of social integration: clarification of a theoretical legacy." *Sociology and Social Research* (July): 699–721

DENZIN, N. K. (1971) "The logic of naturalistic inquiry." *Social Forces* 50 (December): 166–182.

DURKHEIM, E. (1964) *The Division of Labor in Society.* G. Simpson (Trans.) New York: Macmillan.

ELKIN, F. (1946) "The soldier's language." *Amer. J. of Sociology* 51 (March): 414–422.

ERIKSON, K. (1966) *Wayward Puritans: A Study in the Sociology of Deviance.* New York: John Wiley.

FEIGELMAN, W. (1974) "Peeping: the pattern of voyeurism among construction workers." *Urban Life and Culture* 3 (April): 35–49.

FITZPATRICK, J. (1974) *Underground Mining: A Case Study of an Occupational Subculture of Danger.* Ph.D. diss., Ohio State University.

GARFINKLE, H. (1956) "Conditions of successful degradation ceremonies." *Amer. J. of Sociology* 61 (March): 420–424.

GOFFMAN, E. (1961a) *Asylums.* New York: Doubleday.

——— (1961b) *Encounters.* Indianapolis, IN: Bobbs-Merrill.

GOLD, R. (1958) "Roles in sociological field observation." *Social Forces* 36 (March): 217–223.

GOULDNER, A. (1954) *Patterns of Industrial Bureaucracy.* New York: Macmillan.

GRAVES, B. (1958) "'Breaking out': an apprenticeship system among pipeline construction workers." *Human Organization* 17 (Fall): 9–13

HAYNER, N. (1945) "Taming the lumberjack." *Amer. Soc. Rev.* 10 (April): 217–225.

HOMANS, G. (1941) "Anxiety and ritual: the theories of Malinowski and Radcliff-Brown." *Amer. Anthropologist* 43 (April-June): 164–172.

HUIZINGA, J. (1955) *Homo Ludens.* Boston: Beacon.

INVERARITY, J. M. (1976) "Populism and lynching in Louisiana, 1899–1926: A test of Erikson's theory of the relationship between boundary crises and repressive justice." *Amer. Soc. Rev.* 41 (April): 262–280.

JANIS, E. (1968) "Group identification under conditions of external danger," in D. Cartwright and a. Zander (eds.) *Group Dynamics.* New York: Harper & Row.

KEESING, F. (1958) *Cultural Anthropology: The Science of Custom.* New York: Holt, Rinehart & Winston.

KEMPER, T. (1972) "The division of labor: a post-Durkheimian analytic view." *Amer. Soc. Rev.* 31 (December): 739–753.

LUCAS, R. (1969) *Men in Crises.* New York: Basic Books.

MEAD, G. (1934) "Mind, self, and society from the Standpoint of a Social Behaviorist," edited by C. W. Morris Chicago: University of Chicago Press. This appears in a posthumous book of articles written by Mead.

McCARL, R. S., Jr. (1976) "Smokejumper initiation: ritualized communication in a modern occupation." *J. of Amer. Folklore* 89 (January-March): 49–63.

MILLS, C. W. (1940) "Situated actions and vocabularies of motive." *Amer. Soc. Rev.* 5 (December): 904–913.

NYDEN, P. (1976) *Miners for Democracy: Struggle in the Coal Fields.* Ph.D. diss., Columbia University.

PIAGET, J. (1962) *Play, Dreams and Imitation in Childhood.* C. Gattegno and F. M. Hodgson (Trans.) New York: Norton.

REISS, A. J. (1961) "The social integration of queers and peers." *Social Problems* 9 (Fall): 102–120.

ROBERTS, J. M. and B. SUTTON-SMITH (1962) "Child training and game involvement." Ethnology 1 (April): 166–185.

ROETHLISBERGER, F. J. and W. J. DICKSON (1947) *Management and the Worker.* Cambridge, MA: Harvard University Press.

ROY, D. (1960) "Banana time." *Human Organization* 18 (Winter): 158–164.

———— (1953) "Work satisfaction and social reward in quota achievement: an analysis of piecework incentive." *Amer. Soc. Rev.* 18 (October): 507–514.

SMITH, D. L. and R. SNOW (1976) "The division of labor: conceptual and methodological issues." *Social Forces* 55 (December): 520–528.

STEELE, P. D. and L. ZURCHER (1973) "Leisure sports as 'ephemeral roles.'" *Pacific Soc. Rev.* 16 (July): 345–356.

STODDARD, E. (1968) "The informal 'code' of police deviancy." *J. of Criminal Law, Criminology, and Police Science* 59 (June): 201–213.

STONE, R. (1946) "Status and leadership in a combat fighter squadron." *Amer. J. of Sociology* 51 (March): 388–395.

SULLIVAN, H. S. (1977) quoted on p. 72 in L. Zurcher, *The Mutable Self.* Beverly Hills, CA: Sage.

TURNER, R. (1967) "Types of solidarity in the reconstituting of groups." *Pacific Soc. Rev.* 10 (Fall): 60–68.

Van GENNEP, A. (1960) *The Rites of Passage.* M. B. Vivedome and G. C. Coffee (Trans.) Chicago: University of Chicago Press.

WARDELL, M. L., D. L. SMITH, and C. VAUGHT (1979) *Coal Miners and Coal Mining in Southwestern Virginia.* Blacksburg, VA: Agricultural Experiment Station.

WEISS, M. (1967) "Rebirth in the airborne." *Trans-Action* 4 (May): 23–26.

YOUNG, F. (1965) *Initiation Ceremonies: A Cross-Cultural Study of Status Dramatization.* Indianapolis: Bobbs-Merrill.

ZURCHER, L. (1979) "Role selection: the influence of internalized vocabularies of motive." *Symbolic Interaction* 2, 2: 45–62.

———— (1978) "The airplane passenger: protection of self in an encapsulated group." *Qualitative Sociology* 1 (January): 77–99.

———— (1970) "The 'friendly' poker game: a study of an ephemeral role." *Social Forces* 49 (December): 173–186.

———— (1968) "Social-psychological functions of ephemeral roles: a disaster work crew." *Human Organization* 27 (Winter): 281–297.

———— (1967) "The naval recruit training center: a study of role assimilation in a total institution." *Soc. Inquiry* 37 (Winter): 85–98.

———— (1965) "The sailor aboard ship: a study of role behavior in a total institution." *Social Forces* 43 (March): 389–400.

———— D. W. SONNENSCHEIN, and E. METZNER (1966) "The hasher: a study of role conflict." *Social Forces* 44 (June): 505–514.

# 6

## Dancing with Identity: Narrative Resistance Strategies of Male and Female Stripteasers

*Carol Rambo Ronai and*
*Rebecca Cross*

### SAMPLE AND PROCEDURE

In this work, we analyze the life narratives of 14 female and 10 male strip-tease dancers to develop a critical understanding of deviance as a component of biographical activity. Carol Rambo Ronai developed an interest in the biographical work of exotic dancers while reflecting on data gathered in an ongoing field study of striptease artists (1992a, 1992b, 1994, 1997; Ronai & Ellis, 1989). Rebecca Cross, as Carol's graduate assistant, helped to code the data Carol had gathered, and she developed a parallel interest in biographical work. Together, they analyzed the dancer's narratives noting the framing devices each used in their life history narratives.

In total, 10 men and 14 women, all stripteasers in the southeastern United States, participated in tape-recorded "life history" interviews. Eighteen of the dancers were White, three were African American, two were Hispanic, and one was Asian. Each of the 24 dancers in the sample had participated in one or more types of striptease: revues, strip-o-grams, topless/table dancing, and nude dancing.

A revue is a traveling striptease show, consisting of all women, all men, or both women and men. The shows begin with each dancer performing an individual striptease routine, and they conclude with all the dancers participating in a choreographed dance performance. Some shows feature activities such as Jell-O® wrestling or boxing. Female traveling revue dancers usually strip down to a string bikini, occasionally appearing topless for extra money. In any form of striptease, the men strip down to a T-back strap that conceals the genitalia and exposes the buttocks. Dancers often find revues more exciting than other forms of striptease and enjoy receiving a flat rate-plus-tips as payment. However, revue dancers often complain of receiving lower tips than topless/table dancers or nude dancers.

Strip-o-grams are usually performed at a birthday party or other celebration. The person who "sends" the strip-o-gram selects a dancer from a photo album. The dancer appears at a designated time and place to perform a striptease dance for the recipient. Male strip-o-gram dancers often appear as a character such as a delivery person, a police officer, or a lost motorist. The female strip-o-gram dancer often arrives wearing a revealing outfit and strips down to a string bikini or lingerie. The stripteaser dances very close to the strip-o-gram recipient, and physical contact, such as caressing or kissing, may occur. The pros and cons of strip-o-grams are similar to those of traveling revues, with the added disadvantage of the danger inherent in entertaining in private homes. Dancers use a variety of methods to ensure their safety: they call management when they arrive at and leave a site, have a friend wait in the car outside while performing, or have a friend attend the performance with them.

Topless and nude dancing take place in strip bars designed for the activity. In topless bars, where alcohol is served, dancers wear pasties and a T-back strap. Customers make physical contact with the dancer during a routine called a "table dance," although ordinances vary on how much contact is allowed. In settings where dancers are totally nude and no alcohol is served, customers are not permitted to touch dancers except to tip them on stage. If the customer is interested in more, dancers can conduct dances for them behind private Plexiglas® booths.

The advantages and disadvantages of topless and nude dancing vary considerably from those of revues and strip-o-grams. For example, most topless and nude dancers rely solely on tips. Strip clubs are thought to be more boring than other forms of striptease, because dancers have a set schedule. However, the club setting is the safest place to work because there are bouncers to look out for the dancers' safety. Nevertheless, it is easy for anyone who wants to harm a dancer to follow the dancer home.

Knowledge of the different occupational forms furthers our understanding of how deviance is constructed by exotic dancers. Dancers who engage in one form of striptease often regard group members who engage in other forms as deviant. The form of the occupation serves as an important way to organize the discourses that dancers use to narratively resist deviance attributions.

## NARRATIVE RESISTANCE AS BIOGRAPHICAL
## WORK, DIALECTICS, AND MAPPING

When an interviewer asks a subject to narrate a biography, the subject and the interviewer jointly negotiate the subject's identity. The subject relies on at-hand categories and typifications to retrospectively construct the "life." Subjects seek to "frame and organize one's character and actions, selecting and highlighting the defining aspects of one's past" (Gubrium, Holstein, & Buckholdt 1994, p. 157). These verbal management techniques are "biographical work."

Jaber Gubrium, James Holstein, and David Buckholdt (1994, p. 156) define biographical work as the "ongoing effort to integrate accounts of a person's life," which the authors argue is "continually subject to reinterpretation because it is always the biography-at-hand." Narrated biography is a stationary process rather than a static product. The elements of biography change because of time passage and the context of the social situation in which the account is told. For Gubrium et al. (1994, p. 155), "Much of the work of assembling a life story is the management of consistency and continuity, assuring that the past reasonably leads up to the present to form a life-line." Biographical work is an activity in which a subject attempts to "make sense" of his or her life experiences.

In this project, we use the discourse of exotic dancers to highlight one form of biographical work: narrative resistance. "Others have the ability to threaten our opinion of ourselves by suggesting negative categories to define ourselves by" (Ronai 1997, p. 125). This threat is experienced as "discursive constraint" (Ronai 1997, 1994) by the individual. For instance, a child who is being sexually abused may be told that she is a slut and if she speaks about the abuse others will know the "truth" about her. This form of discursive constraint simultaneously controls the child's behavior (stay silent so others won't know) and her narrated biography as she tells it to herself (I am a slut and that is why this is happening to me), thus setting her up for future abuses. If she does not have an alternative stock of knowledge which enables her to resist this definition of self, she may incorporate the negative label into her identity.

Narrative resistance is a response to discursive constraint which dialectically emerges from and constitutes an alternative stock of knowledge within a stigmatized group. Narrative resistance is an active speech behavior which serves to decenter the authority of specific individuals or society to dictate identity. The narrative resistance strategies presented here are forms of biographical work which cast self in frameworks which make use of the language of deviance, but reshape it in such a way as to resist taking on the negative identity for oneself. In reshaping the resources that the mainstream stocks of knowledge offer a stigmatized group, the group in question is remapping both their individual identities and their collective place in the terrain of social space.

Each time an individual narratively resists discursive constraint and another group member incorporates that particular strategy into their own stock of knowledge, that strategy eventually emerges as a part of the local or alternative stock of knowledge. These alternative stocks of knowledge, intersubjectively shared by the community, in turn, serve to positively alter the mainstream stocks of knowledge regarding the group in question. For instance, many of the dancers interviewed expressed that they were either supporting themselves through school or supporting a child. One has only to listen to television or radio talk shows on the topic of striptease to hear non-strippers reproducing these discourses.

"Well at least Allen is in school" or "Midnight does it to support her children" are remarks that represent a small shift in the public's perception of striptease. These discourses still make use of the language of deviance—"If someone strips for a living and she or he is not in school or supporting children, then she or he is doing something wrong." Now, however, instead of viewing striptease as always wrong in all contexts, there are occasionally fields in the common stocks of knowledge where stripping is understandable or even acceptable. This mainstream discourse, in turn, intersubjectively circulates back to striptease dancers as a resource for their use in future instances when they are called to narrate accounts of self.

## NARRATIVE RESISTANCE STRATEGIES

This article focuses on a form of narrative resistance that uses images of deviance as negative exemplars—standards of comparison—to avoid negative identity assignments. The dancers in this study made use of a wide variety of narrative resources while constructing their biographies for our life history interview, many more than we could discuss in a single article. Therefore, we limit our analysis of identity construction and narrative resistance to two particular strategies where images of deviance are used as exemplars: sleaze and immersion.

### Constructing Deviance Exemplars

Exemplars, as defined by Gubrium and Lynott (1985, p. 353), are "products of the collective work of representing experiences . . . recognizable means of sharing particular collective representations." For striptease dancers, the collective representations of their experiences are deviant images. Dancers construct deviance exemplars which delimit identity by serving as a narrative "straw man" or "straw woman" by which to compare oneself. A dancer practices biographical work to define her or himself as an exception to the average striptease dancer. Her or his identity emerges narratively by resisting the deviant role that the exemplar represents. By engaging in this pattern of discourse, a dancer defines the deviance frame as acceptable for some people, but not for herself or himself. Dancers, both male and female, triangulate their "selves" relative to the selves of other dancers, thus mapping identity claims in social space as they narrate their biographies. Through this process of comparison, they map their own position in the social world relative to other dancers.

Garcia, a 26-year-old strip-o-gram dancer, uses a deviance exemplar to describe another dancer whom he did not respect:

> I know a guy who is fool enough, he got accepted to medical school, because his father wanted him to be a doctor, but while he was doing his undergrad, he started stripping. He got accepted, and I think he did like three semesters of medicine school, and he went back to stripping and that is what he is doing now. So, like, to me, that is a pity. He could have done a lot of good to a lot of people, being a doctor. Now, he is a stripper, what good does he do? I don't see it as a job, but a way to get money. I think it should be the means to an end, not the ends to a mean.

Garcia constructs an exemplar, a model of someone who is treating the occupation of stripping as a permanent job. He defines himself conversely by stating that, for him, exotic dancing is only a "way to get money."

Nina, a 22-year-old revue and strip-o-gram dancer, gossips about a rival troupe, "In the Raw":

> Everyone knows about them. We know what's up. How do I say this? [Giggles.] They's hos [euphemism for "They are whores"]. Say "Hey ho" and those bitches'll turn around and answer you "What?" [Giggles.] Our group can't make the money they do because we don't *fuck* [her emphasis as she laughs out right] everyone we dance for. We may not make the money they do, but we aren't total sluts either.

Nina constructs "In the Raw" as the comparison group or exemplar by describing them, and then designates her troupe as superior because they do not engage in the same behavior. This time an entire group is set up as the triangulation coordinate by which to map and narratively resist a deviant identity.

Jessica, who is 25 years old, White, a senior in college and a revue dancer, displays a native awareness of how deviance exemplars are constructed and used:

> Other girls spend a lot of time talking about who they aren't by talking about someone else. I'm sure you got a lot of dancers to talk to you and I'm sure you

got them talkin' trash. It's bad for the industry. You won't get trash from me. I'm one of the people that don't fall into the category of the misconception that dancers come from bad homes or are doing it out of some sort of sexual need or things like that. But that's the public talking. I don't see dancers as bad. And I don't need to badmouth to tell you who I am. Dancers are so catty, back stabbing, always talking 'bout other dancers. I hate it.

Jessica engages in some of the identity management practices for which she chastises other dancers. She constructs an exemplar and narratively distances herself from its deviant status. She tells us what "other girls" are like, she tells us gossip is harmful, and she distances herself from them by telling us what she is like. Jessica's typification of "other girls" was common. Most of the dancers interviewed joked that they talked behind each other's backs, wanted to know what others had said about them, and told us gossip about other dancers.

As deviance exemplars are constructed and narratively distance the self from deviance, they are used with the understanding that some dancers match the negative characteristics defined by the emergent, multi-dimensional, non-Cartesian map of identity. Male dancers use some of the same exemplars as female dancers use, as both groups are subject to discursive constraint and a negative identity. Exotic dancers create identity maps from the narratively shared knowledge of exotic dancing, and restructure that knowledge by avoiding locating their own identities at deviant map coordinates. Dancers locate themselves in social space by specifying, among other things, sleaze and immersion as exemplars.

## The Sleaze Exemplar

Dancers engage in biography work, specifically narrative resistance, by locating themselves relative to "sleaze." Sleaze is a deviance exemplar that serves to constitute a form of narrative resistance which helps map a dancer's claim to a location in social space. The type of exotic dancing a stripteaser engages in can determine how she or he constructs her or his identity relative to sleaze. Most revue dancers remarked on how sleazy they think nude dancers are, which serves to narratively resist deviance by portraying themselves as less deviant in comparison. Garcia specifies this dimension of identity in his text:

If you go all the way naked, which I never do, there is only so much you can do, offer to them. And from an exotic, appealing, sexy dancer, you become something that they are just looking at. What is this guy going to do now? Unless you can pull rabbits out of a hat or something—overkill.

Nina, a White revue dancer, also states, "I'll never go nude. I just can't." Garcia and Nina both believe they are less sleazy than other dancers because they don't undress completely.

Connor, a 19-year-old, White, female, nude dancer, expresses similar sentiments when sharing with us her experiences from when she first started stripping and was trying to figure out how she was supposed to dance in the private booths. She concludes, "When I first started working there, I sat there for ten minutes and watched the guy. And you see everything. And me, I never show everything." Even though Connor is a nude dancer, she specifies sleaze as an exemplar in a manner similar to revue and table dancers. She sets up nude dancers as the deviance exemplar and narratively resists the deviant identity by explaining that she is not like the typical nude dancer who exposes it all.

By specifying physical contact with customers as closer to sleaze relative to nudity, nude dancers use this exemplar differently from revue and table dancers. They assert that nude dancing is superior to topless or revue dancing because they are not touched by the audience except to receive tips. For example Madeline, a 20-year-old nude dancer, stated the following: "I would only work in a place where there is no contact involved." Ashley, a 36-year-old nude dancer, parrots Madeline when she says, "I feel like if they will pay me to look at me naked, they can't touch me, they can't screw me, I am safe."

Sometimes narrative resistance is practiced by establishing another dancer's behavior as an exemplar by locating it as sleazy and placing one's own conduct in opposition to that behavior. Stephanie, a 21-year-old nude dancer, illustrates this as she describes what goes on in a private dance booth:

> I have known some girls like that. They will bring Vaseline, and jelly, but the extent of bringing things in there, sometimes I will bring ice in there. They are supposed to be simulating masturbation, and I don't do that.

Stephanie narratively constructs public masturbation as sleazy in order to narratively resist assigning to herself the deviance she attributes to the women who simulate masturbation. Her claims about her own behavior distance her from sleaze.

Madeline, a nude dancer, relayed a similar story:

> One girl asked me to do a dance with her in the private dance booth. And whenever you walk by the booth and she's doing a dance in there, you always hear a vibrator going off. That is so sleazy. I could not do that in front of somebody.

By disapproving of the girl who uses a vibrator, and claiming to be unable to use them in front of people herself, Madeline narratively resists what she considers to be "so sleazy" and distances herself from it. To make her point more explicit, Madeline went on to discuss a situation, which took place earlier in the evening before our interview:

> I don't know if you noticed it, but tonight there was a lot of tension because there was one girl that was out on stage and I couldn't believe it, and every girl I talked to was like, their faces just dropped. She grabbed the bars and flung her head down until it was almost on the floor exposing "the pink."

The phrase "the pink" refers to the labia and/or clitoris. Exposing the pink by lifting one's leg, and spreading one's legs, or bending over is illegal and is considered by the dancers to be desperate and a way of "upping the ante." If one dancer does it, the customer will expect the other dancers to do it, or they won't tip. Furthermore, according to Madeline, "A girl like that gives all dancers a bad name." Not only does Madeline narratively distance herself from sleaze, but she also demonstrates an awareness of the implications of this dancer's behavior for the collective identity of dancers and distances the occupation from her also.

Hudson, a 23-year-old, White, male, revue dancer, uses a technique similar to Stephanie's and Madeline's when he talks about raunchy stage behavior: "Like a fake sixty-nine. I wouldn't do that on stage, but I have seen people do that." Hudson attributes a label of deviance to male dancers who perform acts such as a fake sixty-nine (pretending to engage in mutual oral sex), and then narratively resists the deviant label by stating that he could not behave that way.

Sleaze is also specified through the vocabularies of gender and race. It is taken to be common knowledge among female dancers that male dancers are sleazier. Kitty comments, "Guys get away with murder on stage. A woman would never do that stuff, wouldn't want to." Many other female dancers echo this sentiment. Only one of the 10 males interviewed, Ron, hints that he thinks women can be "sleazier" than men. He states, "Some women can be even more sleazier on stage than the most sleaziest man, but not usually."

The rest of the men are somewhat defensive about sleaze as they apply it to their own gender's participation in the occupation. Often, the sleaze exemplar is specified by male dancers in such a way as to distance themselves from the "sleaze" they believe typically applies to men in their field. Hollywood, for instance, talks about how he finds erections on stage to be objectionable:

> Yea, there was one guy that I danced with, he always got a hard on while he was out there. But it was gross. . . . I guess some girls would like it, but I guess most girls, the majority, thought it was disgusting.

Likewise Hudson reported the following:

I wouldn't want to have an erection when I was dancing. . . . I think the girls would get turned off by that. . . . A lot of them really grab for that area when you are up dancing close and stuff like that when you are up close to them, but I don't know if they would like it that far.

Race, as a vocabulary, appears to intersect gender as a way to do biographical identity work and narratively resist the sleaze exemplar. It is taken to be common knowledge among Whites that African American male dancers are sleazier than all other dancers. The two African American male subjects did not speak of race in any manner when specifying the sleaze exemplar. When Rachel, a White female dancer, hears that Carol will interview a Black male revue dancer named Kareem, she feels obligated to issue this warning:

You gotta watch out for him. I don't think he will try anything, but he might. He likes blondes so, it ain't no big deal, just watch out for him. If you saw this guy on stage, actually all the Black guys are like this, they are so N-A-S-T-Y [spelled out]. Nasty. I know it sounds racist, but it's true.

Ron makes a similar remark regarding Kareem as he discusses himself:

You need to come see me dance. When I do it, I do it for the ladies. I don't put it [his groin region] in their face. No chick likes that crap. And if they do, I ain't interested in spending too much time with them anyway. Now Kareem, he'll put it right up in their face. I watch their faces when he does that. I'm a professional and I say they don't like it. All the Black guys do that shit.

Ron sets up Kareem and "Black guys" as the sleaze exemplar. He is White so he can distance himself from the sleaze attributed to male strippers by specifying his race. Ron elaborates on the intersection of the vocabularies of gender, race, and sleaze at another point in his interview. He remarked on three practices: "tying off" (tying something around the base of the penis after stimulating it to produce a tourniquet effect), "stuffing" (placing something in the groin region to produce the appearance of an erection), and injections (injecting a vasodilator into the penis to increase the blood flow and consequently the size). He explained, "Usually it's the Black guys doing it. No one needs a hard-on to dance. I get embarrassed when I spring one, and wait for it to go down if I can." Hollywood, as noted earlier, is similarly uncomfortable with men having erections on stage and stated, "I would never stick no needle in my dick." These practices, particularly the injections, are discussed in very hushed and conspiratorial tones. When Hudson is asked if he knows anyone who does things to enhance the appearance of their penises on stage, he commented, "Whites will sometimes tie off or stuff, but it's the Black guys that get radical. They inject. They have a reputation for having a big one to maintain."

No dancer specifies African American or Hispanic females as sleazy. The first author has heard White customers classify both racial groups as sleazier than Whites, however. Twice, male Hispanics were classified as sleazier or more vulgar, on the average, than other dancers. Ron, when he learns Carol is to interview Garcia, commented the following:

> He's a spic, Cuban or something. Don't do his alone. No, do it alone, and if he tries anything with you call me, I'll set him straight, I'll kick his ass. In fact tell him at the start of the interview that I said I'd kick his ass if he tried anything. Then you'll be safe.

Almost a page of transcription material covered this topic. The first author's subsequent experiences with both Kareem and Garcia were very positive. While Kareem was mildly flirtatious during his interview, like a couple of the White male dancers and one of the White female dancers, the first author always felt safe. Garcia was a graduate student living in campus married student housing with his wife and child. In both instances, the interviewer found nothing untoward in their conduct.

Sleaze, as an exemplar, forms one dimension of a working identity map where subjects may locate themselves based on who they are and the stocks of knowledge they have access to. By demarcating an identity for themselves relative to the sleaze exemplar, dancers do not reject the deviant stigma others apply to the occupation of striptease dancing as a whole. Indeed, both male and female dancers reinforce it by using it to narratively resist where they stand in relation to it. By practicing narrative resistance, however, dancers actively produce and reproduce an alternate stock of knowledge as an identity resource for themselves as individuals or as a group to draw upon. By exchanging this talk in backstage settings and reproducing it in an interview, dancers are jointly practicing identity as a form of resistance to mainstream society's definition of them—in this case, as sleazy. Sleaze, however, is not the only exemplar that dancers specify when mapping their identities.

## The Immersion Exemplar

Another exemplar dancers appeal to when doing biography work involves describing the degree to which a dancer is immersed in the occupation. Total immersion in the occupation is viewed negatively (no dancer claimed to be totally immersed), so dancers narratively resist constructing identities for themselves which would define them as "too far into it." While they do not draw on medical frames like "rehabilitation" or "recovery," they do appeal to a vocabulary of getting "hooked" or "addicted" to the occupation, the money, or the excitement, as a way to specify immersion. Part-time dancers are more likely than full-time dancers to refer to this exemplar in their narratives.

Jarrod, a 28-year-old, Black, male striptease dancer who has danced on and off for 9 years, uses the vocabulary of addiction:

> I could stop anytime, I could just get out of it at anytime, stop. I hope I don't sound like a dance-aholic, but . . . I'm not at the point of dancing that I have to do it. I don't depend on it for anything.

Helena also uses this vocabulary:

> I'm fortunate that I turned out okay, because people, some people that I hung around with and the way my life was, you know, I'm surprised I'm not into drugs. I mean when I danced at Chez Manique or Cat's, you get hooked on the money and you get hooked to the fun, and I really didn't get hooked and get pulled in.

When asked specifically why she did not get "pulled in," Helena answered the following:

> I think I had more respect for myself and I think I had more, I cared more about things, about what happened in my life than a lot of them.

Helena used others that she "hung around with" as exemplars of who was too immersed in the occupation. She claimed they were "pulled in" while she was not. Describing how she respects herself, and how she cares about what happens to her, we can see her narratively anchoring herself on the identity map in such a way as to prevent her from seeing herself as "pulled in."

Others use this anchoring strategy more overtly to resist the exemplar of immersion. Rachel, a 25-year-old, uses her college and work experience as anchors which prevent her from being immersed too far. She distances herself from this exemplar by stating, "This isn't my life, that this is all I can do. I have my degrees, I'm managing the store now, I'm going to stay in retail. Once I leave [Townsville], I'm not going to do this anymore." Rachel speaks of her dancing as a temporary activity, thereby distancing herself from the total immersion that would be implied if it were a permanent career.

Jessica uses the immersion exemplar somewhat differently from Rachel:

> I am going to stay in college, I will get a degree, and I will seek employment in another field, but I think having the ability to do this, it's something that is there in case, something to fall back on, and that makes me feel secure knowing I have that.

Jessica distances herself from the immersion exemplar when she claims that dancing is "something to fall back on," again offering the temporary nature of the activity to herself and us as evidence that she is not too immersed.

Claiming an intense personal relationship may also serve as a way to narratively resist immersion. Hollywood, a 36-year-old, White, male, revue and strip-o-gram dancer states, "My dad is real close, helps me keep my head screwed on straight so I don't get into it any more like some of them do." Kitty, a White, female, revue and strip-o-gram dancer who claims to be 25 years old (others disputed this, claiming she was 27 or 28), similarly states, "We argue sometimes, we drive each other nuts, but my mom supports me, and she keeps me straight, so I don't get into any real trouble." Neither dancer claims to have activities which compete for their time and attention, but rather they claim a deep bond which serves to firmly anchor the self in such a way as to prevent total immersion.

Other exemplars presented themselves as resources for biographical work and narrative resistance such as attractiveness (who is too old, overweight, awkward or ugly to dance), naturalness (how much does one depend on cosmetic treatments such as breast, pectoral, calf, or other implants, liposuction, hair coloring, and so forth), appropriate attitude (is the person in question too arrogant, vain, or conceited), as well as twenty other categories we noted. By using all of these themes, dancers are able to triangulate and map an identity for themselves through a very treacherous terrain which makes available less than perfect resources for accomplishing biographical work. Bit by bit, over time, through narrative resistance, alternative stocks of knowledge on the identity of dancers emerge, offering a small ray of hope that identity is a contextual matter rather than a stagnant caricature which blankets all stripteasers regardless of their situations.

## NARRATIVE RESISTANCE AND BIOGRAPHICAL WORK

This article contributes to the social constructionist literature on deviance and deviant identities and implements a new theoretical framework (biographical work) within this tradition. By focusing on both males and females, this text has sought to remove certain stereotypes which may have operated in research in this area in the past. The theory of biographical work, applied specifically to alleviate a possible gender and deviance bias in the stripteaser literature, illuminated a specific pattern in the discourses of our subjects. These patterns, in turn, enabled us to develop the concepts of narrative resistance and deviance exemplars, thus expanding the applicability of biography work as a theory.

The use of narrative resistance, in particular deviance exemplars, is not restricted to stripteasers or any group of people who engages in what might be considered "deviant behavior." Narrative resistance is a cultural universal. Everyone in their self talk sets up other individuals and/or groups as examples by which to compare themselves and triangulate identity. If one is a mother who works outside the home, she might say, "I wish I didn't have to work, but at least I make time for my kids, unlike Sally and Sue" or "I may not be the best father but at least I bring home my paycheck and check my kids' homework unlike Bill and Steve."

By recognizing the generalizability of this strategy, then we come full circle to realize that both male and female striptease dancers, like everyone else, are engaged in the work of trying to make sense of their identities. The working mother is told she should be at home; the father is told he should do more for his kids; the striptease dancer is told stripping is wrong. All of these forms of discursive constraint are attempts at domination and control, either as an effort to constrain how a person chooses to self identify or as an effort to change her or his behavior (become an at-home mom, better dad, or stop dancing, and we won't label you). None of these subjects are forced to passively internalize a negative identity. To do so would create a problematic identity. By formulating and consulting an alternative stock of knowledge, subjects develop the resources to resist. The working mother talks with other mothers and taps into the story that as long as you make time for your children, you are still being a good mother. As more and more mothers work, these discourses circulate until finally being a working mother is not considered a problem by anyone anymore, unless you don't spend time with your children. Likewise with the father, the striptease, and everyone else. Through the process of biography work and narrative resistance we become the authors of our identities, charting for ourselves a place in social space which transforms negative discourses into more positive identity resources for ourselves and others to draw upon in the future.

## NOTES

Reprinted from *Deviant Behavior* 19, no. 2 (1998): 99–119. Copyright © 1998 from "Dancing with Identity" by Carol Rambo Ronai and Rebecca Cross. Reproduced by permission of Taylor & Francis, Inc., www.routledge-ny.com.

We would like to acknowledge Jaber Gubrium, James A. Holstein, and Gale Miller for their assistance.

Address correspondence to Carol Rambo Ronai, Department of Sociology, University of Memphis, Clement Hall Room 225, Memphis, TN 38152. E-mail: CRRONAI@CC.MEMPHIS.EDU.

# REFERENCES

Gubrium, Jaber, James Holstein, & David R. Buckholdt. 1994. *Constructing the Lifecourse*. Dix Hills, NY: General Hall.
Gubrium, Jaber, & Robert Lynott. 1985. "Alzheimer's Disease as Biographical Work." Pp. 349–369 in *Social Bonds in Later Life*, edited by W. Peterson & J. Quadagno. Newbury Park, CA: Sage.
Ronai, Carol R. 1997. "Discursive Constraint in the Narrated Identities of Childhood Sex Abuse Survivors." Pp. 123–136 in *Everyday Sexism in the Third Millennium*, edited by C. R. Ronai, B. Zsembik, and J. Feagin. New York: Routledge.
———. 1994. "Narrative Resistance to Deviance: Identity Management among Striptease Dancers. Pp. 195–213 in *Perspectives on Social Problems*, vol. 6, edited by J. A. Holstein & G. Miller. Greenwich, CT: JAI Press.
———. 1992a. "Managing Aging in Young Adulthood: The Aging Table Dancer." *Journal of Aging Studies* 6: 307–317.
———. 1992b. "The Reflexive Self through Narrative: A Night in the Life of an Erotic Dancer/Researcher." Pp. 102–124 in *Investigating Subjectivity: Research on Lived Experience*, edited by C. Ellis & M. G. Flaherty. Newbury Park, CA: Sage.
Ronai, Carol R., & Carolyn Ellis. 1989. "Turn-Ons for Money: Interactional Strategies of the Table Dancer." *Journal of Contemporary Ethnography* 18: 271–298.

# 7

# Careers

*Everett C. Hughes*

Career, the word, has itself had a career. Once a race-course career came to mean figuratively a short gallop at full speed, even a charge of cavalry, the swift flight of a bird in hawking and the course of the sun and stars across the sky hence also full speed or impetus. Those meanings, all obsolete, have given place to this: "A person's course or progress through life (or a distinct portion of life)" A more special meaning is "a profession affording opportunities for advancement," and in a still narrower sense, and without abjectives, it refers in both English and French—to the taking up of diplomatic service as a permanent calling.[1]

Our subject is career in the broad modern sense of a person's course through life and especially through that portion of his life in which he works. That portion however, cannot be understood apart from the whole. In our sense, everyone has a career. Yet, such is the nature of our society, more and more people have careers in the somewhat narrower sense. Ours is called the bureaucratic age; Karl Mannheim said that career, in the strict sense, refers to the progress of a person through a bureaucracy.[2] At each step he receives a neat package of money, authority and prestige, whose contents he knows exactly in advance.

Many people have careers in that sense; insofar as that is true, everyone is in course of becoming an official—a civil servant—if not of a government bureaucrat at least of some other organized system. But not all of us are in such careers yet; perhaps we shall never be. Indeed, it appears that as the formal careers in which one accumulates seniority and social security (which has come to mean money) takes less of a person's living time, people resort to many forms of moonlighting to fill both their time and their pockets.

Apart from that breaking out of the bonds, there are many life-careers not formally organized and consciously defined. Even in those which are so defined that each step may, like the grades of civil service, be given a number, there is more than meets the eye. A mere account of progress of a person through the numbered grades does not tell the full story of life even in the civil service. In such organizational careers, there are many unforeseen contingencies and irregularities of which people in the system may or may not be aware. There are rumored regularities of which people in the system may or may not be aware. There are rumored regularities which those in charge will deny, but which nevertheless may turn out to exist. I start from the assumption that, even where there is no bureaucratic course to be run there are many regularities. The business of the students of careers is to discover those regularities, to find whatever order there may be in the course run by the lives of people as they grow and learn; as they choose, are chosen, rejected or knocked about by circumstances; as they wax or wane in energy, skill and wisdom; as they become more devoted and deeply rooted in their work, or, on the contrary, are bored, frustrated and perhaps flee from one kind of work to another, or from all work (which is defined as psychosis in our society). In the study of careers we deal with the dialectic between the regular and repeated, on the one hand, and the unique on the other; such study is, thus, like all study of society, directed at the meeting of ongoing but changing society and the unique human organism, whose years are few but whose offspring are, of course, so like their parents.

I shall only attempt to indicate some of the dimensions which must be used in analyzing careers; the variables—were they closely enough defined—in terms of which they may be described and ultimately measured. The setting of a framework of dimensions and appropriate concepts is our first problem. Much work has already been done on careers. Every biography is a case study of a career. The careers of people in various occupations have been described and measured by sociologists and psychologists. I shall, in this discussion, refer to the work done but little, and that for illustrative purposes. That does not imply that I consider the work of little value; in more extensive treatment I would certainly give more explicit credit.[3]

The first dimension of a career is biological age; the essence of career is that age changes from moment to moment and that no moment is repeated. For each of us, a moment of our age is also an event in history, a point in the career of institutions or social systems of the professions and occupations we work at, in technology and the labor market, and of the social (racial, national, ethnic, religious, class and sexual) groups to which we belong. I shall come to these points later. The grosser relations of biological with social life cycle have been defined, although much of the work does not distinguish the crude measure by years of life from actual biological development and decline. What is social definition or process is not easy to distinguish from what is biological condition. One thinks of the findings of the ages at which mathematicians and physicists make their discoveries. It is a fact of biology, or has it something to do with changes of economy of attention, energy and time almost forced upon one who has called attention to himself by creative work? Maybe they become less creative because they know too much, or are thought to know too much, or are given other work to do, or all of these.

Consider also the matter of physical energy, speed and physique. Herein lies my interest in the careers of athletes and the actresses who play the Hollywood version of the ingénue, if that old-fashioned term properly designates the starlet who wears bathing suits and new creations with striking effectiveness. "The Final Whistle" is the title of an article which tells how "the Celtics'" Bob Cousy, modern basketball's most exciting player, closes out a 16-year playing career which has made him "The Greatest." Cousy is now 34 years old.[4]

The movie actress likewise cannot play that particular role for many years; she—like the athlete—may take care to avoid the fate warned of in the couplet:

> When the age of forty they come,
> The men run to belly, the women to bum.

The athlete may keep his figure—although he generally doesn't—but he loses his speed and his wind. The actress, too, may still be able to wear the clothes, but her face and her manner betray her. The athlete, the bathing-beauty actress, the aviator barnstorming across an ocean, do, indeed, correspond to the older meaning of career: a short gallop at full speed, a star coursing across the sky.

So much is banality; everyone knows it (as they do much of what is important to social science). These careers are theoretically important mainly because of what happens after the brief gallop. We shall come to that later. These spectacular cases also remind us that, in a less spectacular way, there are probably changes in most occupations attendant upon changes of energy, speed, resilience and even appearance. The airplane stewardess could doubtless keep up the pace longer than she is allowed to; on the other hand, there is some indication that the operating-room nurse finds it both hard and galling to jump at the command of the surgeon after she is thirty-five. The operating room demands physical speed and a stout character. As a school teacher gets older, she may replace the vigor and speed of her first teaching years with wisdom and guile; perhaps with a sharp tongue and a tone of authority. The anthropologist who no longer has the stomach and the stamina to go to the field in the tropics of the backwoods can retire to the museum or the campus to work on his notes.

It is not only in athletes that men engage in work that they cannot keep up for many years. Jeremy Tunstall, in his recent book *The Fisherman, A Study of an Extreme Occupation,* reports that the work of the deep-sea fishermen who sail out of Hull to the North Atlantic is so strenuous, dangerous and even crippling that a man must, by his middle thirties, either have worked and studied his way up to be an officer of fishing ships or must have gone down to miserably paid and poorly regarded work on the docks. We have scarcely, in most lines of work, paid attention to the many changes in speed and style of work which come with advancing age, including the advance from the 20's to the 30's, as well as from the 40's to the 50's and 60's.

The menstrual cycle, pregnancies, and child rearing obviously affect the careers of women; again it is difficult to separate direct biological consequence from taboos and social definition. Some years ago there was a study, which I cannot now find, which showed that white-collar women allowed themselves the luxury of monthly headaches much more often than women out in the factory. One of my research assistants, in the period when I was doing studies of industry, reported that a large proportion of middle-aged Negro and Polish women in the plant she was studying always had a little something wrong with them which they called "female trouble," but that they could not indulge themselves with time off. The student-nurse in a maternity uniform illustrates well enough the change in attitude toward work and appearance in public of pregnant women. It is reported that even in Australia, a man's country, women are getting out to work when their children are still young. Women are, in our world, doubtless healthier than ever before and certainly less subject to taboos than formerly. Yet since society allows women to work, and since many of them want to or think they must, the career interrupted by biological events and their consequences is more common than ever. Previously, although they worked hard, most women left the labor market, if they ever entered it, at marriage—and stayed out. The changes that come in the human organism in its life cycle are then one dimensions of career, a dimension or a facet which we have explored only in the grossest way.

The more crucial problem, however, is what happens after physiological change, or any other change for that matter. What happens to the Marilyn Monroes who stay alive; and to the Bob Cousys who retire at the age of 34? To discuss this we have need of further concepts. All lines of work, except those reduced to some fine degree of repetition of a single motion by industrial engineers, consist in fact of a variety of activities. Often one of them gives the name to the work: machinist, teacher, salesman. In some occupations, the name varies with change in the activity which is considered the fundamental one: clergy are priests, pastors or preachers, according as they emphasize cult, cure of soul or religious and moral pronouncement. The people who are employed by colleges and universities sometimes emphasize teaching, sometimes custody of the young, sometimes research. I have never heard a college teacher call himself a grader of papers, although some of them seem to do as much of that as they possibly can (one way to restrict production of the master activity is to divert effort to chores). Let us then speak of the *core activity* of an occupation; it may also be the one which gives the occupation its name. Any occupation will consist of some combination of this activity with others *auxiliary* to it, either in the nature of the case or because of the industrial organization of the work. Keeping a fire in the stove is not, in the nature of the case, an activity of school teachers; but in the one-room school it was a necessary activity. There was no one but the teacher to do it. In any occupation, and in each phase of a career in any occupation, there will be an actual *economy of time and energy* devoted to its several component activities. There will also be, in many cases, an idealized economy of time and energy; or perhaps several idealized statements of what it is. Implicit in those ideal statements will be a ranking of the several component activities by value and prestige. Observation of people in the occupation may, in fact, reveal that their actual behavior belies their statements about the value of various activities. Furthermore, the economy of time and effort given to the component activities is a function of a division of labor among the people engaged in a line of work, or in the organized system in which the work is done; as one's career progress, it may be that his place in that division of labor changes. He can delegate, or have delegated to him, various of the component activities; he may even delegate, or otherwise escape, the core activity itself.

Characteristically, then, a career consists in part of changes in the economy of time and effort given to the various component activities of an occupation, or line of work, and to other activities which occur in the general system in which one has his career.

Now we return to our athletes, actresses and the Hull deep-sea fisherman, as examples of workers who cannot continue long at the core activity of their occupations. What happens to them? All, or nearly all, kinds of work are done in some system in which there is a variety of kinds of work to be done, and a corresponding variety of social roles. The institutions in which professional athletes work include trainers who keep players physically fit, coaches who teach coming and current players; scouts who smell them out and recruit them to the profession; managers who control them on and off the floor or field; and people who handle money, promotion and higher management. Some players graduate into one or another of these positions in the athletic system. Cousy has already signed up as a coach at a college which emphasizes athletics. But not all players have the qualities of personality or the skills which fit them for any of these positions, high or low. More disappear to get into the news only when they die in poverty than remain to become Branch Rickeys. Only a few actresses graduate to character parts or become Katherine Hepburns. More of the fishermen end up on the park bench and the dole than on the bridge. But there are generally some positions in a work system for those who have had to abandon the core activity.

Still other positions are on the outlying parts of the system, where it meets the public and the larger world. A ballplayer may sell sporting goods; so long as his autograph is still in demand it does not matter whether he knows the goods well or whether he is an effective salesman. He has, to start with, a ready-made clientele as large as his reputation as an athletic hero; this gives him time to develop the other qualities necessary to continued success if he has the makings of them. He may, as Mark Harris's southpaw pitcher, author Henry Wiggins, sell insurance to other ballplayers. There are such positions on the periphery of many work systems; physicians occasionally become salesmen for pharmaceutical companies. Teachers may become lobbyists, or go into the textbook business. Some occupations are carried on in systems which have many connections with related systems and with the public; as a person comes to the end of one phase of his career, he may shift to a place in one of the connected systems. Another possibility is that some work system not in any way connected with one's original occupation may offer a field for exploiting skills and characteristics developed in it. Many Negro union-leaders were first evangelical preachers; the packinghouse workers' union offered a larger congregation and perhaps a greater sense of mission than rural chapels or urban storefront churches. In some cases, the change may be from great to small, as when the unhappy seminarian or disenchanted priest exploits his literacy to pass the examination which will make him a letter-sorter in some huge post office; he joins there other highly literate, disappointed or ruined men in that "tomb of forgotten men."

Part of the study of careers is to seek out the positions to which people may move when they must or do leave the basic or core activity; and to investigate the processes by which people are selected (by self or others) for those positions and take the steps which determine their longer-run futures—whether the movements take them up or downwards in prestige, money and power.

Psychologists, I should imagine, might want to find out whether the qualities required for these alternative positions are related, and how, to these which fitted one for the core activity; and whether the practice of the core activity develops them.

The movement to activities other than the core activity is, however, not due merely to physiology or even psychology. In many occupations and work systems the road to prestige, higher income and reputation turns away from the core activity. Those who remain in it may be looked upon with condensation by those who have left it, when they retire they will be given a watch which they won't need, and praised for faithful and indispensable service. The school teacher, the nurse, the salesman behind the counter, the engineer who becomes and remains an expert draughtsman, may indeed win these small increments of which Mannheim spoke; they do not win the greater prizes. To do so they would have to abandon the basic activity for administration, teaching in professional schools, research, or the higher politics of the profession. Indeed, it has been said with some truth that the lengthening of professional education in most of these fields serves not so much to increase skill in the core activity as to facilitate escape from it. These occupations belong to those in which it is thought that the only people fit to administer, train successors and do research are those who have served a sort of apprenticeship in the core activity. Only so may one become a number of the license in-group. One must first have been a colleague, although after he deserts the core activity he is never fully one with those he has left behind.

There are occupations, however, in which one may scale the greater heights while continuing to practice the core activity; indeed, it may be necessary to continue it if one is to achieve a considerable success. Medicine, law and scholarship are among them. But, given recent developments in the organizational system in which these activities are carried on, the case is no longer clear. Medicine is practiced increasingly in clinics and hospitals; law, in large firms and in government bureaus. The various activities of the higher learning are conducted not only in universities but in a variety of research institutes as well; the universities themselves are much more complicated than in the past. Administrative and promotional activities are multiplying. Who shall do them, and what shall be their places in the system? Already, a separate profession of hospital administrators has arisen; it is not yet true that the administrator of a hospital is the person of greatest prestige, power and income in it. The practice of medicine offers greater rewards. Yet I think it would be found that the physicians and surgeons who become famous and powerful do, in fact, devote a good deal of time to organizational matters. Similar developments may be observed in the law and the academic world, with corresponding elaboration of the complex of activities other than the core one and with a great increase in the number of possible career-lines. These developments make the original choice of occupation but one of a series of choices which continues through most or all of the career; choices of allocation of present and future time among the various activities of the work system, choice of goals to be worked toward, choice of reference group—that is, of the categories of people in the system whose special good will and respect one will cultivate. As one proceeds in his line of work, his previous decisions tend to limit the choices open to him, although in times of rapid change new and unexpected possibilities (and temptations) turn up.

Part of the study of careers is directed toward the great variety of changes in one's distribution of time and effort among the variety of activities in any work system; changes some of which are a function of the physiology of age, others a function of social age as defined in the particular system.

I have thus led to a third dimension of careers: that of moving through a social system of some kind. That point has already been sufficiently illustrated. The social matrix, or system, in which work is done itself changes. Ours is a time of great change in the social organization of perhaps most kinds of work; technological development, the change of scale on which many lines of work are carried out, and social movements, all contribute to change of these systems. I think it has until recently been assumed by those who studied careers, and the choice of careers, that kinds of work outlasted individuals. That assumption certainly no longer holds of many lines of work. People outlive kinds of work; perhaps not some of the older professions and trades, but even in them the social system may change so drastically that a person may, several times in his work life, have a shift from one position in the system to another and to learn new things in order to make the shift.

The study of careers requires that we put these dimensions together in a search for the sequences which turn up in the work-lives of people, and for what determines these sequences. It is evident, and should be taken into account, that it is the fate of a person not merely to be endowed with certain qualities of skill, mind and personality which may be developed in a variety of ways, but also to be born at a given moment in history. He runs his life course through a social maze that is in itself at a certain point in its own career. It is a big order to put all of these things together. If we try to do it all at once, without any division of labor among ourselves, we will certainly fail. If we do develop a proper division of labor, but see to it that all the aspects of the problems are studied and the studies properly integrated, we can make progress.

## NOTES

Reprinted from Everett C. Hughes, *Qualitative Sociology* 20, no. 3 (1997): 389–97. Courtesy of Kluwer Academic/Plenum Publishers.
*Editors' Note:* "Careers" was taught by E. C. Hughes at Brandeis University and Boston College. I have decided to publish it in the original English text unedited. "Careers" appeared in French in E. C. Hughes: *Le Regard Sociologique, Essais choisis, textes rassemblès et presentés par Jean-Michel Chapoulie*, Paris, Éditions de l'EHESS, 1996, under the title "Carrières," pp. 175–185. This French version is translated from the English text. The French version was translated by Jacques Mailhos and revised by Jean-Michel Chapoulie and Cecile Desmazieres.

1. *Shorter Oxford English Dictionary*, Second Edition; and *Nouveau* Petit La-

rousse, *A Dictionary of Americanisms*. The word has an almost identical history in both English and French. The special American addition is the use of the word to distinguish "career" diplomats from those appointed occasionally.

2. Mannheim, Karl. "Über das Wesen and die Bedeutung des wirtschaftlichen Erfolgsstrebens," *Archiv für Sozialwissenschaft und Sozialpolitik*. Vol. 63 (June, 1930), pp. 449–512.

3. Many of you know of the pioneering work of Professor Anne Roe, and of the richly informative and suggestive book on *The Psychology of Careers* by Donald Super. Many of the matters I will touch upon have been treated by them. Given my task of introducing the subject of careers in a rather general way, I shall not go into details concerning their work, and the business of calibrating their terminology and mine. It would not be difficult to do, since neither of them goes in for difficult terminology. W. Lloyd Warner and his associate have studied and are studying the careers of large samples of business teachers and of higher civil servants. A number of my students have studied the careers of school teachers, commercial air pilots, lawyers, and even of plumbers. There is a rich literature on particular occupations, both humble and proud, in which the course of life of people is described although not always systematically. One of the most recent is Tunstall's *The Fishermen*, which tells in detail of the life and work of the fishermen who sail out of Hull to distant waters on strenuous and dangerous voyages. As I present some of the dimensions of careers, such work is in the back of my mind.

4. *Saturday Evening Post*, March 16, 1863.

# 8

# Career Concerns and Mobility Motivations of Orchestra Musicians

*Robert R. Faulkner*

Careers occupy a central position in the life and consciousness of urban man. The meaning of career experiences is derived from the relation between objective and subjective features of work in modern organizations, between the structure of positions ranked in terms of power, prestige, and income, and the socially constructed worlds of actors as they make their way through this hierarchy (Hall, 1948; Goffman, 1961; Hughes, 1958; Glaser, 1968; Stebbins, 1970). The concept of a career is of major theoretical importance because it promises to join structural and organizational considerations to phenomenology. On the one hand, careers are made up of systems of positions, their relation to one another, and typical sequences of movement within and through them. On the other hand, members acquire ways of thinking, feeling, and believing about these arrangements; they orient themselves, positively and negatively, emotionally and intellectually, toward the roles they are paid to perform and the routes they are constrained to pursue. One perspective on careers therefore focuses on these institutionalized routes and positions; another on the occupant's distinctive outlooks towards where they are now, have been in the past, and probably will be in the future. The study of changes in position and role, and the contingencies upon which these depend, is a frame of reference for studying the outlooks, involvements, and identities of actors (Becker and Strauss, 1956; Strauss, 1959; Becker, 1964, 1970).

This paper is about symphony musicians, their personal feelings and ideas about mobility in the orchestra world. The effort will be directed not to a comprehensive description of their organizational career lines but to a detailed consideration of the shared concerns and subjective experiences they generate. By career concerns I mean those experiential turning points, stretches of uncertainty, periods of personal crisis, and occasions for fateful decisions which, from the viewpoint of the musician, impart a characteristic stance and feeling toward where one is situated in an organizational career. These concerns are influenced by the imputed place and meaning of present position in a career line, for a player's current location in the symphony world constitutes a point of reference from which his career progress can be evaluated and future plans assessed. Thus career concerns are social outlooks which have considerable bearing on the mobility motivations of people. They supply a perspective from which decisions are made about remaining in or moving from an organization and about the probable chances for advancement in a career line (Wager, 1959; Glaser, 1964; Goldner, 1965).

Career concerns, so conceived, bear considerable resemblance to a common-sense point of view; in respecting members' own definitions of the career situation, I shall write mainly from their vantage point: the reality of those undergoing these experiences. Three concerns constitute the reality of orchestral performers' careers: (1) advancement and mobility, or a concern with improving one's position; (2) and related, the extent to which circumstance rule out advancement and rule in the occupancy of undesirable positions, a concern with "entrapment"; and (3) the consolidation and strengthening of current organizational involvements, a concern with "making commitments."

The materials on which I base my discussion are drawn from interviews with fifty musicians in a major orchestra in the eastern part of the country.[1] The documentation bearing on the subjective experience of careers has been drawn from those sections of the interviews which dealt with the circumstances of success and failure in the occupation, decisions to stay or move to other orchestras, and organizational involvement in the orchestra. The cited excerpts are verbatim transcriptions from taped interviews lasting from one to four hours; tabulations are based on content analysis of several structured questions asked of these respondents.

## ORGANIZATIONAL SET AND THE SYMPHONY WORLD

Some preliminary words are in order concerning the characteristic features of the occupation and its members. The careers of these musicians, not unlike those of other professionals in urban society, develop within a network of organizations characterized by specialization, mobility, and hierarchy based on technical competence. The institutionalization of these patterns has created a small group of distinguished organizations at the top, a group of second-rank but solidly established competitors, and a large group of third-rank symphonies of poorer quality. As Caplow has suggested, the orchestra world can be viewed as an organizational set (Caplow, 1964: 201–216): a stratification system of two or more organizations where the higher a given organization's prestige, the more influence it has upon the standards of achievement in the set as a whole, and the more eminence enjoyed by those in the upper ranks of the set. Work settings so arranged provide training and testing grounds for each other's talent: career flow, not surprisingly, is in the direction of rewards. The higher a given organization's prestige, the more influence it has and the greater its ability to draw recruits away from the lower and middle ranks toward the top. Organizational stratification systems vary considerably in terms of the number of elite units and other units, as well as in the status differentiation within any one particular and other units, as well as in the status differentiation within any one particular unit. It may be that selection for a position in a leading unit is contingent upon occupancy of a prestigious role in a unit just a few notches below in the set. Moreover, a second-rank competitor can offer distinguished positions to some of the middle ranking members of elite units, thereby drawing away their talent. Thus the hierarchy of organizations, the positions within them, and the chains of recruitment and replacement created by vacancies contribute to our understanding of the generation of ambition and structure of mobility.

The symphony orchestra world is one of the most complex, competitive, and stratified organizational sets in existence. Today there are more orchestras, and distinguished ones, in this country than there are in any other; among the top or first-class units can be found in what is known as the "Big Five." In musical excellence, caliber of musicianship, total contract weeks, weekly basic wages, recording guarantees, and paid vacations, the leading orchestras in this country are the Boston Symphony Orchestra, the Chicago Symphony, The Cleveland Orchestra, the New York Philharmonic, and the Philadelphia Orchestra. Below the big league there are twenty-four established orchestras of varying quality, length of season, and income.[2] The orchestra studied in this paper is located near the top of this minor league set; reasonably prestigious, but no more exemplary than its second-rate competitors.

Musicians in any orchestra differ widely in their career outlooks, motivations, and horizons as well as their paths into the present organization. Some are just starting while others are near the end of their careers. Some have moved into their present position by working up the ranks, taking the difficult route from marginal symphonies to the top of the minor leagues. They may be playing next to a colleague who started his career as a section player in one of the big five, and who then came to this orchestra in order to occupy the more prestigious position as leader of, for example, the violin, cello, trumpet, or percussion instrumental section. Some have grown accustomed to the easy comforts and securities of the setting while others are thoroughly disenchanted and desire to move into the upper ranks of the orchestra world. Not all are equally ambitious or motivated, nor are they on the same level musically, technically, or emotionally. They may despise and envy one another, disagree about music and the merits of conductors, and even be in open competition with their colleagues for prestigious or better positions within their respective orchestral sections. Precisely because the orchestra contains a balance between the mobile and immobile, the restless and the loyal, the study of the meaning of these careers should provide important additions to a current sociological interest in the subjective features of status passage (Glaser and Strauss, 1971).

In setting out to describe this diversity within a minor league setting as well as the subjective experiences of its typical occupants, I do not wish to imply that the concerns of advancement, entrapment, and commitment are found everywhere in the orchestra world—from top to bottom—in like fashion. Much more comparative research within and between orchestras is needed before we can fully understand the outlooks and career problems of those situated in them. What I do wish to suggest is that the shared interests and concerns described here are held by symphony players in greater or lesser degree (compare with Westby, 1960: 227–229). Such concerns are also generalizable to other segments of this organizational set from which our respondents came and to which some of them are going. While the distribution and intensity of concerns may vary, the differences are of degree rather than kind, and they impart a characteristic quality to the professional socialization of orchestral performers.

## CAREER FOOTHOLDS, TIME, AND "MAKING IT"

Most organizational members like to think their careers are moving in a more or less orderly and progressive fashion. One feature of the orchestra world is its well-defined statuses, for positions within an ensemble are ranked into principal, assistant principal, and section desks. All of the 100 musicians have a very good idea about where they are vis-à-vis both their colleagues and players in other orchestras. In making sense out of and assessing whether they are getting ahead or, colloquially put, "making it," players can look at *where* they are located, *how long* it took them to make each upward move, and what the next move might be. Among the ambitious and mobile players there was a persistent, albeit muted, concern with quickly improving their position. In telling about this they described their career paths in the present, the orchestra they left, some of the bridges they burned behind them, and their own timetables for success. For a principal player, his move out of one of the country's most distinguished orchestras was a major turning point.

> Sure, it was a better orchestra, it was larger, the strings were great, the season was longer, and with recording there was more money involved—and I do think I could earn more money there than I am here. But the chance to play principal, with its experience and exposure, is something I thought valuable enough to leave all that I had there. If I ever hope to be the principal of a larger orchestra, the normal move is to go to a smaller orchestra and then to step up into that position. Very seldom does a top orchestra take a principal who hasn't *been* a principal player. I think most musicians when they take a job like this in this caliber orchestra are thinking of it as a stepping stone.

A focal concern of those musicians who moved from a distinguished orchestra dealt with the opportunities for principal, gaining wider personal recognition, and rapidly developing as a musician. They enter a minor league setting, reasonably enough, with some feeling of sacrifice, but with a sense of achievement and mobility. The move down the organizational ladder but up positionally was remembered in the following way by a talented principal player:

> I left A. (a major orchestra) three years ago, I still think it was a good decision. Although this orchestra is not one of the top five, the principal chair is more important to me. It was a really difficult decision because it was a great orchestra with a very fine conductor. But I had to think about what was happening in front of me in the section. My stand partner was an older man, he would retire in another few years and the first-stand people were excellent, and the conductor liked them. The opportunity came up here, and these things don't come along all the time, if I didn't take it, who knows when I might get the next chance, in 10 or 15 or 20 years? Maybe by that time you're too old, you know top orchestras are hesitant about hiring someone over 36, somewhere around in there. You should make your move before you're that age anyway and this was a chance to grow, because you do grow artistically, more than by remaining in the section.

As has been pointed out in a variety of connections (Martin and Strauss, 1956; Wesby, 1960; Roth, 1963) organizational members develop, among other outlooks, an age-consciousness and concern with the temporal aspect of their mobility. Norms and benchmarks develop concerning how old candidates for a given position should be. And performers judge their colleague-competitors' rates of advancement and progress against these expectations. These demands lead performers to subjectively experience their career fate in the problematic terms they do. As table 8.1, section A, indicates, most are

**Table 8.1.  Musician's Views of Their Careers and Work**

| | |
|---|---|
| A.  "Do you have to be at a certain place by a certain time in this type of career?" | |
| Yes, cites age (between 35 and 40) | 66%[a] |
| Yes, cites hiring policies | 42% |
| Yes, cites problem with getting buried in the minor league orchestras | 18% |
| No, mentioned that it all depends on the individual | 10% |
| | |
| B.  Likelihood of remaining in this orchestra | |
| Very likely | 18 |
| Somewhat likely | 13 |
| Somewhat unlikely | 9 |
| Very unlikely | 10 |
| Total | 50 |
| | |
| C.  "If you had the chance of bettering your position in another orchestra would you move?" | |
| Yes, would definitely take the job | 12 |
| Probably, would have to think about it | 9 |
| Probably not, have to give up too much | 14 |
| No, would not move | 15 |
| Total | 50 |
| | |
| D.  Negative consequence of section playing | |
| Skills can deteriorate | 24% |
| You become subservient | 16% |
| Little room to grow as a player | 16% |
| | |
| E.  "For you personally, what are the best features about being here in this orchestra?" | |
| My position (status, musical advantages) | 32%[a] |
| Work itself (performance demands, experiences on the job) | 34% |
| Private sphere (family, house, schools, leisure) | 56% |
| Colleagues (co-workers in section, atmosphere of friendliness) | 30% |
| Students (clientele) | 20% |
| Money, pension plan, retirement benefits | 18% |

*Source:* Robert R. Faulkner
[a] Total percentages greater than 100 because respondents could mention several alternatives.

fully aware of the consequences of staying in a top orchestra but buried in a section of it. Looking ahead to prospective advancement, a shared concern was with time. Throughout the orchestra world there is a feeling that if one does not move from a certain location by a given age, the occupancy of that job will, in effect, rule out and irrevocably condition chances for further mobility.

If some musicians are drawn from major symphonies to the present orchestra by the chance of improving one's position and one's life chances, others come up through the ranks from the minor leagues. Working conditions, pay, the opportunity to improve as a player, and the chance to get a secure foothold on a higher rung account for these mobility motivations.

> Every time I left an orchestra I went to a job which had more musical responsibility, more room to grow as well as financial reward. When I started out I wanted to get as much experience and knowledge as I could and one of the turning points for me was after a few years there (in a minor league organization) I realized that I needed a larger situation to grow in. You see, it was a small orchestra and I knew after the second year I wouldn't make my career there, I felt I had to move.

For this player and his colleagues, advancement is viewed in terms of increasing by favorable working conditions and opportunities for being and becoming a virtuoso orchestral player. Each organization in this set, and each position in an orchestra, is linked with a different arrangement of work contingencies, that is, factors upon which work satisfaction, colleague prestige, and performance excellence depend. One musician nicely summed up his and others' sense of career progress and the related concern with making his mark by a certain age by saying:

> I felt I was going nowhere in that orchestra. Who wants to spend their life in the minor leagues? Who wants to get stuck at 35 in a situation you can't stand? The orchestra was going down and the conductor was stifling the better players, so this was a first-class job, better pay, better orchestra, more professional colleagues. You have to be mobile if you want to advance your career. Anyone would have made the same decision, it was an obvious move up.

As they acquire more experience, confidence, and professional polish they come to feel uneasy and maybe even bored with a particular job. Those who occupied principal positions in less prestigious orchestras felt, in several instances, that their careers and talents were languishing in the lesser or mediocre orchestras in this organizational set. The chance to play within a better ensemble and under skillful conductors, and the incentive that comes from colleague competition, appear to have motivated their departure from these settings. Asked if his move to this orchestra was an advance in his career, a brass player replied it was, but he appeared ambivalent about having given up his principal chair to do so.

> It was really a hard decision to make but I was unhappy about the money there. I didn't get the raise I asked for and I disagreed with the guys in the section stylistically. I decided to take the section job here but I had to make a choice, either to stay there and play first in an area that was more obscure, or come here and play second in a location I thought more ideal.

The place and meaning of a position in a career line is a matter of perspective (Becker and Strauss, 1956; Glaser, 1964). More than 35 percent of the respondents view their present role as a stepping stone toward the top; it is a stop of some consequence, but merely a place for consolidation before moving onward and upward (table 8.1, section B). The likelihood of their staying is perceived as low. For the majority of musicians, however, their mobility aspirations had been realized by succeeding in moving this far up the orchestral career ladder, or they had settled for less and became committed to their present job.[3] Still others came to this orchestra with the idea of staying but then decided after two or three years to leave for greener pastures. This change in perspective was nicely illustrated by a young reed instrumentalist who had just accepted an offer from a top minor league organization. His career climb had been swift, this was his third orchestra in six years, and like his mobile colleagues, each move up was considered an improvement. Career concerns changed as his future location and reference group shifted upward.

> Before I got into this orchestra, I didn't have a realistic appraisal of myself and how far I would go, I was just looking for a job and like everyone else I had the dream of having a first chair in one of the big orchestras but I didn't think that it could ever be a reality. The concern was with getting started and the position here was the next big step for me. It's not a major symphony but it made me think that if I came this far . . . maybe someday I might have a chance at one of those chairs. So I auditioned for two orchestras and didn't make it. I sort of felt that maybe I'm just permanently in a lower class of players, that I'd never be considered for a better job in a better place. But I played another audition and got the job, it's a chance to do a lot more, a better place for me.

These various sentiments and outlooks are representative of the moving perspective in which these men and women interpret career progress. Like other occupational members, this performer can feel relatively successful or a relative failure depending upon his looking down to where he came from or up to where he wants to go in the orchestra world. Making successful moves are contingent on several factors. First, the person has to acquire knowledge about which orchestras and positions are desirable and which are not. As suggested earlier, the organizational set and status hierarchy within any one orchestra embodies this consensus. Second, a performer develops a working understanding of his actual and potential mobility. The development of personal timetables for vertical mobility into a "better" orchestra and a concern with improving one's situation reflect this perspective. Third, one must not have a reputation which will cause a conductor or audition committee to reject one's candidacy for top-level positions. To the extent that invidious comparisons are made around time and location in an occupation, age-grading can rule out occupancy of desired places for certain members (Roth, 1963). This means being situated at or near the top of the occupational esteem system early in a career; for many it meant occupying a principal job in order to be ready to move into a comparable opening in one of the major orchestras. Finally, one has to be patient enough to wait for these openings and endure the uncertainty of playing the audition and putting one's self on the line. These performance demands require that a musician keep on the move to "better his position" and be prepared to seize those opportunities that may come only a few times in a career.[4] For the mobile players there is pressure not to succumb to the easy temptations of settling down in a less desirable but more accessible orchestra. Thus, positions in this stratum of the organizational set contain musicians who have moved to it in order to better their career position. It also contains those who are likely to move out of it, and are on their way up, and for whom a long stay would present a major setback, if not failure.

In characterizing these mobile performers' outlooks, the elements discussed below are or have been present in most respondents. Of course, the relative prominence of each element tends to vary. The meaning of career concerns centers around access to those situations which afford the most desirable setting for coming to grips with these occupational problems.

First, there is general agreement that this occupational world is a competitive one. Stratification within organizations enhances the importance of invidious comparisons among members. To the extent this stance is shared, one's position in the set stands for where one is situated socially and musically. One is occupationally constrained to do something on his own to improve one's position. The frequent expressions of frustration and annoyance over blocked mobility and the concern about getting onto the right organizational terrain and into the right position all point to the subjective effects of this hierarchical system. Positions are assessed in terms of the degree to which they facilitate mobility upward, the extent to which they establish footholds or stepping stones toward the summit.

Second, and closely related, there are frequent expressions of concern with whether mobility to a particular stratum enlarges a player's share of responsibility, control over career contingencies, and allotment of concrete rewards such as money, pension returns, and contract weeks. Advancement thus often means better working conditions, more professional colleagues, and a more rewarding place to be.

Third, there is a common sentiment that one must grow professionally, that one must move towards increasing expertise, not against or away from it. A concern centers around whether career movement conditions the chances for personal development in a given direction, for experienced selves, or for being and becoming more skilled as a player. This comes with persistent and dedicated work in one's calling.

Finally, a concern with advancement is sometimes conceptualized as merely avoiding some of the negative and degrading consequences of organizational involvement. Some found themselves moving and being moved off the main lines of career ascent, they were "getting buried in the minor leagues." This had serious disadvantages, given the pressure of age and mobility expectations. Their move into this setting was interpreted as an advancement as well as a solution to this pressing career concern. They moved because it meant escaping from an undesirable place or situation. As some put it, they started to feel trapped. It is this sense of prospective failure, of finding themselves stranded in a dead-end job that lends a particular tone and temperament to their career accounts.


## ENTRAPMENT


To the mobile player many positions in the orchestral world rule out courses of action which will lead somewhere; being on a certain organizational level limits career options and even maneuverability. This often becomes a clearly understood and deeply felt constraint when attempts are made to leave a position for something better.

A performer can come to find himself engaged in lines of action requiring the adopting of skills and attitudes that constitute a liability for improving his position. It is well known that in work organizations the occupancy of some jobs, usually at the lower levels, results in overspecialization or the acquisition of skills which do not facilitate performance of higher work demands. Players concede that, in some measure, this is unavoidable in a hierarchically ordered orchestra. Without someone playing second section fiddle to the concertmaster's first there would be no orchestra. But they also realize that playing in a section or even second chair to the principal can narrow one's musical development and career chances (table 8.1, section D). Ultimately the trap of section playing can be a state of mind, a job with mild advantages but more serious disadvantages. The outlook can best be introduced by citing a principal musician who avoided being anything but this.

> PM: I think everybody decided that if he is going to be a reed player that he is going to be the first in a major orchestra; I did. My first job offer was second chair in P (top minor league setting) but I didn't take it. After that I got the job in Q as principal.
> Q: Playing first was very important to you, why?
> PM: It's kind of hard to explain but something kind of happens to you if you play in a second position for very long. You must be ready to do whatever the first player does, as far as intonation goes, this playing together, you're subservient in a way. I think after a period of very many years you get in a box of just playing second. People have tried it, have tried to play first after

this but have been very unsuccessful. I think if you want to be a first player, start as a first player, even though it's a lesser orchestra.

It could be said that the phrase "box of playing second," as applied to the experiential outcomes of section work, contains a double viewpoint. Not only are talents circumscribed and restricted—which is the intended observation—but they do not develop beyond a certain point. The second desk in an orchestra is particularly exemplary in this regard. The player is more than an instrumentalist in the ensemble, but in the process of conforming the performance demands in this position, he unfits himself for first-desk positions. A concern with mobility and professional growth along these lines was dramatically put forth by a second desk player in one of the brass sections. His prior job was second principal, he moved to avoid being stranded in a lower orchestra, and some of the consequences of these moves were expressed in the following way:

> I had to get out and move to a better orchestra, now I'm thinking a lot about auditions. I can't stay here. I auditioned for two places this year, I would take any of those jobs as first, they are better jobs, and if you really look at this job here, it's kind of dead-end. I know now I've got to find something else because you look around and see the guys who have been in this place on a job similar to mine for 30 years and I see they're frustrated people. If you play second you lose some of the shine in your playing. I know some guys who have played second and the job for principal opened, their playing had deteriorated. I'm afraid this would happen to me. I can't spend the rest of my life here. You can get pegged as a second, conductors kind of stereotype you if you stay too long playing in the section, I think they might even have reservations about listening to you.

Important and consequential decisions result from both age and occupancy of a position. Occupational expectations provide penalties for those who stay too long either buried in a section or playing second chair. To acquire a reputation of this sort is to predetermine the other possible locations and even musical experiences. Deterioration of skill is one concrete problem for the above player. Another concern is with downward mobility as a musician must in some cases continually compete for his position with those below him. Thus a major turning point can be the experience of getting trapped in a situation where the chances of mobility slowly diminish because of age (Faulkner, 1971: 61–78) and where the possibility of demotion increases with intense competition among the members of the organization.

That these career concerns about mobility are shot through with querulous asides about some colleagues who are living proof of entrapment and its consequences is no surprise. Plagued by self-judgments of professional inadequacy, some saw the slow workings of career fate on others and were making attempts to avoid a similar course. In learning the occupational culture, a player acquires knowledge of problematic locations and their typical occupants. He sees that some are hopelessly stranded. This only reaffirms his concern with extricating himself from the orchestra, with getting a few steps on colleague competitors, and with avoiding a dependency on the conveniences certain work routines can provide. A younger string player expressed it like this:

> The thing that you really have to be careful of is that you don't get into a situation where, if it's less than what you want it to be, that you don't stagnate there. It is very easy, and each one of us has to make his own decision. I don't want this to happen to me, right now I'm looking for a musically better orchestra. If I'm going to move I'd better do it pretty soon.

Those who share this outlook are typically under forty, less committed to this orchestra than their colleagues, see themselves as advancing their careers in a few years, and, not surprisingly, are concerned about the consequences of staying where they are for the rest of their careers (table 8.1, sections B and C).

## "LOSING TOO MUCH": ADJUSTMENT
## AND MAKING COMMITMENTS

The majority of musicians interviewed, however, had career concerns and mobility motivations of a different bent. They would not move if given the opportunity, and around 60 percent are likely or somewhat likely to remain in this setting until retirement (table 8.1, sections B and C). At an earlier stage they feared entrapment. Like their colleagues, they desired advancement. But some of their concerns with advancement and upward mobility had faded. Not infrequently as they remain in this orchestra, changes begin to take place in the musician as well as in the objective chances of moving any further up the orchestra ladder.

For the reasons enumerated previously, a musician comes to find himself being eliminated from top-level positions in other organizations by the operation of occupational expectations concerning age and promotion. One has to move fast to realize a career anchored at the peak of this organizational set. But many of these performers come to feel they have progressed upward to a place which is as high or higher than they had originally anticipated. As they compare themselves with former colleagues still in the bottom ranks, their self-image is one of relative success. For the section principals there is no other position equal in status and desirability; to return to a section would be a demotion. It would be an unwanted return to a sort of dirty work, little autonomy and few responsibilities. They wait or are waiting for that one opportunity, that one shot at the major leagues, but room at the top is scarce. Some are passively on the market; others have removed themselves from the audition scene. Here is a principal who appears to be ambivalent about his continuing stay in the orchestra: he was beginning to redirect his career sights away from his original dream and towards his current work reality:

> My aiming for that big chance, my aspiration isn't quite as great as it was when I took the job here, I wouldn't turn down something like I had in mind when I took the job, my aspiration is towards a bigger orchestra, one of the big ones. . . . But my hope isn't quite as great as it was, I mean my hope isn't any less, it is just that my goals are slightly different than they were then. In the four years I've been here I think now music isn't as much or at least this ultimate desire of mine, this stepping stone thing I was talking about. This isn't as important to me now. I might move to one of the top orchestras but we are settled here now and you have to think about that.

Further, in adjusting his outlook to the particular work culture, a player can eliminate himself from further advancement. Learning the ropes and making music with certain conductors, and growing accustomed to playing in an ensemble with certain colleagues appears to strengthen involvement in the minor league setting. It is the ease of everyday routines and the atmosphere of friendship that some respondents spontaneously mention (see table 8.1, section E). Moreover, the position occupied is interpreted as especially fit to his or her private standards, musical capacities, temperament, and personal style. If the work and career path become a lot less exciting, the current routine and customs make them predictable and controllable. As they stay, they cannot face the prospect of starting again in an unfamiliar organization with unfamiliar performance demands.

> It's comfortable here, it's like being in the womb (laughs). I'm set in my job, my career. If I were to go to another place, I'd have to start all over again establishing the reputation I've built here.

Performers develop a local reputation and derive satisfaction from acquiring it. Moreover, they become accustomed to the perquisites and privileges of the job. A focal concern then centers around losing these rewards.

> I would imagine there's a certain amount of fear as to not wanting to give this up and this is what a move would mean, a move somewhere else. I'd be dishonest if I said there wasn't this fear, I think I'd have to prove myself all over again. I feel perhaps I could, but still it's tough. I'd be faced with being thrown into a major orchestra, a whole new situation, and you have to produce, you have to play.

The tension is there. I could probably make twice as much money, but the pressure isn't worth it. There's not that much pressure here. There was an opening last year and I must say I thought about it at the time; it would have been nice to be there (in a top five orchestra) with more prestige, better pay, a beautiful string section . . . but I thought about the pressure, the schedule, it would be a lot of work.

For this musician, these benefits and opportunities might be lost by moving to a top orchestra. In calculating its advantages and disadvantages, he decided that the cost of taking the audition and possibly the job—in having to learn a new set of ropes, pressure, and so on—was too much. The advantages of successful integration into his present position outweighed the otherwise attractive, and more musically rewarding, possibilities of working in a prestigious orchestra. This respondent is in his mid-thirties, which suggests that such rewards can pile up relatively fast in this occupation. Following Becker (1952, 1960) and Geer (1966), a player becomes committed whenever he realizes that it will cost him more to change his organizational position than it will to remain where he is. Table 8.1, section E, suggests some of the things that have value for these musicians. They constitute some of the valuables by which performers become committed more to making do in the minor leagues than to making it in the majors: perquisites of the job, contribution to pension plan, adjustment to one's way of doing things, rewarding friendships with colleagues, a clientele of music students, and a measure of local eminence. Their accumulation restrains career mobility and increases the likelihood of staying at this orchestral level.

In purposefully carving out a niche for himself in the orchestral work world, a musician often finds that involvements are being deepened for him in other areas as well. He may find himself in the unenviable position of eliminating himself, as well as being eliminated, from further advancement. The process of acquiring these involvements are partially unwitting and unintended, they involve several aspects of mundane existence, and they typically develop as unanticipated offshoots of his job. Taken separately or together it is the family, household, and schools, in short, the features of community localization (see Friedman, 1967) which constitute sufficient value for their loss to be a constraint on the performer. For a majority of those interviewed, the incidental "side-benefits" realized in the *private sphere* (Berger and Kellner, 1964) had a profound effect on dampening motivations to move onward and upward.

The recognition of the persuasive role of sinking "roots" and gradually deepened commitments also forces the realization that their effects are not easily turned aside or undone.

I'm very happy here; I would like to see the orchestra grow and maybe a better conductor and maybe more lucrative for the players, but I'm willing to stay here. I have roots here now. I like the people I work with and also my family enjoys it here, we have a house now, the kids are looking forward to school, I don't think that I would consider an offer from another orchestra, the situation here is a lot.

The "situation" to which he refers is not definable solely in terms of those forms of work satisfaction and dissatisfaction typically of interest to the occupational sociologist. Instead, a persistent theme throughout the interviews (see table 8.1, section E) deals with the overlap of work and non-work domains. Commitment always encompasses a range of interlocking relations between work and other areas of life in which investments are located and from which they cannot be extricated.

As far as trying to maintain a family life, here I go to work and I come home. In a top orchestra you go to work and you may not go home, for three or four days. So that's one positive thing about here, but I guess there are other things that go along with being in a major orchestra, it's an honor, no question. Maybe I should have done it (taken the audition), but there are other things I consider other than the prestige and the money. I can't duplicate what I do here anywhere else.

For several players the combination of individual adjustment to work and relatively large amounts of leisure result in constraining forces for the family: to give them up would be a loss in the private sphere. The interaction between private and work spheres intensifies commitment.

If I were to take that job with a major symphony . . . like the audition three years ago, and my wife and I have had discussions about this, you just have to spend a great deal of time at the job, whereas you don't have a weekend free where you can go skiing or recreation of some kind. It makes it difficult for the family, for the kids. I realize this.

The minor league situation is thus, if not ideal, at least a place in which a lifestyle can be fashioned and considerable predictability achieved. And it is more than a place for making do in a situation of limited and limiting choice. Here is a principal player who turned down a job with a major orchestra

because I wasn't interested, I'd be limited in the other part of my life. When it gets right down to the point of how seriously I would consider leaving here—wild dreams, you think, gee, that could be great—but then if I had a decision to make, it might not look so great. I'm sure there's a very strong feeling of security here, and this would be hard to pull yourself away from.

In redirecting their concerns away from the place of work toward other scenes in their social life, these musicians turn toward those experiences that they can actively shape for themselves, toward those places where they can be somebody special, and where they can retreat from the occupational career struggle as well as some of the duller and even degrading moments of music making in the symphony (Faulkner, 1973). In scaling their aspirations down and in cooling themselves out (Goffman, 1952), these musicians come to defend their present occupational role as well as justify how they managed to end up where they did. More importantly, for our purposes here, in the private domain these players recognize an opportunity and place to produce for themselves and their family a world in which they can feel secure. It is a situated location where they can be at home. Even more, a person belongs where his home is; if a player is, as several put it "in a rut," it is a benign one indeed. "I didn't want to stay permanently," said a middle-aged musician, "but what I've got here is really great, because I have roots here, to move now would be losing too much."

The benefits from this line of adaptation can now be enumerated. First, insofar as he receives support from significant others, the performer is freed from many of the career pressures and risks that accompany upward mobility in this occupation. If the person is unwilling or unable to meet high-level achievement demands, he will find a sympathetic audience of like-situated colleagues who will spare him the negative consequences of censure for not making it any higher up the career rungs. Second, an acknowledged commitment to the conveniences and work ways of the local setting strengthens the world these immobile colleagues have fashioned for themselves. It confirms the shared views, of those who preceded the musicians, about the hazards, difficulties, and even politics of going higher in the ranks. Third, and related to the above, the lowering of career sights often facilitates a shift of interest to the private sphere. This fact has important consequences for the shaping of identity that cannot be pursued here. All that ought to be clear is that the majority of musicians making this turning point confessed relief that their major career decisions, fears, and speculations were behind them. Confronted with the opportunity to move, decisions in both the work and private domains inhibited their departure from their present course of action. Other relationships are made conditional on such resolutions to stay. Family, colleagues, and friends develop expectations which support and amplify what a musician can do and be. In sum, these acquired commitments and perspectives on them enhance organizational involvement while creating a defense against the reawakening of attachment to formerly held mobility motivations.

## CONCLUSIONS

In the description and analysis of career lines we must ask how mobility is objectively structured and distributed in organizations, as well as how it is subjectively perceived and experienced. This study of orchestra musicians has been concerned with mobility motivations and organizational commitment as individual processes, and only marginally with the occupational structures which facilitate them. In so doing, I focused on career concerns as they are subjectively apprehended, the individual adjustments made by the player, the impact of occupational expectations on his career, and some of the unanticipated side benefits which arise as offshoots of his organizational involvement. The expressed career concerns can be regarded as different phases in the life of the minor league symphony player, but the examination of other work cultures may inform the study of careers generally. For example, the chronology of high aspirations, entrapment, and finally scaling down of ambition bears considerable similarity to Chinoy's classic study of auto workers (Chinoy, 1955) while the personal adaptations to blocked mobility resemble Goldner's discussion of making do in managerial circles (Goldner, 1965). Both the humble and the proud need to be studied in the light of career concerns for they may provide insight into the meaning of status passage and a new comparative basis for analysis of occupations themselves.

The study of careers as subjective experience at this level of the orchestra world seems especially called for—given that many of the important realities of the American experience lie not in the major but in the minor organizational leagues. Whether it be in the performing arts, academia, publishing, professional sports, or television broadcasting, we need more studies of the middle ranks of these stratified and highly competitive work settings. It is at this level, moreover, that our opportunity structure is supposed to flourish, and it is here that people come to grips with the disjunction that often exists between personal aspirations for success and the avenues available for their concrete realization. The perspective developed here suggests that in thinking about mobility in work organizations, we might profitably study what the occupational members are thinking, their expressed concerns, what appears possible, which is thought desirable, and the shared ways in which they define a place for themselves in society.

## NOTES

Reprinted by permission from *The Sociological Quarterly* 14 (spring 1973): 334–49.

Reprints of this article may be obtained by writing to: Robert R. Faulkner, Department of Sociology, University of Massachusetts, Amherst, MA 01003.

1. The majority of musicians in the brass, woodwind, and percussion sections were interviewed, and performers in the violin, cello, and bass sections were sampled in equal proportions. In seeking to describe this occupational culture using the information and knowledge that players use in observing, interpreting, and describing their experiences, four musicians were kind enough to serve as informants during the research. Their patience in teaching me what to look for and how musicians classify their career concerns is gratefully acknowledged.

2. The minor leagues in the orchestra world are further stratified by the same criteria resulting in a sort of orchestral counterpart to Double A and Triple A baseball. But unlike the sports scene, I could find little systematic sorting or ranking of the minor leagues beyond an agreement that there were two or three top organizations and five or six lesser or mediocre orchestras in the lower strata. At the risk of imposing more order of their interpretation and definitions of where these orchestras stand in this honor market, I shall forego such invidious comparisons. The organizational stratum is composed of organizations in these cities: Atlanta, Baltimore, Buffalo, Cincinnati, Dallas, Denver, Detroit, Houston, Indianapolis, Kansas City, Los Angeles, Milwaukee, Minneapolis, Montreal, New Jersey, New Orleans, Pittsburgh, Rochester, St. Louis, San Antonio, San Francisco, Seattle, Toronto, and the Washington National Symphony. Below these are the bush leagues composed of semi-pro and amateur symphonies (see Caplow, 1964).

3. It would seem that to the extent that the ranking of minor league organizations is loosely defined, the larger the number of musicians with limited aspirations can be satisfied with playing in what they consider to be either a top minor league orchestra or just a notch below the top. The reluctance to fully acknowledge ranking within the minor leagues is, in itself, revealing. It would appear that all organizational sets have cultural forms and cognitive outlooks that serve to dampen or reduce invidious comparisons. Where colleagues in other, and better, orchestras are envied, elaborate steps may be taken to conceal the expression of envious feelings. To ask questions about organizational ranking may raise fears in the respondent that he may be suspected of envy, he then demonstrates that such feelings are groundless by denying the ranking. Or the loosely defined sorting of orchestras I elicited may be the result of players who feared to admit to themselves that they were in fact envious of players in top minor league orchestras. This admission, most likely, would damage their self-image. Thus while most could agree that a musician should avoid getting stranded in a poor or mediocre orchestra "out in the sticks," or on the bottom terrain of the set, it was less clear if one was, or could be, stranded at the level comprising the middle and upper middle ranks. Some musicians have told me in so many words that they felt pretty well off where they were and that if a player fails to make it into the big orchestral leagues he can, nevertheless, come to view himself in business, the professions, and the academic world, the more flexible a ranking of minor league organizations, the more comfortable members can become with a touch of organizational aggrandizement and with an adjustment in their personal ambitions. Finally, to the extent organizational ranking is loosely defined by musicians, the larger the proportion of minor leagues who can (1) successfully cool themselves out, (2) remain preoccupied with chances of moving within the minors rather than into the major leagues, and (3) move to orchestras at the same level and consider the move a step upward.

4. Musicians' perceptions of mobility possibilities do have an impact on their career concerns. Interviews with first and second desk personnel suggested that there was agreement on several related items: (1) that the rate of turnover in the major orchestras, as well as the top minor ones, was variable, depending on the retirement of personnel; (2) that no more than two to five openings appear for any top orchestra during any season; (3) that politics and preferential treatment of some candidates is inevitable and, moreover, has a lot to do with who eventually secures the position;

and (4) that they had been on both the long and short end of these political machinations.

# REFERENCES

Becker, Howard S.
1970 (ed.) "The self and adult socialization," Pp. 289–303 in Sociological Work: Method and Substance. Chicago: Aldine Publishing Co.
1964 "Personal change in adult lie." Sociometry 27 (March):40–53.
1960 "Notes on the concept of commitment." American Journal of Sociology 66 (July):32–40.
1952 "The career of the Chicago public school teacher." American Journal of Sociology 57 (March):470–477.
Becker, H. S. and A. L. Strauss
1956 "Careers, personality, and adult socialization." American Journal of Sociology 62 (November):253–263.
Berger, P. L. and H. Kellner
1964 "Marriage and the construction of reality." Diogenes 4 (Summer):1–24.
Caplow, Theodore
1964 Principles of Organization. New York: Harcourt, Brace and World.
Chinoy, Ely
1955 Automobile Workers and The American Dream. New York: Random House.
Faulkner, Robert R.
1973 "Orchestra interaction: some features of communication and authority in an artistic organization." The Sociological Quarterly 14 (Spring):147–157.
1971 Hollywood Studio Musicians: Their Work and Careers in the Recording Industry. Chicago: Aldine-Atherton, Inc.
Friedman, N. L.
1967 "Career stages and organizational role decisions of teachers in two public junior colleges." Sociology of Education 40 (Summer):231–245.
Geer, B.
1966 "Occupational commitment and the teaching profession." The School Review 74 (Spring):31–47.
Glaser, Barney G.
1968 Organizational Careers. Chicago: Aldine Publishing Company.
1964 Organizational Scientists. Indianapolis, Ind.: Bobbs-Merrill Co.
Glaser, Barney G. and Anselm L. Strauss
1971 Status Passage. Chicago: Aldine-Atherton, Inc.
Goffman, Erving
1961 Asylums: Essays on the Social Situation of Mental Patients and Other Inmates. Garden City, N.Y.: Doubleday and Co., Inc.
1952 "On cooling the mark out: some aspects of adaptation to failure." Psychiatry 15 (November):451–463.

Goldner, F.
  1965  "Demotion in industrial management." American Sociological Review 30
        (October):714–724.
Hall, O.
  1948  "The stages of a medical career." American Journal of Sociology 53
        (March):327–336.
Hughes, Everett C.
  1958  Men and Their Work. New York: The Free Press.
Martin, N. H. and A. L. Strauss
  1956  "Patterns of mobility within industrial organizations." Journal of Business
        29 (April):101–110.
Roth, Julius A.
  1963  Timetables. Indianapolis, Ind.: Bobbs-Merrill Co.
Stebbins, R. A.
  1970  "Career: the subjective approach." The Sociological Quarterly 11
        (Winter):32–49.
Strauss, Anselm L.
  1959  Mirrors and Masks: The Search for Identity. New York: The Free Press.
Wager, Leonard Wesley
  1959  "Career patterns and role problems of airline pilots in a major airline com-
        pany." Unpublished Ph.D. dissertation, University of Chicago, Depart-
        ment of Sociology.
Westby, D. L.
  1960  "The career experience of the symphony musician." Social Forces 38
        (March):223–230.

# III

# EXPERIENCING WORK

*Work as Practical Accomplishment: Willie's Hand*

This photograph is from a study of an auto and farm mechanic in northern New York. He was a fixer and a maker. One day, he'd be making a cedar-oil still for a neighbor. The next day he'd rebuild a sewing machine and sew a dress for his daughter's confirmation ceremony. He lived on about $7,000 a year, but he lived in a world rich in knowledge and social relationships.

I used photographs to encourage Willie to tell the story of his work. This was his phenomenology found in the small details of everyday life.

Photo: Photo by Douglas Harper from Douglas Harper, *Working Knowledge: Skill and Community in a Small Shop* (Chicago: University of Chicago Press, 1987).

As I sat watching children on a class outing in a park in Hong Kong, I wondered how the educational system had helped create children who were as playful as any, yet were highly focused on tidiness (they carefully placed each wrapper from any snack into the trash receptacles, which were themselves clean) and a kind of group identity that was clearly evident in their demeanor and play. All teachers perform an occupational role that carefully manages their display of emotions. The comparative study of education would lead us to understand the subtle interplay of emotions and culture in the occupation of teaching.

*The Social Construction of Emotions in Work: Hong Kong Teacher*

Photo: Kowloon Park, Kowloon, China, 2002, by Douglas Harper.

Just before dawn in Bologna, Italy, on a Sunday. In Italy, life and work are lived at an odd combination of paces: both frantic and relaxed. People drive fast and talk in a rapid-fire staccato, but linger for hours over coffee and conversation. I was trying to capture some of the ebb and flow of social energy in Italian culture by photographing the city when virtually no one was there: dawn on a Sunday morning. But I'd forgotten, of course, that people who maintain the city often do it during off-hours: cleaning streets, for example, before the rush of traffic.

I made several photos of the street cleaners and sensed the strong camaraderie of the workers. Sociologists have long noted that workers who work when most of the society is at home or at rest develop work cultures based on living topsy-turvy in time.

Photo: Bologna, Italy, 1999, by Douglas Harper.

*Work and Time: Bologna Street Cleaners*

*These photos correspond with the three subsections of part III.*

160

The cultural study of work is derived from phenomeno ogy, which is most simply understood as the study social life. This approach in sociology traces to Weber's int thetic understanding (*Verstehen*). Alfred Schutz, a sociologist who did most of his work in the 1950s, brought the philosophy of Edmund Husserl to the study of everyday social relationships. Sociologists who have studied the "practical accomplishment" of work, using either symbolic interaction or ethnomethodology, are tied directly to the traditions in sociology that were developed by Weber, Schutz, and others such as Herbert Blumer and G. H. Mead.

"Symbolic interaction" alerts us to how humans process information in interaction. The symbolic interactionist understands that an individual gives off information (e.g., words, gestures, and expressions) that is perceived and given meaning as another individual interprets and reacts. A second individual defines the gesture, word, expression, or combination thereof. The key idea is that all meaning is constructed through the process of interaction and is based on interpreting symbolic meaning. Perhaps the best summary of this perspective is Blumer's (1969); however, many of the authors of chapters in this book have also written extensively on the theory of symbolic interaction.

The process of definition is often referred to as a conversation with oneself, though the metaphor suffers because the process is automatic and usually unselfconscious. Still, most recognize this process. William Russo's main character in his novel *Straight Man* is Hank Devereaux. When Hank is about to say something that will get him into trouble, he refers to himself as William Henry Devereaux, Jr., and wonders, "Just who said those words which appear to have emerged from my mouth?" It is an elaboration of this conversation with self to which symbolic interaction refers.

"Ethnomethodology" focuses on the taken for granted aspects of social life, the unwritten and largely unrecognized social rules that guide routine behavior. Here again, we speak of social life as the product of a small association such as a family or of larger groups such as occupations, social classes, or gender groups. Fundamental as are the social rules studied by the ethnomethodologist, they are elusive and difficult to describe. Thus ethnomethodologists early on uncovered tacit social rules by breaking them. This might mean something as prosaic as bargaining for a package of cigarettes at the grocery store to uncover the tacit rules of interaction governing economic exchange. A now famous study by Garfinkle (1967) sought to understand the rules of sexual identity by studying an individual who changed sex. Both symbolic interaction and ethnomethodology inform the studies that comprise part III of our book and bibliography.

# PRACTICAL ACCOMPLISHMENT

Culture is the practical accomplishment of social life, and some, but not a large number, of sociologists have studied precisely how members of society construct meaning and impose order into their work worlds. Sociologists have studied how workers in high-risk occupations use rituals and magic to manage uncertainty, as, for example, in Roth's (1957) study of containing disease contagion. Psathas and Henslin (1967) studied how cab drivers locate places in the routine accomplishment of their job. They studied the meanings behind the patterns of communication between cabbies and dispatchers, one of the very few examples of conversational analysis in the study of work. The ethnomethodological approach was applied in Thorlindsson's (1994) study of how Icelandic cod fisher captains create a science of locating fish through a myriad of factual procedures and intuitions.

The articles we have chosen for part III include a study of constructing truth in the process of creating an encyclopedia (Tomlinson, 1985; see chapter 9), managing uncertainty with rituals (Gmelch's 1978 study of baseball players; see chapter 10), and reducing the complexities of a job, in this case policing, to concrete practices in Bittner's 1967 study of the police on skid row (see chapter 11).

Tomlinson's study uses the autobiographical method to deconstruct and demystify the job practices of encyclopedia writing. Learning the tacit rules involves, in this case, learning how to generate sufficient text to satisfy the bureaucratically organized task of "encyclopedia production." Gmelch's study of how baseball players use rituals to organize reactions to uncertainty makes us aware of how irrational practices underscore the organization of work that is organized around unpredictable outcomes and the very high stakes of professional athletics.

Bittner stresses the ad hoc nature of work on the street, often called the "situational contingencies" of the setting. Although the police officer may formally be trained to "uphold the law" and "arrest lawbreakers," all police officers spend their time on the beat deciding which laws to enforce, which lawbreakers to arrest, and who to protect. Bittner shows us that because the part of the city largely populated by the homeless is so different than other work settings, the basis of the police officer's authority—the ability to arrest—has a profoundly different character. The police officer fashions peacekeeping around this and other situational contingencies. These include intimate knowledge of the setting: knowledge of which individuals may be of danger to what others, of the schedule of the distribution of welfare checks, or knowledge of the informal relationships between individual bar owners, for example, and their typical clients. In other words, the police officer ignores the illegality of public drunkenness and protects a habitually drunk man from would-be predators. The officer's work should be understood as the practical accomplishment of managing these types of contingencies. Bittner's study is perhaps the most accomplished example of this core approach in the cultural study of work.

## EMOTIONS IN WORK

The study of the emotional dimensions of work was not originally recognized as a subdiscipline in the cultural study of work, though the management of emotions figured heavily in such studies as Mayer and Rosenblat's (1975) analysis of how social workers react to danger in the ghetto. The study of emotions in work was revolutionized in 1979 with the publication of Arlie Hochschild's analysis of how airline stewardesses learn to manage emotions on the job, an analysis using the dramaturgical perspective of Erving Goffman as a basis for connecting "feeling rules" to occupational settings. She wrote:

> The smoothly warm airline hostess, the ever-cheerful secretary, the unirritated complaint clerk, the undisgusted proctologist, the teacher who likes every student equally, and Goffman's unflappable poker player may all have to engage in deep acting, an acting that goes well beyond the mere ordering of display. Work to make feeling and frame consistent with situation is work in which individuals continually and privately engage. But they do so in obeisance to rules not completely of their making. (Hochschild, 1979, 563)

The study of emotions in work suddenly burgeoned. Sociologists studied how clerks deal with impatient or uncivil customers (Rafaeli and Sutton, 1990), how service workers manage the momentary but emotionally charged encounters with clients (Wharton, 1996), and how supervisors of workers with limited cognitive ability manage work organization (Copp, 1998). Several sociologists studied how workers in health industries manage the emotional landscape of health care. Perakyla (1991) and Lee-Treweek (1996) are among the most telling.

The question of managing emotions in sports was covered by Gallmeier's study of professional hockey players (1987) and Snyder and Ammons's (1993) study of baseball players getting psyched to play. These researchers taught us that the work of a professional athlete (or any other worker whose job involves maximum performance and uncertainty) requires attaining a certain kind of emotional pitch, maintaining it for the time of the performance, and then recreating it in another setting after a short interlude.

Much "emotion work" involves managing fear. Studies of the American soldiers during World War II showed the importance of peer group pressure in defining and managing the combat situation, a fundamentally fearful work setting in which workers must depend on each other to the point where one's partner's mistakes could cost a worker his or her life. Norms come into existence that define and guide this social interaction.

Sociologists have begun to study nearly all emotions that become part of the routines of work. For example, several sociologists study how love and its assorted feelings such as jealousy and possessiveness guide social interaction in child care and education.

The studies we have included in part III are Raz's (1997; see chapter 12) study of false happiness and pleasure in guide work at Tokyo Disneyland, which draws heavily on Hochschild's pioneering study of airline stewardesses. Jack Haas's (1977; see chapter 13) study of fear among high steel workers was the first to analyze how the pressure of peer pressure group membership mitigates against fear in highly dangerous blue-collar jobs. Finally, we note that several articles comprising other chapters include the study of emotions in the context of work.


## TIME AND WORK

Work exists in time. The relevant dimensions of time, however, are many.

Classic studies of blue-collar work done in the 1950s such as Donald Roy's studies of the assembly line show how workers whose actions are directed by unvarying machine rhythms adjust themselves collectively and culturally. Indeed, these themes were presented cinematically in Charlie Chaplin's 1936 film *Modern Times* and in an ongoing tradition of assembly-line studies. Now that much of this work has been moved to the developing world, the study of assembly-line work must be understood in the context of globalization.

The matter of time and work may include how the time of day influences the organization of social interaction, as in the case of Hood's 1988 study of janitors, which is included in this volume (see chapter 14). One of our students studied this aspect of time in a particularly compelling way, in this instance as experienced in her job as an all-night waitress. Her various clientele included a rowdy crowd who come to eat as the bars close at 2:00 A.M., regular appearances of other night workers such as policemen on their rounds who feel a protective empathy with the night waitress, the occasional trucker or late-night traveler who appears and disappears with little fanfare, and, finally, day workers eating their breakfasts before their workday begins and as the waitress's ends. All of these people treat the waitress differently and are treated differently in turn by her. Some treat her comradely as a fellow night worker, whereas others, who work during the day and only visit the diner as the night workers begin or end their shift, act superior because they belong to the world of day work. The cook and the waitress may ritually drink a cup of coffee during the 4:00 A.M. lull that cements their common identity as workers. It is the time context that gives the work its particular characteristic.

Time also influences the ordering of authority in the workplace. Eviatar Zerubavel (1979) shows us that the nurse's time, for example, is structured into the doctor's. In fact, all support workers as well as patients organize their time to the time frame set by the physician. Ironically, however, the telephone and the beeper now allow the doctor's private time to be easily interrupted, and his or her importance on the job, which gives power during the day, can cause private disruption during the night.

The work of Air Force security specialists studied by Hertz and Charlton (1989) is the constant visual surveillance at a missile installation. The work consists of looking for something—a missile attack—that, in all likelihood, will never appear. This nonwork is, however, among the most difficult to accomplish because of its near meaninglessness and the utter boredom that results. Time becomes an enemy, and it is confronted psychologically and physically with small acts of sabotage. Much modern work is quite boring, like that of the security specialists or customer service phone workers who wait for complaints to come in and are not allowed to interact with each other between calls. Because surveillance work consists of looking for something that will likely never happen, workers speak of time slowing down to the excruciating pace of a snail.

The larger framework of time also figures heavily into the cultural study of work. The matter of careers is a question of how work is structured into the life patterns, so the section in this collection on careers (chapters 14 and 15) might well be considered a subset of the study of time. Hochschild's study of work and home (1997), included in our collection, shows how time has changed its meaning as modern work has escaped the time constraints it used to have (see chapter 15).

These are some, but certainly not all, of the ways in which a phenomenologically oriented sociologist would approach work. But virtually all cultural studies of work are phenomenological to one degree or another. The selections presented here are the most pointed or focused along the lines of practical accomplishment, emotional life, and the nature of time in work.

## CITED AND RECOMMENDED READING

### Theory

Blumer, Herbert. *Symbolic Interaction: Perspective and Method.* Englewood Cliffs, N.J.: Prentice Hall, 1969.

Garfinkle, Harold. *Studies in Ethnomethodology.* Englewood Cliffs, NJ: Prentice Hall, 1967.

## Work as Practical Accomplishment

Casper, Monica J. "Negotiations, Work Objects, and the Unborn Patient: The Inter-actional Scaffolding of Fetal Surgery." *Symbolic Interaction* 21, no. 4 (1998): 379–400.

Engestroim, Yrjo. "Developmental Studies of Work as a Testbench of Activity Theory: The Case of Primary Care Medical Practice." In *Understanding Practice: Perspectives on Activity and Context,* edited by Seth Chaiklin and Jean Lave, 64–103. New York: Cambridge University Press, 1993.

Haas, J. "Binging: Education Control among High-Steel Ironworkers." *American Behavioral Scientist* 16 (1972): 27–34.

Harper, Douglas. "Portraying Bricolage." *Knowledge and Society: Studies in the Sociology of Culture Past and Present* 6 (1986): 209–32.

Henslin, James M. "Craps and Magic." *American Journal of Sociology* 73, no. 3 (November 1967): 316–30.

Lave, Jean. "The Practice of Learning." In *Understanding Practice: Perspectives on Activity and Context,* edited by Seth Chaiklin and Jean Lave, 3–32. New York: Cambridge University Press, 1993.

Lewis, L. S. "Knowledge, Change, Certainty, and the Theory of Magic." *American Journal of Sociology* 69 (1963): 7–12.

Psathas, George, and James M. Henslin. "Dispatched Orders and the Cab Driver: A Study of Locating Activities." *Social Problems* 14, no. 4 (spring 1967): 424–43.

Roth, Julius. "Ritual and Magic in the Control of Contagion." *American Sociological Review* 22 (1957): 310–14.

Thorlindsson, Thorolfur. "Skipper Science: A Note on the Epistemology of Practice and the Nature of Expertise." *Sociological Quarterly* 35, no. 2 (1994): 329–46.

## The Social Construction of Time in Work

Cottrell, Harry. "Of Time and the Railroader." *American Sociological Review* 4 (1939): 60–77.

Epstein, C. F., and A. L. Kalleberg. "Time and the Sociology of Work: Issues and Implications." *Sociology of Work and Occupations* 28, no. 1 (February 2001): 5–16.

Hertz, Rosanna, and Joy Charlton. "Making Family under a Shiftwork Schedule: Air Force Security Guards and Their Wives." *Social Problems* 36, no. 5 (December 1989): 491–507.

Hochschild, Arlie. "The Time Bind: When Work Becomes Home and Home Becomes Work." *Population and Development Review* 23, no. 3 (September 1997): 655–62.

Hood, J. C. "From Night to Day: Timing and Management of Custodial Work." *Journal of Contemporary Ethnography* 17, no. 1 (1988): 96–116.

Roy, Donald F. "Banana Time: Job Satisfaction and Informal Interaction." *Human Organization* 18, no. 4 (1959–1960): 158–68.

Zerubavel, Eviatar. "Private Time and Public Time: The Temporal Structure of Social Accessibility and Professional Commitments." *Social Forces* 58, no. 1 (September 1979): 38–58.

## The Social Construction of Emotions in Work

Copp, Martha. "When Emotion Work Is Doomed to Fail: Ideological and Structural Constraints on Emotion Management." *Symbolic Interaction* 21, no. 3 (1998): 299–328.

Gallmeier, Charles. "Dinosaurs and Prospects: Toward a Sociology of the Compressed Career." In *Sociological Inquiry: A Humanistic Perspective,* edited by K. M. Mahmoudi, 1–21. Dubuque, Iowa: Kendall/Hunt, 1987.

Haas, Jack. "Learning Real Feelings: A Study of Ironworkers' Reactions to Fear and Danger." *Work and Occupations* 4 (1977): 147–70.

Hochschild, Arlie R. "Emotion Work, Feeling Rules, and Social Structure." *American Journal of Sociology* 85, no. 3 (1979): 551–75.

Lee-Treweek, Geraldine. "Emotion Work, Order and Emotional Power in Care Assistant Work." In Veronica James and Jonathan Gabe, eds., *Health and the Sociology of Emotions,* 115–32. Oxford: Blackwell Publishers, 1996.

Mayer, John E., and A. Rosenblat. "Encounter with Danger: Social Workers in the Ghetto." *Work and Occupations* 2 (1975): 227–45.

Perakyla, Anssi. "Hope Work in the Care of Seriously Ill Patients." *Qualitative Health Research* 1, no. 4 (1991): 407–33.

Rafaeli, A., and R. I. Sutton. "Expression of Emotion in Organizational Life." In *Research in Organizational Behavior,* edited by L. L. Cummings and Barry M. Straw, 1–42, 11. Greenwich, Conn.: JAI Press, 1987.

———. "Untangling the Relationship between Displayed Emotions and Organizational Sales: The Case of Convenience Stores." *Academy of Management Journal* 31 (1988): 461–87.

———. "Busy Stores and Demanding Customers: How Do They Affect the Display of Positive Emotion?" *Academy of Management Journal* 33, no. 3 (1990): 623–37.

Raz, Aviad E. "The Slanted Smile Factory: Emotion Management in Tokyo Disneyland." *Studies in Symbolic Interaction* 21 (1997): 201–17.

Rogers, Joy M., Stanley J. Freeman, et al. "The Occupational Stress of Judges." *Canadian Journal of Psychiatry* 36, no. 5 (1991): 317–22.

Smith, Allen C., and Sherryl Kleiman. "Managing Emotions in Medical School: Student's Contacts with the Living and the Dead." *Social Psychology Quarterly* 52, no. 1 (1989): 56–69.

Snyder, Eldon E., and Ronald Ammons. "Baseball's Emotion Work: Getting Psyched to Play." *Qualitative Sociology* 16, no. 2 (1993): 111–32.

Wharton, Carol S. "Making People Feel Good: Workers' Constructions of Meaning in Interactive Service Jobs." *Qualitative Sociology* 19, no. 2 (1996): 217–33.

# 9

# The Social Construction of Truth: Editing an Encyclopedia

*Graham Tomlinson*

Theologians, moral philosophers, and others who grapple with questions of truth have not been especially helpful in the sociological understanding of truthfulness and lying. Some who claim to know the truth advise us never to lie. Others have excused some lies if told in defense of a "higher" truth (Bok, 1978: 7), thereby according priority to this higher truth and exonerating falsehoods perpetrated in its service. Still others would justify falsehoods told to one's enemies for the sake of saving oneself or others.

One recent analysis (Bok, 1978) emphasizes the distinction between truth and truthfulness, between matters of epistemology and matters of ethics. Although "the whole truth *is* out of reach" (1978: 4), determinations of truthfulness centering around questions of intention are more feasible. Truthfulness implies intentional honesty, whereas a falsehood (a lie) is "an intentionally deceptive message in the form of a statement" (Bok, 1978: 15). This article accepts the usefulness of this distinction and is focused on adaptive practices involved in truthfulness and falsehoods.[1]

If one agrees with Bok that the truth is beyond our reach, then we should turn our attention to that which is within reach—the practices that make up the construction of "truth." These practices are of analytic and theoretic interest and can be empirically investigated.

In choosing to study truthfulness, we do *not* have to abandon the study of truth. What we abandon is the positing of one more version of truth in a world already cluttered with truth claims. To wit, we live in a world of truth-claimers in which certain institutions make stronger claims than others.

Advertisers, parents, and professional card dealers will privately acknowledge the precariousness of their truth claims. On the other hand, many religions, the news media, and encyclopedias display little embarrassment when asserting the truth and truthfulness of their claims.

The assertion of truth by an organization is a form of reification. It posits an object with characteristics practically devoid of the human activities that were responsible for its creation. All authoritative sources of truth should be examined through the practices by which that truth is achieved. Theologies should be studied through the practical affairs of theologians and churches; news reports through the practices found in newsrooms (Lester, 1980), television studios, and the activities of journalists on the street; and science through the adaptations employed in the labs and the field (Yearley, 1981; H. Zukerman, 1984). The study of these practices reveal not so much deliberate deception but adaptations to the organizational rhythms, settings, and requirements that come to play a central part in the daily routines of those involved.

Against this background of philosophical and social scientific investigations of truth and truthfulness, this study examines the social construction of "truth" as achieved in writing articles for an encyclopedia. On one hand, there is the final product—the encyclopedia—promoted and perceived as the truth; on the other hand, there are the routine, daily practices of those involved in the processes of creating that product. One would expect a consistency between the two, but this analysis shows gaps of varying widths between them.

## SETTING AND METHOD

During the 1970s, I was employed for 18 months as an associate social science editor for the revision of a major one-volume encyclopedia produced at a prestigious university press. Located in a major metropolitan area, the university press was housed in a brownstone building just off campus. Gentleness and respect characterized the working ambiance among editors, who, despite their varying statuses, treated one another with a kindness that sharply contrasted with the noisy city outside.

The editorial staff was formally divided into four statuses: 2 editors-in-chief at the top, 6 senior editors, a third level of 24 associate editors, and, finally, a number of assistant and copy editors. Senior editors supervised anywhere from four to eight associate editors. In addition to this editorial staff, a number of freelance editors were hired to write specific articles and nearly a hundred scholars (two-thirds of them from the university) received fees from serving as consultants. The editorial responsibilities were formally divided into four areas: geography, humanities, physical and natural sciences, and social sciences. Although my responsibilities were in the general area of social science, I occasionally received assignments in other areas. Within the social science department there were three associate editors in addition to myself.

The final product—that is, the published encyclopedia—weighed 10.5 pounds and contained over 50,000 articles and about 7 millions words. The encyclopedia was the major revenue producer for the university press and supported its other publications. When the first edition was pending in the 1930s, there was substantial opposition within the university faculty. Many professors argued that such a publication under the auspices of their university would tarnish their scholarly reputations. This opposition was easily overcome when many of them were hired on and coopted as consultants.

The encyclopedia enjoys an excellent reputation and is revised about once every decade. Many of the same editors are rehired from edition to edition. The editors are not academicians (although some have advanced degrees) but hire unemployed academics serving either as consultants as freelancers or as full-time employees when positions are open.

When initially hired, I had no intention of conducting research; having just completed a stint in a marketing research job, I was merely looking for a job. But about six months into my employment, as I watched myself and others becoming more and more "creative" in writing articles, I decided to keep field notes on these activities. Initially the notes were primarily descriptive as I recorded editors' adaptive practices in producing articles. During a data collection period of about 12 months I kept field notes on my own practices and those of other associate editors. I also kept notes on the *queries* from the senior editors. Queries were questions, usually written out in memos, addressed by senior editors to articles or parts of articles produced by associate editors. Queries were usually placed in a basket on the desks of associate editors on a daily basis.

The practices that are analyzed in this article involve aspects of the larger generic process referred to as truthful adaptations later in the article.[2] These adaptations may be viewed collectively as the ways that associate editors and senior editors adjust to a variety of organizational and personal constraints in order to carry out their respective jobs.

## LEARNING THE ROPES:
## THE WORK OF ASSOCIATE EDITORS

One of my duties as associate editor consisted of examining "social science" articles (ethnic groups, political and social organizations, prominent figures in the social sciences) from the previous edition to determine which articles should be deleted and which should be retained and perhaps revised. For example, a previous article on "food" was dropped because it was considered too broad a topic. Some of the material from that article was to be subdivided and included in other articles, such as that on milk.

The primary responsibility for deleting or adding articles fell to the senior editors with little consultation with the associate editors. Determining a "major" figure involved a good deal of caprice: Bob Dylan was included but Erik Erikson was not. Little or no revision was required for deceased notables. Selection of major figures often seemed to turn on the particular favorites of the senior editors, or their lack of knowledge about a particular field (my senior editor's background was in English literature). On occasion he would ask my opinion about an addition. Among others, I suggested C. Wright Mills should be included. He had never heard of him, and so Mills was not included. I tried Erving Goffman, with the same result. Eventually, I gave up suggesting additions.

An additional task of associate editors was revising old articles or writing new ones. Each associate editor was provided a book of guidelines containing proofreaders' rules, stylistic rules, and reference rules associated with factual changes. Proofreaders' rules were the standard ones used by newspaper editors. Stylistic rules included such "fashionable" changes as altering the spelling of "Moslem" to "Muslim," or ceasing to refer to various groups of Native Americans as "tribes." Reference rules specified that any factual change must be accompanied by a bibliography card that would be kept on file. My senior editor suggested that I could pick up these rules on my own, but he did emphasize strongly one rule: *Never get information from another encyclopedia or reference book.* Another major encyclopedia had just completed a revision and this might prove a temptation among the editors.

The lines of responsibility were such that associate editors were responsible to only one senior editor. My senior editor had a production quota of 2,000 lines of copy per week due to the editors-in-chief. Each of the associate editors had quotas of 500 lines of copy due weekly. If all the associate editors met their quotas, the senior editor would have his quota. My weekly quota was delivered to the senior editor on Fridays, and his quota was due to the editors-in-chief on Wednesdays.

The senior editor would review my copy and return articles periodically to my desk with queries. Sometimes the queries were simple requests for clarification: One associate editor was asked to clarify why he referred to tennis as a bisexual sport, by which he meant that it was played by both sexes. Others asked only for additional information (the senior editor was well-versed in opera and tended to return all opera-related articles for further information) or for additional bibliographical references (for example, recent books on subjects known to the senior editor but overlooked by the associate editor). Other queries were far more extensive.

The workday began with the editors' irregular arrivals between 8:00 and

9:00 A.M., during which time we drank coffee and read newspapers. Between 9:00 and 10:00 A.M. the editors gradually began to attend to their editing duties. Around 9:30 A.M., I typically left the office and went to one of the numerous libraries located on campus to find and work with relevant references. Normally, I did not return to my office until the following morning.

Initially, I could not meet my weekly quota of 500 lines of copy. I was quite scrupulous, following the guidelines exactly, even working on weekends in an attempt to maintain my quota. My senior editor assured me that all novice editors had this problem and that I would soon overcome it. He insisted only that I work within the guidelines. However, despite my best efforts, I found that I could produce only about 300 lines per week. After a couple of months on the job, I began to sense growing irritability on the part of the senior editor with my failure to meet the stated quota.

One morning, while entering the reference room of the undergraduate library, I was surprised to find two associate editors from another department poring over a volume from another encyclopedia. Initially, the editors were unaware of my presence, and I watched in mild surprise and then in shock; they appeared to be copying from this other encyclopedia. In a joking way I inquired as to whether they were copying or not. One quickly replied that they were merely checking their facts against this encyclopedia. At this point, however, they gathered their materials and left. I doubted his statement and decided to investigate. I mentally noted the article they were working on, removed it from the turn-in basket the following Friday, copied it, and went back to the encyclopedia in the reference room. The two articles matched almost word for word. I then suspected how other editors so easily met their quotas.

There was an initial period of shock, but oddly accompanied a feeling of having obtained some useful information. Conversations with friends about my new-found information produced a range of reactions from shock to "that's the way the world works." With some degree of hesitancy I, too, began "to check facts" in other encyclopedias. When I gradually realized that the senior editors would probably never know of this activity, the "checking" increased.

Over the next few months I began to make systematic observations of the other editors. Periodically I would check the reference rooms of the libraries, noting the frequency with which I saw editors examining other encyclopedias and reference books. As all new material added to the encyclopedia was supposed to be derived from original sources, this seemed a clear violation of the spirit and perhaps the letter of the rule against consulting other encyclopedias. Yet it was also clear that this was a widespread practice; I observed editors from all departments using secondary sources. It was also certain that one's quota could be achieved using these and related methods.[3]

## TRUTHFUL ADAPTATIONS

In subsequently categorizing and analyzing my data, I came to identify and focus on two distinct issues relevant to the production of "truthful" encyclopedia articles. First, associate editors used a series of *circumvention practices* to avoid or prevent the query process; second, the *query process* and *strategies for responding to queries* were subject to a weekly pattern, varying in rhythm and emotional tone.

### Circumvention Practices

Articles, once queried and returned to the associate editor, could not be counted in future quotas. Therefore, queried articles became extra weight. It behooved the associate editor to circumvent this prospect whenever possible.

Associate editors employed a number of circumvention practices to avoid or mute the query process. First, articles that proved particularly difficult because of technical information could be assigned to freelance editors by the associate editors. Typically, the associate editors would allow these articles to accumulate until there were enough to make it worth a freelancer's time and then make the assignment. The university press paid for this work, and the returned articles were allowed as part of one's quota. However, the expense involved and the fact that it reflected poorly on the associate editor's reputation made freelancing a practice that had to be used infrequently. Nonetheless, the use of freelancers had the merit of shifting the responsibility for any particular article away from the associate editor.

Second, associate editors might engage in the practice I came to term *underediting.* Many of the senior editors had worked together on previous editions of this encyclopedia, as well as on editions of other encyclopedias and reference books.[4] Thus, my senior editor had written many of the articles assigned to me from the previous edition. I discovered that changes I made in his articles would often be queried. For example, one article on a well-known black writer asserted, "His writings express the violent hatred of a black man for all aspects of white society." Not only would many people consider this to be an inaccurate statement, but it seemed to me to be inappropriate in an encyclopedia. The senior editor queried and rejected my efforts to change this statement. Or, again, the wine article contained only two sentences on the wines of Spain. My copy expanding the treatment of this topic was rejected on the grounds that Spanish wine was not of worldwide importance (even though I pointed out that Spain was the third-largest wine-producing country in the world). Eventually, it became clear that if I made as few changes as possible in certain articles, the likelihood of receiving queries decreased.

Underlings in any organization soon learn the consequences of challenging those in authority. Although I did not perceive my actions as a challenge—on the contrary, I viewed my editorial suggestions as those of a conscientious editor—they were so perceived by the senior editor. Successful apprentices in trades, graduate students, or students in such professions as medicine and law all learn that their conscientiousness may well prevent their advancement because it is perceived as a challenge by those above them.

Third, associate editors might avoid queries through the practice of *paraphrasing*. Particularly in light of the possibility that articles in other encyclopedias or reference books had been written or edited by these same senior editors, paraphrasing the articles would typically result in their approval and hence in an unqueried article.[5] I quickly found out, for instance, that if I wanted to include additional historical information on organizations, I was well-advised to check and see what information other reference books or encyclopedias included on the organization at issue. Indeed, despite the directive to use only original sources, such sources were in practice distrusted; articles relying heavily or exclusively on original sources were more apt to receive queries than those modeled closely on already published secondary accounts.

A fourth practice, often employed as a last resort, involved *losing* an article, perhaps by hiding it in your desk, perhaps by literally throwing it away. If an associate editor has a particularly difficult article—typically because few references on the topic were available—that article could be deposited in one's desk. The senior editor did not require the return of articles in any particular sequence and kept no systematic records as to which and how many articles had been queried. At any given time an associate editor would have articles on as many as six or seven topics, and the senior editor was unconcerned about which topic one was working on. Only on a few occasions did the senior editor request a specific article. If an article was repeatedly queried, associate editors might, in exasperation, simply destroy the article. This solution befell even a number of articles that had appeared in the previous edition.

Finally, an editor might *thin-air* for an article. This practice involved "creating" some piece of information if such information were not available. For instance, articles on religious groups, ethnic groups, and organizations required current population figures. These figures were not always available and in a number of cases had not ever been compiled. (Many groups of people in Third World countries, as well as Native American groups, for example, had never been included in any systematic census.) The senior editor always insisted that we "search harder" when informed of the unavailability of such data. Although many of these articles were "lost," the fact that each such article needed only a population figure to gain acceptance provided strong temptation to "invent" a number.[6] In the same way that population figures could be invented, so could the references documenting and supporting them.

All of these practices represent practical adaptations to organizational routines and constraints. In one sense they were survival techniques that got the job done, even if they circumvented the stated aims of the organization. Freelancing allowed the associate editor to shift responsibility; underediting and paraphrasing permitted associate editors to "speak the same language" as senior editors and thereby avoid the vulnerability of using original sources. In the more extreme instances, when backed into a corner, associate editors turned to the practices of losing and thin-airing.

### The Rhythm of the Query and Response Processes

The query process possessed its own internal order and temporal rhythm. Hall (1984), Jaques (1982), Zerubavel (1981), and others have distinguished between time as measured by a clock and time as experienced by the person. Clock time in the encyclopedia editing process was imposed by the publication deadline, which was in turn broken down into smaller and smaller deadlines. The senior editor's weekly rhythm was controlled by the 2,000-line quota and that of associate editors by their 500-line quota. The quotas represent clock time. However, experienced time, although constructed within the frame of clock time, possessed its own distinctive emotional tone, reflected in the character of queries. Some queries appeared inconsistent with the generally polite atmosphere of the workplace. Some queries were neutral requests for additional information, whereas others were framed in polite or even pleading language. Still others were sarcastic, sometime even insulting: For example, the death date I put on a biographical article was returned with the query, "Are you sure this is on his tombstone?" After I began to keep systematic records, I soon established that the tone of the queries corresponded with particular days of the week. Comparisons with queries from my senior editor with those from other senior editor showed the same pattern.

On Monday, two days from the senior editor's due date, the tone was usually *neutral*. On Tuesday, the tone of the queries turned *polite*. On the day the senior editor's quota was due, the tone became *pleading*. On Thursday, the day after copy had been turned in, queries tended to be *sarcastic*. By Friday, the tone had escalated to *insulting*. Presumably, the weekend offered enough of a buffer so that senior editors could feel their sarcastic and insulting queries would be forgotten by Monday.

The response strategies to queries by the associate editors were structurally related to these weekly rhythms. The strategies involved compliance and avoidance. Although there were exceptions to the two patterns described below, observations indicated that these were typical response strategies.

On Monday, Tuesday, and Wednesday, when the tone of the queries was neutral, polite, or pleading, the typical response strategy was one of compliance. In addition, on these days the query standards were relaxed. For example, I had an article on concentration camps queried on Monday because of a lack of bibliographical references. On a Wednesday (pleading tone from the senior editor) the article was resubmitted and accepted in the same form as it had originally been presented.

During the first three days of the work week, the working relationship between senior editors and associate editors could be characterized as cooperative. The tone of the queries established a framework for cooperative behaviors by the associate editors. Requests for documented evidence on Friday frequently would be dropped by Wednesday. Circumvention practices typically would not be employed during these times. Associate editors tried to help the senior editors perform their job.

On Thursday and Friday, when the tone of the queries turned sarcastic or insulting, the behavior of the associate editors tended toward avoidance. Associate editors practiced avoidance by failing to respond to the queries. As associate editors' copy was due on Friday, they concentrated their efforts on completing new articles rather than on responding to the senior editor's queries. In fact, many of the queries generated on these two days were hidden away, lost, or destroyed.

## CONCLUSION

I have described a set of adaptive practices that intervene between organizational requirements and rhythms and encyclopedia submissions. Several organizational features stand out as encouraging these practices. First, most of the interchanges between the senior editor and the associate editors were *written*. Senior editors usually placed the queries on associate editors' desks while the associate editors were not there; similarly, copy with completed queries was returned in the absence of the senior editor—associate editors usually made these returns prior to the arrival of senior editors in the morning. Face-to-face interaction centered around the query process rarely occurred, maintaining a distant relationship between the senior editor and the associate editors. Additionally, associate editors and the senior editor worked in different places, the senior editor in the office and associate editors in the libraries. This distance provided a condition under which the kinds of adaptive practices described here could flourish.

Second, quantitative criteria governed editorial relations. With such criteria, meeting quota deadlines tended to become an end in itself.[7] The stated goal of the enterprise—the production of a truthful document—was undermined by the practical pressures to meet the ever-persistent quota deadlines.

Within the kinds of structural constraints mentioned above, a kind of dual fabrication (Goffman, 1974: 83–123) was taking place. From the associate editor's standpoint, circumvention procedures were designed to short-circuit the query process, and if those failed, the avoidance was implemented. Yet another kind of fabrication was occurring, one that linked these micro practices to more macro levels. The final product, the published encyclopedia, is sold to the public as a version of the truth. Yet the practical and organizational constraints that went into its production are repressed and hidden from public sight.

The close links between the practices described here and the final product cannot be overemphasized when organizations are established with the aim of producing the truth, problems will arise because those persons charged with this task must and will develop strategic adaptations to the real, practical constraints to which this organizational production is subject. It is perhaps even the case that those organizations that make the boldest truth claims may also be the ones most imbued with the greatest use of what has been termed, in this paper, *truthful adaptations.*

Many institutions are subject to the sorts of organizational constraints, quantitative criteria, and deadline pressures examined here. The adaptations of encyclopedia editors do not differ greatly from those found in the news media (except perhaps for time frame); Lester (1980) has shown how bargains and negotiations enter into what is considered newsworthy, and Tuchman (1978a, 1978b) demonstrates how organizational and other aspects of the institution generate and shape what the public takes to be an accurate rendering of the world. And untruthful adaptive practices employed to produce the truth have been located in other institutional settings. Human service institutions have been shown to "create" numerical data by fitting questionable behaviors into categories that are available for counting because such data are deemed more valid by those at the top of accountability chains (Gubrium and Buckholdt, 1979). Jacobs (1979) discovered that marketing research was replete with adaptive practices that, although not in accordance with research guidelines, allowed people to get the job done. At the largest level, what is being produced is culture (Peterson, 1976; Tuchman, 1983), culture which may become reified and accepted uncritically by many of its consumers.

## NOTES

Reprinted from Graham Tomlinson, *Journal of Contemporary Ethnography* (formerly *Urban Life*) 15, no. 2 (July 1986): 197–213. Copyright © 1986 by Sage Publications, Inc. Reprinted by permission of Sage Publications, Inc.
*Author's Note:* An earlier draft of this article was presented at the Conference on

Qualitative Research, University of Waterloo, Ontario, May 1985. Since then, I have benefited from critical readings by Sissela Bok, Gary Alan Fine, Thomas Gieryn, Allen Grimshaw, Charles Tucker, and anonymous reviewers for *Urban Life*. I am especially grateful to Robert M. Emerson and Jaber Gubrium, without whose encouragement and critical comments the article would not have evolved into its present form.

Graham Tomlinson is assistant professor of sociology at the Baptist College at Charleston, SC. He has completed a sociolinguistic analysis of the comedic performance. His present interests are in the sociology of culture, especially in the sociology of food. He has completed a study of the organization of recipes and is currently conducting research on food festivals as community performances.

1. Useful studies conducted on issues dealing with truthfulness include Ludwig (1965), Blumenstiel (1970), Wolk and Henley (1970), Knapp et al. (1974), Ditton (1977), Knapp and Comadena (1979), Prus (1982), Lindskold and Walters (1983), Klockars (1984), and M. Zukerman (1984).

2. The development of generic concepts has been a goal for a number of qualitative researchers, including Miyamato (1959), Strauss (1970), Lofland (1970, 1976), Bigus et al. (1982), Couch (1984), and Prus (1985).

3. For the most part, there seemed to be a tacit understanding among associate editors that "everyone" used other encyclopedias. It was not verbalized frequently and, when it was, it was usually done in a joking manner. The longer I remained in the job, the more open other associate editors became in their use of encyclopedias and reference books; that is to say, they made no attempt to hide it when I observed them.

4. Although I was aware that certain occupations were reputedly gay-dominated (e.g., hairdressers), I was surprised to learn of a rather substantial gay component among encyclopedia and reference book editors. My guess is that certain occupations have substantial gay representation, although they are not identified in the public as "gay" occupations. Some occupations may move through a history in which a few gays are initially employed, become tolerated, and then achieve roughly equal employment rates as heterosexuals. Encyclopedia editing in the setting studied seemed to have reached this latter point.

5. Editors achieved job mobility by moving from the revision of one encyclopedia or reference book to the revision of another. When one became an editor-in-chief, he or she had a ready network of previously known editors to draw on.

6. The notion of pulling numbers out of thin air, in fact, did occur. Included in this notion was guessing what the population of an organization or ethnic group might be, based on the latest available figure. However, the latest available figure might be ten years old or from a questionable source, and associate editors had no adequate way of estimating what the accurate figure might be had they increased or decreased. One often did not know.

7. Other studies have demonstrated this tendency in police work (Skolnick, 1978) and war (Chomsky and Zinn, 1972; Halberstam, 1972).

## REFERENCES

BIGUS, O.E., S. C. HADDEN, and B. G. GLASER (1982) "Basic social processes." Pp. 251–272 in R. B. Smith and P. K. Manning (eds.) Qualitative Methods: Handbook of Social Science Methods, Vol. II. Cambridge, MA: Ballinger.

BLUMENSTIEL, A. D. (1970) "An ethos of intimacy: Constructing and using a situational morality," pp. 435–453 in J. D. Douglas (ed.) Deviance and Respectability. New York: Basic Books.

BOK, S. (1978) Lying: Moral Choice in Public and Private Life. New York: Pantheon.

CHOMSKY, N. and H. ZINN [eds.] (1972) The Pentagon Papers: The Senator Gravel Edition. Boston: Beacon Press.

COUCH, C. (1984) "Symbolic interaction and generic sociological principles." Symbolic Interaction 7: 1–14.

DITTON, J. (1977) "Learning to fiddle customers: An essay on the organized production of part-time theft." Sociology of Work and Occupations 4: 427–450.

GOFFMAN, E. (1974) Frame Analysis. New York: Harper & Row.

GUBRIUM, J. and D. BUCKHOLDT (1979) "The production of hard data in human service institutions." Pacific Soc. Rev. 22: 115–136.

HALBERTAM, D. (1972) The Best and the Brightest. New York: Random House.

HALL, E. T. (1984) The Dance of Life. Garden City, NY: Doubleday.

JACOBS, J. (1979) "Burp-seltzer? I never use it": An in-depth look at market research," pp. 133–142 in H. Schwartz and J. Jacobs (eds.) Qualitative Sociology: A Method to the Madness. New York: Free Press.

JAQUES, E. (1982) The Form of Time. New York: Crane, Russak.

KLOCKARS, C. B. (1984) "Lies, secrets, and social control." Amer. Behavioral Scientist 27: 411–544.

KNAPP, M. and M. E. COMADENA (1979) "Telling it like it isn't: A review of theory and research on deceptive communications." Human Communication Research 5: 270–285.

LESTER, M. (1980) "Generating newsworthiness: The interpretive construction of public events." Amer. Soc. Rev. 45: 984–994.

LINDSKOLD, S. and P. S. WALTERS (1983) "Categories for acceptability of lies." J. of Social Psychology 120: 129–136.

LOFLAND, J. (1970) "Interactionist imagery and analytic interruptus," pp. 35–45 in T. Shibutani (ed.) Human Nature and Collective Behavior: Papers in Honor of Herbert Blumer. Englewood Cliffs, NJ: Prentice-Hall.

———— (1976) Doing Social Life. New York: John Wiley.

LUDWIG, A. M. (1965) The Importance of Lying. Springfield, IL: Charles C Thomas.

MIYAMATO, F. (1959) "The social act: Re-examination of a concept." Pacific Soc. Rev. 2: 51–55.

PETERSON, R. A. (1976) The Production of Culture. Beverly Hills, CA: Sage.

PRUS, R. (1982) "Designating discretion and openness: The problematics of truthfulness in everyday life." Canadian Rev. of Sociology and Anthropology 19: 70–91.

———— (1985) "Generic sociology: Maximizing conceptual development in ethnographic research." Presented at the Qualitative Research Conference: An Ethnographic/Interactionist Perspective, University of Waterloo.

SKOLNICK, J. H. (1978) "Clearance rates," pp. 190–200 in E. Rubington and M. Weinberg (eds.) Deviance: The Interactionist Perspective. New York: Macmillan.

STRAUSS, A. (1970) "Discovering new theory from previous theory," pp. 46–53 in T. Shibutani (ed.) Human Nature and Collective Behavior: Papers in Honor of Herbert Blumer. Englewood Cliffs, NJ: Prentice-Hall.

TUCHMAN, G. (1978a) "News net." Social Research 45: 253–276.

——— (1978b) Making News: A Study in the Construction of Reality. New York: Free Press.

——— (1983) "Consciousness industries and the production of culture." J. of Communication 33: 330–341.

WOLK, R. L. and A. HENLEY (1970) The Right to Lie. New York: Peter Wyden.

YEARLEY, S. (1981) "Textual persuasion: The role of scientific accounting in the construction of scientific arguments." Philosophy of the Social Sciences 11: 409–435.

ZERUBAVEL, E. (1981) Hidden Rhythms: Schedules and Calendars in Social Life. Chicago: Univ. of Chicago Press.

ZUKERMAN, H. (1984) "Norms and deviant behavior in science." Sci. Technology and Human Values 9: 7–13.

ZUKERMAN, M. (1984) "Learning to detect deception." J. of Personality and Social Psychology 46: 519–528.

# 10

# Baseball Magic

*George Gmelch*

On each pitching day for the first three months of a winning season, Dennis Grossini, a pitcher on a Detroit Tigers' farm team, arose from bed at exactly 10:00 A.M. At 1:00 P.M. he went to the nearest restaurant for two glasses of iced tea and a tuna fish sandwich. When he got to the ballpark at 3:00 P.M., he changed into the sweatshirt and jock he wore during his last winning game; one hour before the game he chewed a wad of Beech-Nut chewing tobacco. After each pitch during the game, he touched the letters on his uniform and straightened his cap after each ball. Before the start of each inning he replaced the pitcher's rosin bag next to the spot where it was the inning before. And after every inning in which he gave up a run, he washed his hands. When asked which part of his ritual was most important, he said, "You can't really tell what's most important so it all becomes important. I'd be afraid to change anything. As long as I'm winning, I do everything the same."

Trobriand Islanders, according to anthropologist Bronislaw Malinowski, felt the same way about their fishing magic. Among the Trobrianders, fishing took two forms: in the *inner lagoon* where fish were plentiful and there was little danger, and on the *open sea* where fishing was dangerous and yields varied widely. Malinowski found that magic was not used in lagoon fishing, where men could rely solely on their knowledge and skill. But when fishing on the open sea, Trobrianders used a great deal of magical ritual to ensure safety and increase their catch.

Baseball, America's national pastime, is an arena in which players behave remarkably like Malinowski's Trobriand fishermen. To professional ballplayers, baseball is more than just a game. It is an occupation. Since their livelihoods depend on how well they perform, many use magic to try to control the chance that is built into baseball. There are three essential activities of the game—pitching, hitting, and fielding. In the first two, chance can play a surprisingly important role. The pitcher is the player least able to control the outcome of his own efforts. He may feel great and have good stuff warming up in the bullpen and then get into the game and not have it. He may make a bad pitch and see the batter miss it for a strike or see it hit hard but right into the hands of a fielder for an out. His best pitch may be blooped for a base hit. He may limit the opposing team to just a few hits yet lose the game, or he may give up a dozen hits but still win. And the good and bad luck don't always average out over the course of a season. Some pitchers end the season with poor won-lost records but good earned run averages, and vice versa. For instance, this past season Andy Benes gave up over one run per game more than his teammate Omar Daal but had a better won-lost record. Benes went 14–13, whereas Daal was only 8–12. Both pitched for the same team—the Arizona Diamondbacks—which meant they had the same fielders behind them. Regardless of how well a pitcher performs, on every outing he depends not only on his own skill, but also upon the proficiency of his teammates, the ineptitude of the opposition, and luck.

Hitting, which many observers call the single most difficult task in the world of sports, is also full of risk and uncertainty. Unless it's a home run, no matter how well the batter hits the ball, fate determines whether it will go into a waiting glove, whistle past a fielder's diving stab, or find a gap in the outfield. The uncertainty is compounded by the low success rate of hitting: the average hitter gets only one hit in every four trips to the plate, and the very best hitters average only one hit every three trips. Fielding, as we will return to later, is the one part of baseball where chance does not play much of a role.

How do the risk and uncertainty in pitching and hitting affect players? How do they try to control the outcomes of their performance? These are questions that I first became interested in many years ago as both a ballplayer and as an anthropology student. I'd devoted much of my youth to baseball and played professionally as a first baseman in the Detroit Tigers organization in the 1960s. It was shortly after the end of one baseball season that I took an anthropology course called Magic, Religion, and Witchcraft. As I listened to my professor describe the magical rituals of the Trobriand Islanders, it occurred to me that what these so-called primitive people did wasn't all that different from what my teammates and I did for luck and confidence at the ballpark.

## ROUTINES AND RITUALS

The most common way players attempt to reduce chance and their feelings of uncertainty is to develop and follow a daily routine—a course of action that is regularly followed. Talking about the routines of ballplayers, Pittsburgh Pirates coach Rich Donnelly said:

> They're like trained animals. They come out here [to the ballpark] and everything has to be the same, they don't like anything that knocks them off their routine. Just look at the dugout and you'll see every guy sitting in the same spot every night. It's amazing, everybody in the same spot. And don't you dare take someone's seat. If a guy comes up from the minors and sits here, they'll say, "Hey, Jim sits here, find another seat." You watch the pitcher warm up and he'll do the same thing every time. . . . You got a routine and you adhere to it and you don't want anybody knocking you off it.

Routines are comforting; they bring order into a world in which players have little control. And sometimes practical elements in routines produce tangible benefits, such as helping the player concentrate. But what players often do goes beyond mere routine. They become what anthropologists define as *ritual*—prescribed behaviors in which there is no empirical connection between the means (e.g., tapping home plate three times) and the desired end (e.g., getting a base hit). Because there is no real connection between the two, rituals are not rational, and sometimes they are quite irrational. Similar to rituals are the irrational beliefs that form the basis of taboos and fetishes, which players also use to bring luck to their side. But first let's take a close look at rituals.

Most rituals are personal, that is, they are performed by individuals rather than by a team or group. Most are done in an unemotional manner, in much the same way as players apply pine tar to their bats to improve the grip or dab eye black on their upper cheeks to reduce the sun's glare. Baseball rituals are infinitely varied. A ballplayer may ritualize any activity—eating, dressing, driving to the ballpark—that he considers important or somehow linked to good performance. Recall the variety of things that Dennis Grossini does. Pitcher Denny Naegle goes to a movie on days he is scheduled to start. Pitcher Jason Bere listens to the same song on his Walkman on the days he is to pitch. Jim Ohms put another penny in the pouch of his supporter after each win. Clanging against the hard plastic genital cup, the pennies made a noise as he ran the bases toward the end of a winning season. Glenn Davis would chew the same gum every day during hitting streaks, saving it under his cap. Infielder Julio Gotay always played with a cheese sandwich in his back pocket (he had a big appetite, so there might also have been a measure of practicality here). Wade Boggs ate chicken before every game during his career, and that was just one of many elements in his pre- and postgame routine, which also included leaving his house for the ballpark at precisely the same time each day (1:47 for a 7:05 game). Former Oriole pitcher Dennis Martinez would drink a small cup of water after each inning and then place the cups under the bench upside down, in a line. His teammates could always tell what inning it was by the number of cups.

Many hitters go through a series of preparatory rituals before stepping into the batter's box. These include tugging on their caps, touching their uniform letters or medallions, crossing themselves, swinging, and tapping or bouncing the bat on the plate a prescribed number of times. Consider Red Sox shortstop Nomar Garciaparra. After each pitch he steps out of the batters box, kicks the dirt with each toe, adjusts his right batting glove, adjusts his left batting glove, and touches his helmet before getting back into the box. Mike Hargrove, former Cleveland Indian first baseman, had so many time-consuming elements in his batting ritual that he was called "the human rain delay." Both players believe their batting rituals helped them after each pitch regain their concentration. But others wondered if they had become prisoners of their own superstitions. Players who have too many or particularly bizarre rituals risk being labeled as "flakes," and not just by teammates but by fans and media as well. For example, pitcher Turk Wendell's eccentric rituals, which include wearing a necklace of teeth from animals he has killed, made him a cover story in the *New York Times Sunday Magazine*.

Some players, especially Latin Americans, draw upon rituals from their Roman Catholic faith. Some make the sign of the cross or bless themselves before every at bat, and a few like Pudge Rodriguez do so before every pitch. Others, like Juan Gonzalez, also visibly wear religious medallions around their necks, whereas some tuck them discreetly inside their undershirts.

One ritual associated with hitting is tagging a base when leaving and returning to the dugout between innings. Some players don't "feel right" unless they tag a specific base on each trip between the dugout and the field. One of my teammates added some complexity to his ritual by tagging third base on his way to the dugout only after the third, sixth, and ninth innings. Asked if he ever purposely failed to step on the bag, he replied, "Never! I wouldn't dare. It would destroy my confidence to hit." Baseball fans observe a lot of this ritual behavior, such as fielders tagging bases and pitchers tugging on their caps, touching the rosin bag after each bad pitch, or smoothing the dirt on the mound before each new batter, never realizing the importance of these actions to the player. The one ritual many fans do recognize, largely because it's a favorite of TV cameramen, is the "rally cap"—players in the dugout folding their caps and wearing them bill up in hopes of sparking a rally.

Most rituals grow out of exceptionally good performances. When a player does well, he seldom attributes his success to skill alone; he knows that his skills don't change much from day to day. So, then, what was different about today that can explain his three hits? He may attribute his success, in part, to an object, a food he ate, not having shaved, a new shirt he bought that day, or just about any behavior out of the ordinary. By repeating those behaviors, he seeks to gain control over his performance, to bring more good luck. Out-fielder John White explained how one of his rituals started:

> I was jogging out to centerfield after the national anthem when I picked up a scrap of paper. I got some good hits that night and I guess I decided that the paper had something to do with it. The next night I picked up a gum wrapper and had another good night at the plate. . . . I've been picking up paper every night since.

Outfielder Ron Wright of the Calgary Cannons shaves his arms once a week and plans to continue doing so until he has a bad year. It all began two years before when after an injury he shaved his arm so it could be taped, then proceeded to hit three homers over the next few games. Now he not only has one of the smoothest swings in the minor leagues, but two of the smoothest forearms. Wade Boggs's routine of eating chicken before every game began when he was a rookie in 1982, when he noticed a correlation between multiple-hit games and poultry plates (his wife has over 40 chicken recipes). One of Montreal Expos minor leaguer Mike Saccocio's rituals also concerned food: "I got three hits one night after eating at Long John Silver's. After that when we'd pull into town, my first question would be, 'Do you have a Long John Silver's?'" Unlike Boggs, Saccocio abandoned his ritual and looked for a new one when he stopped hitting well.

When in a slump, most players make a deliberate effort to change their rituals and routines in an attempt to shake off their bad luck. One player tried taking different routes to the ballpark; several players reported trying different combinations of tagging and not tagging particular bases in an attempt to find a successful combination. I had one manager who would rattle the bat bin when the team was not hitting well, as if the bats were in a stupor and could be aroused by a good shaking. Similarly, I have seen hitters rub their hands along the handles of the bats protruding from the bin in hopes of picking up some power or luck from bats that are getting hits for their owners. Some players switch from wearing contact lenses to glasses. Brett Mandel described his Pioneer League team, the Ogden Raptors, trying to break a losing streak by using a new formation for their pregame stretching.[1]

## TABOO

Taboos are the opposite of rituals. They are things you don't do. The word "taboo" comes from a Polynesian term meaning prohibition. Breaking a taboo, players believe, leads to undesirable consequences or bad luck. Most players observe at least a few taboos, such as never stepping on the white foul lines. A few, like pitcher Turk Wendell and shortstop Nomar Garcia-parra, leap over the entire basepath. One teammate of mine would never watch a movie on a game day, despite the fact that we played nearly every day from April to September. Another teammate refused to read anything before a game because he believed it weakened his batting eye.

Many taboos take place off the field, out of public view. On the day a pitcher is scheduled to start, he is likely to avoid activities he believes will sap his strength and detract from his effectiveness. Some pitchers avoid eating certain foods, and others will not shave on the day of a game, refusing to shave again as long as they are winning. Early in one season, Oakland's Dave Stewart had six consecutive victories and a beard by the time he lost a game.

Taboos usually grow out of exceptionally poor performances, which play-ers, in search of a reason, attribute to a particular behavior. During my first season of pro ball, I ate pancakes before a game in which I struck out three times. A few weeks later I had another terrible game, again after eating pan-cakes. The result was a pancake taboo: I never again ate pancakes during the season. Pitcher Jason Bere has a taboo that makes more sense in dietary terms: after eating a meatball sandwich and not pitching well, he swore off them for the rest of the season.

Although most taboos are idiosyncratic, there are a few that all ball play-ers hold and that do not develop out of individual experience or misfortune. These form part of the culture of baseball and are sometimes learned as early as Little League. Mentioning a no-hitter while one is in progress is a well-known example. It is believed that if a pitcher hears the words "no-hitter," the spell accounting for this hard-to-achieve feat will be broken and the no-hitter lost. This taboo is also observed by many sports broadcasters, who use various linguistic subterfuges to inform their listeners that the pitcher has not given up a hit, never saying "no-hitter."

## FETISHES

Fetishes are charms, material objects believed to embody "supernatural" power that can aid or protect the owner. Good luck charms are standard equipment for some ballplayers. These include a wide assortment of objects from coins, chains, and crucifixes to a favorite baseball hat. The fetishized object may be a new possession or something a player found that happens to coincide with the start of a streak and that he holds responsible for his good fortune. While playing in the Pacific Coast League, Alan Foster forgot his baseball shoes on a road trip and borrowed a pair from a teammate. That night he pitched a no-hitter, which he attributed to the shoes. Afterwards he bought them from his teammate, and they became a fetish. Expos farmhand Mark LaRosa's rock has a different origin and use:

> I found it on the field in Elmira after I had gotten bombed. It's unusual, perfectly round, and it caught my attention. I keep it to remind me of how important it is to concentrate. When I am doing well I look at the rock and remember to keep my focus, the rock reminds me of what can happen when I lose my concentration.

For one season Marge Schott, former owner of the Cincinnati Reds, insisted that her field manager rub her St. Bernard "Schotzie" for good luck before each game. When the Reds were on the road, Schott would sometimes send a bag of the dog's hair to the field manager's hotel room.

During World War II, American soldiers used fetishes in much the same way. Social psychologist Samuel Stouffer and his colleagues found that in the face of great danger and uncertainty, soldiers developed magical practices, particularly the use of protective amulets and good luck charms (e.g., crosses, Bibles, rabbits' feet, and medals), and jealously guarded articles of clothing they associated with past experiences of escape from danger.[2] Stouffer also found that prebattle preparations were carried out in fixed ritual-like order, similar to ballplayers preparing for a game.

Uniform numbers have special significance for some players who request their lucky number. Because the choice is usually limited, they may try to get a uniform that at least includes their lucky number, such as 14, 24, 34, or 44 for the player whose lucky number is four. When Ricky Henderson came to the Blue Jays in 1993, he paid outfielder Turner Ward $25,000 for the right to wear number 24. Oddly enough, there is no consensus about the effect of wearing number 13. Some players shun it, whereas a few request it. Number preferences emerge in different ways. A young player may request the number of a former star, hoping that—through what anthropologists call *imitative* magic—it will bring him the same success. Or he may request a number he associates with good luck. While with the Oakland A's, Vida Blue changed his uniform number from 35 to 14, the number he wore as a high school quarterback. When 14 did not produce better pitching performance, he switched back to 35. Former San Diego Padres first baseman Jack Clark changed his number from 25 to 00, hoping to break out of a slump. That day he got four hits in a doubleheader but also hurt his back. Then, three days later he was hit in the cheekbone by a ball thrown in batting practice.

Colorado Rockies Larry Walker's fixation with the number three has become well known to baseball fans. Besides wearing 33, he takes three practice swings before stepping into the box, showers from the third nozzle, sets his alarm for three minutes past the hour, and was wed on November 3 at 3:33 P.M.[3] Fans in ballparks all across America rise from their seats for the seventh inning stretch before the home club comes to bat because the number seven is lucky, although the specific origin of this tradition has been lost.[4]

Clothing, both the choice and the order in which it is put on, combines elements of both ritual and fetish. Some players put on their uniform in a particular order. Expos farmhand Jim Austin always puts on his left sleeve, left pants leg, and left shoe before the right. Most players, however, single out one or two lucky articles or quirks of dress for ritual elaboration. After hitting two home runs in a game, for example, ex-Giants infielder Jim Davenport discovered that he had missed a buttonhole while dressing for the game. For the remainder of his career, he left the same button undone. For outfielder Brian Hunter, the focus is shoes: "I have a pair of high tops and a pair of low tops. Whichever shoes don't get a hit that game, I switch to the other pair." At the time of our interview, he was struggling at the plate and switching shoes almost every day. For Birmingham Barons pitcher Bo Kennedy, the arrangement of the different pairs of baseball shoes in his locker is critical:

> I tell the clubbies [clubhouse boys] when you hang stuff in my locker don't touch my shoes. If you bump them move them back. I want the Pony's in front, the turfs to the right, and I want them nice and neat with each pair touching each other. . . . Everyone on the team knows not to mess with my shoes when I pitch.

During hitting or winning streaks, players may wear the same clothes day after day. Once I changed sweatshirts midway through the game for seven consecutive nights to keep a hitting streak going. Clothing rituals, however, can become impractical. Catcher Matt Allen was wearing a long-sleeve turtleneck shirt on a cool evening in the New York-Penn League when he had a three-hit game. "I kept wearing the shirt and had a good week," he explained. "Then the weather got hot as hell, 85 degrees and muggy, but I would not take that shirt off. I wore it for another ten days—catching—and people thought I was crazy." Also taking a ritual to the extreme, Leo Durocher, managing the Brooklyn Dodgers to a pennant in 1941, is said to have spent three and a half weeks in the same gray slacks, blue coat, and knitted blue tie. During a 16-game winning streak, the 1954 New York Giants wore the same clothes in each game and refused to let them be cleaned for fear that their good fortune might be washed away with the dirt. Losing often produces the opposite effect. Several Oakland A's players, for example, went out and bought new street clothes in an attempt to break a 14-game losing streak.

Baseball's superstitions, like almost everything else, change over time. Many of the rituals and beliefs of early baseball are no longer observed. In the 1920s and 1930s, sportswriters reported that a player who tripped en route to the field would often retrace his steps and carefully walk over the stumbling block for "insurance." A century ago, players spent time on and off the field intently looking for items that would bring them luck. To find a hairpin on the street, for example, assured a batter of hitting safely in that day's game. Today few women wear hairpins—a good reason the belief has died out. To catch sight of a white horse or a wagon load of barrels were also good omens. In 1904 the manager of the New York Giants, John McGraw, hired a driver with a team of white horses to drive past the Polo Grounds around the time his players were arriving at the ballpark. He knew that if his players saw white horses, they'd have more confidence and that could only help them during the game. Belief in the power of white horses survived in a few backwaters until the 1960s. A gray-haired manager of a team I played for in Drummondville, Quebec, would drive around the countryside before important games and during the playoffs looking for a white horse. When he was successful, he would announce it to everyone in the clubhouse.

One belief that appears to have died out recently is a taboo about crossed bats. Some of my Latino teammates in the 1960s took it seriously. I can still recall one Dominican player becoming agitated when another player tossed a bat from the batting cage and it landed on top of his bat. He believed that the top bat might steal hits from the lower one. In his view, bats contained a finite number of hits, a sort of baseball "image of limited good." It was once commonly believed that when the hits in a bat were used up, no amount of good hitting would produce any more. Hall of Famer Honus Wagner believed each bat contained only 100 hits. Regardless of the quality of the bat, he would discard it after its 100th hit. This belief would have little relevance today in the era of light bats with thin handles—so thin that the typical modern bat is lucky to survive a dozen hits without being broken. Other superstitions about bats do survive, however. Position players on the Class A Asheville Tourists would not let pitchers touch or swing their bats, not even to warm up. Poor-hitting players, as most pitchers are, were said to pollute or weaken the bats.

## UNCERTAINTY AND MAGIC

The best evidence that players turn to rituals, taboos, and fetishes to control chance and uncertainty is found in their uneven application. They are associated mainly with pitching and hitting—the activities with the highest degree of chance—and not fielding. I met only one player who had any ritual in connection with fielding, and he was an error-prone shortstop. Unlike hitting and pitching, a fielder has almost complete control over the outcome of his performance. Once a ball has been hit in his direction, no one can intervene and ruin his chances of catching it for an out (except in the unlikely event of two fielders colliding). Compared with the pitcher or the hitter, the fielder has little to worry about. He knows that in better than 9.7 times out of 10 he will execute his task flawlessly. With odds like that, there is little need for ritual.

Clearly, the rituals of American ballplayers are not unlike that of the Trobriand Islanders studied by Malinowski many years ago.[5] In professional baseball, fielding is the equivalent of the inner lagoon whereas hitting and pitching are like the open sea.

Although Malinowski helps us understand how ballplayers respond to chance and uncertainty, behavioral psychologist B. F. Skinner sheds light on why personal rituals get established in the first place.[6] With a few grains of seed, Skinner could get pigeons to do anything he wanted. He merely waited for the desired behavior (e.g., pecking) and then rewarded it with some food. Skinner then decided to see what would happen if pigeons were rewarded with food pellets regularly, every fifteen seconds, regardless of what they did. He found that the birds associate the arrival of the food with a particular action, such as tucking their head under a wing or walking in clockwise circles. About ten seconds after the arrival of the last pellet, a bird would begin doing whatever it associated with getting the food and keep doing it until the next pellet arrived. In short, the pigeons behaved as if their actions made the food appear. They learned to associate particular behaviors with the reward of being given seed.

Ballplayers also associate a reward—successful performance—with prior behavior. If a player touches his crucifix and then gets a hit, he may decide the gesture was responsible for his good fortune and touch his crucifix the next time he comes to the plate. If he gets another hit, the chances are good that he will touch his crucifix each time he bats. Unlike pigeons, however, most ballplayers are quicker to change their rituals once they no longer seem to work. Skinner found that once a pigeon associated one of its actions with the arrival of food or water, only sporadic rewards were necessary to keep the ritual going. One pigeon, believing that hopping from side to side brought pellets into its feeding cup, hopped 10,000 times without a pellet before finally giving up. But, then, didn't Wade Boggs eat chicken before every game, through slumps and good times, for seventeen years?

Obviously the rituals and superstitions of baseball do not make a pitch travel faster or a batted ball find the gaps between the fielders, nor do the Trobriand rituals calm the seas or bring fish. What both do, however, is give their practitioners at no cost a sense of control, and with that added confidence. And we all know how important that is. If you really believe eating chicken or hopping over the foul lines will make you a better hitter, it probably will.

## NOTES

An earlier version of this article was printed in *Human Nature* 1, no. 8 (1978): 32–39. Copyright © 1978 by George Gmelch. Revised by George Gmelch and used with permission.

1. Brett Mandel, *Major Dreams, Minor Leagues* (Lincoln: University of Nebraska Press, 1997), 156.

2. Samuel Stouffer, *The American Soldier* (New York: John Wiley, 1965).

3. *Sports Illustrated*, 48.

4. Lee Allen, "The Superstitions of Baseball Players," *New York Folklore Quarterly* 20, no. 2 (June 1964): 98–109, 104.

5. B. Malinowski, *Magic, Science and Religion and Other Essays* (Boston: Beacon Press, 1948).

6. B. F. Skinner, *Behavior of Organisms: An Experimental Analysis* (New York D. Appleton-Century Co., 1938).

## REFERENCES

Malinowski, B. *Magic, Science and Religion and Other Essays.* Boston: Beacon Press 1948.

Mandel, Brett. *Minor Player, Major Dreams.* Lincoln: University of Nebraska Press, 1997.

Skinner, B. F. *Behavior of Organisms: An Experimental Analysis* (New York D. Appleton-Century Co., 1938).

———. *Science and Human Behavior.* New York: Macmillan, 1953.

Stouffer, Samuel. *The American Soldier.* New York: John Wiley, 1965.

Torrez, Danielle Gagnon. *High Inside: Memoirs of a Baseball Wife.* New York: G. P. Putnam's Sons, 1983.

# 11

# The Police on Skid-Row:
# A Study of Peace Keeping

*Egon Bittner*

## THE PROBLEM OF KEEPING
## THE PEACE IN SKID-ROW

Skid-row has always occupied a special place among the various forms of urban life. While other areas are perceived as being different in many ways, skid-row is seen as completely different. Though it is located in the heart of civilization, it is viewed as containing aspects of the primordial jungle, calling for missionary activities and offering opportunities for exotic adventure. While each inhabitant individually can be seen as tragically linked to the vicissitudes of "normal" life, allowing others to say "here but for the Grace of God go I," those who live there are believed to have repudiated the entire role-casting scheme of the majority and to live apart from normalcy. Accordingly, the traditional attitude of civic-mindedness toward skid-row has been dominated by the desire to continue it and to salvage souls from its clutches.[1] The specific task of containment has been left to the police. That this task pressed upon the police some rather special duties has never come under explicit consideration, either from the government that expects control or from the police departments that implement it. Instead, the prevailing method of carrying out the task is to assign patrolmen to the area on a fairly permanent basis and to allow them to work out their own ways of running things. External influence is confined largely to the supply of support and facilities, on the one hand, and occasional expressions of criticism about the overall conditions, on the other. Within the limits of available resources and

192

general expectations, patrolmen are supposed to know what to do and are free to do it.[2]

Patrolmen who are more or less permanently assigned to skid-row districts tend to develop a conception of the nature of their "domain" that is surprisingly uniform. Individual officers differ in many aspects of practice, emphasize different concerns, and maintain different contacts, but they are in fundamental agreement about the structure of skid-row life. This relatively uniform conception includes an implicit formulation of the problem of keeping the peace in skid-row.

In the view of experienced patrolmen, life on skid-row is fundamentally different from life in other parts of society. To be sure, they say, around its geographic limits the area tends to blend into the surrounding environment, and its population always encompasses some persons who are only transitionally associated with it. Basically, however, skid-row is perceived as the natural habitat of people who lack the capacities and commitments to live "normal" lives on a sustained basis. The presence of these people defines the nature of social reality in the area. In general, and especially in casual encounters, the presumption of incompetence and of the disinclination to be "normal" is the leading theme for the interpretation of all actions and relations. Not only do people approach one another in this manner, but presumably they also expect to be approached in this way, and they conduct themselves accordingly.

In practice, the restriction of interactional possibilities that is based on the patrolman's stereotyped conception of skid-row residents is always subject to revision and modification toward particular individuals. Thus, it is entirely possible, and not unusual, for patrolmen to view certain skid-row inhabitants in terms that involve non-skid-row aspects of normality. Instances of such approaches and relationships invariably involve personal acquaintance and the knowledge of a good deal of individually qualifying information. Such instances are seen, despite their relative frequency, as exceptions to the rule. The awareness of the possibility of breakdown, frustration, and betrayal is ever-present, basic wariness is never wholly dissipated, and undaunted trust can never be fully reconciled with presence on skid-row.

What patrolmen view as normal on skid-row—and what they also think is taken for granted as "life as usual" by the inhabitants—is not easily summarized. It seems to focus on the idea that the dominant consideration governing all enterprise and association is directed to the occasion of the moment. Nothing is thought of as having a background that might have led up to the present in terms of some compelling moral or practical necessity. There are some exceptions to this rule, of course: the police themselves, and those who run certain establishments, are perceived as engaged in important and necessary activities. But in order to carry them out they, too, must be geared to the overall atmosphere of fortuitousness. In this atmosphere, the range of control that persons have over one another is exceedingly narrow. Good faith, even where it is valued, is seen merely as a personal matter. Its violations are the victim's own hard luck, rather than demonstrable violations of property. There is only a private sense of irony at having been victimized. The overall air is not so much one of active distrust as it is one of irrelevance of trust; as patrolmen often emphasize, the situation does not necessarily cause all relations to be predatory, but the possibility of exploitation is not checked by the expectation that it will not happen.

Just as the past is seen by the policeman as having only the most attenuated relevance to the present, so the future implications of present situations are said to be generally devoid of prospective coherence. No venture, especially no joint venture, can be said to have a strongly predictable future in line with its initial objectives. It is a matter of adventitious circumstance whether or not matters go as anticipated. That which is not within the grasp of momentary control is outside of practical social reality.

Though patrolmen see the temporal framework of the occasion of the moment mainly as a lack of trustworthiness, they also recognize that it involves more than merely the personal motives of individuals. In addition to the act that everybody *feels* that things matter only at the moment, irresponsibility takes an *objectified* form on skid-row. The places the residents occupy, the social relations they entertain, and the activities that engage them are not meaningfully connected over time. Thus, for example, address, occupation, marital status, etc., matter much less on skid-row than in any other part of society. The fact that present whereabouts, activities, and affiliations imply neither continuity nor direction means that life on skid-row lacks a socially structured background of accountability. Of course, everybody's life contains some sequential incongruities, but in the life of a skid-row inhabitant every moment is an accident. That a man has no "address" in the future that could be in some way inferred from where he is and what he does makes him a person of *radically reduced visibility*. If he disappears from sight and one wishes to locate him, it is virtually impossible to systematize the search. All one can know with relative certainty is that he will be somewhere on some skid-row and the only thing one can do is to trace the factual contiguities of his whereabouts.

It is commonly known that the police are expert in finding people and that they have developed an exquisite technology involving special facilities and procedures of sleuthing. It is less well appreciated that all this technology builds upon those socially structured features of everyday life that render persons findable in the first place.

Under ordinary conditions, the query as to where a person is can be addressed, from the outset, to a restricted realm of possibilities that can be further narrowed by looking into certain places and asking certain persons.

The map of whereabouts that normally competent persons use whenever they wish to locate someone is constituted by the basic facts of membership in society. Insofar as membership consists of status incumbencies, each of which has an adumbrated future that substantially reduces unpredictability, it is itself a guarantee of the order within which it is quite difficult to get lost. Membership is thus visible not only now but also as its own projection into the future. It is in terms of this prospective availability that the skid-row inhabitant is a person of reduced visibility. His membership is viewed as extraordinary because its extension into the future is *not* reduced to a restricted realm of possibilities. Neither his subjective dispositions, nor his circumstances, indicate that he is oriented to any particular long-range interests. But, as he may claim every contingent opportunity, his claims are always seen as based on slight merit or right, at least to the extent that interfering with them does not constitute a substantial denial of his freedom.

This, then, constitutes the problem of keeping the peace on skid-row. Considerations of momentary expediency are seen as having unqualified priority as maxims of conduct; consequently, the controlling influences of the pursuit of sustained interests are presumed to be absent.

## THE PRACTICES OF KEEPING
## THE PEACE IN SKID-ROW

From the perspective of society as a whole, skid-row inhabitants appear troublesome in a variety of ways. The uncommitted life attributed to them is perceived as inherently offensive; its very existence arouses indignation and contempt. More important, however, is the feeling that persons who have repudiated the entire role-status casting system of society, persons whose lives forever collapse into a succession of random moments, are seen as constituting a practical risk. As they have nothing to foresake, nothing is thought safe from them.[3]

The skid-row patrolman's concept of his mandate includes an awareness of this presumed risk. He is constantly attuned to the possibility of violence, and he is convinced that things to which the inhabitants have free access are as good as lost. But his concern is directed toward the continuous condition of peril *in the area* rather than *for society in general*. While he is obviously conscious of the presence of many persons who have committed crimes outside of skid-row and will arrest them when they come to his attention, this is a peripheral part of his routine activities. In general, the skid-row patrolman and his superiors take for granted that his main business is to keep the peace and enforce the laws *on skid-row*, and that he is involved only incidentally in protecting society at large. Thus, his task is formulated basically as the protection of putative predators from one another. The maintenance of peace and safety is difficult because everyday life on skid-row is viewed as an open field for reciprocal exploitation. As the lives of the inhabitants lack the prospective coherence associated with status incumbency, the realization of self-interest does not produce order. Hence, mechanisms that control risk must work primarily from without.

External containment, to be effective, must be oriented to the realities of existence. Thus, the skid-row patrolman employs an approach that he views as appropriate to the ad hoc nature of skid-row life. The following are the three most prominent elements of this approach. First, the seasoned patrolman seeks to acquire a richly particularized knowledge of people and places in the area. Second, he gives the consideration of strict culpability a subordinate status among grounds for remedial sanction. Third, his use and choice of coercive interventions is determined mainly by exigencies of situations and with little regard for possible long-range effects on individual persons.

*The Particularization of Knowledge.*    The patrolman's orientation to people on skid-row is structured basically by the presupposition that if he does not know a man personally there is very little that he can assume about him. This rule determines his interaction with people who live on skid-row. Since the area also contains other types of persons, however, its applicability is not universal. To some such persons it does not apply at all, and it has a somewhat mitigated significance with certain others. For example, some persons encountered on skid-row can be recognized immediately as outsiders. Among them are workers who are employed in commercial and industrial enterprises that abut the area, persons who come for the purpose of adventurous "slumming," and some patrons of second-hand stores and pawn shops. Even with very little experience, it is relatively easy to identify these people by appearance, demeanor, and the time and place of their presence. The patrolman maintains an impersonal attitude toward them, and they are, under ordinary circumstances, not the objects of his attention.[4]

Clearly set off from these outsiders are the residents and the entire corps of personnel that services skid-row. It would be fair to say that one of the main routine activities of patrolmen is the establishment and maintenance of familiar relationships with individual members of these groups. Officers emphasize their interest in this, and they maintain that their grasp of and control over skid-row is precisely commensurate with the extent to which they "know the people." By this they do not mean having a quasi-theoretical understanding of human nature but rather the common practice of individualized and reciprocal recognition. As this group encompasses both those who render services on skid-row and those who are serviced, individualized interest is not always based on the desire to overcome uncertainty. Instead, relations with service personnel become absorbed into the network of particularized attention. Ties between patrolmen, on the one hand, and businessmen, managers, and workers, on the other hand, are often defined in terms of shared or similar interests. It bears mentioning that many persons live *and* work on skid-row. Thus, the distinction between those who service and those who are serviced is not a clearcut dichotomy but a spectrum of affiliations.

As a general rule, the skid-row patrolman possesses an immensely detailed factual knowledge of his beat. He knows, and knows a great deal about, a large number of residents. He is likely to know every person who manages or works in the local bars, hotels, shops, stores, and missions. Moreover, he probably knows every public and private place inside and out. Finally, he ordinarily remembers countless events of the past which he can recount by citing names, dates and places with remarkable precision. Though there are always some threads missing in the fabric of information, it is continuously woven and mended even as it is being used. New facts, however, are added to the texture, not in terms of structured categories but in terms of adjoining known realities. In other words, the content and organization of the patrolman's knowledge is primarily ideographic and only vestigially, if at all, nomothetic.

Individual patrolmen vary in the extent to which they make themselves available or actively pursue personal acquaintances. But even the most aloof are continuously greeted and engaged in conversations that indicate a background of individualistic associations. While this scarcely has the appearance of work, because of its casual character, patrolmen do not view it as an optional activity. In the course of making their rounds, patrolmen seem to have access to every place, and their entry causes no surprise or consternation. Instead, the entry tends to lead to informal exchanges of small talk. At times the rounds include entering hotels and gaining access to rooms or dormitories, often for no other purpose than asking the occupants how things are going. In all this, patrolmen address innumerable persons by name and are in turn addressed by name. The conversational style that characterizes these exchanges is casual to an extent that by non-skid-row standards might suggest intimacy. Not only does the officer himself avoid all terms of deference and respect but he does not seem to expect or demand them. For example, a patrolman said to a man radiating an alcoholic glow on the street, "You've got enough of a heat on now; I'll give you ten minutes to get your ass off the street!" Without stopping, the man answered, "Oh, why don't you go and piss on your own pot!" The officer's only response was, "All right, in ten minutes you're either in bed or on your way to the can."

This kind of expressive freedom is an intricately limited privilege. Persons of acquaintance are entitled to it and appear to exercise it mainly in routinized encounters. But strangers, too, can use it with impunity. The safe way of gaining the privilege is to respond to the patrolman in ways that do not challenge his right to ask questions and issue commands. Once the concession is made that the officer is entitled to inquire into a man's background, business, and intentions, and that he is entitled to obedience, there opens a field of colloquial license. A patrolman seems to grant expressive freedom in recognition of a person's acceptance of his access to areas of life ordinarily defined as private and subject to coercive control only under special circumstances. While patrolmen accept and seemingly even cultivate the rough *quid pro quo* of informality and while they do not expect sincerity, candor, or obedience in their dealings with the inhabitants, they do not allow the rejection of their approach.

The explicit refusal to answer questions of a personal nature and the demand to know why the questions are asked significantly enhances a person's chances of being arrested on some minor charge. While most patrolmen tend to be personally indignant about this kind of response and use the arrest to compose their own hurt feelings, this is merely a case of affect being in line with the method. There are other officers who proceed in the same manner without taking offense, or even with feelings of regret. Such patrolmen often maintain that their colleagues' affective involvement is a corruption of an essentially valid technique. The technique is oriented to the goal of maintaining operational control. The patrolman's conception of this goal places him hierarchically above whomever he approaches, and makes him the sole judge of the prosperity of the occasion. As he alone is oriented to this goal, and as he seeks to attain it by means of individualized access to persons, those who frustrate him are seen as motivated at best by the desire to "give him a hard time" and at worst by some darkly devious purpose.

Officers are quite aware that the directness of their approach and the demands they make are difficult to reconcile with the doctrines of civil liberties, but they maintain that they are in accord with the general freedom of access that persons living on skid-row normally grant one another. That is, they believe that the imposition of personalized and far-reaching control is in tune with standard expectancies. In terms of these expectancies, people are not so much denied the right to privacy as they are seen as not having any privacy. Thus, officers seek to install themselves in the center of people's lives and let the consciousness of their presence play the part of conscience.

When talking about the practical necessity of an aggressively personal approach, officers do not refer merely to the need for maintaining control over lives that are open in the direction of the untoward. They also see it as the basis for the supply of certain valued services to inhabitants of skid-row. The coerced or conceded access to persons often imposes on the patrolman tasks that are, in the main, in line with these persons' expressed or implied interest. In asserting this connection, patrolmen note that they frequently help people to obtain meals, lodging, employment, that they direct them to welfare and health services, and that they aid them in various other ways. Though patrolmen tend to describe such services mainly as the product of their own altruism, they also say that their colleagues who avoid them are simply doing a poor job of patrolling. The acceptance of the need to help people is based on the realization that the hungry, the sick, and the troubled are a potential source of problems. Moreover, that patrolmen will help people is part of the background expectancies of life on skid-row. Hotel clerks normally call policemen when someone gets so sick as to need attention; merchants expect to be taxed, in a manner of speaking, to meet the pressing needs of certain persons; and the inhabitants do not hesitate to accept, solicit, and demand every kind of aid. The domain of the patrolman's service activity is virtually limitless, and it is no exaggeration to say that the solution of every conceivable problem has at one time or another been attempted by a police officer. In one observed instance, a patrolman unceremoniously entered the room of a man he had never seen before. The man, who gave no indication that he regarded the officer's entry and questions as anything but part of life as usual, related a story of having had his dentures stolen by his wife. In the course of the subsequent rounds, the patrolman sought to locate the woman and the dentures. This did not become the evening's project but was attended to while doing other things. In the densely matted activities of the patrolman, the questioning became one more strand, not so much to be pursued to its solution as a theme that organized the memory of one more man known individually. In all this, the officer followed the precept formulated by a somewhat more articulate patrolman: "If I want to be in control of my work and keep the street relatively peaceful, I have to know the people. To know them I must gain their trust, which means that I have to be involved in their lives. But I can't be soft like a social worker because unlike him I cannot call the cops when things go wrong. I am the cops!"[5]

*The Restricted Relevance of Culpability.*    It is well-known that policemen exercise discretionary freedom in invoking the law. It is also conceded that, in some measure, the practice is unavoidable. This being so, the outstanding problem is whether or not the decisions are inline with the intent of the law. On skid-row, patrolmen often make decisions based on reasons that the law probably does not recognize as valid. The problem can best be introduced by citing an example.

A man in a relatively mild state of intoxication (by skid-row standards) approached a patrolman to tell him that he had a room in a hotel, to which the officer responded by urging him to go to bed instead of getting drunk. As the man walked off, the officer related the following thoughts: Here is a completely lost soul. Though he probably is no more than thirty-five years old, he looks to be in his fifties. He never works and he hardly ever has a place to stay. He has been on the street for several years and is known as "Dakota." During the past few days, "Dakota" has been seen in the company of "Big Jim." The latter is an invalid living on some sort of pension with which he pays for a room in the hotel to which "Dakota" referred and for four weekly meal tickets in one of the restaurants on the street. Whatever is left he spends on wine and beer. Occasionally, "Big Jim" goes on drinking sprees in the company of someone like "Dakota." Leaving aside the consideration that there is probably a homosexual background to the association, and that it is not right that "Big Jim" should have to support the drinking habit of someone else, there is the more important risk that if "Dakota" moves in with "Big Jim" he will very likely walk off with whatever the latter keeps in his room. "Big Jim" would never dream of reporting the theft; he would just beat the hell out of "Dakota" after he sobered up. When asked what could be done to prevent the theft and the subsequent recriminations, the patrolman proposed that in this particular case he would throw "Big Jim" into jail if he found him tonight and then tell the hotel clerk to throw "Dakota" out of the room. When asked why he did not arrest "Dakota," who was, after all, drunk enough to warrant an arrest, the officer explained that this would not solve anything. While "Dakota" was in jail "Big Jim" would continue drinking and would either strike up another liaison or embrace his old buddy after he had been released. The only thing to do was to get "Big Jim" to sober up, and the only sure way of doing this was to arrest him.

As it turned out, "Big Jim" was not located that evening. But had he been located and arrested on a drunk charge the fact that he was intoxicated would not have been the real reason for proceeding against him, but merely the pretext. The point of the example is not that it illustrates the tendency of skid-row patrolmen to arrest persons who would not be arrested under conditions of full respect for their legal rights. To be sure, this too happens. In the majority of minor arrest cases, however, the criteria the law specifies are met. But it is the rare exception that the law is invoked merely because the specifications of the law are met. That is, compliance with the law is merely the outward appearance of an intervention that is actually based on altogether different considerations. Thus, it could be said that patrolmen do not really enforce the law, even when they do invoke it, but merely use it as a resource to solve certain pressing practical problems in keeping the peace. This observation goes beyond the conclusion that many of the lesser norms of the criminal law are treated as defeasible in police work. It is patently not the case that skid-row patrolmen apply the legal norms while recognizing many exceptions to their applicability. Instead, the observation leads to the conclusion that in keeping the peace on skid-row, patrolmen encounter certain matters they attend to by means of coercive action, e.g., arrests. In doing this, they invoke legal norms that are available, and with some regard for substantive appropriateness. Hence, the problem patrolmen confront is not which drunks, beggars, or disturbers of the peace should be arrested and which can be let go as exceptions to the rule. Rather, the problem is whether, when someone "needs" to be arrested, he should be charged with drunkenness, begging, or disturbing the peace. Speculating further, one is almost compelled to infer that virtually any set of norms could be used in this manner, provided that they sanction relatively common forms of behavior.

The reduced relevance of culpability in peace keeping practice on skidrow is not readily visible. As mentioned, most arrested persons were actually found in the act, or in the state, alleged in the arrest record. It becomes partly visible when one views the treatment of persons who are not arrested even though all the legal grounds for an arrest are present. Whenever such persons are encountered on and can be induced to leave, or taken to some shelter, or remanded to someone's care, then patrolmen feel, or at least maintain, that an arrest would serve no useful purpose. That is, whenever there exist means for controlling the troublesome aspects of some person's presence in some way alternative to an arrest, such means are preferentially employed, provided, of course, that the case at hand involves only a minor offense.[6]

The attenuation of the relevance of culpability is most visible when the presence of legal grounds for an arrest could be questioned, i.e., in cases that sometimes are euphemistically called "preventive arrests." In one observed instance, a man who attempted to trade a pocket knife came to the attention of a patrolman. The initial encounter was attended by a good deal of levity and the man willingly responded to the officer's inquiries about his identity and business. The man laughingly acknowledged that he needed some money to get drunk. In the course of the exchange it came to light that he had just arrived in town, traveling in his automobile. When confronted with the demand to lead the officer to the car, the man's expression became serious and he pointedly stated that he would not comply because this was none of the officer's business. After a bit more prodding, which the patrolman initially kept in the light mood, the man was arrested on a charge involving begging. In subsequent conversation the patrolman acknowledged that the charge was only speciously appropriate and mainly a pretext. Having committed himself to demanding information, he could not accept defeat. When this incident was discussed with another patrolman, the second officer found fault not with the fact that the arrest was made on a pretext but with the first officer's own contribution of the creation of conditions that made it unavoidable. "You see," he continued, "there is always the risk that the man is testing you and you must let him know what is what. The best among us can usually keep the upper hand in such situations without making arrests. But when it comes down to the wire, then you can't let them get away with it."

Finally, it must be mentioned that the reduction of the significance of culpability is built into the normal order of skid-row life, as patrolmen see it. Officers almost unfailingly say, pointing to some particular person, "I know that he knows that I know that some of the things he 'owns' are stolen, and that nothing can be done about it." In saying this, they often claim to have knowledge of such a degree of certainty as would normally be sufficient for virtually any kind of action except legal proceedings. Against this background, patrolmen adopt the view that the law is not merely imperfect and difficult to implement, but that on skid-row, at least, the association between delict and sanction is distinctly occasional. Thus, to implement the law naively, i.e., to arrest someone *merely* because he committed some minor offense, is perceived as containing elements of injustice.

Moreover, patrolmen often deal with situations in which questions of culpability are profoundly ambiguous. For example, an officer was called to help in settling a violent dispute in a hotel room. The object of the quarrel was a supposedly stolen pair of trousers. As the story unfolded in the conflicting versions of the participants, it was not possible to decide who was the complainant and who was alleged to be the thief, nor did it come to light who occupied the room in which the fracas took place, or whether the trousers were taken from the room or to the room. Though the officer did ask some questions, it seemed, and was confirmed in later conversation, that he was there not to solve the puzzle of the missing trousers but to keep the situation from getting out of hand. In the end, the exhausted participants dispersed, and this was the conclusion of the case. The patrolman maintained that no one could unravel mysteries of this sort because "these people take things from each other so often that no one could tell what 'belongs' to whom." In fact, he suggested, the terms owning, stealing, and swindling, in their strict sense, do not really belong on skid-row, and all efforts to distribute guilt and innocence according to some rational formula of justice are doomed to failure.

It could be said that the term "curb-stone justice" that is sometimes applied to the procedures of patrolmen in skid-rows contains a double irony. Not only is the procedure not legally authorized, which is the intended irony in the expression, but it does not even pretend to distribute deserts. The best among the patrolmen, according to their own standards, use the law to keep skid-row inhabitants from sinking deeper into the misery they already experience. The worst, in terms of these same standards, exploit the practice for personal aggrandizement or gain. Leaving motives aside, however, it is easy to see that if culpability is not the salient consideration leading to an arrest in cases where it is patently obvious, then the practical patrolman may not view it as being wholly out of line to make arrests lacking in formal legal justification. Conversely, he will come to view minor offense arrests made solely because legal standards are met as poor craftsmanship.

*The Background of Ad Hoc Decision Making.* When skid-row patrolmen are pressed to explain their reasons for minor offense arrests, they most often mention that it is done for the protection of the arrested person. This, they maintain, is the case in virtually all drunk arrests, in the majority of arrests involving begging and other nuisance offenses, and in many cases involving acts of violence. When they are asked to explain further such arrests as the one cited earlier involving the man attempting to sell the pocket knife, who was certainly not arrested for his own protection, they cite the consideration that belligerent persons constitute a much greater menace on skid-row than any place else in the city. The reasons for this are twofold. First, many of the inhabitants are old, feeble, and not too smart, all of which makes them relatively defenseless. Second, many of the inhabitants are involved in illegal activities and are known as persons of bad character, which does not make them credible victims or witnesses. Potential predators realize that the resources society has mobilized to minimize the risk of criminal victimization do not protect the predator himself. Thus, reciprocal exploitation constitutes a preferred risk. The high vulnerability of everybody on skid-row is public knowledge and causes every seemingly aggressive act to be seen as a potentially grave risk.

When, in response to all this, patrolmen are confronted with the observation that many minor offense arrests they make do not seem to involve a careful evaluation of facts before acting, they give the following explanations: First, the two reasons of protection and prevention represent a global background, and in individual cases it may sometimes not be possible to produce adequate justification on these grounds. Nor is it thought to be a problem of great moment to estimate precisely whether someone is more likely to come to grief or to cause grief when the objective is to prevent the proliferation of troubles. Second, patrolmen maintain that some of the seemingly spur-of-the-moment decisions are actually made against a background of knowledge of facts that are not readily apparent in the situations. Since experience not only contains this information but also causes it to come to mind, patrolmen claim to have developed a special sensitivity for qualities of appearances that allow an intuitive grasp of probable tendencies. In this context, little things are said to have high informational value and lead to conclusions without the intervention of explicitly reasoned chains of inferences. Third, patrolmen readily admit that they do not adhere to high standards of adequacy of justification. They do not seek to defend the adequacy of their method against some abstract criteria of merit. Instead, when questioned, they assess their methods against the background of a whole system of ad hoc decision making, a system that encompasses the courts, correction facilities, the welfare establishment, and medical services. In fact, policemen generally maintain that their own procedures not only measure up to the workings of this system but exceed them in the attitude of carefulness.

In addition to these recognized reasons, there are two additional background factors that play a significant part in decisions to employ coercion. One has to do with the relevance of situational factors, and the other with the evaluation of coercion as relatively insignificant in the lives of the inhabitants.

There is no doubt that the nature of the circumstances often has decisive influence on what will be done. For example, the same patrolman who arrested the man trying to sell his pocket knife was observed dealing with a young couple. Though the officer was clearly angered by what he perceived as insolence and threatened the man with arrest, he merely ordered him and his companion to leave the street. He saw them walking away in a deliberately slow manner and when he noticed them a while later, still standing only a short distance away from the place of encounter, he did not respond to their presence. The difference between the two cases was that in the first there was a crowd of amused bystanders, while the latter case was not witnessed by anyone. In another instance, the patrolman was directed to a hotel and found a father and son fighting about money. The father occupied a room in the hotel and the son occasionally shared his quarters. There were two other men present, and they made it clear that their sympathies were with the older man. The son was whisked off to jail without much study of the relative merits of the conflicting claims. In yet another case, a middle-aged woman was forcefully evacuated from a bar even after the bartender explained that her loud behavior was merely a response to goading by some foulmouthed youth.

In all such circumstances, coercive control is exercised as a means of coming to grips with situational exigencies. Force is used against particular persons but is incidental to the task. An ideal of "economy of intervention" dictates in these and similar cases that the person whose presence is most likely to perpetuate the troublesome development be removed. Moreover, the decision as to who is to be removed is arrived at very quickly. Officers feel considerable pressure to act unhesitatingly, and many give accounts of situations that got out of hand because of desires to handle cases with careful consideration. However, even when there is no apparent risk of rapid proliferation of trouble, the tactic of removing one or two persons is used to control an undesirable situation. Thus, when a patrolman ran into a group of four men sharing a bottle of wine in an alley, he emptied the remaining contents of the bottle into the gutter, arrested one man—who was no more and no less drunk than the others—and let the others disperse in various directions.

The exigential nature of control is also evident in the handling of isolated drunks. Men are arrested because of where they happen to be encountered. In this, it matters not only whether a man is found in a conspicuous place or not, but also how far away he is from his domicile. The further away he is, the less likely it is that he will make it to his room, and the more likely the arrest. Sometimes drunk arrests are made mainly because the police van is available. In one case a patrolman summoned the van to pick up an arrested man. As the van was pulling away from the curb the officer stopped the driver because he sighted another drunk stumbling across the street. The second man protested saying that he "wasn't even half drunk yet." The patrolman's response was "OK, I'll owe you half a drunk." In sum, the basic routine of keeping the peace on skid-row involves a process of matching the resources of control with situational exigencies. The overall objective is to reduce the total amount of risk in the area. In this, practicality plays a considerably more important role than legal norms. Precisely because patrolmen see legal reasons for coercive action much more widely distributed on skid-row than could ever be matched by interventions, they intervene not in the interest of law enforcement but in the interest of producing relative tranquillity and order on the street.

Taking the perspective of the victim of coercive measures, one could ask why he, in particular, has to bear the cost of keeping the aggregate of troubles down while others, who are equally or perhaps even more implicated, go scot-free. Patrolmen maintain that the ad hoc selection of persons for attention must be viewed in the light of the following consideration: Arresting a person on skid-row on some minor charge may save him and others a lot of trouble, but it does not work any real hardships on the arrested person. It is difficult to overestimate the skid-row patrolman's feeling of certainty that his coercive and disciplinary actions toward the inhabitants have but the most passing significance in their lives. Sending a man to jail on some charge that will hold him for a couple of days is seen as a matter of such slight importance to the affected person that it could hardly give rise to scruples. Thus, every indication that a coercive measure should be taken is accompanied by the realization "I might as well, for all it matters to him." Certain realities of life on skid-row furnish the context for this belief in the attenuated relevance of coercion in the lives of the inhabitants. Foremost among them is that the use of police authority is seen as totally unremarkable by everybody on skid-row. Persons who live or work there are continuously exposed to it and take its existence for granted. Shopkeepers, hotel clerks, and bartenders call patrolmen to rid themselves of unwanted and troublesome patrons. Residents expect patrolmen to arbitrate their quarrels authoritatively. Men who receive orders, whether they obey them or not, treat them as part of life as usual. Moreover, patrolmen find that disciplinary and coercive actions apparently do not affect their friendly relations with the person against whom these actions are taken. Those who greet and chat with them are the very same men who have been disciplined, arrested, and ordered around in the past, and who expect to be thus treated again in the future. From all this, officers gather that though the people on skid-row seek to evade police authority, they do not really object to it. Indeed, it happens quite frequently that officers encounter men who welcome being arrested and even actively ask for it. Finally, officers point out that sending someone to jail from skid-row does not upset his relatives or his family life, does not cause him to miss work or lose a job, does not lead to his being reproached by friends and associates, does not lead to failure to meet commitments or protect investments, and does not conflict with any but the most passing intentions of the arrested person. Seasoned patrolmen are not oblivious to the irony of the fact that measures intended as mechanisms for distributing deserts can be used freely because these measures are relatively impotent in their effects.

## SUMMARY AND CONCLUSIONS

It was the purpose of this paper to render an account of a domain of police practice that does not seem subject to any system of external control. Following the terminology suggested by Michael Banton, this practice was called keeping the peace. The procedures employed in keeping the peace are not determined by legal mandates but are, instead, responses to certain demand conditions. From among several demand conditions, we concentrated on the one produced by the concentration of certain types of persons in districts known as skid-row. Patrolmen maintain that the lives of the inhabitants of the area are lacking prospective coherence. The consequent reduction in the temporal horizon of predictability constitutes the main problem of keeping the peace on skid-row.

Peace keeping procedure on skid-row consists of three elements. Patrolmen seek to acquire a rich body of concrete knowledge about people by cultivating personal acquaintance with as many residents as possible. They tend to proceed against persons mainly on the basis of perceived risk, rather than on this basis of culpability. And they are more interested in reducing the aggregate total of troubles in the area than in evaluating individual cases according to merit.

There may seem to be a discrepancy between the skid-row patrolman's objective of preventing disorder and his efforts to maintain personal acquaintance with as many persons as possible. But these efforts are principally a tactical device. By knowing someone individually, the patrolman reduces ambiguity, extends trust and favors, but does not grant immunity. The informality of interaction on skid-row always contains some indications of the hierarchical superiority of the patrolman and the reality of his potential power lurks in the background of every encounter.

Though our interest was focused initially on these police procedures that did not involve invoking the law, we found that the two cannot be separated. The reason for the connection is not given in the circumstance that the roles of the "law officer" and of the "peace officer" are enacted by the same person and thus are contiguous. According to our observations, patrolmen do not act alternatively as one or the other, with certain actions being determined by the intended objective of keeping the peace and others being determined by the duty to enforce the law. Instead, we have found that *peace keeping occasionally acquires the external aspects of law enforcement.* This makes it specious to inquire whether or not police discretion in invoking the law conforms with the intention of some specific legal formula. The real reason behind an arrest is virtually always the actual state of particular social situations, or of the skid-row area in general.

We have concentrated on those procedures and considerations that skid-row patrolmen regard as necessary, proper, and efficient relative to the circumstances in which they are employed. In this way, we attempted to disclose the conception of the mandate to which the police feel summoned. It was entirely outside the scope of the presentation to review the merits of this conception and of the methods used to meet it. Only insofar as patrolmen themselves recognized instances and patterns of malpractice did we take note of them. Most of the criticism voiced by officers had to do with the use of undue harshness and with the indiscriminate use of arrest powers when these were based on personal feelings rather than the requirements of the situation. According to prevailing opinion, patrolmen guilty of such abuses make life unnecessarily difficult for themselves and for their co-workers. Despite disapproval of harshness, officers tend to be defensive about it. For example, one sergeant who was outspokenly critical of brutality, said that though in general brutal men create more problems than they solve, "They do a good job in some situations for which the better men have no stomach." Moreover, supervisory personnel exhibit a strong reluctance to direct their subordinates in the particulars of their work performance. According to our observations, control is exercised mainly through consultation with superiors, and directives take the form of requests rather than orders. In the background of all this is the belief that patrol work on skid-row requires a great deal of discretionary freedom. In the words of the same sergeant quoted above, "A good man has things worked out in his own ways on his beat and he doesn't need anybody to tell him what to do."

The virtual absence of disciplinary control and the demand for discretionary freedom are related to the idea that patrol work involves "playing by ear." For if it is true that peace keeping cannot be systematically generalized, then, of course, it cannot be organizationally constrained. What the seasoned patrolman means, however, in saying that he "plays by ear" is that he is making his decisions while being attuned to the realities of complex situations about which he has immensely detailed knowledge. This studied aspect of peace keeping generally is not made explicit, nor is the tyro or the outsider made aware of it. Quite to the contrary, the ability to discharge the duties associated with keeping the peace is viewed as a reflection of an innate talent of "getting along with people." Thus, the same demands are made of barely initiated officers as are made of experienced practitioners. Correspondingly, beginners tend to think that they can do as well as their more knowledgeable peers. As this leads to inevitable frustrations, they find themselves in a situation that is conducive to the development of a particular sense of "touchiness." Personal dispositions of individual officers are, of course, of great relevance. But the license of discretionary freedom and the expectation of success under conditions of autonomy, without any indication that the work of the successful craftsman is based on an acquired preparedness for the task, is ready-made for failure and malpractice. Moreover, it leads to slipshod practices of patrol that also infect the standards of the careful craftsman.

The uniformed patrol, and especially the foot patrol, has a low preferential value in the division of labor of police work. This is, in part, at least, due to the belief that "anyone could do it." In fact, this belief is thoroughly mistaken. At present, however, the recognition that the practice requires preparation, and the process of obtaining the preparation itself, is left entirely to the practitioner.

## NOTES

Reprinted from *American Sociological Review* 32, no. 5 (October 1967): 699–715. Used with permission.

1. The literature on skid-row is voluminous. The classic in the field is Nels Anderson, *The Hobo*, Chicago: University of Chicago Press, 1923. Samuel E. Wallace, *Skid-Row as a Way of Life*, Totowa, New Jersey: The Bedminster Press, 1965, is a more recent descriptive account and contains a useful bibliography. Donald A. Bogue, *Skid-Row in American Cities*, Chicago: Community and Family Center, University of Chicago, 1963, contains an exhaustive quantitative survey of Chicago skid-row.

2. One of the two cities described in this paper also employed the procedure of the "round-up" of drunks. In this, the police van toured the skid row area twice daily, during the mid-afternoon and early evening hours, and the officers who manned it picked up drunks they sighted. A similar procedure is used in New York's Bowery and the officers who do it are called "condition men." Cf. *Bowery Project*, Bureau of Applied Social Research, Columbia University, Summary Report of a Study Undertaken under Contract Approved by the Board of Estimates, 1963, mimeo., p. 11.

3. An illuminating parallel to the perception of skid-row can be found in the more traditional concept of vagabondage. Cf. Alexandre Vexliard, *Introduction à la Sociologie du Vagabondage*, Paris: Libraire Marcel Riviere, 1956, and "La Disparition du Vagabondage comme Fleau Social Universel," *Revue de L'Instut de Sociologie* (1963), 53–79. The classic account of English conditions up to the 19th century is C. J. Ribton-Turner, *A History of Vagrants and Vagrancy and Beggars and Begging*, London: Chapman and Hall, 1887.

4. Several patrolmen complained about the influx of "tourists" into skid-row.

Since such "tourists" are perceived as seeking illicit adventure, they receive little sympathy from patrolmen when they complain about being victimized.

5. The same officer commented further, "If a man looks for something, I might help him. But I don't stay with him till he finds what he is looking for. If I did, I would never get to do anything else. In the last analysis, I really never solve any problems. The best I can hope for is to keep things from getting worse."

6. When evidence is present to indicate that a serious crime has been committed, considerations of culpability acquire a position of priority. Two such arrests were observed, both involving checkpassers. The first offender was caught *in flagrante delicto.* In the second instance, the suspect attracted the attention of the patrolman because of his sickly appearance. In the ensuing conversation the man made some remarks that led the officer to place a call with the Warrant Division of his department. According to the information that was obtained by checking records, the man was a wanted checkpasser and was immediately arrested.

# 12

# The Slanted Smile Factory: Emotion Management in Tokyo Disneyland

*Aviad E. Raz*

Since its opening in April 15, 1983, in the Tokyo Bay area, Tokyo Disneyland (TDL) has been attracting a yearly crowd of well over 10 million visitors (16 million in 1996), which makes it the most popular diversionary outing in Japan and relatively more successful than the two Disney theme parks in America. Owned and operated by a Japanese company (Oriental Land Co.), TDL is claimed by its owners to be a 100 percent copy of the original Disneyland. TDL, however, was also carefully edited and modified to cater to Japanese consumerist and cultural predilections. It is, therefore, a unique cultural, organizational and consumerist junction where "Japan" meets "America."

This study is the result of participant observation at TDL which was conducted during 1995–1996. I paid for the many visits from my pocket, and often wandered around in the park like any other visitor. At other times I was chaperoned; I participated in five TDL's official guided tours, as well as in eight unofficial tours guided by OLC employees and by Disney engineers ("imagineers"). Each of the guided tours I attended took about four hours, and they were conducted in various seasons (summer through winter). In order to examine the reception of TDL by its visitors more systematically, I videotaped the rides and discussed them with six Japanese key-informants. These discussions followed the methodology of focus groups research. Following a brief ad I had place in the *Tokyo Classifieds,* I conducted interviews with 30 OLC employees: 21 part-timers (10 of them worked in Foods Division, but I managed to interview at least one employee of each of OLC's major divisions, including Attractions, Merchandising, and Personnel) and nine regular employees. Informal interviews were held in cafes and restaurants, lasted between one to three hours and were usually taped. All the workers I spoke to who were currently employed in TDL requested anonymity, and their names have consequently been changed, or omitted altogether. Additional interviews were conducted with Japanese scholars and journalists. These interviews were conducted in various stages of the fieldwork and covered various issues related to Disney.

To discuss Tokyo Disneyland is to discuss a transplant. When studying Tokyo Disneyland, one in fact studies how Disney has traveled to Japan, how a significant piece of American business, ideology, and fantasy has been remade in Japan. On the face of it, this is a case study in globalization—Disney as the black ship of American leisure and pop culture, and how it conquered Japan. My main argument, in contrast, is that Tokyo Disneyland reveals the opposite—namely the active appropriation of Disney by the Japanese. This can be shown from three angles: Onstage, backstage, and consumption. Onstage is DisneyTalk for the physical design of the park and its rides; consumption deals with the ways in which TDL has been worked into the everyday life of different consumerist age groups. In this chapter I focus the "backstage," the organization, from a perspective of emotion management.

To American managers and businessmen, Disneyland is the Sistine Chapel of service culture: An American model for training and people management. A lot has been written—by business journalists and sociologists—on the Disney University in Anaheim, California, in which all employees—or Cast Members—go through two courses called indoctrination number 1 and 2. There is ample literature on the Disney manuals, in which work procedures and scripts for courtesy talk are meticulously written down, as well as on the emotion management practiced on, and by, the employees of the smile factory.[1] Disney's worlds are a fertile ground for a sensitive and critical sociology of emotions. Indeed, the Disney view of human nature is basically emotional; according to TDL's Trainer's Manual, the correct answer to the question "what moves people?" is "20% reason, 80% emotion."

## WORKING FOR TDL

TDL is a big organization. It has 12,390 Cast Members (as of April 1, 1995); 2,540 of these are regular employees and 9,850 are part-time employees (TDL 1998, p. 2). Every day, over 600 entertainers appear in stage shows, musical performances, and parades. Employees are distinctively divided into two groups: part-time workers (*pato, arubaito,* or more formally, *junshain*), and regular employees (*shain*). OLC managers usually say that these two groups are two different worlds. This division of the work force, it should be mentioned, exists both in WDW and DL employment systems, as well as in local Japanese organizations. My presentation will focus on part-time Cast Members, whose life has been already described in the context of DL (Disneyland) and WDW (Walt Disney World). This provides a relatively solid basis of information for comparing TDL and its "originals." It should be noted that the dual market structure of part- and full-time work is a prominent example of the control exerted by the company on its internal labor market. The difference between part- and full-time workers is particularly blatant in Japan, where the "three pillars" of the Japanese system—seniority system, lifetime employment, and company union membership—are limited to regular workers. The part-timers, therefore, are the first to feel the effects of economic downturn: in the oil shock of 1973, for example, they were the proverbial "first fired" (Nakamura 1981, p. 171; cited in Kondo 1990, p. 275). In general, however, the part-time labor market was remarkably increased in Japan since the end of World War II, particularly with the increased entry of unmarried, as well as married, women into the paid labor force, usually as part-time workers, and usually into the retail and service sectors (Lo 1990; Kondo 1990). For the employer, part-time labor offers savings in wages, a solution to labor shortages (of permanent workers), and flexibility in responding to fluctuations in work pace and in demand for a product or service. For the part-timers, the opportunity to work on a part-time basis usually accommodates the need to earn important supplemental income while keeping another primary loyalty (family, school). Employers, in turn, generally point to these attitudes as justification for hiring part-time workers and keeping them in low-paying jobs with little hope for promotion. Industrial relations are therefore split between regular workers and part-timers. According to the popular image, regular workers are hardworking university graduates reflecting the values of the "old generation," while part-timers are unconcerned housewives and irresponsible students that reflect the lack of values of the "new generation," "the generation that awaits directions" (Sengoku 1985). This split is backed up by real facts. Regular workers usually had the lifetime employment and seniority system (*nenko*) to look forward to and the *kumiai* (enterprise-based union) to lean on. Part-timers were exempted from all these. Regulars were fully socialized into company life, while part-timers were only trained to do their particular job. According to the common assertion, it is only *seishain*, not *junshain*, who became *shakaijin* (society people; adults) by virtue of joining the company.

## EMOTION MANAGEMENT AND
## THE DISNEY WAY

In her influential book *The Managed Heart: Commercialization of Human Feeling*, Arlie Hochschild (1983) coined the term "emotion management" in the context of the service work of flight attendants in Delta Airlines. Emotion management was defined by Hochschild as a transmutation of three basic elements of emotional life: emotion work, feeling rules, and social exchange. These elements are part of everyday emotional life, but employees of service companies are taught to *manage* them in a special way.

First, emotion work is "no longer a private act but a public act, bought on the one hand and sold on the other" (Hochschild 1983, p. 118). It is no longer the individual who decides on the right emotional display, but "the company" as represented by the trainer, the manual, and the management.

Second, feeling rules—social scripts that tell us what to feel and how to express our feelings in various situations—are no longer an unwritten, personal and often vague matter, contingent upon the individuals' upbringing and character. Feeling rules are now spelled out publicly—in the "Tips on Magic" and other Disney manuals, in training programs and in the discourse of supervisors at all levels.

Third, social exchange is forced into narrow channels. It is no longer an improvised, real-time, on-the-spot face-to-face interaction, but a carefully prescribed, pre-scripted and stage-managed "show." In what follows I examine three types of work stories: morality stories referred to as "magic moments," complaint stories about what the company calls "communication," and horror stories. These stories illustrate how the transmutation into emotion management is achieved in TDL, and what is its price.

## Magic Moments

Emotion management begins as early as the first day or orientation, when instructors beseech recruits to wish every guest "a nice day" (*tanoshimi kudasai,* in TDL's spiel). The service motto on the "Tips on Magic" manual is "we create happiness." "Happiness" (*hapinesu*) is also the correct answer to the orientation-quiz question "We TDL Cast Members provide _____ to all the guests." Even more direct emotional manipulation is involved in the prohibition, first uttered in orientation, not to talk with Guests about backstage. Miyo, a young Cast Member: "Trainers say, people have dreams about Disneyland, you cannot break their dream, it would break their heart." And, there are the customary "magic moments" stories. In WDW, the most popular of these is "the popcorn story":

> Emerging from the theatre, a mother buys her young son a box of popcorn from an open-air stand. Seconds later, the lad, who looks to be about four, trips and falls. The popcorn spills, the boy bawls, the mother screams. A costumed Cast Member on his way to another attraction happens by. Barely breaking stride, he scoops up the empty cardboard box, takes it to the popcorn stand for

a refill, presents it to the shattered child, and continues on his way (WDW trainer Robert Sias, cited in Henkoff 1995, p. 115).

I have heard the same story told about ice-cream cones and balloons. Always a child is involved; there are no stories about refilling Mom's spilt coffee. There is always the "spontaneity" with which the magic is performed. A number of interrelated lessons about emotions are instilled in these stories. The first implies that everything in the park should be controlled, every mishap quickly taken care of, because this is the meaning of "happiness." Cast Members therefore learn that everything they do on stage is meaningful, and should therefore be under total control. It is a show, but it must look "real," including the production of "spontaneity" and the stage-management of emotion-conveying behavior such as smiling, welcoming, or thanking. Furthermore, emotion-management training cleverly uses these little stories in two important ways. By emphasizing such "magic moments," trainers try to instill verve in jobs that are otherwise tightly regimented. Secondly, the "magic moment" implies that there is an actual emotional reward to be gained from doing your job, as monotonous as it is. By producing "happiness," you make yourself happy. There is ample emotional conditioning at work here. The "magic moment" teaches the employee that s/he does not work for such mundane matters as getting paid, but for a greater cause—for the "happiness" of Guests, maybe even for one's own "happiness." This is explicitly suggested in "The Tokyo Disneyland Show," a manual handed to Cast Members during orientation, which begins with the following recommendation (written inside a Mickey-shaped frame):

> The key to happiness is communicating with Guests. . . . We also hope you will be able to find your own happiness through working here (signed by Kozo Kato, president, OLC).

Academic cynicism aside, these moments might actually be magical for the "4-year-old child" who dropped his or her popcorn. However, many Cast Members soon realize the magician's sleight of hand behind such stories and the commodification of emotion underlying their work environment. While discussing the "magic moments" stories, a Cast Member said:

> You know, they have a message service in the park, the one you usually hear Disney music coming through. It's not supposed to be used as a message service, though. The Leads realize we know it exists, so they tell us, if a guest comes to you in panic because she hasn't seen her baby for an hour, don't mention the message system. They tell us, using the message system too often will destroy the atmosphere of dreams and magic. It's there only for emergencies, you know. In the bottom line, the "atmosphere" is more important than actually helping out people.

Other workers recalled the strict prohibition against speaking with family members who might be visiting the park: "Leads tell us: you're on duty, don't talk personally. Even if we want to make a phone call to home during breaks, we must do it through the area office telephone, and only emergency calls are allowed. It's like being in jail." Other Cast Members mentioned the accidents manual ("incidents" in DisneyTalk). This manual was directly copied from WDW. Following an accident, the closest employee (usually a part-timer) should first call a supervisor (management) and then first aid. "Why not the first aid first?" I was asked by several naïve Cast Members. The manual then instructs the employees attending the victim to immediately write down any admission uttered by him or her regarding self-carelessness (for a discussion of the similar DL and WDW manual, see Adler 1983; Toufexis 1985; Dryman 1995, p. 121).

Some of the "magic moments" stories were apparently too manipulative. Yamada, a custodial Cast Member in TDL, recounted the following story told during custodial orientation:

> They told us about a young custodian who used to give names to every toilet stool. This way he could work harder. We were laughing, because the trainer used silly names to illustrate this, anyway, the story goes on. The young custodian was thinking of quitting his job, it was too hard for him. But then, OLC sent him for a training visit to Disneyland. We were going *"sugoi!"* (cool!) it's good to know that we too might get to fly to California. Anyway, while in Disneyland this Japanese custodian meets with an American colleague, and he asks the American: excuse me, what do you do to get over the hard work? So the American goes, all these toilets here are my friends. I give them names. I remember thinking, it must be pretty rough out there if these are the best stories they could come up with to encourage us. (A similar "toilet story" is cited in Kano 1986, p. 102.)

## "COMMUNICATION" STORIES

At this point I would like to move from the "magic moments" stories to more mundane work stories, whose common denominator is another hallmark of the Disney language.

### Communication

Many Cast Members experienced their "emotional dissonance" in the context of communication. According to Miyo,

> In front of where I work there's a toilet. Guests come and ask me "where's the toilet," and I point towards the direction. After a few minutes they come back

and ask me in a low voice, "isn't that a restaurant?" You see, the toilet has an English sign saying "rest rooms," and they think "rest" stands for "*resuto*" (a Japanese rendering for "restaurant"). I've asked my leads so many times why they won't change the sign. They replied that it's good for communication.

Many Cast Members are conscious of the stage-management of communication. "We all know why OLC wants us to say '*ohayho gozaiemasu*' instead of '*irasshaiase*,'" said a shop clerk ('merchandising assistant'); "they can call it "communication" if they like. . . . It's just another label, a page from the manual."

While the communication spiel is part of the global DisneyTalk, reactions to it among Cast Members differ locally. TDL Cast Members generally find it easier than U.S. Cast Members to distance themselves from the Disney language because it is, after all, a *foreign* language. "Communication" is conceived as yet another buzzword, a façade, something "imported from America," a trendy slogan which has no contents. For Japanese Cast Members, this holds true in regard to DisneyTalk in general. Disney language, like all language, plays a crucial role in socialization and emotion management (see Eisenberg and Goodall 1993 for a discussion of the organizational role of Disney language). As Kuenz (1995, p. 112) argues, "most (WDW Cast members) have internalized the Disney terms; they *never* say uniform, but costume, just as they always say cast, onstage, and backstage." Smith and Eisenberg (1987) similarly report that in their interviews with DL employees, no one used taboo terms such as "customer," "amusement park," or "uniforms" when talking about their work. In TDL, in contrast, Disney language will always remain ultimately foreign to Cast Members. They learn it, use it, and play with it, but leave it behind them when going home. Many have told me that "using the Disney language when speaking with family or friends will simply require too much explaining."

The reaction to DisneyTalk reflects the overall use of English as a foreign language in Japan. The contemporary Japanese city dweller regards English primarily as a fun language of brand names, TV commercials, and the "new music" designed for the "new generation" of Japanese teenagers and young adults (Stanlow 1992). In *Nantonaku Kurisutaru* (Somehow, Crystal), the 1981 bestseller which celebrated the fashion-driven, commodified urban Japanese society, author Tanaka Yasuo suggested that an item labeled with an English loanword is made special. He gives the example of *rein butsu* (rain boots):

They are just *nagagutu* (boots; literally, long shoes). However, when they are called *rein butsu*, even a rainy day makes us feel real up, and when there is a puddle we try to jump into it with a splash, on purpose (Tanaka 1981, p. 151; cited in Stanlow 1992, p. 67).

In TDL, Disney's "communication" works like Tanaka's *rein butsu*. It is used to make one "feel real up," while at the same time openly acknowledging the illusion. For the Japanese, Disney parlance ultimately consists of loanwords—not organizational metaphors to live by, but rather temporary facades to play with. Most Cast Members I talked with did not use the Disney words "naturally," like Kuenz's (1995) informants or Van Maanen's (1991) ride operators. For example, attraction guides used the Japanese word *serifu* (theatrical text) instead of "spiel," while merchandising assistants talked about *aisatsu* in this context; nobody ever said "spieler," just *joho* (literally "information," the title of the Cast member who spiels in front of a restaurant, for example). In a similar vein, most Cast Members referred to themselves as *junshain* and to their Lead as *senpai-shain*.

DisneyTalk is a major protagonist in the story of communication in TDL. Overall, DisneyTalk in TDL reflects the use of English in Japan, which represents an intriguing case of domestication. While the use of English after the War and perhaps up to the 1960s could be viewed as a symbol of Americanization, or of a strong American influence, during the past 20 years the use of English has developed many characteristics of its own. The Japanese-English vocabulary

> incorporated many elements which are not understandable for Americans or other people who speak English as a native language. The Japanese mass media producers have created their own standards for using English, promoting English as a symbol of modernity (Haarmann 1989, p. 16).

The appropriation of English in Japan usually does not induce linguistic change within the host language. That is, English is increasingly being used, but without changing the structure of Japanese in terms of syntax and semantics. Because of orthography, English itself is being changed: the katakana that Japanese use for writing a foreign word, as Stanlow (1992, p. 70) describes it, "instantly domesticates it by forcing the borrowed term to conform to the Japanese phonological system." The language contact between Japanese and English therefore does not follow a pattern of "pidginization" or "creolization," but rather a kind of "departmentalization" (or maybe "depatoization"). English loanwords and catch phrases, in the (globally incomprehensible) Japanese pronunciation, enjoy a commercial appeal and recognition but their meaning is completely clear "only to a minority" (Haarmann 1989, p. 145). English in Japan is arguably copyrighted language, largely considered as artificial and superficial—the language of the department store, the depato. Because of its cultural adaptation, today it would seem odd to speak of the use of English as a sign of "Americanization." I stressed this point since it is equally relevant to TDL. The use of DisneyTalk in TDL, and the use of English in Japan, both exemplify the way Japan has locally adapted global culture.

## Horror Stories

Another popular type of Cast Members narratives, and perhaps the most creative of them, are horror stories. This intriguing genre is the dark opposite of the bright "magic moments" recounted by the company's trainers. Hirono, a Cast Member in Foods:

> There's this rumor: We have a rest room next to the Plaza Pavilion Restaurant. One day a lady was screaming "help me," her kid was stuck in the toilet. *Shain* went to see what happened and pulled out the kid. She was dead already because it was too late and nobody could help her. It's a tragic story.

Such unauthorized, unofficial, subterranean "urban myths" are a global phenomenon. They can be found in all of Disney's worlds, indeed everywhere for that matter (Goode and Ben-Yehuda 1994, pp. 108–112; Best 1989). They are told as true, and are widely believed, but lack factual verification. According to Kuenz's (1995, p. 1170) respondents, WDW has a much larger and more brute share of horror stories:

> No one (outside the company) had ever heard the story of the young mother whose rented paddle boat was sucked into the wake of the Empress Lily where, before the eyes of her gasping seven-year-old, the ship's paddle wheel chopped her quite in half.

This cross-cultural prevalence of horror stories, notwithstanding their possible factuality, is also a subversive act. First, it subverts the company's prescribed myth of total control over its property, employees and customers. Second, it subverts company rules described as "forbidding anyone even to raise the issue." Some of these horror stories, like Jungian-inspired nightmares, capture the essence of Disney culture, its totems and taboos. It is particularly intriguing when two or more stories, told independently in Japan and America, embody a similar narrative. The following two stories illustrate this.

> A family from Kyushu once came to TDL. Two parents and three big children. The children were determined to see who's inside Mickey Mouse, and they tore off the costume's head. OLC sued them and they had to pay 10 million yen.

The second story, entitled "the first Mickey Mouse," is a WDW horror story recorded by Kuenz (1995, p. 116):

(The first Mickey Mouse) has a bad skin problem. He has cancer of the skin. He got it from wearing the mask of Mickey Mouse—the head gear. His mother sued for him—he'd never been married—and he has a job guaranteed with Disney for the rest of his life. He's in his late fifties at least. But he has to be behind the scenes because of his skin. Nobody wants to look at him.

Although different, the two stories share a similar, obsessive concern with the mask—the head gear—of Mickey Mouse and the real face behind it. The question "who (or what) lurks behind the mask" is a traditional horror-story theme, but its meaning is arguably expanded here. The two stories illustrate that the answer to that question is never pleasant; seeing the forbidden face always involve some kind of punishment or other dire consequences. To tear Mickey's head off and expose the cancer-ridden face behind it evidently reflects a desire to dispel the illusion of Disney. Company rules strictly forbid to remove the head gear until out of public view; doing this under any other circumstances means automatic dismissal. There are various horror stories on Disney characters vomiting inside the head or passing out because of the heat and being left on the float until the parade returns backstage (Kuenz 1995, p. 137). The Disney characters, although invisible inside their costumes, are subjected to the most stringent control. Not only them but all employees are repeatedly warned not to "break character." This warning is turned into a horror story even by the management. Kuenz (1995, p. 137) quotes how

> one management type recounted in a training session the story of taking his visiting niece into the tunnels to find Snow White. When they met her, she turned on them, cigarette and Diet Coke in hand, and told them "Get the hell out of here. I'm on break." The child was crushed, the spell broken.

All these different "mask stories" were told by different people in different times and places. In that sense, their surface similarities are amazing. The stories need to be sociologically located in two larger contexts: the organizational and the cultural.

First, the organization. It is arguably working for Disney—the "iron cage of fun"—that has produced the similar narrative of these stories. The narrative can be concisely defined as a "crime and punishment" formula. It begins with a specific transgression: the need to talk to or about the "real" person inside the costume. This feat is achieved only with much planning and trouble. The quest for the "real" person under the disguise reveals an obsession with the strict company line separating onstage (the mask, the costume) from backstage (the face, the person). The horror stories show how this company rule has been transmuted into and internalized as a feeling rule. To cross the line, to tear off the mask, is to break character. Within the horror story, this obsession is temporarily thrown into relief, and given a cathartic release;

then it is quickly punished. In the end of the day, the mask returns to its place. Nobody wants or dares to look at the real face behind it. This is, in a nutshell, the story of Disney's emotional subjugation. Every horror story always already contains its own self-disciplinary morale.

Reflecting the global reality of working for Disney, these horror stories are also arguably told, with local variation, in every large service company. Hochschild's flight attendants, for example, spoke of "anger fantasies" with a strong oral component, such as "befouling the passenger's food and watching him eat it" (1983, p. 114). The strict feelings rules, drawn by the Disney company between onstage and backstage, yield similar horror-and-morale stories in the United States and Japan. However, such stories should also be located in a second, broader cultural context. Anthropological research on Japanese culture and socialization suggests that the onstage/backstage line is more easily accommodated by Japanese Cast Members than by Americans. The onstage/backstage distinction fits into the traditional and much-discussed Japanese duality of *tatemae/honne*. This paradigm, approximately translated as the difference between public/private and appearance/reality, is not unique to Japan but rather a universal "ideal type" of human psychology (see also Moeran 1989, p. 3). Mead's (1932) famous distinction between the "I" and the "me," two major constructs of Western social psychology, is an example of that universality. However, sociologists of Japan have long argued that Japanese society has taken the "I/me" duality much further and much more for granted. Feeling rules that define and link *tatemae* (onstage) and *honne* (backstage) are more uniformly and closely scripted in Japan than in the United States (Tobin, Wu and Davidson 1989). Given the prevalence of this cultural script in Japan, the implication is that Japanese Cast Members are likely to be less concerned than Americans about "being phony"—a central issue in both Hochschild's (1983) and Kuenz's (1995) studies, the former on flight attendants and the latter on WDW Cast Members. As White (1993, p. 39) argues, "In the American context, appearance and reality are not a matched pair, but a contrasting set, representing not a balance but a flawed contradiction."

Is this cultural conditioning, of appearance and reality as a matched pair, ascertained in the context of Japanese Cast Members? The answer is, to say the least, complicated. Measuring one's "real" resistance to emotional subjugation (if at all possible) is an intricate feat, particularly when "real feelings" are discussed in the artificial context of an interview. The range of Cast Members' reactions was varied and it is difficult to generalize. Overall, however, TDL Cast Members expressed relatively little concern about "being phony." It was taken-for-granted as part of the job, part of the show, and part of social life in general. Furthermore, most TDL Cast Members expressed their frustration not with the "Disney Way," but rather in conjunction with their position in Foods Division (and not Attractions). "Role distance"—distancing one's "private" self from the social, or organizational role with which one is assigned "onstage"—was therefore much less of a problem in the eyes of Japanese Cast Members. A receptionist working for OLC said that she used *keigo* (polite, onstage speech) unconsciously because it has become "second nature." This illustrates how cultural conditioning can provide a better socialization for organizational roles. While deducing someone else's "true" emotional reactions is never certain, I can assert with some confidence that no "redefinition of self," as Hochschild describes it, was necessary for the Japanese Cast Members I interviewed. Rather, it was a "redefinition of job" that was desired by those working in Foods. However, this was not due to emotional subjugation at work, but because of the boredom, physical difficulty, and low status of the job. Those who considered the job too boring or without real chances of promotion, simply quit.

## THE *MANAGED HEART* REVISITED

The analysis of emotion management in TDL has further implications or a sociology of emotions sensitive to its global moment. A double juxtaposition is involved here: comparing TDL (Japan) with DL or WDW (America), as well as comparing the "Disney Way" with other service codes turned into feeling rules. In doing the first type of comparison, local cultural variations have emerged; the second type of comparison focuses on one culture, "service culture," as a global project. While Hochschild's analytical categories (such as "feeling rules") were proved to be very relevant to TDL (thus highlighting the common, global features of "service culture"), this comparison also undermines some of Hochschild's analytical premises. Hochschild's sociology of emotions hinges on the flight attendants' conceptualizations of, and reactions to, "feeling rules" and "emotion management." It sometimes ignores the fact, however, that these conceptualizations and reactions are themselves part of a larger cultural system that goes beyond "service culture," commercialization and capitalism (in this sense I agree with some of Wouters's 1989 criticism). When flight attendants (and Hochschild) worry about "true" and "false" selves in the culture-specific way they worry about them, it is not just because of the "commercialization of human life" and their work in the service sector; it is also because they are American. As White (1993, p. 97) lively puts it in the context of teenage socialization,

> The Japanese teen is, by the end of middle school, acutely aware of the distinction between private propensities and values (*honne*) on the one hand, and correct social performance (*tatemae*) on the other. . . . American teens, too, are aware of this, but *they see more often the distinction as disillusioning: their sensitivity to what they see as hypocritical is conditioned by a cultural norm which*

*favors "being yourself" over an accommodation to others through self-discipline and sensitivity.* (My emphasis.)

This study focused on one organization; it certainly does not purport to serve as a general basis for analyzing all other service settings, which present considerable variance. My comparative analysis will focus on one of the more intriguing of Hochschild's conceptual pairs: surface and deep acting. Surface acting is "simple pretending." "Deep acting," a skill learned in Delta's Recurrent Training course, involves emotional identification. For example, in dealing with passengers who were rude or aggressive, flight attendants would think of reasons to excuse the passengers' behavior and make themselves feel sorry or sympathetic rather than angry. Surface acting is acting "by the manual," acting with the body (prompt and proper outward gestures) but without "the feeling." It is *katachi* (form) without *kokoro* (feeling), in Kondo's (1990) concepts. Deep acting is both form and feeling. It is Stanislavsky's Method acting. It is acting "as if this unruly passenger has a traumatic past" (Hochschild 1983, p. 120).

Surface and deep acting may be a characteristic of flight attendants, who work in a unique service territory where interactions are long-term (a 15 hour flight is not inconceivable) and performed in a narrow and over-populated enclosure (the airplane). In TDL (and many other service settings), the employee usually does not see the same customer again (at least not in the same day). I argue that consequently, the Cast Members I interviewed did not speak about "surface" versus "deep" acting in the same way that Hochschild's flight attendants did. Neither was this distinction (or a similar one) mentioned in the Disney manuals. To be sure, the manuals had a lot to say about the Cast Members' role in the show, and employees took it for granted that they were supposed to be "acting." But it was all one-dimensional acting. It was service acting. Indeed, as Cast Members (and most other service attendants) knew too well, the "acting" and "cast" image was not *real*. It was something the company sold them, a rhetorical façade made to keep them "real up."

I suggest that what we can call "ephemeral service"—part-time, short-term, short-lived, mass-produced and anonymously delivered service—involves another conceptualization of acting, which is different from either surface or deep acting. The mode of service acting that is inculcated and practiced in TDL can be defined as *symbolic typing*. I suggest that this concept is also relevant to other forms of "ephemeral service." Symbolic types are reified paradigms of behavior embodied by participants through a fixed set of performative practices. Their existence is not limited to and did not start in service culture. On the contrary, these are age-old cultural constructs of human society. The harlequin and the rogue, for example, are well-known symbolic types of the Western theater. This legacy is particularly relevant to the symbolic type of Cast Members inside Disney's costumed characters. The concept of "symbolic types" was originally suggested by Grathoff (1970) in order to replace the conventional conception of roles. It was further elaborated by Handelman (1986, 1992) who defined symbolic typing as coming into existence when, and only when, a person ceases to modify his or her behavior in response to the reactions of others. Symbolic types, then, are unique kinds of roles that do and reproduced through interpersonal give-and-take, always constituted through perspectives that combine "self" and "other." Symbolic types, in contrast, are stable, permanent performative patterns of behavior that through their inner consistency, self-referentially and independence of social context, serve to create a reality of their own.

While everyday roles are subject to the social flux and uncertainty that dynamize human interaction, service acting is meant to regulate and control that flux. Many service jobs involve fixed performative patterns. The procedures of symbolic typing are laid out in service manuals. The spiel, the set menu, the Disney smile all enable and dictate ritualized performance. This is why Cast Members are warned never to talk back to an angry customer. Instead, they must alert a supervisor. When reality evades the manual, part-timers are no longer fit to deal with reality (unless they are "empowered" by the company to do so under pre-defined circumstances). Symbolic typing is performed within an atemporal realm. This is "service time"—a cyclical time where linear progression is replaced by routinized cycles and "shifts." It should be noted that part-timers in TDL are not allowed to wear wrist watches, whose presence might impair the standard appearance. This is also a symbolic reminder of cyclical tyranny of time in Disneyland—time as frozen within a myth (Frontierland, Fantasyland), within bureaucracy: the company's clocks, shifts and time-cards, and within behavior: the symbolic typing of service culture.

Service culture, enacted through symbolic typing, is a *patronizing* performance. It habituates and conditions us, the customers (patrons). It colonizes our mind through indulgence. As patrons, we must cooperate with the spiel, follow it and choose from it (try asking for something which is not in the menu, even a combination of items which is not prescribed as such). Social interaction becomes a big Nintendo game, with lots of prizes to score if you push the right buttons and route your character in the pre-designed maze. Otherwise, order is lost and we are back into the flux. Symbolic typing, as inculcated by the service manual, abolishes one of the basic constructs of symbolic interaction: the "looking glass self," a term coined by Cooley (1964, p. 183) to describe how our awareness of our own experience is shaped by what others around us think, say, and do about it. Significant others are the "looking glass" where we see our reflection. In contrast, symbolic typing—and hence service culture—is locked in a *mirror* stage. Service attendants are attentive to our facial expressions and to a basic vocabulary of lin-

224 Aviad E. Raz

guistic expressions, but this "awareness" must be only skin-deep. In symbolic typing, there are no more "looking glass selves," only "mirroring bodies"—Frank's (1991) conceptualization of the body in consumerism (see also O'Neill 1985, p. 23; Falk 1993). This is perhaps the "deep" *consummation* of service culture and its oracle, the service manual. It is a Taylorist world whose influence on the postmodern Self is not all ephemeral.

## ACKNOWLEDGMENTS

Reprinted from *Studies in Symbolic Interaction* 21 (1997): 201–17. Used with permission.

Funding for my research in Japan was provided by the Japan Foundation and for that, needless to say, I am extremely grateful. I am also grateful to The Reischauer Institute of Japanese Studies at Harvard University that provided funding for turning my dissertation into a publishable manuscript.


## NOTES

This article is titled after John Van Maanen's 1991 essay on "The Smile Factory: Work at Disneyland." My study has greatly benefited from Van Maanen's insights and I chose its title as an acknowledgment of my debt. In various ways, this study both continues and extends Van Maanen's original conception of the Smile Factory. I added the adjective "Slanted" in order to differentiate between the two titles and highlight the geographical and cultural translocation of a Disneyland in Tokyo. While "Slanted" carries the risk of sounding derogatorily stereotypical, I nevertheless decided to keep it, at the risk of being accused of Orientalism. "Slanted" also conveys a sense of tampering with, misrepresenting and skewing—things that were indeed part of the adaptation of Disneyland in Tokyo, and were done by the Japanese. It is the Japanese who have "slanted" Disneyland, which—if at all connected to Orientalism—denotes its reversal.

1. Fjellman's (1992) monograph on WDW is the most wide-ranging scholarly treatment of a Disney theme park. The cinematic "Disney Discourse" was examined by Smoodin (1994). Disney and postmodernism are the subject of an anthology (Willis 1993) titled "The World According to Disney," whose contributors later published a treatise on WDW, composed by a collective forum called "The Project on Disney" (1995). Several sociologists have dealt with the indoctrination of Disney values, language, and stories as means of corporate control (Van Maanen and Kunda 1989; Van Maanen 1991; Smith and Eisenberg 1987; Boje 1995). The tremendous success of TDL has similarly spawned a thriving genre of "how does it really work" books in Japanese (for example, Komuya 1989; Tsuromoki 1984; Tadokoro 1990; Awata and Takanarita 1984; Kano 1986; and most recently, Lipp 1994). Many of these books explain the success of TDL in terms of its human resource management and

service manuals. This outline of Disney literature in the social sciences does not include articles, of which there are several hundreds.

## REFERENCES

Awata, F. 1988. "Disneyland's Dreamlike Success." *Japan Quarterly* 35: 58–62.

Blocklyn, P. L. 1988. "Making Magic: The Disney Approach to People Management." *Personnel* 65: 28–35.

Boje, D. M. 1995. "Stories of the Story-Telling Organization: A Postmodern Analysis of Disney as 'Tamara-Land.'" *Academy of Management Journal* 38(4): 997–1035.

Brannen, M. Y. 1992. "'Bwana Mickey': Constructing Cultural Consumption at Tokyo Disneyland." Pp. 216–235 in *Re-Made in Japan,* edited by J. J. Tobin. New Haven, CT: Yale University Press.

Braverman, H. 1974. *Labor and Monopoly Capital.* New York: Monthly Review Press.

Carey, R. 1995. "5 Top Corporate Training Programs." *Successful Meetings* (February), pp. 56–61.

Castoro, A. 1995. "A Passion for Service Excellence," *Credit Union Management* (June), pp. 28–31.

Cooley, C. H. 1964. *Human Nature and the Social Order.* New York: Schocken.

Eisenberg, E. M. and H. L. Goodall Jr. 1993. *Organizational Communication: Balancing Creativity and Constraint.* New York: St. Martin's Press.

Eisman, R. 1993. "Disney Magic." *Incentive* (September), pp. 45–56.

Falk, P. 1993. *The Consuming Body.* London: Sage.

Featherstone, M. 1991. *Consumer Culture and Postmodernism.* London: Sage.

———. 1990. "Global Culture: An Introduction," *Theory, Culture and Society,* Special issue: Global Culture 7(2–3): 1–15.

Fjellman, S. M. 1992. *Vinyl Leaves: Walt Disney World and America.* Boulder, CO: Westview Press.

Frank, A. 1991. "For a Sociology of the Body: An Analytical Review." In *The Body: Social Process and Cultural Theory,* edited by M. Featherstone, M. Hepworth and B. Turner. London: Sage.

Freeman, R. B. (Ed.). 1989. "Bonuses and Employment in Japan." Pp. 249–270 of *Labor Markets in Action.* Cambridge, MA: Harvard University Press.

Freund, P. 1990. "The Expressive Body: A Common Ground for the Sociology of Emotion and Health and Illness." *Sociology of Health and Illness* 12(4): 454–477.

Frost, P., M. Louis and L. Moore (Eds.). 1985. *Organizational Culture.* Beverly Hills, CA: Sage.

Fusaha, A. and T. Takanarita. 1984. *An Economic Study of Disneyland* (Dizuniirando no keizai gaku) Tokyo: Asahi Shinbunsha.

Goode, E., and N. Ben-Yehuda. 1994. *Moral Panics: The Social Construction of Deviance.* Oxford: Blackwell.

Gordon, A. 1985. *The Evolution of Labor Relations in Japan: Heavy Industry, 1853–1955.* Cambridge, MA: Harvard University Press.

Grathoff, R. H. 1970. *The Structure of Social Inconsistencies: A Contribution to a Unified Theory of Play, Game and Social Action.* The Hague: Martinus Nijhoff.

Haarmann, H. 1989. *Symbolic Values of Foreign Language Use: From the Japanese Case to a General Sociolinguistic Perspective.* New York: Aldine de Gruyter.

Haden-Guest, A. 1972. *Down the Programmed Rabbit Hole: Travels through Muzak, Hilton, Coca-Cola, Walt Disney and Other World Empires.* London: Hart-Davis, MacGibbon.

Handelman, D. 1990. *Models and Mirrors.* Cambridge: Cambridge University Press.

———. 1986. "Charisma, Liminality and Symbolic Types." In *Comparative Social Dynamics: Essays in Honour of S. N. Eisenstadt,* edited by E. Cohen, M. Lissac, and U. Almagor. Boulder, CO: Westview.

———. 1992. "Symbolic Types, the Body, and Circus." *Semiotica* 85(3/4): 205–227.

Heise, S. 1994. "Disney Approach to Managing." *Executive Excellence* 18 (October), pp. 18–19.

Henkoff, R. 1995. "Finding, Training and Keeping the Best Service Workers." *Fortune* (October 2), pp. 110–115.

Hochschild, A. R. 1983. *The Managed Heart: Commercialization of Human Feeling.* Berkeley: University of California Press.

———. 1989. "Reply to Cas Wouters's Review Essay on the Managed Heart." *Theory, Culture & Society* 6: 439–445.

Inohara, H. 1990. *Human Resource Development in Japanese Companies.* Tokyo: Asian Productivity Center.

Kano, Y. 1986. *The True Story of Tokyo Disneyland (Tokyodizuniirando no shinso).* Tokyo: Kindaiban Geish.

Karthaaüs-Tanaka, N. 1995. *How Japan Views Its Current Labor Market.* Leiden University: Netherlands Association of Japanese Studies.

King, A.D. (Ed.) 1991. *Culture, Globalization and the World-System.* Binghamton: State University of New York.

Kondo, D. 1990. *Crafting Selves: Power, Gender, and Discourses of Identity in a Japanese Workplace.* Chicago: The University of Chicago Press.

Kazumeki, K. 1989. *Tokyo Disneyland's Amazing Management (Tokyodizuniirando no keiei majikku).* Tokyo: Kodansha.

Kuenz, J. 1995. "Working at the Rat." Pp. 110–163 in *The Project on Disney's Inside the Mouse: Work and Play at Disney World.* Durham, NC: Duke University Press.

Lee, M. J. 1993. *Consumer Culture Reborn: The Cultural Politics of Consumption.* London: Routledge.

Lipp, D. 1994. *The Truth about Tokyo Disneyland's Great Success (Tokyodizuniirando daiseiko no shinso).* Trans. By Kuchika Kimundo. Tokyo: NTT shuppan.

Makoto, K. 1996. *Portraits of the Japanese Workplace: Labor Movements, Workers, and Managers.* Trans. By A. Gordon and M. Hane. Boulder, Co: Westview Press.

Smoodin, E. (Ed.) 1994. *Disney Discourse: Producing the Magic Kingdom.* London: Routledge.

Sobei, A. 1977. *Kadokawa gairaigo jiten* (Kadokawa loanword dictionary). Tokyo: Kadokawa Shoten.

Van Maanen, J. 1989. "Whistle While You Work: On Seeing Disneyland as the Workers Do." Paper presented at the panel on the Magic Kingdom, American Anthropological Association Annual Meeting, Washington, D.C., November 16.

———. 1991. "The Smile Factory: Work at Disneyland." In *Reframing Organizational Culture*, edited by P. J. Frost, L. F. Moore, M. R. Louis, C. C. Lundberg, and J. Martin. Newbury Park, CA: Sage.

———. 1991. "Displacing Disney: Some Notes on the Flow of Culture." *Qualitative Sociology* 15(1): 5–35.

Van Maanen, J., and G. Kunda. 1989. "'Real Feelings': Emotional Expression and Organizational Culture." *Research in Organizational Behavior* 11: 43–103.

White, M. 1993. *The Material Child: Coming of Age in Japan and America.* NY: The Free Press.

———. 1995. "The Marketing of Adolescence in Japan: Buying and Dreaming." Pp. 255–274 in *Women, Media and Consumption in Japan*, edited by L. Skov and B. Moeran. Richmond, Surrey: Curzon Press.

# 13

## Learning Real Feelings: A Study of High Steel Ironworkers' Reactions to Fear and Danger

*Jack Haas*

Sidewalk observers watch in a mixture of respect and awe as, high above the ground, hardhat construction workers perform their dangerous ballet. They watch silently as the high steel ironworkers maneuver into place the tinker-toy-like sections of steel that form the skeletal framework of today's high buildings and bridges. High above the workmen, cranes dangle steel beams that must be caught and fixed into place; far below loom enormous chasms of empty space. These workers are protected from certain death only by their skill in balancing on slender beams, a skill threatened by swirls of weather and wind. One cannot but ask how, when faced with such danger, the high steel ironworkers can so casually ignore the perils of his occupation? The confidence and quickness of the workers is bewildering to onlookers who well note the hazards that beset such an occupation; how can these men walk the emerging structures with such confident aplomb? Are we considering brave men, or are these workers foolhardy, challenged by the very nature of their occupation; alternatively, does the answer to the enigma lie in the fact that these men are innately gifted, specially trained, or culturally conditioned so as to enable them to remain calm in the face of such danger? Questions like this are raised in the observer's mind because he cannot relate to the workers' situation; to most of us, such displays, such defiance of risk and the certain consequences of error are inexplicable.

In this paper I shall describe how high steel ironworkers feel and act toward the dangers inherent in their occupation. I shall explore the seemingly inconceivable attitude and behavior of the workers by a juxtaposition of my own reactions when exposed to the same dangers. I will describe how I came to understand the high steel ironworkers' perspectives toward fear and danger. I found myself (in spite of myself) beginning more and more to act as they did. As I came to know these men they admitted to sharing my fear-laden assessment of their occupational situation. We came to share a definition of the situation, a situation they had developed a perspective[1] for dealing with that I had yet to learn.

During the nine months of observation of the construction of a 21 story office building I was a participant observer in a variety of work and recreational settings. I observed union activities, participated in a formal training program for ironworker apprentices, and ate and drank with them. I focused upon the apprentices and attempted to understand the processes by which they were socialized.[2]

The analysis of the data takes two forms. First, the natural history of the research is described as I came to learn the attitude of the workers toward their perilous work. I found that the ironworkers' perspective toward danger was not revealed in their words or actions, but remained an important, although not overtly communicated, part of their everyday methods of coping with their occupational situation. Workers were expected to act in ways which would convince others that they were not afraid. Second, I describe how ironworkers act out their implicitly accepted perspective about danger, and how, through a variety of mechanisms, both individual and collective, they manage to maintain a control of with whom and when they work. The element of danger depends on the trust they are able to afford their fellow workers, the nature and predictability of the weather, the location of their work activity on the emerging structure, and the risks their particular specialty requires.

## A NATURAL HISTORY OF MY FIRST DAYS IN THE FIELD

My traumatic introduction to the work day realities of high steel ironworking came the day the construction superintendent passed me through the construction gate, gave me a hard hat, and wished me good luck. Directly ahead were five incomplete levels of an emerging 21 story office building. From my vantage point I observed a variety of workers engaged in the construction process. The most visible and immediately impressive group of workers were those on the upper level who were putting steel beams into place. These were the ironworkers I had come to participate with and observe. This chilling reality filled me with an almost overwhelming anxiety.

I began to experience a trepidation that far exceeded any usual observer anxiety encountered in the first days of field research. It was the first time I felt this since attempting to gain entree to do a study of apprenticeship training. I watched the men at the top, the precariousness of their position, and the risks of firsthand observation were profoundly obvious. It was with fearful anticipation that I moved toward the job site.

I had anticipated this day but never so directly and profoundly. I had taken out a $50,000 accident policy to protect my family—just in case. I had not told my wife about the research. She found out when a fellow graduate student blurted it out at a party. I protected her and hid my true feelings from my colleagues. Long before the research started I had expected to convince parties to the agreement that I do the research, by writing a letter forgiving them any liability. In these ways I prepared. But as I looked up, I knew I was not prepared for this. These were the people I had come to study and they were up there, and as I watched them I was dumbfounded and awestruck by their aplomb. They "ran the iron" with seeming abandon. It was apparent from the ground that workers moving so confidently across and up and down beams were unafraid.

There I stood, with work shoes, Levi's, work shirt, and a borrowed hardhat, in controlled terror. I noticed two apprentices at the ground level getting out of a trailer van. My strategy had been to locate those apprentices I had met two days previously at an apprentice welding class and follow them on the job.

I yelled to them:

HI, HOW ARE YOU DOING? (AN APPRENTICE SAYS), What's up? I TOLD HIM THAT I HAD JUST GOT ON THE JOB, AND THAT I WOULD LIKE TO FOLLOW SOME OF THE GUYS AROUND.

By this time another fellow, Bob, came up behind us. We stood and talked for awhile. I said:

I JUST SAW THE SUPERINTENDENT OF SLIPPERY STRUCTURAL STEEL, I HAD TO SEE THEM BEFORE I COULD GET ON THE JOB. HOW ARE THINGS UP THERE? SAFE ENOUGH? (HE ANSWERS), Yeh, it's all right, they've got planking all over. Why don't you come up with us? We'll show you around. FINE, LET'S GO. (BELIEVE ME WHAT FOLLOWS WERE TENSE MOMENTS. WE WALKED PAST WORKMEN PUTTING RODS IN AND SETTING CONCRETE FOUNDATIONS TO A LADDER.)

Tom, using only one hand, while carrying welding rods on his shoulder, went up ahead of me on the ladder and climbed to the second level of the building. The ladder was some 20 feet high, tied securely at top and bottom.

I climbed up behind Tom, my apprehension growing in direct proportion to my height above the ground. It appeared that large sections between the girders were planked, but others were not. Many places were exposed and one had to be extremely careful with his footing. Scared but "poised," I carefully and exactly followed Tom. A large quantity of cable was apparent, most of it running diagonally from beam to beam. I followed up another ladder to more planking and over to a planked work area.

This was my introduction to "running the iron," a traumatic experience I somehow survived. In retrospect it was a critical first step in my understanding of how ironworkers perceived and reacted to danger. Needless to say, it was a most important beginning for developing rapport with the ironworkers. I was an outsider beginning to meet their career-long challenge. I earned some credibility as a person who could begin to appreciate and empathize with the problems of their work situation.

For the first two weeks I was very scared. On the steel (or as I now knew "iron") I was cautious, but not too visibly. I knew I was on stage. We were all on stage and I was concerned about developing rapport and not being defined and mocked as the weak deviant. But, I was really scared. I was afraid but trying not to show it. They were boisterous, boastful, and continually demonstrating, by their actions a lack of intimidation about the same situation of which I was most apprehensive. The discrepancy between my personal reactions to "running the iron" and their unified and contrary reaction to the same situation raised the first important question of the research—why did they act this way?[3] I thought it possibly a difference between them and me (never a matter of genetics, culture, or the Mohawk Indian stereotype, but more likely a matter of experience). I had been told before I went on the steel that ironworkers were in fact a very different and unique group of workers.[4]

The actions of ironworkers from the very first day were quite disconcerting; my feeling was one of great fear, yet their actions belied this approach. I felt, and this proved correct, that in order to establish rapport with these workers I would have to demonstrate a certain willingness to participate in the situation and indicate that I could, and would, accommodate myself.

The discrepancy between my feelings and the lack of meaning of their unusually confident behavior raised a question in my mind; was I attempting to interpret their actions according to my relevance structure? I had assumed that, sharing the same experience, we would have the same feelings about it; their actions, however, suggested we were not defining the situation similarly, and, in fact, they had overlooked what was, in my assessment of the situation, frightening. This perplexing discrepancy between the meaning of their behavior and my own definition of the situation led me to attempt to understand why their behavior would be appropriate to such a situation.

Schutz (1967: 174–175) describes three different approaches for understanding the motives of others. The observer can search his memory for similar actions and can assume his motive for such an action holds true for another's actions. If this approach is unsuccessful, the observer can resort to what he knows about the person's behavior and deduce his motive. Finally, if he lacks information about the person he is observing, he can ask him whether one or another motive would be furthered by the act in question. In this situation, I was not able to compare actions in my past with those I observed, nor did I know much about those I was observing except what I had been told by the contractors' representative. The third approach, of attributing different motives, was immediately relevant, but not immediately obvious to me.

In questioning their behavior, I asked myself whether it could be possible that these workers had gained an immunity to fear because of their constant exposure to dangerous situations. It seemed plausible. The more I walked the high steel, to some degree, the more confident and assured I became. This was relative. Whenever I went up on the steel, fear was a strong emotion but there were peaks and valleys depending on what I was on, and where. If ironworkers' actions belied any indications of fear, I suspected they might, nevertheless, talk about it and also about ways of handling it. I was disappointed. They did not talk about being afraid, although they did talk a great deal about danger.

This questioning process was essentially a process where on the basis of my own experience and perceptions I was attempting to understand the actions of others and to a point it didn't make sense until I realized, I was doing what they were doing. I attempted in this sense to reconcile my reactions with the reactions of others. The consistency of ironworker actions on the high steel and their total lack of discussion about fear (a problem I considered paramount), led me to suspect that they had developed a shared perspective for dealing with the problem of which these particular actions were a part. This was a perspective I was beginning to learn, as I came to realize I was acting like they were.

### SHARED PERSPECTIVE:
### THE DISAVOWAL OF FEAR

I had developed a perspective: fear was a reaction to walking the steel, but it was controlled when running the iron. Either ironworkers were immune to the fear of heights and danger, or as I had, they hid their fears when they went up on the steel. Was this perspective peculiar to me or was it one shared by the workers also?

The working hypothesis was that fear was part of their definition of the situation, and that the collective way they dealt with the problem was to treat it as if it did not exist. Individual workers concealed fear from each other. Collectively these reactions produce a situation of pluralistic ignorance

(Schank, 1932: 102, 130–131; Mayer and Rosenblatt, 1975) in which each worker tended to think he was more frightened than coworkers who convincingly controlled their fears. To test this hypothesis is difficult, particularly if workers feel reluctant to talk about their fear—their reticence, both confirms the hypothesis and denies the testing of the hypothesis.

Faced with this methodological problem, the provisional explanation was that workers cannot express their fears, because such expression would raise doubts of their trustworthiness. In a work situation, where the actions of one can affect the safety and lives of others, workers must inspire trust and confidence. Showing fear is exactly contrary to the development of this kind of trust.

One hint that workers did indeed have the perspective that I was beginning to develop, was their discussion about workers who were afraid. They were extremely critical of such workers, and part of their criticism was that they added to the danger of the situation.

While working near the top of the emerging office building, a journeyman ironworker reveals the problem a fearful worker presents. I say:

I GUESS YOU HAVE TO WATCH OUT FOR THE OTHER FELLOW. (ABE ANSWERS) That's right, most of these guys know what they're doing, but you get some of the fucking apprentices, like that guy over there (HE POINTS TO ROY) who's scared up here, and you have really got to watch yourself, because you don't know what the hell they're liable to do.

The journeyman points out that a worker who is afraid has to be watched. He warns me that a worker who acts afraid is unpredictable. This instruction helps me to learn his perspective about fear. The process of developing shared beliefs and actions about a problem was expressed even more clearly by a journeyman teacher at the apprentice class. He warns apprentices about assumed trust of their coworkers by saying;

There's one thing I want you guys to remember, because in so many ways your life depends upon not doing things in a stupid way. Think out what you're going to do beforehand. Make sure that the guy you're working with knows what the hell he's doing too.

There's no sense working with a dummy, because you can never trust them, you've always got to watch out for them and you're not learning a damn thing. If something's been done by another guy, say he's hung a float for you, or done this or done that for you, and you've got to get out on it, you're a damned fool if you don't check it yourself. Now I don't say this is always the case, if you work with someone, say you're paired up with a guy and you've been working with him for awhile and you know him well, and you can trust him and he's no dummy, then you don't have to be that thorough. But if you come on a new job, you are doing the most foolish thing that you could ever do by not making sure.

In this quote, one may perceive the process by which a group (apprentices) come to learn this shared perspective. Apprentices are told the importance of guarding themselves against untrustworthy workers. They are told how to act by thinking out what they are going to do and making sure that their coworkers do too. Later, the instructor presents a number of possible situations. Each situation is interpreted for the apprentices and the proper action for each situation is described. Interpreting situations and actions for others is part of the process of sharing this perspective about fear and threatening coworkers.

Oftentimes a group will develop a special language or argot that focuses on special problems or experiences that the group might face. During the research, I was struck by the vivid phrases ironworkers used to describe actions that revealed fear the phrases ironworkers used are "to coon it," "to seagull it," or "to cradle it." Cooning it or cradling it (it being the steel beam) involves walking on all fours across the steel, or holding onto the steel while traversing it. Seagulling refers to walking the steel with arms outstretched, as in flight, to provide balance. These phrases are only used criticizing the actions of others.

The importance of this relationship of personal danger to the actions of work associates is reflected in the following conversation with a journeyman ironworker:

HIGH UP ON THE STEEL, I LOOK DOWN AND SAY TO THE JOUR-NEYMAN, PRETTY SCARY UP HERE, EH? (THE JOURNEYMAN RESPONDS), It really isn't that bad, just depends on who you're working with. If you're working with a guy that knows what the hell he's doing up here, it's safe as can be. It's only when you get a guy that doesn't know what's going on that you have to watch out.

A fearful or unknowing worker adds a measure of unpredictability to the work situation and makes it potentially even more dangerous. One who is afraid cannot be trusted to act correctly; he may act rashly, being concerned about his own protection or unsure about how to respond. The worker who is afraid may, moreover, neglect or avoid his responsibilities, and, as a consequence, endanger others. One who reveals his fear cannot be trusted to put his responsibility to others in priority to his emotions.

Considering this, it is obvious that one of the crucial tests one must pass to gain acceptance by his ironworker colleagues is to manage his impressions and to hide his fear. Workers act confidently on the steel and do not express their fears because to do so would damage their prospects for gaining the confidence of others and acceptance as a colleague. Their reputation and employability depends upon being defined as trustworthy.

Fear is taken for granted in that it is not talked about or revealed. It is, however, a personal reaction that ironworkers feel. Worker fear is hidden, controlled, and privately lived. Beyond that, there is little one can do about it. A journeyman at the union hall descries what can be done and, given that, how one must accept danger and fear without allowing it to control or adversely affect his behavior.

> I think it [danger] is something you realize as soon as you step foot on it [the steel]. It is a dangerous situation or at least it can be made so. So in a sense you take every precaution you can, and make the job as safe as you can. And then you don't worry about it. You really don't worry about it. I know that sounds funny with you, but no one is going to make it that sits there and stands there and worries about it all day. You recognize it and you respect it, but you don't let it get to you.

The journeyman explains how each ironworker must deal with this reality. Workers take all the precautions possible. After doing so, they must attempt to submerge their feelings and go about their job.

The journeyman's closing statement is instructive. It is important that the worker doesn't allow his fear to bother him and, hence we might assume, his colleagues. Workers must act as if there was nothing to fear. Hughes (1958: 90–91) makes this same point when he says:

> It is also to be expected that those who are subject to the same work risks will compose a collective rationale which they whistle to one another to keep up their courage, and they will build up collective defenses against the lay world. . . . These rationales and defenses contain a logic that is somewhat like that of insurance, in that they tend to spread the risk psychologically (by saying that it might happen to anyone), morally, and financially.

The collective "whistle" suggest Goffman's (1959) dramaturgical analogy of front and backstage behavior—workers maintain a front of confidence and lack of fear before their audience. In this case, the audience is composed of fellow workers, and consequently there are few backstage areas where their front breaks down. One such backstage area was in private conversation with the observer. Alone and in my confidence, workers would tell me of their fear.

Verifying this perspective—that ironworkers deliberately pretend to be unafraid—was a continuing research interest. Ironworkers I observed throughout the research acted almost with disdain to the dangers surrounding them. As a way of proving themselves to their work fellows, many seemed deliberately to flaunt the situation by taking risks—they showed off by volunteering for the most dangerous work activity, as a way of demonstrating their trustworthiness and enhancing their reputations. The very few who acted afraid were treated as deviants, threats, and objects of ridicule to be driven out of ironworking before they allowed their fear to disrupt the shared perspective.

There were only two occasions where advertently or inadvertently ironworkers revealed their fear-laden feelings. The confessions that were made to me privately and personally were most important. These confessions were made when some ironworkers came to trust me as one who would not betray their confidence to fellow workers. Many of them wanted to quit ironworking but they were hopelessly bound into a network of relationships and a career that was difficult if not impossible to terminate. Leaving ironworking would be tantamount to admitting they were afraid, and that would mean total expulsion from a way of life they had become bound and committed to, despite its anxiety provoking consequences.

The most touching example I encountered was when a highly regarded Indian ironworker literally begged me to open university doors to a new career. We both agreed, in a boozy and emotional stupor, that he could not because his whole life, particularly his honored status among ironworkers and reservation Indians, would be forever altered. Competing with his young brother on the high steel, he knew he was pushing the limits. It was only a matter of time before that competition, and the veneer of fearlessness, would be shattered by one or the other's fall.

The other graphic breakdown of front which corroborates the underlying but conscious suppression of fear is when a worker falls "in the hole" and is killed. Although I fortunately never directly experienced such a situation, an Indian journeyman recounted his first dramatic confrontation with the underlying reality. He says:

> I remember one time when a guy fell in the hole. He hit his head on a piece of steel on the way down, so he was killed instantly. Well anyways, this has an effect on you. Most of times you stop work and quit for the day. I didn't feel too bad. I guess death has got to hit closer to home, like if your brother or father gets it. Maybe, I was too new then, but anyways the older guys up there just froze. They wouldn't move, and they wouldn't come off the iron. I had to go up there and bring them down one by one, and some guys were so scared I had to bring them down almost by carrying them.

When a worker falls and is killed, ironworkers leave the job. They go drinking and reminisce about their lost colleague. The next day, seemingly adjusted once more to the dangers, they return to work.

The above story indicates how their managed impressions and assumed behavior were dramatically confronted. The accident and loss of a colleague stimulates a reevaluation of the worker's socially constructed reality. Contrary to the way they were expected to act and the behavior supposedly consonant with their definition of the situation was the fact there was much to fear. It is not difficult to understand their complete breakdown of front. They are reminded—in the most personally affecting way—there is much to be afraid of.

## TESTING FELLOW WORKERS

Although one should conceal fear, workers do agree that the relativity of danger allows a worker to define for himself situations which are too dangerous. Part of their perspective about fear is the recognition that workers should protect themselves and others from situations which increase their common danger. One way to do this is to test the trustworthiness of their fellow workers.

Workers recognize that running the iron is a managed performance and may not reflect one's true feelings. It is important for workers to know whether a confident front (Goffman, 1959) will break down in a crisis. Workers believe it is important to know as much as possible about the trustworthiness of fellow workers in all sorts of situations and they test this by binging,[5] a process similar to styles of interaction observed in black ghetto youth (Kochman, 1969), white lower-class gang members (Miller et al., 1961), hospital personnel (Goffman, 1951: 122), and perhaps as Berne (1964) suggests, North Americans in general. These studies indicate the many purposes of this form of interaction. Hughes (1945: 356) points out an important use of binging in testing newcomers when he comments:

> To be sure that a new fellow will not misunderstand requires a sparring match of social gestures. The zealot who turns the sparring match into a real battle, who takes a friendly initiation too seriously, is not likely to be trusted with the lighter sort of comment on one's work or with doubts and misgivings; nor can he learn those parts of the working code which are communicated only by hint and gesture. . . . In order that men may communicate freely and confidently, they must be able to take a good deal of each other's sentiments for granted.

In the following quotation, a journeyman, three apprentices, and I engage in a sparring match, on top of an emerging 21 story building. Abe, the journeyman says:

> These fucking apprentices don't know their ass from a hole in the ground. (THE JOURNEYMAN TURNS TO ME AND SAYS) I hope you don't think these guys are representative of the whole apprenticeship. They're a pretty sad lot. (JOINING IN WITH THE KIDDING I SAY) Yeh, I've noticed that. (BUD AN APPRENTICE ADDS), Don't listen to him. He's just a fucking Indian. (THE JOURNEYMAN RESPONDS) Yeh, and he's a fucking nigger. (ABE YELLS DOWN TO THE APPRENTICE BELOW) What the fuck are

you doing down there, playing with yourself? For Christ's sakes get up here and bring that machine up here with you.

The example demonstrates how repartee tests relationships and exchanges information. The style is characteristically earthy, there is little regard for amenities, and the jibes seem deliberately provocative—a verbal challenge. In a dangerous work situation where we expect workers to try to ease conflict, we find deliberate provocation. An Indian journeyman sums up the importance of this form of interaction as he and I drink beer in a bar:

> You see, I don't get upset often. And when I do I forget right after. You've got to figure, if you're going to work with the guy, you can't hold something against him, because he could kill you and you could kill him. You forget fast when you're in this business. What you do is try to see what the guy is made of, because if he gets agitated, and wants to fight over something like this, then you don't know what he's going to do up on the steel if something goes wrong. A lot of times you're responsible for that other guy up there and you can either make him or break him.

Workers use binging to test trustworthiness and self-control—will a man keep cool when subjected to such personal abuse? If he loses his poise, it indicates he may lose control in other threatening situations, e.g., high above the ground. If he takes such kidding too seriously, he may carry a grudge into a situation where revenge could be easy. Binging also conveys information about expected relationships among participants; relationships characterized by constant redefinition, indicated by subtle causes from the participants. Such interaction permits the apprentice to experiment by binging back in anticipation of a favorable response, which shows journeymen consider him acceptable.

The one-sided nature of binging between journeymen and apprentice was apparent throughout the study. New apprentices are called "punks," and their role involves carrying out the most demeaning tasks and the acceptance of the deliberate castigation of veteran workers.

On the top of the building, I talked with a journeyman about his constant kidding of new apprentices, I say:

> LOOKS LIKE YOU WERE BUSTING JERRY, THE FIREWATCH, THE OTHER DAY. (ABE, THE JOURNEYMAN, ANSWERS), That's all right, I used to take it even worse than that. You see, I started pretty young. I used to work summers at this, and they had me doing all sorts of punking, and everyone was on my ass, all the time. I remember one summer, I carried bolts around, and that's all. I got so fucking sick of looking at those bolts, I was about ready to go out of my nut. If I took it these guys can take it. You've got to take it and dish it right back.

This journeyman makes it clear that binging is an institutionalized part of the apprentice's career; it is an initiation all must pass through before acceptance as a peer who can "dish it right back." The process is used by ironworkers to let the trustworthiness and loyalty of coworkers, and apprentices are most subject to it. The mechanism is used to test the self-control of coworkers; ironworkers believe it is useful in measuring a man's ability to handle himself in a dangerous situation. Ironworkers also believe that an apprentice's willingness to accept disparaging and hostile attacks on his person provides predictable evidence that he will commit himself to the interests of the group, over and above any self-interests.

## WORKER AUTONOMY TO REDUCE DANGER

In an attempt to reduce the threats to their safety, ironworkers try to control factors they perceive that add to their danger. Such factors include superiors who have little regard for worker safety and unsafe weather conditions. Ironworkers try to limit the effects of both.

It is not difficult to imagine the kind of havoc the wind can play in the high, open areas where ironworkers frequently work. The wind complicates the worker's problem of keeping his balance on steel beams, which range in width from four to 12 inches. The wind is particularly dangerous when workers are carrying equipment across the steel. For example, the heavy wooden "floats" of plywood, on which the welders sit or stand, act as sails when caught by the wind and workers must take special care not to be blown off the beams. Two workers are usually required to carry a float. In a strong wind they will drag the float across the steel. They carry the float away from the wind, then if a sudden breeze stirs up the float does not push them off for they can let it give and reduce the sail effect. If the wind blows very hard, they can drop the float, grab the ropes, and sit or stand on them while the platform swings free in space. Their other alternative is to drop the float completely, endangering workers below—a last and rarely considered option.

Workers frequently were observed telling stories about unusual and extremely dangerous working situations. The following is an example of a story about the wind told by an ironworker journeyman to other journeymen, three apprentices, and myself:

> I remember when I was on this job putting this bridge over the seaway, and this stupid son-of-a-bitch is up there on the bridge and he had his hat on backwards, as this wind comes and lifts the peak up and the hat starts flying off his head. So this guy comes and reaches up with both hands and grabs his hat and goes overboard with it. I mean this fucking guy should have known better and let the goddamned hat drop. So there he is falling down through the air about 100 feet

still holding on to the goddamned helmet. And then you look down below and there he is swimming and he still had one hand on that goddamned helmet. I don't know how stupid guys can be.

The journeyman warns the others of the problem that the wind presents and suggests that they ensure their safety first, and then worry about their clothing or equipment. In addition to the wind, snow, sleet, rain, and ice reduce the workers' visibility and/or make the steel beams and wood planking slippery. Walking the iron is difficult enough without these added imponderables.

Work, however, continues despite difficult weather; snow is shoveled off the steel beams and wood planking and ice is melted from the beams by a portable heater. During the winter, workers dress as warmly as possible and carry on the work activity. The weather is always a problem because it affects not only worker's safety but also their wages. The values of money and safety are sometimes in conflict. The worker is paid by the contractor for showing up in the morning, whether he works or not. If the weather is too inclement, he is paid two hours "show up time." Oftentimes, there is a difference of opinion between the workers and the foreman as to whether work should continue. Sometimes the workers want to work to increase their wages, and the foreman tells them to take the day off; other times the workers feel the weather has made working too dangerous, but the foreman believes the work should go on. The following discussion by a group of apprentices at the apprentice class indicates some of the problems the weather presents.

NINE APPRENTICES STAND AROUND TALKING ABOUT THEIR WORK WEEK. (DICK), How many hours you guys get? I got forty again this week. (BILL), Twenty-eight hours, can you imagine that? Friday we came in and we worked up there in that fucking blizzard until quarter of ten and then the blizzard starts to stop and then they tell us to go home. That pisses me off. I mean I'm willing to work, I say fuck the weather. You know what they have me do, they go and give me a broom and have me go out and sweep the beams off so the welders can go out there. Friday was a bastard, you couldn't even coon it to get out there. Tel 'em Roy.
(ROY), Well I only got twenty-two hours. They put you up there and you work your show-up time and then things start to clear up and they tell you to go home. You see, you get all these guys from Connecticut. We haven't worked a Friday in the last five weeks. Fucking guys are all getting an early start home, so they tell us to get off. (JOHN), I only had twenty hours. I didn't even get in Wednesday. Did you work Wednesday, Bill? (BILL), Damned right, about froze my balls, but I got in four hours until lunchtime. You know that welder, Joe Walker? Christ he was hanging out in the front of the building. What do you think of this Ralph (TEACHER-JOURNEYMAN)? There he is on the goddamned float and the wind's blowing like hell and it's cold as hell up there and the float is banging away up there. So he's got to hold on to the steel with one

hand to keep the float from banging away, and try welding with the other. So he just said "fuck it" and got off of it, and went down to the Cartel [bar] and got himself some brews.

(DICK) I don't know about you guys. All the decking crew got their forty hours in this week. All the rodmen were down there working. Structural guys, they always drag up. What's the matter with you guys, can't you take it up there? (BILL) Oh, fuck you. You go up there and walk around in that shit. God-damn wind's blowing so hard and it's snowing and you can't see your foot in front of you. It's all right, you guys are down on the bottom. That stuff was starting to freeze on Friday. It's all right if it's slushy. I mean it's slushy. I mean it's still not good, but it's not as bad as when that stuff is freezing up on you. Then you're really on your ass.

These comments point out the varied definitions of safe working conditions. Under ordinary conditions workers are expected to handle their fears and accept the problem of danger. In unusual conditions workers decide for themselves whether or not to work. There are, however, other considerations which they may take into account in defining the situation. Some of the factors which influence their decision are the loss of pay, leaving early, and determining how their action will affect the ability of their coworkers to continue working.

At the end of the apprentices' discussion, an apprentice (Bill) indicates that the problem of danger is a relative one. He commented, "It's all right if it's slushy. . . . It's not as bad as when the stuff is freezing up on you." Some kinds of foul weather are more dangerous than others, and some places and jobs on the steel structure are more dangerous than the others. For example, the tops and sides of the structure are more dangerous than the center and lower areas of the building. The top is more dangerous because it is higher; the sides because there is nothing to break a fall.

The relativity of danger in ironworker's thinking sometimes leads to different interpretations of the situation. Some workers may choose to leave work while others may stay. The important point is the collective support given to workers to choose freely, excepting occasions when their refusal to work affects the group. If the group is burdened by a member's decision to "drag up," he is criticized; otherwise, his action is not rebuked.

In the next example, an apprentice describes how the decision to work or not to work is made.

AT THE APPRENTICE CLASS ONE APPRENTICE SAYS TO THE REST OF THE GROUP (INCUDING MYSELF): I will always go up and take a look at what it is like. . . . I usually go up like I did Wednesday, when it was 26 below—I went up there, and went all the way to the eighth floor and looked around and it was too cold. So, I came back down.

It is the apprentice who goes up to the floor where he will be working and who checks out for himself the working conditions; his decision not to work

is an independent one, not relying on the judgments of others. The decision
to work or not may be a group one; when a decision is made to thwart the
foreman or contractor's usurpation of their autonomy the group will then
invariably act together. On one occasion I followed Ray (apprentice) up to
the top level which was almost completely planked. Because of the planking,
this floor had accumulated between two or three inches of hardpacked snow.
It was quite slippery and treacherous because of open spaces and planing
that was insecurely based. Ray said:

> Most of the guys aren't in today, they all took off. YOU MEAN THEY CAME
> IN EARLIER. (RAY ANSWERS) Yeh, but Bill didn't come in. WHO
> DECIDES WHETHER THEY'RE TO LEAVE? (RAY) They do. Mac (THE
> FOREMAN) asked a couple of them to go and shovel snow and they said "no"
> and took off.

In this example, the foreman directs the worker to shovel snow; the group
chooses not to, and the men leave the job. Other workers remain free to
decide for themselves whether or not to work. The perspective of worker
autonomy is enacted and reinforced.

## CONCLUSION

This paper outlines the major problems ironworkers face in their work environment. The first problem, fear of the work setting, is described in terms of
the author's changing awareness of the problem and the seeming contradiction between my personal reaction and the observable reactions of the men
of the high steel. I thought my reactions to be different at first, even though
I acted as if I shared their definition of the situation.

   Their reaction to danger I saw as being unusual and unexpected, but later
more obvious reasons for their behaving in this way became an important
question for the research. The questioning process resolving these contradictory reactions to danger was important for coming to understand why ironworkers act the way they do. Indeed, despite my trepidation of the situation,
I found myself acting unafraid, because I was also interested in developing
rapport with the workers and proving my mettle to them. The fact that they
didn't talk about their fears, if they had any, was suggestive itself of the possibility that an important understanding was not to reveal one's fear. This
reticence was complimented by acts of bravado on the steel, which were
viewed by me as calculated performances for the audience of fellow workers.

   I developed a concept that when workers are subjected to an environment
where they heavily depend on the trustworthy and competent actions of
others, it becomes necessary for them to make continuous demonstrations

of their fearlessness in their work situation. To act afraid increases the dangers and reduces trust among workers whose security depends on such trust being developed. Thus I came to learn and act out the same perspective toward fear shared by the group, a perspective in which workers deny fear in front of others, but live privately.

The processes of social control I have described—testing and controlling fellow workers and maintaining and enhancing individual and collective control over the work setting—are processes characteristic of occupations where danger is a perceived worker problem. The careful surveillance and testing of colleagues, particularly newcomers, the controlled actions belying any fear and the unified efforts to increase worker autonomy are sociologically relevant outcomes in situations where workers face extreme danger. The processes ironworkers have derived for controlling and directing the behavior of apprentices, as well as journeymen, in many ways parallel those described of pipeline construction workers (Graves, 1958), lumberjacks (Haynes, 1945), miners (Gouldner, 1954; Lucas, 1969), combat personnel (Grinker and Spiegel, 1963; Stouffer, 1949; Weiss, 1967), and ghetto social workers (Mayer and Rosenblatt, 1975).

In dangerous occupations participants are described as engaging in a great deal of horseplay, joking and banter, or, as I refer to it—binging. This form of interaction supports worker efforts to maintain control of their work environment and to evolve rigorous sets of expectations about appropriate behavior and shared worker attributes. This suggests that the perception of danger leads to very similar processes and expectations in very disparate occupational groups. The single characteristic they all share is their perception of danger; this perception produces a set of perspectives around the problem of danger that is rigorously and continuously enforced.

The worker's attempt to increase their control over their work environment and lessen the dangers is the second and related theme of this paper. This perspective emphasizes the ironworker's commitment to increasing worker autonomy and thus a control over their environment. They strive to maintain control by collectively supporting individual and group decisions to judge for themselves safe and unsafe working conditions. They support the actions of fellow workers who decide whether or not to work in inclement weather. Fellow workers accept or reject the judgments of work superiors who may not give precedence to ironworkers' considerations and who could consequently pose a threat to their personal and collective security. Workers who perceive physical danger develop mechanisms to control their reactions and the reactions of others. Individually and collectively they struggle to enhance the security of their situation. Symbolic or real threats bind workers together in an effort to protect themselves. Part of the defense, however, lies in controlling one's personal trepidations and insecurities and maintaining an appearance of fearlessness.

These reactions, I believe, are characteristic of many groups and are only more obvious and dramatic in the observation of high steel ironworkers. Behind the calculated performance and fronts of much social activity is the underlying insecurity and threat of failure. These fears are contained and controlled, because to do otherwise is to admit personal failure and to face ridicule or ostracism.

## NOTES

Reprinted from Jack Haas, *Work and Occupations* 4, no. 2 (May 1977): 147–70. Copyright © 1977 by Sage Publications, Inc. Reprinted by permission of Sage Publications, Inc.

I am indebted to Blanche Geer and Howard S. Becker for their assistance in helping teach me how to do research and how to think sociologically. Thanks to Berkeley Fleming for his editorial suggestions. Thanks also to the local union and contractors' association for permission to do the research. My gratitude and sincere thanks to the ironworkers of this study for their cooperation and friendship.

1. The concept perspective is taken from Becker et al. (1961) and refers to a set of beliefs and actions an individual or group has towards a perceived problem. In this case the perspective is a shared or group one, which has developed out of the interactions ironworkers have about their mutually defined problem.

2. After each observation I dictated in as complete a form as possible all that I had seen and heard in the course of the observation. These near verbatim dictations were typed in full as field notes and alter coded and categorized and serve as the basis of this analysis.

3. An important point is that as a stranger to the situation I did not share the expectations of others. This estrangement on my part made the actions of others more profound and dramatic. See Garfinkel (1957: 37), where he points out that such estrangement is helpful for bringing into view the background expectancies of the participants. See also Simmel (1950: 405), where he makes the point that the stranger role carries with it a certain objectivity, i.e., he is not committed to the "unique ingredients and peculiar tendencies of the group."

4. During the interview phase of the study, when the decision to study ironworkers had not yet been reached, respondents provided me with a preliminary set of expectations which affected my thinking. Having had no experience or contact with ironworkers, their comments provided me with a framework of understanding about ironworkers even though subsequently they were found to be incorrect or exaggerated.

In this example, the contractor's representative tells me about Indian ironworkers:

> You know they're the damnest ironworkers (Indians). I don't care what you say, they can go out Saturday night and get a real toot and Monday morning have the jumping jeepers. But, by gosh, you get them up there and they're not afraid of anything.

This statement by the contractor's representative suggests that Indians are unafraid and that there is indeed something to fear, a very important point for me.

5. The term "binging" was, I believe, first used and described by Roethlisberger and Dickson (1934). They describe workers binging each other by punching others on the shoulder. This action served as a means of social control, a warning to the worker that he had exceeded the work group's informally agreed upon standard of production.

## REFERENCES

BECKER, H. S., B. GEER, A. STRAUSS, and E. HUGHES (1961) Boys in White. Chicago: University of Chicago Press.

BERNE, E. (1964) Games People Play. New York: Grove.

GARFINKEL, H. (1957) Studies in Ethnomethodology. Englewood Cliffs, N.J.: Prentice-Hall.

GOFFMAN, E. (1959) Presentation of Self in Everyday Life. New York: Doubleday Anchor.

——— (1951) Encounters. Indianapolis, Ind.: Bobbs-Merrill.

GOULDNER, A. (1954) Patterns of Industrial Bureaucracy. New York: Free Press.

GRAVES, B. (1958) " 'Breaking out': An apprenticeship system among pipeline construction workers." Human Organization 17 (Fall): 9–13.

GRINKER, R. R. and J. P. SPIEGEL (1963) Men under Stress. Philadelphia: Blakerston Co.

HAAS, J. (1974) "The stages of the high steel ironworker apprentice career." Soc. Q. 15 (Winter): 93–108.

——— (1972) "Binging: Educational control among high steel ironworkers." Amer. Behavioral Scientist 16 (September/October): 27–34.

HAYNES, N. (1945) "Taming the lumberjack." Amer. Soc. Rev. 10 (April): 217–225.

HUGHES, E. C. (1958) Men and Their Work. New York: Free Press.

——— (1945) "Dilemmas and contradictions of status." Amer. J. of Sociology 5 (March): 353–359.

KOCHMAN, T. (1969) " 'Rapping' in the black ghetto." Trans-action 6 (February): 26–34.

LUCAS, R. (1969) Men in Crisis: A Study of Mine Disaster. New York: Basic Books.

MAYER, J. E. and A. ROSENBLATT (1975) "Encounters with danger: Social workers in the ghetto." Sociology of Work and Occupations 2 (August): 227–245.

MILLER, W. B., H. GEERTZ, and H. S. G. CUTTER (1961) "Aggression in a boy's street-corner gang." Psychiatry 24 (November): 283–298.

ROETHLISBERGER, F. L. and W. J. Dickson (1934) Management and the Worker. Boston: Harvard University Graduate School of Business Administration.

SCHANCK, R. L. (1932) "A study of a community and its groups and institutions conceived of as behaviors of individuals." Psychiatry Monographs 43, 2.

SHUTZ, A. (1967) The Phenomenology of the Social World [trans. by George Walsh and Frederick Lehnert]. Evanston, Ill.: Northwestern Univ. Press.

SIMMEL, G. (1950) The Sociology of George Simmel [trans. and ed. By Kurt H. Wolff]. New York: Free Press.

STOUFFER, S. (1949) The American Soldier: Combat and Its Aftermath, II. Princeton, N.J.: Princeton Univ. Press.

WEISS, M. (1967) "Rebirth in the airborne." Transaction 4 (May): 23–26.

# 14

## From Night to Day: Timing and the Management of Custodial Work

*Jane C. Hood*

In 1984, nearly three million Americans worked as janitors and cleaners (Bureau of Labor Statistics [BLS] 1986: 79). Custodial and cleaning work ranks third on the list of 37 occupations with the largest expected job growth and accounts for nearly 3% of total job growth projected for 1984–1985 (BLS, 1986: 12). Despite the occupations' prominence in current labor force statistics, however, social scientists have paid little attention to custodians. Except for Golds's research on apartment house janitors (1952) and Hughes's frequently references to the same janitors' strategies for dealing with dirty work (1958: 49–53; 1974: 280), custodians have been neglected in the sociology of work.

Dirty work as a category, however, has received more attention. Ethnographic accounts of meatcutting (Meara, 1974), garbage collection (Perry, 1978; Walsh, 1975), poultry processing (Bryant and Perkins, 1982), apartment house janitors (Gold, 1952) and psychiatric workers (Emerson and Pollner, 1975) have contributed to the development of several important insights about dirty work and the people who do it. Contrary to assumptions often made about low-status workers, these researchers have found that pride in ones' work is necessary for all categories of workers. Even workers who collect other peoples' garbage, therefore, take pride in their work. This pride may be enhanced by pat ownership in the company, as in the case of the San Francisco Scavengers (Perry, 1978), or conditioned by residence in a poor neighborhood where any gainful employment makes one respectable (see Anderson, 1978; Walsh, 1975: 65–67), but all workers need to maintain their dignity and protect themselves from undermining interactions and experiences. Therefore, when faced with threat to their dignity, all kinds of workers will invent strategies to protect themselves (Hughes, 1974: 280).

Examples of such strategies are found in Meara's work on meatcutters and Gold's study of apartment house janitors. Meara describes how meatcutters define potentially deflating interactions with customers as interruptions that take them away from their "real work . . . work with meat," and one of Gold's (1952) apartment house janitors deftly compares himself to a physician in his building who makes "emergency calls at all hours of the night and never [gets] through with work" (Gold, 1952: 492). Whereas the meatcutters distance themselves for demeaning interactions by asserting that customer service was not their "real work," the apartment house janitor aligned himself with a high-status occupation by pointing out the parallels between his work and the physician's. Both strategies protect self-esteem in otherwise threatening interaction settings.

Goffman's discussion of relative stigma (1963: 2–3, 138–139) suggests that the extent to which physically dirty work will be experienced as socially demeaning depends upon the visibility of that work to others who label the work as undesirable. Studies of daytime domestic workers and night janitors demonstrate that time as well as space conditions social visibility. Thus domestic workers minimize status discrepancies by cleaning houses while their clients are away (Glenn, 1986: 174), and the public building custodians described in this article prefer working at night, unobserved by higher status daytime clientele.

The relative stigma of "dirty work" also varies by occupation and sense of ownership so that work need not be physically dirty in order to be regarded as "shit work" and work that is physically dirty may not be experienced as socially demeaning. Emerson and Pollner (1975), for example, find that among psychiatric workers, dirty work is any work that does not require skills and knowledge commensurate with one's occupational status. Thus, emergency team interventions that do not allow workers to use their therapeutic skills become "shit work" for psychiatric workers, and academics use the same term for administrative duties that take them away from their research. Similarly, working for a company in which one has part ownership (Perry, 1978), or cleaning an area that one identifies as one's own, may infuse physically dirty work with pride of ownership.

This study builds upon previous research by recording the experiences of a panel of building custodians before and after they were moved from night to day shift. The mandatory shift change created new status dilemmas as well as practical obstacles for workers by forcing them to work around students and faculty. This comparison between night and day shift custodial work further illustrates how time can alter social space so that "clean work" done at one time of day may be transformed into "dirty work" when done at a different time.

## THE NIGHT-TO-DAY STUDY

In August, 1979, over 100 night-shift custodians at Urban University[1] began performing their jobs on the day shift. Although management had implemented the shift change primarily in order to save money,[2] moving to day shift created and/or accentuated several noneconomic problems for the workers. In response, the custodians ingeniously developed a variety of strategies and tactics for managing these problems. Nonetheless, the change from night to day transformed some of the basic conditions of their work. In exploring the effects of these transformations, this article illustrates: (1) how the timing of work can affect both control over the work setting and intrinsic work satisfaction, and (2) how work settings mediate the stigmatization of dirty work.

The shift from night to day created two general sets of problems for custodial workers. First, day work brought about a number of significant changes in the organization and supervision of their work. These changes included both a weakening of job control in specific work areas and an increase in direct supervision. Second, day work meant that custodians had to do their work among and around the building's daytime occupants. This change produced a number of problems, ranging from increased social visibility to difficulties in completing work because more people were in the way. Overall, custodians experienced diminished control over both their work and its setting, found it more difficult to take pride in their jobs, and were more affected by the stigma of doing dirty work after moving to the day shift.

## METHODS

When Urban University announced in June 1979 that its 124 night custodians would begin working day shift on July 16, I quickly made plans to collect baseline data in order to trace the effects of the shift change. With the cooperation of both the facilities department and the union, my research assistants and I were able to conduct interviews on the job. Data for this study come from: (1) structured interviews done with a panel of 63 workers before and after the shift change[3] and (2) observations and open-ended interviews with union stewards and supervisors over a two-year period.

Half the workers in the panel had 12 or more years of education. Their average age was 42. Two-thirds were male and half were black. With regard to work history, the custodians were either (1) older migrants from other jobs such as construction, machine tool work, health care, (2) younger workers just entering the labor force, or (3) middle-aged and older workers who had done custodial work at Urban University or elsewhere most of their lives.

Compared to the Bureau of Statistics 1984 profile of janitors and cleaners

(BLS, 1986: 79), the custodians in this study were slightly better educated, somewhat more likely to be male, and considerably more likely to be black. Although the BLS does not say what proportion of janitors belong to unions, union membership is common among public-sector custodians. At Urban University, the custodians belonged to AFSCME (The Association of Federal, State, County and Municipal Employees) and earned between $10,656 and $12,904 (including the night differential) in 1979, which was about average for nonindustrial janitors in metropolitan areas.

In the baseline and follow-up interviews, I used interview schedules containing both open-ended questions such as "How do you think your life will be affected by the shift-change?" and closed-ended, forced-choice items such as "Compared to working nights, how much easier or harder is it for you to get your work done (now that you are on days)?" I conducted several of the interviews myself, but most were done by students whom I had trained and supervised. The quantitative data are reported elsewhere (Hood, 1984). This article is based primarily on the answers to open-ended questions, numerous marginal comments made by interviewers, field notes taken over the course of the study, and tape-recorded interviews with union stewards and supervisors.

## CHANGES IN THE ORGANIZATION AND SUPERVISION OF CUSTODIAL WORK

When Urban University administrators first announced the shift change, some of them justified the move to day work by arguing that the night workers were apt to take naps and even drink on the job. By day, the argument went, the workers could be more closely supervised and would not have as many places to hide. As a section manager put it, "It was easier to goof off on nights. For one or two, this was a problem." Although such statements, especially global ones, incensed workers and may have been unjustified, day work did mean increased surveillance over both their workers and their work.

### Closer Supervision

Compared to factor operatives, nurses' aids, food service workers, and most secretaries, third-shift custodians have both more freedom from supervision and more control over their work pace and work methods. Night custodial work in day-occupied buildings generally involves a great deal of local job autonomy for the individual custodian and a minimal degree of supervision. At night, Urban University custodians had the building to themselves. Night custodians are often supervised only by "leadworkers" (foremen) and are visited just once a night by a white collar supervisor. Each custodian has his or her own area to maintain, with a set of tasks to be done daily (emptying wastebaskets, sweeping and mopping), and others to be done periodically (waxing floors, cleaning woodwork, polishing furniture). As long as their areas pass inspection by the time they leave in the morning, and their supervisors hear few complaints from the daytime clientele, the night workers can usually set their own pace and routine. They can vary the order in which they clean rooms or do daily tasks, and establish their own schedules for waxing floors.

After the shift change, workers saw section supervisors more frequently and most got more feedback from supervisors than they had at night. Some workers complained that management was on their backs more and expected them to look busy even though they could not get into areas that needed cleaning. One section head adapted to the change by devising methods of distinguishing old dirt from new, so that he could tell whether or not the custodians had been doing their jobs:

> On nights, you could inspect any time, usually at the end of the shift. Now, you inspect early and you have to learn to watch for things that have built up. You have to be able to distinguish between a day's worth of dirt and a week's worth. Dustballs don't accumulate in a day. I had to develop grit and dirt tests, because, at first [right after the change] I couldn't tell that people had cleaned.

## Weakened Control over Work Areas

> On nights, we were working for ourselves. There was nobody else around. We owned the place.
>
> —A section manager speaking for himself and his workers

Among the custodians at Urban University, pride in work was closely associated with the ability to get one's work done well without interference from others. Whether or not building occupants respected their work, the janitors took pride in leaving their areas clean at the end of a work period. Workers so strongly identified with the areas for which they were responsible that they resisted being transferred to other areas that "might not be kept up like they should," and that would therefore reflect poorly on the transferred worker. Universally feared were inherited areas that had many layers of old wax and would have to be "stripped down." A conscientious custodian stripped away the old wax each time before applying new. Having their own areas not only protected workers from the consequences of others' bad habits but also allowed them to identify the results of their own work.

At Urban University, custodians felt so strongly about their own areas that some identified with these areas as much as or more than they did with their homes. As one man explained, "I've been working this area longer than I've ever lived in any apartment."

If the area was one's own, it followed that the dirt in it was also one's own, and therefore, custodians did not feel as if they were cleaning up other people's dirt. Indeed, custodians complained about having to clean others' dirt primarily when referring to cleaning areas other than their own.

Because day work diluted their control over and attachment to their work areas, the custodians found it more difficult to take pride in their work. For example, managers organized day workers into teams to clean classrooms between 6:30 and 8:00 a.m. Similarly, in order to clean faculty offices and other rooms during the brief times they were unoccupied, managers organized scrub crews that moved from area to area, cleaning rooms quickly before the occupants arrived or when they were out. The more time workers spent in scrub crews, the less time they had for their own areas. Although they recognized that such team work was necessary, custodians fought one supervisor's attempts to expand the use of teams. As one steward complained:

> He was gonna try and make us work his way and go into other people's areas and do all the work from 7:00 to 9:00 A.M. We grieved it because it wasn't fair. People got work areas and have been working those areas ever since I've been on campus, and all at once, he's gonna [try to] turn it all around.

They filed a grievance against the supervisor and won. Having their own areas allowed workers more control over the work process as well as the opportunity to take pride in their own products. This opportunity was worth fighting for. "Area ownership" was very important to the custodians and appeared to serve much the same function that actual ownership does for other workers (see Perry, 1978).

Finally, moving from night to day work cost the custodians control over the building itself. They were no longer able to make relatively free use of public and private spaces. If the building was not occupied at night, custodians were free to work in any room at any time and to use facilities which belonged by day to their clientele. They could cook their lunches in the office microwave oven, take their breaks while watching a late movie on the television in the VIP lounge, or take a short nap on a lobby sofa. They could also visit with coworkers in comfortable surroundings that by day belonged to others (or were public) but became theirs alone at night.

Working in the same building during the day, however, meant sharing the space with the daytime occupants. VIP lounges became off-limits. Televisions and microwave ovens were no longer accessible, and the custodians had to spend their breaks out of sight in the custodians' lounge or hidden in their custodial "closets."

## CUSTODIAL DAY WORK: WORKING WITH AND
## AROUND DAY USERS

For daytime custodial workers, faculty, staff, and students changed from "absentee owners" to unwanted extra bosses, clients who had to be related to, or active destroyers of work product who had to be managed. Furthermore, day work accentuated status differences between the newly visible workers and their clientele.

### Social Visibility

> "At least you can see the dirt."

Occupying a low status became a particular problem for many custodians when the shift change forced them into contact with higher status people during the day. Not only were custodians less likely to come into contact with professors at night, but those that they did see were apt to be more friendly when only the custodian and the professor were in the building. As Kozak (1974: 56) observed in her study of night nurses, many social barriers are lifted in night-work settings, and night workers share confidences of the sort that one is apt to share only with people one will not see again. Thus night work may reduce the stigma of dirty work not only by making the work less visible but also by conditioning the responses of after-hours occupants who share the night custodian's space (see Melbin, 1978: 16).

One female custodian reported that at least she could see the dirt better now that she was working days. Interviews with other custodians, union stewards, and supervisors lent an unintended meaning to her statement. For example, a 20-year-old white man who liked doing custodial work, but didn't feel comfortable about the title of the job, said that he liked working nights because he could work with minimal supervision. After he had been working days for six months, he still felt unhappy about the change because of comments made by students whom he knew from high school. They made him feel inferior for being a janitor rather than going to school as they were. He didn't mind losing the night differential, and the day hours were much better for his social life, but working around students presented him with both psychological and practical problems At night, his occupational status had been visible to former acquaintances. By day, both the dirt and the dirty work were easier to see. Similarly, a 51-year-old black woman spoke of how embarrassing it was to be a janitor, especially since Urban University had no service elevators. At night, at least the elevators were likely to be empty, but on days, she would have to push her cart and mop bucket onto elevators already crowded with people. To minimize her embarrassment, she planned to be as well-groomed as she could when working days. At night she had enjoyed "dressing sloppy."

Racial prejudices were also more evident by day. Without disguising his shock, a supervisor described how a secretary in one departmental office had made it known that she "did not like being around Black people." Rather than confront her racism, he arranged to have the office cleaned at 6:30 A.M. before she got in. That way, both the dirty work and the worker remained invisible.

## Hurt Pride

Because of the continuous day use of Urban University, day work was a process of cleaning and recleaning. One was no longer able to leave a totally clean area at the end of a work period. One woman complained that cleaning Urban University during the day was like trying to clean a house with seven children running around, and a man said that it was like trying to clean Main Street during the rush hour. On the day shift workers felt that they were not accomplishing anything.[4] For example, a woman who had been working days for over two years had become a union steward in order to help fellow workers deal with the additional pressures of day work. Comparing her work to bread baking, she said:

It's just like if you are making bread and don't have the ingredients. Why bother to even make the bread if you can't do it right? Why bother to try to clean if you can't do it at all?

Another woman said, "It takes all the respect out of your work. It's like we're not doing anything."

A female union steward who had been working days for over a year also thought that the cleaning could not be done properly during the day:

People that know about cleaning can go through these buildings and they can see that the work is not being done properly and professionally, and we're professional people. I'm trained as a professional in my department, and you can't do professional work when you have people wall-to-wall.

Like Gold's janitor who compared himself to the physician, this worker thought of herself as a "professional." She had internalized standards of work performance above and beyond what might be expected from her supervisor. When she could not work to her own standards, her pride was hurt.

## The Wet-floor Problem: Job Conflicts with Day Users

The "wet-floor stories" told by many workers capture both a classic status dilemma and the stigmatization that accompanies it. A white female custodian described her confrontation with a faculty member whom she had asked to avoid walking on the floor she had just mopped:

> I told her to please not walk on the wet floor, and she was going to call in a complaint on me for that. She was letting me know that she was a higher-upper than I am.

A man described a conflict with a woman faculty member who insisted on exiting from the elevator on the spot he had just waxed. When he asked her to get out at the floor above and walk down, she refused. Instead, she walked right over his wax so that he had to redo it. She compounded this display of arrogance by refusing to talk to the custodian for a month after that.

A middle-aged white woman complained that the "Caution" signs management supplied did not distinguish between water and fresh wax. When she would try to tell people that a floor had just been waxed, she said that they seemed to think, "Who do you think you are, telling me that I can't go across that?"

Another worker described how people, not content to simply walk over his wet floor, would even walk right onto his mop. Other workers told the same story. Wet-floor stories were typically set in public places such as hallways or foyers, and underlying each was the refrain, "How can we get those professors and students to listen to us janitors? They don't have any respect for our work."

Whereas status conflicts in public places involved professors and students refusing to accede to custodians' requests, status conflicts in offices and occupied classrooms more often concerned who had the right to be where at any given time. Professors would complain about the noise made in hallways and adjacent classrooms that were being cleaned. One young man tried to clean when professors were not around, but "caught it" anyway:

> Because even if you think the [professors] aren't in, they come in and start bitching about all the noise. And the professors don't care about the cleaning, but the boss does.

A woman spoke of the difficulty of getting into offices without disturbing professors:

> We can't get into offices to clean unless we disturb them. It's really kind of hectic. Go to this office, and someone's there. Go to this office and someone's there. Go to this office and someone's there. Some of them gets kinda mad, like "This is my office. My private office for eight hours a day. If you want to clean, you can clean after I leave." It told him that this is the way the change is, and if he doesn't like people coming in, he should have done something about it before.[5]

Sometimes section supervisors served as buffers between custodians and irritated customers. One well-liked supervisor described how he handled such conflicts:

> The job is demeaning enough as it is. I try to make them feel important. Give them pride. I don't criticize them. I praise them. I tell them, "I don't like doing it either (cleaning up other people's messes), but I gotta eat." . . . I never side with the other side. If someone complains about one of my workers, I say "What did you do to upset him? You must have said something to annoy him, because I've never had any trouble with him."

Although workers appreciated supervisors who backed them in conflicts with building occupants, they also devised their own strategies for dealing with continuous problems posed by day work in an occupied building.

## STRATEGIES AND SOLUTIONS

The extent to which all of these changes decreased workers' autonomy and control depended upon the custodians' own ability to manage their clientele as well as upon the supervisors' strategies for dealing with complaints about workers. In order to get their higher-status clientele to do what they wanted them to do, workers "trained" and manipulated the daytime population in a variety of ways. Some employed "cultivating techniques," while others used various forms of "passive resistance" to get their points across. Cultivated relationships have often been observed between service people and their clientele (see Butler and Snizek, 1976). In an article on milkmen and their customers, (Bigus 1972) described the cultivated relationship as one that is carried out to gain a reward. Although not limited to service relationships, cultivated relationships "are usually asymmetrical, with the less powerful party utilizing cultivating tactics to bring the relationship closer to a state of symmetry" (Bigus, 1972: 131–132).

### Training and Cultivating

A middle-aged black custodian described how he had begun to "train" his clients soon after the shift change:

> Once the Dean's kids broke a flower pot. This was right after the change. Someone came to my office during the morning break and knocked. They wanted me to come clean up the mess. Of course they wanted me to come right then and there, but I just said that I'd come clean it up and I got to it around 2:30 [four hours later] just so they wouldn't think that I was gonna jump to their calls. . . . Everyone can tell you what to do, but you can't tell anyone what to do. . . . Everyone's a custodian's boss.

This worker was a steward who tried to promote harmony between workers and his well-liked supervisor. Nonetheless, he felt that he had to start the day shift by bounding the expectations of his daytime clientele.

Another cultivating technique involved getting to know clients well enough to predict and/or negotiate a cleaning schedule. When we interviewed her in April, 1982, Carol had been a supervisor for two months. She had worked third shift for six months before changing to first in August, 1979. This worker-turned-supervisor spoke of how it was possible to overcome the problem of human obstacles by scheduling cleaning with the building's occupants:

> We found out their schedule and we got used to them, finding out when the best time of day was for going in and cleaning up their office. Some didn't mind if the door was open, we'd clean and then come out. Some preferred that you didn't come in while they were there. Some we'd clean while they were out to lunch break.

A custodian who cleaned dance studios felt compelled to mop the hardwood floors frequently because people danced in their bare feet. However, because of heavy class scheduling and irregular scheduled rehearsals, he was finding it difficult to keep the floor clean. Finally he asked for a copy of the class schedule and arranged with the instructors to let him know in advance when they planned a rehearsal. That way he was able to arrange a cleaning schedule around the multiple uses of the studio.

For these and many other workers, having to plan and negotiate cleaning schedules was a challenge that made it easier to take pride in their work on days even if the work was hard to do. As Carol said, "it's more a creative type work; not a routine cleaning offices." If having to work around wall-to-wall people wounded the pride of many workers, others were able to transform human obstacles into a clientele who could be managed. They then substituted pride in these managerial skills for pride in the once-clean floor.

In addition to access to rooms, cultivated relationships could also yield birthday and Christmas presents in exchange for special favors. Helping a faculty member move a file cabinet, or watering plants while someone was on vacation could mean a $10 tip or a fifth of Scotch. The supervisor described earlier claimed that the workers in this section "made out like bandits" at Christmas. However, unlike waitresses, taxi drivers, and milkmen, the custodians at Urban University used cultivation primarily in order to manage their work environment rather than as a means of gaining material rewards.

## Resistance

In addition to the passive resistance such as that used to "train" the dean whose children broke the flowerpot, workers sometimes resorted to more active forms of resistance. For example, according to some workers' accounts, when the custodians found it impossible to clean the busy library during the day, they created a noise disturbance by attaching dustpans and other noisy paraphernalia to their carts. They then enlisted the support of irate students and faculty in getting the library custodians quickly returned to the third shift.

I encountered another example of active resistance one afternoon as I spent over 15 minutes waiting for an elevator. As the crowd on the first floor grew, speculations circulated about what could be keeping both elevators stuck on the fifth floor. Finally several of us began climbing stairs to the seventh and eighth floors. When we got to the fifth floor, we peered around the corner where we saw two young female custodians guarding their drying floor while both elevators stood idle and open. They had stopped the elevators to prevent anyone from stepping on their floors. This "engineering solution" was far more effective than relying on requests to professors. They also managed to bypass the status-discrepancy problem: "If they walk on your floors, let them climb stairs."

## CONCLUSION

Before the shift change at Urban University, the custodians began their work at 10:00 P.M. after students and faculty had left, and finished at 6:30 A.M. Although custodial work ranks close to the bottom of the NORC occupational prestige scale, night work at Urban University allowed custodians to clean their own areas at their own pace with minimal supervision. Furthermore, cleaning up other people's messes in the absence of the messmakers was far less demeaning than it would have been in their presence. Impersonal dirt that belonged to no one in particular became a "dirty area" which at night "belonged" to the custodian, thus transferring the "ownership" of the dirt as well. Night custodians, therefore, spoke of cleaning others' dirt primarily when referring to cleaning another custodian's area rather than their own.

After the shift change, the janitors had to share their areas with students and faculty who continuously tracked dirt over newly mopped floors. They could no longer take pride in an area left clean at the end of a work period but instead had to devise strategies for gaining access to areas that had formerly belonged to them alone. Workers lost control over work scheduling and methods when supervisors formed scrub crews to clean classrooms between 6:30 and 8:00 A.M. Finally, interactions with faculty and students continually reminded the custodians of their lower status and brought them face to face with the people whose dirt they were responsible for removing. Rather than cleaning "areas," the day custodians were cleaning up after people, many of whom did not respect either the custodians or their work.

This longitudinal case study of public building custodians supports other researchers' findings about work pride, relative stigma, and status management among low status workers. The custodians managed their low status jobs by elevating their own statuses and deflating those of their superiors (see Goffman, 1963; Hughes, 1958).[6] They called themselves "professionals" and referred to their custodial closets as "offices." At the same time, they described their "bosses" as stupid people who did not know how to clean and questioned the common sense of "all those people with degrees." The most effective status-management strategy, however, was not really a strategy at all but rather the night-work environment, which masked the ownership of the dirt and made dirty work less visible.

Contrary to assumptions often made about low-status workers, the custodians valued the intrinsic satisfactions of night work highly, and therefore found day work less satisfying (see Gruenberg, 1980). Given the choice of finding another job or adjusting to day work, however, the custodians who remained at Urban University after the change dealt with day work by managing their clientele through a combination of cultivation and passive resistance techniques.

This study demonstrates that stigmatization is conditioned not only by place and peer cultures, but also by time. In his discussion of stigma, Goffman has given an example of a professional criminal who would not go into the public library until he was sure that none of his associates were watching (1963: 3). The custodians at Urban University were themselves proud of their work and were embarrassed only when confronted with others who devalued custodial jobs. Workers like the young man who had gone to high school with Urban University students were far more likely than others to feel embarrassed on day shift because their low status was then exposed to people whom they knew in other contexts.

Although time transforms the work setting for all night workers, work conditions change far less for factory workers than they do for public building custodians. Factory workers have less supervision at night and enjoy more camaraderie with co-workers, but the nature of the job itself is not radically altered. In an occupied building, however, custodial work becomes a very different job than it would be in an unoccupied place. Whereas the night custodian is a manager of things and materials, the successful day custodian must become a manager of people and schedules. Thus for the custodians at Urban University, changing shifts meant, in effect, changing jobs.

Along with other workplace ethnographies, this shift-change study demonstrates the importance of including the work setting in any study of occupations. Jobs that are all grouped under the same heading in the *Dictionary of Occupational Titles* may differ drastically both by work setting and by the timing of the work. In the case of Urban University custodians, a single schedule change transformed a job done autonomously into one involving both more supervision by bosses and more interaction with and interference from clientele. Workers who learned how to manage their new clientele survived the shift change with pride intact. For most others, the change turned a good job into demeaning dirty work.

## NOTES

Reprinted from Jane C. Hood, *Journal of Contemporary Ethnography* (formerly *Urban Life*) 17, no. 1 (April 1988): 96–116. Copyright © 1988 by Sage Publications, Inc. Reprinted by permission of Sage Publications, Inc.
   Gloria Lessan and Glenn Boehme contributed both ideas about and instrumental help with data collection and analysis. I thank Arlene K. Daniels and Hans O. Mauksch for their insights on dirty work and Arlene K. Daniels, Robert M. Emerson, Beverly Burris, and an anonymous reviewer for their comments on this manuscript.
   Jane C. Hood is the author of *Becoming a Two-Job Family* (1983) as well as articles on work and family roles published in *Family Relations, Journal of Marriage and Family,* and *Personnel Administrator.* She is an assistant professor of sociology at the University of New Mexico.

1. This and all other proper names used in the text are pseudonyms.

2. By eliminating the night differential of 20 cents per hour, the Facilities Department estimated it would save $40,000 annually.

3. Of the 104 workers interviewed in 1979, 76 were working at the university on first shift in August 1980. After an unsuccessful attempt to clean the busy library during the day, the 11 library custodians, with support from faculty and students, won the right to return to the night shift. The remaining 17 were working second shift elsewhere at the university (3), or had quit, transferred out of the university, been fired, or died (14). Thus, of the 76 who had made the change to day shift, we reinterviewed 63 (83%) in 1980–1981. Of the remaining 13, four had not originally given permission for a follow-up interview, three refused a second interview, and six were not located by interviewers.

   Compared to the workers remaining in the panel, the 41 who dropped out included more men and whites, slightly more workers initially opposed to the change (62% versus 53%), and more who planned to avoid working days by transferring to second shift, looking for another third shift job, working days on another job, or retiring (32% versus 8%).

4. Of those on the panel, 76% said that it was harder to get their work done on days and only 10% found it easier. Although 46% of the panel found it harder to take pride in their work, 27% found it easier. On the panel 41% found day work both harder to do and harder to take pride in, whereas 32% found the work harder but experienced no loss of work pride.

5. Before the shift change went into effect, workers tried to enlist the professors' support in blocking the change by arguing that day custodial work would interfere with the workings of the university.

6. Goffman has noted that a stigmatized person "sometimes vacillates between

cowering and bravado, racing from one to the other, thus demonstrating one central way in which ordinary face-to-face interaction can run wild" (1963: 19).

## REFERENCES

ANDERSON, E. (1978) A Place on the Corner. Chicago: Univ. of Chicago Press.

BIGUS, O. S. (1972) "The milkman and his customer: A cultivated relationship." Urban Life and Culture 1: 131–165.

BRYANT, C. D. and K. B. PERKINS (1982) "Containing work dissatisfaction: The poultry processing worker," pp. 100–212 in P. Stewart and M. Cantor (eds.) Varieties of Work. Beverly Hills, CA: Sage.

BUTLER, S. and W. B. SNIZEK (1976) "The waitress-diner relationship: A multimethod approach to the study of subordinate influence." Sociology of Work and Occupations 3: 209–221.

EMERSON, R. E. and M. POLLNER (1975) "Dirty work designations: Their features and consequences in a psychiatric setting." Social Problems 23: 243–254.

GLENN, E. (1986) Issei, Nissei, Warbride: Three Generations of Japanese Women in Domestic Service. Philadelphia: Temple Univ. Press.

GOFFMAN, E. (1963) Stigma: Notes on the Management of Spoiled Identity. Englewood Cliffs, NJ: Prentice-Hall.

GOLD, R. (1952) "Janitors versus tenants: A status-income dilemma." Amer. J. of Sociology 57: 486–493.

GRUENBERG, B. (1980) "The happy worker: An analysis of educational and occupational differences in determinants of job satisfaction." Amer. J. of Sociology 81: 247–270.

HOOD, J. (1984) "When changing shifts means changing jobs: Quality of worklife for custodial workers on the day shift." Unpublished.

——— (1987) "The caretakers: Keeping the area up and the family together." Ch. 6 in Anne Statham, Hans Mauksch, and Eleanor Miller (eds.) The Worth of Women's Work: Qualitative Studies of Women and Work. Albany, NY: SUNY-Albany Press.

HUGHES, E. C. (1958). Men and Their Work. Glencoe, IL: Free Press.

——— (1974) "Comments on 'honor in dirty work.'" Sociology of Work and Occupations 1: 284–287.

KOZAK, L. J. (1974) "Night people: A study of the social experience of night workers." Summation 4: 40–61.

MEARA, H. (1974). "Honor in dirty work: The case of American meat cutters and Turkish butchers." Sociology of Work and Occupations 1: 259–283.

MELBIN, M. (1978). "Night as frontier." Amer. Soc. Rev. 43: 3–22.

PERRY, S. (1978) San Francisco Scavengers. Berkeley: Univ. of California Press.

U.S. Department of Labor, Bureau of Labor Statistics (1986) Occupational Projections and Training Data. Bulletin 2251. Washington, DC: Government Printing Office.

WALSH, E. J. (1975) Dirty Work, Race and Self Esteem. Ann Arbor, MI: Institute of Labor and Industrial Relations, University of Michigan/Wayne State University.

# 15

## The Time Bind: When Work Becomes Home and Home Becomes Work

*Arlie Russell Hochschild*

What are the relationships between work life and family life? How do individuals negotiate the role demands of both social institutions? Arlie Hochschild investigates these questions in her three-year study of a large corporation, called "Amerco." Hochschild interviewed 130 employees, including middle and upper management, clerks and factory workers, most of whom were working parents. Hochschild also talked with human resource specialists, psychologists, child-care workers, and homemakers who were married to Amerco employees. In this selection, adapted from her book, *The Time Bind: When Work Becomes Home and Home Becomes Work* (1997), Hochschild discusses her findings about the changing relationship between work life and home life for many working parents.

It's 7:40 A.M. when Cassie Bell, 4, arrives at the Spotted Deer Child-Care Center, her hair half-combed, a blanket in one hand, a fudge bar in the other. "I'm late," her mother, Gwen, a sturdy young woman whose short-cropped hair frames a pleasant face, explains to the child-care worker in charge. "Cassie wanted the fudge bar so bad, I gave it to her," she adds apologetically.

"*Pleeese,* can't you take me with you?" Cassie pleads.

"You know I can't take you to work," Gwen replies in a tone that suggests that she has been expecting this request. Cassie's shoulders droop. But she has struck a hard bargain—the morning fudge bar—aware of her mother's anxiety about the long day that lies ahead at the center. As Gwen explains, later, she continually feels that she owes Cassie more time than she gives her—she has a "time debt."

Arriving at her office just before 8, Gwen finds on her desk a cup of coffee in her personal mug, milk no sugar (exactly as she likes it), prepared by a co-worker who managed to get in ahead of her. As the assistant to the head of public relations at a company I will call Amerco, Gwen has to handle responses to any reports that may appear about the company in the press—a challenging job, but one that gives her satisfaction. As she prepares for her first meeting of the day, she misses her daughter, but she also feels relief; there's a lot to get done at Amerco.

Gwen used to work a straight eight-hour day. But over the last three years, her workday has gradually stretched to eight and a half or nine hours, not counting the E-mail messages and faxes she answers from home. She complains about her hours to her co-workers and listens to their complaints—but she loves her job. Gwen picks up Cassie at 5:45 and gives her a long, affectionate hug.

At home, Gwen's husband, John, a computer programmer, plays with their daughter while Gwen prepares dinner. To protect the dinner "hour"—8:00–8:30—Gwen checks that the phone machine is on, hears the phone ring during dinner but resists the urge to answer. After Cassie's bath, Gwen and Cassie have "quality time," or "Q.T.," as John affectionately calls it. Half an hour later, at 9:30, Gwen tucks Cassie into bed.

There are, in a sense, two Bell households: the rushed family they actually are and the relaxed family they imagine they might be if only they had time. Gwen and John complain that they are in a time bind. What they say they want seems so modest—time to throw a ball, to read to Cassie, to witness the small dramas of her development, not to speak of having a little fun and romance themselves. Yet even these modest wishes seem strangely out of reach. Before going to bed, Gwen has to E-mail messages to her colleagues in preparation for the next day's meeting; John goes to bed early, exhausted—he's out the door by 7 every morning.

Nationwide, many working parents are in the same boat. More mothers of small children than ever now work outside the home. In 1993, 56 percent of women with children between 6 and 17 worked outside the home full time year round; 43 percent of women with children 6 and under did the same. Meanwhile, fathers of small children are not cutting back hours of work to help out at home. If anything, they have increased their hours at work. According to a 1993 national survey conducted by the Families and Work Institute in New York, American men average 48.8 hours of work a week, and women 41.7 hours, including overtime and commuting. All in all, more women are on the economic train, and for many—men and women alike—that train is going faster.

But Amerco has "family-friendly" policies. If your division head and supervisor agree, you can work part time, share a job with another worker, work some hours at home, take parental leave or use "flex time." But hardly anyone uses these policies. In seven years, only two Amerco fathers have taken formal parental leave. Fewer than 1 percent have taken advantage of the opportunity to work part time. Of all such policies, only flex time—which rearranges but does not shorten work time—has had a significant number of takers (perhaps a third of working parents at Amerco).

Forgoing family-friendly policies is not exclusive to Amerco workers. A 1991 study of 188 companies conducted by the Families and Work Institute found that while a majority offered part-time shifts, fewer than 5 percent of employees made use of them. Thirty-five percent offer "flex place"—work from home—and fewer than 3 percent of their employees took advantage of it. And an earlier Bureau of Labor Statistics survey asked workers whether they preferred a shorter workweek, a long one or their present schedule. About 62 percent preferred their present schedule; 28 percent would have preferred longer hours. Fewer than 10 percent said they wanted a cut in hours.

Still, I found it hard to believe that people didn't protest their long hours at work. So I contacted Bright Horizons, a company that runs 136 company-based child-care centers associated with corporations, hospitals and Federal agencies in 25 states. Bright Horizons allowed me to add questions to a questionnaire they sent out to 3,000 parents whose children attended the centers. The respondents, mainly middle-class parents in their early 30s, largely confirmed the picture I'd found at Amerco. A third of fathers and a fifth of mothers described themselves as "workaholic," and 1 out of 3 said their partners were.

To be sure, some parents have tried to shorten their hours. Twenty-one percent of the nation's women voluntarily work part time, as do 7 percent of men. A number of others make under-the-table arrangements that don't show up on survey. But while working parents say they need more time at home, the main story of their lives does not center on a struggle to get it. Why? Given the hours parents are working these days, why aren't they taking advantage of an opportunity to reduce their time at work?

The most widely held explanation is that working parents cannot afford to work shorter hours. Certainly this is true for many. But if money is the whole explanation, why would it be that at places like Amerco, the best-paid employees—upper-level managers and professionals—were the least interested in part-time work or job sharing, while clerical workers who earned less were more interested?

Similarly, if money were the answer, we would expect poorer new mothers to return to work more quickly after giving birth than rich mothers. But among working women nationwide, well-to-do new mothers are not much more likely to stay home after 13 weeks with a new baby than low-income new mothers. When asked what they look for in a job, only a third of respondents in a recent study said salary came first. Money is important, but by itself, money does not explain why many people don't want to cut back hours at work.

A second explanation goes that workers don't dare ask for time off because they are afraid it would make them vulnerable to layoffs. With recent downsizings at many large corporations, and with well-paying, secure jobs being replaced by lower-paying, insecure ones, it occurred to me that perhaps employees are "working scared." But when I asked Amerco employees whether they worked long hours for fear of getting on a layoff list, virtually everyone said no. Even among a particularly vulnerable group—factory workers who were laid off in the downturn of the early 1980s and were later rehired—most did not cite fear for their jobs as the only, or main, reason they worked overtime. For unionized workers, layoffs are assigned by seniority, and for nonunionized workers, layoffs are usually related to the profitability of the division a person works in, not to an individual work schedule.

Were workers uninformed about the company's family-friendly policies? No. Some even mentioned that they were proud to work for a company that offered such enlightened policies. Were rigid middle managers standing in the way of workers using these policies? Sometimes. But when I compared Amerco employees who worked for flexible managers with those who worked for rigid managers, I found that the flexible managers reported only a few more applicants than the rigid ones. The evidence, however, counter-intuitive, pointed to a paradox: workers at the company I studied weren't protesting the time bind. They were accommodating to it.

Why? I did not anticipate the conclusion I found myself coming to: namely, that work has become a form of "home" and home has become "work." The worlds of home and work have not begun to blur, as the conventional wisdom goes, but to reverse places. We are used to thinking that home is where most people feel the most appreciated, the most truly "themselves," the most secure, the most relaxed. We are used to thinking that work is where most people feel like "just a number" or "a cog in a machine." It is where they have to be "on," have to "act," where they are least secure and most harried.

But new management techniques so persuasive in corporate life have helped transform the workplace into a more appreciative, personal sort of social world. Meanwhile, at home the divorce rate has risen, and the emotional demands have become more baffling and complex. In addition to teething, tantrums and the normal developments of growing children, the needs of elderly parents are creating more tasks for the modern family—as are the blending, unblending, reblending of new stepparents, stepchildren, exes and former in-laws.

This idea began to dawn on me during one of my first interviews with an Amerco worker. Linda Avery, a friendly, 38-year-old mother, is a shift supervisor at an Amerco plant. When I meet her in the factory's coffee-break room over a couple of Cokes, she is wearing blue jeans and a pink jersey, her hair pulled back in a long, blond ponytail. Linda's husband, Bill, is a technician in the same plant. By working different shifts, they manage to share the care of their 2-year-old son and Linda's 16-year-old daughter from a previous marriage. "Bill works the 7 A.M. to 3 P.M. shift while I watch the baby." She explains. "Then I work the 3 P.M. to 11 P.M. shift and he watches the baby. My daughter works at Walgreen's after school."

Linda is working overtime, and so I begin by asking whether Amerco required the overtime, or whether she volunteered for it. "Oh, I put in for it," she replies. I ask her whether, if finances and company policy permitted, she'd be interested in cutting back on the overtime. She takes off her safety glasses, rubs her face and, without answering my question, explains: "I get home, and the minute I turn the key, my daughter is right there. Granted, she needs somebody to talk to about her day. . . . The baby is still up. He should have been in bed two hours ago, and that upsets me. The dishes are piled in the sink. My daughter comes right up to the door and complains about anything her stepfather said or did, and she wants to talk about her job. My husband is in the other room hollering to my daughter, 'Tracy, I don't ever get any time to talk to your mother, because you're always monopolizing her time before I even get a chance!' They all come at me at once."

Linda's description of the urgency of demands and the unarbitrated quarrels that await her homecoming contrast with her account of arriving at her job as a shift supervisor: "I usually come to work early, just to get away from the house. When I arrive, people are there waiting. We sit, we talk, we joke. I let them know what's going on, who has to be where, what changes I've made for the shift that day. We sit and chitchat for 5 or 10 minutes. There's laughing, joking, fun."

For Linda, home has come to feel like work and work has come to feel a bit like home. Indeed, she feels she can get relief from the "work" of being at home only by going to the "home" of work. Why has her life at home come to seem like this? Linda explains it this way: "My husband's a great help watching our baby. But as far as doing housework or even taking the baby when I'm at home, no. He figures he works five days a week; he's not going to come home and clean. But he doesn't stop to think that I work seven days a week. Why should I have to come home and do the housework without help from anybody else? My husband and I have been through this over and over again. Even if he would just pick up from the kitchen table and stack the dishes for me, that would make a big difference. He does nothing. On his weekends off, he goes fishing. If I want any time off, I have to get a sitter. He'll help out if I'm not here, but the minute I am, all the work at home is mine."

With a light laugh, she continues: "So I take a lot of overtime. The more

I get out of the house, the better I am. It's a terrible thing to say, but that's the way I feel."

When Bill feels the need for time off, to relax, to have fun, to feel free, he climbs in his truck and takes his free time without his family. Largely in response, Linda grabs what she also calls "free time"—at work. Neither Linda nor Bill Avery wants more time together at home, not as things are arranged now.

How do Linda and Bill Avery fit into the broader picture of American family and work life? Current research suggest that however hectic their lives, women who do paid work feel less depressed, think better of themselves and are more satisfied than women who stay at home. One study reported that women who work outside the home feel more valued at home than housewives do. Meanwhile, work is where many women feel like "good mothers." As Linda reflects: "I'm a good mom at home, but I'm a better mom at work. At home, I get into fights with Tracy. I want her to apply to a junior college, but she's not interested. At work, I think I'm better at seeing the other person's point of view."

Many workers feel more confident they could "get the job done" at work than at home. One study found that only 59 percent of workers feel their "performance" in the family is "good or unusually good," while 86 percent rank their performance on the job this way.

Forces at work and at home are simultaneously reinforcing this "reversal." This lure of work has been enhanced in recent years by the rise of company cultural engineering—in particular, the shift from Frederick Taylor's principles of scientific management to the Total Quality principles originally set out by W. Edward Deming. Under the influence of a Taylorist worldview, the manager's job was to coerce the worker's mind and body, not to appeal to the worker's heart. The Taylorized worker was de-skilled, replaceable and cheap, and as a consequence felt bored, demeaned and unappreciated.

Using modern participative management techniques, many companies now train workers to make their own work decisions, and then set before their newly "empowered" employees moral as well as financial incentives. At Amerco, the Total Quality worker is invited to feel recognized for job accomplishments. Amerco regularly strengthens the familylike ties of co-workers by holding "recognition ceremonies" honoring particular workers or self-managed production teams. Amerco employees speak of "belonging to the Amerco family," and proudly wear their "Total Quality" pins or "High Performance Team" T-shirts, symbols of their loyalty to the company and of its loyalty to them.

The company occasionally decorates a section of the factory and serves refreshments. The production teams, too, have regular get-togethers. In a New age recasting of an old business slogan—"The Customer Is Always Right"—Amerco proposes that its workers "Value the Internal Customer."

This means: Be as polite and considerate to co-workers inside the company as you would be to customers outside it. How many recognition ceremonies for competent performance are being offered at home? Who is valuing the internal customer there?

Amerco also tries to take on the role of a helpful relative with regard to employee problems at work and at home. The education-and-training division offers employees free courses (on company time) in "Dealing With Anger," "How to Give and Accept Criticism," "How to Cope With Difficult People."

At home, of course, people seldom receive anything like this much help on issues basic to family life. There, no courses are being offered on "Dealing with Your Child's Disappointment in You" or "How to Treat Your Spouse like an Internal Customer."

If Total Quality calls for "re-skilling" the worker in an "enriched" job environment, technological developments have long been de-skilling parents at home. Over the centuries, store-bought goods have replaced homespun cloth, homemade soap and home-baked foods. Day care for children, retirement homes for the elderly, even psychotherapy are, in a way, commercial substitutes for jobs that a mother once did at home. Even family-generated entertainment has, to some extent, been replaced by television, video games and the VCR. I sometimes watched Amerco families sitting together after their dinners, mute but cozy, watching sitcoms in which television mothers, fathers and children related in an animated way to one another while the viewing family engaged in relational loafing.

The one "skill" still required of family members is the hardest one of all— the emotional work of forging, deepening or repairing family relationships. It takes time to develop this skill, and even then things can go awry. Family ties are complicated. People get hurt. Yet as broken homes become more common—and as the sense of belonging to a geographical community grows less and less secure in an age of mobility—the corporate world has created a sense of "neighborhood," of "feminine culture," of family at work. Life at work can be insecure; the company can fire workers. But workers aren't so secure at home, either. Many employees have been working for Amerco for 20 years but are on their second or third marriages or relationships. The shifting balance between these two "divorce rates" may be the most powerful reason why tired parents flee a world of unresolved quarrels and unwashed laundry for the orderliness, harmony and managed cheer of work. People are getting their "pink slips" at home.

Amerco workers have not only turned their offices into "home" and their homes into workplaces; many have also begun to "Taylorize" time at home, where families are succumbing to a cult of efficiency previously associated mainly with the office and factory. Meanwhile, work time, with its ever longer hours, has become more hospitable to sociability—periods of talking with friends on E-mail, patching up quarrels, gossiping. Within the long workday of many Amerco employees are great hidden pockets of inefficiency while, in the far smaller number of waking weekday hours at home, they are, despite themselves, forced to act increasingly time-conscious and efficient.

The Averys respond to their time bind at home by trying to value and protect "quality time." A concept unknown to their parents and grandparents, "quality time" has become a powerful symbol of the struggle against the growing pressures at home. It reflects the extent to which modern parents feel the flow of time to be running against them. The premise behind "quality time" is that the time we devote to relationships can somehow be separated from ordinary time. Relationships go on during quantity time, of course, but then we are only passively, not actively, wholeheartedly, specializing in our emotional ties. We aren't "on." Quality time at home becomes like an office appointment. You don't want to be caught "goofing off around the water cooler" when you are "at work."

Quality time holds out the hope that scheduling intense periods of togetherness can compensate for an overall loss of time in such a way that a relationship will suffer no loss of quality. But this is just another way of transferring the cult of efficiency from office to home. We must now get our relationships in good repair in less time. Instead of nine hours a day with a child, we declare ourselves capable of getting "the same result" with one intensely focused hour.

Parents now more commonly speak of time as if it is a threatened form of personal capital they have no choice but to manage and invest. What's new here is the spread into the home of a financial manager's attitude toward time. Working parents at Amerco owe what they think of as time debts at home. This is because they are, in a sense, inadvertently "Taylorizing" the house—speeding up the pace of home life as Taylor once tried to "scientifically" speed up the pace of factory life.

Advertisers of products aimed at women have recognized that this new reality provides an opportunity to sell products, and have turned the very pressure that threatens to explode the home into a positive attribute. Take, for example, an ad promoting Instant Quaker Oatmeal: it shows a smiling mother ready for the office in her square-shouldered suit, hugging her happy son. A caption reads: "Nicky is a very picky eater. With Instant Quaker Oatmeal, I can give him a terrific hot breakfast in just 90 seconds. And I don't have to spend any time coaxing him to eat it!" Here, the modern mother seems to have absorbed the lessons of Frederick Taylor as she presses for efficiency at home because she is in a hurry to get to work.

Part of modern parenthood seems to include coping with the resistance of real children who are not so eager to get their cereal so fast. Some parents try desperately not to appease their children with special gifts or smooth-talking promises about the future. But when time is scarce, even the best parents find themselves passing a system-wide familiar speed-up along to the most vulnerable workers on the line. Parents are then obliged to try to control the damage done by a reversal of worlds. They monitor mealtime, homework time, bedtime, trying to cut out "wasted" time.

In response, children often protest the pace, the deadlines, the grand irrationality of "efficient" family life. Children dawdle. They refuse to leave places when it's time to leave. They insist on leaving places when it's not time to leave. Surely, this is a part of the usual stop-and-go of childhood itself, but perhaps, too, it is the plea of children for more family time, and more control over what time there is. This only adds to the feeling that life at home has become hard work.

Instead of trying to arrange shorter or more flexible work schedules, Amerco parents often avoid confronting the reality of the time bind. Some minimize their ideas about how much care a child, a partner or they themselves "really need." They make do with less time, less attention, less understanding and less support at home than they once imagined possible. They *emotionally downsize* life. In essence, they deny the needs of family members, and they themselves become emotional ascetics. If they once "needed" time with each other, they are now increasingly "fine" without it.

Another way that working parents try to evade the time bind is to buy themselves out of it—an approach that puts women in particular at the heart of a contradiction. Like men, women absorb the work-family speed-up far more than they resist it; but unlike men, they still shoulder most of the workload at home. And women still represent in people's minds the heart and soul of family life. They're the ones—especially women of the urban middle and upper-middle classes—who feel most acutely the need to save time, who are the most tempted by the new "time saving" goods and services—and who wind up feeling the most guilty about it. For example, Playgroup Connections, a Washington-area business started by a former executive recruiter, matches playmates to one another. One mother hired the service to find her child a French-speaking playmate.

In several cities, children home alone can call a number for "Grandma, Please!" and reach an adult who has the time to talk with them, sing to them or help them with their homework. An ad for Kindercare Learning Centers, a for-profit child-care chain, pitches its appeal this way: "You want your child to be active, tolerant, smart, loved, emotionally stable, self-aware, artistic and get a two-hour nap. Anything else?" It goes on to note that Kindercare accepts children 6 weeks to 12 years old and provides a number to call for the Kindercare nearest you. Another typical service organizes children's birthday parties, making out invitations ("sure hope you can come") and providing party favors, entertainment, a decorated cake and balloons. Creative Memories is a service that puts ancestral photos into family albums for you.

An overwhelming majority of the working mothers I spoke with recoiled from the idea of buying themselves out of parental duties. A bought birthday party was "too impersonal," a 90-second breakfast "too fast." Yet a surprising amount of lunchtime conversation between female friends at Amerco was devoted to expressing complex, conflicting feelings about the lure of trading time for one service or another. The temptation to order flash-frozen dinners or to call a local number for a homework helper did not come up because such services had not yet appeared at Spotted Deer Child-Care Center. But many women dwelled on the question of how to decide where a mother's job began and ended, especially with regard to baby sitters and television. One mother said to another in the breakroom of an Amerco plant: "Damon doesn't settle down until 10 at night, so he hates me to wake him up in the morning and I hate to do it. He's cranky. He pulls the covers up. I put on cartoons. That way, I can dress him and he doesn't object. I don't like to use TV that way. It's like a drug. But I do it."

The other mother countered: "Well, Todd is up before we are, so that's not a problem. It's after dinner, when I feel like watching a little television, that I feel guilty, because he gets too much TV at the sitter's."

As task after task falls into the realm of time-saving goods and services, questions arise about the moral meanings attached to doing or not doing such tasks. Is it being a good mother to bake a child's birthday cake (alone or together with one's partner)? Or can we gratefully save time by ordering it, and be good mothers by planning the party? Can we save more time by hiring a planning service, and be good mothers simply by watching our children have a good time? "Wouldn't that be nice!" one Amerco mother exclaimed. As the idea of the "good mother" retreats before the pressures of work and the expansion of motherly services, mothers are in fact continually reinventing themselves.

The final way working parents tried to evade the time bind was to develop what I call "potential selves." The potential selves that I discovered in my Amerco interviews were fantasy creations of time-poor parents who dreamed of living as time millionaires.

One man, a gifted 55-year-old engineer in research and development at Amerco, told how he had dreamed of taking his daughters on a camping trip in the Sierra Mountains: "I bought all the gear three years ago when they were 5 and 7, the tent, the sleeping bags, the air mattresses, the backpacks, the ponchos. I got a map of the area. I even got the freeze-dried food. Since then the kids and I have talked about it a lot, and gone over what we're going to do. They've been on me to do it for a long time. I feel bad about it. I keep putting it off, but we'll do it, I just don't know when."

Banished to garages and attics of many Amerco workers were expensive electric saws, cameras, skis and musical instruments, all bought with wages it took time to earn. These items were to their owners what Cassie's fudge bar was to her—a substitute for time, a talisman, a reminder of the potential self.

Obviously, not everyone, not even a majority of Americans, is making a home out of work and a workplace out of home. But in the working world, it is a growing reality, and one we need to face. Increasing numbers of women are discovering a great male secret—that work can be an escape from the pressures of home, pressures that the changing nature of work itself are only intensifying. Neither men nor women are going to take up "family-friendly" policies, whether corporate or governmental, as long as the current realities of work and home remain as they are. For a substantial number of time-bound parents, the stripped-down home and the neighborhood devoid of community are simply losing out to the pull of the workplace.

There are several broader, historical causes of this reversal of realms. The last 30 years have witnessed the rapid rise of women in the workplace. At the same time, job mobility has taken families farther from relatives who might lend a hand, and made it harder to make close friends of neighbors who could help out. Moreover, as women have acquired more education and have joined men at work, they have absorbed the views of an older, male-oriented work world, its views of a "real career," far more than men have taken up their share of the work at home. One reason women have changed more than men is that the world of "male" work seems more honorable and valuable than the "female" world of home and children.

So where do we go from here? There is surely no going back to the mythical 1950s family that confined women to the home. Most women don't wish to return to a full-time role at home—and couldn't afford it even if they did. But equally troubling is a workaholic culture that strand both men and women outside the home.

For a while now, scholars on work-family issues have pointed to Sweden, Norway and Denmark as better models of work-family balance. Today, for example, almost all Swedish fathers take two paid weeks off from work at the birth of their children, and about half of fathers and most mothers take additional "parental leave" during the child's first or second year. Research shows that men who take family leave when their children are very young are more likely to be involved with their children as they grow older. When I mentioned this Swedish record of paternity leave to a focus group of American male managers, one of them replied, "Right, we've already heard about Sweden." To this executive, paternity leave was a good idea not for the U.S. today, but for some "potential society" in another place and time.

Meanwhile, children are paying the price. In her book *When the Bough Breaks: The Cost of Neglecting Our Children*, the economist Sylvia Hewlett claims that "compared with the previous generation, young people today are more likely to underperform at school; commit suicide; need psychiatric help; suffer a severe eating disorder; bear a child out of wedlock; take drugs; be the victim of a violent crime." But we needn't dwell on sledge-hammer problems like heroin or suicide to realize that children like those at Spotted Deer need more of our time. If other advanced nations with two-job families can give children the time they need, why can't we?

## NOTES

Reprinted from *Population and Development Review* 23, no. 3 (September 1997): 606–16. Used with permission.

"There's No Place like Work" by Arlie Russell Hochschild. Originally appeared in the New York Times Magazine, April 20, 1997. Copyright © 1997 by Arlie Russell Hochschild. Published in expanded form as *The Time Bind: When Work Becomes Home and Home Becomes Work* (New York: Metropolitan, 1997). Reprinted by permission of George Borchardt, Inc., for the author.

*Author's Note:* Over three years, I interviewed 130 respondents for a book. They spoke freely and allowed me to follow them through "typical" days, on the understanding that I would protect their anonymity. I have changed the names of the company and of those I interviewed, and altered certain identifying details. Their words appear here as they were spoken.—A.R.H.

# IV

# WORK CULTURES AND SOCIAL STRUCTURE

*Cultures of Blue-Collar Work: North Country Guys*

Most of the sociological study of blue-collar work has centered on factory work: deskilled, alienating, often dangerous, and often utterly boring. But blue-collar life also includes skilled trades, such as unionized and well-paid work in building occupations (carpenters, plumbers, and the like). There is another category of skilled blue-collar work seldom studied by sociologists, such as that pictured here. Blue-collar entrepreneurs such as these men own and operate complicated and powerful machinery such as the "picker" being used here to move a tree that fell on my house during a storm. These jobs require great skill: the machines can easily do more damage than good. Often these cultures of skilled blue-collar work are in rural America, and they draw upon and reinforce informal neighborhood and work-related networks.

Photo: Madrid, New York, 1988, photo by Douglas Harper.

273

*Cultures of the Professions, Semiprofessions, and Service Occupations: Chinese Businessman*

For many people of my generation, China's communist revolution represented a heroic battle against injustice, class oppression, and western imperialism. The reality of communist life, however, apparently did not match the lofty expectations of the Chinese social philosophers who created the system. Within the past decade, China has accepted capitalist reform, although in a limited and controlled manner. When I visited mainland China for the first time, on a one-day visit from a research trip in Hong Kong, I saw a strange world of western business suits, gleaming towers of international corporations, huge factories making inexpensive products, and massive pollution.

This photograph seemed to capture the international world of modern capitalism: the businessman's identity is based on his clothes and his body language, as is the businesswoman's: they both march out of traditional China into cultures of globalized work.

Photo: Shenzhen Special Economic Zone, People's Republic of China, 2002, by Douglas Harper.

*These photos correspond with the two subsections of part IV.*

In this part we locate work cultures in the social structure, recognizing that the distinctiveness of work in differing class positions necessitates special consideration. Thus we acknowledge the special character of blue-collar work, and the cultures it creates. We then turn to what Everett Hughes defined as the professional. In Weber's terminology, the professions occupy a status position that many occupations seek to achieve. Professions, rather than reflecting essential characteristics of an occupation, are a claim successfully made by some occupations for special privileges and rewards. Finally, the modern world has given rise to a vast category of occupations typically referred to as service jobs. Like professions, they serve clientele, but in jobs that are noted for their denied status, rather than their rewards. All of these occupations are affected by technology, bureaucratization, and globalization.

## CULTURES OF BLUE-COLLAR WORK

Blue-collar workers make things using their hands, tools, and machines. Through history these workers would have included virtual castes such as blacksmiths, who had special status and privilege in their communities because their skill was esoteric and important.

This type of craft work evolved to factory work, which transformed the cultures of work. The craft worker, whether making a wooden wagon wheel in the fourteenth century, or fabricating a repair by welding steel in the twentieth century, were skilled in mind and body. Often many skilled workers worked together, and thus skilled work was connected through work cultures.

We can imagine this by studying historical novels or examining paintings and drawings from earlier eras. The system was once pervasive: the guild shop made the stained glass windows and iron latches for the hundred-year construction of a medieval cathedral as well as the beer the workers drank.

Work identities were life-long and integrated into families. Guild workers were born into families of workers and worked first as apprentices; in the middle stages of learning their skill they became journeymen; and after long years of training and experience they became masters. Thus skill and mastery are part of.aging. As the body deteriorates, lack of strength and dexterity are balanced against increasing knowledge and the ability to apply it.

With the advent of manufacturing, skill was taken out of the manufacturing process. Making things became repetitive and endless actions connected to the unvarying rhythms of the machine, typically on the assembly line. The computers we type on were made on an assembly line. The automobiles we drive home in were, as well. The clothes we wear and even the food we eat, whether fast food, fresh, or packaged, was at least partially processed and assembled on assembly lines. The modern world itself is a product of the assembly line.

Humans, however, do not adapt well to this kind of work. Karl Marx poignantly and powerfully described the misery and dehumanization that the industrial process created. His concept of alienation in industrial capitalism addressed not only the separation of the worker from the product, but also the separation of the worker from other workers, from the essential self, and from what Marx called the worker's "species being," that is, the qualities that make a human a human. Marx expected that revolutionary consciousness would emerge from these circumstances, and in many situations, he predicted correctly. When the collective mind of revolution, revolt, or strikes arises among workers it is indeed a matter of shared definitions and plans—it is culture.

Sociologists have studied factory work by finding a job in a factory and reporting on their experiences. Others have studied jobs they have had prior to becoming professional sociologists. One of these is Donald Roy, who worked in a machine shop in 1944–1945 in which workers were paid piecemeal for what they accomplished. Roy discovered, counter to what one would expect, that workers did not work as fast as they could to increase their salaries. If they did, the time-motion experts would adjust the rate of their pay downward. Their hourly pay would not increase with greater effort; working harder would only produce harder work. So the workers found ways to restrict their production and to hide this from management. This, indeed, was work culture: workers finding ways to preserve their interests against management (Roy, 1952, 1953). Roy's work on restricted production echoed Everett Hughes's assertion that one of the elements found in nearly all work cultures is a struggle over the control of production.

Sociologists have also studied how shop settings and background cultures influence the cultures of industrial workers. This is shown in Bryant and Perkins's (1982) study of poultry butchers, where we encounter them in the factory:

> Workers must snatch live birds from cages unloaded from tractor trailer trucks and hang them, upside down, on shackles attached to moving conveyor lines. The hanging job may involve 30–40 pound turkeys. The hangers are subjected to wing battering by the dirty, squawking birds who frequently urinate and/or defecate on the workers handling them. As the flopping, noisy birds move down the line, they undergo an electric shock intended to relax all muscles for a thorough bleeding after the throat is cut. This step also results in additional excretory discharges from the birds. All five senses of the workers are assaulted. One hanger who was interviewed revealed that, on weekends, he took six to eight showers trying to rid himself of the stench. (203)

Yet, poultry processing employees managed to accommodate themselves; they were pretty satisfied and sustained morale through a widespread network of social interaction both on and off the job. They liked chicken work. They bought the results of their work in chicken sales and feasted on the product of their hard work. Why? The workers were from a regional culture in which options were limited. They were uneducated and not exposed to opportunities elsewhere. The wages in the poultry processing factory were above average. But, most tellingly, the workers found ways to connect on and off the job to form a culture—a collective that gave their lives meaning. One worker, ill with cancer, lovingly told of how her coworkers arranged a bake sale which produced several hundreds of dollars for her (and some great cake!). The hard and unpleasant work of the poultry factory was part of a culture in which most aspects of life were rather hard and unpleasant, but in that culture people stood together.

Many workers, including those studied by William E. Thompson (chapter 17), must find ways to manage boredom. How can workers make their minds minimally engaged, that is, sufficient to the task, but otherwise available to daydreams, fantasies, and sabotage? Roy (chapter 16) describes how a small group of old-timers endure and even come to enjoy a stupendously monotonous job. "Banana time" has come to stand for the phenomena in which factory workers create routines of mirth and playfulness to make the time go by. But these rituals, as Roy learned, are fragile. A misstated joke, in Roy's case, wrecked havoc on his ephemeral work culture.

Many sociologists find that the circumstances of the job make it difficult to establish human connections, and thus prevents forming cultures on the job. For example, Susan Mulcahy and Robert Faulkner (1977) studied how the physical organization of machines in a shop, the noise, and the structure of the work itself assured that workers remained strangers.

Those who have studied mass production work in the flesh have learned that in some circumstances workers find richness and meaning in human connection even when the work is extraordinarily oppressive. But for most workers who make things in factories, work is no better than it was in the beginning of industrialization. Our factories are now often in countries in which workers are likely to be women and children as well as adult men. The work remains dehumanizing. Some work settings nourish cultures that mitigate the alienation of assembly line work; others do not. The work, in all cases, diminishes the human experience.

## CULTURES OF THE PROFESSIONS, SEMIPROFESSIONS, AND SERVICE OCCUPATIONS

Everett Hughes was the first to define the professions sociologically. Much of what we say draws heavily on Hughes's several essays on professions and occupations.[1] But Hughes pointed out that the topic of professionalization was of interest to the founding figures of sociology: Comte observed that the "same engineer had kept the waterworks of Paris going before, during and after the Revolution." For Herbert Spencer, the professions all "elaborated, extended or elevated life . . . part of the development of society." And Durkheim noted the propensity of professional groups to generate social rules and to become "impermeable to attempts of outsiders to control them." Durkheim also imagined that occupational groups would organize social life and provide the basis for social solidarity in an increasingly individualized world (Hughes, 1971, 365).

Nevertheless, it was not until the developments of the Chicago School of Sociology in the 1920s that professions (and, by extension, service occupations) became the special topic of sociological study. The following summarizes the essential themes of Hughes's study of professions and places it in the context of the study of work cultures.

## DEFINITIONS AND ORIGINS

The earliest professional, according to Hughes, was a person who took (or "professed") religious vows. By the late seventeenth century, the meaning had become secularized and had come to indicate a special degree of qualification necessary for a category of occupation. Hughes defined it as "the occupation which one professes to be skilled in and to follow . . . a vocation in which professed knowledge is used in the affairs of others" (Hughes 1971, 375).

The modern professions developed during the early eras of capitalism in Europe, but they were distinctive in societies increasingly dominated by the logic and spirit of the market. Hughes summed this up by comparing the familiar theme of a capitalist world, *caveat emptor* ("Let the buyer beware"), to that of the professional, *credat emptor* ("Let the taker believe in us").

For Hughes, this became sociologically operational with the concepts of license and mandate. The occupations claimed special license to act and justified it with mandates that justified their special status, autonomy, and privilege. The license to touch, cut into, or dispose of bodies was granted to the medical and funeral professions. The license to instill ideas and values into the minds of children was assumed by the educational professionals. Religious professionals claim the license to judge our sins and to arrange for their forgiveness, and accounting professionals assume the license to learn and manipulate our finances. And so goes the list. Hughes pointed out, however, that with the license to cross these boundaries comes the mandate not to use the knowledge gained by privileged access to further ones' own interests, be they prurient or legitimate. The doctor is not supposed to be ghoulish or sexually aroused by his or her work. The priest is not supposed to become titillated upon hearing the sins of others. Educators are not supposed to preach their private orthodoxy. Of course, professionals and professions are rift with conflict over precisely the forgotten or ignored mandates. The current crisis in the Catholic Church is but one example.

In exchange for providing these services, these occupations expect to be self-regulated. They define the schooling necessary to prepare for the profession and determine what tests and examinations will certify the successful aspirant. They also fight for, and usually win, the right to judge and punish themselves. For example, only a university awards or terminates tenure. In some professions, the autonomy has eroded: for example, individuals have won the right to pit one set of professionals—lawyers—against another—medical doctors—in malpractice suits.

In essence, the concepts of license and mandate indicate that the professional asks to be trusted to act in the good faith of his or her client. This trust is effected within the reality—perceived more fully by the professional than the client—that not all problems are solvable; only some diseases may be cured, and one side loses every legal case.

Professional knowledge is assumed to have such depth that it can be mastered by only the brightest and most dedicated. The knowledge is also distinctive due to its intellectual abstraction: professionals think objectively about matters that are generally in the realm of the sacred, passionate, or personal spheres of life. This translates to many as irreverence, or, ironically, as greater than life, and it creates a distance that sets the professional apart.

Of course, there are those within the professions who deal with the individual and thus use the most concrete forms of professional knowledge (e.g., the lawyer who tries cases), and others in the profession who develop professional knowledge itself (e.g., those who study law for their entire career, teach in law schools, and write philosophically and analytically about the law). As professions become more powerful, their mandate also expands: doctors not only become more skilled and knowledgeable about treating disease but also are called upon to define the nature of health and, by extension, the nature of the good, or most desired, life. Politicians are largely recruited from lawyers, who in that role assume the responsibility to organize society legally.

The independence of thought connected to professional life was once reflected in the social independence of the professional. The archetypical professional worked alone and was contracted individually for services rendered. Hughes reminds us that the original professor of the European university earned the right to teach by gaining the doctoral degree and used the university as a forum for and form of validation: his fees were earned directly from students.

These ideal types are barely recognizable in modern society. Most professions and professionals have become socially, economically, and politically powerful and serve their own interests predominately. The term "professional" has come for many to mean simply those who earn a living doing only an activity, such as professional athletes, who are extravagantly paid and seldom demonstrate any meaningful social altruism. Even the assumption of calling and the attendant expectation of service among professions such as the clergy, teachers, and professors have been eroded by scandals in the church and political maneuvering among the teaching professions. The ease with which people leave the professions for more lucrative occupations confirms the decline of professional calling in modern life.

Finally, we have come to see professions as a contested category rather than as a description of intrinsic qualities of special occupations. Hughes notes that this theme of occupational social mobility was described as early as 1933 in an extensive study of British occupations, and it was also the theme of a defining article on professions in America in 1939 (1971, 365–66). The process of professionalization thus has come to describe the process by which occupations make their case for professional status: these processes include extending the educational preparation required for the profession and often a special degree, establishing professional societies and licensing boards, establishing a research tradition within the profession that defines its special characteristics, and organizing politically to gain legal power. Hughes noted that his many students, encountered over several decades of teaching the sociology of work and professions, described these processes, often in the occupations of their parents or those they imagined for their life's work. We include Lively's 2001 study of the process of professionalization in the occupation of paralegals to illustrate this central theme (see chapter 19).

Hughes also recognized that the category of "semiprofessional" was an indication of professionalization as a social process rather than an intrinsic quality. From this view, semiprofessions are those that have not fully made their claim for professional status, rather than occupations with specifically distinctive characteristics.

When a semiprofession becomes identified with an oppressed group or gender, it is harder to move it into full professional status. This has been the case with occupations such as elementary school teaching and nursing. Because they have been dominated by women, their claims for full professional status have been thwarted by the sexist environment in which the professional claim is made. This is easily seen in comparative studies of occupations and professions, whereby we observe that the same occupations in societies with less or different forms of sexism claim professional status more readily.

The sociological study of professions takes the matter of the professional relationship with clients as a proper matter of study. Professionals take the crises of our lives as their routine. When sociologists look behind the scenes of the professional routine, they see the client–professional relationship as negotiated, constructed, and deriving from norms and assumptions that seem inconsistent with the characterization of a profession as a calling with the clients' interest at the center. Sander's (1994) study of annoying customers in a veterinary clinic, included in our collection (see chapter 18), is one such study.

## PROFESSIONALIZATION AND BUREAUCRATIZATION

The single most powerful force affecting professionalization in modern society, however, is bureaucratization. As noted, the professional originally was an autonomous provider of services. As these services became more available, it became necessary to regulate fees and to spread the paying of fees in such arrangements as payments from insurance companies or state funding. Bureaucratization has been an inevitable consequence because it provides the most efficient means to organize the increasingly complex process through which professional services are allocated and funded. Furthermore, bureaucracies, such as townships, purchase professional services (such as from engineers) that are often embedded in other bureaucracies. Simply managing the interactions of complex bureaucracies becomes the specialty of yet another branch of a profession of law or civil administration. The spreading of costs through medical insurance allowed doctors to vastly increase their fees (most people are startled to realize that before World War II, medical doctors and professors made equivalent salaries), but it has robbed medical doctors of their autonomy. Doctors now operate as employees of bureaucracies as varied as hospitals and HMOs; although they are still well rewarded financially, their work has been routinized and can be as controlled as are the tasks of an assembly-line worker. The essential basis between the client and the professional is eroded in the bureaucratized professional environment: clients complain that their doctors have no real knowledge or care about their individual problems, and doctors also complain of the same problem from the opposite vantage point: they miss being doctors in the old altruistic sense, being full caring people to those they serve.

Although sociologists have studied the professions, few have studied the shared work cultures created in professional environments. This may originally be due to the sense that professionals operate as closed castes or guilds. The earliest professionals, the clergy, lived away from society physically as well as morally and intellectually. This is still the case in rare colleges where faculty occupy housing on campus and give much of their private life to their occupational role. In any case, detailed study of the psychological interior of the professional identity has seldom been done. Rather, sociologists have studied how professions recreate themselves and how they operate in society. Many sociologists have examined the formation of professional ideology in professional training. The idea of professional ideology itself sounds a strange chord in the arena of the professions: ideology suggests the protection of special privilege through the creation of fictions that justify inequality. Becker and Geer's study of medical students, included as chapter 3 of this collection, and several other similar studies focus on the question of how students of the professions internalize the larger-than-life responsibilities their work will entail—in other words, how the ideology will be internalized.

The study of the self and the professional identity was examined in the terms of role closeness, role neutrality, or role distance in a study of classroom teachers (Khleif, 1985). The matter of the professional in organizations has been examined critically in studies of proletarianization, or the routinization of professional work (Larson, 1980), and gender inequality within professions such as law (Podmore and Spencer, 1982).

Finally, however, the matter of professional culture remains enigmatic. Lines between professions and other occupations are blurred and contested. Society's appreciation of professional distinctiveness that in the past justified the profession's special privileges and licenses and that recognized the mandates of professions is vastly diminished, even as the economic inequality that follows the professional faultline increases. Few sociologists have penetrated the professional cultures, a symptom of the sociological tendency to "study down" the social ladder and a reflection of professionals' more pronounced ability to avoid the lens of sociological study. Those sociologists who have penetrated the professional worlds have focused more on the problematics rather than the sociologically generic. In other words, further study of professional work cultures is needed!

## SERVICE OCCUPATIONS

We are well used to the idea that our society has moved from a production economy to a service economy. This means on the most simple level that in the late twentieth century, the suddenly prosperous working class priced itself out of existence in a global economy, and as their jobs fled to countries with less well-paid labor forces, the economy has restructured partly around the delivery of services. Professions, of course, deliver services, but we are speaking of service jobs as the doing of tasks or the servicing of people's needs at the other end of the economic and social spectrum. We might speak of the service occupations as "degraded professions" in that they do not require esoteric knowledge or long periods of training, and they do not assume that the practitioners internalize a sense of license or mandate.

Still, the world of service occupations is sociologically varied and rich for study. At one end of the sociological spectrum are jobs in child care, elder care, or other examples of caregiving that are not strictly in the medical profession. In the United States, these jobs are poorly paid and carry an ambiguous social status. These workers are expected to be motivated by professional ethics but receive few if any of the rewards of a profession. The jobs of family domestics and au pairs—family servants by another name—have special characteristics that have gained sociological attention. They are "paid in smiles" (Murray 2000), and often they compete with natural mothers for the love of their children (Murray 1998). The focus on the sociology of emotions in the cultural study of work has led to several studies of the emotional labor, and often the emotional rewards, of these semiprofessional service jobs.

However, the primary focus on the service world concentrates on the exploitation of service workers in highly rationalized work environments. This is the core of the McDonaldized world: human robots delivering poor-quality products or automatic services to customers who pass by in a blur. The 1994 film *Clerks* captured the oppositional culture that arises in these settings. These jobs, which do not involve selling to but rather servicing customers, are automated out of existence as grocery and other stores find ways to have customers pay for and bag their own food.

However, the matter of selling, that is, making a pitch and trying to snag a buyer, has been much studied. Sales involves manipulating the client's view of her or his needs, and the most successful sales personnel do exactly that. Of course, the more expensive the product, the heavier the game and the bigger the bet. But the matter of interactive manipulation is the same, no matter the level.

Finally, there is a small number of studies of the "craft" of service work, especially in the semiskilled occupations. Lawson's study of barbering (1999; see chapter 20) shows the skill and interactive context in which it is played out. Bell's study of bartending (1980) is one of few studies of the aesthetic character of a service occupation.

For the same reasons that the professionals have largely avoided sociological attention, the service jobs have fallen under greater sociological examination. They are more numerous, and they are also settings in which one gains access more easily. Sociologists study down the ladder when they study the service jobs, whether it is for convenience or necessity. Whatever the reason, we know a great deal more about how the service occupations are collectively experienced and defined than we do about the professions.

We conclude with Everett Hughes's succinct summary:

> Persons and organizations have problems; they want things done for them—for their bodies and souls, for their social and financial relations, for their cars, houses, bridges, sewage systems; they want things done to the people they consider their competitors or their enemies. . . . It is in the course of interaction with one another and with the professionals that the problems of people are given definition. (Coser collection, 72)

Seen this way, the professions and their related poor cousins, the service occupations, are essential to the cultural study of work.

## NOTE

1. Hughes's essays on the professions are best found in his collected works, *The Sociological Eye,* vol. 2 (1971). The page references in this essay refer to articles in that publication, which are also listed below in their original sources.

## CITED AND SUGGESTED READING

*Note:* The suggested readings that follow do not repeat the important themes of socialization for the professions and service occupations, deviant service occupations, and special professions and service occupations in the arts and sports, which are covered in other parts of the book.

### Blue-Collar Work

Applebaum, Herbert A. *Royal Blue: The Culture of Construction Workers.* New York: Holt, Rinehart and Winston, 1981.

Aronowitz, Stanley. *False Promises: The Shaping of American Working-Class Consciousness.* New York: McGraw-Hill, 1973.

Blauner, Robert. *Alienation and Freedom.* Chicago: University of Chicago Press, 1964.

Braverman, Harry. *Labor and Monopoly Capital: The Degradation of Work in the Twentieth Century.* New York: Monthly Review Press, 1974.

Bryant, C. D., and K. B. Perkins. "Containing Work Disaffection: The Poultry-Processing Worker." In *Varieties of Work* edited by P. Stewart and M. Cantor, Beverly Hills, Calif.: Sage, 1982.

Haas, Jack. "Binging: Education Control Among High-Steel Ironworkers." *American Behavioral Scientist* 16 (1972) 27–34.

———. "The Stages of the High Steel Ironworker Apprentice Career." *Sociological Quarterly* 15 (1974) 93–108.

———. "Learning Real Feelings: A Study of Ironworkers' Reactions to Fear and Danger." *Work and Occupations* 4 (1977) 147–70.

Hacker, Sally L. "Women Workers in the Mondragon System of Industrial Cooperatives." *Gender & Society* 1, no. 4 (December 1987) 358–79.

Halle, David. *America's Working Man.* Chicago: University of Chicago Press, 1984.

Harper, Douglas. *Working Knowledge: Skill and Community in a Small Shop.* Chicago: The University of Chicago Press, 1987.

Meara, H. "Honor in Dirty Work: The Case of American Meat Cutters and Turkish Butchers." *Sociology of Work and Occupations* 1, no. 3 (1974) 259–83.

Molstad, Clark. "Choosing and Coping with Boring Work." *Urban Life* 15, no. 2 (1986) 215–36.

Mulcahy, Susan D., and Robert Faulkner. "Work Individuation Among Women Machine Operators." *Sociology of Work and Occupations* 4, no. 3 (August 1977) 303–25.

McCarl, Robert S. "The Production Welder: Product, Process and the Industrial Craftsman." *New York Folklore Quarterly* 30 (1974) 243–53.

Riemer, J. W. "Becoming a Journeyman Electrician: Some Implicit Indicators in the Apprenticeship Process." *Work and Occupations* 4 (1977) 87–98.

Roy, Donald F. "Banana Time: Job Satisfaction and Informal Interaction." *Human Organization* 18, no. 4 (1959–1960) 158–68.

———. "Efficiency and 'The Fix': Informal Intergroup Relations in a Piecework Machine Shop." *American Journal of Sociology* 60 (1955) 255–66.

———. "Quota Restriction and Goldbricking in a Machine Shop." *American Journal of Sociology* 57 (March 1952) 427–43.

———. "Work Satisfaction and Social Reward in Quota Achievement: An Analysis of Piecework Incentive." *American Sociological Review* 18 (October 1953) 507–14.

Shostak, Arthur. *Blue-Collar Life.* New York: Random House, 1969.

Thompson, E. P. "Time, Work Discipline, and Industrial Capitalism." *Past and Present* (December 1967) 56–97.

Weiner, Harney. "Folklore in the Los Angeles Garment Industry." *Western Folklore* 23 (1964) 17–21.

## Professions

Abbott, Andrew. *The System of Professions: An Essay on the Division of Expert Labor.* Chicago: University of Chicago Press, 1988.

Allan, Jim. "The Elementary Teachers." In *Doing "Women's Work": Men in Nontraditional Occupations,* edited by Christine L. Williams, 113–27. Newbury Park, Calif.: Sage, 1993.

Becker, H. S. "Social-Class Variations in the Teacher-Pupil Relationship." *Journal of Educational Sociology* 25 (April 1952): 451–65.

———. "The Nature of a Profession." *Education for the Professions, Sixty-first Yearbook of the National Society for the Study of Education,* pt. 2 (1962): 27–46.

Becker, H. S., Blanche Geer, Everett Hughes, and Anselm Strauss. *Boys in White: Student Culture in Medical School.* Chicago: University of Chicago Press, 1961.

Blankenship, Ralph L. *Colleagues in Organization: The Social Construction of Professional Work.* New York: John Wiley and Sons, 1977.

Blau, Judith R. *Architects and Firms: A Sociological Perspective on Architectural Practice.* Cambridge, Mass.: MIT Press, 1984.

Coser, Lewis A., ed. *On Work, Race and the Sociological Imagination.* Chicago: University of Chicago Press, 1994.

Emerson, J. P. "Behavior in Private Places: Sustaining Definitions of Reality in Gynecological Examinations." In *Recent Sociology,* edited by H. P. Dreutzek, 73–97. New York: MacMillan, 1970.

Freidson, Eliot. *Doctoring Together: A Study of Professional Social Control.* Chicago: University of Chicago Press, 1975.

Haberstein, R. W. "Sociology of Occupations: The Case of the American Funeral Director." In *Human Behavior and Social Processes,* edited by A. M. Rose, 225–46. Boston: Houghton Mifflin, 1962.

Henslin, James, and Mae Briggs. "The Sociology of the Vaginal Examination." In

*Down to Earth Sociology,* 6th ed., edited by James Henslin, 204–16. New York: The Free Press, 1991.

Hoff, T. J. "The Social Organization of Physician-managers in a Changing HMO." *Sociology of Work and Occupations* 26, no. 3 (1999) 324–51.

Hughes, Everett C. "Studying the Nurse's Work." In Everett C. Hughes, *The Sociological Eye: Selected Papers,* 311–15. Chicago: Aldine/Atherton, 1971.

———. "Prestige." *Annals of the American Academy of Political Sciences* 325 (1959): 45–49.

———. "The Professions in Society." *Canadian Journal of Economics and Political Science* 26, no. 1 (1960): 54–61.

———. "Professions." *Daedalus: Journal of the American Academy of Arts and Sciences* 92, no. 4 (1965): 655–68.

———. *The Sociological Eye: Selected Papers on Work, Self and the Study of Society.* 1951–1965. Reprint, Chicago: Aldine/Atherton, 1971.

Imber, Jonathan B. *Abortion and the Private Practice of Medicine.* New Haven, Conn.: Yale University Press, 1986.

Jacobs, Jerry. "Symbolic Bureaucracy: A Case Study of a Social Welfare Agency." *Social Forces* 47 (June 1969): 413–22.

Jurik, Nancy C. "Striking a Balance: Female Correction Officers, Gender Role Stereotypes, and Male Prisons." *Social Inquiry* 58, no. 3 (1988): 291–305.

Khleif, B. B. "Role Distance, Role Closeness, and Role Neutrality of Classroom Teachers." *Sociologia Internationalis* 23, no. 1 (1985): 101–11.

Ladinsky, Jack. "Careers of Lawyers, Law Practice, and Legal Institutions." *American Sociological Review* 28, no. 1 (February 1963): 47–54.

Larson, Magali Sarfatti. *The Rise of Professionalism: A Sociological Analysis.* Berkeley: University of California Press, 1977.

———. "Proletarianization and Educated Labor." *Theory and Society* 9 (1980): 131–76.

Lewis, Linda. "Female Employment and Elite Occupations in Korea: The Case of 'Her Honor' the Judge." *Korean Studies* 21 (1997): 54–71.

Lively, Kathryn. "Occupational Claims to Professionalism: The Case of Paralegals." *Symbolic Interaction* 24, no. 3 (2001): 343–66.

Lortie, D. *The Schoolteacher.* Chicago: University of Chicago Press, 1975.

Macdonald, Keith M. "Professional Formation: The Case of Scottish Accountants." *British Journal of Sociology* 35, no. 2 (1984): 175–89.

MacLeod, Martha, L. P. *Practicing Nursing: Becoming Experienced.* New York: Churchill Livingstone, 1996.

Phelan, Jo, et al. "The Work Environments of Male and Female Professionals." *Work and Occupations* 20, no. 1 (February 1993): 68–89.

Podmore, D., and A. Spencer. "Women Lawyers in England: The Experience of Inequality." *Work and Occupations* 9 (1982): 337–61.

Rogers, Joy M., Stanley J. Freeman, et al. "The Occupational Stress of Judges." *Canadian Journal of Psychiatry* 36, no. 5 (1991): 317–22.

Stein, Leonard J. "The Doctor-Nurse Game." *Archives of General Psychiatry* 16 (1964): 699–703.

Wilson, Robert N. "Teamwork in the Operating Room." *Human Organization* 12 (winter 1954): 9–14.

## Service Occupations

Applegate, Jeffrey S. "Male Elder Caregivers." In *Doing "Women's Work": Men in Nontraditional Occupations,* edited by Christine L. Williams, 152–66. Newbury Park, Calif.: Sage, 1993.

Bell, M. "Tending Bar at Brown's: Occupational Role as Artistic Performance." *Western Folklore* 35 (1980): 93–107.

Bigus, Odis. "The Milkman and His Customers." *Urban Life and Culture* 1 (1972): 131–65.

Bogdan, Robert. "Learning to Sell Door to Door." *American Behavioral Scientist* (September-October 1972): 55–64.

Butler, William R., and William Snizer. "The Waitress-Diner Relationship: A Multimethod to the Study of Subordinate Influence." *Sociology of Work and Occupations* 3, no. 2 (May 1976): 209–22.

Davies, Margery. "Women's Place Is at the Typewriter." *Radical America* 8 (August 1974): 1–28.

———. *Woman's Place Is at the Typewriter.* Philadelphia: Temple University Press, 1982.

Davis, Fred. "The Cabdriver and His Fare." *American Journal of Sociology* 63, no. 2 (1959): 158–65.

Glenn, E. N. "A Belated Industry Revisited: Domestic Service among Japanese-American Women." In *The Worth of Women's Work,* edited by A. Statham, E. Miller, and H. Maukesch, 57–75. Albany: State University of New York Press, 1988.

Glenn, E. N., et al. "Degraded and Deskilled: The Proletarianization of Clerical Work." *Social Problems* 25 (October 1977): 52–64.

Graham, H. "Caring: A Labour of Love." In *A Labour of Love. Women, Work, and Caring,* edited by J. Finch and D. Groves, 13–30. London: Penguin, 1998.

Gunter, Billy G., and Donald Maccorquodale. "Informal Role Strategies of Outreach Workers in Family Planning Clinics." *Journal of Health and Social Behavior* 15 (June 1974): 127–35.

Gutek, B. A., B. Cherry, A. D. Bhappu, et al. "Features of Service Relationships and Encounters." *Sociology of Work and Occupations* 27, no. 3 (2000): 319–52.

Howton, F., and B. Rosenberg. "The Salesman: Ideology and Self-Imagery in a Prototypic Occupation." *Social Research* 32 (1965): 277–98.

Kleeh-Tolley, Karen. "Rationalization of Clerical Work and the Loss of Perceived Autonomy." *Humanity and Society* 20, no. 2 (1996): 25–43.

Lawson, Helene. "Attacking Nicely: Car Saleswomen Adapt to an Incompatible Role." *Sociological Viewpoints* 10 (fall 1994): 1–15.

———. "Working on Hair." *Qualitative Sociology* 22, no. 3 (1999): 235–57.

———. *Ladies on the Lot.* Lanham, Md.: Rowman & Littlefield Publishers, 2000.

Lee-Treweek, Geraldine. "Emotion Work, Order and Emotional Power in Care Assistant Work." In *Health and the Sociology of Emotions,* edited by Veronica James and Gabe Jonathan, 115–32. Cambridge: Blackwell Publishers, 1996.

———. "Women, Resistance and Care: An Ethnographic Study of Nursing Auxiliary Work." *Work, Employment and Society* 11, no. 1 (1997): 47–63.

Leidner, Robin. "Over The Counter: McDonald's." In Robin Leidner, *Fast Food, Fast*

*Talk: Service Work and the Routinization of Everyday Life.* Berkeley: University of California Press, 1993.

MacDonald, Cameron L. "Manufacturing Motherhood: The Shadow Work of Nannies and Au Pairs." *Qualitative Sociology* 21, no. 1 (1998): 25–53.

McCammon, H. J., and L. J. Griffin. "Workers and Their Customers and Clients—An Editorial Introduction." *Sociology of Work and Occupations* 27, no. 3 (August 2000): 278–93.

Mennerick, Lewis. "Client Typologies: A Method for Coping with Conflict in the Service-Worker Relationship." *Sociology of Work and Occupations* 1 (1974): 396–418.

Murray, Susan B. "Child Care Work: Intimacy in the Shadows of Family Life." *Qualitative Sociology* 21, no. 2 (1998): 149–68.

———. "Getting Paid in Smiles: The Gendering of Child Care Work." *Symbolic Interaction* 23, no. 2 (2000): 135–60.

Perakyla, Anssi. "Hope Work in the Care of Seriously Ill Patients." *Qualitative Health Research* 1, no. 4 (1991): 407–33.

Pringle, Rosemary. "Male Secretaries." In *Doing "Women's Work": Men in Nontraditional Occupations,* edited by Christine L. Williams, 128–51. Newbury Park, Calif.: Sage, 1993.

Prus, Robert. "Pursuing Commitments: An Analysis of the Influence Work Involved in 'Closing Sales.'" *Qualitative Sociology* 11, no. 3 (fall 1988): 194–214.

Rafaeli, A., and R. I. Sutton. "Untangling the Relationship between Displayed Emotions and Organizational Sales: The Case of Convenience Stores." *Academy of Management Journal* 31 (1988): 461–87.

———. "Busy Stores and Demanding Customers: How Do They Affect the Display of Positive Emotion?" *Academy of Management Journal* 33, no. 3 (1990): 623–37.

Raz, Aviad E. "The Slanted Smile Factory: Emotion Management in Tokyo Disneyland." *Studies in Symbolic Interaction* 21 (1997): 201–17.

Spradley, James P., and Brenda J. Mann. *The Cocktail Waitress: Woman's Work in a Man's World.* New York: John Wiley, 1979.

Wharton, Carol S. "Making People Feel Good: Workers' Constructions of Meaning in Interactive Service Jobs." *Qualitative Sociology* 19, no. 2 (1996): 217–33.

Whyte, William F. *Human Relations in the Restaurant Industry.* 1948. Reprint, New York: Arno Press, 1977.

# 16

## "Banana Time": Job Satisfaction and Informal Interaction

*Donald F. Roy*

This paper undertakes description and exploratory analysis of the social interaction which took place within a small work group of factory machine operatives during a two-month period of participant observation. The factual and ideational materials which it present lie at an intersection of two lines of research interest and should, in their dual bearing, contribute to both. Since the operatives were engaged in work which involved the repetition of very simple operations over an extra-long workday, six days a week, they were faced with the problem of dealing with a formidable "beast of monotony." Revelation of how the group utilized its resources to combat that "beast" should merit the attention of those who are seeking solution to the practical problem of job satisfaction, or employee morale. It should also provide insight for those who are trying to penetrate the mysteries of the small group.

Convergence of these two lines of interest is, of course, no new thing. Among the host of writers and researchers who have suggested connections between "group" and "joy in work" are Walker and Guest, observers of social interaction on the automobile assembly line.[1] They quote assembly-line workers as saying, "We have a lot of fun and talk all the time,"[2] and, "If it weren't for the talking and fooling, you'd go nuts."[3]

My account of how one group of machine operators kept from "going nuts" in a situation of monotonous work activity attempts to lay bare the issues of interaction which made up the content of their adjustment. The talking, fun, and fooling which provided a solution to the elemental problem of "psychological survival" will be described according to their embodiment in intra-group relations. In addition, an unusual opportunity for close observation of behavior involved in the maintenance of group equilibrium was afforded by the fortuitous introduction of a "natural experiment." My unwitting injection of explosive materials into the stream of interaction resulted in sudden, but temporary, loss of group interaction.

My fellow operatives and I spend our long days of simple, repetitive work in relative isolation from other employees of the factory. Our line of machines was sealed off from other work areas of the plant by the four walls of the clicking room. The one door of this room was usually closed. Even when it was kept open, during periods of hot weather, the consequences were not social; it opened on an uninhabited storage room of the shipping department. Not even the sounds of work activity going on elsewhere in the factory carried to this isolated workplace. There are occasional contacts with "outside" employees, usually on matters connected with the work; but, with the exception of the daily calls of one fellow who came to pick up finished materials for the next step in processing, such visits were sporadic and infrequent.

Moreover, face-to-face contact with members of the managerial hierarchy were few and far between. No one bearing the title of foreman ever came around. The only company official who showed himself more than once during the two-month observation period was the plant superintendent. Evidently overloaded with supervisory duties and production problems which kept him busy elsewhere, he managed to pay his respects every week or two. His visits were in the nature of short, businesslike, but friendly exchanges. Otherwise he confined his observable communications with the group to occasional utilization of a public address system. During the two-month period, the company president and the chief chemist paid one friendly call apiece. One man, who may or may not have been of managerial status, was seen on various occasions lurking about in a manner which excited suspicion. Although no observable consequences accrued from the peculiar visitations of this silent fellow, it was assumed that he was some sort of efficiency expert, and he was referred to as "The Snooper."

As far as our work group was concerned, this was truly a situation of laissez-faire management. There was no interference from staff experts, no hounding by time-study engineers or personnel men hot on the scent of efficiency or good human relations. Nor were there any signs of industrial democracy in the form of safety, recreational, or production committees. There was an international union, and there was a highly publicized union-management cooperation program; but actual interactional processes of cooperation were carried on somewhere beyond my range of observation and without participation of members of my work group. Furthermore, these union-management get-togethers had no determinable connection with the problem of "toughing out" a twelve-hour day at monotonous work.

Our work group was thus not only abandoned to its own resources for creating job satisfaction, but left without that basic reservoir of ill-will toward management which can sometimes be counted on to stimulate the development of interesting activities to occupy hand and brain. Lacking was the challenge of intergroup conflict, that perennial source of creative experience to fill the otherwise empty hours of meaningless work routine.[4]

The clicking machines were housed in a room approximately thirty by twenty-four feet. They were four in number, set in a row, and so arranged along one wall that the busy operator could, merely by raising his head from his work, freshen his reveries with a glance through one of three large barred windows. To the rear of one of the end machines sat a long cutting table; here the operators cut up rolls of plastic materials into small sheets manageable for further processing at the clickers. Behind the machine at the opposite end of the line sat another table which was intermittently the work station of a female employee who performed sundry scissors operations of a more intricate nature on raincoat parts. Boxed in on all sides by shelves and stocks of materials, this latter locus of work appeared a cell within a cell.

The clickers were of the genus punching machines; of mechanical construction similar to that of the better-known punch presses, their leading features were hammer and block. The hammer, or punching head, was approximately eight inches by twelve inches at its flat striking surface. The descent upon the block was initially forced by the operator, who exerted pressure on a handle attached to the side of the hammer head. A few inches of travel downward established electrical connection for a sharp, power-driven blow. The hammer also traveled, by manual guidance, in a horizontal plane to and from, and in an arc around, the central column of the machine. Thus the operator, up to the point of establishing electrical connections for the sudden and irrevocable downward thrust, had flexibility in maneuvering his instrument over the larger surface of the block. The latter, approximately twenty-four inches wide, eighteen inches deep, and ten inches thick, was made, like a butcher's block, of inlaid hardwood; it was set in the machine at a convenient waist height. On it the operator placed his materials, one sheet at a time if leather, stacks of sheets if plastic, to be cut with steel dies of assorted sizes and shapes. The particular die in use would be moved, by hand, from spot to spot over the materials each time a cut was made; less frequently, materials would be shifted on the block as the operator saw need for such adjustment.

Introduction to the new job, with its relatively simple machine skills and work routines, was accomplished with what proved to be, in my experience, an all-time minimum of job training. The clicking machine assigned to me was situated at one end of the row. Here the superintendent and one of the operators gave a few brief demonstrations, accompanied by bits of advice which included a warning to keep hands clear of the descending hammer. After a short practice period, at the end of which the superintendent expressed satisfaction with progress and potentialities, I was left to develop my learning curve with no other supervision than that afforded by members of the work group. Further advice and assistance did come, from time to time, from my fellow operative, sometimes upon request, sometimes unsolicited.

## THE WORK GROUP

Absorbed at first in three related goals of improving my clicking skill, increasing my rate of output, and keeping my left hand unclicked, I paid little attention to my fellow operatives save to observe that they were friendly, middle-aged, foreign-born, full of advice, and very talkative. Their names, according to the way they addressed each other, were George, Ike, and Sammy.[5] George, a stocky fellow in his late fifties, operated the machine at the opposite end of the line; he, I later discovered, had emigrated in early youth from a country in Southeastern Europe. Ike, stationed at George's left, was tall, slender, in his early fifties, and Jewish; he had come from Eastern Europe in his youth. Sammy, number three man in the line, and my neighbor, was heavy set, in his late fifties, and Jewish; he had escaped from a country in Eastern Europe just before Hitler's legions had moved in. All three men had been downwardly mobile as to occupation in recent years. George and Sammy had been proprietors of small businesses; the former had been "wiped out" when his uninsured establishment burned down; the latter had been entrepreneuring on a small scale before he left all behind him to flee the Germans. According to his account, Ike had left a highly skilled trade which he had practiced for years in Chicago.

I discovered also that the clicker line represented a ranking system in descending order from George to myself. George not only had top seniority for the group, but functioned as a sort of leadman. His superior status was marked in the fact that he received five cents more per hour than the other clickermen, put in the longest workday, made daily contact, outside the workroom, with the superintendent on work matters which concerned the entire line, and communicated to the rest of us the directives which he received. The narrow margin of superordination was seen in the fact that directives were always relayed in the superintendent's name; they were on the order of, "You'd better let that go now, and get on the green. Joe says they're running low on the fifth floor," or, "Joe says he wants two boxes of the 3-die today." The narrow margin was also seen in the fact that the superintendent would communicate directly with his operatives over the public address system; and, on occasion, Ike or Sammy would leave the workroom to confer with him for decisions or advice in regard to work orders.

Ike was next to George in seniority, then Sammy. I was, of course, low man on the totem pole. Other indices to status differentiation lay in informal interaction, to be described later.

With one exception, job status tended to be matched by length of work-day. George worked a thirteen-hour day, from 7 A.M. to 6:30 P.M. Ike worked eleven hours, from 7 A.M. to 6:30 P.M.; occasionally he worked until 7 or 7:30 for an eleven and a half- or a twelve-hour day. Sammy put in a nine-hour day, from 8 A.M. to 5:30 P.M. My twelve hours spanned from 8 A.M. to 8:30 P.M. We had a half hour for lunch, from 12 to 12:30.

The female who worked at the secluded table behind George's machine put in a regular plant-wide eight-hour shift from 8 to 4:30. Two women held this job during the period of my employment; Mable was succeeded by Baby. Both were Negroes, and in their late twenties.

A fifth clicker operator, an Arabian *émigré* called Boo, worked a night shift by himself. He usually arrived about 7 P.M. to take over Ike's machine.

## THE WORK

It was evident to me, before my first workday drew to a weary close, that my clicking career was going to be a grim process of fighting the clock, the particular timepiece in this situation being an old-fashioned alarm clock which ticked away on a shelf near George's machine. I had struggled through many dreary rounds with the minutes and hours during the various phase of my industrial experience, but never had I been confronted with such a dismal combination of working conditions as the extra-long workday, the infinitesimal cerebral excitation, and the extreme limitation of physical movement. The contrast with a recent stint in the California oil fields was striking. This was no eight-hour day of racing hither and yon over desert and foothills with a rollicking crew of "roustabouts" on a variety of repair missions at oil wells, pipe lines, and storage tanks. Here there were no afternoon dallyings to search the sand for horned toads, tarantulas, and rattlesnakes, or to climb old wooden derricks for ravens' nests, with an eye out, of course, for the tell-tale streak of dust in the distance which gave ample warning of the approach of the boss. This was standing all day in one spot beside three old codgers in a dingy room looking out through barred windows at the bare walls of a brick warehouse, leg movements largely restricted to the shifting of body weight from one foot to the other, hand and arm movements confined, for the most part, to a simple repetitive sequence of place the die, _____ punch the clicker, _____ place the die, _____ punch the clicker, and intellectual activity reduced to computing the hours to quitting time. It is true that from time to time a fresh stack of sheets would have to be substituted for the clicked-out old one; but the stack would have been prepared by someone else, and the exchange would be only a minute or two in the making. Now and then a box of finished work would have to be moved back out of the way, and an empty box brought up; but the moving back and the bringing up involved only a step or two. And there was the half hour for lunch, and occasional trips to the lavatory or the drinking fountain to break up the day into digestible parts. But after each monetary respite, hammer and die were moving again: click, _____ move die, _____ click, _____ move die.

Before the end of the first day, Monotony was joined by his twin brother, Fatigue. I got tired. My legs ached, and my feet hurt. Early in the afternoon I discovered a tall stool and moved it up to my machine to "take the load off my feet." But the superintendent dropped in to see how I was "doing" and promptly informed me that "we don't sit down on this job." My reverie toyed with the idea of quitting the job and looking for other work.

The next day was the same: the monotony of the work, the tired legs and sore feet and thoughts of quitting.

## THE GAME OF WORK

In discussing the factory operative's struggle to "cling to the remnants of joy in work," Henri de Man makes the general observations that "it is psychologically impossible to deprive any kind of work of all its positive emotional elements," that the worker will find *some* meaning in any activity assigned to him, a "certain scope for initiative which can satisfy after a fashion the instinct for play and the creative impulse," that "even in the Taylor system there is found luxury of self-determination."[6] De Man cites the case of one worker who wrapped 13,000 incandescent bulbs a day; she found her outlet for creative impulse, her self-determination, her meaning in work by varying her wrapping movements a little from time to time.[7]

So did I search for *some* meaning in my continuous mincing of plastic sheets into small ovals, fingers, and trapezoids. The richness of possibility for creative expression previously discovered in my experience with the "Taylor system"[8] did not reveal itself here. There was no piecework, so no piecework game. There was no conflict with management, so no war game. But, like the light bulb wrapper, I did find a "certain scope for initiative," and out of this slight freedom to vary activity, I developed a game of work.

The game developed was quite simple, so elementary, in fact, that its playing was reminiscent of rainy-day preoccupations in childhood, when attention could be centered by the hour on colored bits of things of assorted sizes and shapes. But this adult activity was not mere pottering and piddling; what it lacked in the earlier imaginative content, it made up for in clean-cut structure. Fundamentally involved were: a) variation in color of the materials cut, b) variation in shapes of the dies used, and c) a process called "scraping the block." The basic procedure which ordered the particular combination of components employed could be stated in the form: "As soon as I do so many of these, I'll get to do those." If, for example, production scheduled for the day featured small, rectangular strips in three colors, the game might go: "As soon as I finish a thousand of the green ones, I'll click some brown ones." And, with success in attaining the objective of working with brown materials, a new goal of "I'll get to do the white ones" might be set. Or the new goal might involve switching dies.

Scraping the block made the game more interesting by adding to the number of possible variations in its playing; and, what was perhaps more important, provided the only substantial reward, save for going to the lavatory or getting a drink of water, on days when work with one die and one color of material was scheduled. As a physical operation, scraping the block was fairly simple; it involved application of a coarse file to the upper surface of the block to remove roughness and unevenness resulting from the wear and tear of die penetration. But, as part of the intellectual and emotional content of the game of work, it could be in itself a source of variation in activity. The upper left-hand corner of the block could be chewed up in the clicking of 1,000 white trapezoid pieces, then scraped. Next, the upper right-hand corner, and so on until the entire block had been worked over. Then, on the next round of scraping by quadrants, there was the possibility of a change of color or die to green trapezoid or white oval pieces.

Thus the game of work might be described as a continuous sequence of short-range production goals with achievement rewards in the form of activity change. The superiority of this relatively complex and self-determined system over the technically simple and outside-controlled job satisfaction injections experienced by Milner at the beginner's table in a shop of the feather industry should be immediately apparent:

> Twice a day our work was completely changed to break the monotony. First Jennie would give us feathers of a brilliant green, then bright orange or a light blue or black. The "ohs" and "ahs" that came from the girls at each change was proof enough that this was an effective way of breaking the monotony of the tedious work.[9]

But a hasty conclusion that I was having lots of fun playing my clicking game should be avoided. These games were not as interesting in the experiencing as they might seem to be from the telling. Emotional tone of the activity was low, and intellectual currents weak. Such rewards as scraping the block or "getting to do the blue ones" were not very exciting, and the stretches of repetitive movement involved in achieving them were long enough to permit lapses into obsessive reverie. Henri de Man speaks of "clinging to the remnants of joy in work," and this situation represented just that. How tenacious the clinging was, how long I could have "stuck it out" with my remnants, was never determined. Before the first week was out this adjustment to the work situation was complicated by other developments. The game of work continued, but in a different context. Its influence became decidedly subordinated to, if not completely overshadowed by, another source of job satisfaction.

## INFORMAL SOCIAL ACTIVITY OF THE WORK GROUP: TIME AND THEMES

The change came about when I began to take serious note of the social activity going on around me; my attentiveness to this activity came with growing involvement in it. What I heard at first, before I started to listen, was a stream of disconnected bits of communication which did not make much sense. Foreign accents were strong and referents were not joined to coherent contexts of meaning. It was just "jabbering." What I saw first, before I began to observe, was occasional flurries of horseplay so simple and unvarying in pattern and so childish in quality that they made no strong bid for attention. For example, Ike would regularly switch off the power at Sammy's machine whenever Sammy made a trip to the lavatory or the drinking fountain. Correlatively, Sammy invariably fell victim to the plot by making an attempt to operate his clicking hammer after returning to the shop. And, as the simple pattern went, this blind stumbling into the trap was always followed by indignation and reproach from Sammy, smirking satisfaction from Ike, and mild paternal scolding from George. My interest in this procedure was at first confined to wondering when Ike would weary of his tedious joke or when Sammy would learn to check his power switch before trying the hammer.

But, as I began to pay closer attention, as I began to develop familiarity with the communication system, the disconnected became connected, the nonsense made sense, the obscure became clear, and the silly actually funny. And, as the content of the interaction took on more and more meaning, the interaction began to reveal structure. There were "times" and "themes," and roles to serve their enaction. The interaction has subtleties, and I began to savor and appreciate them. I started to record what hitherto had seemed unimportant.

### Times

This emerging awareness of structure and meaning included recognition that the long day's grind was broken by interruptions of a kind other than the formally instituted or idiosyncratically developed disjunctions in work routine previously described. These additional interruptions appeared in daily repetition in an ordered series of informal interactions. They were, in part, but only in part and in very rough comparison, similar to those common fractures of the production process known as the coffee break, the coke break, and the cigarette break. Their distinction lay in frequency of occurrence and brevity. As phases of the daily series, they occurred almost hourly, and so short were they in duration that they disrupted work activity only slightly. Their significance lay not so much in their function as rest pauses, although it cannot be denied that physical refreshment was involved. Nor did their chief importance lie in the accentuation of progress points in the passage of time, although they could perform that function far more strikingly than the hour hand on the dull face of George's alarm clock. If the daily series of interruptions be likened to a clock, then the comparison might best be made with a special kind of cuckoo clock, one with a cuckoo which can provide variation in its announcements and can create such an interest in them that the intervening minutes become filled with intellectual content. The major significance of the interactional interruptions lay in such a carry-over of interest. The physical interplay which momentarily halted work activity would initiate verbal exchanges and thought processes to occupy group members until the next interruption. The group interactions thus not only marked off the time; they gave it content and hurried it along.

Most of the breaks in the daily series were designated as "times" in the parlance of the clicker operators, and they featured the consumption of food or drink of one sort or another. There was coffee time, peach time, banana time, fish time, coke time, and, of course, lunch time. Other interruptions, which formed part of the series but were not verbally recognized as times, were window time, pickup time, and the staggered quitting times of Sammy and Ike. These latter unnamed times did not involve the partaking of refreshments.

My attention was first drawn to this times business during my first week of employment when I was encouraged to join in the sharing of two peaches. It was Sammy who provided the peaches; he drew them from his lunch box after making the announcement, "Peach time!" On this first occasion I refused the proffered fruit, but thereafter regularly consumed my half peach. Sammy continued to provide the peaches and to make the "Peach time!" announcement, although there were days when Ike would remind him that it was peach time, urging him to hurry up with the mid-morning snack. Ike invariably complained about the quality of the fruit, and his complaints fed the fires of continued banter between each donor and critical recipient. I did find the fruit a bit on the scrubby side but felt, before I achieved insight into the function of peach time, that Ike was showing poor manners by looking a gift horse in the mouth. I wondered why Sammy continued to share his peaches with such an ingrate.

Banana time followed peach time by approximately an hour. Sammy again provided the refreshments, namely, one banana. There was, however, no four-way sharing of Sammy's banana. Ike would gulp it down by himself after surreptitiously extracting it from Sammy's lunch box, kept on a shelf behind Sammy's work station. Each morning, after making the snatch, Ike would call out, "Banana time!" and proceed to down his prize while Sammy made futile protests and denunciations. George would join in with mild remonstrances, sometimes scolding Sammy for making so much fuss. The banana was one which Sammy brought for his own consumption at lunch time; he never did get to eat his banana, but kept bringing one for his lunch. At first this daily theft startled and amazed me. Then I grew to look forward to the daily seizure and the verbal interaction which followed.

Window time came next. It followed banana time as a regular consequence of Ike's castigation by the indignant Sammy. After "taking" repeated references to himself as a person badly lacking in morality and character, Ike would "finally" retaliate by opening the window which faced Sammy's machine, to let the "cold air" blow in on Sammy. The slandering which would, in its echolalic repetition, wear down Ike's patience and forbearance usually took the form of the invidious comparison: "George is a good daddy! Ike is a bad man! A very bad man!" Opening the window would take a little time to accomplish and would involve a great deal of verbal interplay between Ike and Sammy, both before and after the event. Ike would threaten, make feints toward the window, then finally open it. Sammy would protest, argue, and make claims that the air blowing in on him would give him a cold; he would eventually have to leave his machine to close the window. Sometimes the weather was slightly chilly, and the draft from the window unpleasant; but cool or hot, windy or still, window time arrived each day. (I assume that it was originally a cold season development.) George's part in this interplay, in spite of the "good daddy" laudations, was to encourage Ike in his window work. He would stress the tonic values of fresh air and chide Sammy for his unappreciativeness.

Following window time came lunch time, a formally designated half-hour for the midday repast and rest break. At this time, informal interaction would feature exchanges between Ike and George. The former would start eating his lunch a few minutes before noon, and the latter, in his role as straw boss, would censure him for malobservance of the rules. Ike's offbeat luncheon usually involved a previous tampering with George's alarm clock. Ike would set the clock ahead a few minutes in order to maintain his eating schedule without detection, and George would discover these small daylight saving changes.

The first "time" interruption of the day I did not share. It occurred soon after I arrived on the job, at eight o'clock. George and Ike would share a small pot of coffee brewed on George's hot plate.

Pickup time, fish time, and coke time came in the afternoon. I name it pickup time to represent the official visit of the man who made daily calls to cart away boxes of clicked materials. The arrival of the pickup man, a Negro, was always a noisy one, like the arrival of a daily passenger train in an isolated small town. Interaction attained a quick peak of intensity to crowd into a few minutes all communications, necessary and otherwise. Exchanges invariably included loud deprecations by the pickup man of the amount of work accomplished in the clicking department during the preceding twenty-four hours. Such scoffing would be on the order of "Is that all you've got done? What do you boys do all day?" These devaluations would be countered with allusions to the "soft job" enjoyed by the pickup man. During the course of the exchanges news items would be dropped, some of serious import, such as reports of accomplished or impending layoffs in the various plants of the company, or of gains or losses in orders for company products. Most of the news items, however, involved bits of information on plant employees told in a light vein. Information relayed by the clicker operators was usually told about each other, mainly in the form of summaries of the most recent kidding sequences. Some of this material was repetitive, carried over from day to day. Sammy would be the butt of most of this newscasting, although he would make occasional counter-reports on Ike and George. An invariable part of the interactional content of pickup time was Ike's introduction of the pickup man to George. "Meet Mr. Papeatis!" Ike would say in mock solemnity and dignity. Each day the pickup man "met" Mr. Papeatis, to the obvious irritation of the latter. Another pickup time invariably would bring Baby (or Mable) into the interaction. George would always issue the loud warning to the pickup man: "Now I want you to stay away from Baby! She's Henry's girl!" Henry was a burly Negro with a booming bass voice who made infrequent trips to the clicking room with lift-truck loads of materials. He was reputedly quite a ladies' man among the colored population of the factory. George's warning to "Stay away from Baby!" was issued to every Negro who entered the shop. Baby's only part in this was to laugh at the horseplay.

About mid-afternoon came fish time. George and Ike would stop work for a few minutes to consume some sort of pickled fish which Ike provided. Neither Sammy nor I partook of this nourishment, nor were we invited. For this omission I was grateful; the fish, brought in a newspaper and with head and tail intact, produced a reverse effect on my appetite. George and Ike seemed to share a great liking for fish. Each Friday night, as a regular ritual, they would enjoy a fish dinner together at a nearby restaurant. On these nights Ike would work until 8:30 and leave the plant with George.

Coke time came late in the afternoon, and was an occasion for total participation. The four of us took turns in buying the drinks and in making the trip for them to a fourth floor vending machine. Through George's manipulation of the situation, it eventually became my daily chore to go after the cokes; the straw boss had noted that I made a much faster tip to the fourth floor and back than Sammy or Ike.

Sammy left the plant at 5:30, and Ike ordinarily retired from the scene an hour and a half later. These quitting times were not marked by any distinctive interaction save the one regular exchange between Sammy and George over the former's "early washup." Sammy's tendency was to crowd his washing up toward five o'clock, and it was George's concern to keep it from further creeping advance. After Ike's departure came Boo's arrival. Boo's was a striking personality productive of a change in topics of conversation to fill in the last hour of the long workday.

## Themes

To put flesh, so to speak, on this interactional frame of "times," my work group had developed various "themes" of verbal interplay which had become standardized in their repetition. These topics of conversation ranged in quality from an extreme of nonsensical chatter to another extreme of serious discourse. Unlike the times, these themes flowed one into the other in no particular sequence of predictability. Serious conversation could suddenly melt into horseplay, and vice versa. In the middle of a serious discussion on the high cost of living, Ike might drop a weight behind the easily startled Sammy, or hit him over the head with a dusty paper sack. Interaction would immediately drop to a low comedy exchange of slaps, threats, guffaws, and disapprobations which would invariably include a ten-minute echolalia of "Ike is a bad man, a very bad man! George is a good daddy, a very fine man!" Or, on the other hand, a stream of such invidious comparisons as followed a surreptitious switching-off of Sammy's machine by the playful Ike might merge suddenly into a discussion of the pros and cons of saving for one's funeral.

"Kidding themes" were usually started by George or Ike, and Sammy was usually the butt of the joke. Sometime Ike would have to "take it," seldom George. One favorite kidding theme involved Sammy's alleged receipt of $100 a month from his son. The points stressed were that Sammy did not have to work long hours, or did not have to work at all, because he had a son to support him. George would always point out that he sent money to his daughter; she did not send money to him. Sammy received occasional calls from his wife, and his claim that these calls were requests to shop for groceries on the way home were greeted with feigned disbelief. Sammy was ribbed for being closely watched, bossed, and henpecked by his wife, and the expression "Are you man or mouse?' became an echolalic utterance, used both in and out of the original context.

Ike, who shared his machine and the work schedule for it with Boo, the night operator, came in for constant invidious comparison on the subject of output. The socially isolated Boo, who chose work rather than sleep on his lonely night shift, kept up a high level of performance, and George never tired of pointing this out to Ike. It so happened that Boo, an Arabian Moslem from Palestine, had no use for Jews in general; and Ike, who was Jewish, had no use for Boo in particular. Whenever George would extol Boo's previous night's production, Ike would try to turn the conversation into a general discussion on the need for educating the Arabs. George, never permitting the development of serious discussion on this topic, would repeat a smirking warning, "You watch out for Boo! He's got a long knife!"

The "poom poom" theme was one that caused no sting. It would come up several times a day to be enjoyed as unbarbed fun by the three older clicker operators. Ike was usually the one to raise the question, "How many times you go poom poom last night?" The person questioned usually replied with claims of being "too old for poom poom." If this theme did develop a goat, it was I. When it was pointed out that I was a younger man, this provided further grist for the poom poom mill. I soon grew weary of this poom poom business, so dear to the hearts of the three old satyrs, and knowing where the conversation would inevitably lead, winced whenever Ike brought up the subject.

I grew almost as sick of a kidding theme which developed from some personal information contributed during a serious conversation on property ownership and high taxes. I dropped a few remarks about two acres of land which I owned in one of the western states, and from then on I had to listen to questions, advice, and general nonsensical comment in regard to "Danelly's farm"[10] This "farm" soon became stocked with horses, cows, pigs, chickens, ducks, and the various and sundry domesticated beasts so tunefully listed in "Old McDonald Had a Farm." George was a persistent offender with this theme. Where the others seemed to be mainly interested in statistics on livestock, crops, etc., George's teasing centered on a generous offering to help with the household chores while I worked in the fields. He would drone on, ad nauseam, "When I come to visit you, you will never have to worry about the housework, Danelly. I'll stay around the house when you go out to dig the potatoes and milk the cows, I'll stay in and peel potatoes and help your wife do the dishes." Danelly always found it difficult to change the subject on George, once the latter started to bear down on the farm theme.

Another kidding theme which developed out of serious discussion could be labeled "helping Danelly find a cheaper apartment." It became known to the group that Danelly had a pending housing problem, that he would need new quarters for his family when the permanent resident of his temporary summer dwelling returned from a vacation. This information engendered at first a great deal of sympathetic concern and, of course, advice on apartment hunting. Development into a kidding themes was immediately related to previous exchanges between Ike and George on the quality of their respective dwelling areas, Ike lived in "Lawndale," and George dwelt in the "Woodlawn" area. The new pattern featured the reading aloud of bogus "apartment for rent" ads in newspapers which were brought into the shop. Studying his paper at lunchtime, George would call out, "Here's an apartment for you, Danelly! Five rooms, stove heat, $20 a month, Lawndale Avenue!" Later, Ike would read from his paper, "Here's one! Six rooms, stove heat, dirt floor, $18.50 a month! At 55th and Woodlawn." Bantering would then go on in regard to the quality of housing or population in the two areas. The search for an apartment for Danelly was not successful.

Serious themes included the relating of major misfortunes suffered in the past by group members. George referred again and again to the loss, by fire, of his business establishment. Ike's chief complaints centered around a chronically ill wife who had undergone various operations and periods of hospital care. Ike spoke with discouragement of the expenses attendant upon hiring a housekeeper for himself and his children; he referred with disappointment and disgust to a teenage son, an inept lad who "couldn't even fix his own lunch. He couldn't even make himself a sandwich!" Sammy's reminiscences centered on the loss of a flourishing business when he had to flee Europe ahead of Nazi invasion.

But all serious topics were not tales of woe. One favorite serious theme which was optimistic in tone could be called either "Danelly's future" or "getting Danelly a better job." It was known that I had been attending "college," the magic door to opportunity, although my specific course of study remained somewhat obscure. Suggestions poured forth on good lines of work to get into, and these suggestions were backed with accounts of friends, and friends of friends, who had made good via the academic route. My answer to the expected question, "Why are you working here?" always stressed the "lots of overtime" feature, and this explanation seemed to suffice for short-range goals.

There was one theme of especially solemn import, the "professor theme." This theme might also be termed "George's daughter's marriage theme"; for the recent marriage of George's only child was inextricably bound up with George's connection with higher learning. The daughter had married the son of a professor who instructed in one of the local colleges. This professor theme was not in the strictest sense a conversation piece; when the subject came up, George did all the talking. The two Jewish operatives remained silent as they listened with deep respect, if not actual awe, to George's accounts of the Big Wedding which, including the wedding pictures, entailed an expense of $1,000. It was monologue, but there was listening, there was communication, the sacred communication of a temple, when George told of going for Sunday afternoon walks on the Midway with the professor, or of joining the professor for a Sunday dinner. Whenever he spoke of the professor, his daughter, the wedding, or even of the new son-in-law, who remained for the most part in the background, a sort of incidental like the wedding cake, George was complete master of the interaction. His manner, in speaking to the rank-and-file of clicker operators, was indeed that of master deigning to notice his underlings. I came to the conclusion that it was the professor connection, not the straw-boss-ship or the extra nickel an hour, which provide the fount of George's superior status in the group.

If the professor theme may be regarded as the cream of verbal interaction, the "chatter themes" should be classed as the dregs. The chatter themes were hardly themes at all; perhaps they should be labeled "verbal states," or "oral autisms." Some were of doubtful status as communication; they were like the howl or cry of an animal responding to its own physiological state. They were exclamations, ejaculations, snatches of song or doggerel, talkings-to-oneself, mutterings. Their classifications as themes would rest on their repetitive character. They were echolalic utterances, repeated over and over. An already mentioned example would be Sammy's repetition of "George is a good daddy, a very fine man! Ike is a bad man, a very bad man!" Also, Sammy's repetition of "Don't bother me! Can't you see I'm busy? I'm a very busy man!" for ten minutes after Ike had dropped a weight behind him would fit the classification. Ike would shout "Marmariba!" at intervals between repetition of bits of verse, such as:

> Mama on the bed,
> Papa on the floor,
> Baby in the crib
> Says giver some more!

Sometimes the three operators would pick up one of these simple chatterings in a sort of chorus. "Are you man or mouse? I ask you, are you man or mouse?" was a favorite of this type.

So initial discouragement with the meagerness of social interaction I now recognized as due to lack of observation. The interaction was there, in constant flow. It captured attention and held interest to make the long day pass. The twelve hours of "click, _____ move die, _____ click, _____ move die" became as easy to endure as eight hours of varied activity in the oil fields or eight hours of playing the piecework game in a machine shop. The "beast of boredom" was gentled to the harmlessness of a kitten.

## BLACK FRIDAY: DISINTEGRATION
## OF THE GROUP

But all this was before "Black Friday." Events of that dark day shattered the edifice of interaction, its framework of times and mosaic of themes, and reduced the work situation to a state of social atomization and machine-tending drudgery. The explosive element was introduced deliberately, but without prevision of its consequences.

On Black Friday, Sammy was not present; he was on vacation. There was no peach time that morning, of course, and no banana time. But George and Ike held their coffee time, as usual, and a steady flow of themes was filling the morning quite adequately. It seemed like a normal day in the making, at least one which was going to meet the somewhat reduced expectations created by Sammy's absence.

Suddenly I was possessed of an inspiration for modification of the professor theme. When the idea struck, I was working at Sammy's machine, clicking out leather parts for billfolds. It was not difficult to get the attention of close neighbor Ike to suggest *sotto voce*, "Why don't you tell him you saw the professor teaching in a barber college on Madison Street? . . . Make it near Halsted Street."

Ike thought this one over for a few minutes, and caught the vision of its possibilities. After an interval of steady application to his clicking, he informed the unsuspecting George of his near West Side discovery; he had seen the professor busy at his instructing in a barber college in the lower reaches of Hobohemia.

George reacted to this announcement with stony silence. The burden of questioning Ike for further details on his discovery fell upon me. Ike had not elaborated his story very much before we realized that the show was not going over. George kept getting redder in the face, and more tight-lipped; he slammed into his clicking with increased vigor. I made one last weak attempt to keep the play on the road by remarking that barber colleges paid pretty well. George turned to hiss at me, "You'll have to go to Kankakee with Ike!" I dropped the subject. Ike whispered to me, "George is sore!"

George was indeed sore. He didn't say another word the rest of the morning. There was no conversation at lunchtime, nor was there any after lunch. A pall of silence had fallen over the clicker room. Fish time fell a casualty. George did not touch the coke I brought for him. A very long, very dreary afternoon dragged on. Finally, after Ike left for home, George broke the silence to reveal his feelings to me:

> Ike acts like a five-year-old, not a man! He doesn't even have the respect of the niggers. But he's got to act like a man around here! He's always fooling around! I'm going to stop that! I'm going to show him his place! . . .

Jews will ruin you, if you let them. I don't care if he sings, but the first time he mentions my name, I'm going to shut him up! It's always "Meet Mr. Papeatis! George is a good daddy!" And all that. He's paid to work! If he doesn't work, I'm going to tell Joe! [The superintendent.]

Then came a succession of dismal workdays devoid of times and barren of themes. Ike did not sing, nor did he recite bawdy verse. The shop songbird was caught in the grip of icy winter. What meager communication there was took a sequence of patterns which proved interesting only in retrospect.

For three days, George would not speak to Ike, Ike made several weak attempts to break the wall of silence which George had put between them, but George did not respond; it was as if he did not hear. George would speak to me, on infrequent occasions, and so would Ike. They did not speak to each other.

On the third day George advised me of his new communication policy, designed for dealing with Ike, and for Sammy, too, when the latter returned to work. Interaction was now on a "strictly business" basis, with emphasis to be placed on raising the level of shop output. The effect of this new policy on production remained indeterminate. Before the fourth day had ended, George got carried away by his narrowed interests to the point of making sarcastic remarks about the poor work performances of the absent Sammy. Although addressed to me, these caustic deprecations were obviously for the benefit of Ike. Later in the day Ike spoke tome, for George's benefit, of Sammy's outstanding ability to turn out billfold parts. For the next four days, the prevailing silence of the shop was occasionally broken by either harsh criticism or fulsome praise of Sammy's outstanding workmanship. I did not risk replying to either impeachment or panegyric for fear of involvement in further situational deteriorations.

Twelve-hour days were creeping again at snail's pace. The strictly business communications were of no help, and the sporadic bursts of distaste or enthusiasm for Sammy's clicking ability helped very little. With the return of boredom, came a return of fatigue. My legs tired as the afternoons dragged on, and I became engaged in conscious efforts to rest one by shifting my weight to the other. I would pause in my work to stare through the barred windows at the grimy brick wall across the alley; and, turning my head, I would notice that Ike was staring at the wall too. George would do very little work after Ike left the shop at night. He would sit in a chair and complain of weariness and sore feet.

In desperation, I fell back on my game of work, my blues and greens and whites, my ovals and trapezoids, and my scraping the block. I came to surpass Boo, the energetic night worker, in volume of output. George referred to me as a "day Boo" (day-shift Boo) and suggested that I "keep" Sammy's machine. I managed to avoid this promotion, and consequent estrangement with Sammy, by pleading attachment to my own machine.

When Sammy returned to work, discovery of the cleavage between George and Ike left him stunned. "They were the best of friends!" he said to me in bewilderment.

George now offered Sammy direct, savage criticisms of his work. For several days the good-natured Sammy endured these verbal aggressions without losing his temper; but when George shouted at him "You work like a preacher!" Sammy became very angry, indeed. I had a few anxious moments when I thought that the two old friends were going to come to blows.

Then, thirteen days after Black Friday, came an abrupt change in the pattern of interaction. George and Ike spoke to each other again, in friendly conversation:

> I noticed Ike talking to George after lunch. The two had newspapers of fish at George's cabinet. Ike was excited; he said, "I'll pull up a chair!" The two ate for ten minutes. . . . It seems that they went up to the 22nd Street Exchange together during lunch period to cash pay checks.

That afternoon Ike and Sammy started to play again, and Ike burst once more into song. Old themes reappeared as suddenly as the desert flowers in spring. At first, George managed to maintain some show of the dignity of superordination. When Ike started to sing snatches of "You Are My Sunshine," George suggested that he get "more production." Then Ike backed up George in pressuring Sammy for more production. Sammy turned this exhortation into low comedy by calling Ike a "slave driver" and by shouting over and over again, "Don't bother me! I'm a busy man!" On one occasion, as if almost overcome with joy and excitement, Sammy cried out, "Don't bother me! I'll tell Rothman! [the company president] I'll tell the union! Don't mention my name! I hate you!"

I knew that George was definitely back into the spirit of the thing when he called to Sammy, "Are you man or mouse?" He kept up the "man or mouse" chatter for some time.

George was for a time reluctant to accept fruit when it was offered to him, and he did not make a final capitulation to coke time until five days after renewal of the fun and fooling. Strictly speaking, there never was a return to banana time, peach time, or window time. However, the sharing and snitching of fruit did go on once more, and the window in front of Sammy's machine played more prominent part than ever in the renaissance of horseplay in the clicker room. In fact, the "rush to the window" became an integral part of increasingly complex themes and repeated sequences of interaction. This window rushing became especially bound up with new developments which featured what may be termed the "anal gesture."[11] Introduced by Ike, and given backing by an enthusiastic, very playful

George, the anal gesture became a key component of fun and fooling during the remaining weeks of my stay in the shop:

> Ike broke wind, and put his head in his hand on the block as Sammy grabbed a rod and made a mock rush to open the window. He beat Ike on the head, and George threw some water on him, playfully. In came the Negro head of the Leather Department; he remarked jokingly that we should take out the machines and make a playroom out of the shop.

Of course, George's demand for greater production was metamorphosed into horseplay. His shout of "Production please!" became a chatter theme to accompany the varied antics of Ike and Sammy.

The professor theme was dropped completely. George never again mentioned his Sunday walks on the Midway with the professor.


## CONCLUSIONS

Speculative assessment of the possible significance of my observations on information interaction in the clicking room may be set forth in a series of general statements.


### Practical Application

First, in regard to possible practical application to problems of industrial management, these observations seem to support the generally accepted notion that one key source of job satisfaction lies in the informal interaction shared by members of a work group. In the clicking-room situation the spontaneous development of a patterned combination of horseplay, serious conversation, and frequent sharing of food and drink reduced the monotony of simple, repetitive operations to the point where a regular schedule of long work days became livable. This kind of group interplay may be termed "consumatory" in the sense indicated by Dewey, when he makes a basic distinction between "instrumental and "consumatory" communication.[12] The enjoyment of communication "for its own sake" as "mere sociabilities," as "free, aimless social intercourse," brings job satisfaction, at least job endurance, to work situations largely bereft of creative experience.

In regard to another managerial concern, employee productivity, any appraisal of the influence of group interaction upon clicking-room output could be no more than roughly impressionistic. I obtained no evidence to warrant a claim that banana time, or any of its accompaniments in consumatory interaction, boosted production. To the contrary, my diary recordings express an occasional perplexity in the form of "How does this company

manage to stay in business?" However, I did not obtain sufficient evidence
to indicate that, under the prevailing conditions of laissez-faire management,
the output of our group would have been more impressive if the playful
cavorting of three middle-aged gentlemen about the barred windows had
never been. As far as achievement of managerial goals is concerned, the most
that could be suggested is that leavening the deadly boredom of individualized work routines with a concurrent flow of group festivities had a negative
effect on turnover. I left the group, with sad reluctance, under the pressure
of strong urgings to accept a research fellowship which would involve no
factory toil. My fellow clickers stayed with their machines to carry on their
labors in the spirit of banana time.

## Theoretical Considerations

Secondly, possible contribution to ongoing sociological inquiry into the
behavior of small groups, in general, and factory work groups, in particular,
may lie in one or more of the following ideational products of my clicking-
room experience:

1. In their day-long confinement together in a small room spatially and
   socially isolated from other work areas of the factory the Clicking
   Department employees found themselves ecologically situated for
   development of a "natural" group. Such a development did take place;
   from worker inter-communications did emerge the full-blown sociocultural system of consumatory interactions which I came to share,
   observe, and record in the process of my socialization.
2. These interactions had a content which could be abstracted from the
   total existential flow of observable doings and sayings for labeling and
   objective consideration. That is, they represented a distinctive subculture, with its recurring patterns of reciprocal influencings which I
   have described as times and themes.
3. From these interactions may also be abstracted a social structure of
   statuses and roles. This structure may be discerned in the carrying out
   of the various informal activities which provide the content of the
   sub-culture of the group. The times and themes were performed with
   a system of roles which formed a sort of pecking hierarchy. Horseplay
   had its initiators and its victims, its amplifiers and its chorus: kidding
   had its attackers and attacked, its least attached and its most attacked,
   its ready acceptors of attack and its strong resistors to attack. The fun
   went on with the participation of all, but within the controlling frame
   of status, a matter of who can say or do what to whom and get away
   with it.
4. In both the cultural content and the social structure of clicker group

interaction could be seen the permeation of influences which flowed from the various multiple group memberships of the participants. Past and present "other group" experiences or anticipated "outside" social connections provided significant materials for the building of themes and for the establishment and maintenance of status and role relationships. The impact of reference group affiliations on clicking-room interaction was notably revealed in the sacred, status-conferring expression of the professor theme. This impact was brought into very sharp focus in developments which followed my attempt to degrade the topic, and correlatively, to demote George.

5. Stability of the clicking-room social system was never threatened by immediate outside pressures. Ours was not an instrumental group, subject to disintegration in a losing struggle against environmental obstacles or oppositions. It was not striving for corporate goals; nor was it faced with the enmity of other groups. It was strictly a consumatory group, devoted to the maintenance of patterns of self-entertainment. Under existing conditions, disruption of unity could come only from within.

   Potentials for breakdown were endemic in the interpersonal interactions involved in conducting the group's activities. Patterns of fun and fooling had developed within a matrix of frustration. Tensions born of long hours of relatively meaningless work were released in the mock aggressions of horseplay. In the recurrent attack, defense, and counterattack there continually lurked the possibility that words or gestures harmless in conscious intent might cross the subtle boundary of accepted, playful aggression to be perceived as real assault. While such an occurrence might incur displeasure no more lasting than necessary for the quick clarification or creation of kidding norms, it might also spark a charge of hostility sufficient to disorganize the group.

   A contributory potential for breakdown from within lay in the dissimilar "other group" experiences of the operators. These other-group affiliations and identifications could provide differences in tastes and sensitivities including appreciation of humor, differences which could make maintenance of consensus in regard to kidding norms a hazardous process of trial and error adjustments.

6. The risk involved in this trial and error determination of consensus on fun and fooling in a touchy situation of frustration—mock aggression—was made evident when I attempted to introduce alterations in the professor theme. The group disintegrated, *instanter*. That is, there was an abrupt cessation of the interactions which constituted our groupness. Although both George and I were solidly linked in other group affiliations with the higher learning, there was not enough

agreement in our attitudes toward university professors to prevent the interactional development which shattered our factory play group. George perceived my offered alterations as a real attack, and he responded with strong hostility directed against Ike, the perceived assailant, and Sammy, a fellow traveler.

My innovations, if accepted, would have lowered the tone of the sacred professor theme, if not to "Stay Away From Baby" ribaldry, then at least to the verbal slapstick level of "finding Danelly an apartment." Such a downgrading of George's reference group would, in turn, have downgraded George. His status in the shop group hinged largely upon his claimed relations with the professor.

7. Integration of our group was fully restored after a series of changes in the patterning and quality of clicking-room interaction. It might be said that reintegration took place *in* these changes, that the series was a progressive one of step-by-step improvement in relations, that re-equilibration was in process during the three weeks that passed between initial communication collapse and complete return to "normal" interaction.

The cycle of loss and recovery of equilibrium may be crudely charted according to the following sequence of phases: a) the stony silence of "not speaking"; b) the confining of communication to formal matters connected with work routines; c) the return of informal give-and-take in the form of harshly sarcastic kidding, mainly on the subject of work performance, addressed to a neutral go-between for the "benefit" of the object of aggression; d) highly emotional direct attack, and counter-attack, in the form of criticism and defense of work performance; e) a sudden rapprochement expressed in serious, dignified, but friendly conversation; f) return to informal interaction in the form of mutually enjoyed mock aggression; g) return to informal interaction in the form of regular patterns of sharing food and drink.

The group had disintegrated when George withdrew from participation; and, since the rest of us were at all times ready for rapprochement, reintegration was dependent upon his "return." Therefore, each change of phase in interaction on the road to recovery could be said to represent an increment of return on George's part. Or, conversely, each phase could represent an increment of reacceptance of punished deviants. Perhaps more generally applicable to description of a variety of reunion situations would be conceptualization of the phase changes as increments of reassociation without an atomistic differentiation of the "movements" of individuals.

8. To point out that George played a key role in this particular case of re-equilibration is not to suggest that the homeostatic controls of a social system may be located in a type of role or in a patterning of role

relationships. Such controls could be but partially described in terms of human interaction; they would be functional to the total configuration of conditions within the field of influence. The automatic controls of a mechanical system operate as such only under certain achieved and controlled conditions. The human body recovers from disease when conditions for such homeostasis are "right." The clicking-room group regained equilibrium under certain undetermined conditions. One of a number of other possible outcomes could have developed had conditions not been favorable for recovery.

For purposes of illustration, and from reflection on the case, I would consider the following as possibly necessary conditions for reintegration of our group: a) Continued monotony of work operations; b) Continued lack of a comparatively adequate substitute for the fun and fooling release from work tensions; c) Inability of the operatives to escape from the work situation or from each other, within the work situation. George could not fire Ike or Sammy to remove them from his presence, and it would have been difficult for the three middle-aged men to find other jobs if they were to quit the shop. Shop space was small, and the machines close together. Like a submarine crew, they had to "live together"; d) Lack of conflicting definitions of the situation after Ike's perception of George's reaction to the "barber college" attack. George's anger and his punishment of the offenders was perceived as justified; e) Lack of introduction of new issues or causes which might have carried justification for new attacks and counter-attacks, thus leading interaction into a spiral of conflict and crystallization of conflict norms. For instance, had George reported his offenders to the superintendent for their poor work performance; had he, in his anger, committed some offense which would have led to reporting of a grievance to local union officials; had he made his anti-Semitic remarks in the presence of Ike or Sammy, or had I relayed these remarks to them; had I tried to "take over" Sammy's machine, as George had urged; then the interactional outcome might have been permanent disintegration of the group.

9. Whether or not the particular patterning of interactional change previously noted is somehow typical of a "re-equilibration process" is not a major question here. My purpose in discriminating the seven changes is primarily to suggest that re-equilibration, when it does occur, may be described in observable phases and that the emergence of each succeeding phase should be dependent upon the configuration of conditions of the preceding one. Alternative eventual outcomes may change in their probabilities, as the phases succeed each other, just as prognosis for recovery in sickness may change as the disease situation changes.

10. Finally, discrimination of phase changes in social process may have practical as well as scientific value. Trained and skillful administrators might follow the practice in medicine of introducing aids to re-equilibration when diagnosis shows that they are needed.

## NOTES

Reprinted from *Human Organization* 18, no. 4 (1959–1960): 158–68. Used with the permission of the Society for Applied Anthropology.

Dr. Roy is in the Department of Sociology, Duke University, Durham, North Carolina.

1. Charles R. Walker and Robert H. Guest, *The Man on the Assembly Line,* Harvard University Press, Cambridge, 1952.

2. *Ibid.,* p. 77.

3. *Ibid.,* p. 68.

4. Donald F. Roy, "Work Satisfaction and Social Reward in Quota Achievement: An Analysis of Piecework Incentive," *American Sociological Review,* XVIII (October, 1953), 507–514.

5. All names used are fictitious.

6. Henri de Man, *The Psychology of Socialism,* Henry Holt and Company, New York, 1927, pp. 80–81.

7. *Ibid.,* p. 81.

8. Roy, *op. cit.*

9. Lucille Milner, *Education of An American Liberal,* Horizon Press, New York, 1954, p. 97.

10. This spelling is the closest I can come to the appellation given me in George's broken English and adopted by other members of the group.

11. I have been puzzled to note widespread appreciation of this gesture in the "consumatory" communication of the working men of this nation. For the present, I leave it to clinical psychologists to account for the nature and persuasiveness of this social bond and confine myself to joining offended readers in the hope that someday our industrial workers will achieve such a level of refinement in thought and action that their behavior will be no more distressing to us than that of the college students who fill out our questionnaires or form groups for laboratory experimentation.

12. John Dewey, *Experience and Nature,* Open Court Publishing Co., Chicago, 1925, pp. 202–206.

# 17

## Hanging Tongues: A Sociological Encounter with the Assembly Line

*William E. Thompson*

This qualitative sociological study analyzes the experience of working on a modern assembly line in a large beef plant. It explores and examines a special type of assembly line work which involves the slaughtering and processing of cattle into a variety of products intended for human consumption and other uses.

Working in the beef plant is "dirty work," not only in the literal sense of being drenched with perspiration and beef blood, but also in the figurative sense of performing a low status, routine, and demeaning job.[1] Although the work is honest and necessary in a society which consumes beef, slaughtering and butchering cattle is generally viewed as an undesirable and repugnant job. In that sense, workers at the beef plant share some of the same experiences as other workers in similarly regarded occupations (for example, ditch-diggers, garbage collectors, and other types of assembly line workers).

Demeaning work has been studied in several different contexts. For example, while on sabbatical leave from his college presidency, Coleman (1974) worked in a variety of low status jobs and wrote about the experiences of workers such as dishwashers and ditchdiggers. Terkel (1974) interviewed a multitude of people whose occupations fit into the category of "dirty work." Garson (1975) investigated low status, monotonous, and often demeaning work situations. Her study included typists, keypunchers, and factory workers, among others. She also interviewed people who worked on an assembly line in a tuna processing plant and whose work was similar to the work in the beef plant of this study. Garson did not observe the tuna

313

workers for any period of time, nor perform the work herself, but was able to portray the attitudes of the workers about their jobs.

Some studies have focused on one type of "dirty work." Perry (1978), a social scientist, observed and worked alongside garbage collectors in San Francisco. He described not only their daily work activities, but also the way workers coped with the demeaning aspects of their work and managed to maintain their self-esteem. Perry found that these garbage collectors overcame the stigma commonly associated with their jobs partially by forming a co-op type of ownership in which they purchased shares. Therefore, the "dirty workers" were actually part-owners.

Other studies relevant to this analysis have been conducted on assembly line work in major automobile plants. Walker and Guest (1952), Chinoy (1955), Georgakas and Surkin (1978), King (1978), and Linhart (1981) vividly describe the experiences of automobile assembly line workers. Linhart's study, conducted in France, demonstrates that the drudgery and dehumanization experienced by auto assembly line workers are not confined to America.

Beef industry workers have also been studied previously. Meara (1974) describes how American meatcutters and Turkish butchers retain their sense of honor while performing "dirty work." But the meatcutters in Meara's study worked in grocery stores, not large-scale assembly lines. Further, her subjects worked with what beef plant workers view as the "finished product." Meatcutters in a grocery store are far removed from the actual slaughter process where live cattle come in one door and hanging sides of beef go out the other. Her Turkish subjects were butchers who owned their own butcher shops, and basically cut meat to order for their customers. Consequently, there is little similarity between their work and the work performed in the beef plant in this research.

This study attempts to extend the range of sites of occupational research. In addition to studying a previously unexplored occupational setting, it is hoped that this study will also add to the conceptual and theoretical understanding of this type of work.

Couched within the symbolic interactionist perspective, this study focuses on the daily activities of the workers. These activities must meet the work demands of their employer and enable the workers to construct and perpetuate a social world of work in a way meaningful to them. Specially, this study analyzes how workers interact with one another on the job, how they cope with the strains of the work, how they maintain a sense of self-worth, and how they develop and maintain informal norms in regard to consumer spending. These spending patterns lead to a financial trap which prevents most workers from leaving the employ of the plant.

## THE SETTING

The setting for the field work was a major beef processing plant in the Midwest. At the time of the study, the plant was the third largest branch of a corporation which operated ten such plants in the United states. It employed approximately 1800 people. In addition to slaughtering and processing cattle for beef, the plant also produced pet food, leather for the wholesale market, and a variety of pharmaceutical supplies which were derived from various glands and organs of cattle. This particular plant had operated for twelve years and was considered a stable and important part of the community in which it was located.

The beef plant was organizationally separated into two divisions: Slaughter and processing. This study focused on the Slaughter division in the area of the plant known as the *kill floor*. A dominant feature of the kill floor was the machinery of the assembly line itself. The line was comprised of an overhead stainless steel rail which began at the slaughter chute and curved its way around every work station in the plant. Every work station contained specialized machinery for the job performed at that place on the line. Dangling from the rail were hundreds of stainless steel hooks pulled by a motorized chain. Virtually every part of the line and all of the implements (tubs, racks, knives, etc.) were made of stainless steel. The walls were covered with a ceramic tile and the floor was made of sealed cement. There were floor drains located at every work station, so that at the end of each work segment (at breaks, lunch, and shift's end) the entire kill floor could be hosed down and cleaned for the next work period.

Another dominant feature of the kill floor was the smell. Extremely difficult to describe, yet impossible to forget, this smell combined the smells of live cattle, manure, fresh beef blood, and internal organs and their contents. This smell not only permeated the interior of the plant, but was combined on the outside with the smell of smoke from various waste products being burned and could be smelled throughout much of the community. This smell contributed greatly to the general negative feelings about work at the beef plant, as it served as the most distinguishable symbol of the beef plant to the rest of the community. The single most often asked question of me during the research by those outside the beef plant was, "How do you stand the smell?" In typical line workers' fashion, I always responded, "What smell? All I smell at the beef plant is money."

Approximately 350 employees worked on the "A" shift on "Slaughter" and were the subjects observed for this research. The most intensive observation focused on the twelve members of the particular work crew to which I was assigned. Of the 350 employees, approximately one-third were Mexican-Americans, two-thirds were white, and two individuals were Native Americans. No blacks worked on this shift. Only five women worked on the "A" shift: a nurse a secretary, and three federal inspectors; all the line workers were male. A few blacks and several women worked in the process division. The explanation given for the lack of women lineworkers in "Slaughter" was the hard physical labor and the nature of the jobs associated with slaughtering. Although pursued, an adequate explanation for the lack of blacks in the slaughter division was never provided.

## METHOD

The method of this study was nine weeks of full-time participant observation as outlined by Schatzman and Strauss (1973) and Spradley (1979, 1980). To enter the setting, the researcher went through the standard application process for a summer job. No mention of the research intent was made, though it was made clear that I was a university sociology professor. After initial screening, a thorough physical examination, and a helpful reference from a former student and part-time employee of the plant, the author was hired to work on the *Offal*[2] crew in the Slaughter division of the plant.

Due to the nature of the work, it was impossible to use any hardware, such as cameras or tape recorders, or to take field notes during the work period. Mental notes of observations and interviews were made throughout each work shift, and logged in a journal at the end of each working day. The researcher gained full acceptance by fellow employees, was treated like any other worker, and encountered very little difficulty in obtaining answers to virtually all research questions pursued. An effort was made to meet, observe, and interact with as many of the 350 employees on the "A" shift as possible. Admittedly, however, the bulk of the information came from the twelve crew members in Offal.

The use of covert research methods in sociology has been questioned from an ethical standpoint. Humphreys' use of covert participant observation in *Tearoom Trade* (1970) brought a variety of ethical questions to the forefront. This study is not nearly as controversial as Humphreys', in the sense that no laws were broken, no false pretenses of other research purposes were used, and the subjects' personal and private lives were not probed. Still, the overall question of whether researchers should observe and study people who are not informed of the research intent is relevant. In his classic work on sociological field observer roles, Gold (1958) describes four legitimate techniques for field research. In this study, I utilized Gold's role of "complete participant" in which I concealed my research intent in order to become a full-fledged member of the group under study. In this case, I am satisfied that doing the research in such a manner was not only legitimate, but the only way to fulfill the research purposes. As Garson (1975:149) points out:

It is very difficult to see people doing their jobs. It's easy to visit the front office of a factory. And it's not too hard to stop workers at the factory gate. The difficult problem is watching the work itself.

Fearful of industrial espionage and interruption of work activities, it is extremely doubtful that plant management would have approved a research project of this nature. Further, even if amenable, there would be no way to interact with the line workers and clearly comprehend their experiences without simply being one of them. Since it was known by all the members of the crew with which I worked that I was a professor, it is quite possible that some guessed that I was conducting research. In fact, more than one worker suggested it. And, at least two or three, only partly in jest, suggested, "You ought to write a book about this."

In order to protect the anonymity of the plant and the workers, no direct references were made that would necessarily identify either the plant or any of its workers.

## THE WORK

The physical exhaustion of assembly line work at the beef plant was extreme. Certain jobs on the line required more physical exertion than others, but the strain of assembly line work went beyond physical exhaustion. As a worker on the line at Ford put it, "The work is always physically exhausting . . . but the real punishment is the inevitability of the line" (King, 1978:201). The inevitability of the line indeed; the line speed on the kill floor was 187. That means that 187 head of cattle were slaughtered per hour. At any particular work station, each worker was required to work at that speed. Thus, at my work station, in the period of one hour, 187 beef tongues were mechanically pulled from their hooks; dropped into a large tub filled with water; had to be taken from the tub and hung on a large stainless steel rack full of hooks; branded with a "hot brand" indicating they had been inspected by a USDA inspector; and then covered with a small plastic bag. The rack was taken to the cooler, replaced with an empty one, and the process began again.

It would be logical to assume that if a person worked at a steady, continuous pace of handling 187 tongues per hour, everything would go smoothly; not so. In addition to hanging, branding, and bagging tongues, the worker at that particular station also cleaned the racks and cleaned out a variety of empty stainless steel tubs used to hold hearts, kidneys, and other beef organs. Thus, in order to be free to clean the tubs when necessary, the "tongue-hanger" had to work at a slightly faster pace than the line moved. Then, upon returning from cleaning the tubs, the worker would be behind the line (*in a hole*) and had to work much faster to catch up with the line.

Further, one fifteen minute break and a thirty minute lunch break were scheduled for an eight-hour shift. Before the "tongue-hanger" could leave his post for one of these, all tongues were required to be properly disposed of, all tubs washed and stored, and the work area cleaned.

The first two nights on the job, I discovered the consequences of working at the line speed (hanging, branding, and bagging each tongue as it fell in the tub). At the end of the work period when everybody else was leaving the work floor for break or lunch, I was furiously trying to wash all the tubs and clean the work areas. Consequently, I missed the entire fifteen minute break and had only about ten minutes for lunch. By observing other workers, I soon caught on to the system. Rather than attempting to work at a steady pace consistent with the line speed, the norm was to work sporadically at a very frenzied pace, actually running ahead on the line and plucking tongues from the hooks before they got to the station. With practice, I learned to hand two or three tongues at a time, perform all the required tasks, and then take an unscheduled two or three minute break until the line caught up with me. Near break and lunch everybody worked at a frantic pace, got ahead of the line, cleaned the works areas, and even managed to add a couple of minutes to the scheduled break or lunch.

Working ahead of the line seems to have served as more than merely a way of gaining a few minutes of extra break time. It also seemed to take on a symbolic meaning. The company controlled the speed of the line. Seemingly, that took all element of control over the work process away from the workers. As Garson (1975:140) indicates, "The main advantage of the auto assembly line to an employer is not speed but control." However, when the workers refused to work at line speed and actually worked faster than the line, they not only added a few minutes of relaxation from the work while the line caught up, but they symbolically regained an element of control over the pace of their own work.

Occasionally, the line broke down. Mixed emotions accompanied such an occurrence. On the one hand, the workers were happy. While the problem was being solved, we were being paid by the company for doing nothing. Foreman and supervisors viewed the breakdown quite differently, of course, and maintenance crews were pressured to work at a frenzied speed to get the line back in motion. On the other hand, even the line workers could not be totally pleased with a breakdown. The Slaughter crew worked on a quota of killing between 1350 and 1500 steers in an eight-hour shift. Invariably, when the line was repaired after being down for a short period, the line speed was generally increased to compensate for the *down time*. Thus, although a brief unscheduled break was enjoyed, when work resumed one usually was forced to work faster and harder to make up for it.

## WORKER SOCIAL RELATIONS

Worker social relations were complex. As could be expected, the various roles occupied by workers in the plant greatly influenced the types of interaction which occurred among them. The major occupational roles at the beef plant were manager, foreman, nurse, federal meat inspector, and line workers. The hierarchical structure of personnel was clear-cut from the company's viewpoint. Plant superintendent, general manager, and other executives were, of course, at the top of the status hierarchy. However, since their offices were separated from the work floor (and they rarely ventured there), their interaction with labor personnel was virtually non-existent. When interaction did occur, it was usually on a one-way basis—there was a clear superordinate/subordinate relationship.

Management's link to labor personnel was the foreman. He personified management on the work floor. His main duties were to assign jobs to his crew members and supervise their work activities. In addition, however, the foreman was often required to perform physical labor. Thus, he had to know all the jobs performed by his crew. Should a worker be absent or have to leave the line unexpectedly, the foreman was required to take over his responsibilities. The foreman often fulfilled the laborer role and worked alongside the rest of the crew. Ironically, though higher in status and "in charge" of the crew, the foreman periodically performed all the duties of laborer at lower pay.

Foremen worked on monthly salaries, whereas laborers worked for hourly wages. When laborers worked overtime, they were paid "time-and-a-half." When foremen worked overtime, it was gratis to the company. This pay differential was usually compensated for at the end of the year when profit-sharing dividends of foremen far exceeded those of laborers. Since foremen's dividends were based on the production of their crews, they tended to push their crews to the maximum. The foreman role was somewhat analogous to that of the "overseer" on slave plantations in the ante-bellum South (Stampp, 1956). He did not have the status nor reap the benefits of the company owner, yet became the "driver" of those who produced the work and profits. In a sociological sense, the foreman at the beef plant emerged as the classic example of "marginal man" (Stonequist, 1937); he was in fact neither management nor labor, and not fully accepted by either.

The general attitudes of the laborers toward the foremen were those of dislike and mistrust. Even when certain workers knew a foreman on a friendly basis in a social context outside the plant, their relations inside the plant were cool. A scenario I personally saw acted out on several occasions by several different workers involved a foreman stopping to talk to a worker in a non-work related, seemingly friendly conversation. The worker would be smiling and conversing congenially, yet the moment the foreman turned to walk away, the worker would make an obscene gesture (usually involving the middle finger) behind the foreman's back, so that all other workers could clearly see. The overt submission and yet covert show of disrespect was reminiscent of the "puttin' on ole massa" technique practiced by slaves toward their masters in the pre–Civil War South (Osofsky, 1969).[3]

Social relations between laborers were marked by anonymity. While virtually all the workers on the kill floor knew each other on sight and knew who performed what job, it was not uncommon for two workers who had worked alongside each other for ten years to know only each other's first names— and that only because it was written on a piece of plastic tape on the front of their hard hats. As Berger points out, "technological production brings with it *anonymous social* relations" [italics in original] (Berger et al., 1974:31). Similarly, an auto assembly line worker lamented, "I've been here for over a year, and I hardly know the first names of the men in the section where I work" (Walker and Guest, 1952:77). The nature of the work on an assembly line almost negates the possibility for social interaction during the work, and consequently creates a certain anonymity among the workers.

Though anonymous, the workers also shared a sense of unity. Work on the line could best be described as "uncooperative teamwork." Because the assembly line demanded coordinated teamwork to some extent, the work became "one for all." Yet, at the same time, since each worker had a separate specialized task, the work became "every man for himself." Workers occasionally helped each other *out of the hole* when they fell behind, but it was done more because it slowed their own work, than because they wanted to help a fellow worker. Still, the help was appreciated and almost always reciprocated.

Beyond sharing labor occasionally, a more subtle sense of unity existed among the workers; a sense that "we are all in this together." Just as an auto worker indicated, "The monotony of the line binds us together" (King, 1978:201), the beef plant workers apparently shared a common bond. The workers referred to themselves as *beefers* and each individual *beefer* shared something in common with all others. The hard work, danger of the job, and ambivalence toward the company and its management, all seemed to unite the workers in spirit. The line workers in the beef plant constituted an "occupational culture" as described by Reimer (1979:24) in his study of construction workers.

Although through profit-sharing and participation in stock options the workers technically shared in the ownership of the plant, they tended to view themselves as apart from it. Management and the plant in general were always referred to as "they," while the workers referred to themselves as "we." As indicated by Schutz (1967), this contrast between the "we-relationship" and "they-relationship" has tremendous impact upon social relations.

As shown by the classic "Hawthorne Experiment," employee social relations often take precedence over production, efficiency, and promise of material rewards (Roethslinger, 1941).

Another uniting element regarding worker social interaction was the process of sharing meaningful symbols. Language emerged as one of the most important symbols at the beef plant (Mead, 1934). As Hummel (1977) suggests, in most bureaucratic organizations a language exists to facilitate communication among those within the organization and to exclude those outside it. As Reimer (1979:78) points out, "For a worker to be fully integrated into a work group and its culture, he must literally know how to communicate in the language of the group." A brief description of the slaughter process in the argot of a *beefer* will illustrate the point:

> After *herders* send in the beef, a *knocker* drops them. The *shackler* puts them on the chain so the *head droppers, splitters, boners, trimmers,* and the rest of the *chain gang* can do their jobs. As long as *the man* doesn't reject a lot and you don't run into a lot of *down time,* its easy to stay *out of the hole* and get some *sunshine time* at the end of the shift.

Despite special argot, the excessive noise from the machinery and the requirement that all employees wear ear plugs made non-verbal gestures the primary form of communication. Exaggerated gestures and shrill whistles were used to get a fellow worker's attention. The "thumbs up" sign indicated everything was all right, whereas "thumbs down" meant one was *in the hole.* One of the most interesting means of non-verbal communication was to beat knives against he stainless steel tables and tubs used throughout the plant. This clanging signified either that a break in the line was coming or that the men on slaughter had quit "knocking." The first person on the line to see the upcoming gap would begin clanging his knife against metal; the next worker picked up on this, and so on down the line, until the entire line was clanging unbelievably loudly. My work station was situated so that when the clanging began it was exactly 35 minutes until the end of the line would reach me. Since there were no clocks on the kill floor and talk was virtually impossible, this procedure served as an important time indicator for all workers in regard to breaks, lunch and quitting time. This ability to communicate a sense of time to fellow workers also served to symbolically regain an element of control that management had taken from the workers by virtue of not installing any clocks on the kill floor.

Two other worker roles existed on the slaughter side of the plant: the nurse, and the federal meat inspectors. The nurse was one of five women on the Slaughter side of the plant on our particular shift. She was approximately 25 years old and considered quite attractive. Needless to say, she received a great deal of attention from the approximately 350 male workers on that shift. The nurse's office was located between the work floor and the lunch room, so that workers walked directly by it on the way to and from breaks and meals. Workers invariably peered in the little glass window on the nurse's door and often dropped in just to say "hi."

Due to working around excessive amounts of beef blood, even the slightest cut on a worker had to be treated in order to avoid infection. This provided an excellent alibi for the workers to make frequent visits to the nurse. On the other hand, trips to the nurse meant time away from the line. Therefore, workers had to be careful not to get too many cuts and spend too much time in the nurse's office, or a foreman would be suspicious. Each visit to the nurse for treatment was documented and crew foremen periodically reviewed the records of their crew members.

While the nurse was considered attractive, and many sexually suggestive comments were made about her among the workers, she was overtly treated with a great deal of respect. I never heard any rude comments made to her or in her presence perhaps because the importance of her role in the plant was recognized by all, including management, foremen, workers, and inspectors.

The federal meat inspector emerged as the most autonomous role in the plant. While inspectors occupied a significant place in the plant's operational system, they were in a sense outside of and above all the plant personnel. Employed by the federal government, their authority superseded even that of plant management. Their decision to reject a product or order something destroyed was unquestioned. Thus, they held a great deal of potential power. This power was not accompanied with respect however. Virtually every encounter a worker had with an inspector took on negative connotations. The only circumstance causing occupants of the two roles to interact was the rejection by the inspector of the laborer's work. Thus, each encounter with an inspector meant more work for the laborer, plus probably an unpleasant encounter with the foreman. Workers typically viewed the inspectors as arrogant and pompous—or as one worker put it—"a royal pain in the ass." It was extremely uncommon to see workers and inspectors interact in anything other than an official context. Inspectors ate in a separate lunchroom and dressed in a separate locker room. Their clean white uniforms made them immediately distinguishable from the laborers whose "white" uniforms had long since become khaki colored from the constant staining of beef blood and the process of being washed in the plant laundry. Only a new worker whose uniform had not yet been laundered could possibly be confused with an inspector at first glance. Inspectors also wore a badge on their shirt pocket for identification.

Because I had previously had one of the inspectors as a student, I had occasion to interact with him in a different context than most workers. This inspector indicated to me that inspectors tended to view workers negatively.

They saw workers as overpaid, careless, and often sneaky—constantly trying to subvert the federal standards that were supposed to be maintained. Further, he indicated that there was more than a little resentment toward the workers in regard to wages. The workers' starting wage exceeded the starting wage of an inspector by approximately $2.50 per hour. This resentment could be manifested by forcing workers to do a job more than once. All in all, the interactional process between workers and inspectors can be summarized as "mutually hostile."

## COPING

One of the difficulties of work at the beef plant was coping with three aspects of work: monotony, danger, and dehumanization. While individual workers undoubtedly coped in a variety of ways, some distinguishable patterns emerged.

### Monotony

The monotony of the line was almost unbearable. At my work station, a worker would hang, brand, and bag between 1,350 to 1,500 beef tongues in an eight-hour shift. With the exception of the scheduled 15 minute break and a 30 minute lunch period (and sporadic brief gaps in the line), the work was mundane, routine, and continuous. As in most assembly line work, one inevitably drifted into daydreams (e.g., Garson, 1975; King, 1978; Linhart, 1981). It was not unusual to look up or down the line and see workers at various stations singing to themselves, tapping their feet to imaginary music, or carrying on conversations with themselves. I found that I could work with virtually no attention paid to the job, with my hands and arms almost automatically performing their tasks. In the meantime, my mind was free to wander over a variety of topics, including taking mental notes. In visiting with other workers, I found that daydreaming was the norm. Some would think about their families, while others fantasized about sexual escapades, fishing, or anything unrelated to the job. One individual who was rebuilding an antique car at home in his spare time would meticulously mentally rehearse the procedures he was going to perform on the car the next day.

Daydreaming was not inconsequential, however. During these periods, items were most likely to be dropped, jobs improperly performed, and accidents incurred. Inattention to detail around moving equipment, stainless steel hooks, and sharp knives invariably leads to dangerous consequences. Although I heard rumors of drug use to help fight the monotony, I never saw any workers take any drugs nor saw any drugs in any workers' possession. It is certainly conceivable that some workers might have taken something to help them escape the reality of the line, but the nature of the work demanded enough attention that such a practice could be ominous.

## Danger

The danger of working in the beef plant was well known. Safety was top priority (at least in theory) and management took pride in the fact that only three employee on-the-job deaths had occurred in 12 years.[4] Although deaths were uncommon, serious injuries were not. The beef plant employed over 1,800 people. Approximately three-fourths of those employed had jobs which demanded the use of a knife honed to razor-sharpness. Despite the use of wire-mesh aprons and gloves, serious cuts were almost a daily occurrence. Since workers constantly handled beef blood, danger of infection was ever-present. As one walked along the assembly line, a wide assortment of bandages on fingers, hands, arms, necks, and faces could always be seen.

In addition to the problem of cuts, workers who cut meat continuously sometimes suffered muscle and ligament damage to their fingers and hands. In one severe case, I was told of a woman who worked in processing for several years who had to wear splints on her fingers while away from the job to hold them straight. Otherwise, the muscles in her hand would constrict her fingers into the grip position, as if holding a knife.

Because of the inherent danger of the plant in general, and certain jobs in the plant in particular, workers were forced to cope with the fear of physical harm.[5] Meara (1974) discovered that meatcutters in her study derived a sense of honor from the serious cuts and injuries they incurred doing their work, but this did not seem to be the case at the beef plant. Although workers were willing to show their scars, they did not seem to take much pride in them. Any time a serious accident occurred (especially one which warranted the transport of the victim to the hospital in an ambulance) news of the event spread rapidly throughout the plant.

When I spoke with fellow works about the dangers of working in the plant, I noticed interesting defense mechanisms. As noted by Shostak (1980), the workers talked a great deal about workers being injured on the job. After a serious accident, or when telling about an accident or death which occurred in years past, the workers would almost immediately disassociate themselves from the event and its victim. Workers tended to view those who suffered major accidents or death on the job in much the same way that non-victims of crime often view crime victims as either partially responsible for the event, or at least as very different from themselves (Barlow, 1981). "Only a part-timer" "stupid," "careless" or something similar was used, seemingly to reassure the worker describing the accident that it could not happen to him. The reality of the situation was that virtually all the jobs on the kill floor were dangerous, and any worker could have experienced a serious injury at any time.

The company management was very much aware of the danger and posted signs everywhere as constant reminders to wear all safety equipment and to be careful at all times. Yet, speed and efficiency clearly took precedence over caution in actual practice. To fall behind the speed of the line meant one had to work extra fast to catch up. In haste to keep up production, worker safety often took a back seat to speed in performing tasks. As in the auto industry, "the single goal of the company was to increase profit by getting more work out of each individual worker" (Georgakas and Surkin, 1978:60).

The nurse indicated that accidents seemed to increase near the end of a shift and near the end of the week when fatigue combined with the attempt to hurry-up and get finished produced several injuries. It was also her opinion that accidents on the job might be significantly related to workers' problems at home.[6] She pointed out that invariably when she was treating an accident victim, they would describe to her how problems with a spouse, finances, etc., had temporarily distracted them and helped bring about the accident.

## Dehumanization

Perhaps the most devastating aspect of working at the beef plant (worse than the monotony and the danger) was the dehumanizing and demeaning elements of the job. In a sense, the assembly line worker became a part of the assembly line. The assembly line is not a tool used by the worker, but a machine which controls him/her. A tool can only be productive in the hands of somebody skilled in its use, and hence, becomes an extension of the person using it. A machine, on the other hand, performs specific tasks; thus its operator becomes an extension of it in the production process. Further elaboration on the social and psychological distinction between tools and machines has been discussed in the ecology literature (for example, Bookchin, 1972). When workers are viewed as mere extensions of the machines with which they work, their human needs become secondary in importance to the smooth mechanical functioning of the production process. In a bureaucratic structure, when "human needs collide with systems needs the individual suffers" (Hummel, 1977:65).

Workers on the assembly line are seen as interchangeable as the parts of the product on the line itself. An example of one worker's perception of this phenomenon at the beef plant was demonstrated the day after a fatal accident occurred. I asked the men in our crew what the company did in the case of an employee death (I wondered if there was a fund for flowers, or if the shift was given time off to go to the funeral, etc.). One worker's response was: "They drag off the body, take the hard hat and boots and check 'em out to some other poor sucker, and throw him in the guy's place." While employee death on the job was not viewed quite that coldly by the company, the statement fairly accurately summarized the overall result of a fatal accident, and importance of any individual worker to the overall operation of the production process. It accurately summarized the workers' perceptions about management's attitudes toward them.

The dehumanization process affected the social relations of workers, as well as each worker's self-concept. Hummel (1977:2) indicates that bureaucracy and its technical means of production give birth to a "new species of inhuman beings." As noted by Perry (1978:7), "there are dire consequences for someone who feels stuck in an occupation that robs him of his personhood or, at best, continually threatens his personhood for eight hours a day." However, workers on the line strove in a variety of ways to maintain their sense of worth. As pointed out by Perrow (1979:4), the bureaucratic structure of the complex organization never realizes its "ideal" form because "it tries to do what must be (hopefully) forever impossible—to eliminate all unwanted extraorganizational influence upon the behavior of its members." Reimer (1979) showed that construction workers view deviance as a fun part of their work. So, too, *beefers* strained to maintain their humanity, and hence, their sense of self-esteem through horseplay (strictly forbidden), daydreaming, unscheduled breaks, social interaction with other employees, and occasional sabotage.

## SABOTAGE

It is fairly common knowledge that assembly line work situations often lead to employee sabotage or destruction of the product or equipment used in the production process (Garson, 1975; Balzer, 1976; Shostak, 1980). This is the classic experience of alienation as described by Marx (1964a, 1964b). This experience has been most eloquently expressed by an assembly line worker in Terkel's research, who stated:

> Sometimes out of pure meanness, when I make something I put a little dent in it. I like to do something to make it really unique. Hit it with a hammer. I deliberately fuck it up to see if it'll get by, just so I can say I did it (Terkel, 1974:9–10).

At the beef plant I quickly learned that there was an art to effective sabotage. Subtlety appeared to be the key. "The art lies in sabotaging in a way that is not immediately discovered," as a Ford worker put it (King, 1978:202). This seemed to hold true at the beef plant as well.

Although sabotage did not seem to be a major problem at the beef plant, it did exist, and there appeared to be several norms (both formal and informal) concerning what was acceptable and what was not. The greatest factor influencing the handling of beef plant products was its status as food product intended for human consumption. Thus, the formal norms were replete with USDA and FDA regulations and specifications. Foremen, supervisors, and federal inspectors attempted to insure that these norms were followed. Further, though not an explicitly altruistic group, the workers realized that the product would be consumed by people (even family, relatives, and friends), so consequently, they rarely did anything to actually contaminate the product.

Despite formal norms against sabotage, some did occur. It was not uncommon for workers to deliberately cut chunks out of pieces of meat for no reason (or for throwing at other employees). While regulations required that anything that touched the floor had to be put in tubs marked "inedible," the informal procedural norms were otherwise. When something was dropped, one usually looked around to see if an inspector or foreman noticed. If not, the item was quickly picked up and put back on the line.

Several explanations might be offered for this type of occurrence. First, since the company utilized a profit-sharing plan, when workers damaged the product, or had to throw edible pieces into inedible tubs (which sold for pet food at much lower prices), profits were decreased. A decrease in profits to the company ultimately led to decreased dividend checks to employees. Consequently, workers were fairly careful not to actually ruin anything. Second, when something was dropped or mishandled and had to be rerouted to "inedible," it was more time-consuming than if the product has been handled properly and kept on the regular line. In other words, if no inspector noticed, it was easier to let it go through on the line. There was a third, and seemingly more meaningful explanation for this behavior, however. It was against the rules to do it, it was a challenge to do it, and thus it was fun to do it.

The workers practically made a game out of doing forbidden things simply to see if they could get away with it. As Perrow (1979:40) indicates, "One of the delights of the organizational expert is to indicate to the uninitiated the wide discrepancy between the official hierarchy (or rules for that matter) and the unofficial ones." Similarly, new workers were routinely socialized into the subtle art of rule breaking as approved by the line workers. At my particular work station, it was a fairly common practice for other workers who were covered with beef blood to come over to the tub of swirling water designed to clean the tongues, and as soon as the inspector looked away, wash their hands, arms, and knives in the tub. This procedure was strictly forbidden by the rules. If witnessed by a foreman or inspector, the tub had to be emptied, cleaned, and refilled, and all the tongues in the tub at the time had to be put in the "inedible" tub. All of that would be a time-consuming and costly procedure, yet the workers seemed to absolutely delight in successfully pulling off the act. As Balzer (1976:90) indicates:

> Since a worker often feels that much if not all of what he does is done in places designated by the company, under company control, finding ways to express personal freedom from this institutional regimentation is important.

Thus, artful sabotage served as a symbolic way in which the workers could express a sense of individuality, and hence, self-worth.

## THE FINANCIAL TRAP

Given the preceding description and analysis of work at the beef plant, why did people work at such jobs? Obviously, there is a multitude of plausible answers to that question. Without doubt, however, the key is money. The current economic situation, the lack of steady employment opportunities (especially for the untrained and poorly educated), combined with the fact that the beef plant's starting wage exceeded the minimum wage by approximately $5.50 per hour emerge as the most important reasons people went to work there.

Despite the high hourly wage and fringe benefits, however, the monotony, danger, and hard physical work drove many workers away in less than a week. During my study, I observed much worker turnover. Those who stayed, displayed an interesting pattern which helps explain why they did not leave. Every member of my work crew answered similarly my questions about why they stayed at the beef plant. Each of them took the job directly after high school, because it was the highest paying job available. Each of them had intended to work through the summer and then look for a better job in the fall. During the first summer on the job they fell victim to what I label the "financial trap."

The "financial trap" was a spending pattern which demanded the constant weekly income provided by the beef plant job. This scenario was first told to me by an employee who had worked at the plant for over nine years. He began the week after his high school graduation, intending only to work that summer in order to earn enough money to attend college in the fall. After about four weeks' work he purchased a new car. He figured he could pay off the car that summer and still save enough money for tuition. Shortly after the car purchase, he added a new stereo sound system to his debt; next came a motorcycle; then the decision to postpone school for one year in order to continue working at the beef plant and pay off his debts. A few months later he married; within a year purchased a house; had a child; and bought another new car. Nine years later, he was still working at the beef plant, hated every minute of it, but in his own words "could not afford to quit." His case was not unique. Over and over again, I heard stories about the same process of falling into the "financial trap." The youngest and newest of our crew had just graduated high school and took the job for the summer in order to earn enough money to attend welding school the following fall. During my brief tenure at the beef plant, he purchased a new motorcycle, a new stereo, and a house trailer. When I left, he told me he had decided to postpone welding school for one year in order "to get everything paid for." I saw the financial trap closing in on him fast; he did too.

Besides hearing about it from my fellow crew members, this financial trap was confirmed for me by the nurse who indicated she had heard the same type of stories from literally hundreds of employees at the plant. All intended to work a few months, make some quick money, and leave. However, they developed spending patterns which simply would not allow them to leave. Deferred gratification was obviously not the norm for the "beefers." While not specifically referring to it as such, research by Walker and Guest (1952), Garson (1975), and Shostak (1980) indicate similar financial traps may exist in other types of factory work.

## SUMMARY AND CONCLUSIONS

There are at least three interwoven phenomena in this study which deserve further comment and research.

First is the subtle sense of unity which existed among the line workers. Because of excessive noise, the use of earplugs, and the relative isolation of some work areas from others, it was virtually impossible for workers to talk to one another. Despite this, workers developed a very unsophisticated (yet highly complex) system of non-verbal symbols to communicate with one another. Hence, in a setting which would apparently eliminate it, the workers' desire for social interaction won out and interaction flourished. Likewise, the production process was devised in such a way that each task was somewhat disconnected from all others, and workers had a tendency to concern themselves only with their own jobs. Yet, the line both symbolically and literally linked every job, and consequently every worker, to each other. As described earlier, a system of "uncooperative teamwork" seemed to combine simultaneously a feeling of "one-for-all, all-for-one, and every man for himself." Once a line worker made it past the first three or four days on the job which "weeded out" many new workers, his status as a *beefer* was assured and the sense of unity was felt as much by the worker of nine weeks as it was by the veteran of nine years. Because the workers maintained largely secondary relationships, this feeling of unification is not the same as the unity typically found on athletic teams, in fraternities, or among various primary groups. Yet it was a significant social force which bound the workers together and provided a sense of meaning and worth. Although their occupation might not be highly respected by outsiders, they derived mutual self-respect from their sense of belonging.

A second important phenomenon was the various coping methods employed by workers in a dehumanizing environment to retain their sense of humanity and self-worth. "There are high human costs in dirty work for the person who performs it" (Perry, 1978:6). Either intentionally or inadvertently, the assembly line process utilized at the beef plant tended to reduce the laborers to the level of the machinery with which they worked. On assembly lines, workers are typically regarded as being as interchangeable as the parts of the machines with which they work. As an auto worker put it, "You're just a number to them—they number the stock, and they number you" (Walker and Guest 1952:138). Attempts to maximize efficiency and increase profits demand the sacrifice of human qualities such as uniqueness, creativity, and the feeling of accomplishment and self-worth. Meara (1974) found that one of the sources of honor for the meatcutters in her study was that, despite the fact that their job was viewed as undesirable, it was commonly acknowledged that it was a skilled craft and thus allowed control of their work. As she indicates:

> Occupations provide honorable and dishonorable work. Those who participate in a generally dishonored kind of work have the opportunity to find honor in being able successfully to cope with work which others may define as dirty. Honor is diminished when autonomy in the work is restricted by others in ways not perceived to be inherent in the nature of the work (Meara, 1974:279).

The workers in the beef plant experienced very little autonomy as a result of the assembly line process. Therefore their sense of honor in their work had to come from other sources.

The beef plant line workers developed and practiced a multitude of techniques for retaining their humanness. Daydreaming, horseplay and occasional sabotage protected their sense of self. Further, the prevailing attitude among workers that it was "us" against "them" served as a reminder that, while the nature of the job might demand subjugation to bosses, machines, and even beef parts, they were still human beings.

Interestingly, the workers' rebellion against management seemed to lack political consciousness. There was no union in the plant, and none of the workers showed any interest in the plant becoming organized. Despite all the problems of working at the plant, the wages were extremely good, so that the income of workers in the plant was high, relative to most of the community. Even the lowest paid line workers earned approximately $20,000 per year. Thus, the high wages and fringe benefits (health insurance, profit-sharing, etc.) seemed to override the negative aspects of the daily work. This stands in stark contrast with research in similar occupations (Garson, 1975; Linhart, 1981).

A third significant finding was that consumer spending patterns among the beefers seemed to "seal their fate" and make leaving the beef plant almost impossible. A reasonable interpretation of the spending patterns of the beefers is that having a high income/low status job encourages a person to consume conspicuously. The prevailing attitude seemed to be "I may not have a nice job, but I have a nice home, a nice car, etc." This conspicuous consumption enabled workers to take indirect pride in their occupations. One of the ways of overcoming drudgery and humiliation on the job was to surround oneself with as many desirable material things as possible off the job. These items (cars, boats, motorcycles, etc.) became tangible rewards for the sacrifices endured at work.

The problem, of course, is that the possession of these expensive items required the continual income of a substantial paycheck which most of these men could only obtain by staying at the beef plant. These spending patterns were further complicated by the fact that they were seemingly "contagious." Workers talked to each other on breaks about recent purchases, thus reinforcing the norm of immediate gratification. A common activity of a group of workers on break or lunch was to run to the parking lot to see a fellow worker's new truck, van, car or motorcycle. Even the seemingly more financially conservative were usually caught up in this activity and often could not wait to display their own latest acquisitions. Ironically, as the workers cursed their jobs, these expensive possessions virtually destroyed any chance of leaving them.

Working at the beef plant was indeed "dirty work." It was monotonous, difficult, dangerous, and demeaning. Despite this, the workers at the beef plant worked hard to fulfill employer expectations in order to obtain financial rewards. Through a variety of symbolic techniques, they managed to overcome the many negative aspects of their work and maintain a sense of self-respect about how they earned their living.

## NOTES

Reprinted from William E. Thompson, *Qualitative Sociology* 6, no. 3 (fall 1983): 215–37. Courtesy of Kluwer Academic/Plenum Publishers.

An earlier version of this paper was presented at the Midwest Sociological Society annual meetings in Des Moines, Iowa, April 7–9, 1982. For reprint requests, write Department of Sociology, Texas A&M University, Ferguson Social Sciences Building, 210, P.O. Box 3011, Commerce, TX 75429.

1. For an excellent overview of his concept of "dirty work" and its impact upon

those who perform it, see Hughes, 1971; Braverman, 1974; Meara, 1974; and Perry, 1978.

2. Interestingly, not a single line worker in *Offal* knew what the word meant or stood for (I did not ask the foreman). Workers who had been in *Offal* for as long as twelve years did not know the meaning of the term. Officially pronounced as "Off-all," it was often pronounced by the workers as "awful."

3. The analogies to slavery are not meant to imply that the workers are slaves, the foremen overseers, and the management slave owners. The laborers voluntarily went to work at the beef plant and were well compensated financially for having done so. The analogy is used merely to analyze social relations between various work roles.

4. One of the deaths occurred during the second week of my study when a crane operator's skull was crushed between the frame of the crane and a steel support beam.

5. For example, one of the most dangerous jobs in the plant was that of the *shackler,* who reached down and placed a chain around the back leg of a kicking 2,000 lb. steer only seconds after it had been slaughtered. This worker was constantly being kicked or battered with flying steel chains and hooks. The *shackler* was paid 10 cents per hour more than other workers on the kill floor, because of the extremely dangerous nature of the job.

6. Though I had no mechanisms for testing this hypothesis, it seemed plausible. In my opinion, the relation between on-the-job accidents and off-the-job events should be studied. Shostak (1980) implies that non–work related problems may relate to stress on the job for blue-collar workers.

## REFERENCES

Balzer, Richard
 1976  Clockwork: Life in and outside an American Factory. Garden City, NY: Doubleday.
Barlow, Hugh
 1981  Introduction to Criminology (2nd ed.). Boston: Little, Brown.
Berger, Peter, Brigitte Berger, and Hansfield Kellner
 1974  The Homeless Mind: Modernization and Consciousness. New York: Random House—Vintage Books.
Bookchin, Murray
 1971  "A technology of life." Pp. 247–259 in Theodore Roszak (ed.), Sources: An Anthology of Contemporary Materials Useful for Preserving Personal Sanity While Braving the Great Technological Wilderness. New York: Harper and Row.
Braverman, Harry
 1974  Labor and Monopoly Capital: The Degradation of Work in the Twentieth Century. New York: Monthly Review Press.
Chinoy, Ely
 1955  Automobile Workers and the American Dream. Garden City, NY: Doubleday.

Coleman, John R.
1974  Blue-collar Journal: A College President's Sabbatical. Philadelphia: Lippincott.
Garson, Barbara
1975  All the Livelong Day: The Meaning and Demeaning of Routine Work. Garden City, NY: Doubleday.
Georgakas, Don and Marvin Surkin
1978  "Niggermation in auto company policy and the rise of black caucuses." Pp. 58–65 in Kenneth Henry (ed.), Social Problems: Institutional and Interpersonal Perspectives. Glenview, Ill.: Scott, Foresman.
Gold, Raymond
1958  "Roles in sociological field observations." Social Forces 36:217–223.
Hughes, Everett C.
1971  The Sociological Eye: Selected Papers. Chicago: Aldine Atherton.
Hummel, Ralph P.
1977  The Bureaucratic Experience. New York: St. Martin's Press.
Humphreys, Laud
1970  Tearoom Trade: Impersonal Sex in Public Places. Chicago: Aldine.
King, Rick
1978  "In the sanding booth at Ford." Pp. 199–205 in John and Erna Perry (eds.), Social Problems in Today's World. Boston: Little, Brown.
Linhart, Robert (translated by Margaret Crosland)
1981  The Assembly Line. Amherst: University of Massachusetts Press.
Marx, Karl
1964a  Economic and Philosophical Manuscripts of 1844. New York: International Publishing (1844).
1964b  The Communist Manifesto. Translated by Samuel Moore. New York: Washington Square Press (1848).
Mead, George H.
1934  Mind, Self, and Society. Chicago: University of Chicago Press.
Meara, Hannah
1974  "Honor in dirty work: The case of American meatcutters and Turkish butchers." Sociology of Work and Occupations 1:259–82.
Osofsky, Gilbert (ed.)
1969  Putting' on Ole Massa. New York: Harper & Row.
Perrow, Charles
1979  Complex Organizations: A Critical Essay (2nd ed.) Glenview, Ill.: Scott, Foresman.
Perry, Stewart E.
1978  San Francisco Scavengers: Dirty Work and the Pride of Ownership. Berkeley: University of California Press.
Reimer, Jeffrey
1979  Hard Hats: The Work World of Construction Workers. Beverly Hills: Sage.
Roethslinger, F.J.
1941  Management and Morale. Cambridge: Harvard University Press.

Schatzman, Leonard and Anselm L. Strauss
  1973   Field Research. Englewood Cliffs: Prentice-Hall.
Schutz, Alfred
  1967   The Phenomenology of the Social World. Evanston, Ill.: Northwestern University Press.
Shostak, Arthur
  1980   Blue Collar Stress. Reading, Mass.: Addison-Wesley.
Spradley, James P.
  1979   The Ethnographic Interview. New York: Holt, Rinehart, and Winston.
  1980   Participant Observation. New York: Holt, Rinehart, and Winston.
Stampp, Kenneth M.
  1956   The Peculiar Institution: Slavery in the Ante-Bellum South. New York: Random House—Vintage Books.
Stonequist, E.V.
  1937   The Marginal Man. New York: Scribner.
Terkel, Studs
  1974   Working: People Talk about What They Do All Day and How They Feel about What They Do. New York: Pantheon.
Walker, Charles R. and Robert H. Guest
  1952   The Man on the Assembly Line. Cambridge, Mass: Harvard University Press.

# 18

## Annoying Owners: Routine Interactions with Problematic Clients in a General Veterinary Practice

*Clinton R. Sanders*

Service workers—from waitresses to brain surgeons—typically devise typological systems into which they place clients and that they use to structure service interactions. Most basically, clients are judged to be either "good" or "bad" largely based upon whether they facilitate or impede the flow of the service encounter thereby enhancing or hindering the worker's opportunity to draw maximum financial and/or sociopsychological rewards from the exchange (Mennerick, 1974).

Like other medical service workers, veterinarians categorize their clients in this manner. However, special features of the veterinary profession and clinical interactions with clients create distinctive problems and require unique responses on the part of the veterinarian.[1] While all medical encounters are negotiated transactions balanced between cooperation and conflict (Lazare et al., 1987), the triangular nature of the veterinarian's clinical interactions with both a human client and an animal patient make for exchanges which are uniquely challenging to the veterinarian and especially interesting to the sociologist. In essence, the veterinarian and the client cooperate to devise strategies through which the animal is cast in the role of the "virtual patient" (Gregory and Keto, 1991).

Because the animal patient is a non-verbal and relatively powerless actor in the situation, the client and doctor exchange information and observations directed at determining the problem experienced by the animal and devising the appropriate treatment. In this exchange the client calls upon his or her everyday, intimate experience of the animal while the veterinarian primarily employs technical expertise. Ideally, the sharing of these rather differently derived types of information leads to a cooperative interaction and mutually satisfactory clinical outcome. However, conflict may result when everyday and technical evaluations and concerns do not coincide. The strong emotional connection the owner feels for his or her pet enhances the potential for conflict. This means that evaluating and controlling the client are central to what the veterinary literature commonly refers to as the "art of veterinary practice" (See Owens, 1986).

This artistic management of the client requires the veterinarian to devise evaluative typologies which help to situate both the people and animals encountered. While veterinarians' definition and control of their patients is an issue of considerable interest (see Sanders, 1994) and evaluations of patients and clients are related, the following discussion focuses predominantly on clinical interactions between veterinarians and owners. In particular, I examine the various characteristics veterinarians use to differentiate "good" clients (compliant, manageable, profitable, likable, and so forth) from those who are definitely "bad." Because negative and conflictual encounters more often highlight definitional strategies and control tactics employed by social actors than do routine and problem-free exchanges, I will focus primarily on categories of problematic clients.

In short, veterinarians define as problematic clients who are annoyingly ignorant, inattentive, demanding, and apparently neglectful of their pets' physical condition. Additionally, clients who are seen as emotionally over-involved with their animals, or display an overriding concern for the financial aspects of the service encounter as opposed to their animals' medical welfare are relegated to the troublesome category.

## THE RESEARCH

This discussion is based on data collected during approximately 12 months of fieldwork in a major veterinary hospital in New England. Nine veterinarians and approximately two dozen veterinary technicians and administrative personnel worked in the setting.

I had originally entered the clinic as a researcher when engaged in participant observation of a series of puppy kindergarten classes held there (Sanders, 1990). My principal interest in observing clinical encounters in the hospital was to gain access to additional situations in which to watch people interacting with their companion animals. I soon found, however, that the day-to-day occupational routine of the veterinarians was as interesting as were the owner-animal exchanges to which I was privy. My fieldnotes soon reflected this dual focus as I began to observe and interact with the doctors and other hospital personnel as they socialized and worked outside of the six examination rooms within which clinical encounters normally occurred.

I visited the clinic an average of three times a week, typically spending between two and five hours each visit observing, interacting, reading available journals, and—eventually—assisting with the ongoing business of the clinic. In my role as participant, I commonly helped with the tasks usually assigned to veterinary technicians. I restrained animals during exams, "held veins" in animals' forelegs while blood was drawn, fetched equipment and supplies, carried and positioned anesthetized patients in surgery, comforted frightened and injured animals, assisted in limited ways during surgeries and necropsies, and accompanied veterinarians on "farm calls" as they ministered to dairy herds.

In addition to the fieldnotes compiled during my stay in the clinic, I also conducted lengthy, semi-structured interviews with all of the veterinarians working in the setting. As is conventional, these interviews were used to refine and expand analytic "hunches" generated in the course of the fieldwork.

## PROBLEMATIC VETERINARY CLIENTS

### Ignorant Clients

In the view of the vets there was no *necessary* connection between problematic pets and characteristics of their owners. Although aggressively macho, ignorant, or fearful clients frequently tended to have aggressive or out of control dogs, this was not always the case (Antelyes, 1990). Problematic clients with problematic animals were those who either did not exercise effective control over their pet during the clinical encounter or failed to warn the veterinarian that the animal might behave aggressively.

As my experience in the field proceeded, I was frequently struck by the apparent ambivalence of owners' feelings for their animals. As a general rule, clinical personnel saw owner ambivalence as indicating a client who should not be a pet owner and who might present potential problems. Here, for example, is how one vet described a particular ambivalent and fearful client.

There are some people who are just plain difficult and I don't even know why they go to the vet sometime. I had one Saturday. Over the years I have gotten to know her. She is just a difficult person. She likes me more than she likes any of the other vets but she has a rotten disposition, a rotten attitude. She acts like her dog is the kindest, nicest thing and then when it comes out at the end of the visit she will say, "Well, I can't do that. He will bite me." The dog has dry eye and needs all kinds of medication in it. And there happens to be one medication, it's a little expensive but it might actually cure it rather than just have to put stuff in over and over again. But I knew she wouldn't want it because it was expensive. So I said, "Well, why don't we try these other things first, see how you do with them and see if they work. If you are able to get the drops in we can go with the more expensive thing which may give you a cure in the long run." She said, "Well, I can't even do that." Well, sorry. Get a fish.

Owners such as this were viewed with some annoyance by the vets. Dealing adequately with these clients required the doctors to take considerable time educating them about the characteristics of their animals, how to deal with them appropriately, and so forth. When the clinic was not especially busy, when the owner was a regular client, or if there was an obvious problem caused by the owner's lack of knowledge—if the animal was severely overweight or very aggressive, for example—vets did take time to instruct the client or give him or her relevant literature. Some clients, however, were so hopelessly ignorant of the basic requirements of animal caretaking that they were viewed with a sort of sad bemusement. Frequently, these owners were the focus of joking among the staff. Here, for example, is an incident drawn from fieldnotes describing a cat owner whose intensely negative reaction upon discovering that her animal had fleas provided us all with some measure of amusement.

I go into an exam room and pet a small Himalayan kitten brought in by a nicely dressed young woman. She is very agitated because Dick has just informed her that the kitten has fleas. I have a hard time taking this seriously and tell her how incredibly common this problem is. She complains, "You would think that the breeder would have taken care of this. I paid $350 for her and you would think that for that amount it wouldn't have fleas." I jokingly respond, "Well, probably the last 50 dollars was for the high class fleas." The woman is still very upset— "They must be all in my house, in my new sofa! I went to my friend's house and she had cats and I sat on her sofa and fleas were crawling all over me." Later, Martha (a tech) and I talked about the client and I tell about my encounter. She says, "You mean she paid $350 for that cat! She was really strange. She was shaking because the cat had fleas and then she was bouncing off the walls when it was getting an injection (she covers her face with hands to demonstrate). Then she wouldn't let us test the stool sample she brought in because of the added expense. I couldn't believe the stuff with the fleas—'Hey lady, all cats have fleas.' 'Oh no, not in my house.'" She shakes her head in amazement and we both laugh.

### Inattentive and Demanding Clients

Ignorant clients were potentially time consuming. Similar costs were associated with clients who were inattentive during the clinical encounter or so talkative that they had to be interrupted in order for the vet to get information or give instructions. Following an encounter with such an inattentive client, one doctor remarked with considerable show of pique:

> Ones like that really annoy me. Here's someone who comes in here and is paying for my time. He comes in and I can't get a word in edgewise because he is going on and on telling me what is wrong. If I do get a chance to talk he just . . . [he stares absently at the ceiling]. I know that they are totally wrong and they don't agree with my diagnosis, but there is nothing you can do.

While inattentive and ignorant clients cost more time and effort than they were worth, the vets saw owners who were overtly belligerent and demanding as being even more problematic. Their behavior in the clinical encounter was regarded as a direct assault on the doctor's expertise—they impeded the vet's ability to control the situation. Belligerent clients complained, disputed diagnoses, demanded special considerations, and generally did not behave in the compliant and appreciative manner deemed appropriate by the doctors. When asked about aggressive and demanding clients, one veterinarian related the following incident.

> There was one weekend in the Fall when it was really busy on call. My first call was five in the morning. It was this very old, diabetic dog with seizures who couldn't breath. He really needed to be put to sleep and the people weren't ready. The husband was very nasty. First of all they wouldn't leave when I got the dog stabilized. I couldn't get rid of them and I had all these other animals in the hospital. In order to keep the dog from seizing, I basically had to keep him anesthetized. They wanted someone to stay 24 hours and they wanted a second opinion. I said, "Fine if you want to take the dog somewhere else, please take him somewhere else. Take him to the emergency clinic where someone can be with him 24 hours." They made me so miserable the entire day. They just took everything I had to give, were mad at me because their dog was dying. . . . If they weren't happy with me they can go see someone else. I don't have a problem with that. But it was constant. They were either here for hours or they were on the phone all the time. And they would just show up whenever they wanted. This happened for a whole day and finally at 10 o'clock at night we put the dog to sleep.

In contrast to the belligerent, demanding, inattentive, or annoyingly ignorant client, a "good" client was friendly, willing to cede interactional control to the vet, responsive to instructions, and sufficiently knowledgeable to provide intelligible and relevant information about the patient's condition. Here is how one vet described the ideal client.

> The perfect client is the person who really cares about the animal, cares about the welfare and well-being of the animal as much as they care about their own need for that animal to be part of their life. They listen to me and are willing to

spend some money so that I can practice my profession correctly. It's a client who can let the animal go; who is willing to let it go if it is necessary and if there is nothing we can do.

## Neglectful Clients

Unlike the ideally compliant and realistic client, some owners were viewed negatively by the staff because their pets' physical condition indicated that they were neglectful of or indifferent to their animals' well-being. For the most part, the veterinarians maintained that this type of client was rare since the very fact that a person brought their animal for veterinary services demonstrated that he or she feels at least a minimal concern for the creature's health.

Negligent owners were viewed with considerable distaste. Love for animals is the major factor which draws veterinarians and veterinary technicians to their occupations and failure to adequately care for one's pets typically was seen as indicating either ignorance or moral deficiency. Here is a woman vet's description of a bad client whose negligence is compounded by his manipulativeness.

> I had (a bad client) today. It's this old dog and she has been incontinent for a year and they keep her outside. So they brought her in and said, "I think she has maggots on her. I don't know, we clean her up and stuff but I think she had maggots on her." I take her in back and her whole underside is eaten up, she had holes all over her, maggots are crawling in and out. It's not something that happened yesterday. Then I look on the history and it says, "will get maggots, have to watch." So the guy clearly hasn't been taking care of her. I call him up—I'm already kind of mad because I know he is not taking care of her. She's fifteen and he's hoping she'll die tomorrow but he doesn't want to put her to sleep. So I say, "She's infested with maggots and if we are going to pull her through this she is going to need constant care." And he said, "Oh No! If it is going to mean really big surgery put her down, put her down." And I hear his wife start crying in the background saying, "Oh what's wrong, did we do something wrong." And he says, like, "No, just shut up." So I am like doubly mad at this guy because he is just using me to put this dog to sleep. . . . So he's a bad client. He's neglectful and he's manipulative.

Since vets typically saw the client's neglect of her or his pet as due to ignorance or inattention rather than purposive cruelty, when encountering routine and minor problems, they usually gave owners the benefit of the doubt and tried to educate them about treatment and prophylactic measures.

> You see a few cases of apparent neglect. The classic case is the dog that is just left out tethered on a run and you see where the collar had just grown into the skin on the neck. Sometime before they notice it the skin will actually grow

around over the collar so the collar will be buried under the skin. ["What would you do in a situation like that?"] You point out to the client that it is just a case of out and out neglect and you impress upon the client that unless he is prepared to take better care of the animal they really should consider getting rid of the animal—finding another home for it or putting it to sleep.

In contrast to this educative approach, extremely negative responses were reserved for owners whose neglect was seen as purposive and which seriously threatened the life of their animals. Such a response is described in my notes.

I go back into the pharmacy and exchange a few pleasantries with Debra. She catches me up. "You should have been here on Saturday. We did a C section on a golden. She was in terrible shape. The owners just weren't paying attention. ["What was wrong with her?"] It's hard to say. She wasn't up on her shots and it may have been a viral infection. When I opened her up her abdomen was full of fluid and her intestines were inflamed. She had diarrhea and was vomiting for two weeks! She had 11 pups in her. She had delivered 6 at home and was straining for hours. She was very weak when they finally brought her in. We did the C section and saved two of the pups; one was born dead. She hung on for a day but was just too weak." Martha chimes in. "She didn't smell too good. She was full of black water. Linda and I worked on the two puppies but we just couldn't get them to breathe on their own. We worked on them for over an hour, but the time comes when you just have to make the decision. She was such a sweet dog too. We all felt really bad. We couldn't believe that the owners would just let her go like that."

In most circumstances, veterinarians instructed or reprimanded the negligent owner. Severe and ongoing incidents of abuse, however, sometimes provoked clinic staff to take the relatively extreme step of reporting the offending owner to local animal control officials or the Humane Society. Most of the doctors questioned viewed this move with considerable ambivalence since it ostensibly violated the confidentiality of the doctor-client relationship.

In rare instances of repeated abuse, where we have tried repeatedly to impress on the owner that he is neglecting his animal and it hasn't sunk in and he's continuing to do so we have contacted the ASPCA or the Humane Society. It is sort of a ticklish area because it is a violation of the client's trust and your relationship. But sometimes the abuse is so flagrant that you can't let it go on. There is kind of a divided loyalty. You have a threesome there. You have yourself and your patient and then you've got your client. You have to balance the needs of both [the client and the patient]. One of the challenges of the job is trying to draw that balance.

## Over-Involved Clients

On the other end of the continuum from the problematically neglectful owner was the client who was so intensely devoted to a pet that he or she, as one vet put it, "calls us up every time (the animal) sneezes." Veterinarians and staff commonly referred to this type of client as an "animal-nut."[2] At worst, over-involved clients were deemed troublesome because of the extra time and unnecessary attention that frequently had to be devoted to them. This client commonly provided the veterinarian with excessive and overly detailed information about his or her pet's condition and behavior, thus making it difficult for the doctor to determine what was actually going on with the animal. Early in my stay in the field, I asked a vet whether he thought that a talkative and hyper-informative dog owner we had just seen was, in his view, a "good" client. He replied:

> Sometimes it's not good when clients give you a lot of information. Sometimes they'll just give you so much you can't separate the wheat from the chaff. The people we have the most problem with are those that complain all the time. It's usually not because we did anything wrong but because they are so busy telling us what they think the problem is that they just don't listen.

Over-involved clients who were excessively demanding, talkative, hostile, or who became overly emotional during a clinical encounter presented problems for the doctors as they tried to most effectively manage their limited time and energy. Not all "animal-nuts" were defined as problems, however. Frequently, the vets recognized that people who are strongly attached to their animals were the prime consumers of their services. One doctor succinctly summarized the clinic's clientele as follows.

> There are three kinds of clients. Some you never see until their animal is almost dead. We hate them. Then there are the people who are pretty conscientious about things. Then there are the people that drive you crazy calling up all the time and coming in with little things. They're a pain, but it's like [the founding veterinarian] says—they put two of his kids through college.

In addition to providing income for the clinic, clients who were intensely devoted animal lovers often were seen as likable eccentrics. Despite their peculiarities, they clearly loved their animals; were solicitous of their well-being (sometimes to a fault); and generally considered and treated them as unique individuals with personal taste, feelings, and emotions (Sanders, 1993).

## Cost-Focused Clients

Each year Americans spend over $5 billion for veterinary services (American Veterinary Medical Association, 1988:11). Engaged in a fee-for-service occupational activity, veterinarians must ongoingly be concerned with monetary issues. In the large clinic in which I worked, the doctors were separated from the "dirty work" of collecting fees and dunning delinquent clients since this activity was handled by the business manager and his administrative staff. When doctors did exercise some measure of control over fees, adjustments were made to "cool out" belligerent clients or to reward those who were regulars, well-liked, and seen as short on funds.

One important criterion used by the veterinarians to judge whether a client was good or bad centered on how concerned he or she was with economic factors. Clients who were more worried about the cost of the service than they were about the welfare of the animal tended to be negatively evaluated, while those for whom money was a secondary issue were more positively defined as appropriately conscientious owners. One vet focused on clients' economic concerns when asked about the characteristics of "bad" clients during an interview.

> Bad client are people that get mad at you because their dog is sick or they get angry at you because they have to treat them or they have to pay. It's not "I'm unemployed. I really wish I could pay. Look, can I pay later?" It's just, "I don't have any money." The dog is sick and you say, "Well, he needs antibiotics." "HOW MUCH IS IT GOING TO COST?" It's just their attitude and how they talk to you. Hey, do you want to treat your dog or not? Some people are just very suspicious that we are trying to make a buck off them.

## CONCLUSION

The interaction of social performers with very different perspectives and goals presents a situation of considerable sociological interest Encounters between service workers and those with/for/upon whom they work present a particularly engaging form of collective action. One area of service delivery that has received considerable attention involves the situated exchange between physicians and patients (e.g., Reeder, 1972; Schwartz and Kahne, 1983; Stoeckle, 1987). In these interactions the doctor is (ideally) in control, knowledgeable, of higher status, acting within her or his work setting, and focused on occupational interests. The patient, on the other hand, is typically concerned with his or her well-being, of lower relative status, and subservient to the doctor's instructions (see Danziger, 1981). Troublesome patients, then, are those who are not compliant, challenge the doctor's expertise, and/or evidence various forms of moral inferiority (Lorber, 1981).

As the primary consumer of the veterinarian's services, veterinary clients are evaluated on similar grounds. In their dealings with the doctors and clinic staff, troublesome clients are belligerent, demanding, and argumentative. The negatively defined client is also inattentive to instructions, overly talkative, "pathologically" devoted to his or her pet, gives indication that he or she neglects the animal's welfare, or is more concerned with the price of service than the health of the patient.

In short, problematic clients are more trouble than they are worth. They impede the routine work flow of the clinic, require extensive education and stroking, affront the veterinarian's moral sensibilities, and affect the profitability of the enterprise. While some of these problematic characteristics are judged by the vets to be the result of client inexperience or marginally acceptable personal quirks that simply must be taken in stride as an integral feature of veterinary practice, others are seen as indicative of more serious failings. In particular, clients who apparently are unconcerned with their pet's physical and/or psychological health and those who do not overtly acknowledge the veterinarians' expertise and control are judged most negatively.

The discussion above has focused on a facet of the day-to-day occupational problems encountered by veterinary practitioners as they deal with animal patients and human clients. As seen, the relatively commonsensical categories into which clients are relegated form the core of the collection of stories which constitute the ongoing lore of the local occupational culture. The collective lore of medical settings in particular is composed of stories which incorporate fairly clear ethical principles as well as identifying social types and specifying certain techniques which have been found to be more-or-less effective in handling both unique and commonplace problems. The local stories aid regular participants in grounding and justifying the difficult decisions one is forced to make in all medical settings and are presented to newcomers as they are introduced to the practical procedures they can employ and the ethical problems they can expect to encounter (see Herzog et al., 1989).

Like essentially all jobs, veterinary work is predominantly a series of routine events. While all the veterinarians with whom I worked saw their occupational routine as rewarding in its predictability, it was the unique happenings—the unusual cases, the "interesting" surgical procedures—that added spice to the daily round of routine events. Unique cases were valued because they provided veterinarians with new or enhanced experience (cf., Dingwall and Murray, 1983; Becker et al., 1961:329–330), allowed them to make use of and hone their technical skills, and offered opportunities to successfully solve diagnostic problems.

But the rewards of veterinary practice go beyond the ability to use technical abilities, solve diagnostic problems, learn new techniques, and encounter unusual medical situations. Clinical practice is, as we have seen, an intensely social activity made even more powerful by the emotional connection that commonly exists between owner and animal. To be a veterinarian means not only to bear the brunt of annoyance, ignorance, belligerent demands, and whining about the cost of services. Veterinary practice also means that one is often the recipient of fervent appreciation offered by clients who recognize that their animals have been cared for with compassion and skill.

## NOTES

Reprinted from Clinton R. Sanders, *Qualitative Sociology* 17, no. 2 (1994): 159–70. Courtesy of Kluwer Academic/Plenum Publishers.

Direct correspondence to the author, Department of Sociology, University of Connecticut, Department of Sociology, Box U-2068, Storrs, CT 06296.

Portions of this paper were presented at the Qualitative Analysis Conference, Carleton University, Ottawa, May 22–25, 1992.

1. As of the end of the 1980s, approximately 38 percent (34.7 million) of American households included an average of 1.5 dogs, 31 percent (27.7 million) included an average of 2 cats, and 6 percent (5.2 million) included an average of 2.5 birds. Seventy-eight percent of dog owners, 60 percent of cat owners, and 8 percent of bird owners used the services of a veterinarian during 1987 (American Veterinary Medical Association, 1988).

2. Harris (1983) refers to clients who display "overdependence on a companion animal" as "unconventional owners" and estimates that they make up between 35 and 40 percent of veterinary clientele.

## REFERENCES

American Veterinary Medical Association (1988), *The Veterinary Services Market for Companion Animals*, prepared by Charles, Charles Research Group, Overland Park, Kansas.

Antelyes, Jacob (1990), "Client Relations when the Animal Dominates," *Journal of the American Veterinary Medical Association* 196(4):578–580.

Becker, Howard, Blanche Geer, Everett Hughes, and Anselm Strauss (1961), *Boys in White: Student Culture in Medical School*, Chicago: University of Chicago Press.

Conrad, Peter and Rochelle Kern (eds.) (1981), *The Sociology of Health and Illness: Critical Perspectives*, New York: St. Martin's.

Danziger, Sandra Klein (1981), "The Uses of Expertise in Doctor-Patient Encounters during Pregnancy," pp. 359–376 in Peter Conrad and Rochelle Kern (eds.), *The Sociology of Health and Illness: Critical Perspectives*.

Dingwall, Robert and Topsy Murray (1983), "Categorization in Accident Departments: 'Good' Patients, 'Bad' Patients, and 'Children,'" *Sociology of Health and Illness* 5 (2): 127–148.

Gregory, Stanford and Stephen Keto (1991), "Creation of the 'Virtual Patient' in Medical Interaction: A Comparison of Doctor/Patient and Veterinarian/Client Relationships," Paper presented at the meetings of the American Sociological Association, Cincinnati.

Herzog, Harold, Tomara Vore, and John New, Jr. (1989), "Conversations with Veterinary Students," *Anthrozoos* 2(3):181–188.

Lazare, Aaron, S. Eisenthal, A. Frank, and J. Stoeckle (1987), "Studies in a Negotiated Approach to Patienthood," pp. 413–432 in John Stoeckle (ed.), *Encounters between Patients and Doctors.*

Lorber, Judith (1981), "Good Patients and Problem Patients: Conformity and Deviance in a General Hospital," pp. 395–404 in Peter Conrad and Rochelle Kern (eds.), *The Sociology of Health and Illness: Critical Perspectives.*

Mennerick, Lewis (1974), "Client Typologies: A Method for Coping with Conflict in the Service Worker-Client Relationship," *Sociology of Work and Occupations* 1:396–418.

Owens, Jerry (1986), "The Art of Practice," *Proceedings of the 53rd Annual Meeting of the American Animal Hospital Association*, New Orleans, pp. 585–593.

Reeder, Leo (1972), "The Patient-Client as a Consumer: Some Observations on the Changing Professional-Client Relationship," *Journal of Health and Social Behavior* 13:406–411.

Sanders, Clinton, (1990), "Excusing Tactics: Social Responses to the Public Misbehavior of Companion Animals," *Anthrozoos* 4(2):82–90.

Sanders, Clinton (1993), "Understanding Dogs: Caretakers' Attributions of Mindedness in Canine-Human Relationships," *Journal of Contemporary Ethnography* 22(2):205–226.

Sanders, Clinton (1994), "Biting the Hand that Heals You: Encounters with Problematic Patients in a General Veterinary Practice," *Society and Animals* 1(3):47–66.

Schwartz, Charlotte Green and Merton Kahne (1983), "Medical Help as a Negotiated Achievement," *Psychiatry* 36:333–350.

Stoeckle, John D. (ed.) (1987), *Encounters between Patients and Doctors*, Cambridge, MA: MIT Press.

# 19

## Occupational Claims to Professionalism: The Case of Paralegals

*Kathryn J. Lively*

This article bridges the gap between sociologists' understandings of professions and professionalization and workers' understandings of "professional" and "professionalism" by examining how paraprofessional workers (Freidson 1970) use these concepts to describe themselves and others in their daily interactions. Specifically, this article shows that paralegals use these concepts strategically to justify their structurally subordinate positions relative to those of attorneys. It also shows how their understanding of what it means to be professional allows them to conceptualize their acceptance of the more demeaning aspects of their jobs, not as a sign of their lower occupational standing, but as a sign of their increased moral worth. Moral worth can be thought of, in this instance, as an individual's level of inherent goodness, or self-worth, that has little or nothing to do with occupational status or prestige. To these ends, my focus is on two concepts not typically found in the sociological literature on professions, *professional* and *professionalism,* and how they enter the subjective understandings of workers who may or may not consider themselves members of an accepted profession.

To date, the majority of sociological work dealing with professions has been conducted using professions themselves as the unit of analysis (Abbott 1988; Collins 1988). Early work attempted to identify which occupations constituted "true" professions and their corresponding functions (Carr-Saunders and Wilson 1933; Marshall [1939] 1965; Parsons [1939] 1954), while later work focused on the structural conditions that either gave rise to professions or inhibited occupations' rates of professionalization (Caplow

1954; Millerson 1964; Wilenski 1964). In the 1970s and early 1980s monopolists shifted focus by attempting to link professionalization to the desires of professional organizations (as opposed to the desires of individual actors) for dominance and authority (Larson 1977), while culturalists attempted to explain professionalization as a function of occupations' levels of cultural (or societal) legitimation (Bledstein 1976; Haskell 1984). In the late 1980s, in yet another revival of interest, Abbott (1988) posited a systems theory of professions that answered the question of why some occupations are professions and others are not by appealing to their differential levels of occupational jurisdiction. Although different in their specific arguments, these theorists share an assumption of the objective taken-for-granted validity of professional categories.

Whereas these approaches have been good for describing the growth and decline of particular occupations, they failed to take into account the individual actors that comprise the professions that they study. Two noteworthy contributions to the professions literature are typically overlooked by students of professions: Becker's (1970) symbolic interactionist interpretation and Ritzer's (1971) work on "unprofessional professionals" and "professional nonprofessionals." Both authors suggest the potential of a gap between criteria of professional performance and members' actions. Becker (1970:92) introduces "a radically sociological view" in which he questions whether such things as professions truly exist. According to Becker (1970:92), professions are nothing more than "those occupations that had been fortunate enough in the politics of today's work world to maintain possession of that honorific title." Professions, he argues, should be conceptualized as folk symbols that organize the way people think about work and are applied strategically depending on one's position along the occupational continuum.

Ritzer (1971) rejects Becker's radical view. He asks why some professionals are more professional, or conduct themselves with a greater degree of professionalism, than others. In what was perhaps the first attempt to account for differences in individual professional*ism*, Ritzer identified two continua that members of the *accepted* professions adopt: "All occupations may be placed on a continuum ranging from the non-professions on the one end to the established professions on the other. But once you pinpoint the position of an occupation on this continuum, the question remains of the degree of professionalism of the individuals in the occupation" (1971: 61).

My research builds on the work of Becker and Ritzer by offering an interactionist approach to the study of professionalism. Instead of focusing on members of the established professions, however, I show how groups of nonprofessionals construct their own understandings of what it means to be professional and to demonstrate professionalism. They do this, in part, by creating their own definitions of professional behavior, which are divorced from any given occupation or occupational status. They then use these understandings to organize the way that they think about themselves and their work and to cope with the more *un*professional dimensions of their jobs, or with situations in which they are routinely treated in unprofessional ways. Further, this research shows that while these subjective understandings may have benefits for the individuals who are able to attain them, they also have significant consequences for the work-related behaviors of these nonprofessionals and significant implications for the status of their occupations.

## METHODOLOGY

This study is based on semistructured, open-ended interviews with fifty-one paralegals employed in private law firms. Paralegals, by definition, are "a distinguishable group of persons who assist attorneys in the delivery of legal services. Through formal education, training, and experience, legal assistants have knowledge and expertise regarding the legal system and substantive and procedural law which qualify them to do work of a legal nature under the supervision of an attorney" (National Association of Legal Assistants 1984, cited in Johnstone and Wenglinski 1985).[1] As this official definition suggests, paralegals are not autonomous workers. In fact, they are required, by law, to have an attorney review their work, and they cannot dispense legal advice to clients or to other members of the legal community.

The respondents were selected through snowball sampling, a method by which one increases the number of respondents by asking each participant already in the study to recommend others for interviewing (Websdale 1999; Weiss 1994). My two initial contacts were women with whom I had worked when I was employed as a court runner in a midsize law firm. Both women provided names of friends and co-workers whom they believed would be interested in participating. As I was working as a paralegal at the time I began this project, I was also in the position to meet paralegals independent of the original "snowball." Although I have experience working as a legal assistant, this study is based on in-depth interviews with others.[2]

The sample for my study consisted of forty-three women and eight men. Five of the women and one of the men were African Americans; the remainder of the sample was white. One of the male paralegals was gay, and one of the women had breast cancer; while these issues were unrelated to work per se, it became evident that these added identities affected the ways in which they were allowed to do their jobs. The age of the paralegals ranged from twenty-four to fifty-eight. The sample was collected from more than twenty law firms ranging from solo practitioners to organizations with well over one hundred attorneys. Although some of the paralegals worked together, I interviewed no more than five paralegals from the same firm.

## PROFESSIONALISM

According to Becker (1970), folk symbols serve to organize the way individuals think about themselves and society. The symbol "profession" organizes the way individuals think about work; "professional" and "professionalism" constitute symbols that organize how individuals think about their own and others' behavior or status in the workplace, yet to date these subjective meanings have not been linked to the sociological study of professions. Indeed, individuals' folk understandings of professionalism seem divorced from sociological understandings of professions, as evidenced in recent ethnographic studies of women's orientations toward work (e.g., Statham, Mauksch, and Miller 1988).

Statham, Mauksch, and Miller's (1988) collection of qualitative studies suggests that female workers define themselves as professionals as a strategy to minimize personal costs of remaining in unprofessional jobs such as domestic work (Romero 1988), public school teaching (Spencer 1988), and police work (Martin 1988). Although these studies occasionally mention or allude to professionalism, or what it means to be a professional, they give very little systematic attention to processes through which workers claim these symbols as their own or to the consequences that may arise for individual workers as a result of making such claims.

Given paralegals' position in the middle of the occupational continuum, as paraprofessionals they make ideal respondents for studying the appropriation of the symbols "professional" (and the corresponding symbol "unprofessional") and "professionalism" by nonprofessional workers. Paraprofessionals are members of occupations organized around the work of a master profession. They lack the requisite job autonomy and, in some cases, depth of experience or knowledge to be full-fledged professionals (Freidson 1970; Larson 1977). In this case, paralegals are members of an occupation that serves attorneys, but they lack the job autonomy, experience, and knowledge to practice law without attorney supervision.

Whereas Becker (1970) believed that all workers would eventually become cynical about their attempts to become members of a "profession" and therefore shun the title professional. Freidson (1970) argued that paraprofessionals, in particular, would strive to attach themselves to their master profession and its corresponding professional associations. Given these two contradictory predictions, I ask, how do paralegals understand professionalism as it relates to themselves and others? Have they become cynical as Becker predicted? Have they given up on their desire to be members of a profession and therefore actively shunned the symbol of "professional" as well? Or have paralegals, as Freidson suggested, become awed by the attorneys for whom they work and attempted to emulate them to seek professional status for themselves? Or have they perhaps divorced the symbols of being professional and of professionalism from the professions altogether in ways the professions literature had not anticipated? Instead, might paralegals have used these symbols strategically as a means of maintaining their own moral worth, or self-worth, as it pertains to their occupational position, as suggested by Martin (1988), Romero (1988), and Spencer (1988)?

## THE APPROPRIATION OF PROFESSIONALISM AMONG PARALEGALS

Despite Becker's (1970) dire prediction about workers' growing cynicism about professions and Freidson's (1970) belief that paraprofessionals align themselves with their master profession and distance themselves from other nonprofessionals, the paralegals in this study talked often and freely about the importance of professionalism and being professional. They did not rely on being more like attorneys or, as would logically follow, less like secretaries. In fact, paralegals tended to judge attorneys and secretaries as either being professional or unprofessional, using the same criteria with which they judged themselves (Ritzer 1971). Indeed, paralegals in this study openly discussed their own professional behavior and the corresponding unprofessional behavior of attorneys in ways that were reminiscent of Ritzer's work on "unprofessional professionals" and "professional nonprofessionals" but had surprisingly little to do with whether they, as paralegals, were actually members of a profession or with their collective level of professionalization.

Because professionalism was an important part of paralegals' work identity, whenever they used "professional" and "professionalism" I asked them what these words meant to them personally. Although no two paralegals completely agreed about what it meant to be professional, they identified two sets of norms that they used for judging their own and others' behaviors (Martin 1988): being competent in one's work and maintaining a credible front (Goffman 1959).

### Competency

Because one might expect competency to be included in any job description, it is not surprising that paralegals stressed the relationship between competency and professionalism. According to them, being competent required that they possess the requisite knowledge, skills, and ability to perform the tasks demanded of them. While a small number of paralegals told

me they had the knowledge, skills, and ability to "run" their attorneys' practice for "a long, long time" if only they had someone to sign off on things
that *required* an attorney's signature, the majority of paralegals' comments
concerning competency dealt with possessing the requisite knowledge,
skills, and ability to fulfill their *own* job requirements, whether or not those
included managing documents, prepping clients, scheduling depositions,
making copies, or even serving coffee. Although each paralegal provided me
with a different job description, each believed that fulfilling that description
was a key indicator of his or her level of competency and subsequently his
or her level of professionalism. For example:[3]

> I think of a professional as someone who gets the work done and the work is
> done so well that people look at it and recognize it as superior. (Donald Ander-
> sen, African American, age 27, 3 years' experience, midsized firm)
> I just think that professionalism is a lot of competency—knowledge and compe-
> tence—a sense of confidence that we are competent to do what we've been asked
> to do. (Barbara Wyatt, white, age 50, 13 years' experience, small firm)
> My definition of professionalism? My first priority is my attorney. Whatever
> they want me to do—if they want me to sing and dance, that's what I'm gonna
> do. (Alice Kramer, white, age 49, 3 years' experience, small firm)

While Donald's comment addresses the importance of creating a superior
work product, Barbara's and Alice's comments suggest that competency also
requires the willingness to do what is expected, regardless of the nature of
that expectation. Few paralegals in the study went as far as Alice in their
reported willingness to do what was expected of them. However, others also
reported that their ability, and to a certain degree their willingness, to
accomplish even the more rote, clerical aspects of their jobs contributed to
their understanding of themselves as professionals:

> When I meet a client, for instance, the room is set up before they get there. I
> have my legal pad. I have my pens. I have their file. I ask if they want coffee or
> water. I have all that ready even before we come back and start. I ask the ques-
> tions that I need to ask. I listen when I need to listen, and I end it as quickly as
> I can . . . as a professional. I think that it's important that you respect the [cli-
> ents'] space and their time. (Lonnie Smith, white female, age 35, 2 years' experi-
> ence, small firm)

Paralegals' definition of competency broadened the range of job-related
tasks that they could perform and still consider themselves professional. By
defining competency as their ability to do what was asked of them, these
paralegals could redefine even the most potentially demeaning aspects of
their jobs (such as making or serving coffee) as indicators of their level of
individual professionalism.

While paralegals all agreed on the importance of being competent in most aspects of their job, how they made attributions of competency was not always clear. Whereas previous work on professions (Freidson 1970; Larson 1977), defined professionals as individuals who had mastered a complex body of abstract knowledge that they could apply on a case-by-case basis, the paralegals in this study disagreed on the relative importance of formal education versus on-the-job experience. One explanation for this disagreement lies in the official occupational definition of paralegal cited above, which allows for a broad range of educational and workforce experience in the occupational category. For instance, while some of the respondents had received formal training in paralegal studies, others had four-year degrees in unrelated subjects, and still others had worked their way up to the position after having been employed for years as legal secretaries. As might be expected, the paralegals who had formal training tended to give precedence to formal education over office-based experience in defining and signaling competence, while those who had been employed as legal secretaries before being promoted informally to legal assistants typically denounced paralegal certificates as worthless and instead stressed the importance of hands-on experience.

Echoing Ritzer's (1971) analysis, Janice Moorehouse, a thirty-four-year-old medical malpractice paralegal with eight years of experience in a mid-sized firm, introduced the notion of competency as a continuum when she pointed out that there are a certain set of skills, knowledge, and abilities that a paralegal must have to be considered professional. Her statement also suggests not all paralegals necessarily have them:

> [T]o be looked at as a professional in this career, in *this* particular job, you have to really have your smarts. You have to have initiative. You have to be very organized and you have to be intelligent—you have to understand what's going on with your cases. . . . Besides just the skills part of being professional and really having a hold on your job, [you also have to be able to do] what they want you to do, what they *expect* of you.

In addition to the three basic components required to be considered competent, several paralegals discussed the importance of maintaining professional interaction styles in ways that were practically indistinguishable from their ability to perform their jobs.

> I would refer to [professionalism] as a *competent* way of communicating, in a civil manner without being defensive or accusatory—defensive of myself or accusatory of others, you know, without *whining* or complaining. I think professionalism, in general, probably we can write books on that . . . It involves,

certainly, very importantly, it would be a sense of competence to do what we
have been asked to do. (Barbara Wyatt)

To me [professionalism] means not being petty—like saying, 'How come you
gave this to me *now?*' You just take it [and do it]. Professionalism to me, as a
paralegal, is whatever you need—I can help you with . . . that's our *duty* here.
We are here to assist attorneys—that's all. (Jody Baine, white female, age 37, 16
years' experience, midsized firm)

Note that, at least for these paralegals, being competent often meant with-
holding anger, exhibiting civility, and stifling pettiness, which is reminiscent
of earlier discussions of display and feeling rules in the workplace (Hochschild 1983; Lively 2000; Pierce 1995; Rafaeli and Sutton 1990, 1991; Smith
and Kleinman 1989) and the presentation of self (Goffman 1959). Indeed,
one of the most striking observations regarding paralegals' use of the term
"competency" is the degree to which it often contained an emotive element
*in addition to* the basic skill, knowledge, and ability required to perform the
job. This finding implies that my distinction between the continua of competency and one's ability to maintain a credible front may be arbitrary.
Although it makes theoretical sense to separate these continua, the paralegals
themselves did not understand professionalism in this way. In fact, many
paralegals believed that the manner in which they completed their work was
almost as important as *whether* or not they completed their work.

For these paralegals, professionalism, or "being professional," required
not only that they do their jobs but also that they do them with good attitudes (or at the very least with the appearance of good attitudes). However,
also note that they demonstrate being professional while at the same time
respecting the social order of the firm, or their social place "beneath" attorneys (Clark 1990) When Jody Baine told me that paralegals were there to
"assist attorneys—that's all," I jokingly asked, "Is that *all?*" She looked at
me blankly—in what I assume is her professional manner—and then mentioned the most commonly cited component of professionalism: demeanor,
or the ability to maintain a credible front (Goffman 1959, 1967).

## MAINTAINING A CREDIBLE FRONT: MINDING
## THE FRONT STAGE/BACKSTAGE DICHOTOMY

According to Goffman (1967:75). "Demeanor refers to that element of an
individual's ceremonial behavior typically conveyed through deportment,
dress and bearing, which serves to express to those in his presence that he is
a person of certain desirable or undesirable qualities." Goffman (1959)
argued that in "our society" the "properly" demeaned individual displays
such attributes as discretion and sincerity, modesty in claims regarding self,

sportsmanship, command of speech, and emotional control. In the society of private law firms, "professional" paralegals display similar attributes primarily through their ability to maintain a distinction between what Goffman referred to as the "front" and "back" regions of social interactions.

In his discussion of social interaction as a series of performances, Goffman (1959) defined the "front region" as the area where the performance takes place (p. 107) and the back region as "a place, relative to the given performance, where the impression fostered by the performance is knowingly contradicted as a matter of course" (p. 112). Performers can deal with the personal or hidden components of their lives in the backstage areas that have the potential to interfere with or contradict their ability to carry out their performances in the front region in a credible way.

The front region of any given performance can be divided into three traditional parts: setting, appearance, and manner (Goffman 1959:23–24). Whereas the setting involves furniture, decor, physical layout, and other background items that "supply the scenery and stage props for the spate of human action played out before, within, or on it," appearance and manner refer to actors' individual performances, or personal fronts. Despite the way paralegals spoke about being professional, or as *"projecting* a professional image," they gave very little attention to their physical settings. However, a few respondents told me that some paralegal jobs were more or less professional than others because of varying contents and the varying qualities of their office space:

> I know some people that have gotten jobs as a paralegal, [but] they're also doing secretarial work. They're answering the phone. *Those* are people who probably don't consider it a professional job—they don't have an office, they have a cube. I'm lucky—I have an office with windows. (Valerie Schwartz, white, age 37, 2 years' experience, midsized firm)

Nevertheless, the bulk of their comments dealt with their personal fronts, including appearance, manner, and emotion management (Hochschild 1979, 1983).

## Personal Front: Appearance

Goffman defines "appearance" as referring to those stimuli that tell us about the performer's social status. These stimuli also tell us about the individual's "temporary ritual state, that is, whether he is engaging in formal social activity, work, or informal recreation" (Goffman 1959: 24). In terms of professionalism or being professional, most paralegals limited their discussion of appearance to their own or others' mode of dress. Although I did not ask about dress, the paralegals themselves often mentioned it in conjunction with their discussion of professionalism. Notably, they tended to disagree about the importance of dress to professionalism, much in the same way that they disagreed about the relationship between formal education and competency:

> Professionalism *doesn't* mean—what it doesn't mean to me is dressing how I call "little lawyer." I *don't* wear little suits and bowtie shirts and things to work. I wear slacks and casual tops. [What I have on]—that's not professional to me. What's professional to me is how I conduct myself. (Pam Miller, white, age 58, 16 years' experience, small firm)
> You know, I have the knowledge about procedures and jurisdictions—I help them [the clients] get through the maze—that's all I'm doing. Whether I am wearing a suit and a tie or I'm wearing a shirt and a tie or I'm dressed casual just like I am today. (Adam Jacobs, white, age 51, 9 years' experience, small firm)
> My attorney had a secretary who wanted to become a paralegal. She did not have a certificate. She did not have a lot of any kind of *legal* training, but she had a lot of *practical* training in real estate and it was a semidisaster. And part of the reason was she came in and my attorney had told her to look professional. So she got new clothes—new business suits—and started ordering every secretary to type everything for her, which was ridiculous. She didn't understand the difference between—the advice she got from someone else was, "If you want somebody to treat you like a paralegal, as somebody a step *up*, you need to *act* like it." Her version of acting like it was bossing people around and wearing new clothes. (Marion Cartwright, white female, age 40, 18 years' experience, midsized firm)

Ironically, of the nine paralegals who said that dress was related to professionalism, four were wearing jeans. The two respondents cited below, for example, excused their choice of office wear when I probed them for their understanding regarding their use of the term "professional":

> Well, normally I'm not this loose [dressed in a long-sleeved T-shirt and jeans], but there's nobody [no clients] coming by today. (Alice Kramer)
> When clients are present, I feel like I should dress a certain way, . . . for instance, I wouldn't wear jeans or anything like that [as I am now] if I know a client is coming in. (Mandy Howell, white, age 25, 2 years' experience, small firm)

Thus the paralegals had very different understandings about the link between dress and being professional. For some, dress was important; for others, it was not.

Another aspect of dress with particular relevance for female paralegals was the seeming incompatibility of female sexuality and professionalism in the workplace.

> Besides, just the skills part of being professional and really having a hold on your job, [you also have to be able to do] what they want you to do—what they

*expect* of you. [But it's also] the way you act. It's the way you *dress*. You know, there are a lot of paralegals that I think are pretty smart, but I don't think that the attorneys view them as professional, because they wear skirts that barely cover their butt. They walk around in high-heeled shoes with their boobs hanging out—that sort of thing. (Janice Moorehouse)

Today's Friday, so hence the dressed-down outfit. I normally wear skirts with blouses and jackets, or in the wintertime maybe sweaters and skirts. Occasionally slacks, but for the most part I wear skirts, hose. . . . I try to keep my hair in some—you know, *not* everywhere. It's not always braided or always pulled back, but I usually try to keep it kind of professional looking. Nothing really flashy ever, you know, just very—*discreet*, I guess, is the best word for the way that I think about it. (Lonnie Smith)

Whether a reflection of status or sexuality, paralegals' comments regarding dress are reminiscent of Tannen's (1994) argument that women's clothing, in a predominantly male (given that women are "marked" and men are "unmarked") environment, always makes an evaluative statement about the wearer. Specifically, she argued that each detail of a woman's appearance is necessarily heightened, from her dress and makeup, to her shoes, whereas men have the option of going unnoticed. Given that the majority of attorneys in private law firms are male and the majority of secretaries are female, casually dressed females are more likely to be mistaken as secretaries, whereas casually dressed males are more likely to be mistaken for attorneys (on reverse tokenism, see Floge and Merrill 1986; Heikes 1991; Williams 1992).

### Personal Front: Manner

Whereas appearance may be taken to refer to those stimuli that function to tell us of the performers' social statuses, manner most often refers to those stimuli that warn us of the interaction role the performer will expect to play in an upcoming situation (Goffman 1959:24). Although Goffman failed to define the term more specifically, the elements of manner that seemed most relevant to the paralegals' understanding of themselves as professionals were thoughts (or problems), personality or lifestyle, and behavior.

A common refrain throughout the study was the belief that professionals keep some degree of social distance between their personal lives and their occupational role. For some, this meant merely checking their problems or any personal thoughts that would interfere with their ability to do their job at the door.

Professionalism, to me, means . . . keeping a sort of *distance* between your personal life and your professional life. Not bringing your personal problems to the office. (Amy Westphal, white, age 27, 3 years' experience, large firm)

I don't think that people should come in with their [personal] baggage. I mean, you come in and you do what you have to do and go home. I mean everyone comes in—and there are days you don't want to work. There are days that you're not gonna bill as much as you normally do, whatever. As long as you do your job, that's all. [When you're a professional] you come in and do what you do and you go home. (Brooke Lyons, white, age 27, 2 years' experience, midsize firm)

As far as handling myself as a professional . . . I don't really know how to explain it, but I don't ever let there be a question in my client's mind that my personal life—or anything that goes on in the office—*ever* interferes with my job performance. (Lonnie Smith)

Lonnie and Brooke's comments, like Marion's comments regarding appearance, suggest a relationship between competency and one's ability to maintain a credible front. Just as Marion believed that paralegals who dressed in short skirts and low-cut blouses lessened their perceived level of competency (and therefore their professionalism), these three paralegals voiced similar opinions regarding their own and others' ability to keep their personal problems out of the office.

While Amy and Brooke emphasized their ability to keep their personal lives private, Lonnie also mentioned how she routinely altered or suppressed her personality in an attempt to be more professional:

As far as handling myself as a professional, it's almost like being *sterile*, you know . . . ? And I'm not saying that I really don't have a *personality*—I most certainly do, but I don't know how [else] to explain it.

And finally, Donald Andersen, a gay man working in a male-oriented firm, emphasized his need to keep his entire lifestyle hidden for fear of losing his job. Donald hid what he perceived to be a potentially discrediting status (Goffman 1963) by projecting an image of "super-competency"; he referred to himself as "the consummate professional." When I asked him what he meant by that term, he explained:

When I think of a consummate professional, I think of someone who is very task oriented, who is always, *always*, thinking about their job and the best way to do your job. And, you know, when you are at work, you do work. You don't *talk* about your personal life. You do things that are—that get the job done and get the job done well. So for me, being a consummate professional is about making the work the primary focus as opposed to, you know, the social aspects. . . . So I have a set standard, up here [raises his hand over his head], to which I hold myself and my work. It's sort of a closet search for excellence in order for me— because I feel that [if] I don't do that and someone finds out that I am gay, I am going to get fired.

Although Donald painted a picture of the way he acted so as to be professional, the majority of the paralegals in the study discussed the ways they acted to *avoid* being *un*professional. The majority spoke of being professional as "not being loud or rude in the workplace," "not gossiping behind people's backs at work," "not whining or complaining," "not buddying around with the people [they] work with directly," or "not yelling in the workplace . . . because it just wouldn't be right."

A minority, however, also saw professionalism as reflected in their ability to present themselves to the community or to clients *outside* of the office:

> To me, [professionalism] means [conducting myself in a professional manner] when I'm in public—even when it's unrelated to work, because this is actually a *small* town. We're a city with a number of people, but we're a small town [in a lot of ways], and people know me—they know I work for this law firm and that I have for a number of years. So it means that I'm always a representative of that law firm. (Pam Miller)

> I have a lot of interaction with clients, and I have to come off like . . . I'm a professional. Like I'm *there* to take care of my business, and that it's not about hanging out. . . . [T]hat I just want to get the job done. I am representing my firm and I just don't want to put out the wrong image. (Yvonne Sims, African American, age 31, 1 year experience, large firm)

Whether in or out of the firm, with coworkers, clients, or employers, these paralegals linked their ability to monitor and to control any of their behaviors that might be construed as unprofessional or interfering with their ability to be, or appear, competent. The components of maintaining a credible front—setting, appearance, and manner—can all be conceived of as continua on which paralegals may or may not be successful in their interactions with others, just as occasions may arise in which they may be, or may appear, more or less competent in the performance of their jobs. This notion of success or failure, or of being more or less professional, is perhaps most clearly illustrated in the last component of the personal front: emotional management.

### Personal Front: Emotion Management

"Emotion management" refers to the efforts of individuals to bring their emotional displays and feelings in line with existing display or feeling norms that govern emotions in specific contexts (Hochschild 1979). Emotion management for paralegals working in private law firms, therefore, refers to their ability to interact with difficult attorneys or clients with little or no (negative) emotional response (Lively 2000; Pierce 1995). In other words, professional paralegals must be able to engage routinely in acts of successful emotion management in the face of emotionally stressful encounters with attorneys and clients. Although Goffman's (1959) discussion of emotion management was limited to "surface acting" or managing the appearance of emotion, Hochschild (1979, 1983) showed that individuals also engage in "deep acting," or attempts to manage their actual emotions. In her study of college students, flight attendants, and bill collectors, Hochschild (1983) enumerated a number of strategies that individuals are likely to use to bring their emotions within the boundaries of preexisting feeling or display rules. When workers enact these strategies in the workplace, for the benefit of the corporation, these actions are called "emotional labor."

In keeping with Goffman's analysis of facial expression, or surface acting, several paralegals in this study tied professionalism to projecting a certain appearance of emotion that they did not necessarily feel. Tracey Styvers, twenty-nine, who had been employed for five years by an attorney who typically handled "the big money divorces," provided a stark example of surface acting when she was forced to deal with demanding or emotionally distraught clients over the telephone:

> As far as [what it means to be] professional, I would say, you can never let the client see or hear what you're thinking. I mean, I spend a lot of time on the phone and there are times that I'll have my head thrown back on the chair with my eyes closed, thinking, Oh my God, or I'll be reading a magazine if I have to. But the client thinks that I am the most caring person, and I *do* care—but they'll think that I'm hanging on their every word, and sometimes I'm not. It's not that I don't care about what they're saying or what they've done, it's just sometimes you can't take it anymore and you can never let the client see that.

Emily Bennet and Lonnie Smith spoke of the generic, or professional, fronts that they reserve for the bulk of their interactions with clients:

> Usually we're pretty relaxed, but there are times when we have to be professional and—especially when the client is present with us, then we, you know, we have our professional front that we use, just to have a uniform look. *Especially* if we're meeting with opposing counsel and *their* clients. (Emily Bennet, white, age 31, 9 years' experience, midsize firm)
> Most of my clients—I would say about 96 percent of my clients know only the professional, even-keeled, never-get-ruffled kind of person. But every now and then you get one that you just kind of let in on the real world. (Lonnie Smith)

These paralegals stressed the importance of displaying emotions they did not necessarily feel (Goffman 1959); however, a much larger number linked being professional with their ability to manage the emotions that they actually were experiencing (Hochschild 1979, 1983); this was particularly true with negative emotions, such as anger. Donald Andersen described one incident in which he confronted a white associate attorney for making racial slurs about one of the African American secretaries, when he *failed* to live up to his own ideal:

It was one of those situations where I felt very stressed *out* with the situation and *lost* it. I mean, if I was being the consummate professional, I would have—*should* have said, You know, so-and-so, this is really not acceptable behavior, and you should not be saying this about people whom you work with, blah, blah, blah, ad nauseam. Instead, I went *off* on this tirade—for about fifteen minutes. I let him have it.

When I asked one respondent to think of a situation in which she had been really angry at work, she also told me about an encounter she had with her supervising attorney when he had arbitrarily refused her request to work on a more challenging case even though she was the most qualified paralegal in the office. She laughed and said, "It took all the strength that I had in order to sit there and remain professional." When I asked her what that meant, she replied:

To remain calm. One of the things about me that I really cannot do, that I really wish I could do is to be very articulate when I am angry—which I can't. So I have to be quiet, because . . . once I open my mouth . . . I'll wind up yelling. I would *love* to be able to be perfectly, you know, calm—no matter how angry and agitated I am—and express myself in an articulate manner, because that's, to me, the ideal of professionalism. But I can't do that, so . . . I *really* had to hold it. I could not say *anything*—I was *so afraid* because there was so much going on in my head that I *wanted* to say. (Lois Garrison, African American, age 45, 2 years' experience, midsize firm)

Whereas Donald and Lois created ideals of professionalism that they would like to attain or to maintain in their interactions with attorneys, Judy Billings based her understanding of what it meant to be professional on a woman with whom she had worked several years before:

I remember when I was younger and I worked in a law office [with] a girl about ten years older than I was. . . . I would watch her neck just turn *red* from the stress that was going on inside her body, but she stayed totally cool on the outside. She *never* lost her temper, and she was nothing but sweet to everybody she talked to—on the phone *and* in the office—but you *knew* that she was having a nervous breakdown inside, and I admired her *so* much. . . . I look back at her and think, you know, she was a classy woman and very professional. And I always thought I wanted to be like that. (Judy Billings, white, age 44, 25 years' experience, small firm)

Closely related to the issue of anger control is the norm against crying, which was mentioned, unsolicited, in 43 percent of the interviews of paralegals who had almost cried at the office, had actually cried, or had witnessed crying in others.[4] The mandate *against* crying had particular relevance for women, who were more likely than men to report crying when angry. A second and perhaps more compelling reason crying had special relevance for women is that many believed that the attorneys, especially male attorneys, already viewed them as weak on the basis of their gender. One respondent explained:

> I got to that point, and I left. And I think if I would have stayed, I probably would have [cried]. . . . I think that men [especially men in the legal profession]—attorneys, high-powered, strong attorneys—think that women have the tendency to cry at everything and blah, blah, blah. So I think I was *about* to cry when I left. (Norma Richardson, African American, age 38, 9 years' experience, small firm)

And another respondent agreed when I asked her to elaborate on her statement that she would never, under any circumstances, cry in the office:

> Because I just feel that women are already stereotyped as basically weak—in the business world—just in the business world, period. I just feel like *certain* men, and especially my supervising partner, view women as the weaker sex, just basically put on earth to be barefoot and pregnant. And for that reason I'm not willing to let them [see] any weakness really . . . so that they have further ammunition to say, See? She's weak. There she is—look at her. Kick her while she's down. *Look* at her. I just don't want them to have that ammunition. (Mary Ferris, white, age 32, 9 years' experience, midsize firm)

Pierce (1995), in her study of the law profession, where the vast majority of high-status attorneys are male and the vast majority (85%) of paralegals are female, argued that these expectations maintain the overall gender hierarchy in law firms. Typical female emotions (caring and empathy) are devaluated and their corresponding emotional expression is defined as weak or unprofessional. Simultaneously, typical male emotions (aggression and anger) are accepted and their corresponding expressions are viewed as necessary and professional when exhibited by attorneys. Therefore, the occupational and the closely corresponding gender hierarchy become self-supporting. When paralegals (females) engage in attorney-associated (male) displays of emotion, they censure their own reactions out of their belief (and their experience) that anger and its corresponding actions are construed as negative or *unprofessional* and could leave them open to administrative sanctions (Lively 2000; Pierce 1995).

## UNPROFESSIONAL PROFESSIONALS: THE APPLICATION OF PROFESSIONAL NORMS TO ATTORNEYS

Despite Freidson's (1970) prediction that paraprofessionals would emulate members of their master profession, the paralegals in this study did not seem overawed by attorneys; in fact, the majority of stories regarding unprofessional behavior involved attorneys, not paralegals (Ritzer 1971).

Patricia Warner, a forty-year old paralegal with eight years of experience in a large firm, illustrated this point very clearly when she told me about a "particularly ugly encounter" that she labeled the "true test of professionalism." This encounter involved an attorney who had stopped her in the hall, interrupted her work-related conversation with another paralegal, and yelled at her for something that was beyond the control of either. Reminiscent of Lois's earlier remarks about managing her anger, Patricia told me it was all she could do not to respond at his level, which she felt was "totally unprofessional." I asked her why she considered that particular story to represent a true test of *her* professionalism and not his.

> P: Because I don't believe a professional should *yell* at another person. You should be able to ask someone to do something in a tone of voice that still lets the person know there's an immediate need. And for *me* not to spout off at him and say what I was truly thinking—it took self-control to do that. And of all the things that you do, I think, as a professional, you should not *show* your true feelings.
>
> K: Do you think that [the attorney] was acting in a professional manner?
>
> P: Oh, absolutely not. I don't believe that he should have *wagged* his finger at me. I think he should have communicated his desire to get [whatever he needed done] in a manner that was not belittling of me.

Like Patricia, Diane Sandburg also spoke of her own understanding of professionalism in contrast to the unprofessional behavior she routinely witnessed in a particular attorney, whom she identified earlier in the interview as "Tom Gray." Diane's understanding of professionalism entailed being pleasant not just to attorneys and clients but to the secretaries and the support staff as well. Taken in this light, she viewed attorneys who were unpleasant to paralegals and secretaries as being unprofessional, despite their relative positions along the occupational continuum.

> [Being professional] means to put your best foot forward . . . to *do* the work that you're given to the best of your ability, to be able to be relied upon to do that work, and to be held in high esteem by the people who are depending upon you, as well as the people, like the word processing staff, who have to tolerate you every day. I think that you have to treat people well—certainly, being professional means that you do that. I would never want somebody to think that I was [another] Tom Gray and screamed at everybody—I think *that's* unprofessional. (Diane Sandburg, white, age 23, 1 year's experience, large firm)

Donald Andersen also spoke of "unprofessional" attorneys, although he focused his attention on their behaviors as well as more indirect indicators of their disrespect for others (Ritzer 1971). Although Donald did not single out a particular attorney, he criticized the behaviors of attorneys throughout the entire firm, which he perceived as overly macho:

> Patent lawyers are really awful, because they are all ex-engineers. I mean you have to be an engineer with a law degree to be a patent attorney. So, first of all, there are not that many women who go into engineering in the first place, and of the number of women that go into engineering, not that many go get a law degree to become a patent attorney. So because of that . . . there was a lot of locker room humor that went around that I didn't appreciate, because I don't think it's very professional.

And finally, Adam Jacobs, who believed that professionalism was really about how individuals conducted themselves and met the interests of their clients, questioned the behaviors, motives, and integrity of the legal profession as a whole:

> I don't find there's a whole lot of professionalism between attorneys [anymore]. They do terrible things to each other—scheduling, *lying.* There's just too many of them out there—it's not the old house it used to be. There's just too many of them. And too many of them trying to get ahead, because it's so competitive. Sometimes I just don't think there's any—a lot of professionalism in it anymore. They put on the image, but under the table they're all sharks.

The above quotations suggest that paralegals tend to judge attorneys using similar, if not the same, norms of professionalism that they use to judge themselves and one another and that they believe attorneys use to judge them. Thus their use of these symbols is not grounded in their understanding of the professions per se or in the processes of professionalization. Regardless of occupational position, the paralegals in this study applied the same norms of professionalism to themselves and those around them. In fact, the only difference between paralegals and attorneys, from the point of view of paralegals, stems from the consequences that paralegals and attorneys face when caught breaking professional norms specific to interpersonal interaction. For example, while attorneys are able to be rude, lose their tempers, or act in any other way that might be considered unprofessional with little or no effect on their perceived competency, paralegals are not.

## CONCLUSION: SUMMARY AND IMPLICATIONS OF PARALEGALS' CONCEPTION OF PROFESSIONALISM

Even though paralegals are by definition paraprofessionals (Freidson 1970) and have yet to attain the honorific title shared by members of the "true professions" (Becker 1970), many see themselves as professionals (Martin 1988; Romero 1988), or as conducting themselves professionally during the daily performance of their jobs (Ritzer 1971). Despite Becker's claim, they are not cynical as a result of their inability to gain the title officially. They make eloquent statements about themselves as professionals and about their concerted efforts to perform their duties and to interact with others professionally. Nor did the paralegals attempt to achieve professional status by associating themselves with the attorneys with whom they work or the legal profession as a whole (Freidson 1970); in fact, many attempted to distance themselves from attorneys, who they believed were inherently unprofessional because of their inability to adhere to certain interactional norms, or because of their ability to *ignore* those norms with relatively few consequences.

Previous studies on law firms have documented the experiences of paralegals who are routinely treated as invisible in their interactions with attorneys and clients (Lively 2000; Pierce 1995). Ironically, part of paralegals' understanding about what it means to be professional includes their ability *be* nonpersons, or to *remain* invisible, during interpersonal interactions in which they are routinely ignored, insulted, demeaned, or offended (Lively 2000). Indeed, the majority of paralegals see their ability to remain invisible as a sign of their professionalism despite the fact that their roles as nonpersons directly relate to their subordination in relation to the attorneys and automatically carry with them a certain level of disrespect (Rollins 1985).

Despite all these factors, and, one could argue, because of them, paralegals still upheld a standard of professionalism with which they maintained their right to be professional, to be considered as professional, and to be afforded some semblance of professional regard.

Given that individuals holding paraprofessional positions are disproportionately female and individuals holding professional positions are disproportionately male, this study's treatment of credibility as a necessary component of professionalism augments Pierce's (1995) findings that the devaluation of female emotions in privately owned law firms results in the reification of the existing gender hierarchy. While Pierce's study focused primarily on emotions, my broader discussion of professionalism suggests that any characteristic of paraprofessionals' performances has the potential to be devalued to the degree that it interferes with, or is contrary to, the needs and expectations of their status superiors. Thus female paraprofessionals are trapped in a double bind from which they cannot escape. On the one hand, if others view their behaviors, appearances, manners, and emotions as characteristically female, they are labeled as unprofessional relative even to their male counterparts (Tannen 1994). On the other hand, as previous research has shown, if their behaviors, appearances, manners, and emotions are "unmarked" or too similar to the behavior of men, they run the risk of being labeled as "ball busters," "lesbians," "old maids," and so on (Collins 1990; Kanter 1977). Only when female paralegals' behaviors, appearances, manners, and emotions allow them to be nonpersons may they be viewed as professional. Male paralegals, while still held to a certain degree of professionalism, enjoy greater discretion, at least in terms of their demeanor, given that they are less likely to be "marked" relative to the dominant group.

The irony of the appropriation of the term "professional" by paralegals, as well as by any other occupation that lacks the structural authority or power to back its claim, lies simply in their understanding that the more willing they are to meet the needs of their status superiors and the more capable they are of dealing with disrespect and disregard in their daily interactions with others, the more professional they are. In addition, because their definition of professional behavior, or professionalism, applies at the individual level, it also reduces the likelihood of collective action. Because their definition of professional behavior requires them to do whatever is required, and to be invisible while they do it, it also reduces the likelihood that they will make sustained claims for equal or better treatment. So the appropriation of the term "professional" may make nonprofessionals and paraprofessionals feel better about their individual situations or reduce the social costs associated with staying in a job in which they are routinely disrespected or asked to do things they believe fall outside their occupational domain, but it does not change their status. If anything, the use of the term "professional," at least for these workers, simply reduces the likelihood that they will ever demand, and therefore be granted, the professional treatment and the occupational status they seek.

## NOTES

Reprinted from *Symbolic Interaction* 24, no. 3 (2001): 343–66. Copyright © 2001 by Society for the Study of Social Interaction. Used with permission.

Direct all correspondence to Kathryn J. Lively, Dartmouth College, Department of Sociology, 6104 Silsby—Room 103, Hanover, NH 03755.

I would like to thank Kathy Charmaz, the staff at *Symbolic Interaction,* and the outstanding reviewers who helped shape this chapter. I would also like to thank Jason Jimerson, Carrie Lee, Luis Saldanha, Jane McLeod, Sheldon Stryker, Maria Tempenis, Peggy Thoits, and Lori Westphal for all of their support and insight. This research was partially supported by the National Institute of Mental Health's Training Program in Identity, Self, Role and Mental Health, Grant #T32 MH14588.

1. Although I have chosen to use the term "paralegal," the respondents in my sample often used the terms "paralegal" and "legal assistant" interchangeably. Anecdotally, however, it seemed that individuals who had been promoted informally preferred the latter, whereas individuals who had formal training preferred the former. It is also important to note that this study is limited to the experiences of "para-

lifers," a term used to distinguish individuals who made the career decision to become paralegals and were promoted because of years of experience or formal education from those who were recruited from prestigious undergraduate institutions on their way to law school or an MBA program.

2. While I was employed as a paralegal, at the time that the first wave of interviews was collected, I did not keep field notes of my personal experiences. My decision not to document my own experience was based on my original research question of how coworkers manage their emotional reactions to both instrumental and emotional stressors on the job. At the time, I was the sole employee of a solo practitioner and therefore outside the selection parameters of my study.

3. All names of paralegals used below and throughout this article are pseudonyms. First and last names, as well as any other unique identifying information, have been altered to protect the respondents' anonymity.

4. In an informal discussion with a former attorney, who presided over a recent ASA round table at which an earlier draft of this article was presented, I was told that the crying taboo applied not only to paralegals and secretaries but to attorneys as well. She stated that although attorneys are allowed and sometimes encouraged to *exhibit* anger (see Pierce 1995:50–82), they are normatively forbidden to cry or exhibit any show of weakness. Indeed, this discussant suggested that the paralegals' unwillingness to cry might in fact be an attempt for them to be more lawyerlike.

# REFERENCES

Abbott, Andrew. 1988. *The System of Professions: An Essay on the Division of Expert Labor.* Chicago: University of Chicago Press.

Becker, Howard. 1970. "The Nature of a Profession." Pp. 87–103 in *Sociological Work: Method and Substance.* Chicago: Aldine.

Bledstein, B. J. 1976. *The Culture of Professionalism.* New York: Norton.

Caplow, Theodore. 1954. *The Sociology of Work.* Minneapolis: University of Minnesota Press.

Carr-Saunders, A. M., and P. A. Wilson. 1933. *The Professions.* Oxford: Clarendon Press.

Clark, Candace. 1990. "Emotions and Micropolitics in Everyday Life: Some Patterns and Paradoxes of 'Place.'" Pp. 305–33 in *Research Agendas in the Sociology of Emotions*, edited by T. Kemper. Albany: State University of New York Press.

Collins, Patricia Hill. 1990. *Black Feminist Thought: Knowledge, Consciousness and the Politics of Empowerment.* Boston: Unwin Hyman.

Collins, Randall. 1988. "Changing Conceptions in the Sociology of Professions." Pp. 11–23 in *The Formulation of Professions*, edited by R. Torstendahl and M. Burrage. London: Sage.

Floge, Liliane, and Deborah M. Merrill. 1986. "Tokenism Reconsidered: Male Nurses and Female Physicians in a Hospital Setting." *Social Forces* 64(4):925–47.

Freidson, Elliot. 1970. *Profession of Medicine: A Study of the Sociology of Applied Knowledge.* New York: Dodd, Mead.

Goffman, Erving. 1959. *The Presentation of Self in Everyday Life.* Garden City, N.Y.: Anchor/Doubleday.

———. 1963. *Stigma: Notes on the Management of Spoiled Identity.* Englewood Cliffs, N.J.: Prentice Hall.

———. 1967. "The Nature of Deference and Demeanor." In *Interaction Ritual: Essays on Face-to-Face Behavior.* New York: Pantheon Books.

Haskell, T. L. 1984. *The Authority of Experts.* Bloomington: Indiana University Press.

Heikes, E. Joel. 1991. "When Men Are the Minority: The Case of Men in Nursing." *Sociological Quarterly* 32, no. 3 (Fall):389–401.

Hochschild, Arlie Russell. 1979. "Emotion Work, Feeling Rules, and Social Structure." *American Journal of Sociology* 85 (December):551–75.

———. 1983. *The Managed Heart: The Commercialization of Human Feeling.* Berkeley: University of California Press.

Kanter, Rosabeth Moss. 1977. *Men and Women of the Corporation.* New York: Basic Books.

Katzman, David. 1978. *Seven Days a Week: Women and Domestic Service in Industrializing America.* New York: Oxford University Press.

Kleinman, Sherryl and Martha Copp. 1993. "Emotions and Fieldwork." *Qualitative Research Methods,* vol. 28. Newbury Park, Calif.: Sage.

Larson, M. S. 1977. *The Rise of Professionalism.* Berkeley: University of California Press.

Lively, Kathryn. 2000. "Reciprocal Emotion Management: Working Together to Maintain Stratifications in Private Law Firms." *Work and Occupations* 27, no. 1 (February):32–63.

Marshall, T. J. [1939] 1965. "The Recent History of Professionalism in Relation to Social Structure and Social Policy." Pp. 158–79 in *Class, Citizenship, and Social Development.* Garden City. N.Y.: Anchor.

Martin, Susan. 1988. "Think like a Man, Work like a Dog, and Act like a Lady: Occupational Dilemmas of Policewomen." Pp. 205–24 in *The Worth of Women's Work: A Qualitative Synthesis,* edited by A. Statham, E. M. Miller and H. O. Mauksch. Albany: State University of New York Press.

Millerson, G. 1964. *The Qualifying Associations.* London: Routledge.

Parsons, Talcott [1939] 1954. "The Professions and Social Structure." Pp. 34–49 in *Essays in Sociological Theory.* New York: Free Press.

Pierce, Jennifer. 1995. *Gender Trials: Emotional Lives in Contemporary Law Firms.* Berkeley: University of Berkeley Press.

Rafaeli, Anat and Robert T. Sutton. 1990. "Busy Stores and Demanding Customers: How Do They Affect the Display of Positive Emotion?" *Academy of Management Journal* 33:623–37.

———. 1991. "Emotional Contrast Strategies as Means of Social Influence: Lessons from Criminal Interrogators and Bill Collectors." *Academy of Management Journal* 34(4):749–75.

Ritzer, George. 1971. "Professionalism and the Individual." Pp. 59–74 in *The Professions and Their Prospects,* edited by E. Freidson, Beverly Hills, Calif.: Sage.

Rollins, Judith. 1985. *Between Women: Domestics and Their Employers.* Philadelphia: Temple University Press.

Romero, Mary. 1988. "Day Work in the Suburbs: The Work Experience or Chicana Private Housekeepers." Pp. 77–92 in *The Worth of Women's Work: A Qualitative Synthesis*, edited by A. Statham, E. M. Miller and H. O. Mauksch. Albany: State University of New York Press.

Smith, Allen and Sheryl Kleinman. 1989. "Managing Emotions in Medical School: Student's Contact with the Living and the Dead." *Social Psychology Quarterly* 52, no. 1 (March):56–69.

Spencer, Dee Ann. 1988. "Public Schoolteaching: A Suitable Job for a Woman?" Pp. 167–86 in *The Worth of Women's Work: A Qualitative Synthesis*, edited by A. Statham, E. M. Miller and H. O. Mauksch. Albany: State University of New York Press.

Statham, Anne, Hans O. Mauksch, and Eleanor M. Miller. 1988. "Women's Approach to Work: The Creation of Knowledge." Pp. 3–10 in *The Worth of Women's Work: A Qualitative Synthesis*, edited by A. Statham, E. M. Miller and H. O. Mauksch. Albany: State University of New York Press.

Tannen, Deborah. 1994. *Talking from 9 to 5: How Women's and Men's Conversational Styles Affect Who Gets Heard*. New York: Morrow.

Websdale, Neil. 1999. *Rural Battering and the Justice System: An Ethnography*. Sage Series on Violence against Women. Thousand Oaks, Calif.: Sage.

Weiss, Robert. 1994. *Learning from Strangers: The Art and Method of Qualitative Interview Studies*. New York: Free Press.

Wilenski, H. L. 1964. "The Professionalization of Everyone?" *American Journal of Sociology* 70:137–58.

Williams, Christine. 1992. "The Glass Escalator: Hidden Advantages for Men in the 'Female' Professions." *Social Problems*. 59:253–67.

# 20

# Working on Hair

*Helene M. Lawson*

This article is about "managing hair" and the choices available to and accepted by people who want their hair cut or arranged. It is also about change in the field. I have been thinking about researching this subject for some time now. Mostly I hate having my hair done no matter who does it or where or when it's done. When I was little, I was told my hair was "too thin" for "Shirley Temple curls," and when I got older, it was "too naturally wavy" to emulate the swinging straight blond look of Mary in the Peter, Paul and Mary trio. Later on, it was not "curly or thick enough" for an "Afro" or "corn rows." I almost never had anything to say to the people who cut and styled my hair. I felt uncomfortable in salons, I hated their magazines, and I usually washed out the chemicals and goo from my hair the moment I reached home. Goffman (1959) might say I had difficulty with "impression management." I had been convinced by professionals (beauticians) that there was a right way for hair to look, yet I did not have the right hair to project a "face" which would emulate movie stars or persons from other cultures whose hair styles were popular. I was also not comfortable in hair "establishments" (beauty parlors) because they displayed rigid "values pertaining to fashion" throughout their shops that I was not able to live up to (Goffman 1959:240). Although I knew better, I was nevertheless constantly reminded by beauty magazines near the dryers and pictures hung on the walls that "real" women had perfect complexions, long tapered nails and perfectly shaped features. Therefore, I felt alienated in salons.

Taking these attitudes and experiences with me, I recently relocated from an affluent white North Shore suburb of Chicago to a rural blue-collar and even whiter area of Pennsylvania. While in the throes of searching for a salon

I could bear to enter, I started noticing the many small colorful barbershops in the area. Each shop had only one barber, and the decor of the shops reminded me of *Andy Griffith* meets the *Frontiersman*. Where I came from, there were no barbershops that had animal trophies on the wall or gun cabinets for sale. I remember my grandfather going to a barber to get shaved. My father used a barber, too, but there were more workers—usually three or four barber chairs in each shop—and hair tonics for sale like Lilac Vegital to counter the effects of thinning hair (my father used this at home). I was never invited to accompany the men in my family when they got their hair cut, and so by walking past the red and white barber pole outside the shops and peeking in through the windows, I surmised that barbershops were only for white men and boys.

When my son was young, men and boys were wearing longer hairstyles. My husband had his hair styled in an upscale salon by a hairstylist who was a woman. I then thought most barbershops were outdated and used only by older men who didn't want styled hair or poorer men who couldn't afford styled hair. I wanted my son's hair styled, but I didn't want to spend a lot of money, either, so I searched for and found a barbershop that looked like a salon. It was called "Franco and Pino's Barbershop," but there was a manicurist who was a woman and two men and one woman who were barbers working there. Here they washed, cut and styled hair and sold shampoo, hair spray and mousse. My daughter came to my salon and got her hair trimmed for higher prices, but she had much longer hair and went less often, so I could afford it. Still, I wondered what it would be like to go where my wealthier acquaintances in Chicago went, to salons that served wine and had special consultation rooms.

When my son got older, he chose to go to a "unisex" salon mostly staffed by women. He claimed prices were "cheap" and the workers "did more stylish work than male barbers." Furthermore, they took walk-ins. My daughter found herself an "openly gay" man who was a hairstylist, who she said could cut hair "better than any woman. Besides, he's a scream! He wears a tool belt with a lot of scissors and hair tools in it and swings them around."

Through my experiences and those of my family, I have had a relatively diverse experience with the hair management field. Nevertheless, my perspectives are directly limited by my gender, race and class. Most overtly, my whiteness has meant that I have learned little about black hair and the management of it, formally or informally. Only recently, as I conducted this research and interacted with African-American and Indian colleagues and students have I began to examine the issue of race and hair.

In order to understand, on a more in-depth level, why certain people choose to use specific types of hair workers in specific types of shops and the social implications of such choices, I searched for articles on hair work. Although there are many articles on the symbolism and importance of hair throughout history, there are few sociological articles about hair workers. There are, however, related occupational articles that focus on ways in which workers sell themselves to clients. Haas and Shaffir (1978) find that doctors convince clients they are competent by using symbols such as lab coats, medical tools and language to present themselves in the most favorable ways. According to Rubinstein (1973), artifacts such as uniforms, night sticks and guns legitimate police officers' authority over others. Hair workers, however, are service workers, have fewer credentials and rate lower on prestige scales than doctors or police officers. Their artifacts are hair dryers, scissors, clippers, razors, and chemicals. Yet clients respect and depend on their expertise, allow them to touch their face and hair in the most intimate ways and use their services in ever-increasing numbers. Overall, employment of cosmetologists and related workers in the United States is projected to grow 17 percent between 1994 and 2005 (Mittelhauser 1997). In 1997, the occupation employed 748,000 cosmetologists and 79,000 barbers (Ilg 1998). In this article, I analyze the importance of hair management. To ground my study, I begin with a brief history of hair work and workers. This history reveals the ever-changing nature of the hair management field and individuals' and groups' attitudes toward hair and hair care. I then present interviews with and observations of barbers, cosmetologists, and clients, and conclude with a discussion of my findings.

## METHODS OF RESEARCH

The data for this paper are based on observations in 16 barbershops, 12 beauty salons (10 are midrange [$17.00 to $25.00 for a wash cut and blow dry], and two are upper-range [$25.00 and up]), eight unisex chain salons and two beauty schools. Within these locations, I conducted in-depth interviews with 17 barbers (13 white and two black men and two white women). When studying cosmetologists I interviewed 15 white men and 15 white women. I also interviewed four white beauty salon owners (two men and two women), one white man who owns a beauty school, four white beauty school teachers who are women, and six white beauty school students (five women and one man). In addition, I spoke with 40 adult clients (15 white women, 15 white men, three black men, three black women, one Indian man, one Indian woman, one Puerto Rican man and one Puerto Rican woman), who frequent various types of shops and salons in rural northwestern Pennsylvania; Chicago, Illinois; and Los Angeles, California. I also interviewed nine children (five white boys, one Puerto Rican boy and three white girls), who were brought to hair establishments by their parents.

The interviews with workers were conducted at their places of employment, such as barbershops or beauty schools, when things were slow. Sometimes I arrived early for an interview appointment with a barber in order to listen to barber-client conversations. I had my hair washed, cut and styled in four different salons and followed friends, colleagues, family and students to shops where they had their hair done. I visited relatives in Chicago and Los Angeles to get data on unisex chains and upscale salons. The interviews with clients were conducted at various locations. Some clients were colleagues or acquaintances and spoke with me over lunch or dinner. Students or friends referred other clients to me. Because my primary research was conducted in the predominantly white area of northwestern Pennsylvania, this study centers on shops and salons dominated by white owners, stylists/barbers, and clientele. I address issues of gender race, and class within these white-dominated spaces; however, I leave the important work on black or other non-white owned and operated salons and shops to other researchers.

## THE IMPORTANCE OF MANAGING HAIR

Hair arrangement has been an important part of culture and tradition since antiquity. Aside from concern over the length and visibility of hair, photographs and epithets prove that over the centuries, women's and men's hair has been arranged, styled, curled, and colored in a very conceivable manner and enhanced with every kind of embellishment, including wigs. In fact, men have taken as much care over their hair as women and tended to wear wigs more often than women (Yarwood 1978). Levine says humans have always believed hair, like nature, needs taming: "it grows by itself and is part of our physical selves," but "unlike other parts of the body, is often more serviceable when pruned, trimmed, or tied up in some way so as to allow for comfortable vision" (1995:88). Schwartz says there are even larger issues at stake than comfort or vision because hair is symbolic as an area where culture and nature interact. To study the management of hair is to become "entangled in wider cultural meanings and ideas about generativity, procreation, power, [and] religion" (1995:10) as well as gender, race, and class identity.

Throughout history hair has been a powerful symbol of individual and group identity. Mercer, discussing African-American hair styles, points out that head hair managed by humans "socializes hair, making it the medium of significant 'statements' about self and society" (1994:249). All cultures work out an equilibrium between too much hair and too little hair, how hair should be worn and by whom, and who should manage it. Perspectives shift over time according to cultural desires based on gender, class, race, religion and other institutions (Levine 1995; Synnott 1993; Yarwood 1978).

The hair of gods and goddesses as well as mortals is described in Greek epics, for example, with adjectives such as "abundant, unfettered, untamed, wild, rampant, flowing free, long, rich and fair" (Levine 1995). Homeric representations equate long untamed hair for men with heroic strength, political power and youth. According to Levine, "The only biblical commands regarding men's hair are prohibitions against cutting it" (1995:89). Cultures, such as Greek, Roman and Jewish, have manipulated and managed women's hair through use of wigs and veils. For instance, when women marry, rules for managing their hair change because, in women, hair is a mark of "fertility and sexuality primarily associated with generative vitality," and "female sexuality is tolerated, if not encouraged, in traditional patriarchal societies for only a brief period immediately prior to marriage." At this time "public display of hair serves as a sexual stimulus and an incentive and inducement for men to marry" (1995:95–96).

In addition to such use of hair as a symbol of gender inequality, hair management is related to economic status and racial identity. People with little money generally arrange their own hair and have always done so. Yet this is not always about economic hardship. People of all races and cultures evolve intricate hairstyles related to climate, hair texture, and social class. Within each culture styles may be used as symbols of power, signs of rebellion, or to emulate those who have more prestige. White and White exemplify this cultural symbolism of hair in their study of slave hair and African-American culture. The authors describe the intricate "centuries-old hair styling arts" of "cutting, shaving, wrapping and braiding of hair" enacted by African-American slaves (men, women and children) in Mississippi in the 1800s (1995:49–50). That slave owners by and large allowed freedom of hair styling to slaves reveals an important "slippage in a normally tight system of slaveholder control" that allowed for reflection of tribal affiliation, status, sex, age, occupation, and other aspects of enslaved individuals' "identities" (1995:49). Slaves also shaved and combed their masters' hair in intricate rituals that signified their relative social positions as did slave owners' tendency to refer to slaves' hair as "wool," likening Africans to animals (1995:56). When slaves were liberated, many straightened their hair to copy white hairstyles, further illustrating the relationship between hair and inequality. Yet, after the black power movement of the 1960s, large numbers of African-Americans began to wear hair styles such as Afros and dreadlocks to celebrate the natural texture of their hair and rebel against assimilation to white norms. Soon after, values regarding hair texture and styles changed. "Woolly" hair was now envied, and other cultures began to emulate and adopt African-American hairstyles. Post–civil rights America seems again dominated by the "supposedly superior white variety" (White and White 1995:56) of hair, particularly for women, illustrating the constant change in displays of hair identity politics. The role of hairstylists involves similar issues of class values and change over time. Whereas hair management in the United States holds little status for men or women, in Nigeria, hairdressing is a "notable" occupation for women. Moreover, specific styles are worn by different classes of men and women. For example, members of the royal family generally wear "Awoyoyo" and "Agogo," styles that are painstaking to arrange and very expensive (Ogunwale 1972).

## HISTORICAL DIMENSIONS OF COSMETOLOGY AND BARBERING

In the contemporary United States, hair arrangement is divided among several types of workers. Cosmetology is the study of cosmetics and their use. Hair cosmetics include hair conditioners, mousses, sprays, styling lotions, straighteners, permanent waves, dyes, bleaches and shampoos (Robbins 1997). Cosmetologists, also called hairdressers, hairstylists and beauticians, are licensed workers who are trained in basic cosmetology training which includes fundamentals of hair cutting and styling, nail care, skin care, and makeup application. Cosmetologists primarily shampoo, cut and style hair, but they also dye, straighten or permanent-wave hair, give manicures and facial treatments, and provide make-up analysis. Cosmetologists can specialize in any of the above areas, or they can train or be certified in all. Most European hairdressers serve an apprenticeship. In the United States students take a six-to-twelve-month course at a state licensing school. The competency-based instruction in cosmetology has curricula for 1,000- 1,500- and 2,000-hour programs. Students can pick and choose (Miller 1995). Approximately 85 percent of wage and salary cosmetologists are employed in beauty salons or parlors. The remaining 15 percent work in department stores, health clubs, nursing homes, drug stores and funeral parlors. On average they change employment every four years. And, in spite of the growing number of men who have become cosmetologists in recent years, the share of women in the occupation has grown—90 percent of cosmetologists are women (Mittelhauser 1997). Cosmetology has low earnings for entry-level workers. Based on data from 1994 Current Population Survey, the median annual earnings of entry-level cosmetologists rank among the lowest for any occupation, about $14,800 compared to $24,300 for all workers. Yet, more experienced workers can fare much better. About 40 percent of cosmetologists are their own bosses. They rent chairs or booths, paying a set fee to a salon to lease a space to perform their services. The fee varies based on the location of the salon and the service it provides. The success of chair renters depends on the clientele they are able to retain (Mittelhauser 1997).

Though current practitioners have low social status, cosmetology is an ancient skill and custom. Men and women have used cosmetics for thousands of years. They were originally natural substances, such as plant dyes and clays. The ancient Egyptians applied perfumes and anointing oils to the body as early as 4000 B.C. They used these cosmetics for decorations, protection against the hot dry climate and also for religious reasons. The Egyptians, Greeks and Romans made cosmetics from plants. They also used powdered minerals to make face and eye makeup and hair dyes (Robbins 1997). Attempts to wave and curl hair also date back to early human civilization. Egyptian and Roman women applied mixtures of soil and water to their hair, wrapped it on crudely made rollers and baked it in the sun (Yarwood 1978). The ancients also used plant dyes on their nails, regarding long, colored fingernails as a mark of distinction between aristocrats and common laborers. By 1100 A.D. the use of cosmetics spread to Western Europe. Africans of about the same period painted their bodies for war and for magical ceremonies. In North America animal fats were used by Native Americans for protection against cold and as body decorations (Robbins 1997).

During the First World War, white western women began to use more chemicals on their hair. Yarwood (1978) suggests that one of the reasons these women also cut their hair short during this period was the invention of modern techniques of permanent waving which gave body to limp hair and made it easier to manage for long periods of time. When large numbers of white middle-class women went to work in war plants, they found short permed hair easier to manage. Women who could afford coloring or permanents along with haircuts went to cosmetologists trained in this new chemical technology. When the home permanent was invented in 1932, poorer and braver white women bought over-the-counter products and helped give each other permanents and dye jobs at home (Yarwood 1978). With the use of ever more services and products, the hair industry and the need for cosmetologists, particularly for white middle-class women, continued to grow.

While cosmetology focuses on the use of chemical cosmetics to manage hair and promote bodily attractiveness, barbering focuses on the use of precision instruments, such as razors, to manage hair and shave customers. The word barber comes from the Latin word "beard," and barbering has been dominated by white men since its beginning. To barber is to dress, cut, shampoo, style or shave head and face hair (Bureau of Labor Statistics 1998). Today very little shaving is done in barbershops because the straight razor has been replaced by shaving devices that most men can use on their own (Dobson and Walker 1979). Although throughout history long or fairly long hair has been more usual than a "short-back-and-sides" for white men, for much of the 20th century white men have worn their hair short (Yarwood 1978:215). Even so, Neimark (1994) claims barbers with limited services are currently less in demand because recent high-style appearance norms for men often require specialized services such as dyes and toupee work that most barbers do not provide. In most states barbers can be licensed to perform all the duties of cosmetologists, except skin and nail treatment, if they want to train and be certified for them. Most United States barbershops are one-person operations (approximately three out of four barbers are self-employed and work alone) (Bureau of Labor Statistics 1998). The median annual income for entry-level barbers is similar to that of cosmetologists ($15,080) and varies according to size and location of the shop, numbers of hours worked, customers tipping habits, and competition from other shops and salons. More experienced barbers with a large regular clientele can earn a good deal more (Bureau of Labor Statistics 1998).

Barbering, like cosmetology, has been done for thousands of years. Excavations of early Egyptian tombs revealed that abrasives such as pumice stones were used to remove unwanted hair on both men and women. Greeks and Romans also followed this practice (Dobson and Walker 1979). Barbershops were common in Greece about 420 B.C. and in Rome in 299 B.C. According to Andrews, early barbers are alluded to in the Book of the Prophet Ezekiel in a discussion of religious practices, such as shaving heads of Jewish mourners with sharp razors (1904:26). In the twelfth century, barbers expanded their trade by taking over monks' surgical duties, such as periodic ritual bloodletting because barbers were experts in the use of sharp instruments and a papal decree forbade the clergy to let blood. In fact the red and white barber pole that remains today is a symbol of bloodletting and bandages. Furthermore, Andrews describes the early barber as "notable tradesman and a many-sided man of business who . . . spread the town news and gave advice" (1904:26). There is also evidence that white "[w]omen barbers in the olden time were by no means uncommon . . . and numerous accounts are given of the skillful [*sic*] manner they handled the razor" (Andrews 1904:16–17). Stagecoach travelers were usually shaved by such women during long journeys. And even black women "shaved with ease and dexterity" (104:17). Yet women did not own shops, command as much respect, or fulfill the upper status positions, such as Master Barbers. For example, there are no women included in the historical listing of Master Barbers and Barber-Surgeons of London who served royalty from 1308 to 1973 (Dobson and Walker 1979).

In the 1400s, these London barbers banded together and formed a guild for social and religious observances. Eventually it became The London Company of Barbers, a trade guild. While women could join the barbers' guild in London, many did not because management consisted of white men and women workers felt they got few benefits from joining (Andrews 1904). Almost a century later in the United States, barbers' labor organizations include women, but they continue to represent men's interests. In the late 1970s, membership of The Journeymen Barbers, hairdressers, Cosmetologists and Proprietor's international Union of America as composed of 97 percent men. The president of this union claimed there were different contracts for barbers that guaranteed them more because barbers, unlike beauticians, headed households and were willing to work longer hours and support pension deductions (Howe 1977).

In the 1990s, there are many newer professional hair workers organizations such as The National Beauty Culturists' League and The National Hairdressers and Cosmetologists Association. Furthermore, titles such as barber, hairdresser, cosmetologist and hairstylist require similar qualifications and in many cases are interchangeable. Yet, these titles remain gendered and hierarchical and continue to separate hair workers. The label barber still symbolizes man and the label beautician still symbolizes women with little differentiation regarding race. For example, Hair International, the oldest professional association for barbers, was originally The Association of Master Barbers and, as its current website (www.hairinternational.com) proclaims, is still proud of its "history of men, for it was men who brought the Association into being. The ladies, in the persons of our beautician members of the gentler sex, came later. But it was men, barber shop owners, who saw the need for such a national organization and who took the steps necessary to raise it from the dark realm of hope and desire into the light of actuality and accomplishment." And cosmetologist and hairdresser are more elite labels than beauty culturist, barber or beautician. This is probably why men who work in salons are called "hairstylists" rather than "handsomenessians," and their shops are not called "handsomeness salons" or "handsomeness parlors." Connell argues that gendering and "definitions of masculinity are deeply enmeshed in the history of institutions and of economic structures. Masculinity is not just an idea in the head or a personal identity, it is also extended in the world, merged in organized social relations" (1995:29). Trade unions (such as the barber's union) "adopted the breadwinner wage objective, at the price of driving divisions between male and female workers" (1995:29). Yet barbershops are declining in number (5.1 thousand in 1990 to 4.8 thousand in 1993), and beauty salons are increasing (76.1 thousand in 1990 to 83.2 thousand in 1993) (Bureau of the Census 1996). In 1997, there were 748,000 cosmetologists across the nation and the vast majority (676,000) were women. In the same year, there were 79,000 barbers across the nation, and the vast majority of these (61,000) were men (Ilg 1998). In addition, since the 1960s, salons have been splitting in two economic directions aimed either at the upper end of the market or concentrating on economical cutting services at the lower end of the market (Mittelhauser 1997). The fancier salons, aimed predominantly at white customers, offer services such as tanning beds, facial make-overs and massage and relaxation technique classes. According to industry reports, these have emerged in reaction to the growing demand for more services for women of privileged economic class, emphasis on higher appearance standards for men, and the "convenience of having a number of needs met under the same roof" (Mittelhauser 1997:36).

Salons at the lower end of the market are exemplified by franchised chains labeled "unisex," i.e. servicing both men and women. These stores offer a basic haircut and styling for around $10.00. They are the McDonald's of hair care, generally found in shopping malls in large cities. Methods of operation in unisex shops combine the practices used in barbershops and those used in beauty parlors. Similar to barbershops, they are economical and operate with a first-come, first-served approach. Unlike barbershops, they sell products such as shampoo and spray but carry a much smaller line than can be found at beauty salons. Similar to the beauty salon, unisex shops offer a complete line of services, such as dyes, permanents and styling, but each service costs extra, and most customers come for a quick cut (Mittelhauser 1997). Unisex shops hire recently certified hair workers, 80 to 90 percent of whom are women (no racial demographics given) (Mittelhauser 1997). These workers make a low salary and get a small commission once they make their quota. Generally, the personnel are transient and move on to more autonomous higher-paying work situations (Mittelhauser 1997). A major factor in the success of unisex shops has been the growing number of men who prefer them to traditional barbershops. In fact, a large California-based chain has a clientele that is about 70 percent male (no racial demographics given) (Mittelhauser 1997).

An additional change has occurred in beauty schools where gendered language has been removed from the major text used in cosmetology schools across the United States, Milady's Standard Textbook of Cosmetology. Originally published in 1938, the text referred to workers as "she" in almost all cases. The only place "he" was used was at the beginning of the text where it referred to easy access into higher level positions for men in the field. The revised (1995) text refers to all cosmetologists as "the worker." It also uses labels such as hairstylist and salon rather than beautician and beauty parlor (Miller 1995).

Changing gender demographics and language in the industry are indicative of fidelity. The field of hair management has changed and will continue to do so in ways significant to gender, race, and class norms and structures. With this history in mind, the following pages examine interaction; in a specific group of barbershops, salons and unisex chains.

## BARBERSHOPS

The majority of barbers and clients in barbershops are men. Conversations between them focused on agreed upon perceived differences between men and women. These differences put women in a diminished light and separated them from men. The decorations and atmospheres in these shops also helped to separate men from women. Joseph, a longtime local barber, along with five other barbers I interviewed, had animal heads mounted on their walls (see figure 20.1). Joseph also sold hunting guns and gun cabinets in his shop. Hunting is a popular working-class sport dominated by men in northwestern Pennsylvania. These trophies and artifacts are negotiated symbols of "masculinity" and provide a comfortable atmosphere or space where discussions about hunting separate men from women. Joseph said he looked forward to "harvesting a six-point buck this year" and was willing to undergo "cold, damp and uncomfortable conditions for long hours" to achieve this goal. He complained that his wife and other women who attempted to accompany their husbands usually "turned back," or slowed men down because:

> Women don't know how to hunt or take full advantage of the region's resources. They haven't been taught to hunt as kids and so they would rather sit in the woods and read a book. Besides, the women that do hunt can't shoot worth a damn and if they do manage a kill, we [men] end up having to gut and clean it for them. They're too squeamish.

Aside from being labeled squeamish and poor hunters, women, in exception to men, were expected to look young. Marc, a middle-aged white barber who owned a newer shop, said: "I don't mind it on guys, but I really hate seeing gray hair on women. They should be more concerned with their appearance." His slightly graying client agreed wholeheartedly, seemingly reassured by this discourse that he need not change his own hair (Marc did not do dye work in his shop, anyway) and encouraged to value and trust his barber's perspective on women and aging. This customer continued the conversation reflecting his agreement with his barber on other gender issues, complaining because his daughter preferred observing nature to playing sports like his son: "She's not like my son. She's more interested in chasing butterflies than catching the ball." The barber agreed that "women are usually like that," further solidifying his role as confidante and gender-informed peer.

Women were not supposed to be interested in business, either. Fred, a 50-year-old white barber, offered two old torn leather couches, business and money magazines, and local newspapers. He could usually be seen through the window during slow times, sitting on one of the couches discussing local business happenings and what was in the paper that day with local men. Fred said information of importance to men was being relayed:

> We talk about business, what's going on with companies in the area, whose business is in trouble, if they are selling it and so on. We discuss money and deals, guy stuff.

In other shops, women were also berated, looked upon as objects, or not wanted around. Tim, white 60-year-old barber, kept "dirty magazines" hidden in a drawer. He joked about the attributes and failings of naked women's bodies with familiar clients. Moreover, a colleague who had his hair cut by

**Figure 20.1.** The decor of this barbershop reflects masculine interests.

Photo by Helene M. Lawson

Tim said that Tim did not want women customers because they "get in the way when men want to talk." In fact, most barbers openly discussed their dislike of having women invade their space and some said they would not do women's hair. John, another popular barber, was glad that his shop was behind a pool hall because he felt fewer women would come in:

> No women come in here because they would have to go through the pool hall and they don't want the men to stare at them. That's fine with me. I went to barber school and then cosmetology school, but I did not ever get the hang of doing women's hair. I felt clumsy about it, so I just cut men's hair. I felt like I was all fingers when I was cutting and rolling hair in school. I started in 1950 and cut hair all my life, but I never did women. My clients like it that way.

There are few women barbers in rural northwestern Pennsylvania. I did, however, find two, Susan and Jane, sisters who own their own shop. It was obvious that these barbers also reinforced differences between men and women that were not essential, natural or biological:

> We like working on men. They are more fun, they joke more. We like to talk sports with 'em. We don't color hair and we usually do short cuts. We are barbers after all!

This shop was a typical-looking Pennsylvania barbershop with hunting and sports magazines around and nature pictures on the walls. Their prices were comparable to what other barbers charged and, there were no products for sale. Also, like other barbers, Jane said she had only a few women customers and they got "short cuts" similar to the men's.

In fact, all seventeen barbers interviewed said they disliked and would not style long hair, even if it was on men. They linked long hair to femininity or homosexuality, and bonded with clients by mutually articulating their dislike of "fags." For instance, Gus, an older white barber, bragged about what he did to a long-haired newcomer who came in for a short cut:

> So this fag came in with really long hair tied back in a rubber band and he says he wants to get a shorter cut. I had that ponytail off and on the floor before he could take the rubber band off. Wouldn't want my other customers to see that.

The creating of this particular type of segregated gendered space that took place at this establishment is an interactional accomplishment that results in a place of business being turned into a hang-out for "real" men.

Children in northwestern Pennsylvania who went to barbers also made a connection between going to the barber and being "manly." For example, Rocky, a white five-year-old who got a "buzz" haircut, was greatly influenced by the ambiance in the barbershop:

I play fireman. The barbers have a fire engine that I sit in. They give me suckers when they are done shaving my head. The barbershop is the best place for boys to be.

Andy, a white seven-year-old, came to a salon with his mother and 10-year-old sister when they got their hair styled, but had never had his hair done there. He also wanted to be a "man," and the men stylists at the salon confused him. He asked one of the workers:

Why do you dress like a girl? Only girls have earrings in their ears. My dad says boys who wear rings in their ears are sissies. I would not like to get my hair cut here. I go to the barber shop with my dad. My dad says boys go to the barbershop and girls to the beauty parlors.

Dougie, a six-year-old, also came into a salon with his mother when she got her hair done, even though more often he visited the barber with his dad. His experiences were also somewhat confusing because, once in a while, he got his hair cut by a man who was a stylist. He called the hairstylist a "barber":

He is a barber because he's a man and he cuts hair. I think it would be fun to be a barber when I grow up, but I would only like to cut men's hair because I do not want to touch women. No girls get their hair cut where my dad takes me.

Even though Paul, a young Puerto Rican son of a colleague, went to a local hairstylist with his father, his father was also concerned with his son being considered "manly" and had certain rules for what was okay and what was not. When I asked the father why he went to a hairstylist instead of a barber, he said that barbers had long disappeared from the scene in Puerto Rico. He said Americans were "behind the times" because "all hair workers in Puerto Rico are hairstylists." And his son Paul added, "I go to a hairstylist, but I would never sit under a dryer. Those things are for women."

Class and racial differences are also relevant to the barbershop experience. One barbershop I visited in Chicago was in a culturally diverse, working-class area and another was downtown in a large hotel. The lower-class shop was owned by Ross, a 45-year-old black barber. I saw sports magazines on a table, and there were two older black men sitting around talking. I saw no white men in this shop, but I did find a black woman waiting for her son to get a haircut. She knew the other men in the shop and talked with them and the barber about local gangs and a recent armed robbery in the area. The camaraderie between the woman and the men differentiates this urban shop from the rural shops in Pennsylvania; however, both locations share a working-class tendency toward use of the shop as a site for community interaction and racial segregation.

In addition, an Indian customer, Raj, told me about a particularly bad experience he had in a Pennsylvania barbershop. While getting his hair cut, Raj heard two white male customers whispering loudly about his "brown ass." The barber did not react to or stop the racist comments. This reaction helped to code John's place as safe for the bigoted clients, reinforcing their confidence in him as an individual who shared their perspective on racial differences.

The hotel shop, in Chicago, was somewhat different; it was run by a black barber but owned by the hotel. Further, it was cleaner and had a wash basin. Haircuts, shaves, and moustache and beard trims cost more money ($15.00 and up) than in the Pennsylvania barbershops I visited. There were business and news magazines on leather chairs. The customers were white men who wore suits and ties. They spoke to each other rather than include the barber in their conversation. Their conversation centered on the unseasonably hot weather, and the Chicago Bulls' recent two-game loss. The customers had come to the hotel before and said they knew the barber. Yet, in their relationship with the barber, they were unwilling to view the barber as peer, either for racial or class differences or both.

More generally, class is relevant to the barbershop experience in terms of cost. Male customers who go to barbers usually explain their reasons for doing so in terms of practical necessity and economics. Tom, a white 40-year-old construction worker, said, "I go to a barber to be neat and combed and presentable, not as an asset for attracting women or making money, like yuppies." Similarly, Frank, a white 45-year-old balding math professor, said, "I go to a barber. Look at my hair—what would you do? Besides, it's cheaper." And Joe, a white 49-year-old gas station attendant with very short hair, said, "I go to a barber. Doesn't my hair look it? Why would I need a hairstylist?" Thus, economics played a leveling role in the class choices of both university professors and blue-collar workers.

## BEAUTY SALONS

As previously stated, cosmetology is dominated by women (90 percent of workers are women). The mid-range salons particularly reflected it. They were filled with beauty products for women, such as shampoos, hair clips, ribbons, and specialty objects, such as jewelry and earrings. There were pictures of stylized women hanging on the walls and women's magazines such as *Elle* and *Redbook* on racks near the hair dryers (see figure 20.2). One upscale salon had *Money* magazine as well as magazines on antiques, gardening and decorating. Another upscale salon had prints of famous works of art on the walls and sculpture displayed around the waiting room. In addition, in all the salons I visited, there were complex interactions between the white hairstylists and their diverse clients that differed significantly from those between the barbers and their clients. First of all, there was more flirting and teasing than I witnessed in barbershops. Jerome, a 28-year-old openly homosexual stylist, liked flirting with women:

> I tell women that I love them, and how beautiful they are, and they love it. I wear revealing clothes—tight pants, you know. . . . I get women that pick up on me all of the time, but I never take them up on it.

Gloria married a client:

> Some of the guys who come in to get their hair styles are quite good-looking. In fact, I married one of my customers. He's ten years younger than I am, and he kept coming in to get his hair cut when it didn't even need it. He kept asking me out, and I felt it wouldn't work, but he was cute and I kept playing around and teasing and stuff, so he would wait around after work, saying, "Couldn't you just go to dinner with me? Give me a chance." So I finally did, and it worked, and we've been married for a year now.

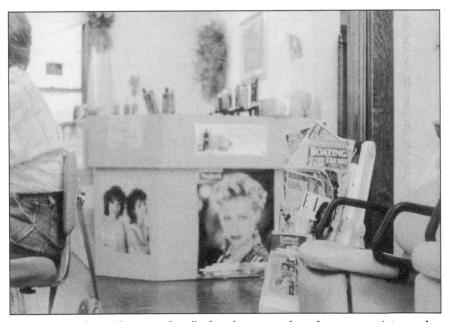

**Figure 20.2.   This mid-range salon displays beauty products for women, pictures of women's hair styles, and magazines appealing to women.**
Photo by Helene M. Lawson

And Steven, a young, white student cosmetologist, was engaged to a client. He said, "I met my girlfriend here. We started kidding around, and now we're serious."

There was also greater intimacy. Men and women hairstylists claimed to act as psychologists, giving advice and listening to personal problems. For example, Ann said she helped women with their "wedding jitters and divorce stresses":

> So Mary comes in and we talk about this guy she's going with. What a mess! He's using her and he knows it but yet she doesn't know it. I try to help her look real good so she has more confidence and maybe she'll drop this guy. Guys talk about their girlfriend troubles, too. They use us as shrinks. You know, people get their hair done before important events, weddings, divorces. They are usually stressed and need a place to talk. We seem to fit the bill.

Roger, a young hairstylist, also listened to women's problems:

> Men stylists talk to women clients about personal things. We do not think of it as gossip. We're more like social workers. The other day this woman starts telling me she is thinking of having an abortion. It's hard to deal with, but you do.

Thirdly, less homophobia and more acceptance of gender difference existed in the salons than in the barbershops I visited. As previously stated, barbers and their male clients made negative comments and jokes about gay men. By contrast, Emma, a 31-year-old customer of hairstylists, was complimentary:

> I go to a (openly) gay stylist. He has a swishy ponytail. Gay men want things nice. They are creative stylists.

There was, however, competition between men and women stylists based on stereotypic gender attitudes. George, an experienced hairstylist, believed men hairstylists had an advantage because women clients were like Cinderella, looking for a prince:

> I think that men have an advantage because women love to be handled by a man. They love it when a man tells them that they look good. They do not want to hear it from a woman. A hairdresser can be their fantasy man. A man has always got that flair.

Larry, a 32-year-old cosmetologist who owned an extremely elite Michigan Avenue salon in Chicago, said men were not only viewed as lovers but as better workers:

I think that when a woman sits in a man's chair she believes anything he says. I feel that a woman in a man's chair feels like he is superior. They feel better with a man, so they feel like men know what they are doing. Look at all the famous stylists. They are mostly men. They do make-up and hair for the stars. They do platform work [work at the trade shows and represent manufacturer's products and do hair styling skills on stage in front of other stylists].

Moreover, Ted, who worked in an upscale salon in Los Angeles, also firmly believed men were superior to women as workers:

Men have a much easier time controlling their women clients because they are men and women think we know more. But we are [also] better technicians than women. In fact, I think that only men should be in this business.

And, Gina, a white 40-year-old, married client who preferred using men stylists, believed that women could not be trusted to do a good job on other women because they competed with women for men:

I think men are better technicians. I think this is because men when doing women's hair go that extra mile because they want women to look good. I think there is a competition factor between women hairdressers and their customers. I do not think with men there is.

In such attitudes we see, as Williams explains, that "qualities associated with men are more highly regarded than those associated with women . . . even in predominantly female jobs. This is partly because men tend to monopolize positions of power in these occupations, and they can make decisions about employees that favor other men. But also, this fact reflects a widespread cultural prejudice that men are simply better than women" (1993:3). Loretta, an experienced stylist, addressed the falseness of this cultural prejudice. She said she had worked with men stylists and found they were no different from women as a category: "It all depends on the individual and their schooling." In fact, no stylists told me they thought the sex of hairstylists was related to his or her ability.

Clients, however, may feel differently, reflecting biases of their own. An Indian colleague of mine told me she thought that women hairstylists in India were much superior overall to any Indian or American hairstylists: "Only women can do the hair of other women, so hairstylists in India are more experienced and very capable. I miss being able to go to them. They do wonderfully intricate hairstyles." Similarly, six white women clients said they preferred going to women stylists because they were more comfortable with them. Helen said, "Women know what other women want; they are on the same wave length," and Joanie said she used women workers "whenever I can. My doctor and dentist are women."

I also spoke with three white men clients who went to white women hairstylists at mid- and upper-range salons for their views on women hairstylists. Ron was a neighbor of a woman who owned a Pennsylvania salon. He went there to have his hair dyed because he "trusted Mary to do a good job." He talked about a trip he was taking to Florida and teased her about making him a "hot number" so he could "get lucky." Mary kidded along and agreed with Ron on how "hot" he looked, providing the flirting behavior I found common in interactions between stylists and clients. Michael, an older client, also had his hair dyed. He complained the whole time about the high school being across from this house and the problems he was having with "kids owning cars and driving over my grass." Mary listened with interest and sympathy, here enacting the role of nurturer also commonly seen in men and women stylists. Later, Michael told me Mary was "the best . . . a good colorist and a concerned friend" who made his thinning hair "look natural."

The third customer was a younger white man with a full head of hair who had it dyed at a salon by Marge. George said Marge was "terrific":

> I am a baby boomer. I do not want my gray hair showing. I want a stylist who is good in color—that is, able to color or highlight my hair—because I want to remain youthful looking in order to compete in the job market. Marge is terrific. She really knows her stuff.

Confidence in women's technical skills in managing hair is not limited by class. Ira, a 52-year-old male CEO living in California, went to a salon in Hollywood. He wore a full-head wig that was worked on by both men and women cosmetologists:

> It costs me about $9,000 a year to maintain my wigs. I go every two weeks for a trim. I turn over one of the hairpieces to a [male] stylist and he cleans and revives it. When I return two weeks later, he fits my wig and a [female] hairstylist cuts my own hair to fit in with the wig.

Ron, Michael and George, who went to women stylists, thought they were technically competent and enjoyed flirting or talking with them. Ira, who used both men and women stylists, felt his concerns with skill could equally be met by men or women technicians. In fact, Ira also added that, at his salon, "I get served wine and usually there are some hors d'oeuvres when I'm waiting to help pass the time. It's a pretty pleasant place."

Some children who were brought to beauty salons made a connection with going to the salon and being "womanly." Jana, who was eight, said:

> I learn girl stuff, you know, how to be pretty. I want a Braun [butane-fired] hot comb for Christmas. I want my hair dyed blonde when mom says I'm old enough.

Some young white boys were also curious about and attracted to beauty salons. Even Dougie, who did not want to touch women, wanted to understand what they used and did. "I like to come here with my mother because I like to look at the things that are in this place, the hair clips and jewelry and fancy ribbons." And Andy, who was seven, had figured out that barbers couldn't do women's hair:

> My mom says barbers cannot fix her hair because they do not have the lotion to curl her hair. I have never seen that lotion in the barbershop. I like coming here to watch what they are doing to my mom's hair.

Yet, Drew, a nine-year-old, went to a stylist to get his hair cut:

> My mom says she has taken me here since I was three years old. I have never been to a barber. I do not want to go to a barber. I like the way Frank cuts my hair. My mom and dad say barbers do not cut hair as good. Frank cuts my dad's and brother's hair too.

Although children such as Andrew, Dougie, Jana and Drew go to barbers or salons with their parents, their curiosity and changing conditions may mean that as they grow older, they will eventually visit "unisex" shops.

## UNISEX CHAINS

All the owners and workers in the beauty salons I visited said their shops were "ambidextrous," i.e., they serviced both men and women. Yet, according to their records, the clientele in beauty salons were mostly women (approximately 80 percent). The eleven unisex chains I visited claimed to have a much larger percentage of men clients (50 to 70 percent) and all had the word unisex displayed. In addition, all eleven chains were owned and managed by men. None of the stores had demographic breakdowns for race, but anecdotal evidence and personal observation made clear that there was a predominance of white stylists and younger clients. I did not see any persons of color in 10 of the unisex shops I visited. One unisex shop in Evanston, a culturally diverse suburb of Chicago, had one African-American woman worker, and I saw three black men clients sitting in the window.

The ambiance and decor in these salons were different from those of barbershops and beauty salons. Three salons had bare walls and sold no products. Eight salons had large photographs of young romantic white couples holding hands or riding bicycles and Caucasian parents with young children. There were no drapes, sculpture, paintings, animal trophies, jewelry, or hair ribbons displayed. Customers waiting for appointments sat in straight-backed chairs near windows where everyone who passed by could see them (see figure 20.3). The atmosphere was therefore not private, warm, cozy or inviting in any of the shops I visited. Yet the unisex trend has taken hold in shopping malls across the country, where its economic driving force is apparent. Sam, the owner of a unisex salon in Chicago, discussed the appeal of his business:

> Unisex chains are transitional places where people go when they are young and looking for a place they can afford. Otherwise, we get people who are unhappy with the services of their current barber or cosmetologist, need a haircut and don't know where else to go. These customers also don't want to spend a lot of money on their hair. I think we have a good market niche.

Workers in these salons, however, were not satisfied with their niche. As previously stated, 80 to 90 percent of unisex cosmetologists are newly certified women. Marie, a 20-year-old white cosmetologist, described the negative aspects of her job:

> I would like to move to a better salon or own my own salon, one day, but it is hard to get a stable of steadies you can bring with you when you work at one

**Figure 20.3.    In this unisex salon, a customer waits in full view of passers-by. The decor is neither masculine nor feminine.**

Photo by Helene M. Lawson

of these chains. I am not encouraged to consult with customers before cutting because it is better to get customers in and out. You make more money that way and you don't have many regulars anyway because we don't take appointments. People take a number and wait till their number comes up. When it does, we work on whoever is next in line. I don't talk much or get to know customers. They are usually in a hurry.

This experience is different from that of salons where workers said intimacy between client and worker is common, or even from barbershops where conversation and gossip are important rituals. Yet all eight male customers interviewed preferred the fast service and economy of the unisex chains to other choices. Dan, a white 50-year-old who retired early on a pension, was anxious to explain why he gave up the masculine culture of barbers, how he tried more expensive upscale hairstylists and why he has ended up using economic unisex women "barbers":

I used to go to Mac, the corner barber. I was about ten and he used to drink; and when I came in I used to check if he was sober. I knew the difference because when he did my sideburns and had too much to drink he would cut me with his straight razor. He kept Bloody Marys in a refrigerator. I kind of admired him. I stopped going to barbers when my wife started cutting my hair, and she was real good at it. Once in a while I tried different barbers. Then my hair got thinner, and I got divorced. A friend of mine said I should go to Old Town [an upscale area] to a stylist. Businessmen went there. They really catered to you. He said they would cut and style my hair to make it look like I had more hair. Well, I went and they put perfume and lotions on me. It was totally a rip-off. I didn't need all that catering and all that money. They didn't make me look any better. I had to make an appointment way in advance. They charged me $40.00 for a stupid haircut, and I had half the hair of other guys. I had to pay $8.00 for parking and give the guy a $5.00 tip. I only went there once. I never went back. That's when I decided to go to Super Cuts. I tried different barbers [female workers] there. I found that some cut my hair nicely and some badly. They were all women. I originally felt funny. When I was younger I always went to male barbers. Why do I call the women "barbers"? I guess because I still feel funny going to a woman.

George, a 32-year-old white graduate student living on a research assistant's limited income, told me about his experiences at a unisex shop in Chicago and that the "cheap" cost was a draw for him:

I don't make appointments, but if you are willing to wait, you can get who you want to cut your hair. They used to charge $2.00 extra for that, but now there are more chairs and they don't. I don't talk to the women much. They use first names and call you when your name comes up. It's like an assembly line. They ask me what I want. Generally, I just have it wet down and cut. It's pretty transient. I have never developed a relationship with the barbers [women who cut hair at Heads Up]. I'm there to get a hair cut really fast and cheap as possible.

Vince, a white 65-year-old living on social security in Los Angeles, reminisced about a hairstylist he went to in the past. He cannot afford hairstylists now, and he does not particularly like unisex shops, but he prefers them to L. A. barbers who he says give even less service:

When I first retired out here, I went to a barbershop. There were three old men, and they charged $9.00 without a shampoo. It was like a bunch of old men sitting around, and they read the papers and talked about sports. They had a TV on all the time and all they used were electric clippers. In the Chicago suburb where I used to live, I went to a hairstylist it was a fancy place. They had little rooms. One was a nail salon. They had a little boutique where they sold jewelry, mousse, shampoo and stuff. They had a wig room. Stylists would use add-ons and try to make people with thin hair look good. Anyway, I don't like the barbers here in L.A. There are hundreds of unisex shops, so they are never really crowded, and I never have to wait. At Cost Cutters the workers look real young to me, and I don't think they are well trained, but they charge $9.95 for a shampoo and haircut, and I can get in and out without much talking. I just don't let them touch the top, and they do okay with the rest.

By contrast, Carol, a white 45-year-old secretary, said she went to a unisex shop once and wouldn't go there again because the workers were not as experienced or qualified as in regular salons. However, her teenage daughter does:

My daughter goes because she can get her hair cut real plain, nothing fancy. She has no problems and just gets a straight cut. She is a teenager on a budget. I am a woman, and I want something a little fancier, and I am willing to spend more time and money.

Most of the clients I observe in these shops were approximately thirteen to twenty years old. They did not speak to each other or the hair stylists in any personal way that I could observe.

## DISCUSSION

I undertook this research in an attempt to understand the importance of hair management, focusing on the choices available to and accepted by people who wanted hair cut or arranged. I also wanted to search for possible change in the occupation. I believe I have uncovered interesting answers to both of these questions as well as additional clues for the future of work in general.

To begin with, both hair workers and their clients are concerned with identity management and hair is one way people display their identifies. Hair is a symbolic indicator of gender, race and class status. Details of its shape, color, and texture and length are seen as clues about age, ethnic background, personality and even values of its wearers (Goffman 1961). In fact, according to Gerson (1985) some of the most extreme displays of womanly and manly natures may occur in settings that are usually reserved for members of a single sex category, such as locker rooms or beauty salons. Evidence of this can be seen in the shape of the lettering on barber shops and salons, the pictures in their windows and especially in the shop environments which contain obvious displays of gender, class and race. It is with these symbols in mind that customers attempt to choose a hair service provider that will preserve their sex, class and race categories. Furthermore, these displays are quite in keeping with the attitude of social life in which people take appearances at face value unless they have special reason to doubt (Bernstein 1986).

But, to display one's identity is not sufficient not make it solid or permanent. It must continually be reinforced, constructed and accomplished. (Connell 1995; West and Fenstermaker 1995; West and Zimmerman 1987). According to Cahill (1989), children especially exemplify this process:

> Sex-class related appearance management socially invests infants with sex class identities. It also promotes young children's identification of both others and themselves. In addition, others' responses to children's experimentation with identity transforming . . . appearance management encourages them to embrace behaviorly their ascribed-class identities. They consequently begin to align their sartorial expression with conventional standards of sex-class related identities to others. They thereby become gendered persons to themselves as well as to others. (1989:298)

In my research for example, children who visit hair establishments claim the identity of "girl" or "boy" and develop behavior committed to reinforcing their sex category. Girls are already aware that being beautiful is good, and women with dyed blond hair are looked upon favorably. Boys know they should have short or "buzz" cuts to be "cool." Thus, children are "leery of other displays that might furnish grounds for questioning their claims" (West and Zimmerman 1987:142). And, to that end they continue to test acceptable gender behavior by showing curiosity about men who sit under a hair dryer or wear earrings and women who style their hair with lotions and chemicals not used by men.

Adults also base their acceptance of providers on class, race and gender displays. And, they continue to use and produce these categories in their chosen hair establishments. I barber shops in rural northwestern Pennsylvania, barbers and adult customers, mostly men, promote separation between the sexes, classes and races through male-oriented business gossip, sexist jokes, homophobic and racist comments and other segregating activities. To a lesser extent, mid-priced salons in the same geographic location also promoted separation of the sexes. They have mostly women workers and sell products for women. In addition, many of their customers still cling to stereotypes that men are better technicians or women don't want other women to look good. Some men customers refuse to use labels such as "hair stylist" and call women hair workers "barber."

Although this study shows how gender is produced in these social situations, it also shows how change can occur. The diminishing numbers of single-sex segregated barber shops, the transformation of beauty parlors into less gendered styling salons and the rise of ungendered unisex shops show change in the most extreme examples of gendered workplaces. The industry is currently encouraging more men to become cosmetologists. Now many men and women customers in salons interact with the worker without concern for gender. Customers of either sex category confide intimate personal stories to whomever does their hair on a regular basis. Although upscale salons in urban areas such as Chicago and Los Angeles continue to segregate by class through higher-status symbols such as artwork, appetizers and wine, and high prices, these symbols are ungendered. Both sexes are represented among workers in these salons. Topics of discussion are more likely to be cultured rather than sexist. Apart from the new arrival of men as customers, perhaps upscale salons were always this way. Lastly, unisex chain shops emphasize an ungendered economy in a deliberately sterilized environment. Because their clientele includes a large percentage of young people who do not energetically engage in producing gender while in the shop, the unisex environment has tempered the extremity of gender display in the field of hair work. Clients do not appear to be suffering on this account. And this may have portents for the future of work.

## NOTES

Reprinted from Helene M. Lawson, *Qualitative Sociology* 22, no. 3 (1999): 235–57. Courtesy of Kluwer Academic/Plenum Publishers.

## REFERENCES

Andrews, William. (1904). *At the Sign of the Barber's Pole.* Yorkshire: H. R. Tutin.
Bernstein, Richard. (1986). *France Jails Two: An Odd Case of Espionage. New York Times.* May 11.

Bureau of Labor Statistics. (1998). *Occupational Outlook Handbook,* Bulletin 2500. U.S. Dept. of Labor.

Bureau of the Census. (1996). *Statistical Abstract of the United States.* U.S. Dept. of Commerce. Oct.

Cahill, Spencer E. (1989). "Fashioning Males and Females: Appearance Management and the Social Reproduction of Gender." Pp. 281–298 in *Symbolic Interaction.* Vol. 12(2).

Connell, R. W. (1995). *Masculinities.* Los Angles: University of California Press.

Dobson, Jessie and R. Milnes Walker. (1979). *Barbers and Barber Surgeons of London.* Oxford: Blackwell Scientific Publications.

Gerson, Judith. (1985). *The Variability and Saliance of Gender: Issues of Conceptualization and Measurement.* Paper presented at the annual meeting of the American Sociological Association, Washington, DC, August.

Goffman, Erving. (1961). *Asylums.* Garden City, N.Y.: Doubleday Anchor Books.

Goffman, Erving. (1959). *The Presentation of Self in Everyday Life.* Garden City, N.Y.: Doubleday and Co. Inc.

Haas, Jack and William Shaffir. (1978). "The Professionalization of Medical Students Developing Competence and a Cloak of Competency." Pp. 71–88 in *Symbolic Interaction.* Vol. 1(1).

Howe, Louise K. (1977). *Pink Collar Workers: Inside the World of Women's Work.* New York: Putnam's Sons

Ilg, Randy. (1998). Telephone Interview. Bureau of Labor Statistics. U.S. Dept. of Labor.

Levine, Molly Myerowitz. (1995). "Gendered Grammar of Ancient Mediterranean Hair." Pp. 76–130 in *Off with Her Head!* edited by Howard Eilberg-Schwarta and Wendy Doniger. Berkeley: University of California Press.

Mercer, Kobena. (1994). *Welcome to the Jungle: New Position in Black Cultural Studies.* New York: Routledge.

Miller, Laura V. (ed). (1995). *Milady's Standard Textbook of Cosmetology* (Revised). New York: Milady Publishing Co.

Mittlehauser, Mark. (1997). "Cosmetology: A Career on the Cutting Edge." Pp. 34–41 in *Occupational Outlook Quarterly.* Vol. 40. No. 4, Winter.

Niemark, Jill. (1994). "The Beefcaking of America." Pp. 33–40 in *Psychology Today.* November/December.

Ogunwale, Titus A. (1972). "Traditional Hairdressing in Nigeria." Pp. 44–45 in *African Arts.* Spring.

Robbins, Clarence R. (1997). "Hairdressing." Pp. 11–13 in *The World Book Encyclopedia.* Vol. 4. Chicago: Scott Fitzer.

Rubinstein, Jonathan. (1973). *City Police.* New York: Farrar, Straus and Giroux.

Synnott, Anthony. (1993). *The Body Social: Symbolism, Self and Society.* London and New York: Routledge.

West, Candace and Sarah Fenstermaker. (1995). Doing Difference. Pp. 8–37 in *Gender and Society.* Vol. 9, No. 1, February.

West, Candace and Don H. Zimmerman. (1987). Doing Gender. Pp. 126–151 in *Gender and Society.* Vol. 1. No. 2. June

White, Shane and Graham White. (1995). "Slave Hair and African American Culture in the Eighteenth and Nineteenth Centuries." Pp. 45–76, in the *Journal of Southern History.* Vol. LXI. No. 1. February.

Williams, Christine L. (ed) (1993). *Doing "Women's Work."* California: Sage Publishing Co.

Yarwood, Doreen. (1978). "Hairstyles." Pp. 215–222 in *The Encyclopedia of World Costume.* New York: Bonanza Books.

# 21

# Women, Resistance, and Care: An Ethnographic Study of Nursing Auxiliary Work

*Geraldine Lee-Treweek*

Research on traditional male industries has highlighted conflict, union activity and sabotage, whereas women have often been portrayed as a relatively compliant workforce. In addition, research on paid care has made assumptions about the nature of the work and the workers' motivations for undertaking it. Paid care workers are often presented as driven by altruistic motives. However, there is evidence to suggest that this work, especially in the current economic climate, may, for some women, be undertaken for instrumental reasons, and be perceived by those who do it as hard labour for a wage, rather than as a vocational choice (Bates 1991; Lee-Treweek 1994, 1995). It is only when paid care workers are perceived firstly as workers, and secondly as "carers," that the potential for resistance can be revealed.

This chapter uses empirical material from a study of work in a nursing home for older people to present an interpretation of the ways in which female nursing auxiliary workers used resistance as an everyday strategy to get through, and exercise some control over, their work. As has been shown for other working class occupational subcultures (Beynon 1973; Willis 1979; Pollert 1981) the resistance displayed by nursing auxiliaries was based around defying the official status and formal definitions of their work. This chapter argues that, for female care workers, forms of resistance are as essential to getting through the work as they are to car assembly workers. Most contemporary discussions of care labor fail to address these issues (for instance, see Willcocks et al. 1987; Hockey 1990). This paper will argue that there are strong reasons why they should.

## PAID CARE WORK AND RESISTANCE

Sociology has had an interest in caring, both in informal and formal settings, for a number of years (Finch and Groves 1983; Graham 1991; Bates 1991). However, paid care work has rarely been presented as a work-oriented issue. Despite Oakley's (1974) exposition of housework as similar to factory labor, informal care and work in the private sphere has never really made the grade as a worthy topic for the sociology of work. Paid care shares a marginalized status with informal care in terms of its perception as a work activity.

The sociological study of paid care, by failing to address the problematic nature of paid caring as work, tacitly accepts assumptions about its status. For example, it assumes that women are equipped to deal with bodily substances, that they are sympathetic, can provide for others emotionally, and that they enjoy this work as an extension of their "natural" role and engage in it by choice. Paid care work has been perceived as those activities involved with the response to, and compliance with, the needs of others; an extension of women's domestic roles. This has resulted in research which ignores that paid care is a work activity and as such may be shaped by factors similar to those affecting other low-status occupations. There are some exceptions to this neglect (Lawler 1991; Mackay 1989; Bates 1991; Lee-Treweek 1995). For example, Bates's (1991) study indicated that young women on the Youth Training Scheme involved in care of the elderly found the work physically and emotionally taxing. Her research illustrates that these workers are not naturally endowed with the necessary skills and that the realities of undertaking paid care often come as a shock.

Over the last few decades paid care has undergone a number of changes which mean that it is increasingly important to understand it as work. During the early 1980s the availability of such work expanded rapidly and the sector was also affected by market forces in a similar way to other industries. Paid care has become big business in the private sector, providing residential and home-based services. The care of older people in registered residential homes can be used to illustrate this. Laing and Buisson's (1991) market survey of all registered homes shows that in 1980 there were 3,165 local authority, 2,400 private, and 1,346 voluntary sector registered residential homes. By 1990, there were six fewer local authority homes, while there were 100 more in the voluntary sector. The private sector, on the other hand, had added more than 7,000, an increase of 390 per cent, taking their share of provision from 35 per cent to 67 per cent. Overall public sector provision of institutional care has been declining slightly since the mid-1970s, whereas private provision of all forms of care (institution, domiciliary, etc.) increased dramatically in the 1980s and still continues to do so, if at a more modest rate (Laing and Buisson 1991).

The numbers of women working in care settings has increased with the expansion of the private care sector. The vast majority of paid carers employed in this sector are female and untrained (Clough 1986). In some homes, especially those providing residential rather than nursing care, there may not be any professionally trained staff. In private nursing settings a focus upon creating an "efficient" skills mix often involves an extensive use of lower grade, less-qualified staff. This can mean each dayshift having for example, only two trained nursing staff and six untrained nursing auxiliaries to care for 30 patients, and at night this may be reduced to one trained nurse and two untrained auxiliary staff. In the last decade, growth has also taken place in the number of private care agencies whose business lies in providing home helps, trained nurses, domiciliary workers and trained/untrained "hands on" care staff to individuals in people's own homes (Laing and Buisson 1994a).

This chapter focuses on the work of nursing auxiliaries who form a central part of the workforce of paid carers, in both the public and the private sector. The work is "hands on" care labour; heavy, dirty and low paid. It has similarities to many male working class jobs. It is labour framed by difficult conditions that are created by others: management; nursing home owners; and trained nurses. The move towards more private homes over the last ten years has brutalised the work setting of nursing auxiliaries. Wages in the private sector, where most auxiliaries work, are very low. Rates can be as low as £1 an hour in unregistered non-officially recognised homes, whereas in well-established registered settings an auxiliary may earn £3–4 an hour. Auxiliaries in local authority care homes or public hospitals are paid slightly more at around £5 an hour. The work is often physically heavy (involving lifting weights which would be unacceptable in male-dominated industries), physically dirty (involving tasks such as washing soiled bodies) and highly repetitive. The low levels of pay and the poor working conditions might suggest that these workers would be better off taking up shop work, which has commensurate pay levels and does not usually entail such strenuous labour. However, it is clear that employment in this sector has advantages for some women. Clough (1986) notes that such employment often has flexible hours, is part-time and provides the opportunity to work close to home.

Like their male counterparts, women construct subcultures which defy the official remit of their workplaces, to make work bearable. The lack of references to resistance in the paid care literature might be taken to suggest that paid carers in the private sector are rarely involved in institutionalized formal types of resistance. Our knowledge of resistance strategies is limited due to a lack of detailed ethnographic accounts of paid care labor. Gottfried (1994) argues that women workers often resist on an everyday level and clearly this will be less readily perceptible than resistance of a more formal nature. There is a need to redress the lack of critical ethnographic research on paid caring as a work activity and indeed in the context of women's work more generally.

Resistance in male industries has traditionally involved reconstructing meanings through work subcultures and resisting the work through the material of the job. Resistance in care seems on the outside to be plausible. The materials of care are the recipients of care—the patients. The shopfloor is the context of that care—the wards, the bedrooms and other spaces labored in by paid care workers. Yet, I will argue, the work context of the female paid carer is nonetheless an arena for worker resistance as much as the care plant or packaging factory.

The empirical material used in this chapter illustrates that the subcultures developed within the "caring" work place can have strong similarities to those identified in research on male subcultures (Willis 1979; Beynon 1973; Nichols and Beynon 1977; Cockburn 1983; Burawoy 1979) and in women's non-care labor (Pollert 1981; Cavendish 1982; Westwood 1984). By recognizing women's paid care work as being affected by similar factors to other forms of labor, and by considering the production of the body along the same lines as the production of objects, a new perspective on women's care work becomes visible. This demands a reconsideration of our perceptions and constructions of the nature of "women's work." Many low-level care occupations are peopled predominantly by working class women who have no formal training. As their numbers increase and the job market for paid carers expands, the exhibition of formal and informal resistance to work is more likely to occur as groups seek a clear role in this changing setting.

## THE SETTINGS AND THE STUDY

This chapter focuses on the work of nursing auxiliaries in a private nursing home. There are around 5,000 registered nursing homes for older people around Britain, the majority of them privately owned (Laing and Buisson 1994b). Nursing homes, unlike residential homes, have to employ trained nursing staff to provide nursing attention. However, trained staff make up a minority of those who work in homes, and much of the work is done by nursing auxiliaries or assistants with little or no training (Clough 1986). Many of these workers are now undertaking levels one and two of the National Vocational Qualifications in Care "on the job." These staff carry out much of the contact care with patients, theoretically under the supervision of trained staff.

This chapter draws on ethnographic research undertaken at a nursing home which I will call Bracken Court, a privately run 32 bed establishment sited in the south west of England. The patients at Bracken Court needed a high level of help with basic activities such as washing and using the toilet. Many were unable to communicate verbally. The nursing auxiliaries' job was to provide "hands on" care.[1]

## CONDITIONS FOR RESISTANCE: HIERARCHY AND CONTROL

The home was organised hierarchically. Nursing staff, ranked in order of formal qualification and status, were: one Matron (a Registered General Nurse), three other Registered General Nurses, four Enrolled Nurses (with some agency Enrolled staff often being used) and 20 nursing auxiliaries (10 part-time and 10 full-time). The trained nursing staff were most visible in the "clean" public areas, working in the office, organising coffee and talking with patients and visitors. These presentational tasks were legitimate and important aspects of their work. The trained nurses judged how well the nursing auxiliaries were doing their work by the physical state of the patients but were not generally involved in "hands on" care. There were also staff who were considered as domestics—three cooks, two cleaners, and two laundry women. Nursing staff had little verbal contact with the non-nursing groups who worked relatively autonomously. They had their own territories, including the kitchen, the laundry room and the domestic stores, and they were largely free agents organising their own time.

In contrast, the nursing auxiliaries worked in the "backstage" areas of the homes, generally in the patients' bedrooms, undertaking physical care under strict temporal constraints. The auxiliaries' role was the care of the body, the control of dirty substances and the general organisation and ordering of patients. Pride was grounded in doing these activities successfully, especially since the work often had to be undertaken without the proper equipment because of management economy measures. The auxiliaries' work load was often defined by factors outside their control. Major disruptions, such as sickness, incontinence or death, could change the order of events.

These traditionally "private" spaces in theory belonged to the patients, and, according to Bracken Court's brochure, privacy and individuality were respected. But for the auxiliary, this area was a work space. In these places the everyday physical construction of patients, the containment of disruption, and the ordering of distress or aggression was carried out. Despite the auxiliaries having a small staff room, its use during work hours was banned in order to discourage avoidance of work. Thus, with little temporal or physical space of their own, and a low status dirty job, the nursing auxiliaries were the lowest status workers in the hierarchy.

## Paid to Care

Nursing auxiliaries were recruited from the local neighborhood, commonly through adverts in shops, local papers and by word of mouth. At the time of the study all the auxiliaries employed in the home were white working class females whose ages ranged from 20 to 50. Although one worker had two "A" levels, the majority had few formal qualifications. In 1993, day auxiliaries were paid £2.75 an hour and night auxiliaries £3.25 which they considered to be comparable to the rates offered by other private homes in the local area. The job description was presented as "caring for the needs of elderly patients."

Although initially auxiliaries made references to being a "caring person" to describe their reasons for taking up the work, a few weeks into the research (once a stronger rapport had been formed with them) they began to produce different accounts which emphasized a more instrumental view of the work. For example, care work was often described as being taken up when money was needed, rather than being a planned choice.

> Delia: We needed extra money and one of the mums down the school gate said there was night work going here. I came up and Matron said I could start the next day.

Care work was also perceived as easily obtainable with a very informal interview process.

> Sally: My mother worked at Summerville [dementia unit] and when I was 18 I got a job there too 'cos Matron knew me.
> Julia: Worked in a bank when I left school, stopped when I had the kids. My mum had done care [residential home work] and evening shifts fitted in with them [her family].

Many workers had links with care labor through female relatives who already undertook paid care work. There was an informal process which often led to daughters, sisters or nieces being asked to help out part-time and ending up full-time. Therefore many of the auxiliaries came into paid care work almost by chance, rather than as a planned move.

All the nursing auxiliaries expressed their main motivation as earning a wage. However, conveying this view to those outside the job was noted as extremely problematic.

> Siobhan: When I first started I would tell people straight, I was doing it for the money, but that doesn't go down well so it's better to say that you love the old dears.

The instrumental career was a role that the women found impossible to explain to the outside world. However, within the nursing home it was acceptable to express these views with colleagues who also experienced the same difficulties. As one auxiliary working a night shift explained to me,

> Debbie: I hate this place, I hate this job, I wish I'd married someone rich . . .
> I'm not here for the job satisfaction, God knows what I'm here for.

Another worker, a 45-year-old auxiliary with five years' experience in the home, explained her view of the job,

> Sandy: It's no work for these young girls. They should be working in shops, in Debenhams on the perfume counters or something. They shouldn't be doing all this, none of us should really.

It was no job for the younger women, but on reflection it was no job for anyone.

Such feelings were compounded by the social denigration of care work as easy and "natural" labour for women and these views were often held by members of the auxiliaries' own families.

> June: I think my husband thinks we sit here and talk to them [patients]. He doesn't realise its all dirt. There's nothing as germy as old people.

The auxiliaries recognised that their paid *care work* had little to do with *caring* although in the social imagination the two terms are often considered inseparable. They had been socialised for the work, yet its components did not match the unrealistic social conceptions of care as a nurturing vocation. For most workers the reasons for taking up care were instrumental and involved practical concerns: close proximity to home, work which fitted around child-care arrangements and the ease of gaining car work in relation to other jobs. The motivation of the workers and the nature of the job made informal resistant behaviour likely.

## The Process of Care

Resistance to work was also affected by the way the process of caring was organised in a cyclical manner. Although the home's brochure advertised "family-type" care, the pressure to create the clean and orderly individual was far stronger. The main work of the nursing auxiliary was to create a sanitised "lounge standard" patient, fit to be placed in the front stage of the home, from the "bedroom state" of being dirty physically and often mentally disordered. Through the auxiliaries' routines, the normal order of the home was created, predominantly within the bedroom areas, out of sight of both trained staff and visitors. It involved not only the cleaning and dressing of the patients but also the creation of some semblance of gendered normality, through dressing, applying make-up, combing hair, and putting in dentures. The auxiliary's role appeared to revolve around policing the boundaries of the good "lounge standard" patient and to moderate, as far as possible, socially unacceptable behaviours.

The constraints of the job meant that the auxiliaries' work was about process and order, much the same as factory labour. For example, this auxiliary described morning work in the following way:

> Sue: We get them (patients) up, we sit them up, we feed them, wash them, dress and put their teeth in and wheel them down to the lounge.

Once in the lounge patients had to be removed again[2] at regular intervals to be reordered or taken to the toilet. Then they went to lunch, to the toilet, back to bed for two hours, up again for late tea, to the toilet, into dinner, to the toilet, to the lounge, to the toilet and finally to bed. During the night, auxiliaries undertook two-hourly rounds in which each patient was checked and their body ordered as necessary. This type of strict routinized order meant that auxiliaries' work made sure that the patients circuited the home in the correct physical state.

The product of the work was a clean, orderly, quiet resident. The auxiliaries did not express their labour as "people" work but as labour which could be done without too much thought or personal input. Rather than being about patients' needs, it was about the patient as an end product at the conclusion of a long line of caring activities. The good home should "run like clockwork" (Carolynne).

## RESISTING THE WORK: THE RECONSTRUCTION OF ROLE

In theory the trained staff were supposed to organize and supervise the nursing auxiliaries' work but actually spent much of their time in the lounge with patients or visitors, or in the matron's office doing administration. Although the auxiliaries were left to get on with the physical labor, they revered the skills of the trained nurses, often complimenting them on nicely dressed sores or supporting them when a patient was rude. The hierarchy was also important to them.

> Vera: You've got to have respect in a nursing home, there's got to be discipline.
> June: I'm all for Matron, she's very good and keeps everyone in line.

But an ambiguous relationship to authority existed: an acceptance of one's place and yet at other times a resistance to the hierarchy.

Rather than perceiving themselves as the victims of the strict routine, the auxiliaries presented a view of themselves as the prime movers in its construction and maintenance. In comparison, the trained nurses' role was reconstructed as only peripheral in the home organization.

> Maddie: We are the nuts and bolts here.
> Carole: We're the cogs, we keep it all going.
> June: We know these people, we get them up, we dress them, we know what they're about.

But "knowing these people" was not about knowing patients as individuals.

> Debbie: We hardly get to know them personally, we're too busy. . . . I can't say I know any of them that well, only on a superficial level.

This attitude has a parallel in the male working class industrial environment where workers value their mastery of the materials of the job. In this setting, knowing how to use one's materials and having familiarity with them gives the worker a feeling of personal control (Willis 1979: 191). Likewise, the nursing auxiliaries were familiar with the type of work needed to construct patients and how to handle their materials. This knowledge was a source of both pride and resistance to the sheer drudgery and lack of control over the nature of the work.

Furthermore, the auxiliaries' reconstruction of their role involved devaluing that of the trained nurses. They emphasised that their experience of the work was more firmly grounded within the labour process and that their knowledge was more essential than that of the trained nurses. This was particularly true in the case of the trained staff's notions of psychological care, which were regarded as "nonsense" (Sue), but also in their understandings of the health states of patients. Despite the face that the trained nurses had hospital experience, the auxiliaries viewed the trained nurses' role and knowledge as inferior.

> Rita: You can't tell me you can learn this from books, I don't believe it. You see trained nurses in here [who] don't have the sense they were born with.

Or as one young auxiliary who was interested in training to be a nurse commented:

> Zara: I'd like to train as a nurse but it's all college stuff on the diploma. You can't learn this stuff in a university. If I started the course I'd probably know most of it from this.

The trained nurses were not considered as professional carers with "hands on" experience but as managers whose administrative role divided them from the "real work."

To Bracken Court's auxiliaries, care work was an ongoing production process rather than a set of person-centered acts. Therefore, although the trained nurses were qualified and had a higher official status, it was the auxiliaries who could handle patients, who knew the essential tricks of the trade and the way patients behaved. In relation to this view of work, the labour of the trained nurses was denigrated to being non-essential or, at worst, incorrect. It was defined as clean work which was neither real nor necessary. The auxiliaries' concept of real nursing work was obtained from their past experience of trained nursing staff who had encouraged a strict physical order and discipline.

> Zara: The first Matron I knew, we had to have them [patients] all up and beds pristine before nine, no bedsores, everything orderly; that's real nursing.
> Vera: Matron Sharpe was wonderful. Any trouble, sleeves up, she was in there.

An idealised form of nursing underpinned the auxiliaries' belief in their own importance within the home, an ideal which can be said to have much in common with a Nightingale-type older form of nursing. It involved processing and sanitizing the environment and was object-centered rather than patient-centered. Real nursing was hands on, physical, dirty and strictly routinized work. In this labour the routine took precedence over need, either that of patient or worker.

## RESISTANCE TO AND THROUGH THE MATERIALS OF THE JOB

Like their counterparts in other forms of labor, the auxiliaries based their resistance upon the materials they worked with and could therefore control. This material was the patients' bodies, and the processes involved in working on them. The nursing auxiliaries were not unionized and thus had no formal means of representation. The "hands on" resistance to the job reflected their lack of legitimate ways to display discontent and the hidden nature of the tasks involved.

Resistance by non-compliance or selective compliance to patient needs was observed on a daily basis and had become part of the routines of auxiliary labor, a ritualized response to the sheer amount of work. Non-compliance to patients' needs was in direct defiance to lay notions of caring work as nurturing and to the auxiliaries' job descriptions. They had also reconstructed states such as "needy" and "sick" into states of pretence and willful childishness. In this way they normalized patient behaviors and took control though their own ways of interpreting them.

Non-compliance to patient's emotional needs was often justified by the pressure to produce lounge standard individuals as expected by the home and its visitors.

> Carolynne: It's all very well for them [the trained staff] to say we need to be quicker working in the bedrooms but they're not in there watching us slave.
>
> Maddie: If they're [patients] not done properly and down by 10am Mrs Moreham [home owner] does her nut, and she's at it, "Mrs Brownley's [patient] hair hasn't been brushed."

Much of the work involved creating the product for the visual consumption of others. Non-compliance was part of the general resistance to the nature of the job but at the same time it was essential in getting through the work. It created the kind of ordered patient that the home demanded and appeared to induce a similar state to that described by Goffman (1961: 61) in his conceptualization of situational withdrawal. Thus, in Bracken Court total silence was more favorably looked upon than screaming or crying. The successful completion of work for the nursing auxiliaries involved the creation of such individuals.

Another strategy utilized by the auxiliaries to order patients and contain disorder was routine depersonalization of patients enabling them to be considered as objects of work rather than individuals needing care. Detached from emotions and personhood, patients could be swiftly processed through acts of care. Depersonalisation was perceptible in practices such as ignoring the presence of patients even when talking about them. For example, it was common to hear night staff discussing the ill health of patients whilst they were changing them. Derogatory terms which referred to death, such as "popped her clogs" or "snuffed her candle" and terms which related to confused behaviour, such as "lost it" or "off her trolley," were in daily usage.

Communicating with patients was seen as pointless, so when early in my observations I asked one auxiliary what George, a stroke victim, had said, she replied,

> Judith: God I don't know, who would, 'less you speak Russian.
>
> GLT: But you can understand some of it?
>
> Judith: Yes, but you'd be here all day trying to get it out of him.

Providing care for people takes time but the ordering of objects can be undertaken more rapidly. Depersonalisation allowed the work to be done more quickly and made the work less upsetting. As one auxiliary explained, whilst we were in the same room as George,

> Maddie: Poor George, he doesn't know what's going on, damn shame isn't it looking at this lot. I'd like to have seen them ten years ago when they were really people, independent and looking after themselves.

If patients were no longer people but were chores or acts and were not truly conscious of the situations around them, then the work was less psychologically difficult for the workers. Forcing breakfast into someone's mouth every morning, and dressing and washing them in silence, was a resistance to working with difficult things/objects, not a response to working with people and their needs. Care work consisted, in effect, of acts performed on objects in the swiftest ways possible.

Another strategy of resistance utilised by the auxiliaries was the spatial management of truth and lies which involved a distinction between the public and private areas of the home. This was especially clear in the lounge and the bedroom. In the lounge patients would regularly ask to be taken home in front of relatives and other visitors. Here it was imperative that disorder did not breach the image of care and the auxiliaries' strategy was to lie and use mistruths to manage disorder. Patients would be told they were going home "tomorrow," "next week" or "later on." Although the trained nursing staff often answered patient questions with mistruths, they did not utilise truth and lies in order to obtain "good" behaviour. This task appeared to have been delegated to the auxiliary staff.

In the privacy of bedroom and other back stage areas, a quite different strategy was used by the nursing auxiliaries. The truth was used in a cold and detached way which often visibly distressed patients. For example, on one occasion Dilys, who suffered from dementia, had buzzed for the night staff. June, a night auxiliary, arrived and asked her what she wanted.

> Dilys: I want to go home now.
> June: Well you can't, you live here, don't you remember that?
> Dilys: But why can't I leave?
> June: You can't walk or look after yourself, you know that, now go back to sleep.

Walking down the corridors back to the lounge, June expressed the opinion that "that kind of thing" was mere, "attention seeking," not genuine distress.

It was also the auxiliaries' belief that truth-telling (in the appropriate spaces) induced acceptance, which was good for patients. However, use of the hard truth also appeared to induce passivity and withdrawal. This strategy was justified by workers through the notion that patients needed to face facts, as one auxiliary noted,

> Sally: It sounds bad to people who don't know, but you've got to tell them the truth, you can't lie to them.

Despite this comment, lies and truth-telling occurred in direct relation to the spatial organization of the home in an expedient manner, to create and maintain order. The emotional and psychological ordering of individuals in the bedroom spaces produced the form of individual expected, and facilitated the swift processing of patients around the circuit of the home.

The processing of patients from disorder to order was not monitored by others. To cope with the work, the auxiliaries either reconstructed it as a form of kindness or argued that hardness and non-compliance to emotional needs were positive attributed in an auxiliary.

## KEY COMPONENTS OF A NURSING AUXILIARY SUBCULTURE

The auxiliaries viewed their firm behavior with patients as a normal and laudable part of their work. The fact that patients were in the home appeared to indicate to them that they needed such treatment. As Delia put it they were at the "end of the line," relatives and other institutions such as residential homes, hospitals and other forms of care had proved unequal to the task. In this way the auxiliaries spoke of doing what ordinary folk could not deal with and clearly saw themselves as being harder and more able to cope than others.

The auxiliaries viewed themselves as most able to cope with the idiosyncrasies of patients. For example, the auxiliaries appeared to believe that the trained nurses were less used to abuse and should be shielded from it.

> June: Violet told Matron to bugger off and she [Matron] just laughed it off. When she left I said to Vi, "How dare you speak to matron like that, she's not used to that language."

June's account suggests that although Matron should be protected from abusive language, as an auxiliary, she should not.

Another illustration of the auxiliaries' view that it was their job to cope was observable when patients were violent. Violence from patients was experienced on a daily basis and usually occurred when personal care tasks were being carried out. In situations where a trained staff member was present and a patient exhibited violent behaviour, it was the auxiliary who would position herself to take the brunt of it and re-order the situation. Such events were seen as funny, the basis for staff room stories and myth-making. For example, at the end of shifts the auxiliaries often joked about the work.

> Lucy: She [a patient] hit me on the head one morning about five times . . . this morning she punched me in the chest when I was lifting her.

Ann (butts in): Well yesterday I lifted her up and she punched me in the back.

Others gave similar stories which were accompanied by laughter. Such incidents were commonly referred to as "fun."

Night staff prided themselves on being the "hardest" shift; working the longest hours (11), at a time when the patients were in a tired and difficult state. Many had also worked in their own homes all day prior to coming into work. Night staff saw the deprivations of sleep and social life as indicative of having superior strength to the other auxiliaries.

> June: Remember we had that Zara girl, thought she'd get all her hours done on three nights so she could be with her boyfriend, she couldn't hack it, had to give up (said jubilantly).

When all available coping strategies failed many auxiliaries found it necessary to leave. During the block observation period at Bracken Court twelve of the auxiliary staff expressed a wish to leave. Six months after the block observation five auxiliary nursing staff had moved on but a core of older women were left. Interestingly, these were the workers who had the least regard for patients' needs.

The auxiliaries had contact with the other untrained staff who worked as ancillaries within Bracken Court: cooks, cleaners, and laundry women. There was also contact with care assistants working in a neighbouring home (which was owned by the same proprietors) and they were also subordinated within the auxiliary's construction of others. Care assistants were perceived as failed auxiliaries who were in June's words "Soft cows," women who were too soft with those they cared for and not tough enough to cope with auxiliary labour.

> Vera: Don't get me wrong, they're lovely girls, but they don't work as hard as we do.

The auxiliaries considered that it was they who had to cope with the disorder created by care assistants when patients arrived from residential care and were demanding and emotional.

> Judy: Over there [residential home] they're always hugging them [residents] and letting them play up and then they come over here and we have to cope with it all.

It was only the tough style adopted by the auxiliaries that could re-order these individuals.

The cooks and to some extent the cleaners were defined as "clean" workers whose role and chores stemmed from a domestic form of labor. In line with the trained nursing staff at Bracken Court, the auxiliaries constructed the domestic staff and care assistants as a lower rank. Auxiliary staff tended to ignore these groups and maintained a distinction between their own chores and those of the other workers. Interaction was undertaken with the minimum of communication.

## DISCUSSION

This chapter has focused upon the work of women auxiliary workers undertaking paid care in a nursing home for older people. It has presented an interpretation of the main features of the work subculture to identify rituals of resistance. I have indicated that these strategies were central to the process of getting the job done for these workers and that their resistance was aimed primarily at the nature of the work and the drudgery which it entailed. Unlike some industrial workers, these paid care workers did not have formal routes to representation through a union, and the nature of the work ruled out direct sabotage. Their resistance involved a redefinition of the auxiliaries' role and resistance to the materials they worked with—the patients.

Like many other forms of production, this work is disjointed, alienating, personally unrewarding and repetitive and in the process of the work corners could be cut. The auxiliaries perceived the job as a form of process which involved ordering bodies to time and chores constraints, rather than as people work. Pride was obtained by going the distance, getting through the work and laughing about it with your mates. The resistance of the auxiliaries was highly effective as being non-compliant to the patients created the quiet individuals that the trained staff and visitors to the home expected.

One of the key issues raised by this chapter is how women's practices of resistance at work can be understood in relation to those of male occupational subcultures. There is a lack of material which covers thoroughly women's resistance in work settings. Even writers who have produced research on particular female work settings, such as Westwood (1984) and Pollert (1981), have not highlighted practices of resistance to the same extent as contemporary pieces of work about male labour. In the case of paid care labour resistance is rarely mentioned.

There remains an underlying social expectation that women undertake paid care because they enjoy it and that it involves altruism and nurturance rather than choice and skill. To suggest instrumental motivation on the part of some paid carers could be interpreted as throwing stones at angels, but for many paid carers there is a gap between the image of the work and their experiences. This is reflected in the auxiliaries' difficulties in explaining to others why they did the work and what it meant to them. In addition, there is increasing business orientation within the care market, which appears to make paid care more like other forms of labour. All these factors are sources of tension for paid carers.

Research on male forms of resistance has emphasised that working class masculinity is embodied and enacted in work subcultures. But toughness is not a male prerogative in working class culture and acceptance of hardship can also be seen in research on working class women's ideas about health. Blaxter and Paterson (1982: 33–4) found that coping with hardship and getting on with life regardless was perceived by women as a matter of one's moral fibre. Great importance was placed upon not giving in and appearing weak to those around. Cornwell's (1983) work on working class women's attitudes to health also illustrated virtue in struggle, particularly in resisting one's own physical health needs.

Coping and forms of "toughness" may also be seen in other all-female work cultures relating to health care. For example, in the case of nursing, Mackay (1987) and Ashley (1982) have noted that trained nurses value tough behaviour and undervalue the importance of support and care for those in the profession. The auxiliaries at Bracken Court illustrate the way a female work subculture can elevate personal hardship and coping to a level which is self-defeating. For example, the auxiliaries' construction of patient violence as a joke avoided its recognition as an important issue and one which was not acknowledged or addressed by management. Personal toughness had been elevated to a position of importance and this was most visible in the mythology around staff room stories. In these, auxiliaries performed great lifting feats, often alone, dealt with physical assaults by patients and spoke of unending physical care tasks. It may be the case that toughness at work, rather than being the preserve of males, is fundamental to working class occupational subcultures, both male and female.

I am not arguing that all paid carers do not enjoy their work. One has to acknowledge that for many women paid care offers opportunities for independence and camaraderie they cannot get elsewhere. In the future paid care will need to expand further to cater to the needs of an aging population and as this sector develops the potential for resistance within care will grow. More research needs to be undertaken on the work subcultures of different forms of paid carers; the meaning the work has for them, and the ways in which they interpret the tasks they are expected to undertake. The sociology of work should embrace paid care labor as an increasingly important source of work for women in Britain, at the same time as it has to resist the assumptions that have marginalized it along with informal care labor.

## ACKNOWLEDGMENTS

I would like to thank Ian McIntosh, David Stopforth, Angus Erskine, Sue Scott, and Huw Beynon for their help and encouragement with this chapter.

## NOTES

Reprinted by permission of Sage Publications Ltd., from Geraldine Lee-Treweek "Women, Resistance and Care: An Ethnographic Study of Nursing Auxiliary Work," in *Work, Employment and Society* 11, no. 1 (1997): 47–63. Copyright © BSA Publications Ltd. (1997).

1. The study focused upon auxiliary work and utilized participant observation (179 hours of intensive data collection) and in-depth interviews. Less intensive data collection and a close relationship with the home was maintained for over two years. For further details of the home and the methods used in this research, see Lee-Treweek 1994.

2. I use "removed" to emphasize that there is movement involved, for all but two patients, use of a wheelchair, i.e., they were wheeled around by the auxiliaries rather than under their own steam.

## REFERENCES

Ashley, J.A. (1980) 'Power in Structured Misogyny: Implications for the Politics of Care,' *Advances in Nursing*, Vol. 2, Part 3, 3–22.

Bates, I. (1991) 'A job which is right for me' in I. Bates and G. Riseborough *Youth and Inequality*. Milton Keynes: Open University.

Beynon, H. (1973) *Working for Ford*. Wakefield: E.P. Publishing

Blaxter, M. and Paterson, E. (1982) *Mothers and Daughters: A Three Generational Study of Health Attitudes and Behavior*. London: Heinemann.

Burawoy, M. (1979) *Manufacturing Consent*. Chicago: University of Chicago Press.

Cavendish, R. (1982) *Women On the Line*. London: Routledge and Kegan Paul.

Clough, R. (1986) 'Staffing of Residential Homes' in K. Judge and I. Sinclair (eds.) *Residential Care For Elderly People*. London: HMSO.

Cockburn, C. (1983) *Brothers: Male Dominance and Technological Change*. London: Pluto Press.

Cornwell, J. (1983) *Hard Earned Lives*. London: Tavistock.

Finch, J. and Groves, D. (1983) *A Labor of Love, Women, Work and Caring*. London: Routledge and Kegan Paul.

Goffman, E. (1961) *Asylums*. London: Penguin.

Gottfried, H. (1994) 'Learning the Score: the Duality of Control and Everyday Resistance in the Temporary-Help Service industry' in J.M. Jermier, D. Knights and W.R. Nord, *Resistance and Power in Organizations*.

Graham, H. (1991) 'The Concept of Caring in Feminist Research: The Case of Domestic Service.' *Sociology* 25: 61–75.

Hockey, J. (1990) *Experiences of Death*. Edinburgh: University of Edinburgh Press.

Laing and Buisson (1991) *Review of Private Health Care 1990–91*. London: Laing and Buisson.

Laing and Buisson (1994a) *Review of Private Health Care 1993–1994*. London: Laing and Buisson.

Laing and Buisson (1994b) *Care of Elderly People, Market Survey 1994*. London: Laing and Buisson.

Lawler, J. (1991) *Behind the Screens, Nursing, Somology and the Problem of the Body*. U.K.: Churchill Livingstone.

Lee-Treweek, G. (1994) *Discourse, Care and Control: An Ethnography of Nursing and Residential Elder Care Work*. Unpublished PhD thesis: University of Plymouth.

Lee-Treweek, G. (1995) *Understanding Paid Care: Towards a New Critique*. University of Manchester Occasional Papers.

Mackay, L. (1989) *Nursing a Problem*. Milton Keynes: Open University.

Nichols, T. and Beynon, H. (1977) *Living with Capitalism: Class Relations and the Modern Factory*. London: Routledge and Kegan Paul.

Oakley, A. (1974) *The Sociology of Housework*. London: Robertson.

Pollert, A. (1981) *Girls, Wives, Factory Lives*. London: Macmillan.

Westwood, S. (1984) *All Day Every Day*. London: Pluto.

Willcocks, D. Peace, S. and Kellaher, L. (1987) *Private Lives in Public Places*. London: Tavistock.

Willis, P. (1979) 'Shop Floor Culture, Masculinity and the Wage Form' in J. Clarke et al., *Working Class Culture*. London: Hutchinson.

# V

# DEVIANCE IN WORK

*Deviance in Work: Tramps Waiting for Work*

Many years ago, I wrote my doctoral dissertation on the culture of railroad tramps. I studied tramp culture by participating in it, riding freights, camping out in hobo jungles, and picking fruit with tramps who became agricultural migrants.

I learned that although tramps may seem like a deviant culture, they are, in fact, an important part of the mainstream economy. As agricultural workers, they ride to the harvest towns on the freights to wait for the harvest, and they work in the orchards until the harvest is complete. When they are no longer needed they leave, generally on freights, and usually without the money they had earned in the orchards.

This photograph was taken in an apple harvest town in northern Washington State. I had ridden freights to the town with a tramp named Carl, whom I had met in a Minneapolis freight yard. We waited by the employment office in the decrepit trailer, with the other tramps pictured here, nearly a week before we were hired to pick apples.

Photo: From Douglas Harper, *Good Company*, (Chicago: University of Chicago Press, 1982, by Douglas Harper).

Some work is indisputably deviant in the sense that it is cruel, violent, or systematically in violation of generally accepted laws or norms. Our selection by Patricia Adler (1985, chapter 23) on the organization of illegal drug selling falls into this category. Other work exists in a gray area: not illegal, but related to illegal activities and outside the pale of general social norms because it services the deviant desires of nondeviant clients. Our previous chapter on exotic dancers (Ronai and Cross, 1998, chapter 6) explores this theme. Much work is partly legal and partly illegal, such as the sale of used and sometimes fenced materials on the streets of New York City, which has been analyzed by Duneier (2001). Other workers live on the fringes of society, breaking many laws on a daily basis but performing important work in the meantime. The tramps that Harper (1982) studied rode freight trains thousands of miles to take on the important work of the apple harvest. Finally, we note that deviance is integrated into many normal jobs, such as making up truth when editing encyclopedias (Tomlinson, 1985, chapter 9), cheating customers (Ditton, 1977), and stealing from bosses in a chain restaurant (Grey et al., 1994). Dabney and Hollinger's 1999 study of illicit drug use among pharmacists is included in our volume to reaffirm this point (see chapter 22).

It is clear from these examples that "deviant" is part of the normal and that the lines separating the two must be drawn carefully. Sociologically speaking, however, these examples of deviant work have important similarities to nondeviant work. To begin with, we recognize that deviant work is but one of many ways that people establish regular activities through which they get their living. We must remember that the quality of being deviant is a social process rather than an intrinsic property of human acts. As Howard Becker and many other sociologists have reminded us, an act is considered deviant because enough people in a group or society have convincingly labeled it that way. Killing for hire seems to be among the most despicable of jobs, yet when one works for any of several governments (including that of the United States), one may be hired to do exactly that. Although the government may call this "covert action," the reality is that one earns a living by killing others in the same kind of "cold blood" of the Mafia hit man. Or, when we label the work of the drug pusher deviant because of the laws it violates, we must recall that the laws themselves are a production of social processes, and that although some drugs are indeed illegal, others (some of which are more dangerous) are not or were not in the past. Although such discussion does not tell us about the cultural process of deviant work, it forms an important backdrop for our study.

Deviant work is often organized rationally and often even bureaucratically. The deviant worker often confronts his or her job with the same long-term planning and the same kind of understanding of rewards and sacrifices that nondeviants have of their careers. The safecracker studied by Bruce

Jackson (1969) employed a lawyer to get him out of jail when he was inevitably arrested and considered such costs as normal expenses. Jackson described the rational behavior of this criminal as beginning with a carefully researched investigation as to which types of crimes have the lowest arrest records and the lightest sentences, and then gaining skills to become successful in the same way most people organize themselves for their work.

We have known for decades that much of the crime in society is organized into criminal syndicates. The syndicates provide services to the public like gambling, prostitution, cheap goods, and substances such as drugs that are not easily otherwise available. Defenders of organized crime often say that without public appetite for these materials, there would be no organized crime. Whether or not this is the case, it is true that crime syndicates are organized into regular sets of duties, responsibilities, lines of reporting, and hierarchically organized patterns of authority. Crime syndicates are successful for the same reasons that bureaucracies in the nondeviant world are. They work well because they are managed efficiently.

All organized crime, however, must control itself without formal rules, the threat of dismissal, laws, courts, and jails. When a member of the criminal organization begins stealing from the organization, he may be warned by having his legs broken by an enforcer from within the group. If he continues stealing, he will probably be killed (although the criminal organization prefers to call the killing an "execution"). The hit man is thus performing a service in a regular way, which makes it possible for the organization to continue.

Indeed, one often has a "career" in crime—a life built around carefully orchestrated behavior within a formal organization such as exists in syndicates. Many of the same qualities that move people ahead in the nondeviant world advance the deviant. These include such qualities as resourcefulness, cunning, hard work, imagination, and responsibility. Harper recalls, as a young man from a fairly innocent part of the country and upbringing, moving to an East Coast city and befriending an ex-junkie and pusher who, fresh from the streets, became his apartment mate for more than a year. As we began taping discussions for what they hoped to be a book on the culture of heroin distribution, he was struck by his friend's assertion that life as a pusher in the Lower East Side of New York was a challenging and demanding job. Although it is outside the current discussion to consider whether any addictive substances should be sold on legal or illegal markets, it was clear that getting and distributing the drug was intellectually difficult and very dangerous. The career of the pusher was often short-lived overall because of human greed at various levels of the network, and error was not protected and limited by a bureaucratic organization. But for the time that the pusher procured and distributed his wares—that is, he solved the problems of a client population—he worked in a network of delicately balanced human associations. The pusher survived because he built a reputation among customers for fair price, quality product, and predictable availability. When competitors invaded his territory, he responded with better prices or, ultimately, violence. This point is made in contemporary studies of drug distribution, such as in Simon and Burns's study of a low-income neighborhood in Baltimore (1997).

These are some of the ways in which deviant work resembles the worlds of work most of us depend upon. There are, as well, profound differences. Note that we have stressed, in these comments, the "career" deviant rather than the impulsive crime of the teenager who steals a car or the spouse who kills in a jealous rage. The following comments continue in this perspective.

First, although most occupations develop an ideology, those developed by deviants are often chilling, boldfaced rationalizations of violent and corrupt ways of life. The killers studied by Mary Lorenz Dietz (1983) justify their acts by saying that they are protecting their reputations or self-esteem or that they are ridding the world of undesirable characters. The fact that not all violent criminals kill leads us to suspect that even these rationalizations do not operate evenly throughout the criminal world.

The violent criminal must "get himself psyched up" for his actions, but the level of violence the killer routinely engages in surpasses what virtually everyone else in society will ever experience. One must only reflect upon the struggles of conscience experienced by returned combat veterans (who kill out of self-protection with a fully developed ideological justification and strong peer pressure and support) to realize that humans do not normally kill each other without remorse. Those of us who do are somehow categorically different than those of us who don't. As Dietz shows us, even among the violent criminals, many draw the line at murder.

The drug salespeople and the professional safecrackers also operate with a set of rationalizations that do not always bear up well. Many criminals are attracted to their work out of quite dispassionate analyses, which show that the benefits of a life of crime are quite attractive indeed. The work is exciting and challenging in the way of few jobs in modern society. A successful criminal career brings more status than one would normally achieve in a blue-collar job, material possessions, and a lot of leisure time. Yet one senses in the justifications and rationalizations of a criminal, even one so articulate as Jackson's safecracker, a certain hollowness that suggests the norms and values of the larger society still create, for the criminal, a sense of guilt over a life led outside the mainstream. Indeed, since the source of the wealth must always be hidden, the status gained in a life of crime is limited to what are often pretty sleazy peers.

In these comments, we have suggested that crime bears fundamental similarities to other forms of work. The activities of the job (whether we admire them or not) require skill, knowledge, and the willingness and ability to use

violence successfully. The criminal's work is often organized into large organizations that are run rationally. The ideological rationalizations of criminals
remind us of the rationalizations of many workers. Still, however, we must
recognize that the work of crime often takes the individual into parts of the
human experience that defy explanation. Ultimate violence becomes a fright-
ful routine for many, and we are no closer to really understanding how it
happens than we have ever been.

## CITED AND SUGGESTED READING

Adler, Patricia A. "Wheeling and Dealing: An Ethnography of an Upper-level Drug
    Dealing and Smuggling Community." *Journal of Sociology and Social Welfare* 28,
    no. 1 (March 1985): 139–62.
Bryan, J. "Occupational Ideologies and Individual Attitudes of Call Girls." *Social
    Problems* 13 (spring 1966): 441–50.
Charlton, Joy, and Rosanna Hertz. "Guarding against Boredom: Security Specialists
    in the U.S. Air Force." *Journal of Contemporary Ethnography* 18, no. 3 (October
    1989): 299–326.
Dabney, Dean A., and. Richard C. Hollinger. "Illicit Prescription Drug Use among
    Pharmacists." *Work and Occupations* 26, no. 1 (1999): 77–106.
Dietz, Mary Lorenz. *Killing for Profit: The Social Organization of Felony Homicide.*
    Chicago: Nelson-Hall, 1983.
Ditton, Jean. "Learning to Fiddle Customers: An Essay on the Organized Produc-
    tion of Part-time Theft." *Work and Occupations* 4, no. 4 (November 1977): 427–49.
———. *Part-time Crime: An Ethnography of Fiddling and Pilferage.* London: Mac-
    Millan, 1977.
Duncier, Mitch. *Sidewalk.* New York: Farrar, Strauss and Giroux, 2001.
Forsyth, Craig J., and Tina H. Deshotels. "The Occupational Milieu of the Nude
    Dancer." *Deviant Behavior: An Interdisciplinary Journal* 18 (1997): 125–42.
Grey, Mark A., and Wendy Ryan Anderson. "Serving and Scamming: A Qualitative
    Study of Employee Theft in One Chain Restaurant." *Security-Journal* 5, no. 4
    (October 1994): 200–211.
Harper, Douglas. *Good Company.* Chicago: University of Chicago Press, 1982.
Heyl, Barbara. "The Madam as Teacher: The Training of House Prostitutes." *Social
    Problems* 24 (June 1977): 545–55.
Hong, Lawrence, and Robert W. Duff. "Becoming a Taxi-Dancer: The Significance
    of Neutralization in a Semi-deviant Occupation." *Work and Occupations* 4, no. 3
    (August 1977): 327–42.
Jackson, Bruce. *A Thief's Primer.* New York: MacMillan, 1969.
Miller, G. *Odd Jobs: The World of Deviant Work.* Englewood Cliffs, N.J.: Prentice
    Hall, 1978.
Ronai, Carol Rambo. "Sketching with Derrida: An Ethnography of a Researcher/
    Erotic Dancer." *Qualitative Inquiry* 4, no. 3 (1998): 405–20.
———. "The Next Night Sous Rature: Wrestling with Derrida's Nemesis." *Qualita-
    tive Inquiry* 5, no. 1 (1999): 114–29.

Shaw, Clifford R. *The Jack-Roller.* Chicago: University of Chicago Press, 1930.

Sieh, E. W. "Garment Workers: Perceptions of Inequity and Employee Theft." *British Journal of Criminology* 27 (1987): 174–90.

Simon, David, and Edward Burns. *The Corner: A Year in the Life of an Inner City Neighborhood.* New York: Broadway Books, 1997.

Sutherland, Edwin H. *The Professional Thief.* Chicago: University of Chicago Press, 1937.

Thompson, William E., and Jackie L. Harred. "Topless Dancers: Managing Stigma in a Deviant Occupation." *Deviant Behavior* 13 (1992): 291–311.

# 22

## Illicit Prescription Drug Use among Pharmacists: Evidence of a Paradox of Familiarity

*Dean A. Dabney and*
*Richard C. Hollinger*

A heightened level of social status and respect accompanies membership in an occupational profession (Greenwood, 1957). An example of this is the pharmacy profession. Ten years of public opinion polls consistently rank pharmacy as the most honest and ethical occupation, even above the clergy (McAneny & Moore, 1994). This elevated social status can be partially attributed to the specialized training and knowledge that pharmacists possess about the intricacies of prescription medicines and their pharmacological effects on the human body. Given their level of expertise, society freely yields its respect, trust, and admiration to those who are believed to be authorities on the safe and effective use of prescription drugs and medicines.

Pharmacists are granted the primary jurisdiction over the day-to-day dispensing of a variety of controlled pharmaceuticals to the public. This dispensing function is accompanied by numerous privileges and responsibilities. For example, pharmacists are expected to serve as the front line of defense against the inappropriate use or unauthorized acquisition of prescription medicines. Furthermore, they serve as mediators between the prescribing doctor and the patient, guarding against potentially undesirable health consequences such as adverse drug interactions, allergic reactions, or inappropriate and unnecessary prescription medication use. Pharmacists are accorded virtually unrestricted access to a cache of potent drugs and medicine far exceeding that of any other member of society. Collectively, these responsibilities and privileges act to further solidify the pharmacist's position as society's drug expert. As the above-mentioned integrity polls suggest, Americans seem to be quite satisfied with the ways in which pharmacists exercise their knowledge, training, and access to fill 1.6 billion prescriptions annually (Wivell & Wilson, 1994).

The present analysis identifies a potential negative effect that can result from the technical training, expertise, and familiarity that pharmacists have with prescription medicines. In particular, factors related to the process of being and becoming a practicing pharmacist can be linked to the most serious form of professional misconduct that faces the profession today—illicit prescription drug use.[1] Interviews with 50 pharmacists recovering from prescription drug abuse demonstrate how a pharmacist's self-confidence, knowledge, and virtually unrestricted access to prescription drugs can contribute to the eventual abuse of these substances.

Our data suggest that pharmacists must contend with a paradox of familiarity. The educational, occupational, and professional socialization processes associated with being and becoming a pharmacist can lull druggists into a false sense of confidence about their ability to self-medicate without ever first consulting with a doctor. Thus, for some pharmacists it appears that knowledge and familiarity breed consent not contempt, and as such, can contribute to progressively greater involvement in prescription drug use.

## LITERATURE ON ILLICIT DRUG USE AMONG PHARMACISTS

In 1982, the American Pharmaceutical Association (APhA, 1982) issued its first ever policy statement acknowledging that substance abuse is a problem among its membership. However, given the sensitive nature of this problem, we are left without accurate incidence or prevalence data on the problem—only rough estimates. The National Association of Retail Druggists (NARD, 1988) estimates that profession-wide, one in seven pharmacists will succumb to chemical dependency at some point in their careers. A survey conducted among the licensed pharmacists in a New England state (McAuliffe et al., 1987) found that 46% of the 312 practitioners responding had admitted to the use of some form of controlled substance at least once in their lives, 19% within the past year. Moreover, more than 20% of the respondents had engaged in illicit prescription drug use. The McAuliffe et al. (1987) data also offer estimates of the problematic effects of drug use as 2.3% of the respondents admitted drug dependency,[2] 8.9% reported experiencing adverse effects in their private or professional life due to their usage, and another 6% were identified as being at risk of drug dependency. Thus, the authors conclude that 18% of the respondents were already dependent on drugs or at risk of future drug dependency.

Another study conducted among practicing North Carolina pharmacists ($N = 1,370$) revealed that 24% of the respondents had worked with a colleague who they believed was either abusing or addicted to drugs (Normack, Eckel, Pfifferling, & Cocolas, 1985a). This study estimated that 21% of the respondents admitted to personal behaviors that placed them at risk of chemical impairment.[3]

Extrapolating from the available estimates of drug use/abuse onto the overall population of more than 190,000 U.S. practicing pharmacists nationwide (Martin, 1993), one can conservatively estimate that tens of thousand of pharmacists presently engage in some form of illicit prescription drug use. Moreover, the prevalent data suggest that a considerable segment of this subpopulation of drug-using pharmacists engages in high levels of usage or experience personal or professional problems as a result.

Pharmacists are not the only people who use drugs while at work. Data from the National Household Survey on Drug Abuse (NHSDA) show that 3.1% of full-time U.S. employees older than the age of 12 have used some form of illicit prescription drug in the past year (Hoffman, Brittingham, & Larson, 1996). The larger NHSDA data set that includes a random sample of individuals older than age 12 (employed or not) shows that 10.1% had used illicit prescription drugs within the past year (Substance Abuse and Mental Health Services Administration, 1996). Self-report studies that ask various samples of U.S. employees about their substance abuse behaviors (Decima, 1990; Lehman, Holcom, & Simpson, 1990; Schneck, Amodei, & Kernish, 1991) show that 1% to 3% report some level of illicit prescription drug use in the past year. Studies that analyze the results of employers' drug testing of job applicants (Normand, Salyards, & Mahony, 1990) or current employees (Lehman et al., 1990; Sheridan & Winkler, 1989) show that anywhere from .2% to 7% of employees test positive for prescription drug use. None of these estimates, however, approach the above prevalence estimates for the pharmacy profession (McAuliffe et al., 1987).

Growing concern over the problem of illicit drug use among pharmacists has spawned a number of other studies that inquire more deeply into the nature and dynamics of this form of employee deviance. Bissell, Haberman, and Williams (1989) asked a sample of 86 drug-recovering pharmacists to describe their substance abuse experiences in hopes of explaining drug use within this special population.[4] These researchers found that 24% of the interviewees focused their drug use on nonnarcotic prescription drugs, 22% preferred mild narcotics, and 31% chose strong narcotics. Ingestible medications such as benzodiazepines and amphetamines were among the most popular, whereas injectable drug use was rare. It was not uncommon for respondents in the Bissel et al. study to report using remarkably large amounts of prescription medications on a daily basis. Moreover, significant numbers of the abusing pharmacists reported that they engaged in complex consumption patterns and had progressed into the latter stages of the substance abuse process (i.e., exhibiting visible signs of mental, physical, and emotional problems) before they entered treatment.

Laypersons are often surprised to learn that the pharmaceutical profession is confronted with problems of drug use among its ranks. They expect that druggists, perhaps more so than any other members of society, should know better than to engage in such self-destructive behaviors. They assume that pharmacists' respect for the dangers of potentially addictive substances coupled with their professional ethics will protect them. The flaw in this logic is that it assumes that greater knowledge about the effects of medications should prevent illicit prescription drug use by pharmacists. We contend that the opposite may actually be true.

## INSIGHT FROM THE EMPLOYEE
## DEVIANCE LITERATURE

The employee deviance literature offers considerable evidence that occupational and professional socialization processes can, on occasion, encourage deviance. Several researchers have considered the ways in which organizational culture and the nature of one's job can facilitate occupational trust violations (Benson, 1985; Cressey, 1953; Dalton, 1959; Ditton, 1977; Geis, 1967; Gouldner, 1954; Hollinger, 1991; Horning, 1970; Mars, 1982; Sieh, 1987; Tatham, 1974). Although each of these studies takes a slightly different theoretical orientation and focuses on a different work setting, in sum they illustrate how the normative definitions of the work group culture enable employees to violate rules by neutralizing their violations of organizational trust.

A review of the existing literature on substance use within the various health care professions reveals significant evidence to support the premise that social factors can and do facilitate profession-specific substance abuse. For example, the American Nurses Association (ANA) estimates that 8% to 10% of the 1.7 million practicing nurses in this country are dependent on drugs or alcohol (ANA, 1984), and the Michigan Nurses Association (MNA, 1986) estimates that one in every seven nurses will abuse drugs during his or her career.

Dabney's (1995a, 1995b) research links nurses' deviant drug theft and use to informal nursing work group norms. Interview with 25 nurses from various critical care settings found that on-the-job therapeutic drug use (i.e., self-medication) was common and accepted within nursing work groups studied. These behaviors were excused on the basis that they were therapeutic in nature (i.e., helped the nurse perform his or her work duties) and involved what were perceived as less addictive nonnarcotic prescription medications. Note that there are other studies that relate organizational norms to nurses' drug use (Bissell & Jones, 1981; Bogardus, 1987; Green, 1989; Hood & Duphorne, 1995; Hutchinson, 1986; Moodley-Kunnie, 1988; Poplar & Lyle, 1969; Shaffer, 1987; Smith, 1989; Sullivan, 1987).

Considerable research has also addressed the issue of controlled substance use and abuse among doctors. The most widely cited studies include Carlson, Dilts, and Radcliff (1994); Hughes, Conrad, Baldwin, Storr, and Sheehan (1991); and McAuliffe et al. (1984). Again, these researchers find that doctors' drug use is generally centered on therapeutic self-medication rationalizations. Various occupational factors are associated with doctors' drug use. These include complete autonomy, a lack of accountability, easy access, high stress, and peer group approval. Moreover, numerous characteristics associated with the profession of medicine are attributed to doctors' drug use, namely, a sense of invincibility, a proscribed faith in the healing powers of medicines, and weak social control mechanisms within the profession (Hankes & Bissell, 1992). In sum, the literature on drug use within the medical profession—much like the pharmacy and nursing literature—identifies a series of factors within the professional culture that facilitate the onset and progression of substance use and abuse among its membership.

## INSIGHT FROM THE PHARMACY PROFESSIONAL SOCIALIZATION LITERATURE

The pharmacy professional socialization literature also offers support for our central premise that being and becoming a pharmacist can contribute to substance abuse among these professionals. For example, research on the pharmacy school experience reveals inadequate levels of substance abuse education (Baldwin et al., 1991; Bissell et al., 1989; Kurzman, 1972; McAuliffe et al., 1987; McDuff, Tommasello, Hoffman & Johnson, 1995; Miederhoff, Allen, McCreary, & Veal, 1977), the existence of permissive student attitudes toward recreational drug and alcohol use (Baldwin et al., 1991; McAuliffe et al., 1984; Miederhoff et al., 1977; Normack, Eckel, Pfifferling, & Cocolas, 1985b), evidence of instrumental drug use to facilitate studying (McAuliffe et al., 1984), and cognitive dissonance associated with their new-found access to powerful prescription medications (Bissell et al., 1989; Hankes & Bissell, 1992). Collectively, this body of research suggests that pharmacists in training are exposed to mixed messages about prescription medicines. Their course work focuses on the technical aspect of prescription drugs—glossing over the dangers of substance abuse—and prescription medicines are praised for their healing potential. At the same time, research (McAuliffe et al., 1987) suggests that pharmacists are immersed in a social atmosphere that encourages experimental drug use and self-medication practices. These situations potentially contribute to pro-drug use attitudes or early instances of experimentation. Several scholars (Hankes & Bissell, 1992; Winick, 1961) have gone so far as to suggest that this familiarity and knowledge can leave the individual feeling immune to drug abuse.

Research on post-pharmacy school socialization in processes identifies additional drug-related risk factors. For example, several inquires (Chi, 1983; Epstein, 1990, 1991; Sheffield, O'Neill, & Fisher, 1992a, 1992b) have found evidence that pharmacists, similar to other health care professionals, are often hesitant to report known drug use behavior by a colleague or peer. Chi (1983) reports that more than one third of the retail pharmacists surveyed claimed that they knew a fellow pharmacist who was working under the influence of controlled substances. Of these pharmacists who were aware of an impaired colleague, less than one half chose to report or act on their knowledge of the wrongdoing. By not reporting known or suspected drug use by a peer, pharmacists tacitly are encouraging such behaviors, thus allowing the drug-using individuals to misconstrue silence as a sign of approval of their deviance.

## RESEARCH METHODS

The data for this analysis were drawn from a larger multimethod data collection effort[5] that took place between 1993 and 1995 (Dabney, 1997). The present analysis focuses principally on personal interviews with recovering drug-abusing pharmacists. These interview data offer firsthand accounts of the attitudes and behaviors of pharmacists who use drugs; thus, they provide an important first step toward understanding its complex social problem.

The face-to-face interviews were designed to examine the personal life histories of a random sample (Berg, 1998) of 50 pharmacists who were in recovery for past prescription drug abuse. The process began with the development of a loosely structured interview guide. This interview guide was divided into 13 topical areas that allowed the interviewer to probe various aspects of the individual's pharmacy career, paying particular attention to the intertwined dynamics of his or her personal drug use.

Interview participants were recruited with the assistance of leaders in the recovering impaired pharmacists' movement. Most every American state has developed a recovery network for impaired pharmacists. Although organizational structures, funding sources, and other administrative aspects differ from state to state, each of these social assistance networks is committed to serving as a liaison between drug- and/or alcohol-using pharmacists and the governing social control and sanctioning bodies (e.g., state board of pharmacy, pharmacy employers, Drug Enforcement Administration [DEA]) that oversee pharmacy practice. Three key figures in these networks were enlisted to implement our sampling strategy.[6] Each individual was asked to contact members of his or her recovery network and make them aware of the research project and a forthcoming data collection trip to the area. The recruiters provided program participants[7] with contact information and encouraged interested parties to call the researchers for further information and/or to schedule an interview time. This process was continued until 50 pharmacists with prescription drug problems had initiated contact and the interviews were completed. None of the participant-initiated contracts resulted in a refusal to participate. All of the interviews were conducted by the senior author.

The interviews took place in 1994 during four data collection trips to pharmacy conferences and recovery network locales. They were conducted in a wide variety of physical locations (i.e., hotel rooms, dormitory rooms, public parks, restaurants, respondents' homes, respondents' places of employment, meeting rooms). Each interview involved only the interviewer and the voluntarily participating pharmacist.

The fifty interviews were completed with pharmacists from 24 different states. The tape-recording of each one was transcribed verbatim. Thematic content analysis (Berg, 1998) was used to analyze the data. First, the paper copy of each interview transcription was coded by hand. This involved identifying general thematic categories within the interview conversations. These mundane categories included but were not limited to the various topical areas contained in the above-described interview guide. Eight-symbol codes were handwritten in the margins to mark conversational excerpts that illustrated the given thematic category. Once general themes were developed and labeled within the interview transcriptions, the process was repeated using more specific thematic categories. For example, prescription drug use with medicinal motivations (i.e., self-medication) was a general theme that was identified and labeled in the original coding pass. Subsequent coding passes further delineated the self-medication issue by affixing codes that specified the type of ailment or condition that the self-medication was intended to treat (e.g., work stress, physical pain, insomnia). By sorting and resorting from general to more specific themes, we were able to search for and identify more specific themes in the data. Several phases of this sorting and coding process were conducted until we developed a comprehensive classification of all interview data. At this point, all codes were entered into the Qualpro computer program, thus allowing us to organize and retrieve data more easily. This program allowed us to visualize thematic patterns in the data, determine the prevalence of a given theme, and save the direct quotations for each theme into separate computer files.

## DRUG USER DEMOGRAPHICS

Table 22.1 presents data that compares the demographic characteristics of pharmacists who have been detected engaging in illicit prescription drug use to the overall population of practicing U.S. pharmacists. The far left column of table 22.1 provides demographic data for the 50 drug-recovering pharmacists that we accessed and interviewed using the above described research methods. In an effort to provide the fullest possible profile of drug-using pharmacists, we include demographic data from all of the data sources in our larger inquiry (see Note 5). The second column of table 22.1 provides demographic data for the 89 pharmacists who were implicated in the above-mentioned incident reports, and the third column provides similar data for the 312 survey respondents who reported five or more lifetime episodes of prescription drug use.[8] For comparison purposes, the far right column of table 22.1 presents demographic data for the entire population of U.S. pharmacists.

Table 22.1 suggests that there are several demographic characteristics that set drug-using pharmacists apart from the larger professional pharmacist population. For example, notice that more than three fourths of the drug-using pharmacists in the personal interview, incident report, and survey samples are males (78%, 88.8%, and 77.9%, respectively). Yet, the data in the far right column show that the overall population of practicing pharmacists is less than two thirds male (64.2%). Disproportionate male gender distributions have also been observed in the previous studies where samples of drug-using pharmacists were involved. The sample of 89 recovering pharmacists that were interviewed by Bissell et al. (1989) was composed of 83% males and only 17% females. Similarly, Gallegos, Veit, Wilson, Porter, and Talbott (1988) found that 89% of the pharmacists that entered drug treatment in Georgia from 1975 to 1987 were males.

These gender differences become more dramatic when compared to the available estimates on chemical dependency among all U.S. citizens. For example, Levers and Hawes (1990) estimate that the population of chemically dependent people in this country is composed of 40% females. Thus, all indications suggest that male pharmacists become drug abusers more often than their female colleagues.

We turn to the occupations and professional literature for several possible explanations of these gender disparities. Kanter (1977) and other feminist scholars (Apter, 1993; Harris, 1995; Steinberg, 1984) have argued that women working in traditionally male dominated professions are held to higher productivity and discipline standards than are their male counterparts. Studies of female doctors (Allen, 1994; Briles, 1994; Candib, 1996; Lorber, 1993; Riska & Wegar, 1993; Secundy, 1996) suggest that the health professions may be especially prone to this one-way assimilation process. Thus, it may be that

**Table 22.1.   Demographic Characteristics (%) of Drug-using Pharmacists from Three Data Sources and the Population of Practicing U.S. Pharmacists**

| Variable | Interview (N = 50) | Incident Report (N = 89) | Survey (N = 312) | All U.S. Pharmacists (N = 179,445)[a] |
|---|---|---|---|---|
| Gender | | | | |
| Male | 78.0 | 88.8 | 77.9 | 64.2 |
| Female | 22.0 | 11.2 | 22.1 | 29.2 |
| Unknown | — | — | — | 6.2 |
| Race | | | | |
| White | 96.0 | 87.5 | 94.3 | 81.9 |
| African American | 2.0 | 6.3 | 1.6 | 2.4 |
| Hispanic | 2.0 | 4.2 | 1.6 | 1.4 |
| Asian | — | 2.0 | 2.5 | 3.3 |
| American Indian | — | — | — | 0.5 |
| Unknown | — | [b] | — | 10.7 |
| Age | | | | |
| 0–29 | 8.0 | 21.4 | 15.7 | 6.3 |
| 30–39 | 38.0 | 32.9 | 20.5 | 28.6 |
| 40–49 | 36.0 | 25.7 | 22.5 | 25.2 |
| 50–59 | 12.0 | 12.9 | 23.0 | 15.2 |
| 60+ | 6.0 | 7.1 | 18.3 | 16.2 |
| Unknown | — | — | — | 8.3 |
| Degree status | | | | |
| Bachelor's | 84.0 | — | 82.4 | 84.1 |
| PharmD | 4.0 | — | 11.5 | 6.2 |
| Master's | 12.0 | — | 5.8 | 4.7 |
| Other | — | — | 0.3 | 1.4 |
| Unknown | — | 100.0 | — | 3.5 |
| Practice setting[c] | | | | |
| Hospital | 36.0 | — | 22.4 | 23.6 |
| Chain retail | 26.0 | 100.0 | 59.6 | 33.1 |
| Independent retail | 28.0 | — | [d] | 32.6 |
| Home infusion | 4.0 | — | 3.5 | — |
| Nursing home | 4.0 | — | — | 2.2 |
| Temporary contract | 2.0 | — | — | — |
| Other | — | — | 14.5 | 8.4 |

a. These data were obtained from the Pharmacy Manpower Project (Martin, 1993).
b. Race data was unavailable for 41 (46.1%) of the cases in the archival component. However, for comparison purposes, the above percentages do not include these cases.
c. The practice setting percentages for the interview participants represent their principal practice setting during their drug use years.
d. The survey instrument did not differentiate between chain and independent retail settings; they are presented together.

female pharmacists are scrutinized more or feel as though they are scrutinized more by their peers and supervisors. These added expectations or social controls could offer female pharmacists less opportunity to commit occupational deviance of any kind, especially such serious violations as illicit prescription drug use.

It is also possible that the gender disparities observed in table 22.1 may be due partly to the masculine ideals that have been shown to pervade all health care professions. Macho terms such as "God complex" and "the invincible doctor" have long been associated with the health care professions. Similarly, customary male personality characteristics such as competition and strong-willed determinism are standard criteria that define a successful health care practitioner. Several researchers (Becker, Geer, Hughes, & Strauss, 1961; Bloom, 1973; Freidson, 1970, 1975; Haas & Shaffir, 1987; Konner, 1987) have provided evidence to support the notion that many health professions (e.g., medicine, pharmacy, dentistry) take on definitive androcentric cultural characteristics. It seems logical that drug use, especially forms of a treat-it-yourself self-medication are well suited for this male dominant mind set.

As table 22.1 also shows, the vast majority of the drug-using pharmacists in the personal interview, incident report, and survey samples were Caucasians (96%, 87.5%, and 94.3% respectively). Past studies (Gallegos et al., 1988; McAuliffe et al., 1987) have also found Caucasians to make up the vast majority of reported drug-using pharmacists. Referring to the far right column of table 22.1, however, notice that the findings of the Pharmacy Manpower Project (Martin, 1993) estimate that only 81.9% of the overall population of practicing U.S. pharmacists are Caucasian. Thus, it appears that the percentages of Caucasians in samples of drug-using pharmacists are consistently higher than the larger professional population.

Moreover, note that the race distributions in table 22.1 are significantly different from those seen in the overall population of drug-using Americans. For example, recent National Institute of Justice research (NIJ, 1997) indicates that minorities—not Caucasians—tend to make up disproportionate numbers of apprehended drug users. The slightly higher Caucasian drug use figures in all three samples of pharmacists suggest that being and becoming a pharmacist may somehow contradict the traditional race/drug use trends.

The data on age (see table 22.1) show that drug-using pharmacists tend to be older than the overall population of U.S. pharmacists. Again, we offer several possible explanations for this finding. The high incidence of drug use among older pharmacists may represent a sign-of-the-times artifact in the data. Most middle-aged pharmacists went to school during the 1960s and 1970s, a time when permissive attitudes toward recreational drug use were popular. Moreover, pharmacists who went to school prior to 1970 were exposed to the relaxed dispensing practices that were commonplace in the pharmacy profession before self-regulation and more strict federal guidelines (Controlled Substance Act of 1970; see Shulgin, 1992) ushered in a more conservative approach to prescription medicines. Pharmacists who were educated and professionally socialized during this time may hold more permissive attitudes toward drugs and drug use and, as a result, be more likely to engage in either the recreational or therapeutic use of prescription drugs.

There are other factors that likely contribute to the age differences shown in table 22.1. For example, the personal interview data suggest that it usually takes several years for pharmacists' drug use to progress to the point that others become aware and begin negative sanctions against them. Finally, the interview data suggest that many pharmacists use drugs to alleviate physical pain. It may be that age, along with the wear and tear of a longer pharmacy career, lead to more physical pain and thus precipitate more self-medicating behaviors.

## PHARMACISTS' DRUG USE TRENDS AND PATTERNS

Each of the 50 pharmacists who were interviewed spoke at length and in detail about their personal drug use histories. As expected, there were many unique aspects to each individual's past drug abuse; however, the thematic content analysis revealed several consistent trends and patterns in their drug use behaviors.

## NATURE AND EXTENT OF DRUG USE

Each recovering pharmacist's past was marked by an extensive drug addiction history. All 50 individuals recounted daily drug use. All showed clear signs of being chemically dependent on one or more prescription drugs. The constant presence or threat of physical withdrawal was the most obvious indicator of chemical dependency. Most described a pattern of progressive drug use situations wherein even short periods of abstinence would lead to withdrawal symptoms. For example, one 39-year-old male pharmacist said,

> Two years before I sobered up I was really reaching my bottom. I would chase these delivery trucks down in the morning because I didn't come to my store until midafternoon. I was in withdrawal in the morning, and I was without drugs, so I had to have it—I was just going nuts. Many mornings I had gone to work sweating. It would be 30 degrees, it would be January, and the clerk would say, "You look sick," and I would say, "It's the flu."

Almost all of the respondents spoke about a conscious or unconscious recognition of their chemical dependency, especially the coinciding threat of physical withdrawal. To counter this threat, most other pharmacists maintained a near perpetual state of chemical intoxication. They generally designed a tightly structured and continuous drug use pattern to avoid physical withdrawal. This trend was demonstrated in the following comment made by a 38-year-old female pharmacist: "During the last 4 years of my use, I used every single day. Day in and day out, all the time to try to stay out of withdrawal and just maintain."

Many individuals described how they had progressed to dosage intervals of an hour or less. One 45-year-old male pharmacist said,

> It was just crazy. . . . I just kept taking more and more stuff because I loved it. . . . Percosets [narcotic analgesic], you know. CIIs, it was unbelievable. And I would be popping these things, and 30 minutes later I'd have to pop some more. It just really snowballed fast on me until I wasn't knowing what I was doing. . . . Oh gosh, I was probably doing 20 Percoset a day at work.

Only 10 of the 50 interviewees described a drug habit that focused on a single type or class of prescription medication.[9] Three of these individuals engaged in heavy, daily use of cocaine (up to 5 grams per day). The other eight individuals claimed that their drug habit was exclusively focused on narcotic analgesics.[10]

The remaining 40 respondents can be described as poly-drug users.[11] Their daily drug use behaviors included multiple types and classes of controlled substances. Thirty-two of these 40 poly-drug users were regularly using at least one type of narcotic analgesic. However, their narcotic analgesics habit usually coincided with the use of some other class of prescription medication, such as amphetamines (e.g., Dexedrine, Ritalin), barbiturates (e.g., Seconal, Phenobarbital), or benzodiazepines (e.g., Valium, Xanax). As a 45-year-old male pharmacist explained, "I was taking amphetamines, not necessarily every day but occasionally. The opiates [narcotic analgesics] I was taking every day. And the benzodiazepines I was taking sporadically . . . daily. So, it was mainly opiates."

It also should be noted that many of the interviewees chose to mix alcohol with prescription medications. In fact, a considerable number of the respondents described daily or weekly drinking habits. Most of the alcohol consumption can be described as being drinking behavior wherein the individual drank a high volume over a short period of time. Similarly, a number of respondents indicated that they sometimes mixed illegal street drugs with the prescription drugs. For example, five of the respondents described occasional marijuana use. In most cases, the street drug use was not daily but rather taken weekly, monthly, or on a special occasion.

## GARBAGE HEADING

Each poly-drug user was asked if he or she considered him- or herself to be a "garbage head." This is a term used within the drug treatment and support group communities to refer to an individual who is not particular and will use any type of drug to which he or she can gain access. Thirty of the 40 poly-drug users characterized themselves as garbage heads. They routinely described extensive drug use experimentation. For example, a 48-year-old male pharmacist explained that his Narcotics Anonymous sponsor once required him to write down the name of every drug type that he had used over the course of his 15-year career. He claimed that this exercise yielded a list of 144 different medications. The following interview excerpts are indicative of the types of responses that were received when asking about the breadth of garbage head practices. A 43-year-old male pharmacist said,

> I did it all. You know we were kind of garbage cans. My drug of choice was codeine. I did a lot of acetaminophen with codeine. I started out with aspirin and codeine, like Empirin, but the Empirin hurt my stomach. So, you know, being really dumb I went to Tylenol with codeine and stayed strictly with that [all narcotic analgesics]. But I was not a downer lover, I didn't like to be zoned out like pot made me. I liked to be up and fired up and moving. Codeine did that to me. Unlike others, it didn't cause the drowsiness, it gave me a surge. But still, I had to try other things to see what worked best together.

Similarly, when asked what types of drug he preferred to use, a 42-year-old male pharmacist replied, "Anything. In the beginning anything. No matter what it was. If it had that 'C'[12] with the little lines in there . . . CII, CIII, CIV . . . I had to go and do it."

Most of the respondents described how they would ingest large amounts of drugs each day. Only a small minority engaged in what would be considered or recommended dosage levels of the myriad of prescription medications that they were taking. Some pharmacists recounted staggering daily dosage schedules. For example, one pharmacist described how he was injecting 500 mg of Demerol each day. Several other respondents described how they were injecting in excess of 100 mg of a narcotic per day. Intravenous users were not the only ones who displayed heavy drug use patterns. Several individuals were ingesting more than 100 Percodan or Percoset pills each day. Two separate cocaine users explained how their habits had progressed to a daily intake of an impressive 5 grams per day.

## TITRATING

An interesting trend emerged from the inquiry into the development of drug tolerance. Early in the interview process, pharmacists began speaking about a drug use practice called *titrating*. This term refers to a practice whereby individuals apply their pharmaceutical knowledge to manage their personal drug use, enhancing or neutralizing specific drug effects by ingesting counteracting drugs. In effect, they would walk a chemical tightrope that allowed them to remain high, function, and disguise the obvious physical signs of drug abuse. For example, one 44-year-old male pharmacist said,

> When I was out partying I could drink. See, I didn't drink at work. That's one of the ways that I got heavier into the benzos [benzodiazepines] and the barbs [barbiturates]. . . . You could take something like that and get the sedative effects, but it wouldn't smell on your breath. So I would not drink, but basically I had to wake up. . . . I would put about four Percosets [narcotic analgesic] and four biphetamine 20 mg or Dexedrine [amphetamine] with the Percoset. When it was time to roll out of bed, to try to get work, I would swallow all that and wait a little bit until it would start to kick in. And then I would just compulsively swallow whatever Percoset I could get my hands on. And swallow amphetamines as needed to titrate my energy levels to being productive and not to appear impaired from the opiate.

This pharmacist used his titrating knowledge to achieve three different goals: (a) physical euphoria, (b) avoidance of negative side-effects, and (c) avoidance of detection. All three of these themes were found in varying degrees among the 28 pharmacists who recounted titrating practices.

Regardless of the origin, there is clear evidence that titrating behavior evolves from pharmaceutical training. Most pharmacists did not hesitate to state that they had learned how to titrate by applying what they had learned in class lectures or by reading books or articles on pharmacology. This is illustrated in the following exchange between the interviewer (I) and a 56-year-old male pharmacist (P).

> I: It seems like you were really putting your expertise to work there?
> P: Yep, all my knowledge of pharmacology so I could get perfectly titrated. And I'd go in there [to work], and 15 minutes later I could be snowed over.

Widespread presence of garbage heading and titrating offers important support for our assertion that being and becoming a pharmacist affects the individuals' drug use. Clearly, these pharmacists were exploiting their access to prescription drugs and applying their educationally acquired knowledge to enhance and inform their drug use.

## PARADOX OF FAMILIARITY

Without exception, every interviewed pharmacist saw his- or herself as a drug expert. They argued that pharmacists, more so than doctors, were best prepared to dispense and counsel patients about the nature and dynamics of prescription drugs. For example, a 33-year-old male pharmacist said,

> You are the guardian of their health. The doctor might not know what they're doing. It's your idea to make sure that the right meds are used. We are supposed to question the doctors in a good way. We say "Hey look, don't come off arrogant, but hey doc, why are you doing this?"

This individual emphasizes the important role that pharmacists play in the large health care delivery system. This was a common sentiment offered by many respondents.

The naïve observer might expect that a strong professional identity as well as extensive knowledge regarding the effects of prescription drugs should be the perfect deterrent against abuse. However, we found that this was not always the case. Often, addicted pharmacists described how their intimate familiarity with prescription medicines actually was a contributing factor to abuse. In particular, the interview data show that the professional socialization process exposes pharmacists to a dangerous combination of both access to drugs and detailed knowledge about them. This professional pharmacy socialization process produces what we wish to call a paradox of familiarity.

The seeds of this paradox can be traced back to the pharmacy school experience. The interview data reveal that pharmacy school offers students very limited training in the dangers of addiction. For example, when asked about his addiction education, one pharmacist offered up the following types of responses:

> I had no [drug abuse] education. I was a drug expert and knew nothing about the [addictive effects of these] substances.
> It was just that junkies shoot heroin.
> Never did we ever have a class like "addiction." Never did anyone ever come in. Absolutely not. That was not even considered. That never came up.
> That was the sum total of pharmacy education on substance abuse. "Keep your hands off the stuff, ha, ha, ha." That's it, that's all I ever learned.

What little drug education training these pharmacists did receive was usually quite technical and rudimentary. For each drug type, they were made aware of the addiction potential ratings that are contained in the Controlled Substance Act of 1970 (Shulgin, 1992). Pharmacy students were provided general information about the signs of abuse that accompany various controlled substances. This is not to say that pharmacists in training are not told about the dangers of drugs. On the contrary, instructors did stress that people can and did get addicted to prescription medicines. However, the message was conveyed on a very general and impersonal level. Rarely were they told that pharmacists just like them could get addicted to prescription medicines. This can be seen in the comments of a 59-year-old male pharmacist:

> In school it was cold, clinical—"Yes, this can be habit forming and addictive." But as far as the addiction process is described in detail, you know, the mental and the physical part of it and how those interact, and all those self-esteem issues, that's totally lost in it. It's just totally clinical. . . . they did touch on it, actually, but from a legal and a clinical standpoint. "If you do this you will get in trouble. There are the penalties, this is what they'll do to you. This class of drugs have this addiction potential."

The insufficient and abstract nature of the drug addiction awareness is also expressed in the following exchange between the interviewer (I) and a 46-year-old male pharmacist (P):

> I: Do you think that they teach you everything that you need to know about substance abuse?
> P: Substances of abuse? Absolutely not.
> I: Did they teach you anything? I guess would be the better question?
> P: Let me tell you, we went on rounds to [a hospital], which was the alcoholic ward. And we saw society's [alcohol problem], we learned how to manage it. We learned about drugs that we used for DTs [delirium tremors] and that was about it. And I think that many classes even after that received very little more than that, basic stuff such as. . . . "This is addiction and how to treat it." Not even that, "These are the physical effects of alcoholism, etc. And this is the medical management of those physical effects." No treatment of the disease at all, ever.

Drug use in pharmacy school is further exacerbated by the presence of other educationally related factors. For example, we found widespread evidence that pharmacy school helped foster benign attitudes toward prescription drugs. This belief system was affected by easy access to prescription medication, relaxed attitudes toward occasional drug use, heavy social drinking and drug use in pharmacy fraternities and other social get-togethers, and exposure to drug-using pharmacy mentors (i.e., internship preceptors).

A major element of the paradox of familiarity is rooted in a pharmacist's constant exposure to prescription drugs. Throughout a pharmacist's career (both during and after college), his or her every day is filled with repeated contact to a host of prescription medicines. This continued exposure to pharmaceutical company representatives and their sample medicines effectively erodes the individual's fear of drug addiction danger. For example, a 41-year-old male pharmacist commented,

I: You say that work desensitized you further. How so?

P: Because of pharmacy school, I didn't realize the dangers of the chemicals, and I see so many prescriptions for Valium [benzodiazepine] and codeine [narcotic analgesic] . . . that over a period of years it seemed okay. I wasn't smoking marijuana, I wasn't doing anti-Baptist alcohol, so I was okay.

The combined effect of constant access to prescription drugs is also seen in the remarks of a 52-year-old female pharmacist:

Well, the accessibility helped. I mean, I used the profession because you're accessible to all these drugs. And I mean, I know. I'm a trained pharmacist. I know what can make you feel good, and what can make you feel quiet, and all the different kinds of drugs, so my drug knowledge helped me pick the best one for me.

The situation is exacerbated by the multimillion-dollar drug marketing offensive waged by the pharmaceutical companies. Pharmacists in training are constantly being told about the powerful, therapeutic effects of the prescription medicines that they dispense. This reinforcement comes from a variety of sources, such as patient consultations, coworker discussions, professional organizations, and especially personal interactions with sales representatives from the pharmaceutical industry. A few examples of this positive, prodrug reinforcement are offered below. A 44-year-old male pharmacist stated,

P: That's the way I grew up. . . . If there's a problem—if you have a headache— you can take a pill. If there's a stomachache, you can take a pill. There was a pill for everything.

I: Like, "better living through chemistry"?

P: I think that that's right.

I: Did you buy into that?

P: I think I definitely did. If there was something wrong, regardless if it was one of my kids or whoever it was, we made something that could take away anything that you had. I mean any problem that you had. It wasn't looked at like it is now. Now it's "say no to drugs" and blah, blah, blah.

Similarly, a 34-year-old male pharmacist said,

I: A lot of people talk about that [a "better living through chemistry" mentality] as being an age when everyone was just so mesmerized by the healing potential of these drugs and not really the side effects hadn't caught up to— you know—people were just so impressed by what they can do. Is that what you're kind of talking about?

P: Yeah. Exactly. Xanax, for instance, was touted as the greatest drug ever. I remember going to an UpJohn [a drug manufacturer] lecture in probably the late '80s. The lecture was at a local pharmacy group. He said, "It's not habit forming. Basically, when you stop taking it, the symptoms of anxiety that reoccur are the original symptoms coming back of why you took the drug." This was a guy representing UpJohn doing that lecture. I mean, you laugh now, but I came home and told my dad, "No, no." that's what I told him, I said, "It's not habit forming." He was like, "Naa." I don't know why he knew or thought he knew, but he had always said it was okay. Later on, we learned from psychiatrists and psychiatrists that Xanax was very habit forming. . . . I believed the [UpJohn] guy.

I: So coming out of pharmacy school you bought into that kind of relaxed orientation towards the medicine?

P: I would say so.

Exposure to marketing propaganda about prescription drugs was clearly one-sided in nature. The positive aspects of the drugs were never tempered by any real effort to educate the pharmacists about corresponding dangers. For example, a 46-year-old male pharmacist said,

Yeah, what we learned back in the '70s, was "Yes, this was indeed a problem for society. Isn't it fortunate that pharmacy doesn't have it?" We know too much. We know what these drugs will do, so obviously it could never happen to a pharmacist.

Respondents described how this combination of open access and positive professional reinforcement led to a feeling of familiarity and closeness toward the drugs. Pharmacists eventually let their guard down and began to adopt a benign belief system toward prescription medicines. They believed that these drugs could only improve lives; and therefore, they dismissed or minimized the dangers. Self-medication became a viable and attractive form of medicating every problem. The paradox of familiarity is clearly articulated in the following exchange that occurred between the interviewer (I) and a 40-year-old female pharmacist (P):

P: But as far as respect for the medications, yes, I had that right out of school. A lot of respect for the power of good that the medications could do.

I: What do you mean by that?

P: Well, we have a lot of people who are alive today that would not be alive without some of the pharmaceuticals that we have. And that I think is [a source] of respect.

I: What about substance abuse? Did you know anything about it at that point?

P: Zero.

I: Nothing in school or at work?

P: Right, Pretty scary, huh?

The interview data clearly demonstrate that pharmacists were able to deny the dangers and maintain an attitude of invincibility when it came to the issue of drug addiction. As professional pharmacists, they thought that they were immune to drug addiction. For example, a 33-year old male pharmacist said,

> P: I felt that I could handle it better than the average layperson. Because, after all, I'm a professional. So yeah, it was a very cavalier attitude towards drugs. Very cavalier.
>
> I: So you bought into that "I'm a professional" thing?
>
> P: Yeah, and I know what I'm doing. I know what the edge is, and I'm not going to go over the edge, but clearly I was well over the edge. In the end, I got very paranoid, and I got very out of control. And it's hard for me to talk about it, because it's a shameful thing. Because I do consider myself a professional, and I let myself down, and I let a lot of people down. But for me it was a very cavalier—kind of, "I can handle this"—kind of attitude. I know what I'm doing.

Similarly, a 43-year-old female pharmacist said,

> I don't know that I really thought about it. I figured, well yeah, I know more about these drugs than anybody, so maybe that justified my use and perhaps I thought being an educated, intellectual type person that I would be able to detect any problems. . . . Yeah, that's about it. I know what all these things do, I can handle it. Absolutely. I knew all about the drugs and I could quit any time I wanted to. That was a real liability. Because that's where I rationalized it out. I'm a pharmacist. I know about these drugs, and they're not going to bother me. I can quit any time I want.

In all, 46 of the 50 pharmacists interviewed spoke directly about this paradox of familiarity. All expressed little doubt that this dangerous combination of access and knowledge contributed to the onset of their drug use. This paradoxical mind-set did not simply affect pharmacists' decisions to start using prescription drugs. It also seemed to offer the pharmacists a convenient rationalization to continue and even increase their drug use. For example, it was not at all uncommon for interviewees to describe how they continuously broadened their definitions of acceptable use levels. This is seen in the comments of a 33-year-old male pharmacist.

> I was on the hospice team and did patient consultations, evaluating their pain situations and figuring out ways to use drugs to control their pain. One of the ironic things is that I was an expert in the use of narcotics. I knew how to administer them for patients. I guess I felt that I knew so much about them that I would not get into trouble with abusing them myself. But there's a difference between knowledge and understanding. I thought that figuring out milligrams and durations and intervals that I would protect myself. None of that protects you in the long run. . . . You end up with your thought processes in one area,

in another area you're impaired. Before long, you're not following the rules you set down. So you change the rules. You change them because they don't apply to you anymore. I had rules like "never two days in a row," but that was probably the first rule that I had made that I broke. Once I didn't take an opiate two days in a row. I would be okay. You can't become an addict if you're not using all the time. I kept that rule for quite awhile. Recreational use, lower level of use for quite awhile, not doing it every day.

In many cases, pharmacists even described how they used their pharmacy knowledge to fine-tune their drug use, maximizing the drugs' pharmaceutical potential. This tendency can be seen in the comments of a 47-year-old male pharmacist.

P: Yeah, because now that I knew more, I knew how to be more careful about it. To fine-tune my taste. I knew what to stay away from and what to go towards. I knew how to keep from overloading my own system. I knew when I was starting to get toxic, and I could adjust my drug use. Because I was still at the point where I hadn't quite crossed that line yet.

I: So it didn't slow down your use, it didn't cause you to think, "Oh, this is bad." It allowed you to see more exactly how to do it and do it better.

P: Exactly right. For example, access to the pharmaceuticals. If I didn't steal Percodan [narcotic analgesic], I knew that I could take a Tylenol #3 [narcotic analgesic] and something else and enhance the high. I knew how to create that synergistic effect so that much inventory wouldn't be missing. Because it wasn't always Percodan. I would sometimes do a Tylenol #3, and those were so liberally kept, sold by the thousands for a week type of thing, it was such a big mover. So I could keep myself high and keep myself from developing the toxicity by combining other drugs and that sort of thing.

Similarly, a 41-year-old male said,

I used my training to its fullest potential. Fullest potential. . . . Do you remember John Lily? The guy did a lot of work, experimental work with dolphins. He had a book called the *Center of the Cyclone*. In his book, he made a statement that one cannot consider oneself a true researcher unless one is willing to experiment, do the experiment on oneself. I said, "Exactly." That was one of my defining moments. So I would take that statement. . . . If you didn't try it, you can't consider yourself a true researcher. That's how I viewed myself. I always believed in constant improvement.

As these pharmacists progressed into the later phases of their drug abuse period, they were forced to ponder the significance of their drug use habit. At some point, they came to the realization that they had a drug problem. However, very few individuals voluntarily sought help. Instead, they kept their problem a secret, reasoning that their knowledge would again afford them the vehicle to get themselves out of any predicament that they were in. To them, only uneducated street addicts needed professional drug treatment. This characterization can be seen in the comments of a 33-year-old female pharmacist.

> Yeah, I didn't think that it would happen to me. I was pissed. I thought those [drug abusers] were people that lived under bridges. People who didn't have college educations. People who . . . I guess I was just kind of a snob.

Even when they got caught for stealing or using drugs, many pharmacists still maintained their shield of overconfidence. In the following quote, a 39-year-old female describes what happened when she was hospitalized for drug related health problems.

> P: I was judgmental too. You know I [thought] those [drug abusers] were people who had no self-will. In the ER [emergency room] they did treat me like an addict and I'd get very angry, very angry.
> I: Why?
> P: Well, because I wasn't an addict. I would say things like, "Don't you know who I am? I am a pain specialist in this hospital; I know when I need narcotics," and they, you know, looking back on it, it must have just been humorous.

## DISCUSSION

The above excerpts from personal interviews demonstrate how pharmacists' professional expertise contributes to the detriment of their health. These druggists were all aware that their drug use was wrong. They knew that their employers and the federal law made it illegal for them to remove drugs from pharmacy stock or ingest drugs while on the job. However, they were adept at developing vocabularies of adjustment (Cressey, 1953) or techniques of neutralizations (Sykes & Matza, 1957) to offset negative normative judgments. They came up with a series of excuses or justifications that served as post hoc rationalizations and a priori justifications for their behaviors. Faced with a growing drug problem, they convinced themselves that they were capable of controlling it without any outside assistance. Without exception, these behaviors and their accompanying vocabularies of adjustment were rooted in the experiences and expertise that they had gained while becoming a member of the pharmacy profession.

The above outlined interview data raises some very troubling suggestions about the ways that being and becoming a pharmacist can inadvertently produce deviant drug habits. We have been able to identify a number of aspects within the educational, occupational, and professional socialization proc-

esses that seemed to contribute to the initial onset, progression, and maintenance of these individuals' illicit prescription drug habits. The occupational
and professional literature offers several possible insights into our findings.

The central argument of this article is that drug abuse among pharmacists
does not solely have its origins in the problems of individual actors; but
rather, it is rooted in the nature of the profession itself. Numerous scholars
(Freidson, 1970; Greenwood, 1957; Pavalko, 1971) have described how the
professional socialization process instills neophyte members with a sense of
perceived power and authority over the knowledge and social objects that
are unique to the profession. In applying his concept of "professional dominance" to the professional socialization process that affects doctors, Freidson (1975) and others (Becker et al., 1961; Bloom, 1973; Haas & Shaffir,
1987; Konner, 1987) have documented how medical professionals routinely
overestimate the limits of their professional knowledge or abilities. As an
example, note that members of the medical profession routinely use the term
*God complex* to refer to a doctor who thinks he or she is capable of curing
any physical ailment regardless of the circumstances. In the same way that
some doctors think that they can remedy any physical ailment, it is possible
that some pharmacists may reason that they are capable of self-medicating
with any prescription drug without putting themselves in significant risk of
drug dependency.

The potential for a pharmacist to abuse his or her professional power may
be exacerbated by yet another issue. It has long been argued that pharmacy
is merely an occupation or, at best, a marginal or quasi profession. This is
because it has failed to exercise strict controls over its object and the behavior
of its members (Denzin & Metlin, 1968). Pharmacists have always had great
difficulty in convincing others that they are really society's drug experts
because it is the medical profession that controls the disbursement of medications to the general public (i.e., via an authorizing prescription). Denzin
and Metlin point out that, almost like a machine, the pharmacist merely fills
the prescription order that the patient's medical doctor has dictated.
Although contemporary pharmacists would like us to believe otherwise,
doctors still provide the "primary medical advice" to the sick and ailing
patient (Denzin & Metlin, 1968, p. 379).

Moreover, pharmacists do not provide a "service" as much as they simply
sell pharmaceuticals and patent drugs that are viewed by most people as a
"product" rather than an "object" to provide services. This distinction has
long been held as one of the essential differences between an occupation and
a profession. Granted, pharmacists do limit the public's access to many controlled substances; however, they still have "not been able to gain exclusive
control over the social object" central to their daily work (Denzin & Metlin,
1968, p. 379).

All professions engage in a monopolization of the knowledge and social objects that define their professional identity (Greenwood, 1957; Pavalko, 1971). Members attempt to convince themselves and others that they are best equipped to interpret, control, and administer all aspects of professional knowledge and their given social object. However, as Denzin and Metlin (1968) have pointed out, a subservient position to doctors has kept the pharmacy profession from ever satisfying all of the requirements of a professional identity. As a result, pharmacy remains a frustrated, quasi profession. Thus, in trying to compensate for their low status as members of a frustrated profession, pharmacists may be especially prone to thinking that they can control their own prescription drug use. For some pharmacists, permissive drug use attitudes and behaviors may reflect an effort to compensate for their frustrated professional identity.

Another distinguishing difference between an occupation and a profession is that the latter attempts to exercise some level of quality control and enforce ethical standards over its members (Greenwood, 1957; Wilensky, 1964). This is accomplished first by screening out unqualified applicants and then by purging known deviants from among their ranks. It is clear from these data that the pharmacy profession has not been able to either effectively prevent existing substance abusers from entering the profession or to adequately deter those who later choose to violate its code of ethics.

Greenwood (1957) has argued that the "principal function of professional schools is to identify and screen individuals who might not possess the highest quality of characteristics and thereby prevent deviants from entering into the professional culture" (p. 54). Quite to the contrary, our interviews with drug abusing pharmacists provided evidence to suggest that the pharmacy school subculture may actually attract those with addictive personalities and even encourage (or at lease passively tolerate) illicit drug use while at work. Perhaps it should not be surprising that in this type of occupational environment, a poorly screened, acculturated, and inadequately socialized neophyte pharmacist can become an abuser of prescription drugs.

We fully recognize that the conclusions of this study must be qualified by several caveats. Several limitations in the methodology significantly limit our ability to draw definitive causal conclusions. First, the data in this study are cross-sectional in nature. Moreover, the data collection process relies on retrospective accounts of past behaviors. This poses serious temporal ordering problems. Specifically, the post hoc nature of these data leaves us unable to determine if reported attitudes and behaviors existed prior to the respondent's initial illicit prescription drug use behaviors or if they reflect the individual's postdeviance reconstruction of past events.

Interview data are especially vulnerable to this temporal ordering criticism. All of the pharmacists were well into their drug abuse recoveries when they were interviewed and at the time were participants in various 12-step programs. Several constructionist oriented scholars (Alasuutari, 1992; Denzin, 1987; Rudy, 1986) have documented how the structure and content of 12-step programs significantly shape the way in which recovering individuals think and talk about their past drug (or alcohol) use, attitudes, and behaviors. Hence, the interviewees' exposure and willing participation in these groups will undoubtedly affect the way they tell their story. When the recovering pharmacists were left to direct the flow and content of the interview, they often spoke about how factors such as their early childhood experiences or a high incidence of drug and/or alcohol abuse within their immediate family helped shape their own personal drug abuse. We found this tendency to be widespread among the interviewees. However, in every such occasion, the interviewer consistently shifted the focus of the conversation and asked the individuals to consider the ways in which various social and occupational factors were related to their drug abuse history. This strategy proved to be especially successful at getting the interview respondent to speak freely and candidly about a variety of sensitive issues.

Although we made every effort to force the interviewees to reflect on various social factors that affected their past illicit prescription drug use, there is no way to determine the extent to which their involvements in 12-step programs has shaped the substance of their interview accounts. One possible future remedy for this situation would be to identify and conduct interviews with pharmacists who are currently beginning to use drugs, have just recently come forward, or have been apprehended for their drug use, and then compare the nature and content of their untainted accounts.

Despite the above-mentioned limitations, these data offer vivid descriptions of how pharmacists can and do allow their professional position and expertise to perpetuate their illicit prescription drug use behaviors. This study joins a large body of employee deviance studies that show how occupation/professional norms and privileges can encourage rule- and law-violating behaviors. This study documents how occupationally socialized deviance can permeate even the highly respected profession of pharmacy; thus, society's drug experts have become the "drugged experts."

## NOTES

Reprinted from Dean A. Dabney and Richard C. Hollinger, *Work and Occupations* 26, no. 1 (February 1999): 77–106. Copyright © 1999 by Sage Publications, Inc. Reprinted by permission of Sage Publications, Inc.

1. In the context of the present study, the term *illicit prescription drug use/user* represents a legal distinction. This concept is meant to refer only to the illegal use of prescription medications as outlined in the Controlled Substance Act of 1970 (Shulgin, 1992). It includes the use of mind-altering, prescription medications when such use is done without a legitimate prescription order that has been signed or authorized by a licensed, FDA-approved physician. The use of prescription medications without

an authorizing prescription order constitutes illicit prescription drug use regardless of whether such medications were procured from pharmacy stock, from a street level drug dealer, or any other illicit market source. Our use of the term illicit prescription drug use does not refer to the use of those mind-altering controlled substances that are deemed to have no medicinal purposes and thus are classified as Schedule I substances under the Controlled Substance Act of 1980 (e.g., marijuana, hashish, heroin, industrial inhalants, and hallucinogens such as LSD; see Shulgin, 1992). Moreover, the term illicit prescription drug use does not include the use of prescription medications when such use is done in accordance with the instructions on a physician authorized prescription order, regardless of how substantial or prolonged the use may be. The term illicit prescription drug use does not include the use or abuse of alcohol. Also, note that this concept carries no functional distinction. It is not intended to speak directly to any physical, emotional, or mental consequences or resulting states of behavior/consciousness associated with an individual's use of any prescription medicine. Issues related to an individual's drug-related behavioral or mental functionality will be referred to under the headings of drug abuse, impairment, or problematic drug use.

2. Pharmacists in the McAuliffe et al. (1987) study were asked to offer a self-assessment of drug dependency to any one of a number of psychoactive controlled substances. This list included prescription as well as nonprescription medications. Individuals were classified as being at risk of drug abuse if they reported more than 100 total drug use episodes and experienced more than one drug-related interference with functioning (as determined by a standard checklist of items such as calling in late to work due to substance use, seeking treatment, etc.).

3. Normack, Eckel, Pfifferline, and Cocolas (1985a) used a scaled usage inventory that sampled the presence and frequency of an individual's use of a variety of substances to establish their criteria for impairment risk. Similar to the McAuliffe et al. (1987) study, they did not limit their inquiry to prescription drug use. Anyone scoring more than a 2 on the usage scale that ranged from 0 to 4 was identified as being at risk.

4. The researchers used a broad definition of drug use, stating that they were interested in "pharmacists recovering from alcohol and other drug addictions" (Bissell, Haberman, & Williams, 1989, p. 21). Similar to the above studies, they have not limited their analysis to pharmacists' use of the substances that they are responsible for dispensing.

5. Three separate data sources were used in the original inquiry to achieve a more comprehensive inquiry into pharmacists' illicit prescription drug use behaviors. These data sources included (a) in-depth interviews with pharmacists who were recovering from illicit prescription drug use behaviors; (b) incident reports detailing officially discovered cases of pharmacists' drug related wrongdoings occurring in two major retail pharmacy chains; and (c) a self-administered, anonymous survey of a random sample of practicing pharmacists.

6. These recruiters functioned as present or past coordinators of their respective state recovery network. They had access to the names of all current and past network members and were able to contact them without violating the confidentiality agreements that are cornerstones of the recovery movement.

7. Recruiters were explicitly asked to refer only pharmacists who had a past history of prescription drug use. Several individuals who contacted us or were interviewed had no prescription drug use history (i.e., they used alcohol or street drugs only). These individuals were not included in the present analysis.

8. The membership list of the American Pharmaceutical Association was used to generate a random sample of 2,000 practicing U.S. pharmacists. Completed surveys were returned by 1,016 individuals (50.5% response rate). The data presented in table 22.1 include only those 312 respondents who reported five or more lifetime episodes involving the illicit use of one of the following 10 addictive substances; cocaine, amphetamines, other stimulants, barbiturates, benzodiazepines, narcotic analgesics, nonnarcotic analgesics, inhalants, muscle relaxants, and antidepressants. Data on marijuana/hashish use and antibiotic use were available. However, given the fact that these two do not fit the description of mind-altering prescription drugs, we chose to exclude them from our analysis. We maintain that the presence of five or more lifetime use episodes is indicative of a relaxed approach to unauthorized drug use, thus suggesting that the individual has progressed past the experimental or one time occasion of drug use.

9. The term *drug class* refers to the groupings of drugs that have similar psychoactive effects. For example, the narcotic analgesic drug class includes all opiate-based medications. All drugs of this class are prescribed principally for pain relief. Some of the other drug classes that will be discussed in this paper include amphetamines, barbiturates, benzodiazepines, stimulants, and nonnarcotic analgesics. Each of these drug classes has its own distinguishing characteristics. The term *drug types* refers to the different medications contained in each drug class. Each drug type is assigned its own generic or brand name. Examples of drug types that fall into the narcotic analgesic class include Percodan, Morphine, Demerol, and Dilaudid. Note that there are often hundreds of drug types within each drug class.

10. The term *narcotic analgesic* is commonly used to refer to opiate-based medications. All narcotic analgesic drug types are classified as CII substances under the Controlled Substance Act of 1970 (Shulgin, 1992). Each of these substances is a highly addictive pain medication and is subject to the most strict inventory and dispensing controls. Narcotic analgesic drug types include morphine, Dilaudid, Demerol, Percodan, Percoset, Codeine, and Hydrocodone.

11. The term *poly-drug user* refers to an individual who routinely uses multiple types or classes of drugs and alcohol. Poly-drug use behaviors usually result in states of cross-addiction as the body develops a tolerance and dependence on multiple forms and combinations of drugs. This advanced type of drug habit is generally very difficult to reverse or control and treatment becomes a very complicated detoxification process.

12. The letter C is commonly used to abbreviate the word *class*. The Controlled Substance Act of 1970 (Shulgin, 1992) classifies prescription medications in five separate classes or schedules according to their medicinal purpose and addiction potential.

## REFERENCES

Alasuutari, P. (1992). *Desire and craving: A cultural theory of alcoholism.* Albany: State University of New York Press.

Allen, I. (1994). *Doctors and their careers: A new generation.* London: Policy Studies Institute.

American Nurses Association. (ANA). (1984). *ANA cabinet on nursing practice, statement on scope for addiction nursing practice.* Kansas City, MO: Author.

American Pharmaceutical Association. (APhA). (1982). Report of the American Pharmaceutical Association Policy Committee on Professional Affairs. *American Pharmacy, NS22,* 368–380.

Apter, T. E. (1993). *Working women don't have wives: Professional success in the 1990s.* New York: St. Martin's.

Baldwin, J. N., Light, K. E., Stock, C., Ives, T. J., Crabtree, B. L., Miederhoff, P. A., Tommasello, T., & Levine, P. J. (1991), Curricular guidelines for pharmacy education: Substance abuse and addictive disease. *American Journal of Pharmaceutical Education, 55*(4), 311–316.

Becker H. S., Geer, B., Hughes, E. C., & Strauss, A. L. (1961). *Boys in white: Student culture in medical school.* Chicago: University of Chicago Press.

Benson, M. L. (1985). Denying the guilty mind: Accounting for involvement in a white collar crime. *Criminology, 23,* 583–607.

Berg, B. L. (1998). *Qualitative research methods for the social sciences* (3rd ed.). Needham Heights, MA: Allyn & Bacon.

Bissell, L., Haberman, P. W., & Williams, R. L. (1989). Pharmacists recovering from alcohol and other drug addictions: An interview study. *American Pharmacy, NS29*(6), 19–30.

Bissell, L., & Jones, R. W. (1981). The alcoholic nurse. *Nursing Outlook, 29*(2), 96–101.

Bloom, S. W. (1973). *Power and dissent in the medical school.* New York: Free Press.

Bogardus, D. E. (1987). *Missing drugs.* Salt Lake City, UT: Medical Management Systems.

Briles, J. (1994). *The Briles Report on women in healthcare.* San Francisco: Jossey-Bass.

Candib, L. M. (1996). How medicine tried to make a man out of me (and failed, finally). In D. Wear (Ed.), *Women in medical education* (pp. 135–144). Albany: State University of New York Press.

Carlson, H. B., Dilts, S. L., & Radcliff, S. (1994). Physicians with substance abuse problems and their recovery environment: A survey. *Journal of Substance Abuse Treatment, 11*(2), 113–119.

Chi, J. (1983). Impaired pharmacists: More programs move to handle the problem. *Drug Topics, 127*(47), 24–29.

Cressey, D. R. (1953). *Other people's money.* Glencoe, IL: Free Press.

Dabney, D. A. (1995a). Neutralization and deviance in the workplace: Theft of supplies and medicines by hospital nurses. *Deviant Behavior, 16,* 313–331.

Dabney, D. A. (1995b). Workplace deviance among nurses: The influence of work group norms on drug diversion and/or use. *Journal of Nursing Administration, 25*(3), 48–54.

Dabney, D. A. (1997). *A sociological examination of illicit prescription drug use among pharmacists.* Unpublished doctoral dissertation, University of Florida, Gainesville.

Dalton, M. (1959). *Men who manage.* New York: John Wiley.

Decima. (1990). *Final report of transport Canada on the results of the substance use and transportation safety study.* Toronto, Canada: Decima Research.

Denzin, N. K. (1987). *Recovering alcoholic.* Newbury Park, CA: Sage.

Denzin, N. K., & Metlin, C. J. (1968). Incomplete professionalization: The case of pharmacy. *Social Forces, 46,* 375–381.

Ditton, J. (1977). *Part-time crime: An ethnography of fiddling and pilferage.* New York: Macmillan.

Epstein, D. (1990). Theft: How safe are your pharmacies? Part I: The chains. *Drug Topics, 130*(47), 12–23.

Epstein, D. (1991). Theft: How safe are your pharmacies? Part II: The independents. *Drug Topics, 131*(1), 13–25.

Freidson, E. (1970). *Professional dominance.* Chicago: Aldine.

Freidson, E. (1975). *Doctoring together.* New York: Elsevier North-Holland.

Gallegos, K. V., Veit, F. W., Wilson, P. O., Porter, T., & Talbott, G. D. (1988). Substance abuse among health professionals. *Maryland Medical Journal, 37*(3), 191–197.

Geis, G. (1967). The heavy electrical equipment antitrust cases of 1961. In M. B. Cinard & R. Quinney (Eds.), *Criminal behavior systems: A typology* (pp. 139–151). New York: Rinehart and Winston.

Gouldner, A. (1954). *Patterns of industrial bureaucracy.* New York: Free Press.

Green, P. (1989). The chemically dependent nurse. *Nursing clinics of North America, 24*(1), 81–94.

Greenwood, E. (1957). Attributes of a profession. *Social Work, 2,* 45–55.

Haas, J., & Shaffir, W. (1987). *Becoming doctors: The adoption of a cloak of competence.* Greenwich, CT: JAI.

Hankes, L., & Bissell, L. (1992). Health professionals. In J. H. Lowinson, P. Ruiz, R. Millman, & J. G. Langrod (Eds.), *Substance abuse: A comprehensive textbook* (2nd ed., pp. 398–908). Baltimore: Williams & Wilkins.

Harris, A. M. (1995). *Broken patterns: Professional women and the quest for a new feminine identity.* Detroit, MI: Wayne State University Press.

Hoffman, J. P., Brittingham, A., & Larson, C. (1996). *Drug abuse among U.S. workers: Prevalence and trends by occupation and industry category.* Rockville, MD: U.S. Department of Health and Human Services.

Hollinger, R. C. (1991). Neutralizing in the workplace: An empirical analysis of property theft and production deviance. *Deviant Behavior, 12,* 169–202.

Hood, J. C., & Duphorne, P. L. (1995). To report or not to report: Nurses' attitudes toward reporting co-workers suspected of substance abuse. *Journal of Drug Issues, 25*(2), 313–339.

Horning, D. (1970). Blue collar theft: Conceptions of property, attitudes toward pilfering, and work group norms in a modern industrial plant. In E. O. Smigel & H. L. Ross (Eds.), *Crimes against bureaucracy* (pp. 46–64). New York: Van Nostrand Reinhold.

Hughes, P. H., Conrad, S. E., Baldwin, D. C., Storr, C., & Sheehan, D. (1991). Resident physician substance use in the United States. *Journal of the American Medical Association, 265*(16), 2069–2073.

Hughes, P. H., Storr, C., Sheehan, D. V. Conn, J., & Sheehan, M. F. (1990). Studies of drug use and impairment in the medical profession. *Addiction and Recovery, 10*, 42–45.

Hutchinson, S. (1986). Chemically dependent nurses: The trajectory toward self-annihilation. *Nursing Research, 35*(4), 196–201.

Kanter, R. M. (1977). *Men and women of the corporation.* New York: Basic Books.

Konner, M. (1987). *Becoming a doctor.* New York: Penguin.

Kurzman, M. G. (1972). *Drug abuse education in pharmacy schools.* A report prepared for the Drug Enforcement Administration by the American Association of Colleges of Pharmacy, Washington, DC.

Lehman, W. E. K., Holcom, M. L., & Simpson, D. D. (1990). *Employee health and performance in the workplace: A survey of municipal employees in a large southwest city.* Fort Worth, TX: Texas Christian University, Institute of Behavioral Research.

Levers, L. L., & Hawes, A. R. (1990). Drugs and gender: A woman's recovery program. *Journal of Mental Health Counseling, 12*, 527–531.

Lorber, J. (1993). Why women physicians will never be true equals in the American medical profession. In E. Riska & K. Wegar (Eds.), *Gender, work and medicine* (pp. 62–76). London: Sage.

Mars, G. (1982). *Cheats at work: An anthropology of workplace crime.* London: George Allen & Unwin.

Martin, S. (1993). Pharmacists number more than 190,000 in United States. *American Pharmacy, NS33*(7), 22–24.

McAneny, L., & Moore, D. W. (1994). Annual honesty & ethics poll. *The Gallup Poll Monthly, 349*, 2–4.

McAuliffe, W. E., Rohman, M., Fishman, P., Friedman, R., Wechsler, H., Soboroff, S. H., & Toth, D. (1984). Psychoactive drug use by young and future physicians. *Journal of Health and Social Behavior, 25*(3), 35–54.

McAuliffe, W. E., Santangelo, S. L., Gingras, J., Rohman, M., Sobol, A., & Magnuson, E. (1987). Use and abuse of controlled substances by pharmacists and pharmacy students. *American Journal of Hospital Pharmacy, 44*(2), 311–317.

McDuff, D. R., Tommasello, A. C., Hoffman, K. J., & Johnson, J. L. (1995). Addictions training for physicians and other licensed health care professionals in Maryland. *Maryland Medical Journal, 44*(6), 453–459.

Michigan Nurses Association (MNA). (1986). *Fact sheet: Chemical dependency of nurses.* East Lansing, MI: Author.

Miederhoff, P., Allen, H. D., McCreary, G. J., & Veal, A. F. (1977). A study of pharmacy students' attitudes toward drug abuse. *American Journal of Pharmaceutical Education, 42*, 129–131.

Moodley-Kunnie, T. (1988). Attitudes and perceptions of health professionals toward substance use disorders and substance dependent individuals. *The International Journal of the Addictions, 23*(5), 469–475.

National Association of Retail Druggists (NARD). (1988) *NARD'S guide to programs for the impaired pharmacist.* Alexandria, VA: Author.

National Institute of Justice. (NIJ). (1997). *1996 Drug use forecasting: Annual report on adult and juvenile arrestees.* Washington, DC: Author.

Normack, J. W., Eckel, F. M., Pfifferling, J., & Cocolas, G. (1985a). Impairment risk in North Carolina pharmacists. *American Pharmacy, NS25*(6), 45–48.

Normack, J. W., Eckel, F. M., Pfifferling, J., & Cocolas, G. (1985b). Impairment risk in North Carolina pharmacy students. *American Pharmacy, NS25*(6) 60–62.

Normand, J., Salyards, S. D., & Mahony, J. J. (1990). An evaluation of preemployment drug testing. *Journal of Applied Psychology, 75*, 629–639.

Pavalko, R. M. (1971). *Sociology of occupations and professions.* Itasca, IL: F. E. Peacock.

Poplar, J. F., & Lyle, W. (1969). Characteristics of nurse addicts. *American Journal of Nursing, 69*, 117–119.

Riska, E., & Wegar K. (1993). Women physicians: A new force in medicine? In E. Riska & K. Wegar (Eds.), *Gender, work and medicine* (pp. 77–94). London: Sage.

Rosenthal, M. M. (1995). *The incompetent doctor: Behind closed doors.* Philadelphia: Open University Press.

Rudy, D. R. (1986). *Becoming an alcoholic: Alcoholics Anonymous and the reality of alcoholism.* Carbondale: Southern Illinois University Press.

Schneck, D., Amodei, R., & Kernish, R. (1991). *Substance abuse in the transit industry.* Washington, DC: Office of Technical Assistance and Safety.

Secundy, M. G. (1996) Life as a sheep in the cow's pasture. In D. Wear (Ed.), *Women in medical education* (pp. 119–126). Albany: State University of New York Press.

Shaffer, S. (1987) Attitudes and perceptions held by impaired nurses. *Nursing Management, 18*(4), 46–50.

Sheffield, J. W., O'Neill, P., & Fisher, C. (1992a). Women in recovery: From pain to progress: Part I. *Texas Pharmacy, 8*(1), 29–36.

Sheffield, J. W., O'Neill, P., & Fisher, C. (1992b). Women in recovery: From pain to progress: Part 2. *Texas Pharmacy, 8*(2), 22–34.

Sheridan, J. R., & Winkler, H. (1989). An evaluation of drug testing in the workplace. In S. W. Gust & J. M. Walsh (Eds.), *Drugs in the workplace: Research and evaluation data* (NIDA Research Monograph 91). Rockville, MD: National Institute of Drug Abuse.

Shulgin, A. T. (1992). *Controlled substances: A chemical guide to the federal drug laws.* Berkeley, CA: Ronin.

Sieh, E. W. (1987). Garment workers: Perceptions of inequity and employee theft. *British Journal of Criminology, 27*, 174–190.

Smith, H. C. (1989). Substance abuse among nurses: Types of drugs. *Dimensions of Critical Nursing, 8*(3), 159–167.

Steinberg, J. A. (1984). *Climbing the ladder of success in high heels.* Ann Arbor: University of Michigan Press.

Substance Abuse and Mental Health Services Administration. (1996). *National household survey on drug abuse: Main findings, 1994.* Rockville, MD: U.S. Department of Health and Human Services.

Sullivan, E. J. (1987). Comparison of chemically dependent and non-dependent nurses on familial, personal, and professional characteristics. *Journal of Studies on Alcohol, 48*(6), 563–568.

Sykes, G., & Matza, D. (1957). Techniques of neutralization: A theory of delinquency. *American Journal of Sociology, 22*(4), 665–670.

Tatham R. L. (1974). Employee views of theft in retailing. *Journal of Retailing, 50*, 49–55.

Wilensky, H. L. (1964). The professionalism of everyone. *American Journal of Sociology, 70*, 137–158.

Winick, C. (1961). Physician narcotic addicts. *Social Problems, 9*, 174–186.

Wivell, M. K., & Wilson, G. L. (1994). Prescription for harm: Pharmacist liability. *Trial, 30*(5), 36–39.

# 23

# Wheeling and Dealing: An Ethnography of an Upper-Level Drug Dealing and Smuggling Community

*Patricia A. Adler*

## BACKGROUND

Awaiting the outcome of each successful smuggling run was a community of dealers ready to begin the process of distributing the drugs on a wholesale level. There were many more people who specialized in dealing than in smuggling; a stateside funnel shape beings to form. . . .

There were two basic forms of drug dealing: straight dealing and middling. Straight dealing involved purchasing drugs in one quantity and dividing them into smaller units to sell. Southwest County cocaine dealers thus bought in kilos and sold in pounds or bought in pounds and sold in ounces to dealers at lower levels. . . .

The second type of transaction that upper-level dealers engaged in was middling. Here, individuals sold the drugs they purchased intact, without separating them into smaller units. Middling generally occurred under one of two circumstances. Occasionally, a dealer with a load to sell found a single customer who wanted to purchase the entire amount. The ease and convenience of this type of deal caused many dealers to ask around when they were offered drugs for sale, to see if they could set up a simple transfer by finding a buyer interested in purchasing this same amount. Then, they simply transported the merchandise from their supplier to their customer and extracted a profit for filling the function of middleman. Although the middleman, in effect, deprived the first supplier of the additional profit he or she could have earned by selling directly to the final customer, most dealers did not mind (or even preferred) working through middlemen, because it provided them with an extra layer of insulation from strangers. This first type of middling was precipitated, then, by the supplier's offer of merchandise.

The second type of middling was customer-initiated. Dealers were often approached by people looking to buy a specific amount of drugs. In this case, potential customers let it be known that they had cash available for a purchase. Upon hearing such a request, most dealers shopped around to see if they could fill this order from someone else in town. If they matched a source of supply with a cash purchaser, they boosted the price and made money on the transfer. Because this was such a common practice, considered a service to both sides, middlers might even discuss their profit margin openly with one or both parties. They might elect to receive their payment in cash or in kind (or both). The one thing they could not do was to reveal the identity of the two parties to each other. This second type of middling was the most common form and occurred within all dealing levels and circles. . . .

A third type of activity which developed and became increasingly popular among Southwest County residents . . . was the commercial production of high-potency domestic marijuana. . . . In the Southwest County marijuana fields and greenhouses, I observed several sophisticated cultivation techniques designed to maximize marijuana's THC content and appearance, from genetic cross-breeding to fertilization, prevention of seed-formation, pruning, growing, hydroponics, harvesting, curing (drying), and manicuring.

Because of the common product these two industries shared, some individuals sidestepped into the cultivation business from dealing, while others attempted to move into dealing through cultivation. But marijuana growing was a time-consuming and dangerous business. Planting, irrigating, fertilizing, and pruning required that the grower exercise responsibility and remain close to the fledgling crop. Harvest seasons required the most vigilance, as the incidence of ripoffs was high. All growers, especially those with outdoor fields, had to guard their near-ready crops both day and night until the process of cutting, preparing, packaging, and distributing was completed. And unlike dealing, where violence was less common, a successful cultivation business required carrying and occasionally using shotguns, handguns, and rifles.

A very different range of activities was thus called for in this enterprise, overlapping occupationally only at the sale of the finished product. There was therefore only limited cross-involvement, as beyond their common drug world membership and the sympathetic nature of their industries, dealers generally stayed out of large-scale cultivation and growers usually lacked the orientation toward or interest in more full-time dealing. . . .

## THE FAST LIFE

The life-style associated with big-time dealers and smugglers was intemperate and uninhibited. Dubbed the fast life, or "flash," it was characterized by a feeling of euphoria. So pleasurable was life that nobody worried about paying the bills, running out of drugs, or planning for the future. Dealers and smugglers plunged themselves fully into satisfying their immediate desires, whether these involved consuming lavish, expensive dinners, drugging themselves to saturation, traveling hundreds of miles to buy a particular item that caught their eye, or "crashing" (sleeping) for 15–20 hours at a time to make up for nights spent in unending drug use. Those who lived in the fast lane sought an intensity that disdained the boredom of security and the peace of calm quietude. They were always on the run, rushing back and forth between partying and doing business, often intermingling the two. Schedules and commitments were hard to maintain, since people were apt to pursue the unexpected at any time or get caught in a run of drug consumption that could last for hours or even days. One coke dealer commented on the frequency of his partying:

> When we're sitting around the house with friends that are into dealing it always turns into a party. We do a lot of drugs, drink a lot, and just speed rap all night. . . . It's a full time thing; we're basically decadent 24 hours a day.

Those who lived the fast life were the *beautiful people*, bedecked with expensive adornments such as flashy clothes, jewelry, and sports cars. When they entered a restaurant or bar they ordered extravagantly and tipped lavishly. They grew up to retain a childlike innocence by escaping the unpleasant responsibilities of adult life, while seizing the opportunity to surround themselves with anything money could buy. In their own eyes, they were the ultimate "in crowd."

The dealers' and smugglers' fast life emulated the jet set with all of its travel, spending, and heavy partying. Private planes were diverted to carry a smuggler's entourage off for a week in Las Vegas, where they all drank, gambled, and saw the shows. At other times it was off to the Pacific Islands for sunbathing and tropical drinks, to the mountains for skiing, or to famous spas, where they luxuriously exercised and rejuvenated themselves. In contrast to those children of inherited wealth, though, dealers and smugglers had to work for their money. Their life-style was characterized by a mixture of work and play, as they combined concentrated wheeling and dealing with unadulterated partying. Yet, like jet-setters, they ultimately became bored and sought ever greater excitement, usually turning to drugs for their most intense highs.

Members of the "glitter crowd" were known for their *irresponsibility* and *daring*, their desire to live recklessly and wildly. They despised the conservatism of the straight world as lowly and mundane. For them, the excitement of life came from a series of challenges where they pitted themselves against the forces that stood in their way. Although they did not create arbitrary risks, dealers and smugglers were gamblers who enjoyed the element of risk in their work, being intoxicated with living on the edge of danger. They relished more than just the money; they reveled in the thrill-seeking associated with their close scrapes, their ever present danger, and their drug-induced highs. Gone was the quiet, steady home life of soberly raising children and accumulating savings, as they set themselves on a continuous search for new highs. They exalted freedom, the ability to pick up and "blow" without having to answer to anybody. One dope chick who had spent the past several years moving from relationship to relationship with various big dealers discussed her sense of freedom:

> Now I can do anything I want and not have to worry about someone telling me not to do it. One day I just woke up and said to my little girl, "Honey, pack your clothes. We're going to Hawaii."

Drug dealers lived for the present, surrounding themselves with the maximum pleasures they could grab. They did not, as the middle-class ethos suggested, live in reduced comfort so that they could enjoy the fruits of their labor at a later date. In fact, the reverse was true. The beautiful people seized their happiness now and deferred their hardships for the future; they lived for the moment and let tomorrow worry about paying the tab. One dealer's old lady elaborated on this *mañana* effect:

> It was always like, tomorrow, tomorrow. You write a check, you think you'll cover it tomorrow. It was like that. We went through a lot of stuff like that.

*Money* lay at the base of their exhilarating madness, more money than most could ever have imagined. The gigantic profits that could be accumulated after even a short period of smuggling or heavy dealing could run into hundreds of thousands of dollars a year,[1] which seemed like an endless supply to most participants. Sometimes they became so overcome by their material wealth that they just gloried in it. One novice dealer exclaimed:

> We were like little children in a big fancy palace playhouse. We'd dump all our money on the living room floor and we'd roll in it.

Most initiates could not imagine how to spend this much at first, but they soon learned. After even a short period they found themselves laughing when hundred dollar bills came out of laundered shirt pockets, crumbled and torn from the wash. By then money had become something to be spent without care on the fulfillment of any whim. One member of a smuggler's crew recalled:

Money meant nothing to me. Like, if some guy gave me a $100 bill I'd go out and burn it or cut it in half for all I cared.

This overabundance drove them to generate new needs, to search out new avenues of spending. As one dealer illustrated:

At the height of my dealing I was making at least 10 grand a month profit, even after all my partying. When you have too much money you always have to look for something to spend it on. I used to run into the stores every day to find $50, $60 shirts to buy because I didn't know what else to do with the money, there was so much.

*Drugs* were also a big part of the fast life. Smugglers and dealers took personal consumption for themselves and their entourage as a basic cost of doing business, to be siphoned out before profits could accumulate, so drugs flowed freely, without care for expense. High-potency marijuana and hashish were smoked in moderation by many, most noticeably among the marijuana traffickers. Alcohol, particularly wine and champagne, was consumed regularly, often along with other drugs. Cocaine, however, was used heavily, its presence pervading the entire dealing community. They typically "coked" themselves to saturation, and it was not uncommon for a dealer to snort more than an ounce a week (market value: $2,000–$2,200) during periods of heavy partying. One cocaine dealer estimated how much he and his old lady took out for their "own heads":

As much as we wanted, which was a lot. We used a couple of grams a day at least, that was nothing. We could go through a quarter [of an ounce], you wouldn't believe it. We used big ziplocs, the large size, for our personal stash. We'd stick a big spoon in it and just dump it out on the mirror. One time I dropped an ounce down the front of my shirt when I went to take a toot [snort] and the bag ripped. I just brushed it off, it was nothing.

One of the reasons dealers and smugglers went through large quantities of cocaine so quickly was that they built up a short-term tolerance to its effects. Early phases of contact with the drug usually brought on a subtle rush of warmth, and feelings of affection for surrounding people. This might be accompanied by a brief seizure of diarrhea, a loss of appetite, and a feeling of acceleration. After a half hour or so the warmth faded and the speed effect intensified. The usual reaction was either to moderate this overintensity with alcohol or marijuana or to pass around another series of "lines" and snort some more. This pattern could continue for hours or days until the participants became so "wired" (tense) that they found themselves gritting their teeth and passing up further offers. Sleep usually came only with great difficulty, and then often did not last long, as individuals awakened, often exhausted, with a slightly bitter drip down the backs of their throats.

After people had been exposed to heavy cocaine use for a period of weeks, they usually noticed a slight change in its effects. They required larger quantities to generate and sustain that buzzing feeling of warmth ("the rush"). Their loss of appetite and sleeplessness diminished, so that people who used it to loose weight soon noticed a reduction in its effectiveness. These changes, although indicative of a shift in individuals' patterns and quantity of usage, were not associated with any physical withdrawal symptoms when the drug was unavailable, such as heroin and barbiturate users experience.

The great appeal of cocaine snorting rested on two main characteristics of its effects: internal and interpersonal. Psychologically, individuals achieved a sense of happiness and well-being. They felt as if their problems were temporarily solved and that everything was wonderful, that they could do no wrong. This was associated with great sensations of safety and power. However, coke was even more strongly a social drug, helping to facilitate intimate lines of communication between people. One pilot voiced a commonly held opinion concerning cocaine's aphrodisiac effects:

> Coke and chicks! Yeah, man, whenever I have some I make sure all the ladies know, cause it really turns them on, they really dig it.

Beyond these casual relationships, serious coke users used the drug to enhance interaction with others. One ounce dealer described the effect it had within his group of friends:

> Coke helps you get past the stupid front games. Our little sessions at night with coke show the closeness that comes from the coke raps. You have such tight friends in such a short amount of time—it's all right there.

Another dealer discussed how cocaine affected his relationship with his wife:

> She and I have such a severe communication gap that it's probably 50 percent of the reason cocaine persists the way it does. When we get together in the evenings it smooths the way for us to relate, for us to have our special time together as lovers. We probably couldn't go on together for long without it.

Dealers and smugglers began consuming cocaine in even larger quantities in the late 1970s when "freebasing" became a popular fad. This involved altering the refined drug's condition into a smokable state. Chemical kits which contained the solvent that transformed coke into base became widely available in headshops. Jean described her fascination with this drug experience:

You start by mixing the coke with the solvent. You pour it out with an eye-dropper onto the dish and it fluffs up like little white trees—like snow, it's pretty. Half of the Jones [the high] is watching that stuff form, scraping it up, putting it into the waterbase pipe—you have to use a torch to keep the heat on it all the time—it forms oils and resins. And as it drops down through the pipe it starts to swirl—half the Jones is in that whole process of smoking it. The other half is in the product. It's like you got hit by a train, it hits you so heavy, but then it goes away so fast that you use so much.

Yet along with the intense highs came some equally intense lows. An experienced freebaser recalled some of his more unpleasant episodes:

Lows? It's like when you can't get up to go to the bathroom and your mind goes by itself. When you're up pacing the floor—your mind, but your body's not. When you're so wired and exhausted and you just want to sleep but you can't. You lie there staring at the ceiling for about 24 hours straight. You're so fucked up you're embarrassed to go out of the house. Falling asleep in public bars. I've been so fucked up I couldn't go in to work and my six-year-old kid had to call in sick for me.

Getting into the habit of consistently freebasing (called "being addicted" by some) broke several dealers and smugglers in Southwest County. Many individuals, once introduced to freebasing, found it increasingly difficult to moderate their drug use. It was an allure that compelled continuing use more than any other drug popular with this subculture. Because larger and more frequent doses of cocaine were used when smoking base, two people could easily consume a quarter to a half ounce of cocaine during a single night's "run" (sitting of continuous usage). Some heavy users freebased for as long as seven or eight days straight without sleep. One person I knew went through $20,000 worth of cocaine in a week this way, while anther used $60,000 worth in a month. Only the richest and most successful dealers and smugglers could afford to sustain such an expensive drug diet. Freebasing, however, could become all-consuming,, leaving little time for the business of earning money. Thus some people committed themselves to sanitariums for rehabilitation when they realized that they had reached this level of involvement. Still others quit the business altogether (some with the help of Narcotics Anonymous), as one former pound dealer explained:

Once I got into base I realized I could never deal again, because you can't have the product or you might get into doing it again.

Another component of life for Southwest County's beautiful people was the *casual sex scene*. Although many members of the community were married and had children, they openly broke the bonds of marital fidelity to explore their sexual urges. Casual attractions, although not the only mode of sexual fulfillment, were a commonly accepted part of life. This open sexual promiscuity was legitimated by the predominance of the hedonistic ethos which infused the dealing and smuggling community. The ease with which they engaged in casual sexual relations indicated their openness toward sexual self-indulgence as a subculturally accepted norm, overriding the contrary sexual mores of the greater society.

Many male dealers and smugglers went out with their male friends to pickup bars, looking for one-night stands. Some kept old ladies on the side and set them up in apartments. They also played musical old ladies, shifting from one to another as they got tired of each one. Extramarital flings were not limited to the men, though, as married women frequently went out for a night with the "girls" and did not come home until sunrise. Marital relationships often became taken for granted in the light of this emphasis on immediate attractions, and divorce was common.

Dealers' old ladies formed an interesting part of the drug scene, because although their role was occasionally active, it was more often passive. Some women ran their own drug businesses. Of these, most entered dealing through the connections they made while living with a male dealer. Typically, after a breakup, these women needed money and realized that they had the knowledge to attempt doing business on their own. Not all women who tried to establish themselves as drug traffickers were successful, however. This lack of success rested, in part, on certain qualities essential to the profession and in part on the reactions men had to working with them. Blum et al. offered a discussion of why there were fewer women dealers in their sample which is relevant to my sample as well:

> Dealers suggest first that women do not always have the personality for it, that they are too paranoid. They also say that women are victims of the double standard; their being in the dealing business is generally disapproved. Some observed that women are less business-oriented in general and so are less likely to be entrepreneurs in peddling drugs. Some contend that women are in general less competent; others hold that women, as the girl friends or sexual partners of dealers and users, can get their drugs free and need not worry about drugs or money. Finally, some of our dealers point out that women cannot do as well in dealing because men, who comprise the majority of the business network, are not comfortable dealing with them or do not trust them. . . .

Women . . . were also used by male dealers and smugglers as employees. Smugglers felt that women were less vulnerable to the suspicions of police or border agents. Positions in which women were often employed included transporting money or drugs, locally, around the country, or across international lines, and operating stash houses.

The majority of women in Southwest County's drug world took a more passive role, however. A crowd of dope chicks formed part of the entourage

which surrounded big dealers and smugglers. Universally beautiful and sex-
ily clad, they served as prestigious escorts so that dealers could show them
off to other members of the community. . . . In return, they were expected
not to intrude on any of their companions' social or business relations. One
dope chick offered this explanation of the reciprocal relationship.

> I guess he just wanted someone to look pretty and drive his Pantera, so that
> people would say, hey so-and-so's got a real foxy-looking chick.

A major coke dealer was frank about his colleagues' attitudes on this
point:

> The guys want a chick who will hang on their arm and go places with them and
> they don't really have to relate to her, because they would actually prefer if the
> chick was dumb enough to where they could leave her with a couple of bottles
> of wine and say I'm going out to do some business, I'll see you in the morning.
> They want a chick who will accept where she's at and have enough brains to
> know when to shut up.

*Children* of the drug world experienced an upbringing that was very different from children of the larger culture. When their parents went out to a
party they were often left home alone. Some were enrolled in boarding
schools to offer their parents greater freedom. In divorced households they
were often bounced back and forth from one parent to the other as the adults
fluctuated in their financial and household stability. When parents dealt or
partied in the home, only slight efforts were made to hide their actions from
the children. However, as the party progressed or the children aged and
became more aware, it was increasingly impossible to disguise what was happening. Other parents made no attempt to camouflage their promiscuous or
drug-related activities. They took their children with them when they slept
around or partied, allowing them to view what went on without censorship.

The result for this treatment was generally a premature precocity and
independence on the children's part. Given the responsibility for viewing,
understanding, and accepting this adult behavior, children adapted rapidly.
They learned about the nature of drugs: what they were worth and what
effects they generated. They also learned to amuse and take care of themselves in the absence of parental protectiveness.

In some cases, their experience with drugs came firsthand. From earliest
infancy these children were "tinydopers," becoming passively intoxicated
through the inhalation of smoke in the air. As they got older, however, they
were permitted to take an occasional toke on the communal marijuana cigarette. Parents varied in how regularly they gave their children drugs. Some
made marijuana available to children whenever it was requested, either bringing them into the smoking circle or rolling "pinners" (tiny, thin joints) for

the youngsters to smoke on their own. One dealer, when queried about the possible dangers of offering drugs to young children, replied:

> What the hell! It grows in the ground, it's a weed. I can't see anything wrong with doing anything, inducing any part of it into your body any way that you possibly could eat it, smoke it, intravenously, or whatever, that it would ever harm you because it grows in the ground. It's one of God's treats.

Other parents offered marijuana to their children only occasionally. These parents made the decision to let their children have access to marijuana for one of the following special reasons: (1) as a reward for a child's good behavior in the past, present, or anticipated future; (2) out of guilt, to compensate children for neglecting them in other ways; (3) as a source of adult entertainment, because children behaved amusingly when under the influence; or (4) as a medicinal aid, to help children fall asleep or to alleviate their cranky moods.

Children of the dealing crowd eventually outgrew their cuteness as tiny-dopers, however, and some graduated to become "tinydealers." Moving into junior high and high school, thirteen- and fourteen-year-old dealers were capable for making large sums of money by selling ounces of marijuana and grams or half-grams of cocaine to their peers. One smuggler commented on this second generation of dealers:

> Those are kids who've been raised with this life-style, easy money, drugs around all the time—their parents are still heavy dealers now. All these kids and tall their friends have access to the drug and they're ripping off their parents. Or else they're dealing on their own through their parents' connections or through their parents' friends' kids. . . . What the hell are the parents going to do? They're not setting the example themselves so what can they do? They have no relating to the kids anyway.

Thus these children grew up in their parents' image. It is not unusual to see a community transmit its norms, values, and occupational preferences from one generation to the next. In fact, this commonly occurs with some regularity, even when that community constitutes a subculture that stands off from the norms of the greater culture. The unusual thing here was the fact that drug use and drug trafficking, acts which are usually reserved for more mature members of a community, were allowed for children, a sacred group in most societies. This violation of a cross-cultural taboo further stigmatized the drug dealing subculture as highly deviant.

## NOTES

Originally published as "Wheeling and Dealing: An Ethnography of an Upper-Level Drug Dealing and Smuggling Community," *Journal of Sociology and Social Welfare* 28, no. 1 (March 1985): 139–62.

1. I sat down once with a commercial marijuana smuggler and we figured out that if he did one run per week (which was his average frequency) during the prime season of October to April and incurred no unexpected losses due to arrest, theft, or accidental mishap, he could clear a profit of $800,000 per year. This figure did not include a deduction for the expense of his personal drug consumption (and that of his crew or entourage), because most dealers and smugglers considered this a prerequisite of the business rather than part of their net profit. This salary represented the upper end of the profit scale, since commercial marijuana smuggling was the most lucrative type of operation I witnessed. There was a vast difference between how much dealers and smugglers earned. When compared to legitimate work, dealer's profits were quite high, but the big money was always in smuggling.

# Index

# About the Editors

**Douglas Harper** is professor and chair of the Sociology Department at Duquesne University. His books include three studies of work: *Good Company*, about railroad tramps who harvest fruit in the American northwest; *Working Knowledge*, a biography of a small-town mechanic, and *Changing Works*, which explores the social meaning of agricultural change. Harper has published extensively in the area of visual sociology and has taught visually inspired sociology in Holland, Italy, France, and Switzerland, as well as in the United States.

**Helene M. Lawson** is professor of sociology at the University of Pittsburgh, Bradford. She is also program director of sociology and coordinator of the Gender Studies Program at the University of Pittsburgh, Bradford. Lawson is author of *Ladies on the Lot: Women, Car Sales, and the Pursuit of the American Dream*, as well as articles on hair workers, conservation officers, and equality in working-class families. She is currently working on trust in Internet relationships, rural culture, and animals. She is also preparing a book about small-town dance studios.